MAGIC

ALSO BY ROLAND LAZENBY

Michael Jordan: The Life

Showboat: The Life of Kobe Bryant

Jerry West: The Life and Legend of a Basketball Icon

The Show: The Inside Story of the Spectacular Los Angeles Lakers in the Words of Those Who Lived It

Mindgames: Phil Jackson's Long Strange Journey

Blood on the Horns: The Long Strange Ride of Michael Jordan's Chicago Bulls

MAGIC

The Life of Earvin "Magic" Johnson

ROLAND LAZENBY

SEVEN DIALS

First published in the United States in 2023 by Celadon Books,
a division of Macmillan Publishers

First published in Great Britain in 2023 by Seven Dials,
an imprint of The Orion Publishing Group Ltd
Carmelite House, 50 Victoria Embankment
London EC4Y 0DZ

An Hachette UK Company

1 3 5 7 9 10 8 6 4 2

A CIP catalogue record for this book is
available from the British Library.

ISBN (Trade Paperback) 978 1 4746 1331 6
ISBN (eBook) 978 1 4746 1333 0
ISBN (Audio) 978 1 4746 2236 3

Designed by Michelle McMillian
Printed in Great Britain by Clays Ltd, Elcograf S.p.A.

MIX
Paper from
responsible sources
FSC® C104740
FSC
www.fsc.org

www.orionbooks.co.uk

To Larry Johnson
and the millions of others caught up
in the school-busing crisis of the 1970s,
aimed at integrating public education in America.

In memory of Earvin Johnson Sr.

In memory of Matthew Prophet, Jr.,
who rose from buck private to lieutenant colonel
in the U.S. Army while serving combat tours
in both Korea and Vietnam, who then
upon retirement from the service became an educator
who played a major role in those integration efforts.

In memory of George Fox.

In memory of Billy Packer, friend and mentor.

I get out on the break, and I just get crazy.
That's when I'm at my highest point.
And I feel it crazy down to my knees.

—EARVIN "MAGIC" JOHNSON, 1986

Contents

AUTHOR'S NOTE

Yes, this is a long book, but Earvin Johnson has lived a very big life, to the point that after five years of working on it, I was still down to the wire on the final page proofs, hustling to add in that Johnson was part of a group aiming up the largest deal ever for a sports franchise—to buy the National Football League's Washington Commanders for six billion dollars.

The time editing the book was also marked by the passing of key figures and witnesses to Johnson's career, including his father, Earvin Sr., and his high school coach, George Fox.

Fox alone patiently granted me more than fifty interviews, allowing me to dig into the richness of Johnson's quite singular adolescence. Numerous others, such as Fox's assistant Pat Holland and Johnson mentor Charles Tucker, did much the same. Their memories, along with those of lawyer George Andrews and agent Lon Rosen, are among the more than four hundred hours of interviews that I and my friend, veteran NBA reporter Gery Woelfel, did in building the Johnson story.

The book itself is a culmination of my own forty-five-year writing career, a tenure marked in the early days by my motoring across the

American basketball landscape in a 1984 Chevette diesel as I covered games and conducted interviews.

Financially strapped in 1992, I was sleeping in my rental car in the parking lot of the media hotel while covering Johnson's appearance at the All-Star Game in Orlando. Yes, I had my media credential and thus access to do interviews, but I experienced little of the supposed glamour of the NBA.

In 2020, my wife, Karen, digitized my archive of more than three hundred cassette tapes of interviews from 1982 to 2000, which turned up numerous overlooked recordings from 1990, of my talks with Magic Johnson, Pat Riley, Mychal Thompson, and other Lakers figures—long-forgotten interviews, never before transcribed, that became a rich contribution to this effort.

I first began writing about the Lakers in 1988 and in the time since have produced several books that told the story of the team in one fashion or another.

In so doing, I was afforded opportunities to do classic interviews with so many key figures, from George Mikan and the early Lakers to a variety of personalities involved with the Showtime era, including Johnson, Kareem Abdul-Jabbar, Jerry West, James Worthy, Michael Cooper, and others, a number of whom—Jerry Buss, Jack Kent Cooke, Chick Hearn, Bill Sharman, and others—are now since departed.

In producing this biography, I leaned heavily at times on those classic interviews and my earlier writings and research.

In the end, I have relied on everything I can bring together in attempting to tell this most unusual story of Magic, the tall boy who dared to dribble.

MAGIC

PROLOGUE

The fear comes with the moment.

How does a man that size move that fast with that high dribble, twisting one way, then the other, selling each turn so completely?

You can watch it all you want on videotape without finding a clue or even a dab of solace. It always seems to come to that instant where he'll look you dead in your eye, a suddenly fixed gaze, a quizzical expression that sends the jolt of panic.

What next?

Then, there it is, the blinding, truth-telling flash when he's all perfectly downhill on helpless you, you who have retreated in that noble effort to somehow do what the voice always tells you.

Stay in front of him.

And then it happens. His whole face blows up, cheeks full of air, the gaze finally completely narrowed on you, merciless as he almost nonchalantly flips the ball over his shoulder to the trailer coming directly behind him—*How in hell did he see that?*—and the dunk rains down on you the cold realization that he has put you just where you don't want to be, that there are witnesses and no place to hide, and you're thinking, *Motherfucker. Where are the cameras? There's gonna be evidence.*

Meanwhile, there's Lakers broadcast legend Chick Hearn, jumping on the pile of your misery and talking radio trash about it to the known world: *God and all his apostles could not have stopped that move!*

All you have to do is inhabit that moment once, and if you somehow managed to miss it before, you now understand the nickname so fully and completely that all questions are smashed.

Magic.

Earvin Johnson is prancing legs high on the break in one of his fancy, legendary, over-the-top summer all-star charity contests at UCLA's Pauley Pavilion, and he's got Larry Bird on the wing to his right, blond hair flying, running and straining to fill the lane like it's Game 5. Suddenly at full speed, what now looks like a six-nine, two-legged tarantula, a blur of impossibly long and lean, Johnson uncorks a high right-handed hesitation dribble all while looking off poor Larry, which helps open a gap to cross the ball over and dive left into the retreating crowd at the basket just as Larry begins to converge from the right, hands up, thinking he just might dunk it.

As Johnson rises up in the lane, knee lifted high, he flips the ball to his right hand to give one final tease of a look to Larry that freezes every defender in the process, then flips the ball back to his left to sort of finish a double clutch in the paint—*an assist to himself!!!!*—with everybody around him left slack-jawed and gawking.

Poor Larry, too.

"A 6-9 point guard, a one-man fast break," Bird would say when he first met Johnson. "I'd never seen that before."

No one had ever seen anything before remotely like Earvin "Magic" Johnson, Jr.

Oh, how dear Earvin loved to serve it up at high speed on the break, stretching his long arm out, offering the ball on a platter, letting the defender almost drool on it just before flipping it left to the teammate converging from the wing or pushing it right or wherever because everybody learned long ago to run with Magic, fill the lanes, eyes and hands ready for the gift, a gift that absolutely nobody foresaw or even thought possible.

"Earvin knew they were open before they knew they were open," sportswriter Fred Stabley, Jr., who covered the early years of Johnson's career, explained in 2019. "I always thought it was like he knew he was better than you and he was going to show you."

Nothing, it seemed, was ever the same with Johnson. Always different. *Always* different.

"Magic put on performances you can't believe," offered Doug Krikorian, longtime L.A. sportswriter. "Michael Jordan was dominant in the '90s when ESPN and cable were big. *USA Today* was big, when cable hit. People forget that cable wasn't that big in the '80s. Magic was phenomenal. Every game he played, he played great. He didn't give a damn about stats. He played in the NBA twelve seasons, and they were in the NBA Finals nine times. Does that tell you something about Magic?"

Only in the rarest of human occasions is the revolution so profound, so overwhelmingly obvious, that all that comes after it, all the decades of astounding play and evolution, can't touch it.

Magic.

In defiance of the physical world.

Finite. Complete. Perfect. Open only to pale imitation.

Jimi Hendrix in low-cut Chucks with a crazy-strung, left-handed, upside-down guitar, screeching and wah-wahing and wailing away into eternity. Rare true greatness is immune to the future like that.

Oh, it pays homage to the past. Marques Haynes. Cousy. Black Jesus. Pistol. Magic.

MAGIC!

To see that kind of showboating basketball leaves the impression that it is all easy and natural, all God's own perfect gift. All . . . fun.

No wonder the smile and the joy were so big. It's the "Gotcha!"

"I don't think," teammate James Worthy would say, "there will ever be another six-nine point guard who smiles while he humiliates you."

Trash talk? He didn't have to say a word. Just showed you his teeth.

The sheer embarrassment of it all helps explain why the showboaters were not welcome in the game, which for decades was lorded over by the stubbornest of people, false prophets touting false fundamentals.

After all, Bob Cousy, the game's great early showboater, got cut three times from his New York high school team.

Repeat. Bob Cousy got cut three times from his New York high school team. By a "dean" of coaches.

The early efforts of American pro basketball persisted through years of empty seats and failed franchises until the stubborn men broke down and began staging doubleheaders in Madison Square Garden with the Harlem Globetrotters.

Now, people would pay to see that, would come again and again to watch all the fun trickeration with amazed delight.

Just as they would later form a gathering delirium in the Great Western Forum in Los Angeles to watch . . .

Magic.

The patron saint of The Show.

"I never knew which place to look," recalled longtime NBA photographer Andrew Bernstein, perched on the baseline for so many of his games. "I never knew what Magic was gonna do every time he came down the court. The excitement in the Forum was incredible. Every game. Constantly."

The zebras were left with the same confusion, trying to track Johnson at high speed. "As a referee on fast breaks, you kind of read the player to where the ball was going," recalled ref Don Vaden. "With Magic, you couldn't. You never knew where it was going to end up."

"He made people want to see an NBA game," said former Utah Jazz coach Frank Layden. "He made it Showtime. He's glowing. He comes right at you."

"He understood that the game was about entertainment," explained Buck Williams, a seventeen-year NBA veteran who first encountered Earvin Johnson as a thirteen-year-old on summer vacation where he wowed a packed crowd at a public park in North Carolina. "From day one, when he picked up that basketball with a smile, he knew how important entertainment was. It's not just a game of basketball, of passing, shooting, and dribbling. It's a game of entertaining folks and how it translates into finance. He understood how entertainment equated to the bottom line."

Yet Johnson somehow presented all the flashiness the seeing eye could absorb and merged it with a pure and unbending desire to win . . .

Yep, Cousy did that, too.

"There was only one guy running a fast break who could do it better than Cousy," Cousy's own coach himself, Red Auerbach, once averred. "And that was Magic Johnson."

Far beyond that, Earvin "Magic" Johnson opened up the blue-sky vistas for the future of the sport by overcoming decades of coaching prejudice and stubbornness to weaponize the big man in ways never imagined. He did it against the game's deeply entrenched best inclinations, blowing right through every caution sign and flashing warning light that coaches could muster, converting hearts and minds at every little step along the way, despite his own nagging insecurities that only began to abate with his arrival in L.A., where he built a savvy alliance with the Lakers' great stoic of a center, Kareem Abdul-Jabbar, and with their coach, Pat Riley.

"It was a beautiful time," Johnson would recall of the era his ball wizardry instantly created known as Showtime. "We had graceful, beautiful players. Kareem with his skyhook. James Worthy with the beautiful floaters and finger rolls. Byron Scott with his beautiful jump shot. Michael Cooper with the way he played defense and the alley-oop for the Coop-a-Loop. Those are the type of things that we did that made Showtime. And they also changed basketball."

"Magic Johnson could make the simple plays look like they were the hardest in the world," said Lakers Hall of Famer Jerry West. "And he'd do them in a simple manner. He really wasn't flashy. Magic Johnson very rarely threw a pass behind his back. He just made the right pass at the right time."

Oh, sweet timing.

Johnson's charismatic presence, the way that he could literally dance through a game, produced a dramatic and seemingly instant success, first with a state championship for his high school team in 1977, followed by leading Michigan State to the mythical national college title in 1979, then capped it all by taking the Lakers to a dramatic pro championship as a rookie in 1980, a succession of victories that, in turn, brought him a raw and unprecedented power that he soon used to stun the sports world after just two seasons in the NBA by essentially firing his own championship coach.

At the time, no player in the history of American professional sport had wielded influence so publicly and so ruthlessly, yet he managed to survive the widespread fan outrage by producing yet more charm and victory, all with deft moves that presaged the coming age of great player power in the twenty-first century.

Virtually everything about him ultimately proved different, unprecedented right down to the tragic early end to his playing career.

In many ways, Johnson's greatest alliance was with his nemesis, Larry Bird. Together, they formed the grandest rivalry in the history of the sport, from college right on through the professional game. "Earvin changed a lot of things," observed Charles Tucker, the Lansing, Michigan, school psychologist who befriended an adolescent Johnson and eventually became his advisor/agent. "He and Bird changed the game on the floor, the way people viewed it off the floor, from a relationship point of view, from a business standpoint. It became a business for TV. The TV audience got much bigger. Every time him and Bird played it got high ratings, whether it was in college or the pros. They changed things. And they were smart enough to know what kind of power they had, too."

"Magic meant so much to the game," observed Lakers teammate Michael Cooper, the high-flying finisher on what seemed an endless array of Johnson's dramatic assists. "The key with Magic, and what makes a star turn into a superstar, a star is gonna shine by himself. A superstar is gonna make other people shine. That's what Larry Bird and Magic always did. They made the league what it is today."

The Controller

Johnson began this march to supreme success by fashioning his genius in pickup games on the courts of his hometown, Lansing, Michigan. It was there that Dale Beard first grasped the truth—if he was going to get anywhere in basketball, he better learn to mold his own game to the unorthodox, high-speed approach of the tall, smiling guy who seemed to have spent his whole life dribbling.

"He would say, 'Hey, you know what? I get the rebound, just fill the lanes, and if you don't look, you gonna get hit upside the head with the basketball,'" Beard recalls Johnson telling him with that broad, happy face that turned suddenly serious when he repeated the instructions as a warning.

"If you're not looking, you're going to get hit."

Beard's eyes grow warmer at the memory on a gray late-winter day in Lansing in 2019.

"It's just been incredible to have seen that and how that developed at a young age," he says. "People that didn't really see that, they couldn't even believe it, they wouldn't even believe that, because you just never saw big guys doing what he done on a playground.

"So, he would get the ball off the rim as a rebounder and we would just fill the lanes . . . left wing, right wing, and we'd just go," Beard says, animated by the memory. "And sure enough, he'd get you the ball where you wanted it, in stride, on time. It was just something you could cling on to, to say, 'Okay. I know what he's going to do. I know how he's going to play. So I gotta adjust to what he wants me to adjust to. I can't play my game.' So you had to do what he asked you to do or you weren't going to play."

Or you weren't going to play?

No point guard, no player, would ever dictate the game the way Earvin "Magic" Johnson did. To the point that he altered even coaching itself.

In articulating that experience again, Beard marvels at the supreme control Johnson discovered in the pickup laboratories of Lansing, a control he would extend to all the major and minor figures of his fast break of a basketball life: the coaches, the teammates, the rivals, the managers and owners, the locker room staff and ball boys, the ushers in the buildings where he played, the media figures drawn there to conjure up stories about him, the fans who read and saw them. They were all on his string.

Such control would mean everything to him from his earliest days playing the game, allowing him to fend off all the many questioners who said over and over again over the years that tall boys weren't allowed to dribble the basketball. From a young age, Johnson dug in his heels, determined to show anyone who doubted him, critics and rivals alike.

Thus, the growing tally of his control itself inspired the early awe and wonder, especially as witnesses grasped the art and speed and rhythm with which he delivered it. "There isn't anything singularly impressive about Magic Johnson," observed Bobby Knight, who coached against him and watched him interrupt the victory march of Knight's great University of Indiana teams. "He's encompassingly impressive."

From grade school on, Johnson's signature would be the no-look pass, just the sort of innovative fun that could vex coaches and teammates alike into sleepless nights.

No one could explain this talent better than another of the game's premier point guards, his onetime friend Isiah Thomas: "He's the only guy that I've ever seen that would look at a guy, time him, measure his speed, look away for about three seconds, look you off, and then hit that guy on the dime without even looking at him."

As grand and new as it all was, however, Johnson's story would ultimately prove to be much larger than his game, larger even than his own life, first as an emblematic presentation of race in America and how he used his gift and the basketball experience to peel away some of the layers of ugliness and misunderstanding. The backdrop for this was Michigan, where so many Black families had sought escape in the Great Migration away from the harsh and violent racial climate of the South.

It was in the midst of the charged atmosphere of the 1970s conflict over court-ordered busing to achieve integration that an adolescent Earvin Johnson first came into his shine.

From his early role in the school integration issues to his pairing with Bird to his later capturing of business success based on Black consumer preferences, Johnson's life would be infused with race. In many ways, that was the thing he cared about most, explained Lon Rosen, his longtime friend and agent.

"Race is a theme that binds much of Johnson's success," *Los Angeles Magazine* would declare in 2003. "With that smile—the feature for which he is so widely praised—he is white America's ideal of a nonthreatening black man, an image integral to his canonization, alongside the ultra-pale Larry Bird, as one of the NBA's twin saviors."

Magic

He was just fifteen when the nickname appeared in the local paper. It was the kind of thing that set off alarms with Christine, his deeply religious mother.

Magic?

A name like that left her cold.

It was blasphemous and immediately unsettled the world that she and her husband, Earvin Sr., had worked so hard to establish for their seven children. A name like that opened the window to the thought that things might not be just in God's hands, but in the devil's, too.

The nickname presented its own collection of problems, one that, as she feared, would stretch to forever.

In her spiritual journey, she had read the Bible often. Magic was not a word that held power there. Her world was about faith, love, and forgiveness, things that everyday people could have and hold and bring into their lives to help them endure the things that couldn't be endured.

Magic?

"She worried that the name would put bad ideas into my head," Johnson would say.

Bad ideas? Somehow it all eventually led to the notion that he could have unprotected sex with literally any and all that he met. And the record would show that he "met" many.

The mere nickname led his mother to glimpse all the wonder and heartache that lay ahead. She shuddered at the thought of it. Sure, he loved basketball, loved it every second, minute, hour of his life, which had been such a good thing, a blessing that he had it. But now this?

Magic?

A name like that set her to praying.

As for her son, a name like that was another sort of flashing neon sign, his reward, as a mere teen, for turning a dead, empty, soulless gym into ground zero for celebration.

Not surprisingly, the crowd picked up the sobriquet almost immediately. It rolled from the news pages right onto their tongues.

Magic!

It became a chant then that would ring through the decades in arenas all over the world.

Even if you left God out of it, a name like that came with warning signs all over it. His father knew that people in general were not to be trusted with that kind of control over your life. If they built you up, they could take you right down at their whimsical pleasure.

With a name like that, good wasn't nearly enough. You had to be almost perfect. Given a little time, a name like that could turn to ridicule, the kind that could haunt a lifetime.

What could Christine Johnson really do but pray?

Magic?

"Curse" might have been another word, if his mother had been the brooding sort.

As it was, she did all she could every day of the week. She lived her life as she was supposed to, and turned the rest over to God.

Nobody at the time could have possibly seen the vast, unimagined temptation that lay ahead. It was an era when recreational drugs and alcohol had gripped the youth population like never before. Yet those vices, despite all the pressures from his immense ambition and resulting fame, would hold no sway over him.

His addiction, beyond basketball, would quickly prove to be the human touch. Christine Johnson's sweet young boy would discover what the alpha male comes to know early in life, that his gift was an astoundingly magnetic attraction, the kind that could prompt seemingly rational everyday people to abandon caution to find some means of embracing him, the more intimately the better.

And so he would become, in the vernacular of that increasingly promiscuous era, Mr. Magic Johnson, the double entendre of which so often left him chuckling, gloating even.

"Let's face it," he would boast, "'Magic' is a romantic, sexy name."

It was certainly that, until finally it wasn't, until his long trail of carelessness with sexually transmitted disease caught up with him and snuffed out his playing career and turned his great smile into a deeply furrowed brow.

It was then, at the end of a long and much celebrated youth, that the man in full began to emerge, when for a second time his story became bigger than his own life, with a diagnosis that thrust him into the midst of the global AIDS crisis.

It would lead to his eventual transition to the full entrepreneurial life, which allowed Johnson to fashion his own sort of Black power. The Smithsonian Channel would highlight the weight of this power in a documentary called *Afrofuturism*, in which professor Damion Kareem Scott of the City University of New York described the emotion of watching the end credits roll for the 2018 film *Black Panther*, in the Magic Johnson cinema on 124th Street in Harlem.

Oh so quietly, subtly, the sense of history sank in. Scott rose, got another bag of popcorn, and watched the film again and contemplated all that it meant.

Which leaves us now to ponder, chief among the many questions about the mystery that is Earvin "Magic" Johnson, Jr., how?

Just how did it all happen?

PART I

LANSING

1

BOOM, BABY

By March 1990, Jerry West had had a good long look at Magic Johnson, had witnessed it all up close, first the transformation Johnson had brought to the Los Angeles Lakers a decade earlier, and then all that followed: the championships, the MVP seasons and performances, the virtual onslaught of victory and success, the building-pumping celebrations at timeouts after every fast-break run, the high fives and hugs and general glee that shook both Los Angeles and the National Basketball Association out of the deep slumber and ennui that had settled over the American pro game like a blanket in the late 1970s.

All that Jerry West had witnessed unfolded in sharp contrast to his own Hall of Fame career that saw West and his Lakers team mates suffer through the agony of seven straight losses in the league's championship series between 1962 and 1970 only to finally succeed on the eighth attempt, a seemingly joyless victory in 1972 that had been met by numbness and confusion and conflict in the locker room afterward.

With all the winning in the 1980s, Johnson had helped a bit to shoo away the pesky ghosts and demons that for far too long occupied the belfry of Jerry West's personal torment. Johnson and West had quietly formed a partnership over the years, the executive's agony balanced by Johnson's great joy and success.

That contrast, in part, was the reason this writer had traveled that March of 1990 to interview West over two days in a hotel room in Dallas, where West had gone to scout college basketball talent in search of the next good player for the team.

By that time, West, the self-appointed guardian of the Lakers, was on his way to becoming what many considered the game's top front office figure. West "could spot talent through the window of a moving train," *L.A. Times* columnist Jim Murray would declare during the era.

West, indeed, was a manic genius and a nearly impossible perfectionist. He could see so many things in the furious action on the court and was known as an "active" general manager, the kind who never hesitated to address problems he saw with Lakers players. Just how "active" was West? One former Lakers head coach, Del Harris, explained in a 2004 interview that the team was never really his, but Jerry's.

During the Showtime era, West the GM was both vigilant and instructive with so many players, but he revealed over that weekend in 1990 that over the years he had hardly ever said a word to Johnson about his play and even then only if he thought Johnson was becoming "predictable."

The great Magic predictable? You might just as well have accused Marilyn Monroe of lacking her steamy charm.

At that moment in 1990, Magic Johnson was perhaps the sporting world's most widely admired and successful star. Over the years, it seemed that just about everybody had come to love Magic. And that had included a high school junior in Wilmington, North Carolina, way back in 1980, by the name of Mike Jordan.

Yes, as a teen, the once and future king of basketball had had one true idol—Magic Johnson. Even then, Jordan's competitive nature rendered him absolutely unsparing in his disdain for rivals and other players. Yet Jordan tried to mimic so many things he saw in Johnson's play that for a time he even fancied himself a point guard, attempting in high school practice each day the no-look passes and brilliant fast-break play of his idol.

How great was the infatuation? Jordan gave himself the nickname "Magic Mike" and by his senior year in high school had a vanity plate by that same title for his very first car. Jordan drove all over his hometown proudly telling the world that he was Magic Mike. Yet when Jordan got to the University of North Carolina as a freshman the next fall, coach Dean Smith promptly advised him to lose the nickname.

There was only one Magic, Smith supposedly explained.

Jordan, of course, went on from there to become what fans worldwide would call "the God of basketball."

At times over his career, Johnson himself had occupied a similar roost in the hierarchy of the sport. In fact, his accomplishments and infectious style of play defined the great Showtime era of Lakers basketball with a team that so often seemed to play beyond the reach of everybody else. As such, Johnson came to occupy a status as the game's last great analog star, one who finished his playing career in the early 1990s only to watch the digital world rapidly overtake the game as well as its messaging and marketing, just in time to lift up that kid from Wilmington who once considered himself Magic Mike.

These circumstances help explain a belief among many serious students of the game as well as among many, many fans that Magic Johnson, along with Jordan and others, should be in the conversation as perhaps the greatest basketball player of all time.

"I never quite understood why he's never been involved in the conversations for the greatest player ever, what he brought to the game," remarked longtime NBA coach Alvin Gentry, a comment echoed many times over by numerous veteran observers of American pro basketball.

The argument goes that if Michael Jordan is indeed the so-called God of Basketball, at the very least, Johnson is the Other God, one who accomplished so much in addition to presiding over what many consider to be the greatest era in the history of the game, the 1980s.

For others, such lofty status seems an odd place for a player who, by his own admission, never jumped all that high; who was considered to have a suspect jump shot; who by far prized winning over scoring or acrobatics, who came into the NBA with what many experts considered a weak left hand, a serious limitation for anyone attempting to survive as a point guard in the league, especially a tall person with an impossibly high dribble ripe for the plucking.

"I still had doubts about myself," Johnson himself would confess, looking back on his early days as a rookie in 1979. "I wasn't sure I could make it in this league."

Which, in turn, helps explain why that March of 1990, long after he had seen it all, Jerry West revealed that he wasn't convinced in 1979 that the Lakers should have taken Magic Johnson as the number one overall pick in the NBA draft.

Speaking for recorded interviews, West said Johnson's great run of leadership and success would remind him of a conclusion about scouting talent: You could see what players could do on the floor, their physical capabilities, but you couldn't always read their hearts.

"I thought he would be a very good player," West admitted. "I had no idea he would get to the level that he did. No idea. But, see, you don't know what's inside of people. Physically, you can see what they can do on the court. The things you could see you loved. But you wondered where he was going to play in the NBA, how he would be able to do it."

That comment then pretty much summed it up: Earvin "Magic" Johnson was defined as that unseen quality, that great mystery of human performance that made the business of talent scouting seem so uncertain.

West paused a moment in the interview, searching for an answer to his own question about Johnson's greatness, then added, "Through hard work, he just willed himself to take his game to another level. I don't think anyone knew he had that kind of greatness in him. The athletic ability is the easiest thing to see, but it does not constitute what a great basketball player is."

Asked to expound on greatness, West observed that while there were a number of very good players at any given time in pro basketball, truly great players could be counted on one hand.

Looking back on the 1980s, West said, "Obviously Magic Johnson is one of them. Larry Bird.

"Obviously Michael Jordan," West added, then let the thought trail off from there.

The tremendous challenge to being a truly great player is hard for the public to understand or even see, West finally offered. "It is a burden."

As for the nature of Johnson's particular greatness, West said, "It's like a macho thing. Magic Johnson had a macho-ness that came out in him, a desire that 'No one is gonna beat me.'"

Johnson would display that quality night after night over many seasons, that vast intangible factor, prima facie evidence that he possessed perhaps the biggest heart in the history of a game of very big hearts.

The Scene

In explaining himself in 1990, Jerry West struggled with several observations to explain what exactly allowed Johnson to find greatness before finally settling on this: "When he was born somebody did sprinkle a little extra dust on him."

Perhaps, then, that was it, the answer to the mystery, one that decades later would still stand as the best possible conclusion. Extra magical dust at birth, a supernatural influence of the highest order, falling all around a special child.

The record shows that Johnson was delivered into the world on August 14, 1959, a Friday, in Lansing, Michigan, the fourth of seven children and the youngest of three boys in the family of Earvin Sr. and Christine Johnson.

Maybe the supernatural influence came that weekend from the electrical storm and slashing rain that saw a tremendous bolt of lightning strike a massive transformer, resulting in a booming explosion that startled residents of the city and left many without power.

Maybe little baby Earvin had gotten an extra charge from a bolt of that lightning.

Or maybe it was the news story on the front page of the *Lansing State Journal* that very morning, about the birth of a chicken with three hearts.

After all, the child would one day earn the nickname Magic, so it stood to reason that his formula might include a little voodoo or a taste of the occult.

Another thought is that the timing of his arrival presented another strong indication of his impending stardom. That very weekend of Johnson's birth, school officials in Lansing were hosting an open house at a brand-new version of Everett High School with its fancy 1950s state-of-the-art basketball gymnasium, a gym that would someday bear his name.

Understandably, baby Earvin couldn't make an appearance to christen the gym that weekend. It would take fifteen years and a series of unexpected events before he showed up to make the hardwood there one of the hallowed sites in the history of American basketball.

No, the events of that day pose just one of the many mysteries of his great life, observed Lon Rosen, his longtime friend and agent. "For example, why was he, the third male child in the family, given the name of Earvin Johnson, Jr.? That name usually goes to the oldest male."

Perhaps Earvin Sr. and Christine sensed that this gangly newborn was going to be something special, although that seems unlikely because the Johnsons adamantly considered each of their seven children special.

Actually, if you had to settle on one single thing that drove the life of Magic Johnson to astounding success, it might well be the scene at the hospital that day of the exhausted young mother, Christine, holding close the swaddled child, with his father, Earvin Sr., sitting dutifully, quietly, happily at her bedside.

One of the first things the nurses and staff had noticed about the mother was the smile, the dimples. Christine Porter Johnson had been gifted with a genuine and profound sweetness long steeped in abiding faith, the kind that calmed people in her presence and just about always summoned the better angels of their nature.

She loved to put people at ease, to project her genuine sense of caring, to allow the emotion of her religious devotion to flow with its quiet force. Neither did it hurt that she enjoyed a good laugh and a warm embrace. She had learned from a young age that life was dear and you had to hold on to it. After all, she had been hugged many times in her life by her own mother.

If there was something else that the staff noticed about Christine Johnson it was probably her regularity. She had pumped out son Quincy first in 1956, followed by baby Larry in 1957, then daughter Lily Pearl in 1958.

And then, right on cue, was this baby, Earvin Jr., in '59.

It was the kind of output that had been prized by farm families for centuries, only Christine Johnson was no longer working the North Carolina soil where her family before her had toiled away in futility for decades.

At seventeen, she had watched her beloved mother, Mary, waste away with kidney disease until she finally passed at age forty-seven in late 1953, leaving Christine to raise her two younger siblings, circumstances that, as Christine would reveal later, led to her becoming a teenaged mother herself, just as her mother before her had done. It was so typical of the subsistence farm life, where so many women died young, either from childbirth or lack of medical care, circumstances that often doomed their daughters to become mothers too soon.

Christine's mother, Mary Della Jenkins Porter, had lived a hard, short life as the wife of a sharecropper and tenant farmer. Yet her struggles against privation and poverty seemed in many ways to matter little because she met them with a faith and love of spiritual worship that she instilled in Christine and the rest of her large family, the kind of faith that had been passed down to her through the generations of a family that faced little but unrelenting misery decade after decade after decade, lives devoid of anything that resembled the sort of victory Christine's baby Earvin would come to know.

Indeed, if there is any fact or theme that emerges from the study of Magic Johnson's life and legacy, it is an indomitable spirit that stretches across the generations of his family all the way back to his great-great-great-grandfathers born in the 1830s in North Carolina in the times of slavery, a collective will that reveals Johnson's story and that of his family to be one of the human spirit, a sustaining strength that allowed them to endure heartbreak and failure and calamity, sometimes of an epic nature.

The untimely passing of Christine's own dear mother in 1953 had been one of those moments.

It wasn't too long afterward that the tall, quiet soldier came into Christine's life, when her cousin, who was stationed at a North Carolina army base, brought one of his buddies home one weekend.

Christine was soon intrigued by this shy stranger from Mississippi, a young man named Earvin Johnson. She would later confide that something about him made her feel sorry for him.

It seemed only a matter of months before he was out of the army and she had packed up and said goodbye to the farm life to head north with him to Lansing, Michigan, where he had the promise of a job in an auto plant. Soon it would seem like she had boarded a time machine that had whisked her away from the tenant farm life and into another universe, one with flush toilets and running water. It wasn't long after that, she once recalled, that she was headed into her own crash course in motherhood.

Now, on this Friday in August 1959, her husband sat beside her in the hospital room, his joy tempered only by his thoughts of how he was going to feed his beautiful young family. After all, he had fathered three other children before he met and married Christine, and those children would remain a part of his life, often coming from their lives in the South to stay with the Johnson family in their cramped Michigan home.

With all that was to unfold in the coming years Earvin Sr. would come to be known in the Lansing community as a man of few words, offering a silence that many considered off-putting, creating at times a sense that he was ill at ease or even perhaps possessed of contempt.

To his family, however, he was a man of a steady but low-key joy and humor, a father willing to work two jobs while starting a trash-hauling business on the side to provide for his children.

"Once you've met Earvin Sr., you don't know if you've met him," a family friend would later explain to *Inside Sports* magazine.

"He's an old-school, southern guy, born in Mississippi," explained Greg Eaton, a Lansing businessman and family friend, in a 2020 interview. "He came here as a young man. I think he got here when he was around twenty. I was in high school when they came, that was 1955. Then, in '58, I worked in the Fisher Body plant with him. Hardworking guy. He got hired and never left there. In '55, General Motors, Oldsmobile . . . you could come here, walk across the street and get a job. Jobs were that available then.

"Earvin Senior's a big guy. He's about six-four, with big hands. Strong. Real strong. I remember how he would throw big, heavy things on the truck like they were nothing."

Because he was so quiet, people tended to underestimate Earvin Johnson, Sr., but his silence hid much complexity, said Charles Tucker, the Lansing school psychologist who became a family friend and then, surprisingly, the son's first agent and advisor. "He could see right through you."

Actually, that would prove true of Christine as well, Tucker added in a 2019 interview. "Both parents were very quiet and very deceiving. But once you got to know them it scared you how knowledgeable they were, how patient and how smart they were. . . . They knew how to deal with people. You think that you might be fooling them or running something by them, but they're way ahead of the game. And the problem is, they won't let you know it."

Time would confirm the father's gift for reading the complexities in the quickly evolving world of his son.

"My father taught me strength," the son would later say.

Strength, indeed. Earvin Sr.'s conservative, measured relationship with his celebrated son would serve to assure a magical, almost perfect timing that would change the course of global basketball history, which would be their own secret delight for many years, the quiet hum of a joy father and son shared only between themselves.

So many athletes lack guidance, a friend of the Johnson family once observed. "Magic had all the direction in the world."

2

SMILE

The chuckles and grins for Christine Johnson's newest baby boy came so often and brought such delight to all who witnessed them that there was no way they could just be attributed to mere gas.

Nope. The laughter and grins were decidedly real, which meant his parents and siblings and grandparents and cousins, whoever was around really, found so much joy in them that it soon enough became the business of nearly everybody to greet him with a funny face or a noise or toss him up and down until he squealed and giggled and cackled.

People seemed to try to outdo each other in terms of who could get the most delight out of the chubby giggle box in the crib.

Thus, his happy countenance was reinforced every time he gazed into his mother's loving, welcoming face, which in turn became sort of his own mirror of smiles.

"His mom has a beautiful smile," Greg Eaton offered in his 2020 interview, repeating an impression that quickly registered among family and friends that baby Earvin from the start surely had not just his mother's smile but later would add her warmth and personality to their list of similarities. "She's just a beautiful person. She's a hugger," Eaton explained.

"Man, when she hugs you, you know you've been hugged," agreed Missy Fox, another family friend.

Of her family's many precious heirlooms, the embrace was a special one that baby Earvin would one day take from his mother out into the basketball world and use it to infuse the competition with theretofore unrealized levels of emotion.

But it would be the smile that held everything together. Earvin Johnson would have one of the two greatest smiles of the twentieth century, *Sports Illustrated* would declare in 1996. The other? Louis Armstrong.

His great charisma was all mostly wrapped as a gift from Christine.

"My mother likes to have fun," Johnson himself would say many times over the coming years. "She loves to talk, and I got that from her."

This natural connection between mother and son meant that often in those early days, if she smiled, he smiled. That his or his mother's smile survived at all seems miracle enough considering Christine now had four children under five years old and would soon add reinforcements, three more girls, including a set of twins.

In fact, the Johnson household had quickly transformed into baby central, a juggling act of diapers and feeding sessions and activity and mayhem that drove young Christine through a punishing schedule.

Fortunately, her husband's mother, Lillie May Johnson, soon relocated to Lansing, as did Christine's younger brother James, to help a bit in keeping the assembly line of child-rearing up and running, with the boys in one bedroom, the girls in another, and the parents in a third with whoever the current infant happened to be.

Young Earvin apparently chuckled through it all, which revealed the essential truth of life for a child born with an easy and infectious smile. The more they laugh, the more people are eager to make them laugh. For the blessed few in those circumstances, the smiles and laughs feed on the smiles and laughs, creating mostly a happy cycle of days.

Some might argue that his smile became the primary force driving the life of Earvin Johnson, Jr., one that was constantly competing with the hugs to gain an edge in the emotional power he put forth. There would be so many other forces, of course, but this smile would be the first, and in many regards the main one.

It meant that people wanted to please him. That would be the primary truth of his life. And, in turn, he wanted to please them back.

Even later, as a child, young Earvin seemed intent on pleasing his mother, even when she spanked him, his siblings would recall. His tears would hardly be dry before young Earvin would come back around her, smiling and trying to regain her good graces.

From his earliest moments, the smile had helped soften any opposition he encountered.

Soon enough the baby teeth had come in to fill out the countenance, which so perfectly balanced the broad nose and warm, expressive eyes captured in the early photographs of his kindergarten and primary days. He was so sweet then, his head tilted often in that sudden tenderness that only the truly innocent possess.

It would be only a matter of time before he discovered the mysterious allure of the game. "Smooth floor, round ball," Boston Celtics legend Red Auerbach once offered in describing the perfect physics of basketball.

Everyone who has ever loved "hoops" knows there are many stages of learning to play before a baller actually discovers Auerbach's nirvana on a wooden gym floor.

Rolled-up socks, for example, and other laundry fashioned into a ball provided a good start, especially for young lads faced with that tricky Michigan weather and their mother's strict rules about bouncing balls in the house. Good luck dribbling rolled-up socks. Thus, there was little question that that earliest stage of the game first required imagination. That meant a pencil mark high enough on the wall could work as a basket. No dunking allowed. That would come first on the family's wastebasket or empty clothes hamper. Still, the parameters of the game were first established there and drummed into him again and again while he was going against his older brothers indoors on wintry days, a competition stirred by the basketball-loving Earvin Sr., whose rare quality time with his growing sons usually came on Sunday afternoons before the TV set watching that era's limited selection of NBA games and other sports.

The women in the household would have preferred some other programming, sister Lily Pearl once recalled with a laugh, but on Sunday afternoons in basketball season the men ruled.

Those sessions showed all the stars of 1960s pro basketball as giant figures to emulate: Wilt Chamberlain, Bill Russell, Jerry West, and a host of others, all of them presented as wondrously talented competitors complete with commentary from Earvin Sr. for his children on how to play the game.

Perhaps no one ever took such an introduction to heart the way young Earvin Johnson, Jr., did, for it remained hallowed in his memory. And with good reason. For the first time in hundreds of years of American culture, televised sports and other programming had begun displaying the competence of Black males, countering a systematic and overwhelmingly negative presentation in virtually every form of media the culture produced: newspapers, handbills, magazines, minstrel shows, public speeches, silent films, then talking movies, the entire works, a nonstop flood of hateful messages.

In truth, the NBA's presentation of this competence was far more of a fascinating revelation for Earvin Sr., who had been raised in the harshly enforced racial caste system of Mississippi, than it was for his young children. For Earvin Sr., a man who took everything in life in measured silence, a man who had come of age in the early 1950s as his home state ran through one spasm after another of violence against Black males, Sunday afternoons offered a moment, seemingly innocent and nonchalant, flickering on a black-and-white TV screen, one that few in America could articulate or describe at the time, but it was clearly a moment that quietly reached deep into hearts in the Johnson household and far beyond.

Down on Main Street

As the childhood years passed, they brought with them an unspoken acknowledgment of the status of Earvin Jr., which, among a number of things, led to the terms of endearment accorded him early in life. Being a junior, he was soon called Junebug or EJ or just E, or Junior, each name a layer of meaning and identity for his young persona and certainly critical practice for the day when he would have to manage being both Earvin and his alter ego, Magic. His would prove to be a life with an array of fashionable and fun nicknames.

Having been properly instructed by his father, it wouldn't take long for his basketball-crazy world to come fully alive, never mind the forecast, just shovel the snow off the court.

And then when the weather broke?

The light could flash so harshly on those bright, warm Michigan days, as if the sun itself knew the time was short so it had to cram as much intensity as possible into each moment, with skies so blue and clear it seemed many days like they were wrapped in cellophane. All across his neighborhood there came to be a sense that no one rolled through these blessed days quite like young Earvin, his high right-handed dribble pinging off the sidewalk everywhere he went, even on errands to the store, never mind the bag of groceries carefully balanced on his left arm or the uneven nature of the concrete sidewalks and pavement that defined his world around the family's yellow three-bedroom, one-bath house on Middle Street, not far from where Earvin Sr. endured long shifts at the plant pounding out Oldsmobile bodies each night in the "grinding boot," where he worked as a spot welder with sparks flying.

Although the true impact would come much later, when his children had time to contemplate it, the father's example had already begun to frame the lives of each of his offspring, his long hours at work in the plant, the burn holes in his clothes and other evidence of the intensely physical nature of his employment, the second efforts he made at extra part-time jobs and then starting his own trash-hauling business, his utter exhaustion arriving home in the wee hours, often falling asleep in the tub at the end of another long run. Then rising each morning to haul trash, relieved a bit by a three-hour break before heading into the plant at three for another long shift. And if providence somehow ever allowed a day off, good luck trying to sleep in a bit on mornings with the young, energetic brood bouncing around the household and fighting over use of the single toilet.

"Hardworking family, a big family," recalled Greg Eaton. "I think there was seven in the family, three boys and four girls. His dad worked at the Fisher Body plant and worked on the line and they had a truck to pick up rubbish, which Earvin worked on too and the boys worked on."

Johnson would later share that memory with George Fox, his high school coach: "So, he'd go around to different places and pick up their trash and haul it off to the trash dump. Earvin was telling us one time, when we got to talking about how hard he works and everything, and Earvin told us, 'When I was a little guy, I used to ride around on my dad's pickup, and we'd haul trash. One day I picked up this barrel and dumped the goods out of it, and my dad was in the truck and he looked back. And he says, "Earvin are you finished with that barrel?"' Earvin told his father yes. And then he recalled, 'My dad says to me, "Earvin, we don't leave property looking like that. You go back over there and you pick up that trash and all that stuff laying around where that barrel is sitting." He made me go back over there and pick up every piece. That's the first and last time he ever had to tell me that.' Earvin said that carried over every day in his work life. Don't do the job halfway; do it right. And Earvin told us that was the most basic thing anybody ever taught him."

The father often backed up each lesson with his own pithy saying about work ethic and embracing personal responsibility. "You got a choice," Earvin Sr. was known to say. "You either root and be a hog, or you die a pig."

His determination to work and work and work some more had almost killed him by the time the younger Earvin was twelve. No matter how much it hurt, the father was intent on ignoring the pain in his side, until he almost died from a burst appendix, just as he ignored the blurred vision and dramatic weight loss and constant urination, all because he was trying to get in as many hours as possible at the auto body plant—until he was diagnosed with diabetes. His thought never seemed to be for himself but only for what he could do to provide for his family.

"He always hoped we'd do something in life, you know," the son would say of the father. "He didn't want me to ever join him, hammering them bodies. He wanted something better for me."

These lessons and sacrifices of the father soon were burned indelibly into family memory, as were Christine's efforts to raise and manage and direct her handsome troop through the constantly shifting stages of seven different childhoods (a number that jumped to ten whenever Earvin Sr.'s three children from a previous relationship came to stay in the household). And that was before all the children turned school age and Christine added the job of school custodian and then cafeteria worker to her impossible household schedule.

Each day was a nonstop whirlwind, the comprehension of which could easily overwhelm either parent even later when they had pause to look back on it, the thought of all of them crammed into the cramped frame house with its one bathroom (as Earvin Jr. recalled, you learned at a young age to take care of business quickly on busy mornings).

The parents' diligence and sacrifice registered not just with the family but with the entire community as something to behold. "When you work that hard and you have that many kids and raise them, and all of them came out great . . ." Greg Eaton offered. "That takes a heck of a man, it takes a heck of a marriage with him and his wife and their faith in God."

The house may have been impossibly crowded, the days a blur of activity, but beneath all of the chaos and motion sat a rock-solid platform.

For the parents the only respite in these double-shift lives came on Sundays, and that only after putting in their time at Lansing's Union Missionary Baptist Church, where the services refilled their tanks and recharged their emotional batteries with the faith that made the whole thing happen in the first place.

Eaton, who would go on to become an immensely successful businessman and community pillar in Lansing, got a view of the Johnson operation through his work at the Fisher Body plant with Earvin Sr.

"When I went into the plant, I was just eighteen and we always talked sports," Eaton recalled.

Johnson, who rarely revealed much to anyone he met, opened up about his own days playing the game in Mississippi. "We talked sports all the time. We went to games. He liked basketball, but he liked all sports."

And Earvin Sr. loved cars, loved Oldsmobiles, loved making them despite the challenges and pressures of feeding his family with what amounted to double shifts five or six days a week, all of it undertaken for that pleasure of a little personal time on Sunday afternoons.

It stood to reason that young Earvin, the namesake with a heart so obviously full, would hasten out into the world eager to do his father's bidding, and not in a small way.

The family movie camera seldom found Junebug in those days as the 1960s unfolded, but when it did, he knew how to find it back, directing his profoundly happy gaze into the lens, the smile deepening as he proudly stretched out the dribble high and then low, his tail dropped in a stoop, his head up as he let the ball rise again and then fall, his personal yo-yo. And then he was off once more, with neighbors fussing at the eternal annoying thump of the rubber ball when he was up and out early in the morning, headed out to the courts at nearby Main Street School, where he would often spend his summer days lost in the game and deliriously happy about it, breaking only to go home for a quick lunch and then back at it, again and again and again, his young life seemingly one with the ball.

"People thought I was crazy," Johnson would say, looking back. "They really, seriously did. It would be 7:30 and they'd be going to work, and they'd say, 'There's that crazy Junebug, hoopin'.'"

"It was always basketball, basketball, day and night," his father once explained. "We never had to worry about his whereabouts, just go to Main Street School and he'd be there with his buddies."

"I've had a basketball in my hands since I was seven years old,"

Johnson would say at age sixteen. "My dad played in Mississippi and my two uncles were good. I guess they started me out."

Being a large child had its challenges, but you couldn't tell it from his class picture, with Earvin standing in the back row with his broad smile revealing a missing tooth. "I was big for my age, even then," Johnson once remembered. "But I still wanted to play with kids my own age."

He did a lot of watching in third and fourth grade as the older players in school went at it on the court. "When the older kids would leave the playground, I'd go out and try to imitate what I'd seen them do," he once told sportswriter Fred Stabley. "Pretty soon they were pushing me into the games."

He cited two older boys, Charlie Ford and Bob Riddle, as being the lead culprits to get him to join their games because of his size. "They dragged me out on the court with the older kids," he recalled. "I was scared to death. They'd just play and beat on me all the time and make me cry."

It was an odd reaction, considering he had older brothers, but the pattern had been established for his formative years—always playing against older, better talent at virtually each stage of his development.

"I got beat up pretty good, but I learned," Johnson once explained.

The school's playground was hard by the busy roadway, and the atmosphere included the seemingly constant roar of trucks rolling down nearby I-496, the *Lansing State Journal* would later report. "A cracked asphalt basketball court not much bigger than a patio. The nets sagged, the rims wobbled and a bad pass meant you'd be dancing with traffic passing by the Main Street School."

On some occasions, Earvin Sr. found a little time to slip away there for a game of one-on-one, his son once recalled. "I'd never beat him. . . . Look, he taught me a valuable lesson: Don't play your father! 'Cause . . . it's no fouls unless he calls them. And he's got all the tricks—holding you with one arm, then shooting with the other one. He'll hit you, then shoot, then foul on you. But I'll tell you what, I loved him for it, because that made me tough. I knew I couldn't beat him crying and whining, and that was his whole purpose."

Junebug could also coax brother Larry or even Quincy or younger sister Evelyn there to play, and that was what passersby from the neighborhood would often see, Earvin and brother Larry going at each other. Yet if one of his siblings wasn't available, it didn't matter.

"When I was a kid, I would play myself, one on one, full court during the summer," Johnson explained.

His world came fully alive for the 1966–67 NBA season when the family watched rookie guard Dave Bing breathe life into the moribund Detroit Pistons. Earvin, like all the other boys, wanted to be somebody on the court down on Main Street.

"I'd be Dave Bing on Detroit and then maybe Wilt on the Lakers," he recalled. "I'd be saying to myself, 'Here comes Dave. He shoots the jumper. Good!' Then I'd be Wilt and, 'There he goes with the finger roll. Yeah!' I'd always hit the last shot for the team I wanted to win. It helped me learn a lot of different things. How to dribble and rebound and shoot the ball. I'd watch a game on TV and I couldn't wait to try new things out."

"He liked Wilt, you know," his father recalled of his son's grade school days. "Wilt was who he wanted to be." Wilt, the tallest, most powerful and dominant figure in the world of the basketball gods on TV.

Main Street School wasn't just Johnson's basketball court. It was the place where he first engaged with the world, as both the school and Lansing in general offered him fascinating opportunities as the 1960s wore on.

Eaton himself was half of a pair of older mentors, who soon caught young Earvin's eye due to the example they set as aspiring young businessmen and community figures.

Johnson also met the other half of that duo of young Black businessmen, Joel Ferguson, at Main Street School. In time, Ferguson would go on to become a prominent civic leader in Lansing and a longtime trustee at Michigan State University. But back then, in the 1960s, he was merely the young man in charge of the playground and summer activities at Main Street School.

"That's where Earvin learned to play basketball," Ferguson said proudly in 2020.

The circumstances sound almost made-up, as if someone might

be trying to concoct in retrospect a seemingly perfect, revisionist youth for Earvin Johnson, but closer examination confirms that his formative years were amazingly organic, from Main Street School to his many hours at the local Boys Club.

They weren't drama-free, however, nor short on good fortune. At age nine he nearly drowned until a lifeguard pulled him unconscious from a swimming pool, an incident that left him with a lifelong fear of wading beyond waist deep in any water.

Yet beyond that, most of the contrary incidents in his young life seemed mild and familiar. His father, for example, once discovered Junebug had pilfered some candy from a nearby store, paddled him, and sent him back to confess his crime. And as Earvin moved into adolescence he became practiced in the art of slipping away from his lawn-mowing chores to play yet more basketball, the typical deception of youth.

Both mother and father frequently declared over the years that their son hardly ever gave them any trouble or concern, so much so that Johnson sometimes seemed too good.

"He wasn't perfect," Charles Tucker would offer, but it would be hard to prove it from the recollections of Tucker himself and many others from Lansing who witnessed the era.

Early in his grade school experience he encountered his first true rival, Jay Vincent, a large child in his own grade in a school from the east side of Lansing, presaging Johnson's career blessed by a run of extraordinary competitive relationships, from Larry Bird to Isiah Thomas to Michael Jordan. But after his own brothers, the first rival was the tall boy from across town.

"I met Earvin Johnson way back in third grade," Vincent recalled in a 2019 interview. "He was playing for Main Street. He was nine years old and I was nine years old. I was playing for Holmes Street, and they came over and they played us in a game, which I still tell to this day. We ended up winning the game by one point and then Magic went over there and talked to the scorekeeper, and just like that, it was a magic trick or something. Because they changed the score and they won. So I tell that story all the time. We just laugh about it and laugh about it. But that happened before he was Magic, he did that magic trick."

Those early contests proved to be a preview, in small scale, of a rivalry that would carry through high school, right up to the point they became college teammates.

In third grade, Junebug was already showing a penchant for peeling the rebound off the boards and heading upcourt, Vincent recalled. "We were about the same height. We were pretty young, almost nine years old, maybe a little bit under five foot. We were pretty tall for our age. But he was a really skinny guy. I always had more meat than he had, you know."

Taken together, these things reinforced the fact that, more than anything, Main Street was the place where he began to display character and deep emotional intelligence and cunning, traits that came back again and again to his mother in narrative, just about everywhere she would go in Lansing.

Christine Johnson recalled running into one of Earvin's grade school teachers in 1992 who had a tale about his time in a class that had descended into mayhem. "She laughed and started telling me a story about him," the mother recalled. "It was the first day of school in her first year of teaching. Earvin stood up and told his classmates to get in their seats, to behave, to listen to the teacher. She said everybody stopped and did just what he said to do."

The teacher with the story was likely Greta Dart, who taught him in fifth grade. Young, blond, and blue-eyed, she was just barely five feet tall and quickly came to favor Earvin, who would later remember having a crush on her. Her husband, Jim, drove a beverage truck. The Darts, who had no children, were his first serious encounter at becoming close with white people.

When the boys in school wanted to start a team and needed an adult to supervise, Jim, a basketball fanatic in his own right who played in the city's rec leagues, became what Johnson would later call his first coach.

"Jim Dart helped coach me in sixth grade and he's really meant a lot to me," Johnson would tell the *State Journal* as a high school junior. "He's really meant a lot to me. He sent me to a couple of camps and I was able to learn a great deal."

Soon enough, Dart was taking young Earvin along with him on his route delivering beverages to area stores and would joke that his route took much longer because Earvin was always engaging the people in the stores in conversation.

"I hired him to mow the grass once, and I assumed it was getting done because I could hear the mower," Jim Dart once told writer Joseph Dalton. "And when I looked, there was the mower going around in circles at one end of the yard, and Earvin at the other, talking to somebody."

Over the years, the Darts would grow to seem almost like a second family to him—Johnson came to describe them as his godparents—driving him to events, helping to pay for camps and other opportunities, taking note of his academic work, among other things, and helping to provide a bit of relief from the often cramped life in the house on Middle Street.

It takes little time for public school teachers to identify their allies and pets in the classroom, which meant that word of the overwhelmingly positive nature of this large child named Earvin spread quickly through the school's educator ranks from his earliest days there.

"He was an easy-going boy, a good student," one of his teachers, Dorothy Tomaschek, once told the *Lansing State Journal*.

By fifth grade he was five-six, pushing five-seven and moving on up. His size meant there was almost a foot race between his personality and the game he loved, and soon enough it would be hard for just about anyone to distinguish between the two. That's just how deeply he would become invested in the game as a youth.

Yet there would be times where a priority would have to be established, a chore that soon fell to Greta Dart. When his grades began to suffer, she insisted he miss a youth league championship game to make up work he had failed to turn in.

"She disciplined him pretty good," George Fox, who later coached him in high school, recalled in 2019. "He always told the story and it got around that she wouldn't let him play in a championship basketball game because he was not doing well in the class."

It's important to note that the adolescent Johnson would tell this story about himself to his high school coaches, his early emotional intelligence at work, with the simple act of retelling the story establishing the fact that he was both self-effacing and eager to demonstrate shared values with his coaches. It's striking that a high school player would feel at ease sharing this much of his personal story with his coaches.

More important, it was an early power move by Johnson, who was testing to see if his personal will could overcome the dictates of his teacher. Johnson recalled that he showed up at the game and tried to play, only to be rebuffed and instead left to sit on the sideline watching and stewing.

He recalled his anger and disappointment growing to the point that his relationship with Greta Dart suffered for the next month, yet there was no question the message had registered. He would eventually make amends, with an enhanced appreciation of her concern for his overall well-being.

Yet another factor also registered. His love for basketball was total and complete. And whatever got between him and the game could bring negative reactions.

Changes

His mother's spiritual focus in those days was Lansing's Union Missionary Baptist Church, a staple of her family for generations, but one day she answered a knock on the door to greet a woman proselytizing for the Seventh-day Adventist Church. Christine Johnson had long made Bible study central to her busy life, and her discussions with the woman at first intrigued her, then soon led to major changes for her life and that of her family's.

The Seventh-day Adventist Church is largely a Protestant denomination of Christianity that is said to draw on Lutheran, Wesleyan-Arminian, and Anabaptist strictures, among other elements, including Orthodox Judaism. Its largest focus, however, is on interpretation of scripture, which leads to the belief that Saturday is the seventh day of the week and thus the Sabbath.

Observance of the Sabbath essentially begins on Friday sunset and ends on sunset Saturday. The faith requires a lifelong effort to understand the Bible, to be productive and to avoid eating meat from pigs, certain fish, and other animals that the Bible cites as unclean.

Christine Johnson soon seized upon the Seventh-day Adventist lifestyle as a deeper approach to her faith, with a resulting turmoil that cast her carefully choreographed family life into chaos. Her daughters apparently lined up with their mother in this change while her sons stood with their father, who found himself clinging to his Baptist faith, ham biscuits and all.

The Johnsons' world had been built on laboring nonstop six days a week, with church on Sunday. Earvin Sr. was serious and comfortable in his faith (his father, Jesse, back in Mississippi, was a church deacon). The mother's new faith recalibrated their lives to a strict Saturday Sabbath (basically no activity from Friday evening until Saturday at five).

Their son's overwhelming focus on basketball centered often on Saturday morning youth league games, and Christine's new faith threatened both his attendance at Friday night high school games and Saturday youth events.

For months, it was as if somebody had dropped a bomb into their lives, until Earvin Sr. finally settled on a solution. He decided to go to church with his wife on Saturday and then go again to his Baptist service on Sunday, which allowed their union to move forward with a newfound harmony born of shared sacrifice for each other, all to their children's great relief.

It seems no surprise then, that the conflict appeared to leave young Earvin confused in his own spiritual life for a time. His coaches later in high school could not recall him making any overt statement whatsoever about religion, nothing about prayer before games or any activity that would denote devotion of one sort or another. It was almost as if he was avoiding the subject in the aftermath of the family crisis.

"Some people talk religion, others live it," family friend Charles Tucker said in cautioning any attempt to read too much into Johnson's avoidance of an overtly religious approach to his basketball.

After all, his time at church with his father appeared to be a different matter. He attended as his family life had always required. Leon Stokes, who was in fifth grade, a year behind Earvin, recalled being in Sunday school classes with him at Union Missionary Baptist during that time. "Quite frequently, if our teacher asked a question, it was usually Earvin or me raising our hand to answer it," remembered Stokes, who would go on to be president of the National Honor Society and a teammate of Johnson's in high school.

Johnson even sang in the choir with Earvin Sr. In fact, his love of music and singing seemed so strong from his youth that his mother came to hope that would be his calling. He sang everywhere beyond choir. On the street corner chiming in as a backup with his friends making their a cappella run at the great soul numbers of that era. In the shower. Anywhere really around his family and friends, he was likely to break into song.

"We thought we were really great on 'My Girl,'" he would recall of those days at age eleven, singing with his friends at the corner of Middle and Williams Streets, complete with the Temptations' choreography. "We always had to do all the steps—cross your legs, step, kick. And, of course, when it came to your turn to sing the part that goes 'my girl,' you had to cross your hands to your shoulders, to cover your heart."

Despite his early discomfort with the Seventh-day Adventists and teachers who made him miss basketball games, his was a happy, healthy life, from just about all accounts.

It all began then, a merging of his game and song and rhythm into the singular way he approached performing. "It was nice, because the people get off on you," Johnson would explain to writer Joseph Dalton in 1980. "Either you're good or you're no good. Either one or the other—you can't be in between. You can tell when you're no good because the crowd will be blah. They'll be standing there. But if you got them dancing all the time, that's when you can tell. That's a big part of me. My music."

In that vein, his elementary school basketball and playground presence were beginning to bring him a taste of prominence and he loved it, loved being known as the kid who loved basketball and played it all the time.

In addition to going to church with Johnson, Leon Stokes recalled watching him on the playground as a sixth grader. "I vividly recall Earvin throwing no-look passes right on the money at that age," Stokes said in a 2020 interview, adding that such passes weren't something you saw often at the time and certainly not on grade school playgrounds.

Indeed, Johnson's confidence with the game seemed to grow daily, even as his confidence in other areas began to sag. Those who knew him then have described him as being decidedly inarticulate, a condition mitigated and hidden somewhat by his smile and demeanor. And there was another creeping issue beginning to stalk his sense of worth in quiet ways that he sought to keep hidden.

It was becoming increasingly clear to his teachers, however, that young Earvin had reading issues, defined as dyslexia, issues that he would recall had left him profoundly embarrassed at certain points in his early schooling. By junior high, the dyslexia would leave him almost two full years behind in reading level tests. Researchers were just beginning to understand that dyslexia stemmed from perception issues rather than a lack of intelligence. But he didn't know that as the issue unfolded and it left him with no small amount of insecurity.

He would later recall that at one point Greta Dart suggested he go to summer school to close the gap in his reading. That wasn't something Earvin wanted to do. Summers were his special time. But he agreed to do it to begin to deal with his issues.

Throughout his early life, he would also counter this reading difficulty time and again by revealing an exceptional level of both maturity and emotional intelligence. His innate sense for understanding people and how to relate to them allowed him to function at a high level in everyday life. For example, his high school coaches were surprised to learn many years later of his dyslexia. To them, he represented an amazingly efficient learner, one who could process complex information and then help pass it along to his teammates, a trait based on his obvious ability to listen closely. The coaches never recalled an instance where they had to tell Earvin Johnson something more than once. He absorbed things immediately, part of what made him such a joy to coach.

Experts had come to see that adjusting to dyslexia could be facilitated if a child had high-interest pursuits. Obviously, for young Earvin those early high-interest pursuits were basketball and music, both augmented by the love of the emerging medium of television that marked just about everybody in his late-baby-boom generation. And it wasn't just NBA and college games and other sports. He and his siblings sat enthralled by the array of options, regularly watching the many shows of the 1960s and '70s that featured mostly white-only casts and story lines: *Mannix, The Man from U.N.C.L.E., Barnaby Jones,* and others. Then the networks had begun offering shows that focused on Black lives, such as *Sanford and Son, Julia,* and *The Flip Wilson Show.* Or Johnson could settle in on a Saturday afternoon at the local movie theater, eyes wide at the big screen, for him an immense happy place set to loom large in his future.

Like the rest of his generation, the film and TV offerings helped stoke his ideas and dreams. Just as important for an African American youth as the 1970s opened, the sitcoms and dramas and specials gave him a stronger sense of what a white-dominated world felt like, which proved to be perfect timing. Before he even had time to contemplate it, that world, drawn by his "music," would soon be much upon him.

3

GET ON THE BUS

Over their years growing up together Earvin and brother Larry clearly sported a healthy sibling rivalry, and not just in basketball. The two overly large adolescents shared a bed in the crowded Johnson household, which meant that many a cold Michigan night found them in a tug-of-war over the covers or in a fuss over just who was kicking who awake in the middle of a sweet dream.

But when it came to basketball, their relationship bordered on the profound.

Larry was more than two years older but Earvin was taller. Spurred by their father's obvious love of the game, they both attacked the sport with the sort of unbridled passion that had long defined the best players. That was made clear by their skill sets—always a clue for coaches as to which players had devoted long hours to playing the game and experimenting with all its different facets. In short, Earvin and Larry went at it.

As with any good sibling rivalry, this one also delivered tremendous synergy. After all, Larry had been Earvin's main sparring partner in so many of his early forays onto the outdoor courts, and as such, deserved credit for major contributions to Earvin's game, including the all-important notion of style.

"Larry was a good player himself," recalled Dale Beard, Johnson's friend, high school teammate, and the eventual best man at his wedding in 1991. "Earvin always wanted to be Wilt Chamberlain, and Larry wanted to be Earl 'The Pearl' Monroe." Or Walt Frazier or whatever guard happened to be starring on TV that week. Certainly, Earl the Pearl, aka Black Jesus, had caught Larry's eye—and soon enough Earvin's—with his array of moves that presented something quite new and bold in that era.

"I used to watch Larry on the playground," said Leon Stokes, one of Earvin's high school teammates who as a child had spent lots of time watching the older players on the court at Main Street School. "He was the second-best Earl Monroe player, next to Earl Monroe himself. Larry could really, really play."

"Those two kind of played a lot together on the playgrounds," Dale Beard said in a 2019 interview. "He saw in his brother Larry how Earl the Pearl used to do the spin move and the double clutch and the double pumps and all that kind of stuff. Earv kind of saw that. He said, 'Hey, you know, Larry wants to be Earl Monroe. I want to be Wilt Chamberlain.' So he kind of was mixing his game up from both players."

Soon Earvin had his own intriguing thoughts about Earl the Pearl, which were stimulated further when one of his father's friends told him that Monroe was also nicknamed Black Magic.

Johnson would later explain that when he played himself in one-on-one full-court, he would be Wilt at one end and Earl the Pearl at the other. Those moments opened his mind to a broader notion of how he liked to play the game, Dale Beard explained. "I think by doing that, being as tall as he was and developing the skills of a guard, it just carried over."

Carried over, indeed. It formed the essence of Earvin Johnson as a player.

In retrospect, it was extraordinary that the oversized, rapidly growing Earvin had somehow been able to avoid much of the normal clumsiness of his age to incorporate such moves into his own game. He had reached six feet as he entered seventh grade and shot up from there, to six-five at the end of junior high two years later. He had escaped those ungainly days, he later explained, because he was literally playing basketball all the time.

And in so many places in Johnson's life there would stand Larry, offering both a constant test and a regular example to emulate. Best of all, this rivalry would form the basis of a brotherly love that Earvin and Larry would share over a lifetime.

Sadly, it would also provide the roots of a deep pain that would dog the family for decades and fill Earvin's young life with big, complex problems to solve.

As youths, both brothers held a strong sense of anticipation about someday playing at Sexton High School, the center of the community in many ways that was just a short walk from their house. One of their joys was going to basketball games at Sexton, the only Lansing-area school to have won two state championships, back-to-back, in the early 1960s under famed coach Clayton Kowalk.

The gym at Sexton was rowdy and alive on game nights, and the two brothers could clearly see themselves stepping into the spotlight and starring there. It was just the kind of thought they could take to bed each night as they snuggled into their youthful dreams.

All of that changed, however, when big social change rolled into their lives with the news that the older Johnson siblings—Larry, Lily Pearl, and Quincy—would have to get up early each morning to get on a bus and ride across the city to attend nearly all-white Everett High School. The move was part of a plan by the Lansing city schools to advance racial integration by busing Black students. The move was even more puzzling to the Johnsons considering that Sexton, the school next to their home, already had an admirable racial balance in its student population.

This big change also came as the Johnson family was still adjusting to Christine's new faith, which only added to the already substantial turmoil in their lives. But the city school board said they had to get on the bus, and get on the bus they did. Earvin's older siblings would join a group of about one hundred African American students each day headed to Everett High, which had a student body of about 2,500 that was 99 percent white at the time.

The specific aim of the busing was to begin the process of having Black students and white students share classrooms together, to become teammates, to learn more about each other by going to school together. The school system's plan called for an increasing number of Black students to be bused to Everett High each succeeding year, something of a toe in the water testing integration.

Many other school systems across the northern and western United States were under federal court order to bus students to integrate schools. Lansing itself was under no federal court order at the time, but school officials had initiated the busing in anticipation of needed change. The dawn of the 1970s may have brought an effort to eradicate segregation uniformly across the country, but in many places the mere idea of busing would be met with sporadic episodes of anger and violence. In Lansing, the plan also involved the integration of elementary schools that had traditionally been tied strictly to neighborhoods.

Neither Black people nor white people were happy with the solution. In fact, Lansing's school board itself would face a recall election over making the move, and a majority of the members would lose their seats.

The trouble started almost immediately at Everett when some white students threw rocks at the first buses carrying Black students. The incident left many of them, including the Johnsons, asking why had they been uprooted from their friends to face such hostility in an alien place. The elements of racial animus would plague Everett High for years through a tough period of adjustment. The early fights and racial troubles understandably increased the concerns of many parents, including the Johnsons.

Despite their reluctance and the conflict, the Johnson children had been instructed by their parents to be good students and good citizens at Everett. Indeed, the members of the Johnson family were already becoming known in the community for their forthright approach to school and work. Even so, Lily Pearl, a future educator herself, and her brother Larry would come home each day and talk about how much they disliked the Everett experience. Larry, in particular, had begun having trouble adjusting to the new school almost immediately. He despised it, leaving him to withdraw emotionally and physically from schoolmates. He was said to have been almost chronically late to class and had skipped some of them altogether.

One early bright spot for the Johnson children was that they had made a connection with Everett's varsity basketball head coach, George Fox, who also taught social studies. During a series of interviews in 2019, Fox recalled that the Johnson siblings would encounter him in the hallways and proudly offer a scouting report about their tall younger brother who was gaining citywide fame as a player at Dwight Rich Junior High.

"They kept coming up to me and telling me about him and what he was doing," Fox recalled. The situation for Larry seemed to improve briefly that late fall of 1972, when he made the final cut for Everett's junior varsity basketball team as a sixteen-year-old sophomore. The good vibe didn't last long.

Just days before Christmas, word came that the coaching staff was considering dismissing five Black boys, including Larry, from the jayvee roster. The news stunned the entire Johnson family, with a timing that seemed particularly harsh considering that the boys were among the very first Black athletes ever to compete for Everett. Earvin was left immediately furious by the situation and began worrying that he, too, might be bused to Everett in two years when it came time for him to enter tenth grade. (In those days, high school in Lansing began in tenth grade.)

So began a drama that would drag on for months and then haunt the Johnson family for decades thereafter with unanswered questions about a decision that would send Larry down a dark path in life.

Larry's removal from the team did not involve lackluster effort, his coaches revealed in interviews, looking back in 2019. In fact, Larry played quite hard in practice and in games, according to the recollection of his coaches. Neither did it involve surliness or some sort of mutiny against the coaching. Although, his coaches would also recall, in no way was Larry as talented as his taller younger brother. Then again, who was?

As for their dismissal, the five players had apparently been late to practice or missed it often enough without excuse to bring their coach, a social studies teacher named Pat Holland, to initiate steps to remove them from the roster.

Holland recalled that first he consulted with Everett's varsity head coach George Fox, his boss, about the boys missing practice without giving notice, and it was decided that they had to go. It was just Holland's second season coaching the junior varsity and serving as an assistant to Fox for the varsity. He was also coaching the first group of African Americans in his life.

Faced with dismissal, the five players had asked that Charles Tucker, a doctoral candidate in psychology who worked part-time for the Lansing schools, be called in to mediate the matter.

Pat Holland figured the request was reasonable. He was friendly with Tucker, who was popular among the students. Plus, the psychologist seemed the ideal figure to mediate the issue. Besides his academic work, Tucker had an impressive basketball résumé, from All-City in high school in Kalamazoo to junior college All-American at Kellogg Community College, followed by a somewhat disappointing stint at Western Michigan, then flings in several pro basketball camps before getting cut and deciding to return to school for graduate work at Western Michigan. Even as he went to school and worked, Tucker kept a busy nighttime and weekend calendar playing in various basketball leagues.

The psychologist was still very much on a mission to prove that he remained an excellent player, as jayvee coach Holland had discovered the hard way in a student-vs.-faculty game the previous school year.

"I'm just running down the court and Tucker throws me the ball, hits me right in the head with it," Holland recalled. "It was the first time I ever played basketball with him. I knew he had a good reputation as a player."

Holland was embarrassed and upset by the incident and fussed a bit with Tucker, who admonished him to always be on the lookout for the ball, which only irritated Holland further. However, it wasn't long before the two men were able to laugh about it. "It was funny," Holland recalled. "He was apologetic. He wasn't trying to show me up or anything."

Still in his midtwenties, Tucker had been deployed by the school system during the early stages of busing to serve as a resource for students and educators in solving problems with integration and helping them better understand the situation. In a short time, the psychologist had earned a reputation as a fixer of problems, as a person with a sense of fairness and perspective. Trust seemed extremely hard to come by in those first years of busing, but there is no question from the record and from the memory of the people there that Tucker earned his substantial share of it.

The boys on Holland's team wanted to tell their story directly to Tucker without the coach intervening, and Holland had no problem with that. A quietly keen observer of the variety of people in the school's environment, Tucker hadn't detected any sort of racial animus from Holland. "He was a good coach and a good guy to try to work with and mediate with the kids," Tucker explained in a 2019 interview.

After all, Holland's expectations of players making all practices on time and ready to work were fairly standard procedure, a value Tucker himself had long shared as a high school, college, and pro player.

Considering the times, Holland seemed to feel he was fortunate to have a resource such as Tucker to help him deal with the issue. Even so, Tucker presented a very different sort of figure in that era. Obviously smart and perceptive and successful, Tucker would spend decades in the Lansing school system all while making little attempt to adopt the diction that represented the highly educated man he was.

His work would be highlighted at the time in both the Lansing and Detroit papers, where he explained his approach to language. He offered that the language used by African Americans in the South was a legitimate dialect, that the school system failed when it set up standard English almost as a barrier to Black students, leaving them to face working under what seemed like constant criticism from their white instructors.

His plan was to remove the barrier of language while helping students to adjust. Tucker told a Detroit reporter in 1972 that he still upheld the value of standard English but sought a better means for students to find a comfort level in the new environment of integration.

It was clearly a bold position for a young Black academic to put forth in the early 1970s, but Tucker himself talked the talk, so to speak. What made it work was that he also walked the walk. He was successful at what he did, which was to provide an array of students with frank guidance about the basic circumstances they faced with integration.

As Tucker saw his mission, his primary job was to be able to relate to many of the "kids" coming through the system. Thus, he took great pride in having what he called a "street" image. Time would show he had a quick mind for analyzing people, their fears and motives and behavior, and he used those abilities to calm and assure both sides of the racial divide in the city's schools.

Tucker was six feet tall but described himself as hardly an imposing figure. Some considered him standoffish, even contemptuous at times, but that's not what his actions evidenced. If he had a major fault, it was that his confidence and an aura of cool would sometimes lure him into being a little light on details in some circumstances. But in retrospect, many of his peers and coworkers would look back and consider him absolutely essential to the good things that eventually happened at Everett in the 1970s.

Pat Holland recalled having absolute trust in the psychologist to mediate the issue. "Tucker was, like they say, comfortable in his own skin," the coach said. "I mean, he was not afraid to rule against those kids, you know, obviously. He wasn't there to prove that I should give them another chance or whatever because he's Black and they're Black. He was there to make a fair decision. I fully expected him to and I thought I had an open-and-shut case."

Those who knew him better understood that Tucker's life was also largely guided by his faith, to the point that he not only talked freely of Christian love but sought to use it to guide his actions in his professional practice as a psychologist. Tucker had encountered intensely negative speech and even violent racism in his life and was quite aware of it, yet was also seemingly locked in on an approach tempered by an understanding that many people at the time were blind to their own racist attitudes.

Tucker, like the Johnsons and many of the African American families in the Lansing community, had migrated there from Mississippi, where they had borne the full brunt of that state's harsh racial climate. The life they had found by moving to Michigan wasn't perfect, but it was better.

In 1972, Tucker was just beginning a role that he would keep throughout Lansing's intense integration battles and far beyond, for decades actually, to the point that he was still working as a psychologist for the Lansing schools in 2019. His first decade in the schools would be marked by periodic outbreaks of racial conflict, fights, and other problems, at times serious enough to require that certain schools, in addition to Everett, be closed for several days at a time to let emotions subside.

"It was going on all over the country, a lot of busing going on, segregation type stuff," Tucker recalled in 2019. "And a lot of attitudes. And, of course, everybody wanted to stay in their own communities, around their own environment. That was all over the country, because of the rules and the laws. People didn't want to change."

Many of the teachers in the system in the early 1970s were not unlike Pat Holland, well intentioned but facing a new and challenging task with integration with no real cultural reference points. And the same could be said for the students like Larry Johnson who found themselves retreating from a school climate they found threatening and frustrating.

Tucker saw the atmosphere at Everett and the other schools as fraught with misunderstanding.

"It was a new time in the world, a new day with relationships," Tucker remembered. "It was kind of tough. The parents were different. The kids were different and society was different. And a lot of things were going on. The country was just in a rage itself. So you're asking kids to be bused to another area. Whether Black or white, it doesn't matter whatever color it is, they were being uprooted."

Playing into the mix of the experience was the fact that, in his heart of hearts, Tucker remained an unabashed and unrepentant basketball addict on a mission to prove that he belonged in pro basketball. He virtually inhaled the game as often as he possibly could. That and his religion and his educational training and his street cunning guided his life. And they would soon come to guide—some would stay steer—the life of young Earvin Johnson, although in 1972 Tucker was merely curiously aware of him, having taken notice of the tall young boy who seemed to spend each entire summer day on the court at Main Street School.

At the time he was called in to mediate the issue with the Everett junior varsity, Tucker had no idea that one of the players was Earvin's brother, just as he had no idea of the Johnson family and its particular character.

But Tucker would soon enough learn all of that.

He spent much of his free time in Lansing playing lots and lots of pickup basketball, just about anywhere he could find a high-test game. In the vernacular of the era, Tucker had an abundance of street cred and wasn't shy about deploying it.

"That was my specialty at that time," he explained. "I was a psychology guy and I was a street guy. And I had my religion, of course. I had my ways. It helped me. My hand was always on the pulse because I was always with the kids. That was my life. I didn't want no administration job. I didn't want no principal's job. I could have had all of them. I just wanted to be with the kids because that's what I enjoyed. Some of it I did for selfish reasons because it kept me young, you know, it kept me competitive. . . . And I wasn't married and didn't have no family or nothing. So, I enjoyed it."

Pat Holland, like many, had his own experiences with race. The junior varsity coach was from Saginaw, Michigan, a place that was viewed as somewhat backward in the matter of race relations, but the coach had gained greater understanding while in the service a decade earlier, as he recalled. In fact, in 1959, as Earvin Johnson was just coming into the world, Holland was traveling down south to Virginia with a Black army buddy.

Holland was headed to Fort A.P. Hill for training and his buddy had decided to visit family there, so they traveled together in the man's car. When it came time to pull over and get a hotel room, Holland's friend explained that it wasn't likely that he would be allowed to check into a hotel in the South.

The man told Holland that he would sleep in the car and that Holland could get a hotel room. Holland declined, saying that wouldn't be right, so they crashed in the car, then rose the next morning and finished their drive to Petersburg, Virginia, where they stopped at the bus station. Holland was promptly informed that he was on the "colored" side of the terminal and should go to the other side.

The trip proved to be an eye-opening experience for Holland, which would help him immensely in public education. Lansing at the time was in the first stages of opening up the power structure in the schools to include African Americans. A Black deputy superintendent of schools had just been hired. And the white superintendent, I. Carl Candoli, had begun hiring and deploying key figures to help the system change. One of those was Charles Tucker.

The five jayvee boys were eager to explain the situation to Tucker themselves, why they were in trouble, Holland recalled. "Tucker had a deal with those kids. He told them that if they were going to tell him something, they better tell him the truth. So, we sat down at the meeting with Larry and these other kids. They told their story, and Tucker asked me if that was accurate."

Holland told the psychologist the players had been "one hundred percent accurate."

"He said, 'Fellas, I'll tell you one thing. Mr. Holland made one mistake. He should have kicked you off sooner,'" Holland recalled. "And that was it. They said, 'Okay.' They told it just like it was."

Holland felt he had given Larry ample warnings, and Tucker had confirmed that to him.

In dismissing the players, Holland had made it clear that they would be welcome for tryouts the following year. But none of the players ever returned to the program.

Four of the players accepted Tucker's decision without complaint, both Holland and head coach George Fox recalled. But Larry Johnson was anything but accepting. He angrily vowed that day that his younger brother Earvin would never play for Holland or Fox, or Everett. Then he told Fox the same thing.

"Larry hated me for that," Holland said. Both Holland and Fox knew that for a fact because that day Larry told them so.

Larry's response was not a single outburst of anger limited to that day, but a message he would offer the coaches often over the next two school years when he ran into them in the hallway or other places.

Holland recalled clearly that Larry was two years ahead of Earvin because "he spent a lot of time telling us how much Earvin was never going to come to Everett.

"Any chance I would run into him, he would have some choice words for me," Holland recalled. "He said I ruined his life because he couldn't play basketball."

If Larry never failed to express those feelings to his former coaches over the coming months, he clearly also articulated them to family members at home for quite some time. Earvin would recall that Larry began lobbying him almost immediately to set his mind against going to Everett, encouraging him to refuse to attend there. How close and frequent was Larry's lobbying about Everett High basketball? Considering their sleeping arrangements and with Larry's anger fresh and sizzling, there were times his complaints were the last thing Earvin likely heard at night before falling asleep, although he wouldn't face a decision on the matter until the summer of 1974, nearly two years later, when he would be entering the tenth grade.

Everett's coaches were typical of those at other schools in that they tended not to coddle players, explained Dale Beard, who later played for Holland. "Back then they ran a straight ship, you know, no skipping school or missing practice or you knew what the result was. If you missed school you weren't going to practice. If you missed practice you weren't going to play. I mean, that was just the nature of the beast. When you're that age, you know, and get into a lot of things, you think you're invincible. At that time, they were real particular about who was on the team, regardless of whether you could play or not. You know, they just wanted you to do the right thing. Pat felt that Larry was kind of a troublemaker guy, but he wasn't. He was just being a teenager."

A teen who had been caught smack-dab in the middle of America's busing crisis of the 1970s.

In an interview nearly five decades later, Tucker offered an understandably different perspective, one perhaps tinged with some regret. "Larry wasn't a bad kid at all," the psychologist said. "He was like just about any Black kid at that time, being put in that type of situation. He wasn't going to change the way he did things. Some of the things he was doing weren't one hundred percent bad. They were just different."

The first steps of integration had left the school's new students faced with a situation that was easy to misread, Tucker explained, adding that young males in particular didn't want to act like they were afraid or that they could be cowed.

"There were a lot of problems in general," Tucker remembered. "The jarring emotion of that rock throwing had sort of leaked out into everything in the school. If I was to put the blame on what happened to Larry and some of those guys, I would put at least 80 percent of it on the situation. He didn't have those issues at the other school. Not that he had a lot of issues. He should have played basketball."

Saddest of all, he added, "Larry could play. He had a lot of stuff now. He had a lot of tricks, so he could play. He wasn't a chump."

"That was a tough one because Larry had a love for the game," Pat Holland agreed in 2019. "You could see it, you know, but it didn't translate into some other things that it should have for him."

What it did translate into was a persistent anxiety for young Earvin. He had no idea what he was going to do about playing basketball at Everett. Like the rest of his family, he considered the optics absolutely terrible of Larry getting kicked off the team. White coaches dismissing five Black boys? Surely the place and the people were totally racist. Beyond that, he just didn't like the feel of the school. The gym was never rocking. The teams were mediocre, at best.

The immediate choice for Earvin was easy. He knew that he had to find a way out of being forced to go there when it came time for high school.

Junior High Warrior

As the drama with Larry unfolded, Earvin had headed into his eighth-grade season like the power that he was, turning heads and raising eyebrows with the early signs of his very unusual and effective game.

His seventh-grade basketball experience had brought revelations when his coach, Louis Brockhouse, faced an estimated one hundred boys for tryouts and decided to have them line up, right-handers on one side, left-handers on the other. He ordered the righties to dribble in and make a left-handed layup and the lefties to do the same with their right. Few could accomplish the task.

Like that, Brockhouse had managed to cut the team down to twelve, and Earvin was left feeling grateful that Jim Dart had stressed so much using the left hand, just one of the reasons Johnson would mention the coach at his own Hall of Fame induction decades later.

"In seventh grade, I was six feet and played guard," Johnson himself would recall just a few years later.

In much of what he did, Johnson showed an eagerness to have the ball. It is likely that at least part of the time Brockhouse let him, an early experience that helped drive Johnson's growing view of how he wanted to play the game.

By the eighth grade, Johnson had begun to pull more of the elements of his game together and quickly became something of a force in junior high. Perhaps realizing his relationship with Larry's younger brother was in question, Everett coach George Fox began taking more time to attend games at Dwight Rich Junior High, as encouraged by Johnson's siblings. In retrospect, it was almost as if the bait was being set for some sort of trap.

Fox's daughter Missy recalled a big first moment: "I will never forget my dad having a conversation at dinner one night when he says, 'Hey, there's this kid over at Dwight Rich and he's a really good basketball player. He may be coming up to Everett. I want to go watch him.' And so we all piled in the car and went to this junior high school basketball game. This kid was so good. We had a blast just watching him play and he's in junior high, and my dad was getting so excited like, 'This kid's gonna be really good.' So that's when I was first aware that he was going to be something special. I remember walking out of there and thinking, 'Now we're what? Eighth grade?' And he just flowed. I just remember walking out of there thinking, 'Well, that was fun.' And how many middle school or junior high games do you go to that you think are fun, right? They're kind of boring. He was fun to watch from a young age."

The varsity coach's early assessment of the eighth grader was that he tended to jack up suspect jumpers. Unknown to Fox, Johnson's eighth-grade coach had encouraged him to focus on scoring and shooting and rebounding. Johnson apparently had the green light to develop his offensive game.

"He was skinny as a rail, liked to stand outside and shoot," Fox remembered in a 1980 interview. Gary Fox, the coach's son, was a high school sophomore at the time, playing for another team in the suburbs, but he tagged along frequently with his father to see the unusual player at Dwight Rich. Gary Fox himself would become a high school coach in Michigan and clearly recalled those early trips to scout Earvin. At six feet in the eighth grade, Johnson was impressive, Gary Fox recalled in 2019. "He just didn't have the size but he was handling the ball for sure."

Johnson intrigued George Fox, but the coach began wondering if Johnson had any ability to play inside. "We didn't know how well he could post up," Fox recalled. But the coach saw something else that was extremely promising: "We knew this: when he shot and missed, he usually ended up with the ball."

When he shot, he showed startling quickness to retrieve the miss. Or if he drove and missed, he had an answer there as well, George Fox remembered. "There was a quickness and a big step. He would take that big step and go up with it. If he missed, by the time he would land he was on the way to get the recovery and put it back in. He was amazing at that. How fast he could get up and down."

Johnson's competition with Jay Vincent had continued apace through grade school but then fell off early in junior high when a chubby Vincent failed to make his junior high team in seventh grade, then sat the bench in eighth grade while Earvin helped drive the team at Dwight Rich Junior High to big wins.

"He was a little bitty skinny guy, and then of course, we both grew into our frames," Jay Vincent recalled in 2019, "but he more or less grew into like a deer and just kept dribbling the ball."

"I remember people telling me he didn't have an outside shot and that it would hamper him in college," Dick Rosekrans, who coached Johnson in both eighth and ninth grades, once offered. "Well, I'll tell you one thing, he had a great shot. I saw it in seventh grade. When he had to have it, it was there."

As a junior high player, Johnson could now find small stories about his play and his games in the *Lansing State Journal,* which understandably thrilled him. Yet the newfound status didn't seem to affect his demeanor, recalled Dr. Tom Jamieson, the team physician for a number of Lansing-area schools, in a 2019 interview. "When I first met him he was an athlete at Dwight Rich Junior High, where I was the team doctor. Earvin was always easy to be with and was always a gentleman, even in junior high school."

Such a gentleman, in fact, that when Fox brought his family along to help scout his eighth-grade games, the young player turned on the charm, flashing the smile, holding nothing back in engaging the coach and his family, even though he privately despised the idea of going to Everett and spent many days trying to think of ways of getting out of having to attend the largely white school. But Earvin was also obviously pleased and intrigued by the attention Fox was now showing him. Young Earvin was clearly a budding showman. And he craved that attention.

Even as an adolescent he rarely let emotions rule him. Like his parents, he wasn't going to let people know what he was thinking.

4

TOBACCO ROAD

Yes, sir, Earvin Sr. loved manufacturing those Olds, loved seeing them roll down the assembly line and right onto the highway, loved showing up at work every single night shift and doing his part to have them parked in every driveway in America. After all, they were "The Escape Machines," as ads in the 1960s proclaimed. But truth be known? Earv Sr. ranked them behind another General Motors product, his ultimate heartthrob, the Buick Electra 225, often known by its term of endearment, the "deuce and a quarter," the 225 standing for the car's length in inches, 5,715 millimeters of pure unadulterated land yacht, complete with a full-throated V-8.

No wonder the father so loved the Electra, washing and waxing it in the Michigan sunshine on weekends, treating the vehicle like the family jewels, trading in one model for another every few years or so to keep things fresh and bright and up to date. It was almost like Earv Sr. was polishing a championship trophy, and it likely was, considering the degree of effort it took to keep his family clothed and fed and headed in the right direction.

Best of all, his Electra offered plush bench seating, a necessity for when the Johnsons crammed in (in that era before seat belt and car seat laws and before minivans, for that matter) and headed south, back home to either North Carolina or Mississippi, either journey alternately sprinkled with hope and darkness along with plenty of stories about the strangeness and wonder of life in the South, emphasized for the kids when they stopped to eat in rest areas rather than risk the trouble and embarrassment of trying to get served at a restaurant.

Old habits, born out of necessity, died hard, it seemed.

Christine, for example, was fond of recalling that as a girl she had two dresses she washed every other day to wear to school, which she attended only after she worked in the fields in the morning and then walked four miles to get to the classroom. For years her life unfolded in a typical tenant farm existence of six children, her parents, and grandfather all packed into a three-room house, no plumbing, no running water, no electricity, none of it until the day the modern conveniences finally, miraculously came into their lives.

When the Johnsons and their children headed to Mississippi, Earv Sr. offered up memories of his boyhood after his father went away, leaving him and his brother to help fend for the family, picking cotton and tobacco as youths, just getting by with the life of a farm laborer.

Young Junebug would often sit in the front seat while the old man drove and talked. He and the siblings took in every word their parents offered. Those rides down South for the Johnsons provided a glimpse into that past and the opportunity for family stories and lessons about life, along with warnings about the necessity of caution around southern white people, especially in Mississippi. After all, Earv Sr. had come of age in the summer of the murder of Emmett Till, the Chicago teen killed in Mississippi allegedly for winking at or briefly interacting with a white woman, and in the same state in the same summer the blatant public murders of two Black veterans, both farmers, for simply attempting to register to vote. All were homicides that went unpunished.

Mississippi had always seemed to produce every type of sordid racial violence, but in the 1950s America had begun to awaken, to gain the slightest sense of the unmitigated ugliness of it all, the lynchings and beatings, that had gone on for years against southern Black populations. For decades, African Americans across the South had been powerless against this violence. With the shock and horror of the lynching of a family member or neighbor, their only choice was to retreat to their homes to weep in grief, and to pray, as laid out in Isabel Wilkerson's prizewinning book *The Warmth of Other Suns,* a work that explained the momentum behind the Great Migration, when millions of Black people left the South as a refugee population during the first half of the twentieth century.

The Johnsons, like so many, dealt with such darkness in small doses, explaining the facts to their children but never dwelling on them. Beyond the revelations about the past, the trips south themselves drove thoughts of the families of Earv Sr. and Christine, memories of their parents and grandparents and all the many relatives, the people who had somehow fashioned a life in impossible circumstances.

Even further beyond family memory sat the story in public records that reached back into slavery and revealed a complex narrative, for Christine Johnson's people lived out mostly in and around Tarboro, in Edgecombe County, North Carolina.

Certainly, so much of Johnson's rise in basketball would come from his singular talent and his determination to control the proceedings. Yet another absolutely essential portion of his success was clearly the product of precious values set in motion by the people who came before him, people with names like Jenkins and Porter, as well as, sadly, people with no last name at all, people who lived well beyond even his own family memory.

Who were they? The research to answer this question turns up a family saga filled with many surprises. Largely, they were people who lived on what would come to be known affectionately in basketball jargon as "Tobacco Road" in North Carolina, the heart of college basketball's famed Atlantic Coast Conference. Yet the Tobacco Road that Johnson's ancestors knew offered a life that featured little in the way of quaint notions about sport.

Ferebe

During the Great Depression, as part of Franklin D. Roosevelt's Works Progress Administration, writers were hired to go through the South interviewing formerly enslaved people about their experiences, an exercise that turned up any number of recollections of long grinding days of labor in the hot fields under enslavers who often provided scant little provisions. Even the food that was available was routinely of terrible quality, conditions that led to many enslaved people sneaking away in the night to steal corn from surrounding farms or wherever they could find it just to sustain their families.

We know these accounts to be true because in North Carolina and other southern states there came to be laws that said if planters abused and poorly fed the people they enslaved, who were then found subsequently to have stolen corn, then the enslavers were responsible for the cost of the stolen corn and could be fined.

This treatment of enslaved people helps explain perhaps an enduring maxim of race relations in America: Desperate people are forced to take desperate measures.

Far worse than the hunger was the fact that slaveholders often would claim ownership to any children born to those they enslaved as personal property—an abhorrent yet routine practice.

Records show that Magic Johnson's great-great-great-great-grandmother was an enslaved woman known simply as Ferebe. Her unusual name turns up listed among more than 250 enslaved people in the 1854 will of a very powerful North Carolina figure, James Smith Battle, who owned numerous plantations, including his home, the famous Cool Spring Plantation.

All of the many assembled records of North Carolina show that Ferebe was also the name of one other enslaved woman, who lived on North Carolina's coast and was listed as a twenty-five-year-old runaway in a local newspaper account on Christmas 1795.

Which presents a primary question that remains fascinating but unanswerable. Was this earlier runaway in 1795 Magic Johnson's fifth great-grandmother? If so, she possessed no small measure of spirit. According to several accounts from the era, this earlier Ferebe was threatened by her enslaver with a severe beating to which she responded with a declaration of righteous indignation that she would not be cowed. When her enslaver attempted to follow through on his threat, she promptly subdued him and issued her own beating, which left him seriously injured and crying out for help.

Was the woman Ferebe who wound up in James Smith Battle's will six decades later her relative?

Slave records are notoriously difficult to track, but what is established in record is that Johnson's fourth great-grandmother of the same unusual name resided at Cool Spring, the home of James Smith Battle.

"As a boy, my earliest recollections are connected with the shady grove around the home at Cool Spring and the broad shimmering cotton fields spreading in every direction almost as far as the eye could see," wrote Battle's grandson George Gordon Battle in a memoir that would document the generations of the Battles, a wealthy North Carolina family.

The record is also clear that both of Magic Johnson's maternal great-great-great-grandfathers were born into what was surely slavery during the extremely troubled 1830s. One of Johnson's great-great-great-grandfathers, Willis Staton, was born to Ferebe on or about 1834. He thus became James Smith Battle's property at birth.

Records suggest that it's likely Magic Johnson's other great-great-great-grandfather, Ben Jenkins, was also raised at or near Cool Spring, which sat about halfway on the road between Tarboro and Rocky Mount.

The Battle clan apparently owned a collection of local farms and plantations with names like "California" and "Walnut Creek" and "Penelo" and "Shell Bank" and "Elm Grove." But "Cool Spring" was the main digs for James Smith Battle. His was a vast operation, with an elegant main house that was said to feature an Egyptian marble fireplace. The farm was staffed by a number of highly skilled workers—among them likely Magic Johnson's ancestors—identified in accounts as spinners, weavers, tailors, carpenters, and masons, an array of enslaved people who provided the Battles with amazing "self-sufficiency"; people who made by hand all the clothes, wagons, carts, farm implements, virtually every single item that enabled the lives of the "masters," lives documented in the letters of that era as "beautiful" and "lovely."

Those same letters documented that when Battle women needed to learn to cook, they learned it from the people they enslaved. The plantation also was known, again from letters at the time, as a place that offered lively music and merriment almost nightly, music surely often provided by the enslaved.

In his memoir, George Gordon Battle readily acknowledged the great evil of slavery, but that didn't prevent him from recalling fondly and in detail the bygone life on the plantation, a place where all the enslaved people were said to be proud, handsome, and happy, supposedly much like the Battles themselves.

Such blatant romanticizing of an operation in human trafficking would only serve to bolster a cold and callous notion that the buying and selling of humans was somehow imbued with a southern nobility. At its height, Cool Spring alone enslaved between four and five hundred people, estimated by George Gordon Battle to be about forty families.

Raw numbers from the times suggest an even colder truth. Records show that the market value of a mature enslaved man in that era ranged between $500 and $800, a sizable amount, considering that most land sold for 25 cents, 50 cents, sometimes even a dollar an acre, meaning that the life of a single enslaved person could equal literally thousands of acres. Obviously, from such an equation, it becomes clear that it was the enslaved person working that land who made it valuable. The equation also made clear just how deeply slavery sat at the heart of the southern economy, an immense value to owners who increased that value every time the people they enslaved produced children.

Such a system rapidly led to a deepening, ever twisting and sinister corruption. The profit alone led to an immense rise in the number of enslaved people in North Carolina. Census records show the presence of just 5,000 enslaved people in the state in 1790, a population that would explode to more than 200,000 by the 1830s, a growth that would certainly create the many problems that defined the age inhabited by Ferebe and her baby son.

James Smith Battle was prominent as a person eager to acquire more and more land and more and more enslaved people as their numbers grew with the times. In addition to their collection of North Carolina plantations, Battle and his relatives also owned thousands of acres and vast plantation holdings in Florida and Mississippi, which all required the forced labor of hundreds more enslaved people.

Battle was a complicated figure. When one of the men he enslaved killed a white overseer in the 1830s, Battle was convinced the enslaved man had acted in self-defense and hired two lawyers to fight the enslaved man's death sentence all the way to the state supreme court, where Battle prevailed, setting a legal precedent of sorts. Apparently nowhere had an enslaved person ever been acquitted of killing a white man before. It was all part of a famous and profound drama surely witnessed and deeply felt by Magic Johnson's ancestors.

The linchpin to slavery were the laws holding enslaved people under the total control of their enslavers, a factor immediately threatened when the North Carolina Supreme Court overturned the enslaved man's conviction, declaring him guilty only of manslaughter and returning him to Cool Spring.

The case, known as *State v. Mann,* went a long way toward establishing an enslaved person's rights under the law, one of the first legal cases setting out their human rights in some form, thus limiting the rights of an enslaver. The decision meant "the negro and the white . . . were now placed under the very same law," Joseph K. Turner and John Bridgers wrote in their exhaustive history of Edgecombe County, published in 1920.

The outcome ignited an instant outrage. "This case occurred soon after the Nat Turner insurrection in Southampton County, Virginia, in which a number of white persons had been killed in a servile uprising," George Gordon Battle would write. "Naturally there was much uneasiness among the slave owners and my grandfather was severely criticized by some of his friends and neighbors for defending a slave who had admittedly killed his overseer."

It's also important to keep in mind that farm life in North Carolina in the 1830s was defined in many ways by the staggering news of Nat Turner's slave rebellion in Virginia in 1831, which resulted in many killings and struck holy terror into the hearts of white people in neighboring North Carolina and across the South.

David Dodge, a white writer from that home region of Johnson's ancestors in North Carolina, penned an article for *The Atlantic* in 1886 that looked back on the era and the role that the reaction to Nat Turner played in driving the white fear and violence that have long marked race relations in America.

Enslavers, Dodge recalled of the society he knew well, were already known to be "excessively suspicious and susceptible to panic."

Such panic, Dodge added, drove the mania of an "era of rigorous laws and cruel, unnatural punishments the world over. Scourgings and brandings, maimings and hangings, were as a rule inflicted for offenses now deemed trifling."

The 1830s were marked by the appearance of regular citizen patrols, or militias, around Tarboro to roust enslaved people in their quarters at night to search for weapons and other contraband and, yes, corn, according to historians. In the middle of this nightmarish mix stood the Battles, who stirred an unwelcome controversy amid that fear of the 1830s, the same Battles who controlled so much of the lives of Magic Johnson's people.

Beyond his farm operations, James Smith Battle also became the builder with one of his cousins of the Wilmington and Weldon Railroad and apparently had no moral reservations about using as many as 150 of the people he enslaved in cutting a path over difficult terrain to build long sections of the railway. The odds suggest that one or more of Magic Johnson's ancestors worked clearing the land and laying the rails for the Wilmington and Weldon.

In those days, North Carolina had slave courts, created mostly to reimburse enslavers for accidents or financial disputes involving enslaved people. But the courts also adjudicated criminal charges against enslaved people and even on occasion allowed them to be granted freedom as a reward for years of faithful service, which helps explain how census records show that by 1860 North Carolina had a surprisingly large population of "free" Black people, about thirty thousand.

The animosity between the white community and the Battles smoldered on, however, and would soon have more fuel. The Battles were people of some faith, mostly Baptist and by marriage occasionally Episcopalian, and they would soon enough begin holding services at Cool Spring for the people they enslaved. Such a practice was apparently not all that unusual, even though it was against the law to teach enslaved people to read, or to allow them to preach sermons, for that matter.

In another development apparently related to white fear, records show that across much of North Carolina, white people oddly began recruiting both enslaved people and free Black people to worship together in the 1830s. At face value, it might seem a sign of progress that whites would welcome Black people to worship together to hear sermons from white ministers. After all, the practice lasted more than three decades, until the Civil War, when Black members left white churches in droves, according to church records from the era.

Historians, however, have pointed out that the white ministers of that era tended to preach sermons that stressed the loyalty of servants to their masters.

What would prove to be perhaps a key moment of impact on the life of Magic Johnson and that of his family came in the 1830s, just as emotions were stewing in that region, when Amos Johnston Battle, a close relative of James Smith Battle, left his own plantation near Cool Spring to spend three weeks riding down to Florida on horseback at age twenty-four to visit another of the family's plantations.

As he rode through Georgia, he was said to have stopped at a simple country church and decided to take in a service where he heard the sermon of a Missionary Baptist preacher (the Missionary Baptists had gained their identity following a split with Primitive Baptists in the early nineteenth century). The Missionary Baptists were unique in the South in that era in that they were known to be rigorously opposed to slavery. What Amos Battle heard that day apparently led him to a dramatic conversion and a blinding moral clarity, so to speak. On the way back to North Carolina from his Florida plantation weeks later, Amos Battle was said to have stopped again at the Missionary Baptist church to be baptized and would indeed later become a minister of that faith.

Amos Battle, who came to reside in nearby Wilson, North Carolina, was likewise a man of wealth and power and soon became a substantial benefactor of the Missionary Baptists, so much so that, according to records, he left his sons embittered that he eventually gave away his wealth in "negroes, lands, stocks and bonds." In or around 1834, the young Amos Battle staged a Missionary Baptist conference in Tarboro that further angered the region's white residents, leading to an editorial in the local paper calling him a "bigot" for promoting his new faith that opposed slavery.

The beliefs of the Missionary Baptists would draw over time the interest and the allegiance of many African Americans, including the generations of Magic Johnson's family, as would other branches of the Baptist faith that spread across North Carolina. Amos Battle, meanwhile, would become a major benefactor of Wake Forest College. While Amos Battle held himself thenceforward as a man of morality, some historians have pointed out that his wife, Margaret, owned thirty-two enslaved people bequeathed by her father, an ownership that was tied up for two decades in a court battle over the will. Amos Battle had embraced the blinding light of truth against the lure of the easy wealth and comfort that enslavers could steal from other people's lives. After all the slaves were freed in 1865, Amos Battle was apparently happy and nearly destitute, to the point that Margaret had to rent out rooms in their house to make ends meet.

Jenkins

How fitting would it be that Magic Johnson, the purveyor of racehorse basketball, would have a cavalry sergeant for a great-great-great-grandfather?

Records suggest that Ben Jenkins, Johnson's other great-great-great-grandfather, would later find his way to fight for the North in the Civil War. His name turns up in military service records as a sergeant in the First Colored Cavalry in the Union Army in 1863.

The Ben Jenkins listed in army records was born in North Carolina in the mid-1830s, and there is not another Ben Jenkins among records of the era to contradict this assumption. Still, the question persists: How could Ben Jenkins, working in or near the Battle plantations and farms, turn up in the Union Army? After all, the Battles in their memoirs and letters would claim an immense loyalty from the people they enslaved during the conflict, even as their farms produced goods to support the Confederacy.

One answer would be that the Battle claim was perhaps false. The Union Army began making raids in 1863 into North Carolina with the express purpose of freeing enslaved men and recruiting them to join the Union cause. Historians reported that a number of enslaved men left the Tarboro area after Lincoln's Emancipation Proclamation on January 1, 1863, and made their way to join the Union Army. Some estimates say that as many as 200,000 Black men served in one form or another in the Union Army and were considered by experts to be a major factor in the North's ultimate victory.

Records show that Ben Jenkins joined up at Fort Monroe, Virginia, in December 1863. There were "colored" units formed in infantry, artillery, and even the navy, but the fact that Jenkins was taken into the cavalry suggests that he was an able horseman. The vast majority of officers for the colored units were white, which means that Jenkins achieving the rank of sergeant made him one of the highest-ranking Black men serving in the conflict.

Frederick Browne, a white second lieutenant in that cavalry, recalled in his own memoir that the First Colored Cavalry "trained arduously until May" 1864 and then stepped into a very serious campaign as Union forces pushed to secure victory in a war that had been going on for three bloody years.

The story itself of the First Colored Cavalry, as detailed in both service journals and the memoir of Browne, shows that the units performed well in combat in Virginia and North Carolina over the final fifteen months of the war, engaging Confederate forces in various skirmishes and battles while taking considerable losses. At times, the cavalry unit would spend twenty-four hours straight in the saddle, Browne remembered.

With the Confederacy's surrender at Appomattox, Virginia, in April 1865, all the various units of African American soldiers were combined into one larger unit and ordered south to Texas, where Emperor Maximilian of Mexico, backed by the French, was threatening the border.

That June, the units of Black soldiers were loaded onto steamer ships in the James River south of Richmond, Virginia. Soon word spread among the ranks that they were being taken to Texas to pick cotton to help pay off the nation's massive debt in the wake of the war.

Browne recalled the officers trying to reassure their troops that wasn't the case, but the conflict itself had left Black troops with many reasons to be distrustful. The wartime experience had found them caught between a federal army that was openly prejudiced against them and a Confederate army that considered them traitors and threatened their execution if captured.

Paid less than half of what white troops earned, poorly equipped, and often disrespected by white people in the Union ranks, the experience had left many Black troops embittered.

Restlessness among the troops on the steamers headed to Texas grew so great that first night of the journey that the next morning the officers docked the ships at Fort Monroe in Virginia, marched the units ashore, assembled them on the beach in ranks at attention, and ordered them to surrender their arms.

The moment was tense, Frederick Browne recalled, as some of the men hesitated a bit, then followed orders.

The next night, some of the troops on one of the steamers mutinied on the way to Texas, an incident that ended after an officer shot and killed the leader of the mutiny.

The mutiny quelled, all of the steamers made their way first to the mouth of the Mississippi River, then to Brazos Santiago, Texas, a coastal area of the Gulf along the border where the Black troops, as Browne recalled, were deployed with the overwhelming task of unloading the many ships of the large force dispatched there to protect the border against invasion from Mexico.

While the great unloading was being completed, the African American troops were charged with building an apparently segregated camp in a swampy section of the coast described as "malarial" and "god-forsaken," which in turn soon produced dire reports of an epidemic among the Black troops. The medical officer for the expedition was quoted in records as reporting "a great deal of sickness among the troops. . . . The mortality is quite large," conditions made worse, the officer added, by the remoteness of the location and the absolute lack of medical supplies and personnel to treat the many sick Black soldiers. Through all of this, Sergeant Ben Jenkins somehow survived this ugly, disgraceful, and thankless end to the service of America's first Black troops.

Records show Jenkins and other surviving African American soldiers were finally discharged nearly a year after the war, in Texas, in February 1866.

Census records from 1870 show that Ben Jenkins was back in North Carolina to take on just about the only work available to Black men across the South, the life of a sharecropper and farmworker, in many cases alongside white neighbors who were Confederate veterans.

Ben Jenkins and his wife, Gracie, would have a large farm family. Among their many children would be a son, Joseph, who would be Magic Johnson's great-great-grandfather. Joseph's daughter Arsena, or "Sena" Jenkins, would marry a man named Glass. But Sena's first child, Mary Della, Earvin "Magic" Johnson's own grandmother, seemed particularly attached to the name Jenkins. She would be known in her adult married life as Mary Della Jenkins Porter, indicating that Jenkins was a name she bore with great pride.

The Senator

Ben and Gracie Jenkins would have a daughter, Ella, in 1867, who was Magic Johnson's great-great-aunt. She would grow up to marry a prominent state senator in 1891, later giving Johnson's ancestors something they likely never imagined: a taste of political power and even an alliance of sorts with a new generation of the Battles.

In 1891, Ella Jenkins married state senator Dred Wimberly, who had been born in 1849 at Walnut Creek, another of the Battles' plantations, and was just a teen when the Civil War ended in April 1865. By then, the plantation was run by Kemp P. Battle, who was both a cousin and a son-in-law to James Smith Battle and would go on to fame as a prominent Confederate, a celebrated lawyer and scholar, a strong advocate for the University of North Carolina, and a partner of James Smith Battle in the railroad business.

Dred Wimberly would later recall Kemp Battle one day coming down to the fields where Wimberly was working. The slaveholder called all the workers together to tell them the war was over and they were free to go, or that they could stay and have a job.

The young Wimberly thought about it a bit and took the job. Soon, he was in charge of marketing all the produce grown at Walnut Creek. Wimberly would have the produce loaded onto large wagons for the two-day journey to the market in Raleigh. Once in Raleigh, he would sell the produce, then go to stores to purchase supplies, load them on the wagons, and return to Tarboro, in the process basically serving as a quartermaster for the Battles' still expansive plantation operation.

After several years, however, Wimberly longed to go into business for himself as a carpenter building houses and parted ways with the Battles on good terms in those precarious years after the war. By the time he was nearing thirty, Wimberly was approached by the Republican Party about running for North Carolina's House of Commons. Wimberly replied that he didn't think he was qualified. He thought nothing more of it, only to learn the Republicans had nominated him anyway and he had won without so much as being aware of his own campaign, which seems to indicate the esteem with which he was held in the community.

He served several terms in the House beginning in 1878 and then gained election to the Senate nearly a decade later. In the interim, he joined a Kemp Battle initiative and cast the deciding vote providing critical funding for a struggling University of North Carolina during the period, even though Battle was apparently a Democrat.

"I voted for Dr. Battle's appropriation because Dr. Battle had said voting for the University would help everybody," Wimberly once explained. "It might somehow help the colored folks too."

A twentieth-century editorial in the Raleigh *News and Observer* offered this about Wimberly and other Black legislators: "They upheld education when no one else did. They laid the foundation for the common schools where the schools had few or no friends."

The Battles would long confirm Wimberly's story about his critical vote (he also played a key role in funding what would become North Carolina State University plus numerous other important public projects), but a Raleigh newspaper reporter in 1935 doubted that Wimberly actually cast the UNC vote because records of his early legislative service had apparently been lost.

However, some North Carolina newspapers from the 1870s had published the full roster of the state assembly, and there in newspaper accounts Wimberly was clearly a member positioned to cast the major vote.

In a time of great conflict during Reconstruction, when thousands of Black male voters joined the rolls and Black people were elected to public office amidst a charged political atmosphere, the distinguished-looking Wimberly established a reputation for downplaying conflict and seeking to work with the opposite party.

Yes, Magic Johnson's people were farmworkers, sharecroppers barely eking out a living in the decades after the Civil War, but one of their own was married to not just a senator but one of standing with both parties. It's not hard to imagine the great pride they took in such a development. Yet any hopes the Jenkins clan had of enjoying any political benefit from Ella's spouse were already on their way to evaporating in the 1890s. White supremacists in the Democratic Party had long complained that Black people were not qualified to vote and certainly not qualified to serve in the legislature. Their arguments that Black people were ruining government seemed clearly in opposition to the facts. Democrats had long held an overwhelming majority in the legislature.

Regardless, Democrats would soon crush the Republican Party and in particular the basic right of Black people to vote. It had long rankled Dixie's Democrats that northern Republicans had merged political forces with southern Black people after the war, a development that spurred change in many places but especially in Wilmington, where many freed enslaved people had been drawn by opportunity. By the 1890s, the place was on its way to becoming a peer of Atlanta, with an emerging Black upper class, two Black newspapers, a Black mayor, an integrated police force, and an array of Black-owned businesses enjoying the prosperity that came to a busy port city.

By the 1890s, Democrats had been able to maintain white political control over much of the rest of North Carolina following the war and Reconstruction, but Wilmington and the coastal plain stood apart, largely on the strength of more than 120,000 Black male registered voters.

The Democrats' answer was to foment rebellion in Wilmington with a race riot on November 11, 1898, in which a white militia, called the Red Shirts, stirred by Democratic political rhetoric, took to the streets to burn a Black newspaper that had dared to challenge the Democrats, who used the irrational fear of Black males raping white women to stir up working-class votes.

The local morgue reported receiving fourteen bodies, thirteen of them Black, the next day, but others claimed the death toll ran as high as ninety. As the violence spread, terrified Black people fled with their families into the nearby swamps, where the Red Shirts were said to have pursued them to execute many more, whose remains were never recovered.

Determining a body count became difficult because the second phase of the well-planned rebellion began the next day as the Red Shirts escorted prominent Black people—clergymen, business leaders, politicians—to the train station and packed them out of town for good.

The resounding victory for white supremacy would secure the doctrine and prevent Black people from voting for decades to come. It had been led by the rhetoric of Democrat Charles Aycock, who would be elected governor in 1900. He had begun preaching in May 1898 that Black people in North Carolina needed to be removed from power.

"There shall be no progress in the South for either race until the Negro is removed permanently from the political process," Aycock had declared.

As governor he would set a legislative agenda that followed through on the riot's violent message with Jim Crow laws to limit Black voter registration. Within four short years, the number of Black males on voting rosters would plummet to fewer than six thousand. Removing Black people from politics across the South and other regions was a process that would escalate throughout much of the twentieth century. By the 1940s and '50s, for example, there were counties that had only one or two Black voters. Not only were Black people trapped in a culture based on ruinous sharecropping, the Jim Crow laws had taken away any legal means whatsoever they could use to change it.

Sharecropping

Records show that for decades after the Civil War, deep into the twentieth century, Magic Johnson's people faced the dead-end prospects of sharecropping and tenant farming in those days when the South offered little other options for Black families. For the longest time, such subsistence farming had brought a peasant existence, often mired in debt and servitude, just footsteps from slavery itself.

Sharecropping and tenant farming were not new systems. They had been in place around the globe for centuries for a human population often trapped as starving and downtrodden peasants with no political power whatsoever.

That, too, became the next plight of the vast majority of formerly enslaved people. Census records show millions of African American families with no equity at all in their lives decade after decade over the years of sharecropping, this after centuries of slavery likewise making building equity an impossibility.

In 1922, the North Carolina Board of Agriculture finally released an extensive report based on its study of one thousand farm families in the state confirming what had been known forever, that landless farmers, sharecroppers, and tenants, whether they be Black or white, were doomed to a life of debt and penury, often working twelve-hour days growing and harvesting tobacco and cotton, earning just a few pennies each day, if anything at all, and faced with borrowing money just to eat, all the while hoping at the end of the harvest for a thin share of the profits, always calculated by the landowners themselves with little or no accountability of crop sales.

Nobody made money sharecropping, the report said. Instead, it was a license to get cheated, an outcome confirmed time and again over the decades.

"It was an established fact," recalled Sandra Jones King, the daughter of an Edgecombe County, North Carolina, farmer, "that if you were a sharecropper, around December of the year the person whose farm you worked on would say something like, 'Well John, I don't have anything for you this year. We just broke even.'"

Sharecroppers were almost powerless in the equation, their only choice being to pack up their lives, move out of the tarpaper shack they were living in, and look for another landowner somewhere in the hope he would be honest.

If sharecroppers wanted to get agitated with the system, there was always the reminder that North Carolina had more Klan members than all the other southern states combined.

The North Carolina Board of Agriculture report came just eight years before the Great Depression began crushing agricultural prices and sending farm families, already facing a marginal existence, into full-fledged disaster.

It was in the midst of the Great Depression that both Earvin Sr. and Christine Johnson were born, he in 1934, she two years later.

After the Deluge

Magic Johnson's ancestors had soldiered on in North Carolina, their survival driven by a long line of women, their silhouettes marked by a noticeable stoop, left from their bending into the never-ending task of cutting the firewood and hauling immense amounts of water, performing the toil that the daily lives of their families required. And when the menfolk grew ill or died, the women in Johnson's heritage would step forward to assume command in the fields to assure that crops were planted, tended to, and harvested.

Willis Staton, Magic Johnson's great-great-grandfather, the son of Ferebe, went from life at Cool Spring to being a sharecropper after the war, just like almost every other former slave. He married a woman identified in records only as Charlette, almost half his age, a woman like so many of Johnson's ancestors who would bear the brunt of the subsistence farm life.

In that time and place before any real health care or birth control, women lived perilous lives, often worn down by their troubled maternities amidst a world of toil. They seemed destined to birth large families, a succession of labors that defined the wretchedness of farm life in rural North Carolina in the late nineteenth and early twentieth centuries.

It was a life wrought with ceaseless difficulty for women in that age before rural electrification. Pregnant year after year, all the while faced with the staggering workload of a farm woman, the cooking, washing, cleaning, cutting wood, and tending stove fires day in and day out, Charlette somehow raised the many children needed to scratch out a life from the thin options her family faced.

"Living was just drudgery then," a farm wife from that era once told writer Robert Caro. "Living—just living—was a problem. No lights. No plumbing. Nothing. Just living on the edge of starvation. That was the farm life for us."

Willis Staton, eighteen years older than Charlette, would pass on near the turn of the century, leaving her a widow running her large, extended family both by working in the fields and doing all the intense labor as a farm wife, a herculean task she had somehow managed for years, like so many among Johnson's ancestors.

Her daughter, Ida, too, would face a life of sharecropping. And she would also marry a man twice her age, Richard Porter, on February 10, 1897, in Edgecombe County, a fact that would make the couple Magic Johnson's great-grandparents.

Typical of the perils that farm women faced, Ida would die long before her older husband, likely due to the fact that she birthed seven children.

One of those children was a son, Isiah Porter, born in February 1905, who like those before him inherited the life of a sharecropper. He would marry Mary Della Jenkins on New Year's Eve 1927, in Edgecombe.

Mary Della Jenkins Porter had as many as eight children. She and Isiah Porter would spend their lives trapped in cotton and tobacco, struggling through infestations of boll weevil, the collapse of cotton prices, the Great Depression, storms, and crop failures, every sort of calamity. They were like the generations of the family who came before them, rising every day to face the daunting task of feeding their large families. Nowhere in the records of more than 170 years of Johnson's ancestors is there any indication whatsoever that even one of them shirked this duty.

As they carried on, neither Isiah Porter nor his wife, Mary Della, nor any of the family who came before them, could have possibly fathomed the wealth and power and fame that awaited their own grandson.

Magic Johnson's mother, Christine, the daughter of Mary Della and Isiah Porter, was born in 1936 just as big changes were finally coming to her family.

Amidst all of Franklin Delano Roosevelt's New Deal programs during the Depression there was one that aimed to address the shameful plight of sharecroppers. It was an experimental program that in select locations bought up vast acreage of former plantation land and turned it into hundreds of forty-acre farms where sharecroppers, Black and white, were allowed to purchase their own operations, complete with a modest new farmhouse.

In essence, the program was offering the basic "forty acres and a mule" that had been promised to formerly enslaved people during the last days of the Civil War by Union general William Tecumseh Sherman, in Georgia at the end of his famous March to the Sea.

Tragically, Sherman's order stood for just six months, until President Andrew Johnson, a southern sympathizer, rescinded it.

Census records show that during the Depression, Christine's family—she was just an infant—uprooted their lives near Tarboro and moved thirty miles north to Tillery, in nearby Halifax County, where the government had established one of its resettlement programs over an estimated twenty thousand acres.

The program in Tillery was one of 113 rural "experiments" in resettlement that the federal government had created across the country. Of those, apparently only fifteen included Black farmers. The Tillery Resettlement Farm was renamed Roanoke Farms in 1936.

The idea seemed dreamlike until reality swiftly arrived with the challenge of hundreds of farm families abruptly relocating there, creating newly reconstituted communities and subsequent chaos. Ultimately, conditions would prove impossible, especially for the Black sharecroppers.

Federal administrators for the program had arrived in Halifax County to discover that a good portion of the twenty thousand acres set aside for the resettlement program lay in a floodplain of the Roanoke River. Those assigned to the flood-prone areas were mostly Black farmers, records show.

Even worse, the federal agents tended to leave the white farmers to their own designs while insisting on micromanaging the operations of the Black farmers, men who had decades of experience working the fields of North Carolina.

The 1940 census recorded a pregnant Mary Della Jenkins Porter and husband, Isiah, living in the Dawson portion of the resettlement program with their six children, including four-year-old Christine.

Much of the resettlement project was doomed almost from the start, according to Charlie Thompson, an agricultural economics expert from Duke University who later helped make a film about the resettlement program.

"If you've been a sharecropping family, you're going to try it," Thompson said of the people who packed up their lives and bought into the program. "They've been making nothing and then there's some promise of owning something and making your own way and having your own land. That is attractive enough to risk everything, and that's what they did."

After decades of marginal subsistence farming, Black farmers could finally see an opportunity to gain something for all their years of backbreaking labor, only to discover the game had again changed.

"By the time the thirties come around the deck is already stacked," Thompson explained. "Agriculture had already begun to mechanize."

At the same time the Roosevelt administration initiated the resettlement program, it also launched the United States Department of Agriculture (USDA), which began offering farmers crop loans and price supports, new devices in the agriculture markets, Thompson pointed out in a 2020 interview. "Basically, this begins the U.S. government's involvement in encouraging farms to grow in size."

The focus of the federal government became the creation of larger, corporate farms that could achieve an economy of scale.

"So they're doing that in the Midwest and farms are starting to mechanize and tractors are starting to be a reality for many farmers," Thompson explained. "At the same time, they're saying to African Americans, 'We promised back in the Civil War when Sherman went through the South that we would provide forty acres and a mule. It's time to do that.' So they're providing forty acres and a mule to people who live in these resettlement communities. But they were competing against what were already starting to be called 'bonanza farms' of the Midwest. And so the grain prices are set according to the large-scale production, not to small farm production. And so already structurally small farming is behind the eight ball. They can't possibly compete with it. Their raising forty acres just can't provide enough for families. And so here we are. We're trying to put these farmers on the land. They are raising field crops and trying to sell those, and there's just not enough money in it for people, plus they're doing it with mules when tractors are starting to be a reality."

After centuries of slavery and eight decades of sharecropping, Black farmers were finally offered what was supposed to be a remedy for all the abuse they had suffered only to find the remedy itself was nearly worthless.

The sharecroppers came to the resettlement program in phases, said Gary Grant, whose family participated in the resettlement and managed to prosper despite the odds stacked against them.

In addition to the agricultural changes, many other factors brought failure for the farmers, including difficulty in adjusting to hastily assembled farming communities, plus land that was of poor quality.

Yet with each group that failed, there were a few farm families that made it work, Grant explained in a 2020 interview. "The New Deal was successful in ensuring independence of some blacks. Land-owning certainly put them into another dimension. However, whites knew that independence meant no more free labor for them and thus it had to be stopped."

For a Black population that had been denied every sort of connection with mainstream society for decades beyond slavery, change itself had become a major enemy, because the society that virtually imprisoned them in poverty had rendered so many of them ill-prepared for change.

The resettlement farmers had some tractors that they could share. "But poor land plus racism really put these families at a disadvantage," Thompson explained. "They had to borrow money. This was not a gift. So in many cases there was paternalism. They would go into the office and there would be this white guy who would ask for the payment and they would just say, 'This is impossible. We can't make the payments. We had a crop failure or the price was so low that we couldn't.' I'm speaking generally but those are big reasons why."

The census taken that summer of 1940, as Europe was plowing deeper into the Second World War, shows the Porter family—Magic

Johnson's grandparents and their children—managing to survive on the land with Mary Della again pregnant.

It was in the middle of August when the deluge would sweep into their world, a great hundred-year flood, driven by tropical storms that first ravaged communities in the North Carolina mountains to the west, then gathered momentum to swell the Roanoke River to thirty-one feet above flood level on its way to an all-time record crest of fifty-eight feet, according to the Associated Press and the *New York Times*. The deluge struck the resettlement farm floodplain on August 17, 1940, and wiped out crops and farms and houses for just about every farm family in the floodplain. Two men drowned trying to cross a flooded road.

"At Tillery, near here, about 1,000 persons, mostly negroes, were removed by boats from a government rehabilitation project," the Associated Press reported. "The refugees were quartered in schools and mills on high ground."

It's not hard to imagine the difficulty Mary Della Jenkins Porter, then thirty-six and in a late-term pregnancy, would have faced during the evacuation of her large family on boats with everything they had worked so hard for now literally swept away. The Raleigh *News and Observer* estimated that three thousand people had been left homeless in the flood zone.

Just days after the evacuation, Mary Della Jenkins Porter gave birth to her eighth child, James. The loss of their farms, their crops before harvest, their new lives, was absolutely devastating for so many farm families, just about all of them African American.

In what was perhaps a sign of the family's desperation in the aftermath, thirty-six-year-old Isiah Porter signed up for the draft and even appeared to fudge his age, making himself five years younger in hopes of getting into the service. He was not selected. The great loss could have easily resulted in a deep, paralyzing, forlorn bitterness settling over the family. Somehow Mary Della Jenkins Porter did not let that happen.

After the disaster with the resettlement project in Tillery, public records next find the Porter family back down in Edgecombe County, from whence they had originally come, in farm country near

Tarboro, once again trying to eke out a living in the losing game of sharecropping, now more impossible than ever.

Time froze for so many farmworkers during World War II, except for the thousands who joined the continued Great Migration north looking for any sort of job that actually paid something.

For those who stayed behind on Tobacco Road, including Christine's family, time continued to move along measured in twelve-hour workdays and marked by a wondrous faith that somehow allowed them to shoulder the seemingly unbearable.

5

THE BIKE RIDE

If Earvin Johnson's adolescent years were the subject of a film, the soundtrack would surely have to include an early '70s Motown number, say "Mama's Pearl" by the Jackson 5. The song could help segue to the part of the story where he spent summers in and around Rocky Mount, North Carolina, visiting relatives, his mother's people, marking the young pilgrim's own first big appearance on Tobacco Road.

That's where future college and NBA star Buck Williams had occasion to first encounter Earvin Johnson. "I lived in Rocky Mount and Magic's aunt and uncle lived in Rocky Mount, and he would come down from Michigan during the summers," Williams remembered in a 2019 interview. "He would come down there and stay two, three weeks at a time."

People in the community soon heard about the young stranger who had shown up at a local park to take on Cleveland Howard, nicknamed Tubac, a six-four specimen at Rocky Mount Senior High, where he had starred with the great Phil Ford. Howard was quite an athlete and a legendary player on the courts around Rocky Mount. He had been a four-year two-way starter in football in high school as well, but in basketball he was an extraordinary leaper with something of an outside shot. Some in Rocky Mount even believed Howard was better than Phil Ford, recalled Reggie Barrett, who frequented the playgrounds at the time.

The thirteen-year-old Johnson and the eighteen-year-old Howard didn't have to spend too much time at the park before they were drawn to what would become a legendary one-on-one showdown.

"It was really competitive, really intense," Buck Williams, who was eight months younger than Johnson, recalled. "It was a very grueling game because it pitted our best player from Rocky Mount against this guy named Johnson. They called him Buck at the time."

"I only saw the first game," recalled Reggie Barrett in 2019. "Magic won the first game. It was a best-of-three games. It was for $20, which was a lot of money in 1973 or when they played. Cleveland was playing at Merced [California] Junior College at the time. After Merced, he went into the air force. When they played, he was home for the summer."

What seemed in memory like a throng at Hillsdale Park came alive with the showdown between the two exceptional athletes, and soon enough the moment found a place in the region's basketball lore.

It was startling to see a young player with Johnson's size handle the ball so smoothly, especially against an older player with a rep and his own top skill level, Buck Williams recalled. "Magic won, but it was an unbelievable game. I was twelve, thirteeen at the time and it was one of those moments in time where you don't know how significant it is. Thinking back on it, it was crazy. One of the greatest players to ever play the game came to Rocky Mount and was pitted against one of the greatest players in Rocky Mount. People there still talk about that game to this day. That was my first introduction to Earvin Johnson."

Williams remembered being awed by "how Magic's talent stood out and how he had a unique style to his game. He was very smooth, very fluid, very slick. He had a natural flair to his game. And he had incredible confidence. Even then, he was incredibly confident. That was my introduction to the guy named Earvin Johnson."

Home Again

Johnson returned home that summer of 1973 to find his ninth-grade season in junior high awaiting him along with the lingering uncertainty over his high school future. In another age, say two or three decades down the road, the family of Christine and Earvin Johnson, Sr., would have had an entirely different set of options, a different level of power, in responding to the situation Larry Johnson had faced.

If Earvin Jr. had been born in 1979 or 1989 instead of 1959, he would have found himself faced with all kinds of people eager to offer him enticing alternatives to playing high school basketball. In another few decades, a fourteen-year-old with Earvin Johnson's obvious talent would be the absolute darling of the basketball recruiting world, with college offers galore and elite club teams sponsored by shoe companies bidding to jet him around the country to play basketball.

Yet almost none of that was available as 1972 turned to 1973 and then to 1974.

Young Earvin had little power and almost zero options as to where he played basketball. That was likely true for his parents as well. Yet power didn't seem to be anything that concerned Johnson's parents as the matter unfolded. It's fair to say that Earvin Sr. and his wife were far more a function of their strength rather than any sort of power.

Indeed, in retrospect, you could argue that over the course of the 1970s, the Johnsons offered up the kind of personal value system that would steer not just their son but the course of the sport of basketball itself in unseen ways.

Even his strength, however, was something that Earvin Sr. projected quietly rather than trumpeted. Yet he was hardly a pushover. He could get righteous in a hurry if the situation called for it. But he constantly showed that he operated from a lower, steadier gear.

"I believe in doing the right thing, not the might-be-okay-to-do thing," he once explained in one of his rare public utterances about anything related to himself. "You know what I mean?"

Such an approach would prove critical as his son's talent began to gain clarity in the public mind. Even the keenest observers of basketball in Lansing weren't sure what to make of young Earvin, except for one, Clayton Kowalk, the athletic director for Lansing's schools.

Dr. Matthew Prophet, Lansing's new deputy superintendent for schools, a Black man, went to work in the city in September 1972, and clearly recalled, looking back in 2019, that on his second day on the job, Clayton Kowalk had come into his office and introduced himself. During that initial meeting, Kowalk told Prophet about this junior high player named Earvin Johnson. Kowalk declared that Johnson was on his way to becoming one of the greatest players in the history of the game.

In many ways it was an outrageous statement, but Kowalk had Hall of Fame credentials. As head coach at Sexton, he had won those two state championships back in the early 1960s, the only two Class A state titles ever won by a Lansing school in that era.

Kowalk averred to Prophet that he knew the game, had seen up close all of Michigan's great players, amateur and pro, over the years. Johnson would be as good or better than any player to ever come out of Michigan, which had long been a virtual fountain of basketball talent.

It would be quite a while before others would make such declarations about Johnson, but they were coming.

The ninth-grade season would rest in memory for many as the true beginning of the revelation. Gary Fox, George's son, was a high school junior that year. He had seen Johnson play in the eighth grade and was impressed. When he and his dad took in one of Johnson's early ninth-grade performances, he was curious to see if the kid had gotten better.

"By ninth grade when I went into that game, I didn't recognize him," Gary Fox remembered. "They were doing warm-ups and I'm looking around and wondering where's that little Johnson kid? All of a sudden here he stood head and shoulders above everybody."

Johnson had shot up, from a little over six feet to six-five. When the game started, it was immediately obvious that Johnson was a man among boys. Gary Fox recalled watching Johnson "against his peers as an eighth grader when he was a good player, but as a ninth grader, he just dominated the game. He had grown. I recall he could jump center and bring the ball up and hit the open man. He dominated."

Although he didn't yet know Earvin, Charles Tucker also observed plenty about his game in that ninth-grade season. "He was so big, at that time," Tucker explained in 2019. "When you're big and you're playing with kids at your own age, you can kind of control them. . . . He did that very well. He was able just to keep on running over little kids because he was so big. He just kept controlling the ball all the time."

Dale Beard, at the time an eighth grader playing for Pattengill Junior High, had occasion to watch Johnson. "I thought, 'Wow, you know, this guy is incredible,'" Beard recalled. "You know, bringing the ball up the court and then directing traffic. I'm talking about fourteen years old. That was remarkable back then. You never saw that. He had a lot of special talents for somebody that size and that age."

Looking back in 2019, George Fox said that if the rules at that time had allowed ninth graders to play varsity ball, Earvin Johnson would have been the best player on the Everett varsity.

After that early-ninth-grade game, Earvin was his usual cordial self while visiting with George Fox and apparently gave no hint of how he really felt about Everett or the basketball program. The fact remained, however, that Larry Johnson had vowed his brother would never play for Fox or Everett. The passage of time had done little to soften that vow, which now quietly sizzled on the family agenda. Earvin obviously felt the growing pressure, and would admit as much later.

Larry's problems at school had only worsened with time, prompting Earvin Sr. to get involved, Charles Tucker recalled. "I remember his dad came over to the school a couple of times. He was laying down the rules to the principal and to Larry, too, you know, in a positive way."

As much as young Earvin disliked the idea of attending Everett, he was obviously pleased with all the attention the varsity coach was paying to him. What young player wouldn't respond to positive feedback from a coach? And Fox was a smiling and friendly sort. It seems obvious in retrospect that the seeds of their chemistry were developing then.

The circumstances, however, also suggest perhaps that Larry and his younger brother would also work together to shift their tactics later that junior high season in their effort to play some mind games with the Everett coach.

In 1980, George Fox recalled, "One day his brother came by and said, 'Hey, Coach, Earvin says to come to the game today. He's going to set a junior high scoring record.'"

Prompted by Larry, Fox went to the game that day and was treated to a spectacle. Almost like Babe Ruth, Earvin had called his own shot. Johnson scored 48 points against Otto Junior High, rung up in three six-minute quarters until he sat happily on the bench for the final six minutes of the fourth of the 89–25 blowout.

It almost seemed as if that ninth-grade scoring outburst was Earvin Johnson's first statement game of sorts, that the Johnson brothers were delighting in saying to the coach, "Look at this, look at what you're losing because of how you treated Larry."

Earvin would set three city records in that 10-game junior high season. He scored 227 points and pulled in 138 rebounds. His team's 89 points against Otto was also a junior high record. His photo looked out of place in the *Lansing State Journal* next to a story about a junior high student. In the headshot, he looked mature enough to be a college or even an NBA player.

For all the hoopla, that gaudy ninth-grade season would wind its way to an unexpected conclusion in the city championship bout with his early rival, Jay Vincent, who was no longer consigned to the bench.

"We beat them in ninth grade at their place," Vincent crowed with a chuckle in an interview nearly a half century later. "We beat them for the city title. That's why Magic never says they won the ninth-grade title, because we beat them."

The loss in the championship galled Earvin no end. He recalled spending weeks crying about it off and on, bringing a realization of just how much he hated losing. Three years later, when a reporter asked him about scoring 48 points in a single game, he would be almost dismissive of the event, saying, "Yeah, but we lost the championship."

The loss also left some observers wondering if he was really that good, or was it simply the competition he played against that made him seem so advanced? "Ninth grade is when he really came forward," George Fox remembered. "But again, you know, it's against junior high competition. So, it's not always good for you, but you can see he would sweep a rebound and he just had a knack for getting clear of all the traffic and heading up the floor."

Watching the ninth-grade version of Johnson prompted George Fox to start making plans for the next season, to the point he told assistant Pat Holland, "One thing we got to do with that big fella, we really got to work on him on posting up and rebounding around the bucket because he will be a dominating player."

"I never really thought much about his unbelievable passing," Fox admitted in 2019.

The one thing Earvin knew coming out of that loss was that once he got the rebound, he never wanted to give up the ball, never wanted to give up advantage again, not if he could help it.

Tuck

It wasn't too long after that ninth-grade season that Charles Tucker set himself up to learn more about the big kid he had seen playing so often outdoors at Main Street School. "I was counseling in the Lansing school district when I was working on my doctoral degree," Tucker recalled in 2019, "and I was dealing with kids that somewhat couldn't make a good adjustment in a classroom situation. Maybe they were struggling with some little minor behavior problems. And so, one of my ways of counseling those kids, I found out you could have some success if you mixed some of the good kids with some of the kids that might be having some behavior or adjustment problems."

Earvin Johnson had been recommended to Tucker as a student he might want to mix in with the group because he was well known for having a positive influence on other students.

"I needed that type of student in there," Tucker recalled. "It fulfilled those needs and he mirrored that. It was a blessing that I had him in there. He was extremely important to that group for his behavior and all the other things that were necessary."

Johnson remembered that, after the group session, he was playing on the school's outdoor courts with his friends when Tucker, in a seemingly bizarre development, suddenly showed up, no longer wearing a shirt and tie but now dressed in athletic shoes and gym wear. And the psychologist challenged Johnson to a game of one-on-one, which he won by shoving the taller teen around physically, holding and pushing him, a twenty-five-year-old man going up against a mere boy, embarrassing him in front of his friends.

"Nice game," Tucker said afterward, which infuriated Johnson and his friends. Then Tucker told Johnson he needed to learn to play "the pro game."

It didn't take long before the psychologist had arranged to challenge Johnson on the court in regular pickup games that marked the beginning of a most unusual relationship, played out in lots of one-on-one battles, where they discovered they shared some intensely competitive traits, evidenced by the fact they were constantly accusing each other of cheating.

"Earvin always wanted to win now," Tucker recalled. "I know that because we used to fight. I didn't want to lose. And he didn't want to lose. He'd do anything to win. He'd cheat a little bit and accuse you of cheating." Tucker himself was known for bending whatever rule he could in his own favor. Already a budding practitioner of gamesmanship, Johnson soaked up the advanced tutelage.

"We understood each other," Tucker recalled. "We knew how to win. I always knew how to win, especially playing pickup ball." Some players might have taken pickup games lightly. Neither Tucker nor Johnson apparently ever even considered such a notion.

"I don't care what kind of ball you were playing, Earvin always knew the score," Tucker remembered. "He knew how to win, how to play the game."

Such an approach involved the studied practice of calling a foul at the end of a tied game if you missed a shot, Tucker said, his voice cracking with a chuckle. "He'd do this all the time. People talked about him and me like dogs. The last basket? Don't give it to Tucker. Don't give it to Earvin. Because we'd figure out a way to get a foul if we didn't make the basket."

Which meant they learned early how to litigate furiously sometimes with each other if they were playing one-on-one. The psychologist and the junior high player were soon constantly in search of challenges on the courts, with their relationship quickly evolving to become one of fellow junkies for the game.

The situation also cast the relationship between Tucker and Johnson in an unusual framework. By numerous accounts, the psychologist quickly became a mentor to Johnson in literally every phase of his life. Tucker owned a nice suburban home in which he would soon have a bedroom reserved for Johnson to stay over some nights, obviously a break from the crowded quarters on Middle Street with Johnson's large family.

Tucker would also become an extension of sorts of Johnson's parents, taking a major role in guiding and supervising various phases of his life, even though he had never actually met either Big Earv or Christine. Neither did it hurt that Tucker had what appeared to others to be a collection of nice cars. In those early months together, Tucker would drive Johnson to pickup games around the city. And on special occasions, Tucker would take Johnson and a friend to pro games in Indianapolis and Chicago and Detroit. Tucker showed that he knew the players and could get into the locker rooms, where he would introduce Johnson to his idols.

At Cobo Hall in Detroit, Tucker introduced him to Kareem Abdul-Jabbar, by first working the atmosphere cautiously, watching while standing aside, taking the moment when it arose to step in and address Kareem, then calling Johnson over to meet the great stone-faced center and shake his hand.

Afterward, driving back to Lansing, Tucker told the teen that someday young fans would line up to greet him in a pro locker room, the mere notion of which seemed surreal and distant, but it gave Johnson something to think of when he wanted to dream and to think about things that excited him.

At the time, Johnson was going through an estrangement from his father, who was working all the time. For their trips together, Tucker always insisted that Johnson's father knew where they were going. Johnson would reply that his father didn't care about him, didn't care where he went. That wasn't true, Tucker assured him.

It would be some months before Tucker would meet the parents. When he did, Tucker was so taken by the father, as he would say later, that he fell in love with the guy almost immediately. It didn't hurt that they were both Black men from Mississippi.

"That's what I was used to being around," Tucker explained. "Later on, you look back at it and it's amazing. But not at that time. Because that was just the type of guy that he was. He didn't know what the outcome was going to be as far as Earvin later on in life. He just did it because that's what you're supposed to do. I didn't pay it close attention at that time. I just knew he was a hard worker."

As the days peeled away, more and more powerful people would coalesce around Johnson's son, but Tucker would later look back and recognize that the most powerful among them all was Earvin Sr. himself. For a person who played his cards so close, it was remarkable that the father was never out to impress anyone nor did he attempt in any overt way to exert influence.

"He was the real deal just by being himself, you know," Tucker observed in 2019.

After the two men met, it wasn't too long before Tucker, the psychologist, made the unusual move of offering to go along late at night when Earvin Sr. was making runs with his cleaning service and trash truck.

"I had worked every place, all kind of jobs," Tucker explained. "Just because I had a degree didn't mean anything."

In fact, of his many sweet memories of working with the Johnson family, some of the best remained his time hanging out with Earvin Sr. Tucker was aware that people didn't quite know what to make of him as a highly educated Black male taking the approach he did. But Tucker had always found an easy connection with the everyday working world that Earvin Sr. inhabited. Tucker recalled being struck by the fact that even though Earvin Sr. worked very hard he still found a way to have a major impact on his children.

"He had an impact on me too," Tucker said of those days in his late twenties. "He was more like a true friend. He was just a good example of what I was used to being around. He was just so bright, so smart. I looked at him that way. It really didn't have anything to do with Earvin Jr. That's how our friendship became so strong. I was closer to him than I was with Earvin Jr. He had a big impact on me. I could talk to him about everything and anything. We could laugh. We'd talk about business. And school. Because he had other kids in school besides just Earvin. Earvin Sr. knew the streets very well too."

As a psychologist, Tucker loved to observe people, a particularly important thing to do in those painful days of integration in the public schools. He was struck by how Earvin Sr. camouflaged so much about himself.

"He'd try to play that dumb role," Tucker recalled. "But when you got to know him, he was very bright, so bright it was scary sometimes. He impressed me because he never asked people for anything. He was just a hard worker. We used to have fun when we'd go out at night, when he'd pick me up and I'd go out there with him to clean places. Sometimes we'd have so much fun clownin' around out there we'd be out there thirty minutes longer than we should have been because we were out there seeing who could sweep the fastest, who could lift the most, tellin' jokes and all kind of stuff. I just got to know him. Once you knew how smart he was and that he was for real, you could go to him for help."

It would take longer for Tucker to get to know Christine Johnson. She was more emotive than Earvin Sr. Yet as parents they just about always operated in lockstep, going about their lives with an absolute minimum of fanfare.

Young Earvin obviously soaked up their approach, and the situation with Larry clearly was maturing him into a new assertiveness. As the days passed, he began looking around for options, for an answer, for some sort of power that would prevent him from being forced to go to a school against his will.

Contact

Slowly the facts began to stack up to a realization that late spring, that Earvin might just have to attend Everett High, no matter how much he hated the thought of it. Yet even then he staunchly held out, seeking to balance the facts in his fourteen-year-old mind. He sensed he needed more information.

It was then that he turned the matter over to his instincts, a portion of his nature that was just beginning a lifetime of serving him well. He took a bike ride on a pretty day, far from his home in downtown Lansing out into the suburbs. The cover for his mission was to play yet more ball at a park way out in the country. The important fact was that it was just around the corner from George Fox's home. Johnson apparently wanted to know more about this congenial guy who had been coming to his games with his family tagging along, the very same guy who had kicked Larry off the team. Perhaps Johnson wasn't taking the bike ride as a conscious move. Sometimes powerful instinct can operate so silently that a person doesn't even recognize the reason behind his actions. However, Johnson's life would reveal his inclination to decisiveness and this trip to the suburbs was simply an early expression of that.

Sure enough, when Johnson got out to the street where George Fox lived, he discovered that the coach had a driveway with a hoop over the garage, perfect for him to stop and take some shots. Strangely enough, the hoop wasn't regulation height, which meant he liked it even more because he could dunk on it without having to struggle too much.

At the time, not much was thought about Johnson showing up at the house of the Everett High coach to shoot baskets. Yet, in retrospect, it was an extraordinary move at relationship building by a mere adolescent, whether fully conscious or not. Psychologist George Mumford, who would work extensively with both Michael Jordan and Kobe Bryant, looked at the circumstances years later and said they provided an early revelation of the substantial emotional intelligence that would come to mark Johnson's professional life.

Johnson would recall that he was the only kid in his neighborhood with a bike because most of the other families couldn't afford one. Thus, Johnson remembered, he hardly ever rode his bike because he didn't care to ride alone. It would seem then that there was nothing casual about this effort to ride miles away to the home of the man who was supposed to be his new coach.

Charles Tucker looked back on the moment and offered that it was even more remarkable considering the social barriers a fourteen-year-old Johnson was crossing in an age marked by racial tension.

Fox's daughter Missy, herself a teen at the time, didn't think all that much about it and just considered it an unusual appearance by that kid she had seen create so much fun in a mere junior high game.

Johnson's unannounced arrival at her house was something that Fox's daughter would easily recall years later, in a 2019 interview. "I remember thinking, 'That kid lives down by Sexton and he is riding his bike all the way here? He's kind of young to be doing that.' I knew it was that kid from the gym. He was probably going to be going to Everett. He's not high school yet; he's still in junior high school. And he would ride his bike way out here from where he lived? If you knew where he lived, it wasn't like we were neighbors."

There's no question Johnson's big visit was somewhat risky, Charles Tucker said, looking back in 2019. "Many times, in those situations rather than having a good experience like that, it might be a bad experience."

To come to the Foxes' house on a bike required a significant effort, and it raised an interesting question. How did Johnson even know where the coach lived?

"He would ride down our street to go to the park," Missy Fox explained, "and he would stop, and we had this little basketball hoop that was just attached to the garage so he could dunk on that." He was welcomed and invited into the house. Johnson didn't make the trip only once. He returned several times.

"He would just come and sit at the table and wait for my dad," Missy recalled, "and he just looked real polite and nice and very respectful to my mom and my sisters and I. He was just a really nice kid. I think that he was pretty young when he and my dad started a relationship, knowing that he was coming up. At the time they were starting busing, so he had to come over to my dad's school."

The other indelible impression left on the coach's daughter was the countenance. "Oh my," she said. "Look at that smile, right? That is the one thing he's always had, that smile. And so that just draws you in because when he would smile now . . ."

She let the thought trail off, then said, "He was very shy. He would not talk unless talked to, but we would ask him questions, you know, and he would just have that smile. He would just glow with that smile, but we didn't know that he was like a big deal. You know, we just thought here's another basketball player. This kid is just a nice kid, just a really nice kid."

Even though the visits were unusual, the coach's daughter and family were obviously pleased by them. "I'm glad he did because then we got to know him," Missy said. "We had no idea though. I didn't picture what was going to happen eventually, what happened to him. It was just unbelievable."

"He used to come over," the coach recalled in 2019. "He'd go by and he'd stop once in a while to play in my driveway. I had a basket that was about maybe nine feet, and he'd stop there. I'd be out maybe playing ball myself in a driveway with some kids and he'd stop and play a little bit with us."

Although the shorter goal offered the opportunity to dunk, in no way was that guaranteed, the coach recalled. "He really couldn't dunk till he grew up a little bit and got bigger. I don't know if he ever dunked in the eighth or ninth grade. He might have, but it took him a run to get there, you know, maybe like off a fast break or where he'd steal the ball and go lay it up. I remember when he did start dunking, he'd take three or four dribbles and had to get his speed up to get up in the air."

Told in 2019 about Johnson's unusual effort to get to know the coach at such a young age, Charles Tucker said it only made sense, in light of the ongoing racial issues at Everett, that Earvin was obviously feeling out just how he would be accepted by the coaches who had rejected his brother.

"I think you have to be accepted fully both ways," Tucker observed. "The coach had to accept the player and the player had to accept the coach." As logical as it seemed, such a conclusion was far from guaranteed, no matter how well Johnson's visits went.

The Summer League

It's not clear if the Everett coaches were aware at the time that they were being played a bit by Larry and Earvin. If so, the coaches would not admit to it in interviews decades later. Both George Fox and Pat Holland insisted they never had the slightest doubt that Earvin Johnson was coming to Everett.

That certainly wasn't because young Earvin didn't try to get out of it. Over the summer of 1974, as he was set to enter tenth grade, Earvin recalled, he wrote to the city schools administration asking to be allowed an exception to attend Sexton High. He even explored moving in with another family to change his residence. In one form or another, city officials said no.

It wasn't just that city officials said no. Johnson's parents said no as well, telling their son the school board had determined that he had to go to Everett and that was where he was going.

Which made logical the next step in his relationship with George Fox, which came when Johnson agreed to play for Everett's summer league team. That, in turn, brought a revelation.

"I watched Earvin in practice," Fox explained, "where we practiced in the summer, and I never realized how good he was until we started playing summer games."

Fox had been running summer league games for his teams for a few years. Because he had several other sophomores coming to the team with Johnson, the coach decided to schedule games against smaller, lower division schools. They were good teams that were more rural, a bit whiter, rather than the tougher upper division schools.

"I didn't want to take the sophomores who I just got and throw them to the wolves of Detroit," the coach explained. "I just didn't want to do that. I didn't want to play Saginaw and I didn't want to play some of the Flint schools. I didn't want to go into Detroit because we weren't ready for that."

At the end of the first quarter of the first summer league game, "we were ahead like 25 or 30 to two or three," Fox recalled. "I mean I just couldn't get over it. I never liked to press so we did not press. We just demolished a fairly reputable school when they crossed half-court. And so that's the thing I remember most about our summer league in 1974 was that we just beat teams up bad."

It was Fox's first experience in how Johnson could multiply the talent around him. "So that's the thing I remember most about my early experiences with Earvin, how the other players because of Earvin, they just played better too," the coach said. "He made them better players. I think he's done that all the way through college and pro. He brought the best out of guys. They knew if they worked hard and got open, they were going to get the ball. So, he created that atmosphere beginning when he was going into the tenth grade."

When his team won the second game in similar fashion, Fox told his players he would have to schedule better competition for the next summer.

"They all liked that and we did," he said.

It was in that first summer league that Fox, who had starred on a state championship team himself when he was in high school, was struck with the idea that now as a coach he had the makings of a title team. There was only one problem. The coach had no idea just how much Earvin Johnson was still opposed to the idea of going to Everett.

Jenison

Late that summer, the coach learned from his son Gary that Michigan State players and other top talent were gathering for top-shelf pickup games at Jenison Field House on the school's campus.

"I went out and played," Gary Fox recalled, "and I told my dad about it, that it was just a great experience for local kids to go play against, you know, guys like Lindsay Hairston and Benny White, Bill Kilgore, and Bob Chapman. And they had a kid named Terry Furlow who was really good. So those guys were in that upper gym at Jenison."

The coach quickly suggested that his son invite Johnson to go along the next time he went.

"I stopped and picked up Earvin and we went out and played against the Michigan State kids. It was just old-school open gym. It was all man-to-man. There was no zone, no gimmicks, no box and ones and things like that. The Michigan State kids would take on all challengers."

Johnson, Gary Fox, and some local kids took the floor as a team.

"Now the games were pretty short as I remember," Gary Fox went on. "They were maybe to 9 or 11 baskets, win by two. If you win you get to stay on the floor. The five of us walk out and Earvin wants Furlow. He's like, 'I'm going to go to the best player on the floor.' That's right. There's a high school kid, fifteen years old, never even played in a high school game and he's going to match himself up with the best player in the place."

The game took off at a good pace, up and down. "We were hanging with them and then Earvin brought the ball across half-court and Furlow picked it clean away and headed down to the other end."

In those days, dunking was illegal in college basketball, so "Furlow just went in, laid it off the glass and Earvin came from behind and swept it right off the board and went the other way," Gary Fox recalled. "I remember there's almost like a pause in the house. You know, some high school kid just swept it off the board and headed the other way like it was nothing against the best player there. Furlow, you know, was headed to the NBA."

It was definitely a moment. "Earvin just had a knack for timing, you know, whether it be a big play or whatever. It was just different. If you had a special moment, he could fill it."

With such a big splash, the local group made plans to return. The next time they arrived with Reggie Chastine, a lightning-quick point guard at about five-five, a rising junior on the Everett varsity. Gary

Fox and his friend drove a small pickup, so Johnson and Chastine just jumped in the back.

"When we got out there that time Furlow had an opening on his team. So when we walked in, he grabbed Earvin right away," Fox recalled. "So now Earvin's running up and down with the State kids instead of against them and they held the court most of the day."

When it came time to go, Johnson told Fox he was going to hang around.

"So, he and Reggie found their own way home that day," Gary Fox said. "But it was just amazing to see a fifteen-year-old that had never played high school ball, he's out there in the purest form. It was just up and down the court for pure joy. You could just see the determination and joy in his eyes. That's what Earvin was all about. He wanted to play the best."

Johnson himself recalled other incidents in getting to know the Michigan State star, that Furlow called him "big boy" and "my boy," that soon Furlow began appearing at Johnson's high school games, a pretty girl on each arm. Before long, Furlow was inviting him to college parties where there would be college girls smiling right back at him.

With Furlow, young Earvin, earnest pilgrim that he was, had found another sort of mentor to come into his life, one who wouldn't just battle him on the floor but would introduce him to a bit of the sweet taste of the player's life and a view of all that lay ahead.

6

MISSISSIPPI

Dr. Matthew Prophet, Jr., would long remember the cross burned in his family's yard back in his hometown of Okolona, Mississippi, in the 1930s, all because his father had tried to register to vote. And his father was reasonably well liked in the community of two thousand or so, at least for a Black man. Heaven knows what might have happened if his father had been disdained. Violence could erupt in a flash in Mississippi.

Prophet himself brought an impressive résumé to Lansing, Michigan, in 1972 when he arrived to begin serving as deputy superintendent of schools. He had been drafted into the U.S. Army in 1950 as a buck private and rose steadily through the ranks while serving combat tours in both the Korean and Vietnam Wars, to become a lieutenant colonel, all while obtaining his undergraduate and master's degrees.

After Prophet retired from the military in 1970, he went directly to Northwestern University to earn a doctoral degree in education that focused on his traveling around America and Europe to study various approaches to integration. That included a trip back to his hometown in Mississippi to revisit the grim conditions there.

Upon completion of his studies in 1972, Prophet had been hired by Lansing, where he and the superintendent of schools, I. Carl Candoli, set out on a mission to change the world, or at least to integrate the schools properly, a herculean task that would require many assets, not the least of which was a tall adolescent named Earvin Johnson.

As Prophet would explain in a 2019 interview, Lansing school administrators had begun to include Johnson in their integration plans well before he was ever nicknamed Magic. In time, Prophet would go on to become the highly celebrated and innovative superintendent of the Portland, Oregon, school system, as well as a longtime friend of the adult Magic Johnson. But before all of that could happen, the school administrator and the high school basketball player had important roles to play in the cauldron of Lansing's racial issues over busing and integration in the 1970s.

The experience wasn't hurt by the fact that Prophet, like other key figures in Earvin Johnson's life, was a Mississippian who, like Earvin Sr., had emerged via the U.S. Army from that state's ugly racial climate.

"It was fully and totally segregated without fail," Prophet recalled of the culture that he and Earvin Sr. and so many others endured growing up during the 1930s and '40s.

"There were certain mores and expectations in terms of behavior on the part of Black men, particularly if you were walking on the sidewalks, which were narrow. If a Black male were to meet a white woman approaching him, the Black male must step off the sidewalk and go walking in the street until he gets around the white woman."

If a Black male failed to show such deference, or if he made a move that was somehow perceived as being aggressive around a white woman, "he could be hanged," Prophet said. "Or if in fact he was accused of any other kind of illegal activity he could be hanged."

Mississippi was known for its lynchings and violent acts against Black males, but many hangings were not lynchings. They were executions authorized by the local courts and carried out for what often were seemingly trivial offenses with much fanfare in the town, as Prophet recalled. The executions would draw crowds of white people, often dressed up for the occasion. Meanwhile, Black people understandably gave these events a wide berth.

So many other incidents of violence against Black males were carried out in the backwoods, usually not reported by newspapers, events that traveled only by word of mouth, whispered oh so carefully.

In their time working together, Tucker and Earvin Johnson, Sr., had addressed their lives in Mississippi, the psychologist recalled. "Listening to some of the things that Earvin Sr. had said about the South, his situation was somewhat like mine. A lot was going on, and we heard little bits and pieces. We were very educated about how to respond to them with the upbringing of our parents."

Earvin Sr. at age seven watched his mother leave his father and load him and his brother up to move to Chicago to live with relatives, an experience that ended some months later when his mother sent both sons back home to Mississippi to live with their grandparents. Back in Mississippi, the boys lived the sharecropping life, in and around their schooling. By his late teens, Earvin Sr. had moved back to Chicago, where he would first learn about the abundance of jobs in Lansing. He had headed there to begin his career, only to be drafted into the army, which would eventually put him on the path to meeting Christine.

Yet, like so many African Americans, their experiences in Mississippi traveled with them and shaped them.

Beyond family experience, survival in the southern state had required strong community knowledge and whispered warnings about the dangers of interaction with white people, Charles Tucker explained. "People in the South, they had extended family. They really wasn't blood family, but they learned a lot about what was going on and why it was going on. Those people that would tell us why and how to deal with it really wouldn't say it out in public because of the fear of people really taking it the wrong way, with the Emmett Till stuff and stuff like that that was going on."

In Lincoln County, Mississippi, the home of Earvin Sr., a well-respected Black farmer and veteran had been shot to death in broad daylight on the courthouse lawn in 1954, simply because he was trying to register to vote. The shooting happened in full view of the local sheriff.

"There was stuff like that going on probably in every county in Mississippi," Tucker said in 2019. "Things like that affected a lot of people then. It still affects them now."

It was the reason why many people went north. "A lot of people did in those days," Tucker said. "A lot of people became fearful of the supremacy-type thing going on. So you leave for better reasons."

It wasn't as if they were greeted elsewhere with milk and honey, a situation that had been known for decades. A fight over the segregated beaches of Lake Michigan had resulted in a Black youth drowning when a white crowd stoned him from the shore, which helped ignite the Chicago race riot of 1919.

Earvin Sr. himself had traveled back and forth as a teen in the early 1950s, living for a time in Chicago, then having to return to Mississippi, then back to Chicago, then back south. The 1955 murder of Emmett Till came just as Earvin Sr. was turning twenty.

Till's murder was unique in the sense that it suddenly became a national scandal when so many others had gone unnoticed and unpunished for so long. It had to play on Earvin Sr.'s young emotions, just as it played on the headlines, something of an early George Floyd moment in the public mind. Some civil rights activists would come to consider the Till case a breakthrough because it became national news after years of such violence not mattering, much of it never reported at all.

Race South, Race North

Charles Tucker's family had moved north to Michigan when he was a teen, and his father found a good job in Kalamazoo with the Upjohn Company. "They were not necessarily good jobs, but better," Tucker offered, adding that the racism in some ways "was worse in the North than it was in the South, just in a different way. The end result was still bad, both physically and mentally."

The battles over busing in the North during the 1970s were infused with the idea that white people would pack up and move out of the cities to avoid Black people.

"All over the country, when you had integration, people moved, period," Tucker related. "It doesn't matter where you have it. In high school, you had some that moved, just by virtue of the fact that there would be more blacks going to a school. They weren't afraid, or anything like that. And it didn't take anything out of their pockets. It's just the way they were, mentally. They just didn't want their kids participating with, or associating with, blacks. Period. It wasn't for any particular reason, just the skin color."

The school officials who were moving ahead with the highly emotional act of using busing to achieve integration in the schools weren't naïve. When Prophet first met I. Carl Candoli, the Lansing superintendent was speaking at an education event in Chicago about the ideal of every American child having the opportunity for a top education where the races learned to get along together. The all-white crowd booing Candoli in response was a significant moment in Prophet's racial journey.

The men trying to make busing for integration work in Lansing were quite aware that they were basically going up against centuries of racial animus.

That knowledge guided Tucker's approach in wading into racial disputes in the schools. "If you treat everybody right, then more people are going to be all right," he recalled. "But if you just take one side, then you can't solve the problem. There were also blacks who didn't want to be with whites. And whites who don't want to be with blacks. Even females who don't want to be with males. The conflicts didn't have to do with color all the time. There were a variety of attitudes."

And even the fights and other incidents in the school's halls weren't always racial, Tucker added. "Sometimes they were just fights." A knowledge of the variety of racial attitudes, even within the African American community, guided all of them.

In a series of 2019 interviews, Matthew Prophet acknowledged that his family was privileged, at least in terms of Black people in the South in the 1930s. An only child, he and his parents were among a group of relatives who lived in a house across the street from the home of the family who had once been their enslavers.

Apparently the long-ago enslaver had held Prophet's family in some esteem. "He brought them into this little town of Okolona," Prophet said. "And they were the head of their class in terms of class between Negroes. We would be what you call kind of like a different class."

As such, his family lived in a house surrounded by white families, he explained. "My father and my mother and others of our relatives lived in the house across from our previous family's slave master. In the house we stayed in, there were about eight or nine people from my one family in this one house the slave owner had built for us because he had brought my family in from the fields. They were not sharecroppers. My father was accepted because he had grown up working there and so forth. He had met a lot of Caucasians. And Caucasians really, really liked my father."

Hearing Prophet's recounting of how the white community treated the Black people they favored left one to wonder just how other, less-favored African Americans were treated. Even though they were treated better, that didn't mean Prophet's father didn't have the same failsafe as other Black families—the shotgun under the bed, explained one of Prophet's cousins, Chuck Green, himself a PhD, in an interview.

'We were the only Black family on that street," a collection of about a dozen houses near a commercial district of about twenty stores, Prophet said.

The racial indoctrination started early. "They called us all pickaninnies," Prophet said. "At the time if you were a Black boy or Black girl you were a pickaninny.

"And the way to earn extra money would be to go up to the stores. . . . We would go and dance for pennies. A nickel was a lot of money back then. We'd go dance for pennies as pickaninnies. The only ones who could really afford to pay pennies, one or two pennies, were Caucasians. Blacks could never really afford that kind of money at the time. That was during the Depression."

Prophet's father worked at a variety of handyman jobs. He was a paper hanger and a carpenter, and he played drums in a popular band that performed around the region. In addition, his father worked at a nearby mercantile, or general store, for one of their neighbors, "a Jewish man who was very, very good, a very kind man, one of the most beautiful men that I've ever known in my life. He was very, very good to us."

One day the store owner told Prophet's father that the family had to move. The reason, the merchant said, was that young Prophet would soon be turning eleven.

"This Jewish person came to my father and warned him that even though I was only a boy I was a Black boy," Prophet recalled. "He told him, 'You must move from this house before your son reaches eleven years old because Black boys cannot be in the presence of white girls because they're both reaching puberty.' I was the only young Black male in the neighborhood."

Such proximity would be too dangerous, warned the merchant, who was also a landlord, which allowed him to help the Prophets find a small house in a Black neighborhood. The house sat across an empty lot behind the jail, where the hangings occurred on an outdoors gallows. It was after the family moved that Matthew Prophet snuck through the brush on the vacant lot to witness his first hangings while hiding and watching events from afar.

"The entertainment on Saturdays was hanging," he recalled of Okolona, a place long known for particularly violent racism. "I saw it when I was eleven years old."

When Prophet graduated high school in 1947, he and one of his female classmates applied for a full academic scholarship offered by the Pepsi-Cola Company in a nationwide contest. Both Prophet and his classmate were awarded the scholarships with the provision that the local mayor would need to sign off on them as an endorsement of the recipient's character.

When notice of the scholarship came in the mail, it was addressed to Mr. and Mrs. Matthew Prophet, which delighted his parents because it was the first time in their lives anyone had addressed them with the appropriate respect.

"All blacks never had a title beyond 'boy,'" Prophet remembered. "The highest promotion you could get, they called you 'boy.' Otherwise you were called a n-i-g-g-e-r. That's all in the thirties."

Perhaps it shouldn't have been a surprise then that the Okolona mayor declined to endorse the scholarship for either student, saying that their getting the grants would deny opportunity to deserving white students.

Prophet was understandably embittered, but his parents turned to their siblings—Prophet had six aunts who were college graduates, Chuck Green recalled. Many of those educated siblings had long left Mississippi behind, including an aunt who lived in Washington, D.C. The siblings loaned Prophet's family the money for him to attend Howard University. He was there three years later, heading into his senior year in 1950, when he was drafted into the army.

Soon, he had completed the army's Officer Candidate School and found himself in Korea in charge of an ammo dump in a combat zone, the kind of routinely dangerous duty typically assigned to Black troops, except Prophet was in command of an integrated unit. In fact, he had one white soldier from Pennsylvania who seemed to reek with racist attitude.

Then came the day when a mortar barrage from Chinese troops fell on the ammo dump, which had a river running next to it. Across the river, a truck with a Black driver was hit and ignited, leaving Prophet and his men unable to rescue the man, only to see the white soldier who had seemed so racist jump into another truck and drive across a nearby bridge, braving the fire to rescue the Black driver.

In 2019, Prophet described the event as a profoundly transformative moment in his life, witnessing the act of bravery and camaraderie, considering Prophet's own experience with race. He recalled serving a combat tour in Vietnam when he received a letter from his father announcing that he had finally been allowed to vote in Mississippi.

Prophet had gone on from there to complete his distinguished military career before finding himself two decades later in Lansing, where Black and white school officials were working together, dedicated to a goal of integration, led by Candoli, whom Prophet quickly grew to admire.

Good People

The superintendent and his new assistant superintendent shared a similar philosophy of management and administration—find good people and put them in a position to do their jobs with autonomy, the same principle that Prophet had operated under in the military for years.

Using that approach in public education administration in Lansing in the early 1970s was groundbreaking, an approach that would not gain widespread following until nearly the twenty-first century under the name "site-based management." A good example of the practice had been the hiring of doctoral candidate Charles Tucker to assist the process of integration in the schools. Tucker lived in the same general neighborhood as Prophet, as well as Candoli and George Fox. Yet Prophet and Tucker hardly knew each other and never discussed integration policy, just as no one tried to tell George Fox how to run his basketball team.

Certainly Lansing had its problems—it would be decades before a top businessman and community leader such as Greg Eaton would be accepted for membership in the elite local golf club—but in the 1970s it featured a white power structure in the public schools that was willing, even determined, to hire Black males and empower them to do their jobs as they saw fit, which stood in contrast to so many other communities across the country.

Longtime Lansing sportscaster Tim Staudt would attribute the positive attitude in the city in part to the impressive presence of Eaton and Joel Ferguson.

It was also the capital of Michigan, housing the heart of the state's government, and it enjoyed the presence of Michigan State University in sister community East Lansing plus the auto industry and its many jobs.

It also helped explain why the city schools had hired Dr. Matthew Prophet, Jr., who was the very picture of competence and who would indeed succeed Candoli as Lansing's superintendent before taking on the larger task of Portland schools.

Prophet hadn't been on the job long in 1972 before he got involved in an outbreak of racial skirmishes at Dwight Rich Junior High, which he chose to address by pulling together a group of student leaders.

"I got the right leaders—two white girls, two white boys, two Black boys and two Black girls," he recalled.

He had worked with the group on racial dynamics for a time, and then one day trouble ignited between white and Black students that left a group of them throwing rocks at each other outside the school.

"The kids are all outside throwing rocks across the street," Prophet recalled. "So I say, 'Let's all walk down the middle together with locking arms.'"

The administrator and the eight students locked arms and walked right into the middle of the conflict. "They stopped throwing rocks," he recalled. "Oh man, it was classic. They stopped throwing rocks and all quieted down."

Like Tucker, Prophet felt he could best effect change through student leadership. But it was also about Lansing officials getting the right leadership in place at the individual schools.

Candoli moved Frank Throop (pronounced Troop) into the principal's job at Everett High just as Earvin Johnson began attendance there in August 1974 because Throop had found success as principal of an integrated junior high, displaying his ability to balance sensitive racial issues while maintaining discipline. They had wisely anticipated that Throop's skills would be needed. Perhaps they hadn't realized just how soon.

7

SOBRIQUET

Earvin Johnson showed up at Everett High School in August 1974 just as he was turning fifteen, encountered a chaotic, racially divided environment, and responded much as his brother Larry had two years earlier.

He would rise early each morning in the neighborhood he loved and the dread would hit him instantly. He was going to have to get on that bus to ride to that strange, cold place. Now in its fourth year of busing to achieve greater integration, Everett High had seen a rise each year in the number of Black students bused to campus, which created a greater opportunity for conflict in the daily operations of the school.

"There was still a lot of tension when Earvin first got there," Pat Holland recalled, adding that incidents broke out in hallways and common areas.

Much like Larry had retracted, Earvin recalled in those first days of school he would get off the bus and hop a fence to head out in search of a kinder place to pass the time.

He simply didn't want to be there, Johnson told *Detroit Free Press* sportswriter Mick McCabe, looking back almost a quarter century later.

"I was mad," Johnson recalled. "I was a Sexton man from Day 1. I used to hop the fence. . . . I wanted to go to Sexton. In basketball Sexton had the team back then."

Plus, his girlfriend at the time went to school there.

In a few short months over the summer of 1974, Charles Tucker had managed to secure the beginnings of a close relationship with Johnson that would eventually grow into a close bond with his family. That, in turn, made Tucker both a witness and a participant as the family struggled with the issues of having their children bused into the racial conflict at Everett. By now, Christine Johnson had a job in the public schools in East Lansing working as a lunchroom supervisor, and Tucker had begun to hear good things about her. The psychologist often traveled to Michigan State in East Lansing, so he made a point of stopping by the school where she worked to get to know her. "We would sit down and talk, you know," he recalled. "The principal at the school was a friend of mine. He always talked about Christine Johnson and how great she was."

Those bonds between Tucker and the family grew stronger in the fall of 1974 as the Johnson children struggled to deal with the school environment. After all, the psychologist had grown into something of a voice of authority at Everett over the two years since Larry had been dismissed from the basketball team.

Yet again, with fights and other confrontations, officials chose to close the school down for several days—some would remember it as a week—until tensions could ease, Pat Holland recalled.

"That kind of carried over to everything in the school," Tucker remembered in 2019. "Some of the teachers had problems too. These just happened to be kids who weren't going to be that passive."

Most of the students and faculty at the school were on their way to adjusting, Tucker explained, but in a flash the entire environment could be set on edge.

"It actually didn't take but one or two in that moment to kill the entire relationship process with everybody," Tucker recalled. "In that moment, that affected everybody. So, everybody takes sides. That type of thing. Then you have a disturbance." In that situation, Tucker remembered, it stood to reason that Black students like Earvin and Larry would recoil.

"Larry wasn't a bad kid at all, not to where you had to try to control him and punish him," Tucker said. "Like a lot of the kids, he missed class."

It was a matter of teaching some Black students how to work with the system when they'd made a mistake and how to work with the system even when it was the system making mistakes. The main goal, Tucker explained, was to find ground for agreement. He would tell students it was good for them to take the first step in being agreeable and cooperative. Form a little bit of trust and see where it leads you.

He remembered the days when Larry would approach him in the hallway after the bell and say, "Tuck, give me a pass."

Tucker's reply would be, "Just tell me the truth. Why are you late?"

A big problem was that Larry and his friends would be late returning from lunch. In those days, students could go off campus for lunch so long as they were back in time for class. Black students were often eager to get away from what they saw as an inhospitable place. And that meant problems when they returned late.

Once Earvin Sr. and Christine Johnson gained an understanding of the situation, they began to deal with it, particularly for Larry, Tucker recalled. "Earvin's dad had to come over to the school and say, 'Larry is fine.' I had Larry in high school personally for about three years because I was in the same building. They all said Larry wasn't going to make it out, but I promised myself he was, and I promised his mom that he'd make it. The fact is I had to get Larry to understand the things that he might choose, they're not bad, but it might be the way you're doing them and the time you're doing them. And that's not all your fault. It's the other people too, teachers and some of the people that you've got to work with. They got the same amount of fault. So, between those two, the misunderstanding made it hard."

Larry's situation had begun to snowball, building off his previous experiences at the school, which led Tucker to make his promise to Christine Johnson that they would somehow get him to graduation.

"I told her that because he wasn't a bad kid," he recalled. "He was smart. He was smart with the books. He knew how to handle himself. He just wasn't a passive kid. Once you get that stigma you don't have to be doing too much before they come down on you." Tucker knew the situation required some adjustment on both sides, with Larry and with the teachers and administrators he had come into conflict with.

"For example," Tucker said he told Larry, "if you're going to miss class or be late, don't let the whole school or the teachers see you outside standing around when the bell rings and then you come in late."

Larry had a friend, another student also having some trouble, Tucker said. "They were kind of tough kids. They weren't bad. They weren't going around jumping on people. They just were tough kids."

Tucker had seen that such an attitude was prevalent among the Black students, who despite growing numbers were still quite a minority at Everett. They weren't going to start trouble, but if trouble came their way, they were prepared to finish it.

It is important to note that many of the Black students were from families that just a few years earlier had come out of Mississippi and other parts of the South where engagement with white people had long been dangerous.

Tucker's strategy with them was to try to clean up the smaller things that generated conflict with teachers. Respect the teacher. Don't get in a big argument. You know you're late. Just go in and sit down and do your work.

As he took this approach, he was mindful of the circumstances. "You're putting kids in an environment that wasn't good," he said. "And the expectations were so high. Some of the kids could adjust but others couldn't."

Looking back decades later, it seemed reasonable to ask: What if Larry had been on the team with Earvin? "Why didn't Earvin get mad?" Tucker asked. "Why did he still play when Larry was taken off the team? First of all, I think that Larry might have had an opportunity to be back on the team. But I think the choice was probably halfway Larry's and halfway the coaches'."

Johnson later recalled that in finally agreeing to go to Everett he told his brother he loved him but he wasn't going to give up basketball. In retrospect, it seems remarkable that Johnson, living in cramped quarters with an older brother he loved and admired, wasn't influenced by him more heavily. Certainly, as much basketball as he was playing with Tucker meant the psychologist was in his ear constantly about how to proceed.

The first crisis came as soon as school started.

With Earvin now jumping the fence in the morning, too, coach George Fox became aware of the situation quickly. Earvin had appealed to his parents, appealed to the school board, looked for places he could move that would allow him to attend Sexton, none of which worked. Now he was turning to rebellion with the idea that misbehavior might induce school officials to allow him to go to Sexton.

"I was trying everything to get out of there," Johnson recalled. "But Mr. Fox said, 'No way.' I came here with a chip on my shoulder."

"When we first got him, he was very upset about not going to Sexton," Fox recalled in 2019. "They lived in the Sexton neighborhood, so I got some shots from a few people that Earvin ought to be at Sexton. There was a little tension at the start."

Fortunately for the coach, open gyms for basketball began just in time. "Once I got Earvin in the basketball, into the coaching and into the training, he warmed up to me pretty well," Fox said.

"I didn't want to be here," Johnson told Mick McCabe. "But once I started playing in the gym with the guys everything was OK."

Yet open gyms were loosely organized affairs arranged mostly for underclassmen and players hoping to try out for the team to get a little floor time. It proved just enough to draw Johnson in further, but there were still issues simmering everywhere you turned in Everett High that fall.

Principal Frank Throop had his hands full.

"That principal was one of those who worked kind of close with me," Tucker recalled. "At that time we had so many problems, we kind of went at them both ways. There were some things I suggested and some things that he allowed to happen. That kind of created a good atmosphere, which kind of allowed us to have more trust with certain kids, more than administrators in those days liked to have. Those kids ended up helping us with the problems."

As Matthew Prophet explained in 2019, Clayton Kowalk, the athletic director for the city schools, had predicted all the way back in September 1972 that Earvin Johnson was going to be one of the greatest players in the history of the game. Prophet recalled distinctly that he spoke with Candoli in the aftermath of Kowalk's declaration, and the superintendent responded as he would about any other talented student in the system.

"Candoli said, 'Get him what he needs,'" Prophet recalled.

Apparently, that did not include a special exception to play at Sexton. By 1974, it certainly seemed that Johnson was seen as far too important in the integration effort, in clearing up the ongoing troubles at Everett High.

School administrators knew they had a gifted young person, one who possessed a certain charisma, whom they hoped might help ease some of the difficulties at Everett.

Those administrators weren't fools. They had individually studied integration top to bottom (Candoli had been an Ohio State professor who had studied the issue). They well knew the power that winning sports teams had in influencing the public mind and how integrated teams allowed the public to see Black and white students working together as teammates.

Perhaps that helps explain why Everett principal Frank Throop invited Johnson into his office that fall to ask him to help with racial issues at the school. In retrospect, it seems like a highly unusual move, for a principal to seek the help of a fifteen-year-old who had yet to play even a minute of basketball for Everett High, much less one who had already shown some difficulties in adjusting to the place.

Throop also invited a white quarterback from the school's football team in to ask him to make the same effort, as Johnson would later recall. Throop's request for Johnson's help was based, in part, on the sophomore's growing reputation. As Pat Holland recalled, Frank Throop had introduced himself at a regional meeting of principals at the start of the school year, and one of the principals had supposedly responded, "Everett? That's Earvin Johnson's high school."

Already the place was branded as Johnson's? That certainly got Throop's attention, evidenced by the fact that the anecdote survived. Johnson was completely aware that the principal was making a huge request of a fifteen-year-old and said as much. Johnson recalled asking just how he was going to pull it off.

"You'll figure it out," the principal supposedly replied.

Johnson's response to the request had an effect almost immediately, George Fox recalled. "When they started that busing, Everett was almost a 99 percent white school. We started bringing all these Black kids from the inner city out into suburbia. We had some difficult days at school. We had some fights and small riots.

"It never made a lot of news [it had long been the approach of public school systems in general, much like businesses, to avoid drawing publicity to incidents of violence or race]," Fox explained, but the city's schools faced a tremendous challenge. "But that's what was so nice about Earvin. Our principal when kids would get in fights, white and Black, the first person he'd call—he didn't call the local police—he'd called Earvin Johnson."

Even at that age, Johnson had a way of seeking out the angry parties afterward, taking them aside, and urging them to remain cool, Fox recalled. "He would control a lot of these local fights, when he was in the tenth grade he would. He was the principal's right arm when it came to quelling these racial scrimmages."

Observing Johnson in those circumstances, Tucker was reminded of Earvin's mother, Christine. "Earvin had a good in-house foundation, as it related to basketball," Tucker said. "We also know that he did socially. His mother had great patience. Earvin was patient in terms of important things. He picked that up from his mom."

Johnson would recall over the years that his experience at Everett left him with substantial confidence in his leadership skills.

Even so, it would also seem easy to co-opt, even corrupt, a fifteen-year-old with a power connected directly to the principal. "But Earvin was no pushover," Tucker said, allowing a bit of pride to creep into his voice.

Johnson himself recalled that the music played in Everett's cafeteria at lunch was mostly white-oriented rock. He asked for some soul music to be played, too, and Throop agreed. Johnson also suggested that students be allowed to dance during the lunch break in one of the school's unused rooms, and the principal balked, supposedly out of concern that the dance sessions would make students late to class. Johnson recalled that he guaranteed they wouldn't, then got fellow students to agree and Throop to sign off on it.

At first blush, these moves related to music seem like minor things. But in another sense, Johnson was making another move to access an important part of his growing personal power, music itself. And business ownership.

Johnson would long extol the influence of Eaton and Ferguson as his role models as Black businessmen. Yet his first unacknowledged model as a businessman was his father's trash-hauling business and cleaning services, a successful endeavor that first brought young Earvin into closer contact with Eaton and Ferguson because they used the services Earvin Sr. offered.

This ideal of a successful Black entrepreneur impressed Johnson at that young age, later to be followed by Johnson's own first foray into business.

Setting up and running these lunchtime sessions around the music he loved served as a simple prelude to his role as a disc jockey at Lansing nightspots, first as a senior in high school and later as an undergraduate at Michigan State. Booking and performing such DJ gigs would provide his first experience as a contractor, securing an agreement to perform services, then delivering that contract to the approval of the establishment that was his customer, the most basic and essential elements of a business. Johnson, of course, would go on to substantial success as a businessman after his basketball life, with a major part of his portfolio involving his lucrative food service contracting business for colleges and other public entities.

His early dance sessions at lunch were also an exercise in entertainment, an immense aspect of his personality both on and off the court, one easily recognized in a variety of settings across his entire career. For example, many years later, in 1989, in Charlotte, North Carolina, there was a typical scene after an NBA game at an immense bar at a Marriott hotel: packed with hundreds of fans with Johnson himself up on the stage, leading the whole place in the Electric Slide. This desire to provide entertainment leadership evidenced itself in a variety of ways over his life, including the legendary parties or events he would take such pride in hosting in Los Angeles.

Most important, his lunchtime music sessions at Everett served to make the place more hospitable culturally for African American students, a huge payoff for the school administrators who wanted him there.

Another key issue that the teenaged Johnson brought up—the fact that no Black students were picked during tryouts for the cheerleading squad—met some resistance, which Johnson recalled he answered by holding Black players out of basketball practice. Somehow, he managed to get a more balanced cheerleading squad without angering Fox, a dramatic departure from how his own brother had been treated for missing practice just two years earlier.

In pointing out the difference between the two brothers, Larry himself would observe years later that he answered the challenge of Everett with anger while brother Earvin took a more constructive approach.

None of his strength in dealing with the school's principal was lost on his fellow students. Dale Beard recalled arriving at Everett the next year and hearing the stories about Johnson's influence. "That sophomore year when a fight or anything broke out, they would go get Earvin because he was so highly thought of," Beard remembered. "They would think, 'Okay. Well, he can make the peace here.' And he did, you know." Almost magically, he gained a reputation for separating angry people and soothing them. In the wake of that, Beard said, even more people were drawn to him, as if there weren't enough already.

"He had a way he treated people," Tucker explained. "You can't make people like you, they say, but Earvin made people like him, even if you didn't like him, because he overlooked the fact that you didn't like him. He was that type of guy."

The entire experience with Johnson in high school, beginning with the racial trouble that first fall, was almost "dreamlike," George Fox remembered in 2019. "Earvin had a big impact on everybody at Everett, including the teachers that liked him so much. Probably if the truth is known a lot of those same teachers went to Earvin if they had a problem in their class. I would say that's a true statement, that he probably talked to some kids. I know that he did. He was a real person to help the whole integration system. We had our problems. I'm not saying we didn't, but at the same time, he really helped and I know he helped."

So many of the ways Johnson broke down barriers were subtle, Tucker explained. "A lot of the gym teachers were hard-core coaches, the old-fashioned tough guys. But they didn't have any experience with Black guys, and they weren't trying to change. But through Earvin's gym classes, and Earvin being associated there—they were all white males in that phys ed department at that time—they learned how to cater to Earvin a little bit. Not only could Earvin play, but he always had a smile and he could articulate. Also, Earvin wasn't going to cater to you, but he wasn't going to get upset over every little thing."

It all added up to an impressive performance from fifteen-year-old Earvin, who still had to weather yet another confrontation and adjustment once the season started.

Fox, Stabley, Holland, Prophet, as well as numerous witnesses to the era, observed that Tucker quickly became a mentor to young Earvin Johnson as he moved through so many challenges as a teen. Tucker quietly acknowledged as much in 2019, but he said the bigger reasons that Johnson could step into such a role were his parents and his persona.

"Earvin was good for both races," Tucker recalled. "He was strong-willed, very strong-willed like he is now. But he always had some integrity in what he did. He had a love for people in general. He stood up for his own race. But also stood up for other races. He was for what was right."

Not, as his father would say, "for what might be the okay thing to do," but what was right.

Tucker also pointed out that even though Johnson made no overt references to religion, either in basketball or in his dealings over race at Everett, there was a sense of faith in how he proceeded, even if the family dynamic had been altered in the wake of Christine Johnson's conversion to Seventh-day Adventist.

"I think that everybody had their ways of getting through," Tucker explained. "His father, like everybody in the South, had been around religion. Because that was our life in the South, how we got our guidance, how we got our schools, how we got our jobs."

And how they dealt with the behavior of some white people.

"That's where the church was a place where we could go to call upon for help on anything," Tucker explained. "Even to have meetings about politics or anything. For people from the South, they always respected the church whether they went physically or not."

At the time he was getting to know the Johnsons, Tucker got the impression the father didn't go to church as regularly as he once had. "Mr. Johnson initially didn't go a lot on a Sunday, I don't think," Tucker said, then added that the father still very much employed spiritual values in his personal conduct, which heavily influenced the son, which in turn influenced how Johnson negotiated the complicated race issues at the school.

"Earvin was the type of person, he always had ways of faith," Tucker recalled. "He always did what the Bible said to do. He respected people. He loved people. He honored people. He didn't do a lot of deviation from that. No drugs or alcohol or smoking. He was probably one of the straighter kids you could see. He obeyed his elders. It's hard to say he wasn't religious just because he didn't go to church physically all the time."

The other huge factor was his mother's particular manner in dealing with just about everything. "She's always been very real, very strong religiously," Tucker observed. "She didn't go around preaching so much. But she could just say one word and you would get the message. She would always say, 'God is good.' She could get her message across."

Ignition

Truth be known, Charles Tucker had his concerns about George Fox heading into the 1974–75 season. Was he going to be a rigid coach more concerned about the number of white players in the starting five than he was about winning? In his time at Everett, Tucker had picked up on some cues that Fox's old-school approach might be problematic.

Tucker wasn't alone in his concern. The two men did not really know each other then, and the era lent itself to suspicion. It was a road that ran both ways. Fox was trying to figure out this odd guy Tucker who wore a sporty porkpie hat, who would prove to wield all sorts of power that others didn't or couldn't even recognize at first.

"Tucker looked after Earvin, probably dating back to his sophomore year," George Fox recalled in 2019. "That's when I kept hearing about this Dr. Tucker. Finally I met him. He was a basketball player. He had played college ball. He taught some classes out at Michigan State. He was on the Lansing payroll for something. We never figured out what he did. I think it had something to do with administration and guidance. A troubleshooter."

Obviously, Pat Holland already knew him reasonably well, but to the head coach (and many others at the school) Tucker was a vague figure, seemingly possessed of undetermined power. The students, on the other hand, held Tucker in immense esteem, as noted by newspaper reporters who happened to stroll the hallways with him, where students greeted him with smiles and intoned his name knowingly. "Tuck," they would say as they encountered him, one after another.

Much of this came into focus for Fox as soon as the trouble started.

Earvin was integrating the varsity team in a major way for the first time. He was young but had that large personality that took over any situation he encountered. His main ally in this was Reggie Chastine, a shorter guard and rising junior. The two had become fast friends, to the point that people began describing them as Mutt and

Jeff, a reference to the tall and short newspaper cartoon duo created in 1907 that had entertained America for decades. Johnson himself described Chastine as being just five-three. Others said he was anywhere from five-five to five-seven, but all agreed that next to Johnson he seemed pretty short.

Johnson took to him immediately because he was feisty and fearless and absolutely determined to routinely inform Johnson he was silly to be insecure about his own abilities.

"I doubted myself back then," Johnson would say later of the huge influence of Chastine and his feistiness and confidence. "He was who I should have been."

In addition, Chastine was for Johnson an early Black friend on a team of mostly white players. Soon, the two seemed inseparable. Already buoyant in personality, Johnson drew great comfort and strength from the attitude of his new friend, whether they were venturing out onto the streets at night or taking on the team atmosphere in the gym that fall as practice opened.

The two remaining seniors on the Everett basketball team had apparently not played during summer league but now returned to the team to find, just as they had suspected, a big new threat in the power structure. Johnson noticed they seemed reluctant to pass to him, thought little of it, then came to realize it was willful. In his 1992 autobiography, Johnson recalled senior Danny Parks looking right at him wide open underneath and instead electing to take a jumper that he missed. As Johnson took more and more control of the team each day, he recalled that Parks at one point demanded, "Throw me the goddamn ball."

Johnson responded with an outburst of his own, slamming the ball off the floor and shouting, "I knew this would happen. That's why I didn't want to come to this fucking school in the first place."

Johnson recalled Parks responding that "you people are all the same," accusing the new big man of trying to take over and reminding him that it was Johnson's job to do the rebounding.

"Let us do the shooting," Johnson remembered him saying.

He moved to punch Parks in the face, but teammates separated them. Fox then sent Parks to the locker room and pulled aside

Johnson, who told the coach this was just what brother Larry had warned him about, trouble with white teammates.

Fox assured him he'd talk to his seniors. The two had just helped Everett to its first-ever district basketball title, at least the first in anyone's memory, just the previous season. Obviously the two seniors returned to the team with the idea that they had earned a dominant role.

"Things will get better," the coach promised Johnson, who was fuming that Fox hadn't taken a stronger approach in dealing with the racial attitude.

Tucker was there in the gym witnessing the entire exchange and ran down Johnson in the hall afterward to discuss it.

Johnson recalled the psychologist pulling him aside and telling him not to make the mistake of thinking the incident was about race. The seniors had just been major figures in the Everett team winning its first district title. Such a reaction would be natural for any player who thought his hard-won success and seniority was now being threatened by a newcomer, Johnson would remember Tucker explaining.

"When Earvin first started out some of the seniors on the team didn't like the fact that he was going to have the ball all the time," Fox said in 2019.

At first, the seniors responded to the blowup with the silent treatment, until one of them, Randy Shumway, ended up in a showdown with Johnson on a distance run in the gym. One by one, their teammates dropped out, but neither Johnson nor Shumway would concede, matching each other lap for lap until they finally agreed to stop together, then walked a victory lap arm in arm.

"They finally both stopped and put their arms on each other's shoulder and walked around a little bit," Fox recalled, "and then took off and ran another lap. I'll never forget that."

Shumway soon reached out on the team chemistry issues and played peacemaker, reassuring Johnson that Parks and other players would come around.

More than anything, the teammates could agree, was that results would matter, and they were about to ring up in spectacular fashion.

It was at this point that a tall, young, easygoing sportswriter entered the picture, admittedly unwittingly. Fred Stabley, Jr., was about to meet Earvin Johnson, Jr., although at the time neither of them realized it was any sort of big deal.

Fred Stabley, Sr., was the longtime sports information director at Michigan State, which meant that Fred Jr. had grown up with an inside view of sports, doing everything from working as a batboy for the Michigan State baseball team to guarding the trophy table during the finals for the state of Michigan's high school basketball tournament, which afforded him the opportunity to watch many of the greats—guys like Dave DeBusschere—in their prime. Stabley had been a paid sportswriter from the ridiculous age of something like eleven or so, but the important background was his being the batboy. In baseball, they give everybody a nickname.

In a series of 2019 interviews, Stabley, an affable sort, explained that he had provided literally everyone in his life with a sobriquet, including about fifty different terms of endearment for his wife over the years.

But the only nickname that mattered, on a global scale, was the one he came up with in the late fall of 1974. By then he was in his early twenties, a graduate of Michigan State himself, and a sportswriter for the *Lansing State Journal* who had been assigned to cover Everett's first game, armed only with a vague notion that the school had a hotshot sophomore who had been something of a star at one of the city's junior high schools.

By 2019 the story was a local legend, worn smooth as a stone pulled from a creek bed.

"This is what I recall," Stabley said. "The score could be off but this is what I've used for forty years when people ask me when Earvin became Magic." It was the era when players wore "Daisy Dukes," or as Stabley called them, "butt huggers." Johnson sported a big Afro, a wiry halo of sorts, that gently waved in the breeze as he motored up and down the court, already a picture of mobile long and lean at fifteen, six-six or so and still growing.

The first game that season was on the road, at suburban Holt High School, south of Lansing. "Holt was a predominantly white school," Stabley remembered, "and Everett . . . I think they started three white kids and Earvin and Reggie Chastine."

If anybody was expecting fireworks from the new young star, it soon became apparent that wasn't going to happen. Johnson was a nervous wreck, all would recall. He was called for four fouls in the first half alone. "They won it 44 to 43," Stabley recalled. "Earvin had 12 points and 10 rebounds and fouled out. And so I go back to the office, and everybody back at the office needs to know about this Earvin Johnson kid. And I'm like, 'Ehh, he'll be a good player one day, you know. He had 12 points and 10 rebounds. He fouled out.'"

George Fox himself had a number of friends who were fans of Holt High School sports. The coach had told them he had a special young player, the kind who would make them forget their own stars of yesteryear.

"When he was coming in his sophomore year in the summer, I just couldn't believe what I saw in practice," Fox recalled. "So I started telling my friends, I said, 'Guys. Just hang on.' Well, the first game we played was at Holt and I think we beat them by one point, and Earvin just played average . . . but he just didn't stand out."

Merely by luck of the draw, Stabley was assigned to cover Johnson's second game, this time in Everett's gym, against Jackson Parkside.

"Jackson Parkside was the preseason favorite in the South Central Conference," Stabley said.

The sportswriter recalled that Johnson had more than 30 points and a huge number of rebounds and assists that second game. Records show that big game came much later in the season, in the second contest against Jackson Parkside.

In the early game that looms as the contest that led to Johnson's nickname he had 21 points, 19 of them in the first half, but he wasn't even the highest scorer on his team. That honor went to fellow sophomore Larry Hunter, a burly, 6-4 sharpshooting forward, with 25. After running up a big lead with his whopping 19 first-half points, Johnson spent the second half using an outbreak of amazing passing to set up Hunter and Parks, who scored 20. Everett cruised to victory by 16 points.

It's easy to assume that it was actually Johnson's unique style of play and the size of the upset that inspired Stabley to search for a poetic nickname. It's apparently one of those moments sealed in memory like an old silent film. Stabley couldn't remember if the crowd went nuts or sat in dumb disbelief. But he was sure of one thing in regard to the folks in the Everett gym that night.

"They had never seen anything like this," he said.

"Earvin just went crazy that night," his coach acknowledged with a chuckle almost fifty years later.

"This is the second game of his high school career," Stabley emphasized. "I'd never seen anything like this before in my life. Everybody just kind of stood there or sat there with their mouths open. People are just amazed."

"Jackson Parkside was the home of Tony Dungy," Fox recalled, "and they were supposed to be the best team in the league and we beat them 86 to 70. And that's when he really blossomed."

Writers who worked high school sports in that age—before personal computers had taken over media work—faced tough nightly deadlines, but Stabley was compelled to find Johnson in the locker room afterward.

"All these JV players, which were many of the kids that came from Dwight Rich to Everett, were gathered around Earvin," Stabley remembered. "So I stood behind him for a second and then finally I went up and introduced myself."

"Earvin, we got to call you something," Stabley told the sophomore.

Johnson just looked at him, so the sportswriter plowed right on.

"Big E's out because of Elvin Hayes," he said. "And Dr. J's out because of Julius Erving."

"And where I came up with it, I don't know," Stabley said, looking back yet again in 2019.

"How about Magic?" he asked the sophomore.

Johnson looked at him again for a moment and replied, "That's okay with me, Mr. Stabley."

"So that was it," Stabley remembered. "I didn't have the guts to call a fifteen-year-old high school kid Magic." At least not that night. And not in the next day's paper.

"I went back to the office," Stabley remembered, "and I gave the report to all. Back then we had a sports staff of six people and I basically told them blow-by-blow what had happened." Then he phoned his friend Tim Staudt, who was just a few seasons into a career of fifty-plus years as a sportscaster for TV and radio in Lansing, and told him the story.

"I'm going to name Earvin Johnson Magic," Stabley declared.

"Noooo, that's too hokey," Staudt replied. "Let's call him 'The Franchise.'"

"Now that's really hokey," Stabley said. "He's just a high school kid."

Whatever you were going to name him, it was definitely not something you could just throw in the newspaper without thinking about it.

"We talked about it at the office," Stabley recalled. "And I talked to another sportswriter who just passed away this year, Dave Matthews. He'd seen Earvin play. He started calling him Magic around the office. But almost a month to the day later I got assigned to go down and cover the rematch, which was in Jackson, about forty miles south of Lansing. Everett won the game. Earvin was excellent as usual."

Indeed, the second game was where he scored 36 points with 18 rebounds and umpteen assists.

"That was the first time about a month later that I put Earvin 'Magic' Johnson in the paper," Stabley said.

There were no personal computers to speak of, no internet with its flood of information, no media accelerant whatsoever, but the name soon gained traction.

"The funny thing was," Stabley recalled, "in about two months when the high school tournaments began in mid-March all you had to do was mention the name Magic in the state of Michigan and everybody knew who it was. All the basketball people knew who it was because he was a phenomenal talent, period."

By that point, Stabley had met Christine Johnson.

"Christine wasn't real happy with the nickname," Stabley said sheepishly.

Johnson's mother never told him that personally. He got the message from both Earvin and George Fox.

"She was a very strict religious person and this had the connotation of extraworldly," Stabley remembered. "But she was always nice to me. She was a delightful lady. Earvin was very fortunate to have great parents like that. He got great genes."

"When you say 'Magic,' people expect so much," his mother would explain much later. "I was afraid it would give him a lot to look up to at some point."

At the time, Tucker, who had an eye for literally everything going on, hardly noticed.

"I didn't think nothing of it," he said. "I thought more of it once it settled in after a while. Because I called him Earv all the time. Sometimes I called him Magic. It depended on where we were."

George Fox remembered Stabley coming to Everett's gym and asking him about using such a nickname.

"George, the way Earvin is playing we got to give him a nickname," Stabley said. "Do you think he would be opposed to that?"

Apparently, Stabley had figured it would be better to discuss the nickname further before going forward.

"Fred, there's only one way to find out," Fox remembered telling him.

"I was all for it," Fox recalled. "I didn't care. He called Earvin over and he sat there with us and he explained it to Earvin and Earvin said, 'Yeah, I kind of like that.' That's how that was started right there in Everett's gym. Then Fred started using it a little bit and then as other writers started writing articles and they started using it and pretty soon it was a household word. But you know what's interesting? Pat and I have never called Earvin Magic. Never did. Still don't today. He is Earvin Johnson or E. That's the way we've addressed him. I never worried about it. I thought it was something that maybe it could live and it could die. It mushroomed and blossomed and we never had a bit of a problem with it and I never had anybody question it."

As for the early opposition to Johnson from the team's senior leadership? "Once they realized, 'If I ever get open on the court, I'm gonna get the ball,' that eased a lot of that, that first awareness of how good Earvin was," Fox recalled. "Once they realized that he's a fully encompassed team player, we got rid of a lot of that."

It wasn't long before players and coaches on other teams took note of the power of the nickname, beginning with how officials called his games. "You couldn't touch Magic back then, especially when, you know, Fred Stabley gave him the nickname Magic," Jay Vincent, who played for Lansing's Eastern High, recalled. "That was the perfect name because he was throwing passes one way while looking another."

You didn't know where Johnson would go with the ball, a development that fascinated Vincent so much he had to ask Johnson when he finally got the opportunity where in the world all of that came from.

Johnson told him that it came from watching the NBA on TV with his father.

"He said he thought he could do it better, which he did," Vincent recalled, adding that opponents would watch Johnson and couldn't help but think, "That looks pretty nice."

Johnson was flashy without appearing to be trying to be flashy, Vincent said. "You wouldn't know which way he was going. He's looking one way like he's going to throw it that way, then throws it the other way. He just perfected that style of play."

Vincent was adamant that Johnson hadn't developed that style to any recognizable degree in ninth grade, which raised another interesting facet of the nickname. Being named Magic obviously spurred Johnson to seek to do more and more magical things to live up to his name. He didn't want fans showing up to games and not seeing the reason for the nickname. It pointed the way for the entertainer he was becoming.

"In tenth grade just a year later, he was doing those look-away passes," Vincent insisted, although Leon Stokes, who went to school with Earvin, maintained Johnson was already adept at throwing the no-looks on the playground in sixth grade. By tenth grade, Johnson had begun to merge his playground antics, his make-believe, with formal basketball. "It was full-court," Vincent said.

Even at that age, Johnson had a better jump shot than people gave him credit for. It was almost a set shot that he seemed to push up one-handed. It made sense, Vincent observed, because Johnson's height meant he didn't have to jump all that much to get off the shot.

None of these developments altered the reception to the nickname.

In fairly short order assistant coach Pat Holland had surprisingly developed what seemed to be a good working relationship with the sophomore Johnson. Never in their three years of working together did the two ever discuss or even mention Larry's dismissal.

Almost overnight the nickname had helped take the atmosphere around the program to a different place.

"I can tell you my perspective of it very quickly," Holland said in 2019. "I personally didn't think it was necessary, but Fred thought so. I wasn't against it or anything like that. I said okay. Tim Staudt famously said, 'That's never going to stick.' And, of course, it did stick except nobody on the team or nobody who knew him well called him that. . . . I never called him Magic in my life and George hasn't either."

Johnson and his teammates were mere high school kids and thus open to such a development. The 1960s and '70s in sports had produced many changes and highlights in an open and freewheeling approach to competition, including a certain normalizing of race where Black males began to acquire terms of endearment among the general population. In many ways, the nickname Magic would serve to sustain that movement.

It stood to reason that if Johnson was called Magic in the paper, then eventually sports radio and TV, limited as they then were, began to push the process.

"It caught on, there's no question," Holland said.

He recalled a moment, what seemed like just a few years later, when he and his wife were watching the popular game show *Jeopardy!* and Johnson's nickname was a question, which left quite an impression.

"But I never heard one of the other kids on the team call him Magic ever, not even once," Holland said. "I mean that was just a showbiz thing."

And Holland could never recall a single instance in those days where Johnson referred to himself as Magic. Even in the billing for his later music events he was EJ the DJ.

Looking back over sixty years of observing sports in the state and region, Holland said, "I don't think there's ever been a crowd like that in the city since or even before that. I mean you better get there early. We would sell out every game."

Did the nickname drive that? "I don't know," Holland said. "He was doing the stuff that he did. He was going to draw interest regardless."

There was a regular sign that began appearing in the packed gyms, Fox remembered. It said, "We believe in Magic."

"I remember seeing that around all over," the coach said.

Very soon the school was able to have pep rallies.

"That gym was really rocking," Fox remembered.

The first wave of change had rolled in with that sophomore year, the coach said. "He started to attract a big crowd. He even attracted a lot of students from the other schools."

Despite this development, the racial troubles weren't over. Far from it, the coach hastened to add. "But that's when he really started to blossom."

Soon enough Everett had a booster club that was rocking right along itself. A half century later Holland still had one of the club's Styrofoam hats displaying a big red E on the front.

Which begged the question then and now, did the E stand for Everett or Earvin?

It hardly mattered. His new identity had been born. Henceforth, he became the Magic Man.

"I don't ever call him that," Stabley reiterated in 2019 of the nickname he created. "I call him EJ or big fella or Earvin."

8

GOONS

At first all anybody wanted was a better look at him. This certainly included the coaches, just about all of whom clung to orthodoxy like a lifeline. And Earvin Johnson was the very picture of unorthodoxy, and this is where his presence in the great basketball revolution would loom so large.

For decades, it had been the same in basketball. Big man gets the defensive rebound. Big man then looks to find the little man, the point or lead guard, to pass him the ball. Big men were not to be trusted with doing a whole lot more. Except for getting their butts down the floor to get into position near the basket in hopes that one of the little guys might throw them the ball, but only if they were close inside and spread wide, ready to attack with one big tricky drop step.

Under no circumstances were big men allowed to dribble. And if they somehow did dribble, it was only for a bounce or two, all with the coach on the bench frowning the entire time.

It was a prejudice that ran deep in the psyche of the game, all the way back to the late 1930s when basketball was mostly all about short guys who took set shots with both feet on the floor.

For the 1937–38 season, the people who oversaw the rules finally got rid of the center jump after every basket. Before that, every time somebody scored both teams would go to center court and the referees would stage a jump ball.

Sort of like a soccer match.

Getting rid of the center jump allowed for a more free-flowing, faster-paced game.

It was only a few years after that, in the early 1940s, that the first big guys were allowed into the sport, guys like George Mikan and Bob Kurland, who at six-ten were absolutely shameless because they dared to play a game thought mostly to be the domain of shorter, quicker men.

The sport had a name for these early giants. They were called "goons," freaks of nature, more suited to the circus than a basketball court. Bob Kurland, who with George Mikan came to prominence as the college game's early big men, recalled in a 1986 interview that Kansas coach "Phog Allen classified me a 'glandular goon.'"

Once again, there was prejudice bumping up against the game.

Because it obviously grew out of the heated competition, it wasn't a fun-loving term, not by any means, but even the coaches eventually figured out that "goons" could help them win. You just had to hold them to a very limited role.

And it meant that teams had to walk up the ball just so a big guy like George Mikan could have time to mosey down-floor and set up near the basket. The game, of course, went on to a succession of spectacular big men, from Bill Russell to Wilt Chamberlain to Kareem Abdul-Jabbar to Bill Walton over the next two decades. The term "goon" had long disappeared from the game by the 1970s, but the fundamental idea that big men were limited in their scope remained a tenet of the sport.

Earvin Johnson would change all of that, would change the very syntax of the game, a change that would begin oh so subtly when he entered high school. He would grow to a shade under six-nine and would come to be seen as a most unusual figure, almost a goonish point guard, the kind that coaches would have to travel to see in those days before the widespread televising of basketball games.

There had been other big men before him eager to dribble and pass and display their own genius, but Johnson would prove to be the one, the single figure with the iron will and supreme talent to impose his vision on the game. Make no mistake, it was all carefully disguised in his quick and easy smile, in his forthright love of competition, but it was there, cold and calculating and undaunted, shockingly easy to see for anyone who inhabited a locker room with him.

Which made him the first, because the very first would have to present problems for which there were no answers.

"A six-nine guard?" longtime Los Angeles sportscaster Jim Hill would remember. "No one had ever seen anything like that before."

The Moment

Early in that fall of 1974, when Gary Fox and one of his teammates from Waverly High School had taken Earvin Johnson over to Michigan State to play with a group of college players, the coach's son had witnessed some surprising things from Johnson that had left him with much to think about.

At the time, basketball itself had evolved to a quite snug and safe place as a game with five distinct positions. You played one of the five positions and you didn't get out of your lane very often.

The point guard was called "number one" for a reason. He was the quarterback, the guy who ran the show. The ball was in his hands. He moved the team. Directed his teammates. Was the coach on the floor, as the saying went, or the "floor general." Meanwhile, the forwards were the forwards. The center was the center. No longer were the two guards just guards. One was the point. The other guard played off the ball.

The off guard was there to score and defend but also to provide relief, an extra ball handler, if the defense provided pressure. But the game was in the point guard's hands.

Even the forwards had their specific jobs. The power forward was a tough defender and rebounder who helped to protect the center's flank. The small forward could do the same, but also crept out to aid the guards on the perimeter.

Earvin Johnson at the time was taking his first steps in turning all of that on its head. There had been some precedents. For example, Jim Pollard, the marvelous forward with the Minneapolis Lakers in the 1940s, was known for his ball handling, for running the screen-and-roll play with center George Mikan, for being something of a point (small) forward, but at six-six Pollard never had the ball full-time as a point guard.

Johnson, who would largely play as his team's center in high school, also played like a supreme power forward. Despite all of that, he was on his way to taking the sport into the liberating age of versatility where players moved in and out of multiple positions and roles, all within the flow of a play or sequence, but that would mostly come after he had drummed his versatile presence into the consciousness of first high school and college and then professional basketball coaches over the course of his career.

In September 1974 in the upper gym at Jenison Field House, Johnson played as a guard, forward, and center in a stunning flow that began with his crafty rebounding as a forward that saw him move right into the point guard role that unleashed his teammates as mobile weapons.

It sounds simple enough in retrospect. It was not. The game was wrapped tight in a convention that had come into play across many sports with the rise of coaching as a profession.

"It was so different," Gary Fox recalled of that first time watching Johnson, not in a formal game as he had seen Johnson before, but in a high-test pickup format. "That was at least the first signs of it."

Johnson didn't become the point guard each and every time down the floor. There were excellent guards in that game, and he didn't try to exert his will over them all the time. "He didn't command or demand the ball like he did later in high school with his teammates," Gary Fox explained in 2019. "But when he got the rebound, he was heading up the corridor with the ball, you know."

Perhaps even more amazing, when someone else got the rebound, that person began outletting the ball to Johnson just as they would a designated point guard, Fox explained. Johnson's presence was speaking the silent language of the sport. He was the point guard and he was demanding the ball. "The ball was in his hands," Gary Fox said. "He was pushing it now, but he encouraged you to run because, you know, if you got down there and you were open, he would get it to you. So I just think he brought everybody to what his level was."

The important observation here is that no one was instructing Johnson to do this. He was operating from his fifteen-year-old store of instinct, emotional intelligence, desire to win, plus his analysis of that desire, all packaged in a will, a determination, to force his own particular view of how the game should be played upon the formal contests that he would be facing in high school basketball.

Because he was young and operating from an instinct based on a deeply held personal belief, Johnson himself was only gradually coming into a clear understanding of what he wanted to be.

This was no small thing. It was a singular vision that would fuel the rise of his personal power in life. As he rose to prominence over the ensuing seasons, he would be taken as an oddity, with little apparent understanding among the basketball public as to just how much his young persona had driven this singular approach.

The fact that the game had no three-point shot perhaps aided Johnson's one-man revolution at the time, Gary Fox observed. "Today when I go watch pickup games, everybody's shooting threes."

There was another hugely important thing Fox noticed about Johnson that day when the action moved into the half-court. "He would kick it to a side. Then he would slide ball-side. If you didn't get it back to him right away, all of a sudden he'd be over on the weak side. So if you shot and missed, he would have position to get a rebound and that's where, again, he was beyond his years as a high school kid. With the weak side rebounding. He just had a knack for it."

In other words, in the half-court offense, he naturally played briefly as a point guard, then redeployed himself as a forward or center.

The weak side was where he feasted, the place from where Johnson launched his growing power over the game. That fact was important to Gary Fox because his Waverly team would have to play Everett in December 1974. Fox and teammate Scott Landstra wanted their coach, John Holms, to know the special effort they would have to make against Earvin Johnson.

As can be imagined, the circumstances themselves set up quite a bit of drama in the Fox household, all of it put in place three years earlier when George Fox had decided it wouldn't be a good idea to coach his own son, a decision likely influenced by Fox's experience with the game, first as a star player on Fowler High School's Michigan state championship team in the 1950s, then later when he returned to Fowler as the head coach in charge of a team that included one of his younger brothers.

The coach at nearby suburban Waverly High was a friend, so Fox sent Gary there to play, which had worked out well. Gary would become a star player as a senior, an All-Metro performer who had just earned headlines that December of 1974 by scoring 29 points in a Waverly victory just as the game between Everett and Waverly was coming up on the schedule.

Gary Fox would go on to have an outstanding senior season, leaving his father to wonder at times just how good Everett might have been if Gary had been on the team as a senior for Earvin's sophomore season. Still, Fox quickly put away any thought of regret about not coaching his son.

That didn't mean the coach understandably wasn't something of a nervous wreck as the game with his son's team approached. "My dad wanted my brother to play really well," daughter Missy recalled. "I remember him talking about it, just kind of nervous."

"I just want you to play really well," Fox told his son several times as the game neared and the tension rose, pushed along by media questions about the circumstances.

Sensing the drama, Fred Stabley did a pregame story in which the father said of his son, "We talk a lot about the game at home. He's always trying to psych me out."

In his three years at Waverly, his team had never beaten his father's. Gary Fox badly wanted a win.

"My brother was pretty good," Missy recalled, "but not compared to what my dad had going on."

What George Fox had going on was some concern. He had been obviously disappointed at his team's early conflict and inconsistency. After Johnson's breakout second game, Everett beat Hill High School in the third game. "We played together," Fox had told reporters, a subtle reference to the early chemistry problems. "I liked the way the open players got the ball."

Yet the early games revealed the foul trouble that would dog Johnson's high school career from the first game to the last. He was truly an exceptional player, but, as an oversized figure with dynamic mobility playing in a high school league, he had to learn to stay on the floor.

Those concerns were just a part of the internal conflict going on as the Waverly game approached. Fox warned his team not to underestimate Waverly, a team of mostly white seniors. "I said, 'Gary will have the ball a lot in the last quarter. He'll possess it so much. And if the game is close, he's going to keep the ball till we foul him,'" George Fox recalled.

The coach obviously took great pride in his son's play, but he was also very competitive. "He wanted to win," Missy remembered. "It was a very big game."

And that air of competition seemed to overtake all other emotions as game time neared.

"That night, it was really pretty tense," Gary Fox said.

"Absolutely," his sister agreed. "We were a house divided."

That sense of competition was palpable as father and son rode to the game together.

"Now in the big picture of it all, you know, Earvin and Everett didn't really know how good they were yet," Gary Fox recalled.

Having heard about Johnson from two of his players and having scouted Everett a bit himself, Waverly coach John Holms came up with a plan that went beyond merely having his players use their rumps to try to box out the Everett big man. The Waverly coach had his players use an unusual technique of countering Johnson with constant face-up defense near the basket, instead of turning their backs to box out and losing track of his startling quickness to the basket at both ends of the floor.

"He was so quick getting around those box-outs and getting to the rebound," Gary remembered, "and he had a knack for where the ball was going. He really was a special player, but we found if you just faced up no matter which side he tried to flip to, just face-to-face him and kind of control him . . . Well, what we did with Earvin that night was, whoever was guarding him they faced up."

Meanwhile, the scene in the gym during the pregame was intense for the Fox family. "There's my mom standing there still not knowing where to sit," Missy recalled. "The gym was full and packed to the rims with everybody who came to watch Earvin play."

Ultimately, the mother chose her son and sat on the visitors' side of the gym.

The game came to its conclusion just as George Fox predicted it would.

"He told his team that once we gained the lead that we would get pretty deliberate," Gary explained. "I would have the ball a lot that night."

Which meant, as the father predicted, that he would be primed to shoot free throws. "I made most of them," Gary recalled.

Fox ended up shooting 14 of 17 from the line despite going just 3 of 12 from the floor. One of the free throw misses was a technical called on his father.

Usually mild-mannered and calm on the bench, George Fox never got called for technical fouls. The one he received that night may well have been the only one of his career, the coach said.

"My father definitely wasn't a screamer and a hollerer, you know," Gary Fox recalled. He would just kind of observe and make his points. He would like to talk to kids once they came off the floor but not to just scream at somebody. I don't remember him ever screaming. . . . So it was an emotionally charged evening. We all had a lot invested in it."

The game was tight at the end with about two minutes left to go when Fox drove for a layup on a breakaway. Johnson retreated to defend and blocked the shot but was called for his fifth foul.

"And then we beat them," Missy said, the *we* being Waverly, where she also was a student. "I remember when the game was over everybody just sat there like, 'I can't believe that happened.'"

Perhaps no one was more surprised by Everett's 65–62 loss than George Fox. "I was devastated," he recalled. "I told those kids exactly what would happen if we got beat. And it happened."

The extra effort to keep Johnson off the boards "was a huge part of our success that night," Gary remembered. "You know our playing with Earvin at Jenison earlier kind of set us up as being able to beat them."

"It was like they couldn't believe that Waverly could beat them," Missy remembered of her father's team. The outcome left her wondering if her brother's team was that good or if the night had been a fluke.

The Meeting

Fox's daughter Missy wasn't the only one with questions about the outcome. The Everett program and the coaches themselves soon faced serious issues. As memory served the participants, someone stole Pat Holland's keys in the days afterward as Christmas neared.

"We basically knew who did it," George Fox remembered. "When we accused the kids, that's when we had this meeting with the community."

Some members of the Black community had been angered by the accusations; some had concerns about the direction of the team. Soon enough Charles Tucker was called in, Fox said. "I says, 'Look, Tuck, we know they took them.'"

The meeting over the direction of the team and the bruised feelings soon followed. "That's where that all stemmed from," George Fox remembered.

"It was intense," Pat Holland recalled.

Another part of the meeting agenda involved how Johnson was being used by the coaches, that the ball needed to be in the sophomore's hands more often, according to Pat Holland.

"He usually found his way to get it anyway," the assistant coach observed.

Those seeking change were not Johnson's parents, Holland said. "Not his dad, not his parents, they were wonderful people."

And Holland never once heard Johnson asking Fox to put the ball in his hands more often. If that happened—and Holland didn't think it was ever even mentioned—then Johnson did it in his private conversations with the head coach, the assistant said. "Some people, fans, people who knew Earvin, thought Earvin shouldn't be playing inside all the time. . . . There were a lot of people that were thinking that should be the case.

"I recall George saying, 'Hey, don't start telling me about basketball.' George didn't get his dandruff up very often. . . . These were like people who knew Earvin or whatever, just fans or whatever. George's statement was, 'There's no one in this room who knows more basketball than I do except maybe Tucker.'"

The meeting could have led to further misunderstanding and an interruption in the team's growth, but the coaches recall Tucker stepping up and addressing the crowd's concerns about the coaching. It was a big moment in terms of Tucker helping to unite the community behind the team, one that would pay big dividends of trust.

Looking back in 2019, Tucker emphasized that calming concerns at the meeting and other steps he took weren't part of some plan. He said he wasn't rising each morning and thinking about going out and serving the cause of integration. He was just a young guy having fun and trying to do the right thing.

"It wasn't nothing special," he said, neither his part nor the part of Lansing's school administration. Except that it followed the administration's philosophy of putting good people in place and trusting them to do the right things. Meanwhile, it was a very big thing for the coaches, even five decades later.

With Tucker's involvement, the meeting went quite well, Fox recalled. "It was also pretty respectful. There was no yelling and screaming. The principal had it under control and so did Tucker."

The coaches explained they had to have the keys back, Fox said. "We weren't accusing anyone of anything. I just said that, you know,

'A lot of you are here to talk basketball. I'm not here to talk basketball.' I said, 'Dr. Tucker's probably the only one in this room that I could talk basketball with because he understands it thoroughly.' He kind of liked that, but it was true. The community bought into what we were saying. The meeting ended up being pretty good. It all just went away and we never heard another thing about it."

"That kind of silenced people," Pat Holland remembered.

The situation also served to showcase Johnson's problem-solving skills. "Earvin got involved," George Fox said. "Earvin just told us when it was all done, 'Don't worry, coach. I'll get those keys back.' And we got them back the next day, no questions were ever asked."

The meeting had also served to deepen the relationship between the coaches and Tucker. As for Johnson, he wasn't just aiding the school's teachers in making their way through difficult circumstances; he was using his deft touch to help his coaches make similar adjustments.

Looking back, Fox acknowledged that a young professional in Tucker's position might not have handled the matter as well and things could have easily gone off the rails at Everett.

"It could have, very much so," Fox said, "and Pat and I understood that. But we had enough trust in Tucker and he in us that we wouldn't go that way. There was some people there that would have liked to question my coaching and again, I think I thanked Dr. Tucker for that many times. It never got to be a loud yelling screaming meeting, but I'll tell you there was a lot of pressure when it started."

It wasn't too long after that that the coaches noticed that Tucker had begun to act almost as if he were Johnson's agent, quietly watching for issues of every sort that might arise. And Tucker noticed that the coaches had a good attitude about making adjustments.

"Tucker was very good and clean with me about basketball," Fox offered, "and the reason is, he knew I was a disciplinarian and Tucker liked that. He knew I wouldn't put up with anything and that I was a fair and fundamental coach. And he said that's what Earvin needs."

"Initially Earvin was so good you couldn't destroy success," Tucker observed. "You either had to mess it up or you had to embrace it."

The coaches had quickly embraced Johnson, Tucker added, but they also had to change focus and avoid making their decisions based on what other people, other coaches, might think. Instead, they had to see that young Johnson was a unique phenomenon who knew how to win in an entirely different way.

"What these fans might think, what these teachers might think, what the sportswriters might think, what other coaches might think, little of that mattered," Tucker said.

"We knew Tucker was on our side," Fox countered. "Number one, he was a very knowledgeable basketball man, and he knew Pat and I knew basketball as well. He respected me. He knew I'd been around basketball all my life, and as a result Tucker never interfered with anything. Whatever we did in basketball we might talk it over with him and tell him what we were going to do, but he fully understood and never made a comment negative about our coaching as far as I know."

Tucker clearly so loved basketball, considered the game sacrosanct, that this gradual merger of Black and white was based on the team values of the sport itself, oddly enough just as young Earvin was beginning his own unarticulated assault on how the game was played.

Tucker saw Fox as a man who had quickly found a comfort level, also unarticulated, with the changes Johnson was bringing. The coach had been in the business long enough to understand what stood for success as a coach. He understood that only part of it was about him. Sometimes coaches let a little success go to their heads. That was not Fox, Tucker said, adding that the Everett coach also warmed to coaching Black athletes, something that little in his experience had prepared him for.

"Fox adapted to change very quickly," Tucker said. "That's what made him successful. He adapted to playing Magic where he should have played him. He adapted to having four or five blacks on the team. He adapted to having to play more than one Black at a time. If you played two or three, it's okay. He adapted to that very well. He adapted to the fact that a kid's gonna talk back sometimes. He adapted to that. He could have fought things and killed all the opportunity he had. He wouldn't have won if that had been the situation. His adaptability was so good."

In amazingly short time, things had begun to add up for young Earvin Johnson. Soon they would begin to multiply with the variety of people around him protecting his interests. "He did kind of grow up in a cocoon," sportswriter Fred Stabley observed. "He had his mother watching one thing. He had his dad watching, and was always there. You had Tucker and you had George Fox. You had those four people that really kept an eye on Earvin. He did have four people that pretty much their whole focus was keeping Earvin on the straight and narrow."

Smile Time

The dreamlike state of the Everett basketball experience unfolded in grand fashion in the winter and spring of 1975 with a long string of wins, making it easy to leave behind the discontent of December. The sophomore Johnson chose the moment to embark on the kind of breakout that Clayton Kowalk had predicted for him. In the first game back he powered his way to 15 rebounds, five assists, and two blocked shots to go with 27 points, the high of his brief career, all to deliver an 82–44 win over Catholic Central.

The moment initiated something of a trend, with Johnson bringing huge smiles to his teammates on the bench at that key moment in the fourth quarter of many games with the Everett Vikings with a comfortable lead and their young star taking an early seat to provide playing time for the subs.

"He's going to be something before he leaves us," said George Fox, sporting an irrepressible smile of his own.

Johnson, however, forced himself to frown afterward. "I should have had a bundle of points," he told *State Journal* writer Bob Gross. "I missed a lot of easy shots in close. And I'm a better rebounder too."

Next up was the team he had so badly wanted to play for, Sexton, which smelled like another statement game, with Johnson scoring another career high, 34 points, many of them unstoppable in transition, while taking 21 rebounds with Everett's gym "bulging at the seams," said writer Dave Matthews.

Even Sexton's fans were cheering for him when it came time to sit.

"Sexton's only consolation was that it could have been worse," Matthews quipped.

Yet the quiet, growing star of the show was Everett's 2–3 zone, perfect for the team's size. Johnson obviously played as the rim protector in the center of that zone, but he had six-four sophomore Larry Hunter on one side and six-three senior Shumway on the other, which left teams shooting lots of jumpers or driving and hoping to draw fouls on Johnson.

"We didn't isolate Earvin to guard anybody," Fox recalled. "We kept him around and near the basket and his stats prove that out. He would help out on everything that came inside. But he had such a good recovery from helping out and getting back to his man. That's what we noticed right away. And we just said we can't have him going out and guarding anybody. He was too good."

Fox had always directed his teams to work hard defensively to protect the baseline, but having Johnson brought a change in that philosophy.

"Finally, I realized, 'Wait a minute. We got a guy that can go up there and block shots,'" the coach recalled. The idea became that if a scorer penetrated the zone along the baseline, it wasn't a bad thing, because Johnson would be there to protect the rim.

Fortunately, the great Bill Russell of the Boston Celtics had taught American coaching that brush blocking a shot to a teammate was better than swatting the ball out-of-bounds. So Fox began running a shot-blocking drill to encourage Johnson to block shots the way Russell had. "So then we got Earvin to change to cupping the ball in his hand a little bit and to start tipping it to somebody, not just slamming it," Fox remembered. "So he started knocking it back out to a teammate. That really helped our fast break when he could do that."

Johnson's presence presented many other new opportunities. His size invited some teams to press him, but that very size was excellent for seeing over the defense and breaking presses.

Everett next beat East Lansing despite three first-half fouls from Johnson, which emphasized another observation for his coaches—Johnson was so outsized, so dynamic, such a motor that the rest of the team struggled whenever he left the floor, which meant his foul trouble was truly an outsized threat.

He scored another 22 against East Lansing, with 28 points in help from fellow sophomore Hunter. Then came another 25 points and 17 rebounds for Johnson in the next win, over Battle Creek Lakeview, 66–47, leaving Fred Stabley to comment in his game story, "He could play guard if need be."

"It's never good enough," Johnson said earnestly afterward. "I have to keep on working so I can keep on improving." That happened with the rematch with Jackson Parkside, with another varsity career high, 36 points, and 18 rebounds.

"I love playing with Earvin because he's not selfish and can do so many things to help you win," Randy Shumway observed afterward. "He throws great passes at the right time, but if we need a crucial basket we can go to him because he'll get it for us. I've never seen a player of his size able to do so many things. He could play guard, I'm sure, and still be effective."

The rout of Jackson Parkside on the road had the Everett-leaning crowd chanting, "We're Number 1," by the end of the game, what would become a refrain for the weeks ahead.

It was all new to the Everett Vikings, this onslaught of winning. Many, like Pat Holland, hadn't even considered the possibility that Everett might win a state championship. After all, the last time a team from Lansing had won a major title was Clayton Kowalk's Sexton teams winning back-to-back state titles in 1959 and 1960.

Besides, the growing joy of it all seemed to override any premature ambition.

Even so, the winning took on a life of its own, much like Earvin Johnson's growing notoriety, as January turned to February, along with his unfolding revolution that was likewise at the time hardly even a consideration because he was in no way clamoring to be the point guard.

Except with the way he played.

Even at age fifteen, he was already quite like a great coach in that he was a control freak, taking charge of as many elements as possible to secure victory.

He did it with rebounds. He did it with passing. He did it with relationships. He did it with the way he played, with a mojo that seized the game's tempo and moved it forward, all of it far more than anyone could ever have expected from a fifteen-year-old.

As badly as he wanted the ball, wanted control, he never pouted about it or rarely even articulated a demand for it.

First of all, the idea of someone his size being the point guard remained unthinkable. "Plus his best friends were the point guards," George Fox pointed out in 2019. That, of course, would mostly be Reggie Chastine, whose camaraderie and presence and defensive quickness were too important to allow Johnson to push such an agenda.

Johnson's point of opening, of opportunity, was his already considerable ability to run a fast break as almost no one else had ever run it.

His personal devotion to the running attack drove the whole thing, Fox explained. "It just made our fast break offense go a hundred percent all the time instead of fifty percent because we always relied on it. On our fast break we tried to get him the ball after the first pass. If we could get it to him on the first pass, we would do that. But half the time he was bringing the ball down off his own rebound."

The fact that Fox had directed his team to get the ball into his big man's hands was in itself beyond precedent. It was all highly unusual and amusing to spectators, especially the surprises Johnson would bring to a routine high school game. It was this routine that first ensnared the coach's daughter Missy. Instead of going to games at Waverly, her own school, she found herself drawn to Everett many nights to watch the whole thing unfold.

"He was having fun at all times," she explained. "Everything was just so much fun and his getting everybody involved made it more fun. The no-look pass he would like to make, they called it putting on a clinic because he loved to choreograph some wild plays, you know."

She soon found herself drawn to just about every game on Tuesdays and Fridays.

"It just was that much fun," she said. "You just couldn't imagine the energy. You never knew what he was going to do. It was just fun to see. What's he going to do now? To watch that unexpected fun? It just was priceless."

Attendance at the school's games had been growing before Johnson, but once he got noticed it wasn't just an Everett crowd. People from across the region came to see him play, she said. "They just wanted to come and see what was going on. These are high school basketball games. They were driving from all over to watch high school games. The gym was filling up because there was just so much energy. The students started bringing all that energy in the student section. It all just amped up because you didn't know what he was going to do, and he was going to do something every time he came down the floor. He would come up with some kind of fun, and he was having so much fun. You couldn't help but have fun every game. That kid was just having a blast. 'Let's get it going. Let's do it. Let's just make some fun here.' And so you were just having fun watching him have fun, too, with everybody else on the floor having fun."

Christine

It was in the midst of this fun that George Fox's wife and daughters began sitting with Christine Johnson during Tuesday games, Missy recalled. "We sat by Christine quite a bit. We got to know her well. Earvin gets his smile from his mother."

In Christine's case, the smile worked well for all sorts of circumstances, including moments when she needed to cloak her personal history. What the Fox family couldn't have fathomed at the time was the world Christine Porter had emerged from, a world in Edgecombe County, North Carolina, that was intent, in just about every possible way, on convincing the next generation of Black people that they were not just inferior, but far inferior, so inferior as to be prevented from coming into any sort of meaningful contact with white people.

Sandra Jones King, who went to high school with Magic Johnson's mother in Tarboro, recalled it as a period of no real warmth from any white person but no real animosity either, except in nearly every single facet of life.

The local drugstore, for example, with its soda fountain, was such an appealing place, King recalled. "I remember very well the drugstore with those gorgeous floors and the tables, but we could not go in and sit down. We could go in and order a Coke or some ice cream, but we were not able to sit down. We had to come outside on the street. So, our Saturday afternoon entertainment at that time was meeting and walking down one side of the street and then coming back up the other side of the street with your friends."

The circumstances were both galling and indoctrinating to young Black teens. King recalled going past a local drive-in restaurant where the waitstaff served food on trays attached to your car. Across the South, and in other parts of the country as well, Black people could not eat in any white-owned restaurant. But they could buy a little something to eat out of the back door of some places. Eating at a drive-in restaurant meant that white people would have to serve Black people, which wasn't going to happen.

It stirred her emotion just to go past the drive-in, King said. "The anger that I remember in driving by . . . and seeing all of the white teenagers with their cars. To me, that was really an affront. I thought, 'Why in the world would we not be able to go there?' There was music. They seemed to be having a good time."

A trip to the movie theater would bring another affront. Black people were confined to the balcony. In thinking about the circumstances years later, King would be irked to remember that the theater's only fire exit was on the first floor.

It was in the midst of this era that Mary Della Jenkins Porter sought to provide perspective to her daughter Christine just as she was coming to a realization of her standing in the world as young, Black, female, and poor. "She'd tell me that nobody was better than anybody else," Christine once remembered, "regardless of how much money people had or whether they were Black or white. I have never forgotten that."

Her mother's words revealed much needed parental insight in that era. "We didn't know how to experience the anger," Sandra Jones King explained in 2020.

Generally, the thought for Black youth in the South remained what it had been for centuries—to avoid white people wherever possible. "Stay in your own place is probably a good way of saying it," King offered.

For Christine's mother, there was only one main answer to the harsh racial caste system she had experienced her entire life, one that her own children faced even as the modern world unfolded. "She said having faith and trust in Jesus was the most important thing there was," Christine Johnson recalled of her mother. "And every Sunday she made sure we all went to church."

Two decades later, the relationship with the white coach's family presented something quite new for Christine Porter Johnson. She loved people and had been eager her entire life to smile and express that love. But how could she not be cautious, as life had taught her?

"She was very quiet," Missy Fox recalled of meeting Christine. And then the games would start, and her son's big fun would just spill out for everybody in the gym.

"She cheered as loud as the rest of us," the coach's daughter remembered. "She didn't say a lot, but, boy, she sure cheered her son on and then, man, when she hugs you, you know you've been hugged. We would stand there and if he'd do great things, we'd just hug each other, and she would hug everybody with cheering and high fiving and fist pumps, you know, everything."

Even if the mother had sought decorum, it would have been almost impossible amidst all the outbursts from the crowd that Johnson's style produced every few seconds.

"We became close friends," George Fox remembered, "and so did his family, especially his mom. I was a man of the Catholic faith. I had some pretty good principles and his mom found that out. So, her and my wife became good friends. When I was coaching Earvin at Everett, I had my kids sitting behind me. Some of my kids would sit behind me because I had a bad back from playing ball all my life, sitting on those hard bleachers. So, I needed something to lean against.

One of my daughters—they would change off—sat right behind me and put her knees in my back. Well, when you're sitting there with three or four of your kids sitting behind you, you got to clean up your act. That's what kind of happened, and I'm sure Christine noticed that. And as a result of her becoming a very close friend of our family, especially my wife, that made it a little easier."

It didn't hurt his relationship with his new star player either, Fox recalled. "Earvin got rid of some of his anxiety because of that connection right there. He trusted me, and he knew I knew a little bit about basketball. I confided with him a lot."

Johnson would quickly come to be known for making his teammates better, but the truth that emerged is that he also made every single coach he played for not just better but dramatically better.

"That was for sure," Charles Tucker said. "He was just that good. And Earvin could communicate. Some coaches want to overcoach and play like they're making all of the decisions because the newspaper or some of their friends or their colleagues will say they're some kind of great coach with all of this control. If you start believing that stuff, you mess up, because you go overboard."

George Fox did not go overboard, Tucker said.

The coach quickly became aware that Johnson's mother was a Seventh-day Adventist. "She couldn't or wouldn't go to Friday night games," Fox said, "so I scheduled a couple of games and changed them to Saturday night. And I remember doing that for her. I knew she was a very Christian-like lady, and that fit in good with our family and my friends because most of them are pretty good people and have common values. That's what she liked about me and my family. She observed it and I'm sure she respected us for that. So, she entrusted me with her son Earvin and that helped."

Another part of the community's racial bonding came with the energizing of the booster club and its postgame get-togethers in the school cafeteria with players and their families and boosters and fans, events that grew in warmth with each successive win.

"When the players walked in, we just made such a big deal of it because they were doing such great things," Missy explained. "It was just great to congratulate those guys and to high-five and clap when they walked in. And all of those kids on that team, every one of them, they were just a bunch of class-act kids. They were fun and they were very engaging. They would come in and visit with everybody and talk about the game and everybody laughed. It was a really fun time.

"Earvin would have four or five of them around him," she added, "because he's always been such a leader. They would take their time and come to say hi. We got to know all those kids because they didn't just leave after that game. They would take the time to come and thank the booster club and the parents. So, it was fun and then they wanted the food. They were hungry and this was free food. The booster club people would bring really nice snacks and sodas and stuff. And those basketball players needed a lot of that food so they would come in and they would eat. And they didn't just hurry through. It was more social and the kids would make the rounds."

Indeed, something was happening just a few months into the season.

Black and white were enjoying their time together, enjoying their joint success together. "It was a team," Missy Fox said. "It was a real team."

Even angry Larry Johnson had come into the fold. As a senior, he quietly became a member of the school's pep club, according to Everett's yearbook.

"He became our friend," George Fox said in 2019.

"He adjusted," Tucker recalled. "He stayed in school. That wasn't a problem."

9

POPCORN TIME

Earvin Johnson's adjustment to the Everett program had certainly produced some happy surprises, but that didn't mean it was all one big joyride. The complaint by some players persisted that Johnson was still freezing them out that season, which would come back to the coaches in whispers. George Fox and Pat Holland saw daily the difficulty their players had in adjusting to Johnson's game. It would remain true throughout his career that Johnson didn't easily suffer teammates missing or dropping or fumbling one of his passes. He wanted them catching the ball, and if one had bad hands, it wouldn't take him long to get on Johnson's list.

"When Earvin was a sophomore you just didn't expect the kid to be able to pass like that," George Fox recalled, adding that in the many passing drills the team ran were constant reminders that players on the wing should turn their heads to be fully aware. "I told those kids running drills in practice, 'Hey guys, don't be surprised, don't get hit in the back of the head with the ball.'"

So much of the team's running style came to life that first season as the coaches realized Johnson was capable of doing extraordinary things with the ball in the open court on the break.

"Nobody will play that way again, not in my lifetime anyway,"

Pat Holland said in 2019. "You hardly ever see it anymore. It was just a thing of beauty. A lot of people don't appreciate how much practice goes into having everybody be in the right place at the right time for that to happen. What an ideal guy. He could throw over people; he could throw under people with the bounce pass."

None of it would have happened without the constant work. First of all, he had that key personality trait that Hall of Fame coach Tex Winter considered so central to truly great players—perfectionism. He never seemed satisfied, rather focused always on what he needed to do to improve. Thus, Johnson would show himself from an early age to be a free and enthusiastic laborer in formal practice, never hung up on the idea that he already knew it all, which, George Fox recalled, was central to everything from the atmosphere in practice to the performance on game nights.

"I can take some credit for Earvin for some things," the coach said, looking back in 2019. "I do think I made him a better passer. Because we ran a lot of passing drills and as he got more efficient at it, it was just a matter of how he delivered the ball, but he wouldn't have needed any passing coaching anyway. I do think I did help him fine-tune it."

"My memories are mainly how thirsty he was to be coached," Pat Holland said. "It wasn't like, 'I already know this.' It was none of that, absolutely zero. He worked so hard at the drills that we ran, and we did a lot of drills. I mean, he would just be in rapt attention when we were explaining something. And that was good for the whole team. You might think I'm exaggerating or whatever, but it's hard to imagine a player with such a thirst for basketball knowledge and such a love for the game."

That included walking into a gym before a game and inhaling the smell of fresh popcorn cooking, something that Johnson loved to do. "He wanted to soak everything in, every night." Holland marveled about the things they learned about Johnson that first varsity season, infectious things that would remain consistent about his personality throughout their three seasons together.

The coach's constant refrain to his assistant coach as they watched Johnson in games became "I can't believe what I'm seeing."

The more he observed, the more Fox wanted to create situations in practice that matched what he was seeing from Johnson on the floor. "As a result of watching him and knowing his skills, I ran a lot of passing drills, quick outlet drills. I was just amazed on how much he picked up and how good he got."

Holland was taken by how many drills Fox designed to build Johnson's already ample ball-handling and passing skills. One of them put him alone with the ball playing keep-away from his teammates, using the entire gym as the game area, including the bleachers. Johnson would move here and there with a group chasing him, trying to get the ball away. Just the joy and laughter that Johnson and his teammates displayed with the silliness was something to behold, the assistant coach recalled.

The interesting thing, in looking back, was that Johnson's Everett teams were not living off forcing turnovers, Holland said. "We never ever pressed anybody to get our fast-break points. Never. Not one time. It all just started with a rebound, then here we'd go, you know. But those kids worked and worked on that to be in those spots to fill the lane."

It was much like the timing between a quarterback and his receivers in football, except that what Johnson was doing was woven into the fabric of the tempo, with no set plays, just a constant improvisation unfolding on the run that would lead the millions who watched Johnson over his career to think of jazz. It was becoming the music he would so often speak of. "My music," he would say often over the years ahead.

"Don't go too fast," the coaches would warn his teammates. "Go too fast and you're there before you need to be. You want to get the ball so you can take maybe one dribble or no dribble and put it in. That's the objective."

There was something in Johnson having to tune his passes to his less talented teammates that obviously prepared him for later in his career when he would be flanked by exceptional athletes capable of finishing a break with breathtaking authority.

The beginnings of all this evolution had obviously been Johnson's own experiences on the playground, but the ignition of it in organized basketball began when his first coaches saw that he had to keep the ball in his hands.

While the drills obviously helped Johnson, they were often aimed at helping his teammates to adjust. "Every kid there had to learn," Holland recalled, "and they learned it quickly. If you were in a position to score and Earvin had the ball, you're going to get the ball. So, you better be ready."

There was another sophomore that year, long and lean Paul Dawson at six-seven, whose hands were so bad the coaches first thought to leave him on the junior varsity. But his arms were so long and his potential so big they brought him up to the varsity and set him to working with the ball off a wall, or throwing the ball with a team manager each day to develop his hands. With all of this extra personal work, Dawson would become a key component for Everett going forward and by the end of that sophomore year he was beginning to show great progress.

"This Dawson kid, he learned," Holland said. "I mean, they all did."

Johnson, too. Like so many young big men Johnson had yet to gain a comfort level playing with his back to the basket in the post, Fox recalled. "I just said, 'Earvin, we got to work with you on posting up.' He said, 'Yep. Okay, Coach, I'd like to do that, too.'"

With the gradual integration of the game, rules-makers had retreated into outlawing dunking in high school and college, which further emphasized the old fundamentals for putting the ball in off the backboard on just about all shot attempts around the basket. Players were notoriously resistant to such fundamentals. But when Fox sought to focus on them in practice, Johnson was more than receptive.

In the twenty-first century, when basketball was radically remade into a game of analytics and three-point shots that eschewed the post-up game as inefficient mathematically, the leader of this movement, American professional coach Mike D'Antoni, cited the lack of ability of coaches to teach the post-up game and an inability of players to learn it.

But that was not the case with Earvin Johnson and George Fox.

They really worked on the back-to-the-basket moves that defined post play. And that included Fox's insistence on putting your in-close shots off the glass.

"I really got him so he could use the backboard," the coach remembered. "A lot of kids back in that day, they forgot there was a backboard."

As Bill Bradley had built his game in the 1960s based on *A Sense of Where You Are*, Johnson through his work developed a knowledge of how to operate from fifteen feet in, a competency that included all of the footwork and pivoting to find the perfect angle to the basket for scoring that took advantage of his length.

It eventually made him quite a weapon in the high post, Fox added. "He could post up, then take a nice long step to drive or take that 15-foot jump shot off from the high-post area going down for the corner. Make sure you get the good angle and put it in. And he used to stand there and take that big step, take that turning jump shot. It got to be almost automatic. Because you'll remember when he got to the Lakers, he could use the board. He always did."

Dunking may have been outlawed, but the power finish remained very much a test in so many players' minds in the 1970s. "You couldn't dunk legally in high school," Fox explained. "So I remember one time Earvin was out there at practice dunking from a high-key area and running and dribbling and taking about two to three dribbles to slam it. So, I just said, 'Hey Earvin, come here a minute.' I set a ball underneath the basket. I said, 'You stand right here and reach over, pick up that ball and dunk it.' He couldn't do it. He got up and hit the outside of the rim. Of course, a lot of his buddies are laughing at him then, but it didn't take him long. That determined him. I'll never forget this. Pretty soon you'd see him down there by himself practicing at dunking. You know, within a few days he was up there. I'll never forget that."

All of these advances were made possible because of Johnson's excessively competitive nature. "That was evident from the first time I met the kid," Fox said. "Earvin was so competitive." That began with the spades he and friends played at lunchtime. Very soon he gained a reputation for being a little crazy about making sure he won. Fox knew this because students would marvel at Johnson and then come tell the coach about it.

"He just didn't want to lose," the coach said.

Which made for an electric atmosphere in practice when the coaches, both good free throw shooters, began taking on the players in contests with malted shakes or soft drinks as prizes. The games expanded from there to all sorts of shots. "I had a pretty good set shot too," Fox said of the sport's long-outmoded field goal attempt. "I could stand out there and win a few malteds off of all of them. And I'd bug 'em about that, but pretty soon they'd get better because they wanted to beat the coaches at free throw shooting or just shooting around the key."

It seems reasonable to consider that Johnson's one-handed push shot, almost a set shot in itself, grew out of these old-school influences from his coach.

As if Johnson wasn't already driven enough, Fox sought to heap more fuel on the fire one day by urging him to think about the world beyond Lansing.

"I told him that there was a kid somewhere in this country, a big six-foot-eight, six-nine kid like him, and he might be outworking Earvin. Earvin later told me when he met Larry Bird, he knew what I was talking about."

End Game

The Everett Vikings toppled every opponent in their path to the state tournament as February turned to March in 1975, with Earvin Johnson's smile getting broader and brighter each step of the way. By then, Fred Stabley and his fellow writers at the *Lansing State Journal* were dotting their stories with references to Earvin "Magic" Johnson. Their late-January walloping of Hill High had taken the Vikings' record to 11–1 overall and 7–0 in the South Central Conference.

Looming on the schedule was the early-February meeting with

the Eastern High Quakers, featuring sophomore forward Jay Vincent, now six-five, much stronger and armed with an array of moves around the basket that had allowed him to score 41 in a recent game. That wasn't even tops on the roster for the season. Eastern teammate Greg Lloyd, a senior who would also play at Michigan State, had scored 51.

Scheduled to be played at Eastern, the game was moved to Catholic Central's larger gym, to accommodate fan interest. Central's facility seated 2,000 but when 2,300 showed up they managed to fit them in every available nook and cranny. At a whopping $1.50 a ticket, they got to see the first truly big game of Earvin Johnson's career.

Boosted by Lloyd's 51 on their most recent trip to Central, the Quakers had just rung up an unthinkable 109 points there and had scored 80 or more points eight times. The team's firepower didn't always translate into victory, though, as evidenced by their 9–6 record.

That stood in contrast to the defense that played a prominent role in Everett's success.

"We've played 13 games, and in eight of those games our opponents haven't gotten out of the 40s," George Fox told the *Lansing State Journal*.

Clearly the anticipated collision was big enough that the contest apparently brought the first radio broadcast of Johnson's career. "They were actually scalping tickets," George Fox told reporters afterward. "Can you imagine that?"

Everett won the battle for tempo through the game, but it wasn't clear the Vikings could win the game itself until the very last second. Johnson led all scorers with 26 and 20 rebounds. Greg Lloyd jacked up 28 shots and made 10 of them.

With the two teams battling most of the way, Everett finally got a six-point lead in the fourth quarter and was up 63–58 late, but Eastern scored four, with the game coming down to Reggie Chastine facing a one-and-one in the final seconds. He missed, and Randy Shumway secured the rebound to allow Everett a 63–62 final edge. The victory pushed the Vikings to a 13–1 record and a fifth-place ranking among the state's top schools.

From there they kept winning right through February, claiming the district regular season title in the process, then let out a whoop when the state tournament playoff seedings gave them an unexpected rematch with Waverly.

"After the drawings came out and Earvin saw that we were in the same side bracket in the districts he got a kick out of that," Gary Fox remembered. "He knew that they would get their shot at revenge."

Waverly's box-out tricks wouldn't work a second time. "By then he had figured things out where he'd take a jab step or two and then explode by somebody," Gary Fox said. "We were able to hang on with him for a bit, but we tried to turn up the pressure a little bit and he went through our press like we were not even there."

The final was 91–53, with Johnson scoring 29 and obviously delighted to have hammered the team that had given them their only loss on the schedule. The victory set up yet another rematch with Vincent and Eastern for the district tournament championship, a title Johnson and his teammates claimed by making their free throws, 31 of a whopping 39 attempts. Johnson scored 26, including 14 in the final quarter, in the 83–76 win.

Writer Bob Byington of the *Battle Creek Enquirer* had heard that Johnson was quite an amazing spectacle so he had decided to catch the game. "Johnson dominated, completely took charge of the flow of the game," he would recall a year later. "He handled the ball cleverly. He broke Eastern's press. He threaded seemingly blind passes to astonished teammates. And he did all of this with an air of quiet confidence with just this much of flair sprinkled in. I hadn't seen a player, on any level, dominate a game like that in a long time."

With a 20–1 record, the Vikings headed off to Kalamazoo, to the regional tournament at Western Michigan University. There they met Battle Creek Central, whose coach, Chuck Turner, sometimes liked to stare down the opponent's best player in the layup line before the game.

"I just stare them down during warmups," Turner confessed afterward to the Everett coaches. "I just glare at them. Maybe shake them up a little bit. So here comes Earvin Johnson. So, I glare at him and I glare at him."

The next time Johnson came around in the layup line, Turner told Pat Holland, "He comes up to me and pats me on the bottom and says, 'Coach, how's it going?' I knew right then we were going to get our asses kicked."

After defeating Battle Creek, Everett took on "powerful" Benton Harbor, which left Bob Byington further astonished. "If you want to witness a mind-boggling sight," he observed, "watch the tallest player on the floor weave and stutter up the floor, gliding by smaller, and supposedly quicker, players. Johnson did this the entire game. Each time he advanced the ball up the floor was a new adventure. I think the magical aura of Earvin Johnson began right there."

Byington said that while covering the state tournament he ran into many "enraptured" by the tall, thin sophomore's unusual style of play.

"Earvin Johnson is a happening," he said.

The Battle Creek writer sought out Fox afterward to ask him about this most unusual player who seemed to make a point when he left each game to congratulate the opposing coach and players.

"He's just a remarkable kid," the coach answered immediately, his smile betraying just how taken he was, just how aware he was, of the "dreamlike" experience of working with a once-in-a-lifetime player.

Everett took a 22–1 record into the state quarterfinals at Jackson, Michigan, against Dearborn Fordson, the state's fifth-ranked team. Everett was ranked fourth, and two of the top three teams had already lost. It seemed like the perfect opportunity to grab a championship right there in Johnson's first varsity season.

That seemed a sure lock with just over six minutes left in the game and the Vikings up 13 at 51–38. There was no shot clock in that era, no three-point shot, no real reason to lose.

Except for foul shooting. Down the stretch Johnson and his teammates missed the front end of five one-and-one free throw attempts, two of them by Johnson. With the Dearborn Tractors pressing furiously and double-teaming the ball, Everett also committed seven turnovers in four minutes.

With 22 seconds left, Dearborn took a 56–55 lead. Everett had to foul, which it did, and Johnson rebounded the missed free throw to give his team one last shot.

Then Johnson called a timeout.

Which his team didn't have.

The resulting technical and two made free throws ended it, 58–55.

"Vikings Go to Pieces," read the headline in the next morning's *Lansing State Journal*.

"We choked free throws in that game," Fox recalled in 2019. "It was sad. We missed five one-and-ones in the last quarter. We had the game won and they were intentionally fouling us. We missed them. Otherwise, they couldn't have caught us.

"We were a better basketball team than Dearborn Fordson," the coach added, "and everybody at the game knew that except Fordson. We should have won that and if we had won, we'd probably have won the state championship."

After all, the state's top-ranked teams had already been defeated.

"That's a sad one," Pat Holland remembered of Johnson's torment. "He was a sophomore. And when we went in the locker room, he didn't want to get dressed. He sat there and sat there and just wanted to soak in how much that hurt, you know. He didn't want to forget that. Finally, we said, 'Earvin, we got to go.' He said, 'Okay.'"

A news photographer had entered the locker room a few minutes later and captured Johnson, just sitting there in street clothes, with Fox standing above him, the coach's head in both his hands, still in disbelief.

"I got that picture somewhere," Fox said in 2019. "I'll never forget it. I'll never forget sitting in there on that bench, just quiet with Earvin and a bunch of other guys."

"I've never seen Earvin hurt so bad that he couldn't have smiled, no matter what, at that point," Pat Holland said. "He just really took that hard."

It became obvious to the assistant coach that even though he hadn't yet considered the fact that Everett might win a state title, clearly Johnson and Reggie Chastine had believed it, and not just a little bit. That was why they were so crushed at the team's collapse. Their tears answered that question.

Fred Stabley had stood there with Johnson in the locker room afterward. "This loss is only going to make me work harder," he promised. "I don't like losing. I really didn't think we'd be as good as we turned out to be this season, but it shouldn't have ended tonight."

In retrospect, the humiliating moment raised a question about the course of Earvin Johnson's life. What if Everett had won the state tournament when he was a sophomore? Even without a title, all that preceded it was enough to blow up anyone's ego like one of those floats in the Macy's Thanksgiving Parade.

What happens when a fifteen-year-old is called in to help quell racial issues at his new school and then he begins playing basketball and is immediately nicknamed Magic in the papers and his team begins having great success? Does it not stand to reason that his ego would become distended and perhaps even insufferable? It's all nothing more than a local sensation in the state's capital city, but it's a sensation nonetheless. A development like that could destroy any team's chemistry in a nanosecond, especially one still figuring out the new rules about race.

"It never happened," Pat Holland said.

Asked at the time about the astounding transformation of his life over the few months of his sophomore year and the publicity it had brought, Johnson replied, "I just take all the publicity and put it out of my mind. I let it go into one ear and out the other. My parents have helped me with my attitude. It's just me. I like to express myself on the court instead of speaking out."

Looking back on the situation in 2019, Dale Beard mused, "Earvin was the mayor of Lansing at sixteen, and by nineteen, he would be the mayor of Los Angeles."

Fox would observe at the time that among Johnson's many gifts, perhaps the greatest was his attitude. It and his family had certainly helped him process the overwhelming amount of power that had come into his life.

Certainly, one of his favorite entertainers, Michael Jackson, had been a powerful Black teenager in a very public way at the time. It could be argued that in a very low-key, under-the-radar manner, Earvin Johnson was becoming another of the most powerful Black teens in America at that moment.

Johnson himself obviously felt it, Charles Tucker recalled. "Earvin was aware of everything going on and he was comfortable and he was having fun. What's important back then, his dad and his mom had such strong vibes around him."

Others agreed. "It comes from his parents and it's his sisters and brothers that were real disciplined people too," observed friend and teammate Dale Beard. "It was something that kind of got rooted into him to be that way."

Watching it all happen made Stabley think of Earvin Sr. and the trash truck early in the morning for a teenaged Johnson maybe feeling his oats and maybe wanting to sleep in and his father there saying to him, "It doesn't matter, you're going. Magic Johnson or not, you're going, baby."

At that exact moment, the coaches oh so subtly were watching the reaction of the team and posing the same question to Johnson's teammates, Holland recalled. "They said, 'No, he's great to play with.' The big thing was Earvin did not care. He would score a lot of points just because the opportunity was there all the time. But that wasn't his objective. I say that with great confidence. When the game started his only objective was to win however it may be done. And the kids all bought into his great ride."

"He could do so many things," Fox said, adding that the circumstances surely could have bred trouble yet wound up producing just the opposite. "For his teammates too. So that tells you how they felt about him."

"I think his teammates were more in awe of how good he was," Stabley offered. "I don't even know how he did some of the things he did. I watched him play probably ninety to a hundred games in the five years I got to be with him. I think he knew how he did it, but I don't think anybody else did."

Those around him wouldn't understand his mystery in its entirety, but that didn't prevent them all from craving and envying whatever it was that he had first displayed that sophomore year.

"He gets the rebound in the fast break and he's on the way," Fred Stabley, Jr., remembered of Earvin Johnson, Jr. "The other guys just took off like racehorses and here comes Earvin with the ball down the floor."

As soon as the action broke, then came the smile, the dimples pushing his cheeks so high, flashing the teeth, his irrepressible radiation of delight, followed by the hugs and high fives.

"You know what?" Stabley said of Johnson's years as a teen in Lansing. "I don't think anything ever stood out about him negatively. He was always polite. He always had this big smile on his face that he carried through college, that he carried through the NBA. I always thought it was like he knew he was better than you and he was going to show you."

The entire package made it so easy for the people he encountered to misjudge Magic Johnson and his cutthroat ways when it came to competing. Only the keenest observers would see the edge around the eyes sometimes when he was smiling, the tightness revealing that he was holding something back, just like his old man.

"He has that great smile, but don't get in his way on the basketball court," Stabley admitted in acknowledging something of an unseen, absolutely calculating agenda that induced people to misread him much as they misread his parents. "The smile belied his deep drive. In addition to having tremendous confidence, he had this tremendous exuberance about him that was money when he was on the basketball floor and also money off the basketball floor. But maybe more so on the basketball floor for just this personality he had. It really blossomed on the floor."

In 1975, it added up to mostly winning numbers for Candoli and Prophet and Throop, and the other education administrators in Lansing.

"Earvin didn't care," Holland remembered. "He didn't care anytime, whether you were white or Black. It didn't matter. He helped bring the Black kids together with the white kids as much as he could, more than you would expect any student to help do that."

"Earvin basically changed the culture himself," Tucker offered. "He was so focused on ball and he still had his friends there. And Earvin was the kind of guy, he wasn't going to try to push himself on you to associate with you, but he was kind enough and wise enough, if you all fit in together with the right intentions, he wasn't going to resist that because you were a different race. Earvin was a fun and jolly guy."

"People couldn't help but fall in love with Earvin Johnson," Holland recalled. "It's hard to even describe, even now, you know."

10

NATURAL HIGH

The pain of his team's and his own meltdown in the state tournament served as quite the cooker over the coming months of Earvin Johnson's life. But it wasn't like he was going to quit basketball, far from it. He played everywhere he could find a game over the summer of 1975, usually with Charles Tucker in tow.

"Once the season was over and we no longer had control of Earvin, that's when Tucker made his biggest move," George Fox recalled. "Then he was with Earvin all the time, telling him where to go, what to do. He didn't mess with him as long as he knew Pat and I had him."

The perils of the age loomed everywhere. It was that time when America's youthful baby boomer population was embracing serious partying as a new norm, even a supreme value. The late 1960s had brought a youthful uprising in America, but in many ways the changes it wrought weren't truly felt across the country until the 1970s. Experimentation with recreational drugs of all sorts settled into the schools as street drugs found better avenues of distribution and became more and more available in small towns and cities across middle America.

Detroit, two hours to the southeast of Lansing, was already well on the way to being absolutely devastated by a culture of drug abuse. This trend affected athletic competition as well, as players from high schools to the pros were quietly known to compete while high—stoned on marijuana or racing with amphetamines or cocaine or even tripping on LSD.

It was an age of experimentation, thus so much of it was brand-new, which left school officials across the country scrambling to understand it and to figure out how to counter the trend. Much of the new culture was tied to popular music, with themes about street drug life constantly in songs on the radio, which remained a popular and powerful medium. Drug use itself was often tied to popularity in high school, with the idea that "cool kids get high."

So many in that generation would soon find their lives in ruin. Young Johnson was seen as mature and wise beyond his years, yet that didn't free him from scrutiny from his elders. Of concern to the coaches and Tucker were the friends surrounding Johnson. Some in that group were identified as bad eggs with the potential to lead the budding young star astray. Johnson would eventually begin to remove certain people from his life, but that would take time.

"Tucker tried to alienate Earvin from a lot of those previous friends because he didn't want them to get him in trouble," Fox remembered. "And he did it out of the good of his heart. That bunch, they were something else. Some of those kids followed him all through school right through Michigan State. They were kids that came from Dwight Rich and they were kids that went through Everett High School with him. They were mostly some of his childhood friends that he grew up with."

Somehow, Johnson managed to avoid making the growing drug counterculture a central component of his young life.

"I credit Tucker for that too," Fox said. "Tucker, he really had control over Earvin after the season was over because I'd hear people complaining about it, friends of Earvin saying, 'Hey, I can't even get to Earvin anymore. Tucker's got him isolated from everybody.' Well, maybe at that time that might have been a good thing."

Time would reveal that many of these relationships were harmless to Johnson, but if it was the age of experimentation and partying, it was also the age of extreme caution and more than a small amount of fear among educators and parents.

And Tucker was clearly an educator, one who was also assuming the role of guardian with Johnson. By his own admission, the psychologist was by then deeply in "love" with the Johnson family as a close representation of his own personal values, of basketball and faith, of seeking to counter the obvious racism everywhere with a firm patience. At the center of this infatuation was the teen with breathtaking talent and a smile that cloaked an iron will.

"Earvin wasn't no perfect kid," Tucker said. "Earvin was tough now, but he also was more competitive than he was tough. I put it that way. He was just coming on. We kind of locked horns a little bit."

Tucker was an influence, but it went deeper than that, Johnson's friend Dale Beard explained. "There was some temptations, but we were just so far from that that there was just no way we would have gotten caught up in that."

In other words, the things that ultimately guided Johnson were his family, his own intense competitive nature, and his community. He was so locked in on winning at all times, he seemed to care little for anything that would get in the way of that.

From numerous accounts, including his own, the teenaged Johnson's idea of fun was laughing and dancing and singing with friends, all of which stemmed from a natural reserve of joy so deep it didn't require much in the way of stimulants to turn it loose.

A common phrase at the time was "natural high," from a popular song by the group Bloodstone. Johnson seemed to be the epitome of a natural high.

One of the potential threats, although perhaps undetected at the time, was his growing relationship with Terry Furlow, a talented player at Michigan State who would have his own dance with the counterculture that would lead to his early death when he was an NBA player in his prime, just five short years after he first met Johnson.

Johnson and Furlow were well matched in their work ethic.

"I've never seen a young man work as hard as Terry Furlow to develop his game," Johnson recalled in 2019. "If it hadn't been for

Terry when he went to Michigan State . . . I was still a young guy just coming into high school and he used to say 'Come on and meet me' at what we used to call the old men's gym."

In retrospect, Furlow would represent an alternate reality to Johnson, an immensely talented player from the state of Michigan who allowed the counterculture—the one Tucker was working so hard to block from Johnson—into his own life.

"We would work out and he would beat me like 15–0 and he beat me a bad 15–0," Johnson said. "I would have my head down and he would say, 'Pick your head up. I'm supposed to beat you 15–0, and I'm going to keep beating you until you finally respond.' So he made me so mad, right? But he improved my game and next year I came back and he only beat me 15–2. He said, 'See, you're getting better.' And then we kept playing."

Johnson would forever treasure the huge role those one-on-one battles with Furlow played in his development as a player. Furlow presented that high-level competition that provided for immediate feedback and growth, a rare influence for a fifteen-year-old prodigy to encounter.

Just as important, Furlow had played a major role in his youthful awakening, taking young Johnson with him to college parties, where Furlow made grand entrances, waving off the cover charges and strolling into the soirees with a girl on each arm and his entourage in tow. It was the age of Super Fly, and Johnson had a front-row seat to what would come to be known as OG style.

Johnson would later maintain that Furlow disavowed drug use and other vices and never tempted him, but Johnson clearly witnessed the bigger appetites reserved for a star and understood the terrain that came with them.

Busy

In retrospect, it would seem that Charles Tucker's unarticulated strategy at the time was to keep Johnson busy during the daytime to help him avoid getting busy at night.

Forget the extracurricular lessons, the value of all the pickup ball they played over the summer showed itself almost immediately, Tucker recalled. "Earvin always knew he could play, but going into his junior year he started to see that he was something special. Most people with that kind of ability, they have some ego and they think they're better than what they are. . . . But Earvin didn't ego trip. He just continued to play."

Fred Stabley obviously was well aware of Tucker's influence behind the scenes, so he asked Johnson about it in an article for the *State Journal.* "I have to give a lot of credit to Charlie Tucker for helping me achieve what I have so far," Johnson said. "He's always talking to me, explaining certain things about basketball and life in general. He's always trying to match me up with people who are better so that I will continue working hard and improve."

Tucker, then twenty-nine, told Stabley that he continually searched all over Lansing to help Johnson find a better quality of competition.

The psychologist may have set out to limit Johnson's exposure to negative influences, but as time passed the experience left Tucker with an even deeper appreciation of the teen's personal strength.

"His maturity, both basketball-wise and as a person, he was just way ahead of the game," Tucker observed nearly a half century later. "He could comprehend a lot of things. He understood. He had the ability. He made the right choices. He was secure. And he didn't get into a lot of bad circumstances. He maintained that all the time. He just fulfilled the things that his dad and his mom had drilled into him and all their kids. On the religion side, the manners side, they just set a good example."

It all had made a nice pairing with what Johnson did on the floor. After averaging 22 points and 17 rebounds his first varsity season, he had been named to United Press International's All-State first team as a sophomore, unprecedented recognition in talent-rich Michigan, so much so that a sports editor at the *Detroit Free Press* grew suspicious of all the votes for this unknown named Earvin Johnson from Lansing. A sophomore from Lansing making first team All-State? Something was fishy. So, the *Free Press* moved Johnson to the second unit of its team and would only later correct the move when it became clear the votes were legit.

"We hadn't heard about him until his sophomore year and then there's no internet or anything," explained Mick McCabe, who covered high school sports for the *Free Press* for decades. "So he was a rumor when he was a sophomore and he ended up getting the votes to make our All-State team. But Hal Schram [a sports editor] thought that it was like a little conspiracy that a bunch of coaches had voted for this kid. He didn't know. No sophomore had ever made the Dream Team so he didn't make it. He made the second team or something like that. We [later] had to put him back where he belonged."

Even though the *Free Press* was a major influence in Michigan, Johnson had made the first team of other major news organizations, which boosted his reputation in the basketball-crazy state, regardless of what the *Free Press* had done. The honors resulted that summer in Johnson being invited to play in Detroit, a sign of the off-season coming-out party that soon made him a big-time draw at any game.

Thus, Tucker also represented another increasingly important development for Johnson. He had wheels. A Mercedes, in fact. Not only did they travel, but they traveled in style. Which more than added to Johnson's growing aura. An All-State sophomore chauffeured around by his own personal psychologist and hoops guru?

To an increasing number of observers, Tucker began to smell just a little bit like a guy who was angling for some kind of payday. Not that it was anyone's business, but the facts over time would show that while Tucker seemed decidedly obsessed with managing young Earvin's life, he lacked one key trait necessary to fit that role. He wasn't all that motivated by money.

"I didn't have no intent, didn't know anything about no agency at that time," he said in 2019 when asked about his early image. "I just loved basketball. I was mentor to a lot of kids at that time, not just Earvin. About two or three hundred kids, not just him."

As a young professional, Tucker already had plenty of nice things in his life, from his house to his automobile to what would become his private practice downtown. The house was rumored to have a basketball court inside and a tennis court out back. Actually, the tennis court was the basketball court, with buckets at each end. Tucker excelled at both sports. But well above whatever wealth the psychologist had, what he truly seemed to crave was hoops cred. And time would show that certainly seemed to serve Johnson and his family quite well.

There was perhaps no one in Michigan more invested in hoop culture than Tucker, which would eventually allow Johnson to meet all sorts of people, including pro players such as Ralph Simpson and George Gervin, who were friends of Tucker's and big-time Michigan hoops figures in their own right.

Tucker had loaded up Johnson and Reggie Chastine and taken them down to Indiana to see a pro game or two, which allowed them to meet Gervin and Simpson, which in turn would lead to Johnson eventually getting on the court with them here and there during the summers. Soon enough, Lansing's high-test competition began to find Johnson was a handful to deal with that summer as he continued to grow, first to six-seven, then beyond, Tucker recalled. "He was competitive. He'd go looking for it. He'd run over you, even at that age. He'd run right over you. He was kind of thin. He wasn't strong at that time, just a competitive kid. But he knew how to get shots off on a guy even if he was getting hit. He always had the ball in his hands, and he dribbled the ball up and down the streets all the time. He knew how to push and shove you, and he knew how to take the ball and go up the court."

His size and mobility presented not only a unique combination but a serious challenge because Johnson had to adjust to a world out of balance, one of the challenges of being the first true big man to play point guard, Tucker recalled. "He always was off balance because he was so big. He was always off balance, and people were always running up under him. He always had someone up under him. So he learned how to play off of that. You learn how to play when you're unbalanced all the time with people all under your legs and stuff."

Johnson learned to absorb contact and still score, Tucker explained.

"That's what he was able to do out of all that contact. He was fast and he was so long too that it was like he was just sprinting. He could go. He could have been a sprinter. People don't realize that."

The speed led him to develop an array of hesitation dribbles, which left him changing gears in stride, an ability that had not been considered the property of a big man, or even a whole lot of little men at the time, for that matter.

The six-four Fred Stabley happened to mosey into this pickup culture, where he encountered not only that dynamic development but the peculiar competition between Johnson and Tucker at an off-season open gym at Everett High School. "I went one morning and I'm on a team opposing Earvin," the writer recalled. "Tuck was on my team. Earvin comes down the floor, the game is tied at the end, win by one, and guess who's back there by himself? Me. It was like, 'Oh my God what am I going to do here?' Earvin pulls up at the edge of the free throw line to make the big move with his left hand, like he's going to pull up and take a jump shot. So flat-footed slow-bread me goes off and tries to check him. And he goes around me like I'm stuck and slammed it with one hand and started laughing. He had that perfect hesitation dribble to freeze the defender. Tucker comes up to me and he's mad and he says, 'How did you let him get that basket?'"

Stabley responded, "What was I supposed to do?"

"Tackle him or something," Tucker shot back.

"Oh, yeah," Stabley said. "Like I'm going to tackle Earvin Johnson and blow his knee out. I'll be a heel forever in the city of Lansing."

Tucker obviously detested losing to Johnson.

"Earvin was so caught up in the love of the game," he explained, "and he wanted to win so much. He developed that just from playing on the playground. He hated playing against me because he knew I was going to try to win at any cost."

"That was the only time I ever went over there," Stabley recalled with a chuckle.

The sportswriter would consider himself a lifelong friend of Charles Tucker's, but there was no way he wanted to get between the competitiveness of those two again.

The off-season pickup games, particularly against better and better talent, began to mark Johnson's path. "From a young age he beat people that could really play," Tucker said. "They weren't in the pros, but they were people at Michigan State University, people in the community that had played ball on a major level. And he was able to handle that."

As George Fox promised, the quality of opposition for Everett's summer league schedule that second year was dramatically improved with tougher teams from Flint and Detroit and Saginaw, teams that were willing to physically challenge Johnson.

In his year in the program, Johnson had never shown much of a temper, except perhaps for his early conflict with a senior teammate. Even for someone operating from a deep reserve of emotion, Johnson had never really let those emotions get away from him, Fox recalled. "If he ever got mad at me, he never showed it. He might have pouted and walked away, but he never showed it."

On the floor during games, Johnson had occasionally pointed a finger in anger at an opponent in a heated moment, but he'd always made sure to walk away rather than jump into a scrap.

During the physical challenge of summer league, an opposing player managed to get a different response. "He undercut him when Earvin was up in the air," Fox recalled. "He cut underneath him. You can really hurt somebody doing that. That kid did that a couple times, and when we had a break, Earvin nailed him. He grabbed ahold of him, and they got into a hassle. Didn't amount to much after we broke it up. I said, 'Earvin, you know, you're in too big of a position to do stuff like that. You got to walk away.' He was really mad. That's the maddest I ever saw him. Otherwise, he had a way of controlling his temper and taking it out on the other teams."

The Showboat

All in all, the summer experience allowed Earvin to elevate both his game and his profile substantially. But it wasn't entirely positive. There had been talk among some Lansing-area coaches that he was a "showboat," a pejorative term that suggested he valued style and flashiness over competitive integrity, a charge that the Lansing newspaper would ask him about that fall before his junior season.

"People have a right to their opinion," he calmly told the paper. "I have never intended to show off. I like to dribble the ball, to shoot, to rebound and to pass off. I'd like to be thought of as a complete player, not selfish but a team participant. If I can do that, I don't really care what others think."

The question made clear it was going to take time for a number of people to accept the way Johnson was intent on playing the game.

Even with his inclination to control the events, to merge his competitive nature with his sense of free-flowing fun in the fast break, neither Johnson nor the people around him were yet open to the idea of him becoming a designated point guard. Instead, he remained very much an oddity, the long, tall product of what instinct was telling him to do.

"He was a showman," Dale Beard observed in 2019, "and Earvin always wanted to put on a good show no matter where he was."

"Earvin just was flashy anyway," Tucker agreed, "because you saw a person who had become creative, who was showing new things that had never been done with a basketball before, particularly with a guy that big. Here was a guy that didn't want to shoot, but he wanted to pass. . . . He could affect the game without even scoring a point, he could affect the outcome of the game. That was different."

Tucker was particularly sensitive to the showboat allegation. In Mississippi at a segregated high school in the early 1960s, he had been free to play with a flashy, open style. "You could go behind your back, do anything you wanted to do, so long as you made the basket. And do it in the name of winning," he recalled. "I came north my senior year. Shit, I went behind my back, which was the way I played, and the coach went crazy."

For many basketball coaches, showboating was nothing short of corruption, taking over the game and diminishing it. Some observers would contend that it was further evidence of prejudice against Black players, but even the earlier all-white version of the game had its fancy dans.

From his earliest days going against brother Larry right on through high school, constantly dabbling in flashy play was a huge part of the playground for Johnson, the time and place where players really took their games to another level in terms of entertaining style, which made sense because they were far away from a coach's disapproving eye.

"We had some games now, no doubt," Tucker recalled of those summer days. "There was a lot of stuff going on. You had people trying to imitate other people with their own talent, imitate Earl the Pearl, or Connie Hawkins. There were a lot of people trying to imitate somebody."

What was happening in those summer pickup sessions would all prove to be essential to the evolution of the game, Tucker offered. "Most players, even now, the ones that are real good, they have some flashiness to their games. They have basic skills, but that charisma, the way they deliver those skills is somewhat flashy. Look at Larry Bird, the way he did all that stuff with the basketball. Look at Magic, how he played with the no-look pass. It was just different. Anybody back then taking the ball behind their back and shooting and talking, the coaches would be paranoid about that."

"We didn't go for too much showboating," Pat Holland confirmed. "That didn't go with us. That was an invitation to take you out of the game when you did that."

At the same time, George Fox wasn't on a mission to squelch Johnson and change him, which Tucker considered immensely important. After all, basketball was in many ways something of a test lab for the merging of race in the larger culture itself. During this same period, Larry Bird was spending his summers in his small Indiana community playing pickup with Black players and white players and building what would come to be considered legendary trash-talking skills, a sign of the merging of values that greater integration would bring. Soon enough, talking trash would be seen as neither a Black nor a white trait but simply a fun sidelight to the competition itself, not the equivalent of a brilliant no-look pass but all the same a part of the growing and changing culture of the game, first on the playgrounds and then in the public mind.

Johnson's approach never involved a lot of trash-talking. It wasn't something his father valued. But Johnson's open and entertaining style was another matter, which bordered on a trash-talking diction all its own with all of Johnson's celebratory responses after big plays. Clearly, it was the "fun" that Missy Fox described, the ability to make surprising and unexpected plays that kept crowds buzzing and Everett winning, just as earlier in the century their freewheeling and comedic style had allowed the Harlem Globetrotters to sell tickets for NBA doubleheaders.

This acceptance of Johnson's flashy play would be made easier by its success. One reason coaches of that era responded so negatively to showboaters was the sheer number of turnovers they produced.

The Celtics' Red Auerbach hadn't even wanted Bob Cousy as a player, and even after Cousy showed that he could be fancy and fun while winning, Auerbach would look back and say in a 1988 interview, "There were a lot of nights he threw the ball into the west wind."

Johnson had his share of turnovers, too.

"But Earvin was pretty much on target with his passing," Pat Holland recalled. "Not every time of course, but the great majority of the time that's where his passes were."

"To see somebody that tall and that big and that young, with the mind to do it, that was what impressed you," Tucker offered. "For him to be so young and so big and to have the presence to do it and to win doing it, that was what was impressive about it. A lot of people can throw a fancy pass, but they can't throw a fancy pass that helps you win. He could throw one that helped you win."

His style and the team's early success had sort of opened the way for Johnson to be the kind of rare player who created his own fundamentals. What was even more telling was that the coaches were not just open-minded about that but soon eager to capitalize on it. Holland recalled sitting next to Fox during games. "One time Earvin made one of those passes and George says, 'Quick, write that down. We got to run a drill for that.'"

Johnson was meeting each moment with his unique skills and adjusting as he went along, Holland observed. "He learned what he could do and what he couldn't do out there."

The same was true for his life in general, as his success on the court had made him a public figure overnight, established that October of his junior year in high school when the *State Journal* did a personality profile on him, illustrated with a cartoon portrait that emphasized his outsized Afro and his beaming countenance, a level of attention driven in part by his new nickname. He had begun to encounter people everywhere calling him Magic.

"They call me that all the time and I kind of like it," he said.

He was asked about the bitter loss that had ended his season. Over the ensuing months, Johnson had become philosophical about it. "That was a big disappointment," he replied. "We had the potential to go all the way but losing taught us all a lesson and that was even with a 15-point lead you can't let up. I think we stopped hustling. I know personally I felt terrible, but I grew up a little."

He likewise was growing literally, which allowed him to eclipse the family around him. Earvin Sr. was six-three to six-four, as was older brother Quincy. His mother was five-ten, as were his younger twin sisters, Evonne and Evelyn, both at the time playing basketball at Dwight Rich, where Evelyn was averaging 22 points a game.

As he surveyed the taller figures around the basketball landscape, Johnson revealed he had a new idol, Julius Erving, aka Dr. J, who had caught Johnson's eyes playing for the New York Nets in the old American Basketball Association.

"I really like to watch Julius Erving," he said. "He's beautiful for the way he can move for being six-seven. I like the way he seems to glide whenever he has the ball."

With the higher profile of the All-State status, a number of college programs had moved to express interest in recruiting Johnson, led by Michigan State coach Gus Ganakas, who had begun describing him as perhaps the best college basketball prospect in the entire state.

Johnson read the letters that coaches had begun sending to him and then put them away in a drawer and out of his mind. He did acknowledge that at the least he was now considered the best player in Lansing. "That's nice to hear," he said, "but I have a lot to learn about the game. I've discovered the fun of winning and the fun of playing together. I look at myself and ask why do people think so much of me as a player? Maybe it's because I try to do everything in the game as well as I know how. There's a long way to go."

Come Together

There to greet him at Everett that fall of 1975 was more racial trouble as a new wave of attitudes was again infecting Lansing, much of it seeded perhaps by an ugly incident at Michigan State the previous season that had put coach Gus Ganakas under intense pressure.

With Johnson playing pickup games frequently at Jenison Field House, the Michigan State coach had soon made his acquaintance and made sure the rising star had tickets to every Spartan home game.

Johnson took in games as often as possible while noting the low-key atmosphere. He began following Furlow and the other players he had gotten to know playing pickup games. Seen as mediocre, Spartan basketball didn't generate a lot of fan interest, so there were always seats available.

Ganakas himself had quickly become a fan of Johnson as a sophomore and, like Missy Fox, began attending games at Everett just to watch. Asked about all the excitement Johnson was creating, Ganakas had quipped that his own team should be playing at Everett while Johnson and the Vikings with their fan following should play their games at Jenison.

During Johnson's sophomore season, Ganakas had inserted a white freshman into the Spartans' starting lineup, a move that was met by a startling protest from the Black players on the team. Ten of them had abruptly walked out of a team meeting just hours before State was scheduled to play a home game against Coach Bobby Knight's Indiana University powerhouse team, forcing Ganakas to suspend them and to field a mix of practice players and walk-ons that day.

The players would quickly return to the program, but the incident would drag out for months in the Lansing newspaper and would eventually result in Ganakas losing his job.

Just how much the Michigan State headlines drove the racial trouble that developed that fall of '75 in Lansing is hard to say. At Everett, there were always other factors to stir up people and polarize them along racial lines.

Johnson somehow just pushed against these negative factors with a natural ease that seemed to grow from his great confidence, observed Bruce Fields, then a sophomore in the basketball program. "He didn't care. The train was going to keep moving with you or without you. When he got there, he started a train of momentum of bringing people together. There's no other way to describe it. It was mostly out of jealousy that people were having a hard time with it. This young Black kid getting all this attention?"

That flew in the face of certain people who were used to doing things a certain way for years, Fields explained. "He was bringing everybody together, especially at Everett High School, but there were those within the school, teachers, not a lot, but a couple that were jealous of him, envious of him, and I think rooted against him. But they were immaterial. They weren't going to stop the train because the train was rolling with or without them, you know."

When racial troubles arose again in school early that fall, Johnson decided to act unilaterally without coordinating with the administration, never mind the fact that he had just turned sixteen. It was clearly a sign of his confidence in his own leadership and peacemaking abilities.

"There were interracial disturbances, not just at Everett but other places in Lansing, too," Tucker recalled of that fall. "There was a group of people who kept things going."

Johnson's big idea was to answer it with his own rally for racial unification, almost an impromptu decision cooked up on the spot one particularly tough day. Tucker recalled that Johnson began telling his friends that he was asking students to leave class to go to the football stadium to talk about the issue.

"It was very risky," Tucker remembered.

Administrators had no warning of the move. Not surprisingly, Principal Frank Throop was not happy with Johnson's big idea.

It wasn't clear that this new outbreak of fights at Everett was entirely about race, but there was little question racial issues were in the air.

Throop and other administrators at the school "thought, at that time, to do something like that was very strong," Tucker recalled. "You can't have kids just doing what they want to do when you have assemblies, when you have group things like that. They could take advantage of that by doing what they want to do, which is run all over the place. At that time, you do something like that, you're normally going to be punished."

After all, racial issues were so tricky, an idea that started with good intentions could easily trigger more fights and violence.

It was especially tricky for that junior year because of trouble in Lansing at large as well as in the school, Tucker said. "It was all over the country at that time, but Earvin took it upon himself one day to tell all the kids after lunch to go to the football stadium. And they all went, and the teachers and the principal, we had no control over it. The principal was nervous and everybody else, too, because it was Earvin doing it. At that time, it looked like he was breaking the rules to do something negative. But he brought all the kids together. There were some kids running all over the place. Word got around quickly that 'we're going out.'"

The logistics of it were stunningly slapdash but perhaps indicative of the leadership Johnson projected to the student body. Not all of the school's 2,500 or so students left lunch and classrooms and went to the stadium, Tucker estimated, but hundreds of them, as many as a thousand, "went to the football stadium, which is about a three-minute walk from the main building. He just had them out there.

"The principal got mad and went out there to tell them to come in," Tucker remembered. "But when he got out there, he stood and listened."

There were a variety of athletes in the assembly. Johnson quickly gained the crowd's attention, Tucker remembered. "He cracked some jokes and then he called a couple of other players up. There was Black and white, in all sports, he was just calling them up, football, basketball, baseball. He just focused on a point, and he wasn't socializing either. Earvin just used the time to say, 'Hey, guys, we're gonna have a good time. We got a game coming up. We got a good team and I want all you guys to come to the game. Hey, we can't have our school turned out. We got to get along with everybody and treat everybody right.' He was real mature in his speech. 'We can do it,' that type of thing."

Once he got the response he wanted from his fellow students, Johnson didn't let things drag out, Tucker said. "He let the kids know, all the athletes, he was just calling on them. 'Ain't that right, Joe?' So everybody, they started laughing. And that eased a tense situation, and that carried back into the school. After that everybody went right back to class and we had no fights or stuff."

"After Earv had that meeting it changed people's perception," Bruce Fields said while acknowledging that students at that age were more influenced by the sense of togetherness than any specific literal message, much like a pep rally for harmony. "That brought things closer together. It wouldn't make it a perfect union, but it made it more tolerable. And people were more inclined to work together and put some things aside for the greater good. Things got a little better for the moment."

It was the moment that Johnson first showed himself to be an "ambassador" on a larger stage, Tucker observed. "That was big-time, the idea that they would follow him. Usually they might use a situation like that to get out of class and clown around. Usually everybody was so taken over by the one or two who might want to start something or be negative. But they were overpowered by the support of the crowd. . . . So that was great."

Johnson wasn't punished for the incident, Tucker explained. "It was funny. Half the people didn't know what it even was. But the key thing was, with them being out there, they didn't cause any problems. They didn't misuse the opportunity."

In that era before social media, a rare figure like Earvin Johnson served to draw people together in real time. Dale Beard had heard about Johnson's impact even before Beard himself got to Everett. And then, like Bruce Fields, when he got there in 1975, Beard began witnessing it firsthand. "I'll tell you this," he said, "when anything went on, as far as any controversy, they would always come to Earvin to settle everything, you know, because he was that type of guy. He was not just the basketball player. I think maybe the guy could have run for mayor at sixteen. They'd come to him. 'Hey, Earvin. Hey man, these guys are down here having a little spat, they're kind of fighting.' He'd go down there, 'Hey, guys, break that up,' or whatever. . . . He was just like an ambassador back then."

Johnson helped build community, Tucker observed. "People started following him, and in following him, they came together and realized they could associate with people who didn't look like them. Then they became aware that they were associating with each other and it was all right. In what he did, Earvin brought people together to associate with one another, people who would never have realized they could associate with one another, without that success and togetherness. If Earvin and the winning he brought hadn't happened, those people would likely have never associated with one another and would likely have never learned that it was possible. How many people would come together if it wasn't for sports, in most cases?"

Earlier in the process, during the previous season, Johnson had first sensed that what he was doing could be of help, Tucker recalled. Ultimately, his sports success drove people to watch and observe him, which allowed him to have a wider impact on other issues.

"He never knew the impact he had on people at that time," Beard said. "The guy never was in trouble."

Thus, the way Johnson handled himself made the impact of the sports even greater, Tucker offered. "Earvin's success each year on the court at Everett led people to focus more on the winning and less on racial differences. As a result, people learned that they could go to school together and they could relate."

Junior the Junior

Despite such troubles, Johnson's junior season began with plenty of joy. Certainly a highlight came with the brand-new warm-ups for the Everett High Vikings, earned by their sudden, unexpected vault into the conversation as one of the state's best teams.

"You should have seen him the day we got our new warm-ups," his pal, Reggie Chastine, told one writer. "He was dribbling around and running around all over. Just like a little kid."

And his teammates?

"I guess everyone on the team can tell he really likes to play," Chastine explained. "He's got a nice personality. Everybody likes him. He's just a regular guy."

Until he got on the court. That junior season would bring explosions of scoring. The first big sign of that came in an early December game, another demolition of Sexton, when Johnson set a city single-game record by scoring 54 points.

The new electronic scoreboard that showed each player's point total built an excitement in Everett's packed gym with the noise growing every time he scored down the stretch. As the old record of 51 grew near, George Fox removed all the starters except Johnson and let him go for the record.

"I remember seeing him and Coach Fox talking," recalled Leon Stokes, then a sophomore on the JV team. "I assumed they were talking about leaving him in."

That was when he really felt the pressure, Johnson admitted afterward, but he broke the record with a pair of free throws, then hit another jumper for the total before retiring with about four minutes left to play. He had scored the 54 points in about 28 minutes of playing time. He also finished with 25 rebounds.

"It was one of those games where nobody could stop him," Leon Stokes said.

"I guess it's nice to say you've set a record," Johnson observed when asked about it three weeks later. "But I hadn't really thought about it before. If it wasn't for the team, I don't think I would have done it. They helped me every way they possibly could."

The very next game he faced serious double-teams, scored but eight points but had a whopping 13 assists. "When other teams try to stop me, that leaves the other guys open," he explained to writer Bob Byington. "I get more enjoyment out of hitting another player with a good pass than I do out of scoring a basket."

Everett ripped off six wins to start the season, and just about all of their fans assumed the Vikings were headed to the number one team in the state. Then, just before the first polls came out, they lost the day after Christmas to Detroit Northeastern, a quick team that played a tight half-court man defense that forced a number of turnovers. The Detroit team also hit an array of jumpers that shredded Everett's much admired zone for a 63–58 win.

The Vikings then rolled through 18 more wins, a streak that ran right through the playoffs and included two more 50-point games from Johnson before a narrow win avenging the Detroit Northeastern defeat in the state quarterfinals.

Next up in the state Class A semifinals was the team that Detroit Northeastern had hammered in the Detroit city title game, Detroit Catholic Central.

On the morning of their semifinal game, it was announced that Johnson had again been named to the UPI All-State first team, with a level of play that had fueled the Vikings' rise as the state's top-ranked unit by the playoffs.

Once again, however, the season came down to an almost bizarre turn of events. Everett and Detroit Catholic Central had changed leads back and forth through most of the game until the final 100 seconds when Detroit went up 57–53.

Johnson immediately rushed the ball up the floor and drove all the way to a layup. The referees called him for a charge but scored the basket, 57–55.

It was only Johnson's second foul. Catholic Central missed the front end of a one-and-one, and Johnson again rushed down the floor to attack the basket where he drew yet another charging foul. Catholic went to the line but again missed the front end of a one-and-one.

Johnson then again drove the court and this time attacked the basket along the baseline and again drew another charging foul, his fourth.

Detroit made one of the free throws to go up 58–55.

Johnson angled to get a good shot on the ensuing frenzied possession but again missed, which brought the final strange sequence.

Detroit Catholic Central rebounded, and although there was more than a minute on the clock, Johnson grabbed an opponent in what appeared to be an intentional foul to stop the clock.

It was his fifth. In about a minute he had acquired four fouls and been disqualified. Despite facing double-teams and a collapsing defense, Johnson had taken every one of his team's shots in the fourth quarter until he fouled out.

"Johnson's a great player, but it takes five," observed Catholic Central coach Bernie Holowicki afterward.

"It was a nightmare, just a nightmare," George Fox told reporters. "I don't know what happened."

Johnson had led all scorers with 30 points but had again come apart in the deciding moments and could only watch from the bench as his team lost. He had somehow managed to play the goat and the hero, all at the same time, *State Journal* writer Dave Matthews commented.

"Boy, that hurt," George Fox recalled five decades later.

Everett finished 24–2. In the locker room afterward, Johnson, his coaches, and his teammates were again holding their heads in their hands in disbelief and asking why. They were also asking how, as in, "How the hell do you draw four legit fouls in about 80 seconds?"

The previous season Johnson had sat in the locker room, saying he wanted to soak in every bit of the pain from the loss. This time, it was almost more than he could stand. Everywhere he went, it seemed he was confronted by questions and comments. No one asked the question more frankly than Johnson himself.

Was "Magic" Johnson becoming "Meltdown" Johnson?

Certainly the Boys Club of Lansing, where Johnson had spent much time in his early life, didn't think so. That spring, the local club nominated him for the nationwide "Boy of the Year" recognition.

"Earvin is just an unusual boy," explained Ron Dumke, the Lansing club's executive director. "I've never seen such openness, friendship and spirit of understanding." The Lansing club summed up those qualities in a twelve-page report nominating him for the award.

"I've never seen such maturity in someone as young as Earvin,"

Dumke said. "He's contributed so much to our program. For the past three summers, he's set up our basketball instruction program at our southside club, and he started our midget basketball league. He also has worked with young kids and chaperoned on our trips and picnics. Earvin has been active in church work, in school with the student council. He has an earnest desire to serve others and, on top of it all, he seems to have the maturity to handle the success he's enjoying in basketball."

Dumke cited Johnson's work on his father's trash truck and closed by saying, "It's just unusual to find a young man who is having so much success who is willing to give so much of his time to others. He is a super kid who is one fine human being."

11

MOURNING BECOMES ELECTRA

The summer of 1976 unfolded in a blur, one of those stressful times that you inhabit almost entirely in retrospect because you're too numb to comprehend it in the moment, in the present tense, when it's actually consuming you.

Grief is like that. It leaves you asking later, "Did that really happen? Was I really like that, doing those things?"

Especially youthful grief.

In the wake of yet another disastrous playoff loss, George Fox had decided to burnish his team with the absolutely toughest summer league schedule he could put together, against all the top teams in the state from all the hard-core hoops cultures available in Detroit and beyond.

Earvin Johnson could hardly wait to get going in those games. Leon Stokes knew that because Johnson phoned him. "I was a five-eleven power forward, the tenth, eleventh, or twelfth man on the team, and he's calling me," he recalled. "Earvin would call me to ask if I was ready."

It didn't seem to concern Johnson that Stokes was a rising junior, fresh off the jayvees, trying to make the varsity. He was part of the group. He mattered. Was he ready?

"He treated everybody the same," Stokes said. "Earvin tried to make sure that you, no matter your status, that you were included."

How many sixteen-year-old basketball stars are running through the phone tree for the entire team to make sure they're pumped up for a summer scrimmage? How many sixteen-year-old basketball stars even have all their teammates' numbers? First of all, this was years before the age when teens had cell phones in an interconnected world. Johnson had to dial up these calls from his home phone.

"Earvin tended to be inclusive in his interactions with people, especially teammates," Stokes explained. "It was not like I was gonna play a lot. I took it as that he just wanted to make sure everyone on that team was ready and dialed in and included. I really appreciated that. It meant a lot."

After all, this was THE Magic Johnson heading into his senior year, and he now could measure his notoriety in media wattage. It didn't matter. He was on the phone, dialing his teammates up to pump them up.

"We went down to Detroit that summer to play—I think it was Southwestern High School," George Fox recalled. "We got there and, my Lord, there were TV cameras there for a scrimmage between high school teams in the middle of summer. Reporters, too. It was an unbelievable thing. I'll never forget it.

"We played almost every good team in the state that summer," Fox said, "and we had no problems with any of them. So we knew we were the heavy favorites going into the season. There wasn't any doubt that we were the best team in the state. Everybody else knew it and so did we. That's why there was so much pressure on us to win it."

That, and the driving force of Earvin Johnson's frustration with how each of his first two varsity seasons had ended.

The basketball itself offered hardly any pause for Johnson that summer of '76, when America was celebrating its bicentennial and festooned seemingly everywhere in red, white, and blue. While Fox had run his gauntlet of a summer league, Charles Tucker was busy setting up some competition on his own that would pit Johnson against pro players in high-test pickup games.

Not only was Tucker nurturing Johnson's dreams but he was trying desperately to keep the coals glowing on his own hopes. After years of hustling around to play minor league basketball on winter weekends and trying out with various pro franchises in the summer, the psychologist had turned those experiences into an array of friends and valuable contacts.

In mid-July, Tucker held what would be the first of his many camps and various all-star games over the years. Billed as Charles Tucker's Basketball Camp, the event, held in Everett's gym, reflected Tucker's suddenly elevated profile and status, based in part on the success of his young protégé.

This first camp in Lansing revealed the formula, with Johnson and Jay Vincent among the camp counselors, with pro basketball stars Ralph Simpson and Steve Mix billed as the luminaries, along with a lineup of college and high school coaches from the region.

The addition of pro players to his lineup each summer added to the aura and publicity of the event, with local sportswriters delighted to have interview access to Simpson and Mix the first year and Darryl "Chocolate Thunder" Dawkins the next.

It was all part of a hoops Camelot that Tucker helped create in Lansing. His camp and the various nightly games played by pro and college stars associated with it came to provide the perfect entertainment for the basketball-hungry region during summer. The events also created the image over the coming years that the place was connected with basketball royalty, which it would be once Johnson ascended to the heights of the professional game and Tucker broadened the number of NBA stars he was advising and representing.

Tucker's summer events also seeded the idea with Johnson that would lead to his later establishing his own Midsummer Night's Magic basketball charity event, held each summer at UCLA's Pauley Pavilion to raise money for the United Negro College Fund, a gala that would blow up into substantial fanfare for Hollywood nights well into the twenty-first century. The whole concept of these summer events, a public spectacle amidst a swirl of pickup games and private fun, began in the busy mind of Charles Tucker.

Some people involved in staging the games would privately complain that Tucker was unbelievably casual about ironing out the details of his events. Pat Holland recalled getting a phone call the night before one of Tucker's early camps was to begin and being informed that he was the director of the camp.

"You had to be ready at any time for a change," Holland said. "And they were big changes."

Then there was Tucker himself, the instructor teaching a move. "He would not quit with a kid until the kid could do it right," Holland said with a laugh.

Again, the extra effort was tremendously admirable, but it played havoc with any schedule, the coach recalled.

It didn't seem to matter, however. The lights would come on, the campers and nighttime crowds would show up, and there would be plenty of hoop on full display as Tucker managed to conjure up his own sort of magic.

Looking back, Dale Beard observed that even if the psychologist hadn't been Johnson's advisor and mentor, the things Tucker did for the community at large in Lansing were impressive on their own, with all of the top basketball figures that he brought to town and all the basketball enrichment he provided for the region.

Tucker's personal reward for this effort clearly was that he could get on the court with stars from pro basketball and Johnson and other top players and display that he could indeed play at a high level. These moments came in the extremely high-test pickup games that Tucker orchestrated. As a teen headed into his senior season, Johnson found himself going up against George Gervin, Campy Russell, and Simpson—all introduced to him by Tucker—and more than holding his own.

That summer of 1976, Tucker's newly minted basketball camp also offered college coaches who attended an early look at Johnson, who was coming to be considered one of the top prospects in the country in an era that was still remarkably casual about such things. Among them was Eldon Miller, who had just been named the new coach at Ohio State.

"There isn't a college coach in the country that wouldn't like to have Earvin," Miller told the writers hanging out at the camp, which had been announced with a news story and ads in the *State Journal*. "He's truly a great player. I don't think I've ever seen anybody with more ability and a better attitude toward reaching his potential."

The word about Johnson's talent and intangibles had clearly gotten out, even though such information often traveled slowly in that era before the internet. By September, Johnson would have more than four hundred inquiries from college coaches across the country. Yes, 1976 was well before the age of robocalls and telemarketing, but the Johnson household, with its number listed in the phone book, was already receiving as many as six or seven calls a night from coaches, all of them requesting an in-person visit. Johnson was polite with them, but the level of interest soon became quite a bother, even if Johnson loved and craved the attention.

He had twice failed in the biggest moments of the absolutely most important thing in his young life. "The biggest thing on my mind now is the state championship," he confessed. "I want it so bad."

Even so, his life wasn't all basketball. His first employment had come the summer before at Quality Dairy, a regional chain that offered milk and ice cream and donuts. He earned the minimum wage, then about $2.30 an hour, and delighted in making his own folding money.

In the summer of 1976, he also began working for local businessman and family friend Greg Eaton, who had among his many businesses Greg's Janitorial that cleaned local offices. Eaton noticed right away that Johnson wasn't looking to skate by, that he wanted to work for what he got.

"Just a rock-solid kid," Eaton would remember. "You told him to do something, and he did it with a smile."

Johnson would later admit to plopping down in the plush executive chairs of the offices he cleaned, propping his feet up on the desk, and daydreaming about being a successful entrepreneur much like Eaton himself.

Somewhere in the midst of his spinning schedule, Johnson found time to play an AAU tournament with a team from Detroit that featured Kevin Smith, a highly regarded rising senior guard from Birmingham Brother Rice, a powerhouse team in Detroit's Catholic

League. Johnson stayed at Smith's home for the event, where the two began hatching the idea that they would sign with the University of Michigan together. In the fall, they would visit Ann Arbor during a football weekend and swear fealty to the idea that they would play ball for Michigan, a team that had just made a trip to college basketball's Final Four.

It wasn't something Johnson announced, but he did make it known to writers that he was displeased with Michigan State for the school's firing of his friend, coach Gus Ganakas. "I have known Gus for years, and I think a great deal of him," he told writer Dave Matthews. "And when he was fired I kind of lost interest in MSU."

As Johnson was warming to the idea of playing for Michigan, George Fox was becoming increasingly fed up with all the time the recruiting process was soaking up. Big-time coaches from across the country were now calling Fox each night to talk about Johnson, addressing Fox by his first name as if they were good ol' friends. Fox had loved basketball from the days he was a high school star himself on a rural state championship team right on through his various coaching jobs across Michigan high school hoops, but he wasn't consumed by the game. He had varied interests, beginning with his wife and family and church and friends and including his love of the outdoors, of hunting and fishing. In the name of self-preservation for himself and Earvin, the coach began talks with his star player about narrowing the schools down to a manageable list in the hopes they could get some of the recruiting bird dogs to stop phoning.

In the meantime, the Michigan coaches, led by Johnny Orr assistant Bill Frieder, were all over Lansing and the recruiting of Earvin Johnson, as were others. Leonard Hamilton was a young assistant at Kentucky and he made an impression on Johnson, as did numerous other head coaches, including Digger Phelps at Notre Dame, Lefty Driesell at Maryland, and Norm Sloan at NC State.

Videotape was in development at the time, but there was no widespread use of it. Coaches could study grainy black-and-white game film on a reel-to-reel projector, but there was almost none available on Johnson. There had been no TV broadcasts of his games. So the coaches began coming around in person that summer and early fall.

Digger Phelps met Johnson and Tucker at an office in downtown Lansing, and Lefty Driesell came to practice and pulled Earvin aside for a conversation, Fox recalled. "Bobby Knight came right to school. He told me he was coming in, and I told him I'd meet him in the teachers' lounge right after school. I said we get out at three o'clock. So at three o'clock, I'm walking down the hall to go to the teachers' lounge and he's leaning up against one of our walls in the hallway. Nobody's talking to him or nothing. I walked up to him and I said, 'Hey, coach, you're a little early.' He says, 'I always like to go to school and walk in unannounced and stand in the hallway and observe the students.' And we went in the teachers' lounge just the three of us. We had a nice visit."

Knight's Hoosiers had just won the NCAA championship over Michigan that spring with a stunningly perfect 33–0 record. He and Orr were the hottest coaches in the country that summer.

"I just felt that Bobby Knight did the best job he thought he could do," Fox recalled. "Again, Earvin didn't say no to him because that was Earvin's personality. He just kind of, you know, talked to him and made some compliments about Knight. And that was about it."

Later, when it was all decided, one of the top suitors would rue the fact that they had not gotten to Charles Tucker and paid him off, Mick McCabe of the *Detroit Free Press* would recall in 2019. Tucker would scoff at similar comments and point out that the real audience the recruiters should have sought was Earvin Sr. Few people, of course, managed to solve the sphinxlike mystery of Big Earv like Tucker himself had.

Meanwhile, back in the spring, Jud Heathcote, the coach at the University of Montana who had been hired to replace Gun Ganakas at Michigan State, had arrived in Lansing without a clue as to who Earvin Johnson was and was soon advised that he better find out in a hurry.

But all of these considerations would quickly become swamped by the grief. It was just two days after Johnson's birthday that August that the dreadful news arrived. Dale Beard recalled his mother woke him to tell him that Reggie Chastine had been killed by a drunk driver in nearby Jackson, Michigan. Beard immediately thought of

Earvin. Johnson had a girl he was seeing in Jackson and had had plans to go there with Chastine but had canceled at the last minute due to a conflict. Upon getting the news that morning from Chastine's brother, Johnson ran out of his house into the street and started running in disbelief and crying as he tried to process the realization. He would recall that he didn't stop running for what seemed like hours.

Like that, all their lives halted and changed direction. The Everett Vikings found themselves facing the sudden and surreal task of being pallbearers for their friend and grieving the kind of loss that made the disastrous playoff failures seem almost silly in their insignificance.

Chastine had died of internal injuries and had looked so young and vital at the viewing, like he could get up out of the casket and go play. "It was very difficult," Pat Holland recalled.

Just before graduation, Chastine had told Johnson that he knew Everett was going to win the state title that next season and that he would come back to share in the celebration.

"Him and Reggie, they were close, man," Dale Beard explained decades later. "Reggie was older. He was a mentor to Earvin. You're talking about a guy who had a full beard and mustache in high school. He even looked older than what he was."

"Reg didn't think he had many friends," Johnson told the *State Journal* that week. "He didn't know just how many people liked him and his popularity showed when he was named Homecoming King."

That honor alone suggested the progress integration was making at the school. Johnson prized Chastine for many things, including his clarity. "He'd keep talking to all of us on the team, trying to keep us alert every game," Johnson said, indicating just how much he had learned about leadership from his older teammate.

Although viewed as quiet by outsiders, Chastine had proved to be quite the competitor whose fire had been an example to Johnson and the rest of the team. The past two years of Johnson's life had been marked by dramatic change and his elevation in status as a public figure. Chastine had been there nearly every step of the way, from the early bus rides each morning to Everett to running around the streets of Lansing with Johnson and through every step of the team's fast-paced success. The little guard had pushed the agenda with feistiness and bravado, all while extolling Johnson's greatness as a player, describing his big talent that Johnson himself didn't fully see, always building him up into his greater self, telling him that it was a sure thing that Johnson was headed to the NBA. In the strife of Lansing's busing experiment, Chastine had also been someone just like him, sharing the experience as Black interlopers on a team mostly of white players.

Tucker, who had seen in Chastine a player he could identify with, was just as shaken as Johnson by the loss. "We had many private talks," Tucker told the *State Journal* at the time. "Reggie was unique. At times people felt he had a chip on his shoulder but he didn't, really. Some things he couldn't understand like when coach Fox would get on him for certain things. He'd say how much he disliked Fox, then five minutes later told of how much he loved the man. You had to know Reggie to understand him. He was a super strong individual who kept searching out for things. He had high respect for people."

Chastine's experiences had revealed the challenge of being Johnson's teammate, of having to follow the agenda set by the coaches and Johnson himself. "He didn't shoot much because that wasn't part of our philosophy," Fox admitted, adding that the lack of shots didn't seem to bother him. "He took it like a man. He knew what his contribution was and it was so valuable."

In the depths of his despair after the news broke, a tearful Johnson vowed to never forget him. And Johnson wouldn't, pausing almost ritually in every big moment of his highly successful career for years afterward to think of Chastine and all that he had done in those early years.

"Reggie Chastine was his best buddy," Missy Fox said.

As the ensuing week unfolded in disbelief, Beard kept thinking of a photo that had been in the local paper. "It was a picture with him and Reggie," Beard explained. "They were at half court and they were discussing something. The paper had called them 'Mutt and

Jeff' there. Earvin's bending over and listening to what Reggie's trying to say to him. Earvin respected him as an older guy. Reggie had been on that team for two years. They had played together for two seasons. So they knew each other real well."

"Reggie was probably Earvin's best friend," George Fox said. "He got killed. Him and his girlfriend, they were driving down a street in Jackson, Michigan, and some drunk hit them and killed him the summer of his senior year after he graduated."

"The guy ran a stop sign, had no brakes on his car," Pat Holland remembered.

"So we dedicated the next season to Reggie Chastine," Fox said. "We just tried to comfort Earvin and everybody on the team because it was quite a blow."

Wheels

Johnson had turned seventeen that August and was soon driving everywhere, it seemed. Dale Beard knew it, because he was there, riding shotgun with him. In another fifteen years or so, he would still be riding shotgun, serving as the best man in Johnson's wedding, a reminder of something that both he and Johnson were aware of, yet something they never discussed.

If Reggie Chastine had lived, he would have perhaps been that best man, an honor that Beard would have gladly relinquished if it meant having Chastine and his fiery spirit still around.

A year behind Johnson, Beard would begin the 1976–77 season as a substitute on Everett's varsity and damned fortunate to be there because George Fox would almost cut him after tryouts that fall. The next year, after Earvin had moved on, Beard would emerge as a first team All-Stater—a dramatic ascension—then would go on to become one of the all-time scorers for his college program and after that a professional overseas.

Yet in many ways, he would always be a sub on Earvin Johnson's team, not in a bad way, but in the very best way, beginning that dreadful late summer of 1976 as a companion as Johnson sought to fill the suddenly huge hole in his heart and his life. Beard and Tucker both were there, helping him to rediscover the lighter, carefree moments that had always come so easily for him on a basketball court.

After all, as a shorter African American guard on the Everett junior varsity, Beard also had seen Chastine as a vital role model, somebody he could look up to and draw confidence from in a high school basketball program that was in transition toward having more African Americans aboard.

Beyond the shock and grief, becoming Johnson's friend and confidant proved a natural transition for Dale Beard. On the jayvee as a sophomore, he had been around Johnson enough and come to admire so many things about him. Johnson was already the big man on campus, yet he reached out to Beard, much as he would treat Stokes, not as some kid on the jayvee but as somebody worthy of friendship and respect. Beard recalled that his relationship with Johnson would soon enough gel playing pickup basketball that late summer and early fall. Johnson now had his own status in the pickup games at Jenison Field House as he had come to serve as something of a pipeline for local talent showing up for those games. "Him, myself maybe and one other guy might go to a playground or go out to Jenison Field House out at Michigan State and play," Beard recalled. "He would come in and see who was there and pick who he wanted on the team. And we would run the table, man."

The vehicle for these sorties to the pickup life was no longer exclusively Charles Tucker's Mercedes. Earvin now had his own wheels.

"His dad had got him an Electra 225," Beard said, again laughing at the memory. "They called it a 'deuce and a quarter.' Yeah, he had a big brown one, man. I tell you."

It made sense that Senior would bestow upon Junior a used version of the car that he loved, just as it made sense that Johnson would wash the car in the driveway, polishing and shining it just like his father. And if the old man pulled up in his own Electra? Johnson would get the keys and pull his ride out to make sure his pops had the primo spot in the driveway.

Beard politely, almost sheepishly, popped the question one day early that fall as the team was beginning open gyms. "I'd say, 'Hey, man, you think I could get a ride home?'"

"Yeah, come on, man," Johnson replied.

"We lived across town from each other, maybe ten minutes from each other, but he would give me a ride home," Beard recalled. "We would get in that car, man, after practice, go by McDonald's and head home, and he'd drop me off."

"See you tomorrow at school, man," Beard would say as he got out. "From that moment, we started getting closer," Beard added. "He would give me a ride home every day after practice."

With that closeness came the full view of Johnson on the playground. "This guy was something," Beard said. "The parks would be packed, just an everyday park, packed just to see him play. The playgrounds was made for us at the time. Earvin was a big playground guy. So every day we're at these playgrounds playing."

They made their way to a revolving door of venues all over the city, a circuit that stemmed from Main Street School to include a playground and park then called the West Side drop-in center for teens, even over to the east side to confront Jay Vincent and his crew.

Going up against Vincent in pickup games became one of the big things for Johnson. The two rivals had become friends, but they had never played much pickup in their younger years, Vincent recalled, "because he was on the west side and I was on the east side. He kind of stayed on his side of town until we started playing against each other in high school. Then he would bring his gang of, well, not gang, but his crowd of five or six, seven guys. As we became stars in our sophomore, junior years, he would bring them to my park. I would get my guys and go to his park, and, boy, there would be a crowd of five hundred people out there watching."

Beard would come away from those playground moments with a view of Johnson's forceful personality. "He was always directing and he wanted the ball in his hand," Beard explained. "He felt like he needed to win every game. To do that, he felt like if he had the ball in his hand and could get everybody else involved that he would win the game, which he did."

"Just roll with it," Johnson would tell whoever was on his team when it came to adjusting to his full-speed style and control.

And Johnson wouldn't hesitate to exert his will over them all, as he had just about everyone else he encountered in basketball. That began with his propensity for calling fouls, just like Tucker had taught him.

As Jay Vincent observed with a laugh, you couldn't touch Johnson back then, not after Fred Stabley nicknamed him Magic. He became the master of the self-officiated pickup game.

New Kid in Town

Gary Fox found him first, a six-three guard, rising senior, an All-Stater at the Class D level for small schools in Michigan, found him while playing pickup ball in Fox's first year of college. The kid, named Jamie Huffman, had everything Gary Fox's father was looking for in a guard to help Everett High and Earvin Johnson win the extremely elusive Michigan High School Class A State Championship. Huffman was tall, athletic, and possessed a defensive ability and overall floor game that would fit in extremely well with Everett's evolving roster, Gary Fox told his father.

Even better, Huffman had an older brother going to law school in Lansing, and Huffman was extremely interested in moving in with his brother and moving up to the Class A level of basketball and trying his skill there.

"I thought it would be so awesome to play with Earvin," Huffman would tell *Detroit Free Press* writer Mick McCabe in looking back on that season. "I knew they were short at guard; they weren't very big there. But I didn't have any idea if I was good enough to play there. I was from a small town. We had two lights."

He recalled shooting around with the team during an early open gym that summer. Everyone was clearly waiting for Johnson, who was on his way to establishing a reputation for being late to nearly everything in his life.

"Earvin liked to make the grand entrance," Huffman said. "Afros were in back then. Earvin was six-eight, but his Afro made him seven feet. I saw him and thought: 'Holy cow!'"

Pretty soon Johnson would be serenading Huffman by butchering the Eagles' plaintive rock song "New Kid in Town," which had gained much radio airplay in that era. It would often happen in practice while the players warmed up. Johnson would break into the song.

"Johnny come lately, the new kid in town," he would croon. "Everybody loves you, so don't let them down."

The sight and the sound of it coming from Johnson drew smiles all around, from the coaching staff to the roster. "New kid in town," recalled Pat Holland. "That was just Earvin kind of trying to make him feel welcome."

As well as a sly way to put Huffman on notice.

Beneath it all came the next phase of integration at the school, a phase that could be seen in retrospect as quiet and cautious, just under the surface. After all, they were about to embark on Earvin Johnson's last chance to win a title. This was serious business. Who was this new kid? Johnson had to find out.

Even so, it all seemed nothing but fun, considering it was chaperoned by Johnson's smile and enthusiasm. He had done yeoman's work breaking up fights and easing attitudes for two years in and around the hallways.

Now, with Huffman on the roster, Johnson turned to taking on the task of trying to mix the races socially, a seemingly herculean task with the very distinct worlds of white and Black still operating with little idea of who the other was or the exact width of the cultural divide.

"We were learning," Leon Stokes remembered of the atmosphere at Everett. "It was something new. We were figuring out how to get along."

Each group tended to hang out with its own kind.

White high school kids occupied a "Dazed and Confused" kind of world of secretive keg parties at remote locations or at the home of any parents foolish enough to abandon the premises for a weekend while leaving their teens home supposedly alone. Events started earlier, around eight for the white students, and involved lots of cold beer.

The Black students, on the other hand, didn't get going till later, around ten, and tended to favor wine and that certain mid-'70s Afro chill and dancing. Johnson immediately decided to take Huffman across racial lines to party and play basketball. It was taken as a generous display at the time.

As Charles Tucker would explain in 2019, the early read on Huffman was that he was quite comfortable competing with and being around Black players. But Johnson had to stress-test him and find out for sure. Could he handle going up against that hard-core crowd of competitors from Detroit and Flint? Could he ignore the trash talk and constant dismissiveness, the mental wall that could be built up around the competition that in some ways brought new definition to the cultural divide? Could Jamie Huffman hang?

"I took him to the west side to play with all the brothers," Johnson told Mick McCabe. "Everybody knew he was 'Earv's boy.' I had to get him used to playing against inner-city guys who talked trash. I had to get him ready. I worked with him because he was the key to our team."

Johnson would recall that at the Black parties, he gave the girls directives to get Huffman up and dancing, which would prove a revelation about both Huffman and Johnson. Everett's Magic Man was sort of a Fonzie figure, the charismatic character from the immensely popular TV show *Happy Days*. As Fred Stabley would observe, Johnson had all the women charmed and the men, too. "He was good-looking, extremely talented, and had that great smile and he was attractive and he attracted guys. Not romantically but he was the alpha male."

Other white players soon found their way into Black parties, then began issuing invitations to Johnson and his friends to come to theirs.

"It was my job to cross that barrier," Johnson said, twenty years later. "When things started, I tried to be in the middle. We got a lot of things accomplished here."

He expressed pride in his role of pulling the school together, pushing for an integration of music at lunchtime and the inclusion of Black students on the cheering squad.

And he did not want to be seen as just a basketball player. He had joined the editorial staff of the school newspaper.

"I worked on the school paper and became editor," he said. "I was the average student to the fullest. I participated in everything."

These efforts served to pull his teammates even tighter around him as the season neared that fall. Larry Hunter would start for three years with Johnson on the Everett varsity after having competed against him in junior high.

"He was a jokester," Larry Hunter recalled for the *Detroit Free Press* in 1997. "He was just a nice person all the way around."

"He was just a great friend," agreed teammate Dean Hartley. "A lot of us hung out and did things together. Obviously, he was our leader."

As he prepared to move up to the Everett varsity early that fall, Bruce Fields recalled that Johnson would motor by his house to pick up Fields and his younger brother for sorties in the Electra out to the available nightlife, including parties at Michigan State.

"My mom loved Earv, she loved her some Earvin," Fields recalled in 2020. "He'd come in and kiss her on the cheek and he'd say, 'You know, I got them. I'll look out for them.'"

They'd embark on high adventures, with the Electra crammed tight and the music bumpin'.

"And my mom didn't have a problem with that," Fields recalled. "It was awesome."

Sure enough they were alcohol-free outings, with Johnson taking extra care at the wheel along with being careful not to leave any of his younger charges at any of their social stops.

"Earv was our ride to the party," Fields explained. "He knew he was responsible for us. We were his boys. He was taking care of us and making sure we got back and everybody just had fun."

Johnson was that personable and charismatic. But he felt he had to find out about Jamie Huffman. Ultimately, the only way to know was the same as the only way to know about your shot in basketball. You had to put it up on the rim and give it a chance.

"He didn't care about Black, white especially when it came to sports and us winning," Bruce Fields said of Johnson. "It was like, 'If you can help us win, let's go.' We needed Jamie Huffman."

In the end, it would all come back to coach George Fox himself. Not the Jamie Huffman question. As Charles Tucker pointed out, Huffman pretty quickly established that he was good to go, no time wasted on insecurity. He just wanted to compete.

The question would arise out of George Fox's anger from the end of the previous season. Johnson's own struggles aside, Fox had come away believing intensely that Everett's guards were too small, too short, too vulnerable to being overwhelmed as the level of competition rose. His general impression of Dale Beard was that he was another short little guy from the jayvees. Yes, Beard had been one of Pat Holland's all-time favorites, and Holland was working hard to change Fox's mind, pointing out that Beard was no longer short, had shot up to six feet and was still growing, that he could shoot, had displayed he could score under pressure and defend.

But the winds didn't seem to change until Johnson got involved.

"It was pretty much Earvin's doing," Beard said of the second chance he got in the mind of the head coach. "I came in as a tryout from JV and they basically pretty much knew who they were going to keep on the team."

Pat Holland didn't believe Fox would have ultimately cut Beard, but it's hard to overestimate the trust level, the mental and emotional partnership, that had formed between Fox and Earvin Johnson over the first two seasons, the obvious and absolute joy the staff had with both Johnson and with the challenge of figuring out how to get him to the promised land.

"It was predicated on Earvin, what he saw in me," Beard said of the decision. "I could have been off that team and you never know what direction I would have went in life from there. I might not have even gone to college.

"He was going to cut me at first. I wasn't going to make the team until Earvin said, 'Listen. We got to keep this guy.' He saw something in me."

Johnson had seen those qualities in him, and ultimately Fox would, too, Beard explained. So was launched another of Johnson's vital partnerships, one that revealed its own curiosities as the relationship developed. First, both of their families had emerged from the same small city in the same troubled county in Mississippi—Brookhaven, Lincoln County, where the Black farmer had been shot to death on the courthouse lawn in 1954 for attempting to register to vote.

Their families mirrored the same experiences in moving to Lansing, Beard explained. "He's like myself. We both came from big families. Our families came from the same hometown. You know, we saw our parents, how they worked."

Like Earvin Sr., Beard's father and mother would find relatively stable long-term employment with General Motors. Johnson's obvious admiration for his father resonated with how Beard felt about his parents.

Adding to the curiosity was their striking similarity in facial features and countenance, including their easygoing manner and smiles. Beard would strike many as a shorter version of Johnson but rocking a similar mojo.

Even so, Johnson's endorsement wouldn't earn Beard a place in the starting lineup, but it was a beginning, which afforded Johnson the experience of instructing his younger protégé.

"We had our talks," Beard recalled. "He was just enlightening me because I was a year younger and all this varsity stuff was new to me. He was just telling me how fast-paced the varsity level was going to be and how it is and what he expected out of me, and I fulfilled it. From there, he and I just started becoming closer and closer."

That didn't mean Beard would be able to avoid harsh exchanges with Johnson on the court in the heat of battle. They had their shouting matches at times. Johnson was a leader who knew what he wanted and didn't hesitate to demand it of people, Beard explained.

The up-close perspective and their time spent talking about the game deepened the mystery of Johnson's acuity at such a young age, Beard suggested. "It was just his IQ of the game. He knew he wasn't, you know, the quickest guy but said he always wanted to outsmart you. And I thought that made a whole big difference in him as a player versus everybody else."

As he watched Johnson more and more, Beard began to realize how thoroughly the big guy was organizing the entire team on the floor.

"Just to see how he would put players in place, you know, was like a coach would, you know what I mean?"

The Electricity

In 2019, Tim Staudt was celebrating fifty years as a broadcaster in Lansing, the dean of sportscasting there on both radio and TV, an experience that afforded him the opportunity to witness up close the breadth of athletics in the state of Michigan, from its two fine Big Ten Conference schools with their accomplished football and basketball programs, to the array of memorable high school seasons and players, to the state's various professional teams. Staudt's on-air tenure included the twenty-some straight trips that Michigan State basketball would make to the NCAA tournament under coach Tom Izzo, the numerous Final Four appearances made and the national championships won by both Michigan and Michigan State.

Staudt had seen it all in terms of sports competition in Michigan.

"I always tell people that my favorite three years by far, funny enough, were the three years that Earvin was here at Everett High School," Staudt remarked in a 2019 interview.

Those three favorite seasons did not include Johnson's college career, although those years would be plenty valuable to Staudt. But millions came to witness Johnson playing in college and the NBA, Staudt explained. "Not nearly as many people saw the kid play as a high school player and what that did to the community."

There was no vast national spotlight on Lansing from 1974 to 1977, Staudt said. "I pretty much have felt going back forty years that I was never going to be around a story or an individual through all those years that compared with what he was at Everett. I enjoyed that more than any other time in my fifty years on the air just because of the electricity that was around here."

Staudt's full conversion had first come during the playoffs Johnson's sophomore season. The broadcaster watched an athletic team from Benton Harbor warm up before a game and thought, "My God, they look just like the New York Knicks." Then Johnson scored big off the opening tip in that game and Everett went on to win in a blowout.

From that point on, Staudt had made sure he was there broadcasting each one of Johnson's games live over the next two seasons.

In the process, Staudt was there to play a vital role in the growth of sports media that Johnson's presence demanded.

"In those days this was all brand-new for the community, was all brand-new every day as his persona intensified and grew greatly," Staudt explained. "I mean, look, it was a big deal. Every place we went it was like going to a rock concert because it wasn't like people were filtering in and out of games, like you see at sporting events today. It wasn't like the field house is half empty."

The broadcaster recalled going to games with the dread of having to fight the crowds just to set up his radio broadcast equipment.

"We would just pray that when we got to the place we weren't going to do the game seated somewhere weird, that we're not sitting in the middle of the crowd, that we don't have a problem getting on the air because there are so doggone many people there," he recalled. "The world was different then in terms of the media. Back then there was no cable TV. There's nothing else but this. This was the whole show in the state of Michigan. And, you know, his nickname had taken hold by then so that everybody knew about him and had to see it. I mean if you wanted to see him, you had to go watch him play and he was that good. There was no question, he was that good in high school around here."

His showboating, entertaining style had grown over his first two high school seasons and then would take off to another level his senior year.

Dale Beard understood how Staudt felt about the experience of Magic Johnson because he felt the same about that senior year. "He and I sometimes talk about those days at Everett," Beard said of Johnson, "and, man, I'll tell you, we still have chills like, you know, forty years later. We still think we're back in high school talking about it."

Johnson himself often said over the years that his high school experiences were more powerful even than all of his later successes. "You were so innocent," he once told Mick McCabe. "You did it for the love of playing the game. You played for all these guys you know. You knew their parents and their brothers and sisters. High school was special. I've got a memory like an elephant and I'll never forget those times."

"It was a storybook year for high school kids," Bruce Fields once explained of Johnson's senior season. "We all know how good Earv was. Earv could do things no one else could do in high school. I felt he could have come out of high school and played right away in the NBA."

"I remember '75, '76, and '77 like it was yesterday," Staudt recalled. "That gym that he played in is still exactly the same, except it's now called Earvin Johnson Gymnasium. It looks exactly the same. It hasn't been changed very much. I can still remember sitting in there with those packed crowds. They always had to have extra police there to help, you know, just because there were people outside in line to get in. There were people trying to get in. I mean the police always wanted to go to watch the games, too."

"Every game was special here," Johnson would tell the *Free Press* two decades later. "If you didn't get here by the start of the JV game, you couldn't get a seat. I'd pull up during the JV game and I couldn't get a parking space. The whole Lansing community seemed to come to our games. I used to get chills coming out to play. I'd see Mom and Dad sitting there. You could smell the popcorn here. When I smelled the popcorn, I knew it was time to play."

It was almost hard to explain how much fun it was to run the floor as his teammate and finish the break with those layups, Fields recalled in 2020, adding that road games brought another sort of ego boost for the entire team. "We would go on the road and play against teams at their own gyms. And their fans would be rooting for us. It was crazy. We'd roll in and start beating up on folks and their fans would start chanting for Earv. We'd beat them by 50 and we were gone. But they saw our show and what we were about and they were happy that they had a chance to see it."

It would all have been difficult to understand if people hadn't gained admittance to see it. That was because in many ways if you just took Johnson, the adolescent, at face value at that time, it might have been difficult to figure just what the big deal was all about.

"I can remember interviewing him in high school and he had enunciation problems, he had diction problems. He was shy," Staudt said in 2019. "If you saw where he was when he was in high school, some of the interviews that he did, he was so naïve and sophomoric, a kid that had no polish whatsoever. I thought he had very limited diction skills by the time he got out of high school."

To see from that what Johnson would become in later life as a public speaker and media figure and businessperson was truly astounding and impressive, Staudt offered.

Yet, despite such observations, there were clearly many things about Johnson's overall presence and approach that allowed him great effectiveness as a leader and public figure even in high school. First of all, he still had the same emotional and social intelligence that had prompted him to ride his bike all the way out to George Fox's house as a ninth grader.

"Sometimes," Charles Tucker observed, "you fall into a situation where you get good at something, and people recognize that, and then you get better and better at it."

Clearly, diction problems or not, there was something happening in the community of Lansing, something driven by Earvin Johnson and the people drawn to his unique presence.

Dale Beard recalled that by Johnson's senior season, the racial turmoil at Everett had quieted dramatically. If there was an issue with racial implications, rather than blown up in the public mind, it was discussed quietly, almost in whispers. Leon Stokes, George Fox, Pat Holland, and others confirmed the quiet that fell over those issues.

That influence spread to the Lansing community at large, Jay

Vincent suggested, looking back. "One thing that brought everybody together was when we played basketball. That was something because there was a lot of racial tension at Everett. There was a lot of racial tension throughout Lansing. There's always going to be racial tension. But back then it was a lot of racial tension."

Vincent pointed out that his own school, Eastern, had problems despite a well-established mix of white, Black, and Latino students. After all, Vincent said, the era unfolded not all that long after the Detroit riots in the 1960s.

"Some of the principals, everybody tried to have Magic calm people down, and he brought a lot of people together," Vincent said. "That was a time when a lot of people, blacks, whites, Mexicans, just wanted to go watch Magic do his thing."

The competition between Everett and Eastern that senior season, he recalled, "brought Lansing together. We knew there was racial tension when we played basketball. But everything was forgotten for those two hours that we were on the court."

Johnson's success in many ways could be measured not in his youthful diction problems but in the absence of racial conflict around the program, the school, and the city his senior year.

"They kind of locked themselves off from what was going on," Charles Tucker said of Johnson and his teammates. "By the time the senior year came, they had so many followers everybody was concentrating on the kids. Nobody was concentrating on negativity. They were the best in Michigan. In that time span, they cultivated everything through that team. If it hadn't been for that team being so good, there probably would have been a lot more trouble. That team helped everything. Because the whole city was locked in for three, four years."

There were still some faculty members who didn't approve of Johnson's presence and power, Bruce Fields recalled in 2020.

"The teachers had the hardest time adjusting," Tucker recalled. "That was the thing. The people like the principal, the coaches, some of the counselors, the basic staff that weren't teachers, they kind of molded everything together. And the kids were socializing at the gym. They were focused on winning and having fun."

Obviously, winning and fun had long been indicators of team chemistry. Tim Staudt thought that the talent around Johnson at Everett High School wasn't all that impressive, at least not in terms of Michigan's other great high school teams, even though several players from the roster went on to higher athletic achievement, including Bruce Fields in Major League Baseball. He was drafted by the Detroit Tigers and enjoyed a career playing and coaching the professional game. Others from the roster, including Beard, Paul Dawson, and Larry Hunter, went on to play college basketball.

Staudt's point, however, was an opinion later repeated time and again about Johnson on every level he played—he made all of his teammates better.

A big factor in that, of course, were the high school teammates themselves, who were very much open to being changed.

"Keep in mind Earvin was the only Black starter at one point," Tucker said. "They had four white kids. They were a little older. They were different type kids. None of them was into that type of stuff. You got Larry Hunter who was a street guy, a Larry Bird type guy. He wasn't fitting in with the core or worrying about race. Then you had Paul Dawson, the six-seven guy, he wasn't caught up in all of that either. Then you had Jamie Huffman. He had been around Blacks before from playing ball. He had been around a lot. That whole team, they were all following Earvin. So you didn't have a kid from an elite situation where you had a parent telling him, 'You don't want to do this or you don't want to do that.' Saying, 'You're a better player than that,' telling the coach, 'Play my kid more.' They didn't have all that."

The roster, according to George Fox, was also led by its reliable reserves, players such as Leon Stokes, the president of the school's National Honor Society, someone who could be trusted when he was inserted into the game to play hard and move things forward and keep them organized.

Certainly not to be overlooked, Staudt said, was Dale Beard, who was never starstruck, was always honest with Johnson, and gifted Johnson with lifelong friendship.

"You know Earvin trusts him," Staudt said. "I think Earvin when he looks back at his life and looks at the people that have been around here from his boyhood friends, those guys from his high school days, guys like Dale who has made a name for himself as a good guy, it doesn't get any better than that."

Staudt pointed out there were a variety of other factors feeding into the Everett success, beginning with one that wasn't entirely celebrated: the coaching staff itself.

That could have been perhaps because the situation with Larry Johnson still lingered, in some ways would always linger. Earvin's brother had graduated Everett and like his father went to work at Fisher Body, but apparently his anger overtook him, which drew him into the graveyard of substance abuse and addiction. It would be then perhaps that the Johnson family's greatest strength would exert itself. With the help of his parents and siblings and Earvin later in Los Angeles, Larry Johnson would find the strength to fight off his demons, a task that required of him substantial personal character to survive, which he did. He became a manager of his brother's business affairs in Los Angeles, became what friends would describe as an immensely dedicated family man, then would return to Lansing to help care for his parents as they advanced through their eighties with a relatively active lifestyle.

Over the years, Larry would come to make many public appearances where he would talk of his youthful inability to accept instruction and learning.

In later life, he was often seen escorting his father to Michigan State games or attending one gathering or another of the people in Lansing who had shared the Magic Johnson experience there. At these gatherings, he would sometimes encounter Pat Holland or George Fox and they would express warmth for another although they knew well never to bring up those harsher days.

Larry also became known for marshaling support for public causes related to addiction or other issues. At one of the gatherings in Lansing, Pat Holland recalled Larry coming over to catch up. Holland said he asked about contributing to Larry's causes, and Earvin's brother declined, saying that his causes were fine financially but please pray for them.

Time had passed, whatever actions that might have been viewed as transgressions were clearly forgiven, but it wasn't difficult to sense that the slightest traces of a deep, long-ago hurt still lingered.

In 2020, Earvin Johnson was astounded to learn that Charles Tucker had advised the coaches on his brother's dismissal, apparently a fact that Tucker himself had never disclosed to the Johnson family. Johnson's reaction upon learning that fact would indicate perhaps just how quietly mindful the family remained about the contrast between Larry's journey and that of his famous brother.

Of all the many accomplishments of Earvin Johnson's joyful rise as a youth in basketball, this eventual healing between Larry and the Everett coaches may have been among the most precious outcomes, subtle as it was.

Much like Earvin Johnson himself, George Fox throughout his life projected a countenance of smiles, framed by his amiable face. To some, he presented as a roly-poly sort of a Howdy Doody character who also like Johnson belied his competitiveness and devotion to the game.

Dale Beard himself admitted to misjudging Fox a bit as a young player in the program. Yes, the word on the coach suggested that the he was something akin to a bumpkin. Beard said he very soon became disabused of that notion while sitting in Fox's reel-to-reel film study with the team, then watching how well the coach's matchup zone defense worked as Everett buzz-sawed so many opponents during Johnson's senior season on their way to their astounding moment of truth in the playoffs in 1977.

"Coach Fox was a great, great coach, man," Beard said, an opinion flavored by his own experience leading a totally different Everett team to within a whisker of a state title the year after Johnson graduated, with the relatively unknown Beard as the team's star. "A lot of people didn't give him a lot of credit. . . . Nobody really knew who this guy was far as a coach until you got around him and listened to him. Then you said, 'Hey, you know what? This guy knows what he's doing.' We played matchup zone and our matchup was just destroying other people. They couldn't figure it out because they were high school teams that usually had just one shooter. The teams we played, we stifled them so bad. We were in their faces, and when the ball rotated over to the other side, we're not letting anybody get in the lane."

Fred Stabley credited the coaching success to vision. "George knew what he had long before anybody else knew what he had," the sportswriter explained. "He let Earvin be Earvin. He knew what he had and let him do it."

Leon Stokes recalled becoming discouraged during Johnson's senior season because he did not see a role for a five-eleven power forward such as himself on the team. His disappointment grew to the point that one day he missed practice without giving notice to the coaches.

"When you were in high school you felt you should be playing all the time," Stokes said of his mind-set.

Upon his return to the team, he and Fox discussed the situation, Stokes recalled. "The thing I liked about him, he listened. At least to me he listened. He gave me voice. After that our relationship was a lot more open."

Stokes gained a sense of just how much importance Fox placed on team chemistry, on how substitutes played a vital role in things. In the aftermath, Stokes decided that his first big value to the team would be his own efforts in practice, doing everything possible to push the overall improvement of the group.

"I found him to be a very organized coach," said Stokes, who would go on to graduate from GM's Kettering University and from there to a forty-one-year career with the auto manufacturer, rising to the rank of director in product development.

"George was a little different," Tucker recalled. "He had had enough ball experience. That helped. Then you had Pat Holland, who was a nice guy."

Holland, like Fox, was decidedly wrapped up in the details of the game but had a low-key personality that seemed to suit Johnson well.

The coaching success was built on the obvious respect Fox had for Johnson's parents, Staudt said. "George was very careful to make sure that he and Earvin's parents were exactly on the same page."

As the months passed, it had become clear that there was something in the Johnson family's strength that made white people like them, even made white people eager to please them that, in retrospect, was far above the norm for that era.

"His family meant a lot to me," George Fox explained to *Inside Sports* in 1980. "Maybe if his mother and father were wheeler-dealer types, I wouldn't have cared."

But the fact was that Fox, like Johnson's "godparents" the Darts and many others in the Lansing community, did care about the Johnsons, and cared about them long before they became wealthy or famous, a caring that clearly found its root in the family's strength of character, something that was tangible to just about all who encountered them.

In essence, the Johnsons were representative of millions of Black families in that era, people firmly tied to their faith, conservative in nature, determined to succeed as persons of color, yet largely unseen and grossly underestimated—and often victimized—by the mainstream culture.

Due to the growing reputation of their son, the Johnsons, however, had moved quickly into the public eye, not any sort of overt presence, but one seen by the many eyes gathered in the gymnasiums where their son performed.

In a short time, it would seem that so many in the community, Black or white, would come to focus on the Johnsons and admire them. And this would include many who knew absolutely nothing about Larry's dismissal. What virtually everyone did see was that the Johnsons themselves were quite the pair.

"I would say he was the quiet type but he's the kind that when he speaks you listen," Fred Stabley, Jr., said of Earvin Sr. and the family dynamic.

"You better hope he doesn't have something to say," Tucker said of the father. "Once he does, you can close the door."

"Just for reference purposes, Mama wore the pants in the family," Stabley recalled in a 2019 interview, "but don't push Dad because when push came to shove, he would let his feelings be known. He always was in the background."

Christine Johnson's personality made her well suited for the foreground, Stabley explained. "When she was around, you knew it because she would smile and she was friendly and she was talkative. Earvin Sr. didn't do a lot of smiling. He was more of a serious guy. I'm not saying Christine wasn't. She was just a very happy person. And Earvin Sr. might have been, too, but he didn't show it like Mama did. From what Earvin told me she was quite a basketball player when she was younger."

As George Fox himself explained, how could he not have a genuine and profound respect for Christine and Earvin Johnson, Sr.?

The presence of businessmen Greg Eaton and Joel Ferguson was also an immense factor in the Magic Johnson story and in the racial understanding in the state's capital city, Staudt said. "Those guys were successful in a white world as business guys. If Earvin had grown up in Detroit who knows what distractions he might have had? But Lansing was perfect."

As were these formative experiences for Johnson. Charles Tucker observed that soon enough in the process young Earvin became aware that what he was doing was bringing people together. "As an athlete, we know he's great," the psychologist said. "People like him and follow him. Everything was right here. And so the whole community had to kind of like be together. When Everett came on the scene with Earvin and them, things became more spread out, more competitive. It brought this community to become more involved."

"Earvin had the ability to pull people together," Leon Stokes observed, "because people tended to gravitate to him. People did tend to pull in line because he asked them to. I do think the atmosphere at Everett High School got better as a result of his play and his popularity."

"Today when I hear someone say that this player's an Earvin Johnson or that player's like Earvin Johnson," Tim Staudt concluded, "obviously anyone that says that was never around here forty years ago. So don't tell me that because I was there. I saw. Michigan is a very good basketball community today. The high schools now are very competitive. But there isn't anybody, anybody that's even gotten close to what this guy did and what he was able to do. To me, he was a once-in-a-lifetime athlete."

It all certainly sounded impressive when they all looked back decades later. But at the time in 1976, there was only one real question: Could they go out and win a title?

12

"GLASS!"

Before games could be played right, Earvin Johnson had to look right. That began with his Afro, Dale Beard recalled with a laugh, and that in turn led to one of those early crevices in the tenuous cultural understanding between Johnson and his coach.

George Fox would get annoyed with his star player on certain days when he insisted on wearing a stocking hat during practice. Fox just as forcefully insisted Johnson not wear the hat on the floor, until finally Johnson would retreat to the sidelines with a pained smile and take it off. Little did the coach realize the confrontations over the cap involved the prep work for the Afro, which in that period remained something of a statement for Black youth that reflected their pride.

"Game days were Tuesday and Fridays," Beard explained, "and we would never want our Afros to look terrible on game day. So we'd always braid them bad babies up, and Earvin would have a hat on because his sisters would braid his hair the day before the games. Pearl was mostly the one that would braid his hair. So on game days he would take his braids out."

Having been braided and then released, the Afros would spring into glorious halos, visions of youthful Black cool. "He and I would be in that locker room and, you know, we're gettin' our Afros together and making sure they were all nice and neat," Beard remembered. "In those days you just had to invest in your hair."

The hair was just one of several things that Earvin Johnson invested in over the 1976–77 season. Others included yet more running. And dunking now that a rule change finally allowed it back into the game. But most especially more winning.

The Vikings of Everett High did that for the first 14 games that season, with sportswriters duly noting that Johnson was dunking the ball two or three times a game, all to the crowd's delight. It served as a new level of fun added to his passing and showmanship as the Vikings threw lots of points up on scoreboards just about everywhere they went. Three times that season they scored more than 100 points in a 32-minute high school game. Six other games they put up 90. And in eight more they ran into the 80s, for an average of 81.9 points per game, not a record in Michigan's rich tradition of high school basketball, but an astounding display of not just pace but efficiency. The entire team shot 49.2 percent from the field for the season.

When they weren't running with Earvin, the Vikings were choking opponents with their matchup zone, which allowed a mere 45 points a game, meaning they nearly doubled the score on just about every team they would face that season.

"Coach Fox had a pretty good relationship with some of the other coaches in town," Leon Stokes recalled. "He used to tell them, 'I know you got a good team, but I gotta tell you we're gonna beat the hell out of you.'"

It was a message delivered with the trademark twinkle in his eye. The coach was often amazed at how difficult it became for opponents to even get off a good shot each possession. And if they did manage to score, Johnson had another surprise for them.

Lansing businessman Joel Ferguson would long maintain that one of the biggest developments that Johnson brought to the game was the concept of running after made baskets, that is, inbounding the ball quickly and getting up the floor in a hurry to put pressure on the defense. That trend was just emerging and gaining momentum in Johnson's final varsity season. Soon enough he would make an art form of it in the NBA.

Dale Beard in looking back would offer that Everett High became "a mini version of Showtime," the great fast-breaking Lakers teams that Johnson orchestrated. Obviously, their athleticism fell far short of those great pro teams, but with their seasons of experience together the Vikings would all play their parts in running Johnson's scheme to great success. They would serve as prima facie evidence of his immense gift for making those around him better over his career, the greater the athlete, the greater the gains at each level.

Shots

The number of shots Earvin Johnson averaged per game had shown a steady increase over his three seasons at Everett High, as might be expected. He took about 16 shots a game as a sophomore, 18 shots as a junior, and a whopping 22.5 shots a game as a senior.

Some of this was a function of his offensive rebounding and putbacks and tip-ins. Some of it was a function of just how much he would have the ball in his hands over the senior season.

Another part of it would be a function of the team mind-set. The Everett Vikings would average 17.8 assists a game for his senior season, and Johnson would provide about seven of those assists per game, which indicates how eager his teammates seemed to get him the ball, despite the fact that two other starters were seniors with size and scoring ability who had been in the lineup beside Johnson for most of their three varsity seasons.

The 22.5 shots per game that he took were 32 percent of the team's overall shots that senior season, which George Fox and Pat Holland considered even more amazing because so many games that year would be blowouts that left Johnson on the bench after playing about three quarters or about 24 minutes a game, meaning many nights he took that average of almost 23 shots in a relatively short time.

First, such volume made sense in terms of analytics, largely a twenty-first-century concept in athletics that was hardly even a consideration during Johnson's high school and college careers. Coaches back then usually operated from what they saw on the floor and a glance or two at the stat sheet.

It didn't take much of a glance to see that Johnson shot 53 percent from the floor, which was aided by two other factors. First, Johnson had been working hard on his outside shot over the summer, which would give him the confidence to take and make more over the season. In addition, as Everett teammate Leon Stokes would point out, Johnson had full command of both right- and left-handed hooks and made good use of them. Stokes would chuckle at claims during Johnson's later career that he had "developed" the hooks as a pro.

"He had that in high school," Stokes said.

Most interesting of all was the dunking, allowed within the rules just in time for his senior season.

"The dunk went into effect," Fred Stabley recalled, "and I remember Earvin kind of laughingly said he's got to work on his jumping."

If possible, his smile grew larger at the mere thought of it. Basketball's "fear" police had banned the practice for more than a decade, even banned it in warm-ups, but now that was over. Soon he and teammates Bruce Fields and Jamie Huffman, both guards, were practicing his calling for "glass," a dynamic and common practice in the modern game but so new in 1976–77 that the *Lansing State Journal* felt compelled to explain it to readers, that if Fields or another teammate was driving for a breakaway layup, Johnson could run up behind them and call for "glass," which would mean the guy with the ball would simply throw it off the backboard rather than scoring it so that Johnson could soar up behind him and dunk the ball off the backboard. It was surely a showboating move, but it was also great fun. And Johnson's adoring crowds loved it.

The move often began with Huffman and a teammate double-teaming an opposing guard, Huffman recalled in 1997. "I had one move when I started turning the guy and put him on a 45-degree angle just after he crossed half-court. If he went behind his back or tried a cross-over move or a spin that's when I'd come around and pick his pocket. Earvin knew what I was doing, and if I got the ball he'd take off. I'd pass it to him and he'd slam it. If I was ahead of him and he was trailing I'd throw the ball off the glass and he'd slam it."

The "glass" dunks were not a favorite of the coaching staff, Pat Holland recalled while acknowledging that they were used for emphasis at key emotional points of the season.

The other great factor in Johnson's rising shot attempts was the almost overwhelming control over his high school team that he enjoyed as a senior star and darling of the community. As the season progressed, he would spend more and more time running each possession and getting his teammates in position.

"He was always directing," Dale Beard explained. "He felt like if he had the ball in his hand and could get everybody else involved that he would win the game, which he did."

Which, in turn, made the rest of the team eager to jump on his coattails and ride along, Beard added. "What made him who he was, you—and I'm not saying that because we were friends—you never saw the guy brag about anything or boast about anything or get the big head about anything. He was just, 'We just want to win.' And the basketball was fun. Every game was fun."

Fred Stabley would highlight fellow seniors Paul Dawson and Larry Hunter in a story that season. Both rapidly acknowledged enjoying their time in the large shadow Johnson cast. "If it weren't for Earvin, there would be no shadow to play behind and none of the great publicity we've gotten," Dawson said. "It's been great playing with him, and I'm going to miss it when this season ends."

Indeed, as the senior season unfolded, the coaches and players all seemed quite aware of just how precious and rare was the experience of winning at a top level and how it would be coming to an end soon. They wanted to make the most of it.

They had been anguished by the playoff losses the previous two seasons, but a theme that buoyed their joyride was a team-wide lack of concern about stats, again led by Johnson, hard as that may seem to believe from a guy taking nearly 23 shots a game.

Charles Tucker would note in 2019 that in his third varsity season, Johnson was operating more and more on instinct and listening less and less to his coaches. That would only make sense, Pat Holland responded, adding, how could they as coaches not trust a player like Earvin Johnson? Indeed, a good portion of his increase in shots that season came at the direction of the coaching staff. "If something works in a game, we would milk it to death," Fox explained. "And that's the way Earvin was on the floor. He was win at all costs. No holds barred."

From their ready agreement that Johnson as a sophomore was going to run the break as he saw fit and that his special skill was going to drive the team's tempo, the coaches had taken the unique approach that they were going to aid the flow rather than try to dam it up and control it. It hadn't always been perfect, but they entered their third season together with a decided sense that things were very much headed in the right direction.

In addition to his emotional development Johnson had fully matured into that perfect basketball body that Fox so often talked about, now up to almost six-nine with a sleek 202 pounds. George Fox entered the season talking about how much strength his team had gained, which was largely a function of Johnson's own growth in strength, even though it wasn't an age where basketball players did a lot of weightlifting, if any at all.

Combined with his mobility and flow and revolutionary playing style and control, all tied in with what observers again and again would describe as his immense poise, Johnson was stepping into nothing other than all-time greatness.

At six-seven with long arms, Paul Dawson's hands had gotten better each season, a tribute both to his own work and to Johnson. That didn't mean Dawson was able to get free from the constant noise. He had heard the complaints from the crowd that other players should be on the floor instead of him. Yet his size, his long arms, his rebounding and defense, and his ability to run the floor and finish on the break became a big part of the team's success and would earn Dawson a college scholarship.

"Even with Paul that way, Earvin would never throw him what would be a 'good pass' that Paul couldn't handle," Pat Holland offered. "When Paul got the ball from Earvin, it was in a place where he could catch it and do something with it. That was Earvin. You can talk about great passers. The greatest ones get the ball to players where they can really do something with it, where they're going to go right into a shot. If you throw a good pass to the wrong guy, in other words a guy who can't catch that good pass, then that's not a good pass. If Earvin gave a pass to Paul or to Larry Hunter or anybody in the wrong place and they didn't handle it, Earvin would be mad at himself."

If one of his teammates fumbled away one of his passes, Johnson's disappointment could be sharp and quick, as Beard described. Yet it was often subtle, often just enough to communicate his frustration without making a show of it, Holland said.

Mostly, though, his bountiful emotion became a feedback machine for his teammates. More than ever, Johnson's game was now about flow. Every practice, every game taught him more and more about how to keep things on the floor headed in the right direction.

Smooth Operator

During his own busy summer, Charles Tucker had managed an off-season tryout with the Philadelphia 76ers and almost made the cut, remarkable considering his thirtieth birthday was now in his rearview. Sportswriters would later question his claims of making a big impression in Philly only to find out from then Sixers coach Gene Shue that indeed the small but very quick Tucker had almost made the team for his defense and his ability to pressure the ball.

As with his other tryouts, the experience only served to deepen his contacts with pro players, thus the use of Sixers Steve Mix and Darryl Dawkins in the debut of his summertime events in Lansing, which in turn aided Tucker in promoting Johnson.

Just before the season, the psychologist had told the *Detroit Free Press* that Johnson had scored 28 in one pickup game against pro competition over the summer. First, who keeps a tally of points scored in a pickup game? But Tucker was ready with that impressive fact and with a quote from Ralph Simpson to bolster Johnson's status. "Ralph told me Earvin was the best high school player he ever saw in Michigan," Tucker told the paper.

Then Tucker quoted George Gervin as saying, "He could play with us right now," a revelation that launched the thought that Johnson might consider turning pro right out of high school, as Moses Malone had done just two seasons earlier.

Johnson himself considered the idea a rich fantasy, even as such news set to churning the stomachs of college coaches in the region. This commentary and Tucker's new higher profile also fed a growing curiosity about the psychologist, *Free Press* sportswriter Mick McCabe would recall in 2019. "He was hard to figure out, you know, what his angle was. Was he angling to be Earvin's agent or something like that? I kept waiting for it. What did he want out of it?"

McCabe noticed that Tucker was often sitting with Big Earv during games, and while others expressed difficulty in engaging Johnson's father in conversation, Tucker seemed to have no problem whatsoever with that.

One thing Tucker wasn't doing was trying to upstage the coaches, McCabe concluded. "It wasn't like he was sitting behind the coaches and yelling instructions at Earvin. Or that Earvin would look over and find him in the crowd so that Tucker could tell him what to do, like you would see with players' parents on other teams. Tucker was always very supportive. He was a positive figure, not just with the team, but with Lansing too."

For a guy who had displayed an impressive ability to snare publicity in the Lansing and Detroit and later the Los Angeles newspapers whenever he needed it, Tucker would display an equally deft touch in working around Johnson's teams at every level of the game.

"Tucker liked to be in the shadow," Pat Holland observed in 2020.

That included his instruction with his star pupil, Johnson. "He always had Earvin's ear," Fred Stabley explained in 2020. "He had Earvin's best interests at heart from the very beginning. He saw something in Earvin early. In many ways, he was the reason Earvin toed the line and avoided getting into trouble."

There was little doubt, however, that his influence was rooted in basketball itself, Stabley said. "Tucker played basketball well into his advancing years. He had considerable basketball ability, which is why Earvin listened to him in the first place."

Leon Stokes remembered as far back as junior high school Tucker's presence, his "speaking to Black students about racial issues and societal issues. He was able to bond with us because he played ball with us."

The psychologist did most of his coaching in the constant conversations he had with Johnson about every phase of the game and life. Later, American culture would settle on the term "career coaching" or "life coach" to explain the concept of intense mentoring to help show a person how to negotiate a career. Behind the scenes, Tucker was Johnson's life coach long before anyone knew what the term implied.

Still, his presence and approach were so unusual it left close observers figuring that Tucker had some scheme in mind. His role was expanding with Johnson's own game, from school psychologist to playground partner to family friend to an avuncular figure taking Johnson to pro games and arranging for him to meet top players to becoming his advisor in negotiating the difficulties of the racial atmosphere in the schools to serving as his career guide—it all seemed to be on the table with Tucker. And he was clearly moving several paces ahead of everybody else in terms of tying all of his basketball and educational contacts to his own growing media presence.

He brought reporters and media figures the kind of high-level contacts they desired in coaches and pro players. When Dawkins was scheduled to come to Lansing to appear at Tucker's camp, the psychologist arranged for "Chocolate Thunder" to phone Stabley for an interview at a set time, and sure enough the Sixers center not only phoned but promised to shatter a backboard while in town, which he did, taking down a backboard at the Lansing civic center with one of his "Thunder Dunks" the second year of Tucker's event, a stunt that not only shocked and excited the community but served to increase Tucker's street cred all at the same time.

Tucker clearly had the relationships to make himself a top source for reporters. As Johnson was emerging, the psychologist was becoming a go-to contact for sportswriters on all sorts of inside basketball information. After all, he knew the game, had played it on all levels, and was confident in his knowledge. Sometimes it seemed to them he may have overstated his accomplishments as a player here and there, but when they saw him on the floor it was obvious Tucker could play.

The problem was, his mystery persisted.

"A lot of people were kind of suspectful about Tucker," George Fox explained in 2019. "I've heard and read or seen some of the negative comments that were made about him. You know, they thought he was hustling Earvin to get to him, to maybe be his agent. And he kind of was his agent at first."

Fred Stabley considered the psychologist both a curious and remarkable figure. The sportswriter recalled running into Tucker at the Lansing airport back in that era on a bitterly cold day. The psychologist was changing a flat tire on his car in the parking lot.

"You should call and get somebody to do that for you," the sportswriter told him.

"No," Tucker replied. "I like to do things for myself."

Amazingly, college coaches made no attempt to turn a connection with Tucker into a deal with Johnson, nor with his father, not that it would have done them any good. On the other side of the equation, Tucker didn't appear to be trying to engage college coaches either. He left most of those dealings to Fox.

"Tucker had his heart in the right place," Stabley concluded. "He was always interested in many players and students, not just Earvin."

But with Johnson, Tucker had the perfect charge, with the perfect timing, in the perfect place.

Neither Tucker nor anyone else could have imagined the direction the game would take in the coming decades. But, at that moment in late 1976, college basketball and its growing money machine, the Final Four with its network TV contract, were just gaining momentum in the public mind and were on their way to an explosion in popularity.

North Carolina coach Dean Smith would point out in a 1987 interview that prior to the 1977 Final Four in Atlanta, the event was rather quaint and insular. That would soon end as the college game and its broadcast seemed to reach an exciting new level that very year, with Marquette and coach Al McGuire gaining an emotional championship victory over Smith's Tar Heels.

College basketball would be off and running as a business property with vast amounts of money making their way into the coffers of colleges and universities, soon creating all sorts of incentives for coaches to cheat and skirt the rules concerning amateur players.

Still, for the most part, things remained relatively low-key in late 1976. For example, the coaching staff at North Carolina seemed to be snubbing and ignoring Johnson, which left Everett's star puzzled.

McCabe recalled a moment when the Tar Heels traveled to Lansing early that December to shellack the Spartans at Jenison. "Earvin was there and bumped into Dean Smith," the *Free Press* sportswriter explained. "They were talking and Earvin says, 'I was wondering if I was going to hear from you guys or not.'"

McCabe concluded that the Carolina coaches had overlooked Johnson because they relied heavily upon the pool of high school stars invited to Howard Garfinkel's Five-Star Camp as a recruiting source. Johnson, for all of his acclaim, wasn't a Five-Star product.

Smith apparently changed course immediately, and soon enough the Tar Heels were on Johnson's list of finalists, along with NC State. With so many aunts and uncles and cousins still living on Tobacco Road in North Carolina, Johnson had been eager to make a splashy impact there.

Once his senior season began, with Johnson playing better and better, many coaches would take to calling him before games to wish him good luck and to keep the recruiting conversation going. After all, he was a big man, and just about all of them saw him playing as a forward in college. Johnson made it clear that he wasn't planning on changing his game at Everett just to please them. The record would show that he didn't have to.

Among the college coaches who would get a look at Johnson that season was Walt Perrin, an assistant at Northwestern who would go on to a distinguished career as an NBA executive evaluating talent.

When their team played at Michigan State, the entire Northwestern staff would make a point of going over to Everett one night to see Johnson play, Perrin recalled. "He was magic at the high school level, taller than everyone else on the court, extremely talented, amazing passing ability, an ability to make his teammates a lot better. Nobody expected that. Nobody thought there'd be anybody like that. Magic came along and kind of changed that."

Yet, Perrin recalled being somewhat disappointed by what he saw that night. "One I didn't think he played very well, to the uniqueness of the player I was watching."

Johnson got a little sloppy handling the ball, Perrin recalled. "Our sports information director came away saying, 'This guy is never going to be any good.'"

Spotlight

Everett romped the first two games of the season with Johnson scoring and rebounding seemingly at will. The third game on the schedule was against Eastern and Jay Vincent, played in a newly renovated arena on Eastern's campus that seated 4,500. Vincent, his old nemesis, hadn't defeated Johnson since ninth grade, and in many ways the season would be much about the growing showdown between the two teams.

The two rivals had actually become good friends over high school, based as much on the pickup games as anything else. "I did go over to his house a couple of times and would make me a sandwich or two if I was hungry," Vincent recalled with a laugh in 2019. "So I knew Mrs. Johnson very well. She was a kind and quiet person. It's amazing how she was quiet, and even Mr. Johnson was quiet." And yet, Vincent said, the two of them produced "this young guy Magic who had come out really, you know, totally different. Not only playing basketball but playing it really well but was really a rah-rah type of guy."

Yes, Johnson was the type who made lots of noise in a variety of ways, especially when it came to Vincent and Eastern High.

Despite the many battles between the two big men in high school, their competition never affected their relationship, Vincent recalled. "We were really good friends in high school. Even though I had a lot of publicity, he doubled my publicity, of course, with his name, with the way he played. I was more of a post-up guy, a scoring guy. He was a flashier guy, but we didn't have any conflict at all."

That was true of the enthusiasm in the community for their battles that season, beginning with their first meeting. Eastern's new building was packed with fans willing to shell out the whopping $1.50 to see the two high-scoring big men square off.

Fox was good friends with Eastern coach Paul Cook, who was on his way to becoming legendary in his own right with his program serving as something of a pipeline to Michigan State for talent. And time would bring Cook his own championships.

On this night, Eastern soon grabbed control of the tempo of the game, which left Fox on the bench wondering why Johnson seemed to stand around the first half with little energy while Vincent's crafty work around the basket gave Eastern a lead. The coach addressed those concerns at halftime and Johnson went on a tear, pushing greater tempo and attacking Eastern's zone to get the game to overtime, where Everett prevailed by eight.

To get the job done, Johnson had run up 45 points, all of which were needed to help the Vikings escape.

A few days later, just before Christmas, Fox floated the idea that Johnson should maybe score a little less, maybe around 28 or 29 points a game. The reason for that, the coach said, was that Johnson was maybe dominating too much, that if he wasn't having a good game and was standing around, the entire team tended to do the same.

Johnson didn't flinch at the suggestion, Fox recalled. "He was, 'Don't worry about me. I'll get my stats. And if I don't, I don't care.' That's the way he was. He made the sacrifice of getting everybody involved instead of scoring 40, 45 a game himself. He cut that way back and that really molded our team. Earvin just played with everybody else in mind. I'm convinced of that. It meant a lot to Earvin that his teammates were happy and as he got older and into the senior grade, I know that was very important for him."

January opened with the *Free Press*'s initial statewide poll that had Detroit Catholic Central as number one. A week later, Everett would assume the top spot after facing another unbeaten team, Niles High School, and leaving them in tatters with a 43–17 lead at the half in front of another whopping 4,200 fans.

From there, the Vikings rolled through the cold, snowy weeks undefeated to a rematch on the last day of the month with Eastern and Jay Vincent, who had risen in the ranks to number eight in the state, a matchup unlike anything in Lansing's history, so big it was moved to Jenison Field House, with its ten thousand seats to accommodate the fans, an astounding turnout for two local high schools going at each other.

"Michigan State was drawing two thousand people," Tucker remembered. "But when Earvin and Jay played against each other, they took it up to Jenison. . . . Earvin and them drew ten thousand. Isn't that amazing? They filled it up. People couldn't get in."

"You think about it," said Dale Beard, "in high school, we were pretty much the main attraction here because Michigan State was terrible. I mean they couldn't fill up Jenison Field House if they were giving away tickets. So we were the hottest ticket in town."

The Vikings had prepped for the matchup two days earlier by walloping Waverly, 103–52, with an impressive display of shooting, led by Johnson's 30 points, 13 rebounds, and nine assists. It was the 10th time in the first 14 games of the season that Johnson had scored at least 30 points.

But the tone and tempo of this showdown would be entirely different. Paul Cook's team collapsed around Johnson in a zone that left the free throw line extended wide open, daring the Vikings to attempt jumpers from the elbows. "I mean they sagged the zone almost to where they were touching each other's hands," Dale Beard remembered.

Fox put Beard in to take advantage of that and watched him score 14 points. It was impressive off the bench, but it wasn't enough. Johnson made six of 14 shots, scored 14 himself, then fouled out with 3:45 to play and Eastern ahead 62–48. After a final flurry of baskets, Cook's team celebrated, 70–62.

"We've lost to them six straight times with our kids playing their hearts out," Cook said afterward.

"We played a little zone, but they made a mistake and had Magic down low," Vincent recalled in 2019. "So we just double-teamed and he couldn't be the Magic man without getting the ball."

In the wake of the loss, which left Everett at 14–1, Fox and Holland decided they could no longer play Johnson exclusively down low in their half-court sets. Fox told reporters that night he was going to move Johnson up top where he could handle the ball more. No longer would the Everett coaches keep him down low where he could be denied the ball at key moments.

It was a subtle thing, Holland and Fox agreed in 2019, but it was a giant step toward making Johnson the team's full-time point guard, although he wouldn't be called that, wouldn't think of himself as a point guard, but it was placing the ball in his hands even more, with the full responsibility for directing the team's half-court offense.

"The next day," Beard remembered, "Coach Fox and Coach Holland came up and said, 'Hey, we're going to start you the next game.'"

He recalled the coaches telling him that they had talked to Johnson and he told them, "You know, we got to start this dude."

Before the state playoffs began in mid-February, Fox took his team for a scrimmage at Detroit Northeastern, which proved an eye-opening revelation about life in the big city for the Vikings, who were locked in a cage until the school day ended and the scrimmage could begin.

"Oh my God, the place was jammed," Mick McCabe remembered.

More than seven hundred people and a collection of media and college coaches—including University of Detroit coach Dick Vitale—showed up for a mere scrimmage. Spectators were stunned to see Johnson take the floor in a pair of University of Michigan socks.

"I remember that Coach Fox wanted us to play a team from Detroit," Johnson told McCabe in 1997. "When we got there, they locked us in a cage and everybody looked at me and said: 'What do we do now, Big Fella?' Then the school bell rang and after everybody left, they unlocked the cage and we went and warmed up. All the guys in Detroit started dunking and the guys said: 'Come on, Earv, dunk a few.' I told them to wait. We ended up blasting that team out."

Johnson and Everett would wallop nine straight opponents after the loss, including a road game at Grand Ledge where Johnson had 32 points and 29 rebounds and was greeted at the end with a two-minute standing ovation from opposing fans, a moment that left him with chills.

"They were sure beautiful," Johnson said afterward as he celebrated with a soft drink. He had been greeted by a throng of kids and adults seeking autographs before the game. The victory allowed the Vikings to finish the regular season at 19–1.

Strangely, the playoff draw wound up producing a rematch with Eastern the very next game, again played at Jenison Field House before an overflow crowd.

Having broadcast the final two seasons of Johnson's high school career on radio, Tim Staudt now turned to television for this final showdown of Lansing's two stars. There had never been a TV broadcast of a high school game in Lansing, Staudt recalled. "That was the very first one in the history of that market. We had to hire the equipment out of Toledo. There was a Toledo production company that did Detroit Tigers games, and we rented their equipment and their staff. We had several cameras and we did have replay."

Ad sales were strong. From the radio broadcasts to this TV experiment, Johnson had proved to be the kind of high school star who created his own media history. "We basically did it with chicken wire," Staudt recalled. "I mean we just kind of held everything up together to get it on the air because our studio was only three blocks from where they played that game, but it was packed. There were college coaches everywhere. Earvin really played a great game that night."

By this time, Eastern had lost its point guard to injury, and the Vikings won handily, ending Jay Vincent's high school career. If Johnson and Everett hadn't been so good, that Eastern team would likely have been considered one of the greatest in the city's history, Staudt observed in 2019. "They were that good."

Wrapped in Johnson's very large persona, Everett's road show rolled through those playoffs, with seemingly the main thing holding it all in place being George Fox's stern avowal that the bus was going to leave at five each game night and if you were late you weren't going to play, a standard that Earvin Johnson had somehow miraculously managed to live by despite a trend of being late for nearly everything else in his life.

Then came the day during their playoff run when Johnson didn't make it, with every face on the team bus growing more anxious as the clock ticked toward five. Just as things looked completely dire, Dr. Jamieson declared that he'd left an item from his medical bag in the school, which bought a few more minutes. Yet when he returned, still no Earvin.

Resigned to their fate, Fox told the bus driver to start the engine. They had traveled about a mile from the school, as memory served, when Dr. Jamieson got up and ran to the back of the bus and began yelling excitedly a car was following them.

It was an Electra.

They pulled over to see Big Earv looking at them from the driver's seat—he had been held up at work, or so one of the versions of the story went—as Earvin jumped out of the car and onto the bus, disaster avoided, and everyone left with a memory to chuckle over for decades to come.

As it was, Everett's momentum carried them through five more playoff wins and into the state semifinal against Saginaw in Jenison Field House, a Saturday contest that had been greeted by five inches of wet snow and slushy parking lots. That hardly deterred fans who weren't going to miss the conclusion of Magic Johnson's quest for a title.

Saginaw was a team that routinely made it to the late stages of the state championship battles in that era. True to form, the Trojans slowed the pace of the game, and used six-three defender Mike Booker to deny Johnson the ball and limit him to 16 points, his third lowest total of the season.

Well into the fourth quarter, Everett had a slight lead, Pat Holland recalled, when Johnson out of nowhere called for a slowdown without consultation with the coaches. Holland was instantly alarmed, felt it was way too soon for such a move, and turned to Fox, who said, "Hold on. Let's see what happens."

The dramatic move resulted in the Vikings scoring the next four baskets, Holland recalled, and they eventually closed out Saginaw, 48–40.

"He had so much intelligence and high IQ for the game," Dale Beard marveled about the teenaged Earvin Johnson. "I look at that after all these years and it leads me now to think, 'Wow, you know, he's doing this back when we were playing high school ball, man.' "

The Vikings' reward for surviving was to advance to the state championship game against, surprise, Kevin Smith's team, Birmingham Brother Rice, which had upset Detroit Catholic Central, the defending state champs, in the other semifinal bracket.

"We had a whole week to think about it," Dean Hartley, a senior on the team, would recall.

Especially Johnson, who would be facing his good friend for the state championship the following Saturday. The game would be played in Ann Arbor, at the University of Michigan's Crisler Center.

Meanwhile, the city of Lansing and Everett High School had a high ol' time waiting for the game, with pep rallies, school prayers, signs on many buildings and stores, and all sorts of community cheer.

Tickets had been tough throughout Johnson's three years of varsity ball, but that third season had brought a new level. Each player was allotted ten tickets per game, which hadn't been nearly enough, with cousins of cousins phoning up from out of town trying to get a seat on the Magic train.

In their last home practice before loading up to go to Ann Arbor, the coaches sat back, watching Johnson work and marveling at the young man who had come into their lives, who had arrived at Everett unwillingly, with so much racial turmoil still in the air at the school. They watched him work those final hours of practice and thought of the effort he had made now for three seasons. And the response he had gotten from teammates and the community.

Considering where it had all started, the moment seemed almost surreal. "When those kids . . . I mean, to throw rocks at a bus," Pat Holland remembered. "I'm thinking, 'Oh, my God, how are we going to get through this?' We closed the school for a week to try and get things settled."

Magically, the darkness had lifted.

"I just think it was a learning experience for both races," Dale Beard said. "Once we have got to playing basketball and the season started, man, it just took off from there. Then everybody didn't even think about it. Everybody was saying, 'This is our team. This is our teammate. This is our classmate.' In the city, people kind of accepted it with open arms and I think that's what made that era good."

"I think it made them forget about a lot of things and focus on having fun," Charles Tucker said.

"He wanted everybody to get along," Pat Holland remembered.

Now, amidst all the pep rallies and community excitement, all the final emotional moments of three seasons, Johnson wanted just one thing—for the whole team to go to Ann Arbor a night early to get ready for the big game.

"We talked Mr. Fox into letting us spend Friday in a hotel," Johnson would say. "We had a great time being together."

"And so we went down there and we're staying overnight," Pat Holland remembered. "George and I had a room, and we hear a knock on the door. All the Black kids on the team walk in in their brand-new suits. Yeah, and one of them, Tony Daniel, said, 'Well Mr. Fox, how do you like the looks of your inner-city Black kids now?' They kind of made a joke like that."

The light moment, however, reflected a sad note. James "Bobo" Lauderdale, a senior substitute who had played well over the season, dropped off the team the week before the championship.

"George said he heard later that Bobo did not have enough money to buy a suit," Holland said. "We didn't know anything about those guys buying suits. We would have bought him a suit. So he wouldn't be left out. We just didn't get a reason out of it, why he didn't come. But he had played the whole season."

Dale Beard remembered the time in Ann Arbor as the team's first experience with the big time, with what it felt like to be a college player, staying in a hotel the night before a big game.

"Being at the University of Michigan, that was kind of neat," Beard said. "The night before we went down to practice on the gym floor. It was quiet. Then we went and ate dinner and everybody kind of hung around for a while in the lobby. Fox said lights had to be out by 9:30 or 10. Sure enough, everybody got to their room. We were disciplined kids, man."

"We were in one room playing cards and bonding," Johnson later told Mick McCabe. "We all talked to each other, and Mr. Fox let us order pizza. Then we got up and had breakfast. That made it special."

With their previous collapses in the state tournament still prominent among their thoughts, with their minds on their dedication of the season to Reggie Chastine, Johnson and his teammates didn't have to be reminded to keep their focus on their late Saturday afternoon game.

Thirteen thousand fans had been drawn to the Crisler Center to see Magic Johnson, and when he walked on the floor that day, they responded, George Fox recalled. "Earvin just magnified the crowd. . . . They were electrified by him."

His teammates soaked in the response as well.

"We just felt like it was our time," Dale Beard said.

Unfortunately, that would not help them avoid trouble or another puzzling performance from Magic Johnson. First, he had four assists, but also six turnovers to go with them.

Most concerning of all, he would take an eye-bulging 34 shots during the game, 10 more than all his other teammates combined took.

And he would make just 14 of those shots, meaning that with his volume of errant shots soaking up most of the offense, the Vikings spent a good portion of the game trailing Birmingham Brother Rice.

"He took more shots in that game than he probably would normally take in at least two games," Pat Holland recalled ruefully in 2019. "But again, they were playing us man-to-man. So that made a difference. Who would you rather have taking them?"

The Vikings had been down a bucket or two much of the game, but with more than five minutes to go, things took a turn for the worse. And George Fox grew despondent. "What does it take to win a championship?" he asked Pat Holland.

It's not over yet, the assistant responded.

Indeed, as Holland recalled, with the Birmingham Brother Rice lead stretched out to seven with 5:20 to go in the fourth quarter the coaches called for the Vikings to step up their ball pressure on Kevin Smith.

Then Johnson hit a jumper, followed by a Dale Beard free throw, then by Johnson breaking away for a dunk. Brother Rice answered with a layup, and Huffman answered with one of his own to bring the score to 43–45 with 2:27 to go.

After Brother Rice scored again and a timeout, Johnson hit another jumper and two free throws to tie it at 47 with less than a minute to go. Everett had the ball after another timeout with 45 seconds to go. Johnson worked the clock down to five seconds and took another jumper.

There underneath the basket and in position was long-armed Paul Dawson to snare the rebound and put it right back in for a 49–47 Vikings lead.

With the crowd going crazy and three seconds on the clock, Brother Rice quickly inbounded to Kevin Smith, who motored to just inside the half-court line and let fly.

It banked off the backboard and into the bucket. Good! From 47 feet.

A look of horror on his face, Jamie Huffman collapsed on the floor and lay very still as the building erupted.

Some in the stands later said they thought he just might be dead.

13

THE GREAT AND THE GRUESOME

Kevin Smith would spend decades musing about the lack of a three-point shot in basketball in 1977. If the rules had allowed a trey, his shot at the buzzer would have put a huge dent in the narrative of Magic Johnson's greatness.

The three-pointer had been a nice feature of the American Basketball Association since the 1960s (and yet another brief pro league, the American Basketball League in 1962), but the ABA had merged with the NBA by 1977 and there was no three in America's major league that year, nor at any other level of basketball.

The NBA wouldn't adopt the three until the 1979–80 season, and college basketball and high schools wouldn't fully adopt it until later, in the 1980s.

Which meant that Kevin Smith's miracle shot counted for just two and the championship game between Everett and Birmingham Brother Rice went to overtime. Fortunately, Jamie Huffman picked himself up off the floor. He had believed his team was ahead by one and thus had collapsed in disbelief and despair, thinking his Vikings had lost.

As the two teams took the floor to start the extra period, Johnson locked eyes briefly with his buddy Smith with his own look of disbelief, the moment fed by that inner voice saying, "Not again." It seemed to be a dreadful voice that would never leave him, no matter how much and how often Johnson ultimately won. Yes, he was learning how to close out the biggest games—what he would happily come to trumpet as "Winnin' Time," yet it would rarely be all that easy and would always come only after he had learned to prevent his vast store of emotion from overwhelming his equally substantial poise in the game's biggest moments.

In Crisler Center that day, Dale Beard scored the first four points in overtime and seemed pretty fortunate to get the ball considering the volume of shots Johnson had taken that afternoon. The Magic Man would foul out with a little more than a minute to go in overtime with his team holding a seven-point margin.

That normally would seem a safe lead, except nothing had been safe about any lead that Johnson's teams had held in the previous big games in the state tournament.

Johnson had scored 34 points on 14 of 34 shooting with 14 rebounds.

For years afterward, sportswriters would chuckle at the scene during the timeout after Johnson had fouled out, with a frenetic Magic immediately taking over the Everett huddle and animatedly telling everyone all at once what they needed to do.

"He was just crazy," George Fox recalled. "He was so full of emotion and excited."

The coach firmly took Johnson and set him aside to calm down, then turned to his team to provide instructions to the players. Then Fox allowed time for Johnson to have his say by pulling his teammates in with his long arms for his own final encouragement and instructions.

The game, however, was clearly no longer in his hands. He would have to rely on his teammates. As it is with many late-game situations, it came down to the free throws. The Vikings started out by muffing two one-and-ones in the first seconds after the timeout, sending the tension higher along the Everett bench and among the crowd.

But Jamie Huffman stepped up and made five foul shots down the stretch to preserve victory and launch the ecstatic championship moment that followed, 62–56.

Huffman and his teammates had delivered the title for Earvin Johnson, Fox would tell reporters in the euphoria afterward.

As it was, they hardly had time to celebrate before Fox and Johnson headed off to the McDonald's All-America game in Washington, D.C., where he joined rising stars such as Gene Banks and Albert King in the showcase event.

"I think that he and Banks and Albert King were considered the three best players," remembered the great hoops writer Dick Weiss. "It was Magic's introduction to the basketball world. I mean, everybody knew who he was in Michigan, but this is the first time they'd actually seen him. He was playing in front of about eighteen thousand people at the Capital Centre in Landover, Maryland, and I remember that he could do just about anything you would want a basketball player to do."

Especially when it came to sending the ball where it needed to be.

"The best thing about Earvin was the way kids on the floor respected him and played with him," George Fox recalled of that collection of all-stars, an event that so often digressed into one-on-one play and selfishness as athletes tried to show their individual skills. "They just couldn't believe a guy could pass like that. One coach came up and says, 'Coach, how did you ever lose a game with him?' And I says, 'Good question. I blame myself for that.' Those kids couldn't believe the way he could pass. It was just the evolution of Earvin becoming known as being a point guard. I don't think the term was even in basketball back in the '70s, was it?"

It was. Many coaches had called the position the "lead guard" in that era. Yet the distinction was still relatively subtle to the general public. When Lakers coach Bill Sharman asked Jerry West at age thirty-three to shift from off guard to lead guard for the 1971–72 season, the press hardly picked up on the change and the huge adjustment it required for West at an advanced age.

Six years later the Magic Man was taking his first steps toward putting his unprecedented skills on the bigger stage. In time, he would no longer be just a local sensation in Lansing and the state of Michigan, just as he would no longer be considered a forward. Yet even Johnson himself was reluctant to think of himself differently.

After the McDonald's event, he would jet off from Washington to Europe to play on a team of American high school all-stars entered into the Albert Schweitzer Games in Mannheim, Germany. Back home his performances made headlines as Johnson scored 20 in the main game to deliver the gold medal to his team. That was all well and good to his many fans in Michigan, but what they really wanted to know was, where the heck was their Magic going to school, Michigan or Michigan State? Everyone was dying to know, including Johnson himself. His decision would be affected by news on the home front discovered upon his return. Kevin Smith had signed with Dick Vitale and the University of Detroit and was no longer available to attend Michigan with him.

Johnson's mother had made her preference known. She still wanted Michigan. It was suspected that his father wanted Michigan State, but the old man refused to say.

At seventeen, Johnson had gotten his head turned by Michigan's success, its field house filled with fans, all the trappings of a "big-time" college program, Charles Tucker explained. "He just felt he could go play at a place with an established reputation and a field house full of fans."

Plus, no group of coaches had matched the Michigan recruiting effort.

"Michigan was so close," Tucker remembered. "They were here every minute, basketball courts, softball field, wherever he showed up, they were there. And they would bring out heavy guns, Michigan sports legends, whomever. A lot of people were on him."

Truth was, Jud Heathcote had never been known as much of a recruiter. Earvin Sr. wasn't really focused much on Michigan State itself but rather on the fact that it was in East Lansing.

"Being in Lansing was good for his son," Tucker explained. "And you had a situation here that you could kind of control."

There were those who suspected the control was more important to Tucker than it was to Big Earv. But Johnson did not want to go to MSU.

"His mind was somewhere else. Definitely," Tucker recalled.

The coaches at Michigan were getting antsy because they had started losing recruits who had been waiting to join Magic in Ann Arbor, an hour's drive southeast of Lansing. And the coaches at Michigan State had no confidence and little real belief because Jud Heathcote had had scant recruiting success on a top level in his first year in the program. Plus, the Spartans were coming off a losing season while the Michigan program was coming off a spot in the national championship game versus Indiana.

Then, just as Johnson was trying to zero in on a decision, Vernon Payne, the veteran assistant at Michigan State, took the head coaching job at Wayne State that week, which was seen as a further blow to MSU's chances. Of the State coaches, Payne was the closest to Johnson, had the best trust with him.

"Vern went to Lansing Everett and got him out of class," writer Mick McCabe recalled.

"Listen," Payne supposedly told Johnson. "Tomorrow I'm taking the Wayne State job."

"And Earvin goes, 'Oh my God,'" McCabe said. "And Vern says, 'Listen, you should go to Michigan State. That's the best place for you. I'm no longer on staff there. But that is the best place for you. Jud is the best coach you could get.' I think that also played the influence."

One by one, the other considerations had fallen by the wayside. Kentucky assistant Leonard Hamilton had confided to Fox that he felt he was in good shape with Johnson. Fox had smiled and advised Hamilton not to be confused by Johnson's personality.

"Leonard, that's the way he comes across to most of the coaches," Fox remembered telling Hamilton. "He just don't want to say no to you, but he's not going to say yes, either."

"I just always assumed he would go to Michigan State," Fox recalled. "It had to do a lot with his personality and his friends in Lansing. He wanted those kids to be able to watch him play."

As free and friendly as he was, Johnson would get riled by the recruiting process. He had long planned to visit UCLA until the coaches there contacted him at the last minute and asked him to reschedule, supposedly because they now had a shot at signing Albert King, a move that was said to insult and anger Johnson.

"He's always told me that his first choice was UCLA," said Lon Rosen, who would become his longtime friend and representative. "But when he was supposed to go on the recruiting trip they canceled it because they wanted to bring Albert King in first and they wanted to reschedule. Earvin said forget it. His dream was to play for UCLA. He told me that."

Johnson certainly could have helped the school extend its dominance over NCAA basketball that had stretched from 1964 to 1975. Mick McCabe and other insiders would long joke with him about the secret chip on his shoulder for King and Gene Banks, players who had been ranked above him in the recruiting process.

Johnson had returned home from playing in Germany on Sunday, April 17, to find the entire basketball fan base in the state of Michigan hanging on his decision, evidenced by an eager and unheard-of crowd of 1,500 gathered that early evening at the Lansing airport—featuring competing groups with signs touting either the Wolverines or Spartans—all waiting for him to come off the plane only to discover he had been delayed by a connecting flight.

As it was, he wouldn't arrive until two hours later, at around 11 P.M. By that time, the crowd had dwindled to about four hundred or so of his heartiest fans, including George Fox and Pat Holland, two guys who never looked to get caught in that sort of crowd. Heathcote was there, and the city's mayor, too. Johnson and his decision were like a great magnet, drawing everyone to him.

Exhausted from his travels, Johnson was stunned to see the crowd and even more surprised that before the delay it had been three times larger.

"I thought there might be a couple of reporters and my family at the airport, but nothing like this," he told the gathered media while wiping away a tear. "It means a great deal to me to see that a lot of people really care about me."

Indeed, many were seeking an answer, but he just didn't have it. Some of his friends would smile and remark that Earvin always knew how to savor the attention of a crowd.

"Earvin struggled with the decision far more than people realized," Tucker recalled.

As is often the case, however, the business of recruiting athletes comes down to what happens behind the scenes. And there, local business leaders Joel Ferguson and Greg Eaton were waiting to help the process along, first with the advice they had offered Jay Vincent during the playoffs that year.

"Jud Heathcote came to me when he was recruiting and he said, 'Help me recruit him,'" Ferguson recalled. "One day, Heathcote said to me that Jay Vincent is going to Minnesota and that Earvin was going to Michigan. So I called Gregory Eaton. Earvin always said he and I were his two mentors. So we fixed a dinner for Jay Vincent and had him over on a Sunday. And I told him he can't go to Minnesota, that they got Kevin McHale and Mychal Thompson."

"If you're going to make the NBA, you can't be sitting on the bench and watch these other guys play. So you got to go to State," Ferguson recalled telling Vincent.

The dinner happened the week that Vincent was set to meet Johnson for the final time in the state playoffs.

"If you play Earvin and if you lose, you got to announce right away that you're going to Michigan State, so you don't end up following Earvin," Ferguson recalled telling Vincent.

"They were rivals," Ferguson said in a 2019 interview. "He was paying more attention to Earvin than Earvin was paying attention to him. So I said, 'You got to announce first so it doesn't look like you're following Earvin.'"

With Vincent in the fold, Heathcote asked Ferguson for another favor.

"After Jay announced, Jud came to me and said, 'Hey, you got to help me with Earvin,'" Ferguson recalled.

Heathcote was scheduled to visit with the Johnson family at home that week of Johnson's return from Europe. The coach asked Ferguson what he should focus his remarks on.

"First of all, it's Christine," Ferguson replied.

Heathcote was puzzled and asked why.

"She's a Seventh-day Adventist," Ferguson recalled, adding that his own wife shared Mrs. Johnson's beliefs. "I see her all the time; she's my wife's best friend and she's been over to the house."

The faith had its challenges for modern families, Ferguson told the coach. "My kids can't wait for me to come home on Friday evenings because they are on lockdown then until the sun changes on Saturday."

Ferguson pointed out that Michigan was playing all of its games home and away on Saturday afternoons.

"Assure her that you'll only play Saturday games at night," Ferguson advised, explaining that was key to allowing Mrs. Johnson to observe the Sabbath and still get to see her son play. Christine Johnson had not been able to see him play the state championship game due to its Saturday afternoon start.

At that time, the coaches still had major control over their team's schedules as opposed to later years when TV executives influenced those decisions. The appeal would also favor many others in the Johnson family, especially the sisters, who like their mother had embraced the new faith. Ferguson pointed out there were many things that Johnson was attempting to weigh in his decision that April, but this was an important one.

It didn't hurt that Heathcote was likable, that Tucker had made sure the coach connected with Big Earv, that Gus Ganakas, the previous MSU coach who remained a favorite of their son's, was still at the school and encouraging Johnson to join Heathcote.

A huge but largely unarticulated barrier to that was what Johnson himself had observed of Heathcote on the sidelines of Michigan State games during the previous season. Heathcote's antics—hitting himself in the head, stamping his feet, and yelling at his players—were considered comical, even endearing, to some. But Johnson often found his behavior distasteful and wondered if he could play for him.

All of these things weighed on Johnson's mind that April, pushing him in a way he did not want to go.

"He didn't like the situation," Charles Tucker recalled, adding that it came to a head in the wee hours one day that week in mid-April as Big Earv and the psychologist were working late.

"We were out there cleaning up a shop that night," Tucker recalled in 2019, "and he figured out that we wouldn't go against what he wanted to do. But he kind of knew our opinion. We were out working at the place his dad cleaned up. All at once we saw this car pull up. One o'clock in the morning almost. In that big ol' car. He came out there standing around. His daddy was very smart. He knew Junior wanted something. So he got to talking about his decision, what he wanted to do. Then he said at the last minute, 'What do you all think?' We didn't go against him. He said to his dad, 'You don't want me to go to Michigan.' His dad said, 'No, no, no. I didn't say that. But this is the logic I see.' And then he kind of listened that way, because his dad had always been A Number One for him."

The psychologist watched in awe of the moment. The son obviously had a choice he wanted to make. His father refused to tell him what to do, which was the opening for Magic Johnson to do exactly what he wanted, yet the son had so much respect for the father that he declined the opportunity to charge ahead. "This guy was almost like a father to me, really," Tucker recalled of Big Earv. "This guy was very patient and trustworthy, but he was tough now. He could be tough. He always had a joke to tell. He didn't deal with a lot of people. And he never had his hand out, you know. You just had to be straight with him. People who really know that family, and know his father, they know that he's the one who Earvin really listens to and respects."

The seventeen-year-old Johnson, who had clearly found a way to force the world of adults around him to submit to his will, paused then at the brink of doing that with his own father.

"That was one decision Earvin really didn't want to do," Tucker remembered. "So he kind of like sprinted out of the shop and said, 'Okay, I'm gonna do it tomorrow. I want to make the announcement tomorrow. Make sure you call and tell the coaches right now. I want to do it right now.' He was like, at once, 'I want to do it now.'

"When he made the decision to go to Michigan State, he was going somewhere else," Tucker explained. "I don't know exactly if it was Michigan or somewhere else, but he told his dad and I the night before he made the announcement, 'I'm going to do this because I know that's what you all like, that's what you all think.' He trusted his dad's kind of nonverbal opinion. And he trusted my nonverbal opinion."

Even though Big Earv hadn't told him, Johnson knew what his father wanted him to do "without his father having to say it," Tucker explained. "It wasn't necessary that he stay here in Lansing, but make the decision for the right reason, you know? So go where you can play. You'll be protected a little more here than you would out of town someplace."

The scene offered the unusual picture of Johnson becoming his own man, not by going against his father's wishes but by taking the time to soak in the reasoning behind them.

"He didn't confide in a lot of people," Tucker said in 2019 of Johnson at that age. "But the one or two that he did, he's going to support their opinion. And he's going to have his own opinion, but he listened. He was a good listener. He listens now. He's going to do what he wants to do, but he'll listen very well. I think that's been his success. He'll listen to you and agree with you a little bit, but then he's always going to go back and consult with somebody before he does anything. Eventually he makes up his own mind."

At the moment, Johnson was attempting to straddle the desires of the state's two major rivals. "His mind was in one place," Tucker explained. "His heart was still here in Lansing. He listened to his dad's thinking. He was disappointed in the decision he made, but he only stayed that way for a second. He didn't know what he wanted to do. He knew what he was *going* to do."

In Stitches

Just when it seemed that the entire state of Michigan couldn't stand another day not knowing where Magic Johnson was going to play college ball, he called a press conference for Friday morning, April 22, and got right to the point.

"Thank God the Suspense Is Over," the *Detroit Free Press* declared in one headline.

A smiling Heathcote was greeted by gifts of champagne and a PowerHouse candy bar at his office.

"There's a new emphasis, a new interest and a new excitement around our basketball program now that we have signed Earvin," the coach told reporters.

Indeed, Tim Staudt was hatching a plan to televise Spartan home games, which had never happened before. Ticket sales for games saw an immediate jump. One local member of the state legislature soon declared he was going to start searching for the funds to build Michigan State a new basketball arena. And the *Free Press* quietly began making plans to cover the Spartans' road games, something that had been considered not worth the trouble due to a lack of interest in previous seasons.

That same night Johnson joined Vincent on a team of Lansing-area all-stars playing Detroit-area all-stars in a charity game. Near the end of the game, Johnson went in for a dunk, caught his hand on the rim, and ripped the pinkie away from the rest of his hand, opening a wound that ran down to his wrist.

"It was just awful," recalled Dr. Tom Jamieson, who was watching from the stands and immediately treated Johnson. "Think about taking your little finger and separating it from the fourth finger and ripping that all the way off down towards your wrist."

In a later age, such an injury would have required an X-ray and immediate surgery. Instead, Jamieson wrapped the hand and pondered what to do. "I took him to my office and sewed that up," the doctor recalled in 2019. "I had to put in several deep sutures. I think it was eighteen deep sutures and sixteen superficial sutures to repair that laceration."

The doctor recalled that he had never seen such an injury and such severity although the resumption of dunking that year had led to reports of several gruesome injuries in Michigan as the game and its players adjusted to the use of the power play, a development that quickly prompted manufacturers to begin designing safer rims.

In examining his notes about the injury in 2019, Jamieson saw a notation that Jud Heathcote had phoned him early the next morning to inquire about Johnson.

"He wanted to know what effects that would make on him," the doctor said of Heathcote. "I bandaged him up and got him so he could play with all those sutures and I checked him twice a day."

Sports medicine, of course, would soon change dramatically, the doctor noted. "Nowadays even a little tweak of an injury at a high level and immediately they're doing MRIs and CAT scans."

Jamieson also noted Johnson's remarkable tolerance for pain.

"You got to do one thing," the doctor told him. "No more dunking, man. You're going to be doing layups for a period of time."

It should be noted that Johnson and nemesis Larry Bird would soon usher in the golden age of pro basketball, yet neither of them made any concerted effort to be dunkers, that the slam was mostly absent from their games, even though they were setting up simultaneously the age that followed, of acrobatic, showboat dunkers such as Michael Jordan, Vince Carter, and Kobe Bryant.

His world was about to become the business of feeding both powerful and athletic dunkers, a level of athletes far above that of his high school teammates.

Johnson, with a cast of sorts on his right hand, soon made an appearance at the informal games of State players in Jenison Field House.

"He had a cast on his right hand, and he shot and played with his left hand," recalled Ron Charles, a freshman on the Michigan State team that spring. "He was shooting jumpers with that left hand. It was a sweet adjustment to his right hand. He did not miss."

Nor was he reserved around his future teammates, Charles remembered. "He took a leadership role. He always took the big circle and was never afraid."

14

THE SPARTAN

Earvin Johnson's hand was soon healed and once again he was facing an insanely busy summer, including leading a team to the national AAU championship for his age group. His schedule included a stop at a tournament in California, where Bill Duffy had a chance to come face-to-face with Johnson's rumored stardom. Duffy himself was a top recruit in the class and was headed to the University of Minnesota to play, where he would also encounter Johnson on the Big Ten circuit. Duffy would later become a prominent NBA agent for an array of players, from Yao Ming to Steve Nash to Luka Dončić.

'We're in Oakland at the Sunshine Classic," Duffy recalled in 2019. "I'm there on a Southern California team and our point guard was a guy named Russell Brown, who is still the all-time leading assist maker at Arizona to this day. Sam Williams, who played in the NBA, was our center. So, we're in the tournament and we're doing well. Well, we keep hearing that Earvin Johnson was coming out and we were all curious to see him. But he couldn't get out there the first day and he couldn't get out there the second day. It was a five-day or six-day tournament. He finally shows up and they put him on a team that hadn't won any games. The point guard on the team was

Ethan Martin, who wound up playing at LSU, who was a very good player."

With what was quickly becoming his trademark cool, Johnson made another of his grand entrances into the gym. "We didn't know that he was a guard," Duffy recalled. "They listed him as a forward in *Street & Smith's* or whatever, so we're thinking he's a forward. I went to watch his first game. Ethan Martin was the point guard."

Johnson wasn't in the starting lineup because the team he joined "already had their flow," Duffy said. "Well, they put him in the game and he kept wanting to get the ball. But Ethan Martin is a six-foot point guard and he doesn't want to give up the ball."

As a result, Johnson didn't do much at first and Duffy began to wonder, "What does he do?"

"About a minute after that," Duffy recalled, "he gets the defensive rebound and Ethan Martin runs to the ball, but Magic just takes off. He goes coast-to-coast and goes into the lane and throws a pass behind his head to the trailer, who comes in and dunks it. And I'm like, 'Okay.' Then, he gets another defensive rebound, waves Ethan Martin off and again, goes coast-to-coast for a layup. And now I'm like, 'Whoa.' And the place goes nuts. The crowd is just going crazy, like, 'Who is this guy dribbling through his legs, around his back, making the right plays, talking to everyone, pointing all over the place, making underhand passes from half-court for lobs?' We were like, 'Holy smokes. He's not a forward; he's a guard.'"

The next day, Duffy's team played Johnson's, and Duffy found himself matched up against Johnson.

"I'm six-four and I'm thinking, 'I can guard this guy, right?'" he recalled. "I was trying to get in front of this guy on defense and I thought, 'Let's see if I can steal the ball from him.' He'd just embarrass you. He was big and rangy, so if you tried to attack his dribble, he'd go between his legs or around his back and you'd end up behind him. You learned that you have to back away from this guy. He was the first guy I had seen who was a guard, who was so big, that he'd pick up his dribble at the free throw line and take one step to the basket where he could make a pass back to a shooter or hit the wing or the cutter. It was just amazing what he did with his size, right?

"By that time, after two games, everybody in Oakland was hearing about him. People were coming from all over the place to watch him play."

Duffy's team played Johnson's again the next day. Afterward, Duffy told Johnson, "Hey, man. You're awesome. I'm going to Minnesota and I'm sure I'll see you down the road."

BMOC

Missy Fox had been at Michigan State a year when Johnson made his grand entrance. "I would run into him," she remembered, "and he always had a bunch of people around him all the time because he's that kind of guy, just so gregarious, just all smiles and welcoming. He was the leader."

Johnson's uncle Jim Porter, Christine's younger brother, worked on campus and became friends with Missy Fox. She and Jim Porter were joggers and used to run together.

"Jim kind of generated energy," Missy Fox said. "We got to know Jimmy really well and we would watch games with him and he kind of kept us up to date on what was going on in Earvin's life."

Keeping up with Johnson's life was a spectator sport in itself and quite an arduous one, considering that the towering, beaming young man arrived on campus with thousands of students only vaguely aware of his presence. That, too, would change quickly as basketball season neared.

Joining Johnson that August in the large freshman class was Earlitha "Cookie" Kelly, a striking young woman from Detroit, set to major in fashion merchandising. It didn't take her long to notice the great stir this guy Magic Johnson was creating among the female population, thousands of young women on the campus, and they all seemed to have quickly gained an eye for Johnson. Kelly, too, was drawn to his casual grace, the aura of cool, the smile, the sensation of his person, all from afar.

Kelly would recall years later in her memoir that there was a decided racial alienation on the campus with white students seemingly unenthusiastic about socializing with Black students, which led the smaller African American population at the school to gather in its own social organizations and at its own student union. It didn't take long for Kelly and Johnson to find each other despite the density of competition of young women angling to put themselves in Johnson's presence. He was soon dropping by her dorm room, even crashing for naps there after practice as she and her roommates became friends with him.

"I was shooting, she was rebounding," Johnson recalled in 2022 of those casual early days together.

Soon enough, it became clear that friendship wasn't his intention. He initiated the courtship with a dozen yellow roses. Little could she have realized then, in those innocent days, just what an impact the dynamic of the crowd's attraction to her new boyfriend would have on her life.

Johnson, meanwhile, was well on his way to fitting in with his new teammates. Among that group was rising junior Gregory Kelser, the next great competitive relationship in Johnson's life. A well-established player with considerable leaping ability, Kelser was also an Academic All-American who, like the other leaders in the program, had helped their coaches recruit Johnson. Kelser and Johnson had known each other for a few years by then, having met at a summer tournament in high school at Detroit's famed St. Cecilia's Gym in 1975.

The two young players exchanged pleasantries that day, and after Kelser graduated and went to Michigan State to play, he and Johnson would renew their acquaintance. "He was very familiar with me, and I was very familiar with him," Kelser, a lithesome six-seven forward, recalled in 2019. "He saw me play in college and he liked what he saw. He felt the two of us would really, really blend and that my skills would benefit from what he did on the basketball court and vice versa. At that time, I was All–Big Ten, honorable mention All-America, and had already gotten some accolades. I was one of the top players in the conference and maybe even around the country coming back. And we had several other guys who were good. Bob Chapman was a very accomplished guard on our team, and we had some younger guys. So it wasn't like he was joining some outfit that wasn't going to be pretty good. He was going to join a good group of players."

When you added Jay Vincent to the mix, there was lots of room for optimism, Kelser recalled. It wasn't a roster with a lot of size, but it had athleticism.

"You could see on paper that we were going to be really, really good," Kelser offered.

Not that anyone outside of Lansing cared all that much. After all, it was Michigan State basketball. Johnson immediately brought all one hundred watts of his personality to the situation, beginning with informal practices and pickup sessions before the formal season began.

Duck Time

When it came to adjusting to the new Magic guy, the early inclination of Ron Charles was to duck. Johnson's no-look passes, brilliant as they were, could whack you upside the head, and it wasn't just the embarrassment that stung. They came with velocity. The tall guy would be looking in an entirely different direction and here the ball would be coming right at you.

"I remember one time in one of his early games, I played with my hands down a lot at that time," Charles recalled in 2019. "And he threw a pass to me that would have broke my nose if I didn't duck. It was coming. It was coming so fast and my hands weren't ready and I ducked."

An athletic dunker, Charles had never really thought all that much about playing with his hands up. But sharing the floor with Johnson would quickly make it a top consideration.

"He pushed everybody, encouraged everybody to do better," Charles remembered of Johnson's early days with the program. "He was always cheerful and he never really got down. And he loved to win."

"He had a great personality," Kelser agreed. "He was fun to talk to, fun to be around. He was always smiling. He loved to have a good time. Whether it was just sitting around, shooting the breeze, or at a party on campus. He always enjoyed having a good time. He loved to dance, loved to sing, loved to play basketball, loved to be around people."

The only early drawback was the sound of music.

"He couldn't sing," Kelser explained. "But you couldn't stop him from trying. That was one thing he wasn't very good at. Back in those days, everything was rhythm and blues. There wasn't a whole lot of rap or rock and roll stuff then. It was rhythm and blues. It was those rhythm and blues groups of the '70s. We all got into that."

There didn't seem to be a song that Johnson couldn't butcher. That's why his DJ work was truly valuable. He was spinning records, not singing them. One of the benefits of staying in the Lansing area was that he could continue to expand his DJ work, including stints at one of the area's popular spots, the Bus Stop.

As for his maturing game, the idea had an appeal that got around in time.

"Earvin won those guys over a little bit his freshman year," remembered Fred Stabley, who had been promoted to begin covering Michigan State for the *State Journal*. "Kelser knew right off the bat this guy's great, this guy is going to make everybody great."

Terry Donnelly, a sophomore guard, saw it, too. "I'd heard about him at Everett High School," Donnelly would later remember, "and I'd even seen him play. But it didn't really hit me until I got in the backcourt with him, on the first day of practice. You're running down the floor and you're open and most people can't get the ball to you through two or three people, but all of a sudden the ball's in your hands and you've got a layup."

None of this meant there weren't major problems brewing. Much like Dan Parks during Johnson's sophomore year at Everett, the Spartans had a returning senior in Bob Chapman, a strong, muscular guard who wasn't too keen on being upstaged by a freshman. And Jud Heathcote may have talked sweetly while he was recruiting Johnson, but he didn't seem all that committed to having the ball in the big guy's hands.

George Fox had noticed that immediately in the early practices. The two coaches had become friendly during the recruitment, and afterward Fox had an open invitation to Heathcote's practices. Heathcote had spent years as a high school coach and he didn't hesitate to consult with Fox about Johnson's unique game.

Fox immediately saw that rather than running the fast break, Johnson had been directed to fill the lanes as a finisher. But Fox didn't address the issue with Heathcote because it wasn't his place.

"Jud, you know, had some restrictions on everybody out there," Fox recalled. "Jud was his own man, and I credit him for that."

Fox was impressed with how Johnson responded and was in fact amazed at how easily his former player had moved in as a leader on a college team right away as a freshman.

"He fit in with those college players the same way he did with our high school kids," Fox recalled, "and I thought, 'Boy, that's remarkable that he can go out there as a freshman and take over a college team.' I just liked the way he functioned, the way he got along with those guys, kidding out there on the floor with them and, you know, just had a good time. One thing about playing with Earvin, if he's got the ball, you're going to get it. Now, if you're a poor outside shooter you might stand over there all by yourself. You're not going to get it. But if that outside shooter makes a cut to the basket, if he's open around the basket, he's going to get you the ball."

As far as Johnson controlling every team he played on, at every level, it wasn't any sort of twisted manipulation that kept him in control, Ron Charles observed. "He controlled everybody with his passing."

"That's the thing that Earvin did out there, and that's all the players that ever played with him discovered," George Fox observed, adding that it was Johnson's love of the game sustaining it all.

Unfortunately, that wasn't how things started his freshman season, when he would need all the love he could muster.

The Run

Ron Charles had been born in St. Croix, in the U.S. Virgin Islands, where he spent his early life until his family moved to New York City, where as an athletic six-seven forward he became a basketball star in what Charles described as a very diverse and comfortable culture. In all that time, no one had ever called him the "N word"—until his freshman season at Michigan State in late 1976 when the Spartans played a game at Central Michigan, where the crowd turned decidedly ugly. The atmosphere that day seemed likely a function of the racial division in the state in that era, for which Michigan State's much publicized walkout a few months earlier had become a flashpoint.

Fortunately, a season later when the Spartans played Central Michigan to open the schedule during Johnson's freshman season, the game was held in the friendly confines of Jenison Field House, although that didn't prevent Johnson's nerves from overwhelming his game that day. Pat Holland and George Fox said Johnson's college debut reminded them so much of his first jittery high school contest three seasons earlier.

Never, the coaches averred, had they seen Johnson more nervous than in those two moments. The Spartans won, but the game and its aftermath left Jud Heathcote with a sting.

"I remember the first game that Earvin played," Heathcote told broadcaster Billy Packer nearly a decade later. "I think he had seven points and about eight turnovers, and everyone said, 'Heathcote's crazy. He's got Earvin handling the ball on the break. He's got him out there playing guard on offense. He's got him running the break. He's got him doing so many different things. Nobody can do all those things.'"

Ron Charles himself recalled the media criticism in the aftermath of that game. It must have been a difficult introduction for a tough-guy coach such as Jud Heathcote, teetering on the brink of the moments that would define his career, in a town like Lansing that had taken Magic Johnson as a favorite son over the previous three seasons.

The coach and his team were faced with a sudden and dramatic realignment. It's worth noting that neither Heathcote nor Johnson's college teammates called him Magic. All of them, save his local pal, Jay Vincent, called him "E." To Vincent, though, he was more Magic than ever, throwing those passes one way while looking another.

Not everyone was completely taken with that approach, however. Between Heathcote's concern that clearly bordered on displeasure and Bob Chapman's stewing discontent, Johnson would find a mixed response in his introduction to college basketball over the coming months.

Next the Spartans played in a tournament at Syracuse's Manley Field House, where they dispatched Rhode Island in their opening game before losing to Syracuse by eight in the championship. Fred Stabley recalled that young coach Jim Boeheim was incensed afterward when Johnson was named the tournament's outstanding player despite being on the losing team.

"He was clearly the best player on the floor," Stabley recalled. "That's the one thing I remember."

Stabley was struck that weekend with the answer to what everybody in Lansing seemed to be wondering: Would Magic still be magic in college?

"I think probably the thing that surprised me was how good he was in college, too, you know," Stabley recalled in 2019. "He could do everything he did in high school, maybe not quite the free wheel that he had. But surely he could score; he could still pass the ball wonderfully."

The "free wheel" would have to come later. Heathcote clearly had mixed feelings about how and when Johnson should handle the ball. Much of that was tied into how the coach wanted his teams to operate. First, Heathcote, like so many then and later, was into running a heavy rotation of called plays, which allowed him to control games and, in his mind, secure victory.

"Jud had a deal where he would hold up signs," Pat Holland recalled of Heathcote's hand signals as he stood on the sideline. "This is what play we're gonna run. Earvin was foreign to all of that."

In high school, his coaches had run some half-court sets, but they had quickly come to trust Johnson's constant running and pushing the ball and scoring as he choregraphed almost nonstop fast-breaking finishes as the core of what the team did.

The attacking style that Johnson had been fashioning his entire basketball life was his uncanny ability to pass off the dribble at high speed while converging on the basket. That was the crux of Johnson's genius, Pat Holland offered. "Earvin could do it strongly. He was pushing the ball with such a level of skill. He would see a play developing and know 'that's the instant I have to get the ball there or the guy's not going to score.'"

The slew of early turnovers seemed to have confirmed in Heathcote's mind that Johnson needed to slow down, to stay on his feet, to put the brakes on his high-wire act.

He had a breakthrough of sorts with 20 rebounds and 19 points against Wichita State the fourth game of the season.

"He kept getting better," Ron Charles recalled of Johnson's freshman season, "but I think we learned by playing with him. I remember he had a lot of turnovers, you know, his first couple of games playing. But the turnovers wasn't his fault. The turnovers was because we weren't ready to catch the ball and we wasn't expecting him to pass. Sometimes he was making some amazing passes which would be a turnover for him, but it wasn't his fault."

When Charles was caught unawares by Johnson's passing, it was Johnson who was blamed. "That's not a turnover for me," Charles recalled of how the statistic was recorded. "It was a turnover for Earvin. But you see that some of that stuff we learned, and so, you know, the turnovers went down and we learned his moves by playing with him more because games were different than practice."

It was in games that Johnson began moving into his singular style of play.

The situation would result in something of a running struggle between the coach and Johnson throughout their two seasons together. The moment would stand in retrospect as a question of innovative genius versus convention, of a traditional coach's much valued and preached-about "fundamentals" versus a new and different Black vision for the sport that was only beginning to gain clarity in the public mind, perhaps the most interesting and subtle of many cultural collisions in the social science experiment that was basketball in the 1970s.

"Jud would get on him about passing off the dribble," Charles recalled, pointing out that Heathcote wanted what was then considered the "fundamental," a two-handed pass.

In time, passing off the dribble would come to be seen as Johnson's genius, but not in his new coach's mind. Heathcote, who had just turned fifty in 1977, had already lived a long coaching life, first for 14 seasons in high schools and then another 14 as a college assistant in the Northwest before being named the head coach at the University of Montana for six years where he directed rosters of mostly white players with the notable exception of the astoundingly versatile and flashy Micheal Ray Richardson, a fact that the coach may have trumpeted a bit in dealing with Johnson.

"It was different," Ron Charles said, "because Jud probably never had as much talent as he had at Michigan State with us. So there was probably a cultural breakdown in the way Earvin played."

Former coach Gus Ganakas as well as other older players on the team talked with Johnson to try to help ease the conflict, George Fox recalled. "I think they convinced Earvin how good a coach fundamentally that Jud was. Jud was a disciplinarian and that didn't bother Earvin. But I do think that Earvin viewed Jud with a little skepticism because of his background, where he came from and just everything about Jud, his coaching style, yelling and screaming and getting after kids and disciplining them. But at the same time he respected Jud so much as a fundamental instructor, Earvin was going to learn and get as much out of Jud as he could."

As for passing off the dribble?

"Nobody can make that pass except for Micheal Ray," Charles remembered Heathcote telling Johnson. "We had never heard of a Micheal Ray. Who is this Micheal Ray he's talking about all the time who is so great?"

Later, when they got to see Richardson with the Knicks, they were impressed, Charles recalled. "He was no Magic. He was good, but he was no Magic."

Like many coaches of that era, Heathcote could be harsh, then back off, creating something of a yo-yo, as Johnson's teammate Mike Brkovich once explained to McCabe. "Brkovich said that one of the things he liked about Jud was that he would just be all over you, just killing you in practice. But before you left the gym he would say something encouraging so you didn't leave with a real bad taste in your mouth."

With the passive-aggressive conflict between Johnson and his coach "they both had to have been crazy," two strong wills going back and forth, Charles observed. "Jud definitely wasn't bending a whole lot. So I think Earvin bent a little bit more. We needed Earvin and Earvin respected his coaches."

Johnson, after all, was used to coaches who built their approach around his unique talents. With Heathcote, that only happened in nibbles, Charles said. "Earvin got his way sometimes. They both needed each other. Coach was an excellent teacher and in order to get better you had to listen to Jud coach. And Earvin, he did listen to his coach. He didn't do anything his own way. It wasn't like he was doing stuff that he wanted to do. In the heat of the game he still passed off the dribble sometimes and did things. Earvin handled that well. Now the assistant coaches might not have talked to Earvin or picked on him as much, you know, as Jud, but Jud was a powerful force, a powerful person."

As he had been with the Everett program, Tucker was a quiet factor behind the scenes, always in Johnson's ear, always close with Big Earv, always working at gaining closeness with the coaches, identifying with them, explaining to Johnson why they wanted what they wanted to the point of subtly siding with Heathcote much of the time.

In return, Heathcote allowed him rare free access around the program, Tucker recalled, "because I understood what Jud was about."

That, in itself, gave the coach a chance to succeed with Johnson, because there were things the freshman needed to learn, Tucker recalled. "For a kid coming in like Earvin, the first thing you had to learn coming in was passing lanes. They were not slow no more. The passing lanes closed in on you now. And you can't commit yourself in the air. Because that was his game, with the ball all the time. He found that he had to get used to guys getting up under you when they guarded you and making you turn your back, to where you can't see the help side defense coming."

Even with Tucker's counsel, the relationship between Johnson and his coach, like any fractious chemistry, teetered on the brink that first season, far from the public eye.

"One time Earvin walked out of practice," Tucker recalled of a dramatic development that was apparently never leaked to the media. "This was his first year. Well, that went on for a couple of days. He missed a pick on the baseline, and Jud hollered at him and said, 'Go sit down over there.' That was the way Jud was. You mess up a couple of plays and he'd sit you on the bench. 'You're not ready to practice, not ready to play.' And then I get a call from one of the assistant coaches, and he said, 'Earvin left and he said he ain't coming back.' So all I did—I didn't say a word to Earvin—I went to his father and said, 'You gotta make a decision.' His dad told him to get back up there."

Johnson's walkout apparently sent a successful message and seemed to alter the dynamic a bit in his favor. Heathcote realized anything he hoped to achieve would crumble quickly if he chased off his star.

"Most of the time Jud would pick on everybody he coached," Ron Charles remembered. "He picked on us a lot. He picked on everybody."

In the aftermath, Heathcote would turn more to his "whipping boys," a common practice in coaching of picking on a substitute or a lesser player when a star player messed up, rather than risking a disaster by berating a star and having him sulk or quit the team.

Heathcote backed away from Johnson and began more often taking his frustration out on other players.

"I was one of the ones he picked on all the time," Charles said, "so sometimes I took some of the heat because of the things that Earvin did."

Jay Vincent himself grew quietly indignant at the approach, as he recalled in 2019. "I thought I was a pretty darn good player myself. Every time Magic and Greg Kelser made a mistake, Coach Heathcote would yell at me. So I'm like, 'Whoa. They made the mistakes, not me.' So everybody used to get a chuckle out of that. But you know, Magic did pout a little bit. But superstars? What are coaches going to do? You could yell at the eighth man or the twelfth man, but you can't yell at the superstar. You could kind of be a little stern with him, but you don't get to pound on him. Why? Because he's Magic. Everybody always says everybody's equal, but there's no equal with the superstars of the team. And Magic was a superstar."

Ultimately, this bizarre but rather normal dynamic would go on between Johnson and his coach over parts of two seasons, a back-and-forth that allowed each of them to make gains in increments, according to various witnesses. Heathcote did succeed in containing Johnson's passing off the dribble a bit and in getting him to avoid leaving his feet while making plays at high speed with the ball in his hands.

"I don't think Earvin bent his will," Charles observed. "I think they both came to a happy medium."

Likely so, but as 1977 was turning to 1978, things were neither happy nor medium in the Spartans' camp, despite a growing win streak. As a result of their struggle, Johnson would come to be considered in the long run an even greater outlier, a unique and thrilling revolutionary, and Heathcote would seem a little less of a curmudgeonly hard-ass. Over time, the coach would manage to endear himself to basketball fans in the region almost as much as Johnson himself.

"I'm from Montana, where all the men are men and so are the women," Mick McCabe recalled fondly of Heathcote's comments from his politically incorrect introductory press conference at Michigan State. "He was fun to laugh at because of the stuff like that, just a terrific sense of humor. And he was really good about passing out praise to other people."

For years, long after Heathcote had moved on from Michigan, McCabe would delight in calling and wishing him a happy Mother's Day, because, as the writer explained, looking back in 2019, the coach was quite a mother.

George Fox understandably followed these proceedings in Johnson's first year with great interest.

"It was important to George Fox that Jud sold himself to Earvin," McCabe recalled. "You know, that Earvin could trust him."

One of the early turning points of sorts in Johnson's twisting relationship with his coach and the college game came later in December in a road contest at the University of Detroit, where Dick Vitale had assembled a high-test roster featuring John Long. Vitale had abruptly resigned in the off-season, leaving the program to assistant Smokey Gaines, a former Harlem Globetrotter. Detroit was ranked 15th in the country that week, and even though the Spartans had rolled through four cupcake victories since the loss to Syracuse, a lot of folks figured they'd find a comeuppance in Detroit.

Smokey Gaines wasn't so sure. He had watched over the previous summer as Johnson and Jay Vincent had teamed up to scorch the competition at Detroit's St. Cecilia's. "People talk about Earvin Johnson and Jay Vincent being freshmen," the coach told Charlie Vincent of the *Detroit Free Press*. "They're not freshmen. They played about 55 games together this summer at St. Cecilia against some very good competition. They are really like sophomores or juniors."

On cue, Johnson brilliantly led the Spartans to a smashing 103–74 rout on the road of a Detroit team loaded with talent. It was an early signature win that left close observers thinking that all of Michigan State's early trials might soon be over.

"I remember Bob Chapman walking by me going to the locker room," Fred Stabley said of the moments after the Detroit game. "He looked at me and stopped and said, 'It must be magic.' It was almost like he accepted Earvin now and he kind of accepted the fact that this guy's the real deal."

Time would quickly show that wasn't exactly the case, nor were George Fox's feel-good vibes about Heathcote's developing attitude.

"By Christmas of Earvin's first year Jud personally told me, 'Coach, I can see what you were talking about. We have to make sure he's got the ball early in our up-tempo game,'" Fox recalled. "So Jud adjusted his fast break a little bit and they started going to Earvin in the backcourt, not the frontcourt, and it made a lot of difference. So that was one area I know Jud accepted from Earvin."

There was never a thought of trying to suggest that Heathcote allow Johnson more room to work, Fox recalled. "I never did. I didn't like to get into a messy part of things because I didn't want to lose any friendship, you know. You hate to exercise your right to give an opinion. Jud told me he never realized Earvin was that skilled as a ball handler until Christmas of his freshman year. He finally realized what he had. Up until then, they just ran their old conventional fast break. He said, 'Well, I'm seeing it now.' And that's when he started letting Earvin handle the ball and run the fast break."

Greg Kelser saw the issues more as a function of the pressure of a program trying to grow from long-term mediocre status to very good in a hurry. "I think there's always pressure to succeed," Kelser said in 2019 of Johnson's first college season. "Absolutely, there was pressure. Our coach, Jud Heathcote, did a great job of probably shielding some of the expectations of the media and the public at large. He provided a nice cover and force field around his basketball program, so all we had to do really was work hard and be coachable and try to get better and the results would speak for themselves, which is exactly what happened."

One thing that had been obvious from the start for all involved was that however Johnson played, he was going to make everybody else dramatically better as they got used to his style.

"He made Kelser and all those guys better because none of them was a ball handler," Charles Tucker recalled. "They had a lot of athletic skills, especially Greg Kelser. And Jay Vincent was big. And he had some skills. Ron Charles was the kind of guy who could get up."

The effect of his presence on the program was likely more obvious to Johnson himself than anyone. After all, he had been going against the State players in Jenison Field House since his early teens.

"He assumed that he was the best, and he was," Tucker said. "But when you transfer that into the Big Ten you're not going to be that great, not immediately. And you found out that those guys on those State teams who were losing, the only reason they were losing is that they needed some more talent. They had talent, but they hadn't had enough to win, because all of them were forwards. If one of them was a guard, maybe they would have won more before he got there."

The effect of his presence would become even more obvious in early January when the Spartans launched into the all-important portion of their schedule, the Big Ten conference games. In that era, only the conference champion went to the NCAA tournament. Some conferences held a tournament at the end of the season, but not the

Big Ten. The regular season meant everything, which left some very good teams each year just short of making what would come to be known as "March Madness." In the wake of John Wooden retiring and the end of the UCLA dynasty in 1975, the Big Ten Conference was on its way to reestablishing its own power in college basketball as a big, strong physical league loaded with talent.

Johnson had his first taste of that competition when Minnesota and his new acquaintance, Bill Duffy, came to East Lansing. Or, perhaps more accurately, the league got its first taste of Johnson.

"We played them in our first Big Ten game that season, our freshmen season," Duffy recalled in 2019. "We had a film session like three days before we played them in the Big Ten opener at Michigan State."

In that session, Duffy warned his older teammates Mychal Thompson and Kevin McHale, both of whom were headed to outstanding NBA careers, "Look, you guys don't understand how good this Magic Johnson is."

"I remember Mychal saying, 'He's only a freshman,'" Duffy said. "And I said, 'No. No. No. You don't understand. Trust me. This guy can play.'"

Clearly Minnesota's team leaders weren't all that impressed.

With his skeptical older teammates, Duffy landed in a new world that January, far from the old one that Michigan State basketball had inhabited for years.

"So, we go to Lansing, Michigan," Duffy recalled. "We fly in and right as we got off the plane and got in a bus to go to the hotel, I see a billboard that said, 'Welcome to the Magic Kingdom.' And I pointed it out to those guys and said, 'See, look at this.' I don't think McHale and Thompson really paid attention to the scouting stuff. They were like, 'Whatever.' So we played Michigan State in Jenison Field House and, when they came out onto the floor for the layup line, the whole student section was on the perimeter of the court. They were all on their knees, bowing down and they were chanting, 'Magic . . . Magic . . . Magic.' Our guys were looking around and saying, 'What is this?' I told the guys, 'You'll see.' And Magic went out and he beat us. Magic was in complete command. At halftime, I told the guys, 'I told you this guy can play.' It was unbelievable."

Johnson had illustrated Duffy's point that day by scoring a season-high 31 with nine rebounds, driving the Spartans to their seventh straight win and a 9–1 record. From there they whipped off six more critical Big Ten wins, good enough to take the lead in the conference and raise eyebrows all across college basketball.

In that streak had come their first conference road win, at Illinois, which left Illini coach Lou Henson impressed. "Michigan State is an excellent team," he told reporters. "It's hard to beat its zone defense and slow down its fast break. In Earvin Johnson, Michigan State has a six-eight freshman who can do things like no other freshman I've ever seen. He's ready for the pros now."

By the time the Spartans won by 10 points at Ohio State in late January, they were 15–1 and ranked seventh in the Associated Press top 25 poll, and a few more basketball fans nationwide were aware of Magic Johnson.

Mick McCabe was walking out of the locker room after the game when Johnson stepped out of the shower with a furtive request.

"Hey," the freshman said, "why don't you do a story on our captain?"

There had been a sense of friction between him and senior Bob Chapman off and on through the season.

"Really?" McCabe said.

"Yeah, that'd be good," Johnson answered. "That'd be real good."

In Johnson's mind, it only made sense. He had been getting so much of the publicity and acclaim. The muscular Chapman had the perfect build for a strong safety in football. He had had a window of opportunity to turn pro after his junior season and had turned it down to return to school and help Heathcote build the team.

"Earvin thought that would be a good ego boost for the kid who needed it," McCabe recalled of the article he would write. "Because he expected to come back and kind of have a great senior year and be the man and he wasn't the man obviously."

Not only had Johnson played forward, center, and guard as a freshman, he was now filling in as a media relations director at an expert level. He knew that team chemistry would benefit from Chapman getting the publicity he deserved. And he conveyed that so discreetly that no one else on the team was ever aware of it.

Chapman and Kelser were the official team captains that season, but obviously Johnson was the team's real leader, Ron Charles said.

"He was a leader and coach allowed him to lead," Ron Charles explained.

With his unbounded enthusiasm for seemingly every nuance of every play, for his length of floor celebrations of passes and rebounds and made shots by his teammates, it might well have been impossible for Heathcote or any other coach to limit Johnson's leadership.

Kelser and Chapman certainly weren't going to do it, although Chapman had been the cooler of the two. Kelser was extremely bright but far from the effervescent alpha that was Johnson.

"Greg was and still is a cool guy, a nice guy," Jay Vincent recalled in 2019. "I mean, he can jump out of the gym, one of the greatest dunkers I've ever seen. He was dominant when it came down to dunking a basketball and showing what he can do. He was a great leader but far as trying to be dominant? No. Greg was just a down-to-earth, cool guy, and he still is."

Like Heathcote, Kelser was willing to allow the freshman to lead.

The team's chemistry and camaraderie would need every boost they could get because the Spartans' joyride would come to an abrupt halt just days after Johnson planted the story idea with McCabe, first with a road loss against a rebuilding Indiana team.

The second blow came against Michigan in Jenison Field House, with Boston Celtics assistant K. C. Jones in attendance to get a look at Johnson. The Celtics had a top pick in the upcoming 1978 draft, and team boss Red Auerbach had some ideas up his sleeve. But first they wanted to get a closer look at Johnson.

A reporter had asked Jones, a big part of the heart of the Celtics dynasty that had won 11 championships in 13 seasons during the Russell era, what it was like to look at Johnson. It was like looking at Bill Russell or Kareem, Jones replied instantly, words that left Johnson glowing when he read them later.

In the meantime, however, Johnson's enthusiasm and that of a jubilant and growing Spartan fan base had been deflated by the last-second loss to Michigan, State's sixth straight loss to its rival with only a single win in the past dozen games.

There was criticism in the press that Johnson was too much of a showboat and that Heathcote was maybe outsmarting himself.

"It was a learning experience," Tucker remembered, "because at that time the Big Ten was really tough. Every night you faced a challenge. Michigan, Purdue. Northwestern was good at that time. Illinois was good. Wisconsin. Every team out of ten teams had a pro on it. Iowa had Ronnie Lester. Every team had at least one future pro on it. Ohio State had two. Indiana had two. Michigan had two. . . . And each team had a name coach. Johnny Orr, Bobby Knight, and those guys. Tex Winter. Gene Keady at Purdue. You had people who could coach against you."

In retrospect, that first Big Ten experience proved to be the training ground for Johnson's greatness. "There are key things that most players have to learn coming into the Big Ten," Tucker related. "Everything's a little tougher, that you're going to get bumped every time. You're going to get caught in the air a lot because that's what they do with point guards. You think you've got that space. And all at once you don't have it once you make your play. Then you think you got to pass. It looks open but then it closes so quickly. Then you think you've got a lane right there to drive through, but by the time you get there that lane is closed. And you got a charge or a trip or something."

The assist that seemed so beautiful in high school just a season earlier was now a Big Ten turnover.

"With him, just adjusting to that level of play," Tucker said, "and adjusting to the individual talent, and going up against the coaching you're going up against, coaches that are setting up things against you, setting up their team against you. They're coaching against your team but they're also coaching against you."

Not only were the coaches very good but they were at the conference's very large universities with the resources for film study and the unfolding technology of videotape. They watched him again and again against retreating defenses, saw the relentless right hand and the high dribble that accommodated his amazingly long strides. They tried to analyze his growing and changing wizardry with the basketball, something that had never been encountered in the entire history of the game and certainly not in the volume that Johnson unleashed it.

"Once he began to understand," Tucker said, thinking back on those beautiful moments, "he didn't have anything on his mind. It was just a learning process."

"He was hard to defend," Ron Charles remembered. "I used to like to defend Earvin in our pickup games to try and figure out what he was doing. I knew he was going right most of the time, but you still couldn't stop him. He was strong."

Johnson and his teammates lashed back from the pair of losses with a good win over Indiana, a tight victory over Iowa, followed by an immensely satisfying win by 11 at Michigan (with Johnson's 25 leading the way) that left Wolverines coach Johnny Orr fussing that this Magic needed to go ahead and turn pro and get out of the conference, which in turn added to all the other commentary that had Johnson dreaming and thinking.

He quickly came back to earth with a 19-point loss to Purdue where the Spartan defense gave up 99 points, but that proved the final jolt needed to reel off four more tough wins to claim the conference championship in a game at Wisconsin, a streak where Johnson scored 32 against Ohio State amidst a whirlwind of Kelser and Charles dunks as Johnson read the floor with astounding insight.

First, it was his size, Ron Charles explained. He was big enough, strong enough, mobile enough, to shift the entire course of the conference by creating matchup nightmares for opposing guards. Big Ten guards had size and strength, but Johnson could see over them. And State's break led to him uncorking all sorts of passes and alley-oops for Kelser to finish.

In the half-court, Johnson had gained an eye for feasting on the weak side, where defenses naturally relaxed just an instant, allowing him to strike with one of his burning no-looks. By then, Charles

Johnson with his parents, Earvin Sr. and mother Christine, far right, along with pregnant wife Cookie, in a joyful moment after the 1992 All Star Game in Orlando. *(Steve Lipofsky)*

Johnson's relationship with Kareem Abdul-Jabbar formed the essence of his career. They are shown here on the bench in 1982. *(Steven A. Roseboro)*

Johnson as a senior in 1977. *(Full Court Press Collection, courtesy of George Fox)*

Seniors and coaches from the 1977 Everett High varsity team. Kneeling in front are George Fox, left, and Pat Holland. Standing behind them, from left, are Dean Hartley, Paul Dawson, Earvin Johnson, Larry Hunter, and Jamie Huffman. *(Full Court Press Collection, courtesy of George Fox)*

Everett High coach George Fox and Johnson in 1977. *(Full Court Press Collection, courtesy of George Fox)*

Michigan State was ready to double-team Larry Bird at every turn in the 1979 NCAA championship game. *(Full Court Press Collection, courtesy of Indiana State Sports Information)*

Michigan State coach Jud Heathcote was known for his sideline presence and antics. *(Full Court Press Collection, courtesy of Michigan State Sports Information)*

After struggling in championship moments in his first two high school seasons, Johnson would come to see himself as the consummate winner. *(Full Court Press Collection, courtesy of George Fox)*

Jerry Buss and daughter Jeanie. *(Full Court Press Collection, courtesy of Jeanie Buss)*

TOP: Philadelphia 76er Julius Erving, Lakers broadcasting legend Chick Hearn, and Johnson. Erving's 76ers would meet Johnson's Lakers for the league championship three times in Johnson's first four seasons. *(Steven A. Roseboro)*

BOTTOM: Johnson's smile soon became another of his trademarks. *(Steven A. Roseboro)*

The acrobatic attacks by Julius Erving always proved a major challenge for Johnson and his Lakers teammates. Erving was Johnson's teen idol. *(Steven A. Roseboro)*

Johnson made each Lakers fast break a classic. *(Steven A. Roseboro)*

Fox's team of leftovers, led by Dale Beard, at Everett High were on their way to challenging for a second state title, operating off what Johnson had taught them about winning and eager to show they could do it without him. They, too, were gaining their first of many experiences of watching Johnson define and dominate the sport at its highest levels. That spring of 1978, they and all of the witnesses in Lansing were gaining their first sense of just what he could do.

"By his own work ethic and his style of play everybody wanted him on their side," Fox recalled of his own amazement that spring. "That's what I remember a lot about Earvin Johnson. How he could just get kids to want to play with him."

Which meant there was now no one grinding on Michigan State's developing team chemistry that spring, not Bob Chapman, not Earvin Johnson, not even Jud Heathcote.

"We didn't have anybody who was bigger than anybody else," Ron Charles explained. "Nobody was hurting the team chemistry. That's another tribute to Coach Heathcote because the chemistry was there. Magic was a leader and coach was a leader."

"Earvin didn't let a lot of things interfere with him because he wasn't involved in a lot of craziness," Tucker recalled of the circumstances. "Sometimes people from the outside can get involved with the guys on a team. There was not as much of that back then as there is now. But there was some of it. They'll tell you when to shoot, when not to shoot, and how you should be coached, what you shouldn't do. And they don't know anything about the game themselves, but they can tell you everything. And so sometimes that gets confusing. You get your friends and people you admire, and they get too close to you for the wrong reasons."

In everyone's mind in Johnson's inner circle it all justified Big Earv's quiet belief that his son should stay close by for this first big step of his career. Earvin didn't have a lot of those debilitating distractions that could derail a season or even a career, Tucker said, "because his dad was there. And then I was in the background. And Earvin had always been smart enough. With certain things, he was only going to communicate with certain people. He was the kind of guy to look you right in your face and say, 'Yeah, I understand.'"

Then Johnson would turn around and revisit what you were telling him with his trusted inner circle.

"We might respond if we had to," Tucker recalled. "Then, being with his dad—his dad was really into sports. And I played every day, two or three times a day. He saw that. He saw how his family was just a good churchgoing family, churchgoing mom, churchgoing dad. So he was raised in that good environment. And then I was kind of like the old-fashioned guy. I didn't do anything. Never did smoke. Never did drink. None of that. I always was just playing ball. And going to work every day. So he was around a pretty good environment."

Combined with Tucker's attempts to keep things close with Heathcote, things pulled together very well that spring, the psychologist recalled. "Jud knew what he could do, and he was smart enough to know he had to make adjustments. And Earvin made adjustments."

The last regular season game was in Minnesota where the Spartans squeezed out a one-point win and Johnson again encountered new friend Bill Duffy.

"I told him during the game, 'Hey, we're going to have a party at my apartment after the game,'" Duffy recalled. "Back then, you didn't fly back home after the game. You stayed the night. So he comes over to the apartment and he starts deejaying. He starts controlling the music. He controls the music for the rest of the night. We're all like, 'Wow. Look at this guy. He comes to our party and takes over. He does it all.'"

Indeed, Johnson had reason to celebrate. He was the freshman who had just led basketball-flaky Michigan State to its first Big Ten title in two decades with a record of 15–3 in the conference (25–5 overall), which resulted in his being touted as the first freshman ever named to the All-Conference team. He had earned that honor while averaging 17 points, 7.9 rebounds, and 7.4 assists per game.

And now he was headed to the Big Dance.

15

ANOTHER PROMISED LAND

After winning the last game of the regular season at Minnesota early that March, Earvin Johnson was greeted at the Lansing airport by a mob of autograph-hungry young fans. He looked around quizzically at all the paper and pens being shoved his way through a small sea of extended arms and urgent faces, signed what he could, then made his escape through a back door.

Nineteen years earlier, Michigan State had won a Big Ten title behind the talents of military veteran Johnny Green, who had shown up on campus as a strange, unexpected gift, Fred Stabley explained. "Johnny Green was a wonderful player. He was in the Marines. A funny story, an assistant coach came down on the floor to tell Forddy Anderson, Michigan State's basketball coach, about him. You just never interrupted Forddy at practice at Jenison in those days."

"Forddy," the assistant supposedly said meekly in interrupting Anderson. "You've got to come upstairs and see this."

Anderson went up to the auxiliary gym, Stabley said, "and there's Johnny Green, about six foot five, I think, from Dayton, Ohio, throwing the ball off the backboard and dunking it. Time and time and time again. Of course, Forddy's eyes ballooned out."

In no time, Michigan State had an African American star, a twenty-two-year-old freshman, for its basketball team. Green would lead the Spartans to that conference championship and the NCAA tournament, perform his student teaching in East Lansing, and after graduation would join the New York Knicks as a twenty-six-year-old rookie. He would go on to average double figures over a 14-year pro career with several teams.

State's basketball fortunes had been mostly thin until Johnson had come along two decades later as the heir to Green's legacy, now with the school's second Big Ten championship in hand. This next level of success had proved to be brand-new and exciting for the school's suddenly ballooning fan base in the spring of 1978, but it would also bring a growing understanding of just how precarious it all would be for Johnson, never mind the image he projected, that everything he did was easy and accompanied by his ever-present smile.

To close observers, the only indication of his dueling emotions was a certain tightness of his face behind that smile, often around his eyes. How could it not have been so for such an effervescent optimist, an extrovert also just beginning to gain a sense of the burden of being Magic, of being a light that was on virtually all the time to comfort and assure those around him? If even a shadow crossed his face, it could set off alarms for teammates and others. Fortunately, if he turned moody, he usually didn't stay that way long.

"He's a showman," longtime friend Dale Beard said, looking back at that time when Johnson was eighteen and trying to rule a bigger world. "And Earvin always wanted to put on a good show no matter where he was. He wanted to win. And I mean, the guy still had the big smile. He was always in a good mood and he just wanted to win, man."

His reward for that was the love and joy and desire he inspired in more and more people, a multiplier in his life, a nourishment that he seemingly craved more with each passing day. And that included his dealings with reporters and writers, just about all of whom were white. A divide could readily be found for any athlete in that interaction, especially Black athletes who often seemed extra wary in their dealings with the media. Not Johnson, who just smiled and turned loose his charisma with responses that allowed reporters to relax and fill their notebooks and stories with his comments. He was blessed with a gift for putting them at ease in an era when just about every time a sports reporter asked a question there was a crossing of the country's racial divide.

It helped that Johnson was part of a second wave of integration of sports in America, the first wave populated by greats such as Jackie Robinson in baseball, Bill Russell and Wilt Chamberlain in basketball, Jim Brown in football, stars who had to deal with what they saw as a frequently contemptuous media that perpetrated a disconnect with the public.

By the time Johnson emerged in 1978, integration of Black stars into American sports leagues had been underway for decades. Even so, the process of racial integration and media relations still had a very long way to go, and Earvin Johnson would quickly become one of the foremost figures quietly leading the way. For years now, reporters and other media figures from Lansing and Detroit, all across Michigan, had found themselves irresistibly drawn to his side. And, now, with his emergence onto the national stage, Johnson found that his charm was working quite well there, too.

As longtime college basketball broadcaster Billy Packer observed, looking back on the era, "Magic just had an incredible personality that, you know, if he hadn't scored a point, you'd still like him as a guy."

At the same time, Johnson was nearing that phase of his life where eluding his own fame would become a growing challenge, especially since he enjoyed that fame so much. After all, it was a measure of his great and growing power, and he flexed it by engaging and interacting irrepressibly with people everywhere he went.

At that moment, however, he remained in one very real sense just a college student majoring in telecommunications. Smack-dab in the middle of the NCAA tournament he would have to take four exams in two days on a Monday and a Tuesday. Already, as Tim Staudt observed, Johnson was showing some progress in the things that had limited him as adolescent, the diction and clarity issues.

His partying at Bill Duffy's place in Minnesota notwithstanding, Johnson told reporters that he preferred the basketball road trips because they got him away from all the distraction of his friends back on campus and allowed him time for a little studying. He would later confirm that he was already deeply into his growing camp of female followers despite a developing relationship with Cookie Kelly. "He was a player," friend and teammate Ron Charles said of Johnson at Michigan State, using the term for males eager to engage the female population, with Charles admitting he himself was much the same. "To be honest, all basketball players will be players and be happy in that place. If you're winning, you know, at that time women were going to be knocking down your door to get with you. It was the late '70s. I don't care if you're Black or white or Hispanic, whatever, if you're an athlete . . . they just want to have fun, right? That's just my belief."

And the more Johnson and the Spartans won, the more the women knocked on those doors. On a campus of 45,000 students, in that era before the consequences of sexual frivolity came crashing down on American culture, there was plenty of fun to be had. Indeed, it was often referred to as "good, red-blooded American fun."

In truth, Johnson was already starting to mourn those carefree college days even before they were over. He had seen the news reports over his first season about pro basketball executives singing his praises and expressing hope that he might claim financial hardship and enter the NBA draft that spring of 1978. The mere thought of that, of the big money and the big challenge of playing in the NBA against the game's best players, all sent his thoughts racing when he lay down to sleep at night. He had been thinking about the NBA since his days of grade school fantasies seeded by watching games with Big Earv. Now, it seemed, with every game he played those dreams moved closer to reality, just as friends and family had long predicted they would.

Based on those dreams, he assumed he knew what was ahead. But he had no idea.

The Madness

While pro basketball executives were very much aware of who he was, Johnson wasn't quite yet "nationwide" in terms of being known by the basketball fan base, although the NCAA tournament that spring would begin to change that. Media organizations had just begun promoting the event as "March Madness," a name that would catch on and help lead to immense growth in both popularity and revenue for the college game.

It was no small coincidence that Earvin Johnson was taking his first small step into the spotlight just as this "Madness" was awakening and that he would soon enough come to be seen as a major force in driving it.

The April day that previous spring that Johnson had committed to Michigan State, Tim Staudt had walked into his boss's office at the CBS affiliate in Lansing and suggested the station put together a package to broadcast Spartan games. The affiliate also owned a sister radio station, and his boss initially thought Staudt was talking about radio.

"No, I mean television," Staudt recalled telling his boss. "In those days, there was no television package for Michigan State basketball."

There was a Big Ten game of the week broadcast regionally on TV, but the Spartans had found trouble gaining much attention there, not with Michigan, Indiana, and other conference powerhouses taking the spotlight.

"And there was no cable," Staudt explained. "There was no ESPN. There was a single Big Ten game of the week. That was pretty much it."

In retrospect, it was a stark media landscape in terms of all that would come later, but at the time the newness of it all made it fresh and exciting, especially for a guy like Tim Staudt.

With a pitch that Jenison seated just under ten thousand and that the audience for Johnson had already proved much larger than that, the station negotiated a rights fee of about a hundred bucks a game, which Michigan State athletic department officials readily agreed to, Staudt recalled. "They bought that."

Not only would fans get to see Magic, but they'd witness him going up against great talent in what many believed was the toughest league in college basketball at the time. And Johnson's first season there had not disappointed in the least.

The quality of Big Ten basketball in that era was unreal, Staudt offered, "because you had seniors playing college basketball, which you don't have today. Today, the good players in college basketball are long gone to the NBA well before they get to their senior year."

The idea that a top player might leave school early for a pro basketball contract was still settling over the game.

As it was, American television likewise offered a nearly barren landscape as far as national college basketball programming in the spring of 1978. Few in the industry had realized the amounts of money to be made by developing the college sport as a broadcast property. Just about the only national broadcast of games was done by NBC, the network that also held exclusive rights to broadcasting the NCCA tournament, a property that in time would generate billions in March Madness revenue for the NCAA and its top college programs.

Thus, the 1978 Mideast Regional final of the tournament would offer Johnson's coming-out party in terms of national television exposure. Indeed, the broadcast would mark the first time that Jerry West of the Lakers laid eyes on Johnson. And West would come away with decidedly mixed feelings about this very unusual young player.

With the tournament field consisting of just 32 teams in that era, seventh-ranked Michigan State needed to win just three games to get to the much coveted Final Four, the holy grail for college basketball programs. First the Spartans flexed their great quickness in beating a Providence team coached by Dave Gavitt in the first round in Market Square Arena in Indianapolis, which sent them on to the regional in Dayton, Ohio. There in mid-March they had faced a Western Kentucky team that had carried a losing record into January only to come alive with a winning surge down the stretch.

The Spartans laid 90 points on the Hilltoppers in a big win that had featured a head-scratching performance from Johnson. On the one hand, he made just three of his 17 shots from the floor. On the other, he passed out 14 assists, his career-high at the time.

"It didn't matter," Johnson said afterward of the 14 shots he missed. "I didn't need them tonight."

Perhaps, but it was tournament time again, where confidence seeded survival, where one situation or another had always seemed to leave him teetering on the brink of failure. That, in all fairness, was the very nature of basketball itself. But a better shooting performance certainly would have been most useful two days later in the regional championship, his first truly high-profile game on national television, a showdown between his seventh-ranked Spartans and the number one–ranked team in the country, the University of Kentucky Wildcats, coached by Joe B. Hall, a large, bespectacled man who always seemed weighed down by some unseen force. If Magic Johnson was the picture of fun and flamboyance in the age of disco, Joe B. Hall seemed a snapshot of unarticulated misery, like an insurance man pondering his mountain of a sales quota.

There, standing courtside to introduce Johnson to the nationwide broadcast, was a savvy, self-assured twenty-nine-year-old host named Bryant Gumbel, another major revelation in his own right in terms of the gradual shifting of public perception of race in America.

The announcing crew for the game was led by play-by-play legend Curt Gowdy, who had played for Wyoming in the early 1940s before spending decades championing and pioneering the TV broadcasts of the tournament. Doing the "color" analysis of the game that Saturday afternoon was Billy Packer, who had played for Wake Forest in the 1962 Final Four. These two gentlemen represented the "establishment" of the sport, bolstered by their elite status broadcasting the sport's biggest games. Packer was on his way to serving for decades as the lead analyst for each year's championship event. Both men were eager to introduce what they called this "eighteen-year-old kid," clearly already a candidate for one of the most unique and intriguing players in the era, which presented only one problem. Gowdy and Packer had run through an entire season of doing games but had not seen Michigan State with its looming specter of a guard play even a single minute. Nor had they seen recorded footage of him playing even though videotape was coming into use in the industry. At the time, there was not a single major national highlight show in American sports television.

"I basically had read about him but had never seen him play until the NCAA tournament his freshman year," recalled Packer, who sat atop the roost of college basketball experts in that era. "I got assigned to their game against Kentucky, which was a regional final. At that point I didn't really know anything about him as a person. Mostly what you heard was his flamboyant style. And you never heard much about any individual techniques other than he was a great passer and he had this flamboyancy about him that was special and obviously that he had played very well as a freshman for Michigan State."

Packer did know Jud Heathcote a bit. The coach had gained some prominence in the 1975 NCAA tournament when his Montana team almost upset the great John Wooden's Bruins in the last season of his UCLA dynasty. The son of a Pennsylvania coach, Packer was considered an intense and highly opinionated analyst in breaking down the game, usually from a coach's perspective, which made sense because college basketball in that era was very much a game dominated by its high-profile coaches.

Johnson's style and size alone had been enough to create a number of skeptics as he broke into the regional spotlight that freshman season. As Packer prepared to broadcast the regional, he was curious to see how a hard-ass like Heathcote managed to coexist with this flamboyant eighteen-year-old. Johnson's poor shooting performance against Western Kentucky had raised a few eyebrows, including Packer's.

Kentucky had a big, strong, tough, veteran team, thus the game had been billed as "Magic vs. The Muscle" in the Lansing paper. As a telecommunications major, Johnson was well aware of what the national exposure meant. There weren't many national games broadcast in that era before cable, but the ones that were available tended to capture the attention of lots of fans.

NBC reported that tickets were being scalped at what was then a whopping one hundred dollars apiece outside the arena that day, with Kentucky's hoops-crazy fans and a new cadre of believers from Michigan State converging on the place.

"Kentucky had a veteran team that was well drilled," Packer explained in 2019. "It was a very tight team. They were under a lot of pressure."

Hall had been selected to succeed the legendary Adolph Rupp at Kentucky, and while Hall had won a series of Southeastern Conference titles, that wasn't enough, Packer recalled. "Anything less than the national championship was not going to be acceptable in the state of Kentucky, and Joe Hall was under a lot of pressure."

As a result, Hall's veteran team was just about always well prepared, recalled Jack "Goose" Givens, a standout on that 1978 team. "Most of our conversation centered on Magic and making sure that we control him and his ability to penetrate and get shots for his teammates. We talked a lot about their matchup zone and a lot of the problems that it could potentially cause us. Of course, Magic was often on the top of that zone."

Indeed, the sight of Johnson's size and length out front on that zone as a threateningly large spiderlike figure gave opponents reason for pause, although Johnson also spent lots of time taking up an interior position in the defense.

For years afterward, the narrative on the game would be that Heathcote's conservative style cost the Spartans dearly that day. It was, however, very much the age of slowdown basketball in the college game, with Dean Smith's Four Corners offense at North Carolina having vexed opponents and infuriated fans across the spectrum. Many claimed that Smith was ruining the game, and indeed the slowdown practices, what was called "taking the air out of the ball," would result soon enough in the college game getting its own shot clock.

In the interim, coaches deployed the tactic freely. And Joe B. Hall, although his ball club could force turnovers and score in bunches, was determined to control the tempo against Michigan State that day. At one point in the first half, the Wildcats would have one possession that ran through two minutes of moving the ball around against the Michigan State zone before taking a shot.

This showdown in terms of style had served to increase the interest in Johnson's first big TV appearance that Saturday afternoon, not that NBC spent all that much time or effort in promoting it. It was not articulated at the time, but to many coaches and fans, Johnson already represented a great hope of an antidote for the slowdown tactics that were choking the fun out of the college game like kudzu.

To their credit, Gowdy and Packer teed up Johnson's appearance and the viewers' expectations appropriately. However, what they witnessed that afternoon was mostly a growing desperation that resulted in a huge flop.

"You're going to have games where you don't play well," Charles Tucker said in 2019.

The broadcasters and the public were straining against hope that day to see the tall, beaming, hand-slapping, joyful rumor of a competitor who promised a much livelier strain of basketball, one who could deliver the sport to an entirely new age, one driven by dizzying passes, astounding finishes, boundless energy, unbridled emotion, and fetching theatrics.

That full iteration of Magic Johnson couldn't be seen yet, but he was coming.

Oddly, Heathcote came out that day with first Bob Chapman and then Terry Donnelly bringing up the ball instead of Johnson. Perhaps it didn't matter. Perhaps the coach had sensed or come to believe that Johnson could be keyed up to the max for big games and that it was better to let him settle in rather than giving him a sense of control over the proceedings from the start.

When Johnson did get his hands on the ball in the first half, he took rushed, awkward shots and gave up several turnovers while trying to display his whizbang passing mojo.

"We played strict man-to-man defense," Givens recalled. "That was our focus. That was what we were good at."

Yet Johnson and his teammates slowly found their way against Kentucky's man defense, good enough to take a five-point lead at the half. Considering the game's pace, the size of that lead threatened to end Kentucky's run. Then the Spartans executed a play to score off the opening tip for the second half.

At halftime, Hall had realized his team couldn't match up man-to-man with State's quickness, no matter how well they played. So, he abandoned his man and went to a 1–3–1 zone for much of the final period.

"Out of the 1–3–1 we were able to double-team a lot, particularly when the ball was up front," Goose Givens recalled in 2019. "And we would force Magic to one side or the other. We wouldn't let him operate from right at the top of the key. So, by forcing him one direction or the other, that gave us a lot of opportunities to double-team the ball. And it forced him to give it up and into a lot of turnovers. We forced them into bad passes a lot, and we were able to kind of keep them under control by doing that."

Abruptly, Michigan State underwent a painful search for shots in the second half against Kentucky's zone. Slowly, Chapman and Kelser showed they could get enough shots to keep it very close.

The real factor came about midway through the second half when Johnson picked up his fourth foul. "We knew we couldn't win with him sitting on the bench," Heathcote recalled in 1986, "so he kept playing and played very conservatively, very cautiously."

More than anything perhaps, the game that day revealed the immense challenge that Johnson faced in pushing the tempo under the college rules of the era. There was no shot clock to push the agenda, no three-point shot. Later, in the twenty-first century, the rules interpreters would hype the sport to push its pace. They would cut the timeline violation to eight seconds from 10; they would trim the reset of the shot clock after an offensive rebound to 14 seconds from 24 to prevent teams from executing half-court offenses.

All of these things were done to allow star players to score more points. The use of analytics brought a new math to dictate how the game would be played, which meant that just about all two point shots except layups and dunks would be eschewed for three-pointers.

In 1978, basketball was merely starting the steps to such a new, juiced-up game, but the ideas behind the move had been around for decades.

Pro basketball had learned since its earliest days that its successful business model was to promote star players who scored lots of points. That was how Eddie Gottlieb, the owner of the Philadelphia Warriors when the NBA was formed in 1946, set the tone for a league that found itself immediately struggling to survive. In those early years, Gottlieb turned loose "Jumpin' Joe" Fulks, a Kentucky hillbilly who wowed fans with his new style of shot, a jumper, to become the sport's first player to average 20 points a game. Gottlieb had made sure Fulks played lots of minutes so he could score lots of points to attract fans. In 1959, Gottlieb deployed center Wilt Chamberlain in the same manner, playing him huge minutes to score lots of points to sell enough tickets to allow his team and the league to survive in that era when pro basketball franchises routinely failed. Gottlieb knew that statistics mattered when it came to generating interest and selling tickets.

It could be argued that on that Saturday in March 1978, eighteen-year-old Earvin "Magic" Johnson stood almost alone as a pioneer, playing a sport with no real sense of its own direction, with a college game trying to find a new level of pace and excitement despite its coaches, with a pro game still struggling mightily through a third decade of doldrums, trying to find a successful business model.

That day, Johnson would be caught in the web of the game, almost like a gossamer-winged creature trying to break free of its cocoon.

He would take 10 shots and make only two of them, thus leaving him a miserable five for 27 in the Mideast Regional. He would have four assists but he gained them by making six turnovers. Even so, his team stayed close, despite the trouble of an array of touch fouls called against Johnson that left broadcasters Gowdy and Packer fussing about the official in the two-man crew who called them. Johnson would play much of the second half with four fouls. Chapman and Donnelly, State's other two ball handlers, would foul out. Even so, the Spartans would keep it close down to the very end before losing 52–49, with Kentucky guard Kyle Macy hitting a number of free throws down the stretch.

Many observers said the Spartans' loss that day came as Macy got untracked with a series of screens set by center Rick Robey, but Heathcote always pointed to his team's struggles offensively in the second half against Kentucky's zone.

"My assistant and I would talk about that game," Heathcote admitted to Billy Packer in 1986, "and thought that if we had done a little better coaching job we would have won a national championship that year."

Nearly a decade later, Joe B. Hall would tell Packer that Michigan State was his team's biggest challenge on the way to winning the national championship that year.

"That was a tough game for us to advance. That's for sure," Givens recalled. "Even with him not playing a Magic Johnson type game. We tried to make him as uncomfortable as we could. When you get a guy with that much talent, no one player's going to be able to stop him, and we understood that going into the game."

Taken with the failure to win the ninth-grade championship, the strange playoff collapses his first two years of high school, then having to watch the closing moments of his team's state championship from the bench, this disappointment against Kentucky sat as something of a pattern for eighteen-year-old Magic Johnson, one that he would be loath to acknowledge over the years in establishing the major narrative of his life as one of the game's all-time great winners. That day, however, Johnson readily confessed.

"He played terrible," recalled Mick McCabe, one of his longtime fans in the media. "He took full blame for it in the press conference afterwards. Earvin said, 'I played horribly.' And Kelser got up there and said, 'I totally disagree with Earvin. It wasn't him. It was all of us. He didn't play that bad; you know stats don't show everything else he did for the team.' But he took full responsibility for that."

Mostly, Johnson sensed he wanted to be done with college basketball, with his mind on the bigger things awaiting him.

Love Land

As it turned out, Johnson wasn't even done with Joe B. Hall. Or the Kentucky roster, for that matter. Or even Billy Packer. The broadcaster had partnered with sports media producer Eddie Einhorn to put together a TV event just days after the Final Four. It would be a three-city, round-robin tour of the United States featuring three foreign clubs, including the Russian national team, large and tough veterans of international play, against an all-star team of American college players, coached by Joe B. Hall. The core of the American team was comprised of players from the University of Kentucky.

Among the deep subs were Earvin Johnson and a six-nine, blond-haired forward from Indiana State named Larry Bird. George Fox had warned Johnson that someday he would meet someone his size who wanted it as badly as he did. Johnson would recall knowing Bird as that guy when he first met him. What Fox hadn't told him was that "the guy" could also handle the ball and pass it with showboat style. Or that he would be white. Or that both of them would change basketball forever. Or that when they met they would be sitting on the bench together behind lesser players in something called the World Invitational Tournament. What Johnson did note about the silent white dude was that he really knew how to rebound.

Johnson was already experienced against Russian teams, having scored 41 points against the Soviets a year earlier as part of a team of high school all-stars.

"Joe would be the coach of this United States team and the five starters of Kentucky would all play on the team," Packer recalled.

There would be a regular bench for all three games that included Bird and Johnson, but for each city the team would also add local college stars to help sell tickets, a format that further limited playing time for Bird and Johnson, who mostly gained a sense for each other's games and styles through limited practice time.

"The games included the Soviet Union, Cuba, and Yugoslavia," Packer recalled. "Now Cuba, this was their first real time to ever play in the United States. So we didn't know anything about their players, but the Soviet Union and Yugoslavia were great international teams. Yugoslavia maybe had as fine a collection of basketball players outside the NBA as there were in the world. So the competition was going to be extremely strong. The first game we played was in Atlanta. The second game was in Chapel Hill, North Carolina, and the final game of the three was in Lexington, Kentucky."

Packer had recommended that Johnson and Bird be added to the roster for the entire tour. "Now Bird already had quite a bit of notoriety and would be coming back for what would be his fifth year in college," the broadcaster recalled. Indeed, Bird would be drafted by the Boston Celtics in the first round that spring under a surprise loophole in the rules and would go on to play his senior season at Indiana State, then sign with Boston. He had enrolled at the University of Indiana as a player for his freshman season only to drop out and return home to his hometown of French Lick, Indiana, where he had worked for a time on the town garbage truck before enrolling at Indiana State.

Also on the roster was Sidney Moncrief from the University of Arkansas, who roomed with Johnson. "He was younger than I was," Moncrief recalled in 2019. "I remember he loved music; I loved music. He loved to sing. He played this one song over and over again."

The song was "Float On" by the Floaters, a soft-spoken Motown quartet with spinning dance moves. Johnson would play the song and sing along, then run it back again and again.

"Take my hand, come with me, baby, to Love Land," Johnson would sing, his voice reaching for the high notes. "Let me show you how sweet it could be, Sharing love with me . . ."

"He played it so much, I still remember it now," Moncrief said with a laugh. "You could tell Magic was raised the right way and you could tell he was serious about basketball. I was always impressed with his maturity, his knowledge on the court, his basketball awareness. That's something you can't teach. He had that instinct of what was going on around him. That's what made him such a great passer.

"What impressed me the most was his size and instincts," Moncrief added. "Those were things you normally don't get as a player that age. And he played so hard. You could see his will to win."

The American college players had no time to practice together before taking on the international teams, Packer explained. The broadcaster had covered a number of Kentucky games that 1978 season and had heard of Bird because he was drawing attention as a high-scoring white star.

"I had never even seen Larry Bird so I knew nothing about him," Packer recalled. "That was my first chance to watch Bird and Magic, but Joe B. Hall never played them. They got in I'd say about three minutes a game. Larry Bird was salty. He was very annoyed. I didn't know him from Adam. He just seemed like a kid that didn't even want to be there. He didn't impress me at all because he didn't get to play, but he showed nothing in the practices either."

Bird would later counter that assessment, recalling that he and Johnson would give the starters fits in practice, which left Hall fussing about how could he drill his team if the second unit ran so much and did all of that unusual passing?

As for Johnson, Packer still considered him a "neat kid, flamboyant, but you didn't know how great of an all-around player he was. To this day Larry and Magic are still pissed off about the little opportunity they had in the World Invitational Tournament. I've heard that Larry still bitches about it if anybody ever brings it up."

The lack of playing time was glaring from the very first game when the Americans destroyed Cuba, leaving lots of garbage time and Hall loath to play Bird or Johnson all that much. Kentucky's Goose Givens was one of the starters on a team of college players that defeated the veteran international teams, all accompanied by news reports in Lansing about how little Johnson was getting to play.

"I know both Magic and Larry Bird were a little upset with that," Givens said in 2019. "But I don't know what they would have expected coach Hall to do particularly coming off of an NCAA championship. I think he wanted to play the players he felt most comfortable with. I don't think his decision needs to be defended as I think he did what any coach in that situation would have done."

The situation would become a curiosity only after the Johnson-Bird rivalry came to redefine—many would say save—the sport of basketball.

Writer Jackie MacMullan would capture the one moment in the experience where the two connected, when after the sixth day, they rose from the dead a bit. In the last game, played in Rupp Arena,

Bird pulled down a defensive rebound and quickly headed upcourt, leading the break from the center with Johnson out and filling the lane on the right and eager for the pill. Bird looked him off to the point that Johnson thought he wasn't getting a touch only to have Bird suddenly whip a behind-the-back no-looker into the right hand of Johnson, who promptly answered right back with a no-look of his own to which Bird replied with a touch pass right back to the Magic Man for the score. The crowd loved the play, and Johnson recalled thinking, "Man, I love playing with this guy!"

On cue, he launched into one of his trademark Magic celebratory jaunts headed back downcourt, hitting this strange, pale partner with a high five. Bird acknowledged the bump with his usual expressionless face that suggested he had a future as a crematory salesman.

It certainly was an odd pairing in an odd week, considering all that was to come later, Packer said, "but I can't say that they were worthy."

The good thing, the broadcaster said, was that the two future generational, transformative leaders of the college and pro games got to spend some quiet time together that week traveling, practicing—and sitting.

How Bird felt about it at the time isn't known. "I don't know because Larry was not a guy that you could even really get a conversation going with him," Packer said.

Johnson, too, had tried turning on the charm but found almost no success in getting Bird to hold much of a conversation (although Bird would later admit to being quietly taken with Johnson). He did talk, however, once he got back home to Indiana, telling his teammates that he had just seen the best player in college basketball, this guy named Magic Johnson.

Goin' to Kansas City?

The gold rush was said to have officially started with a phone call to Big Earv, with the news that the Kansas City Kings were seriously interested in drafting Magic Johnson if he would declare hardship by late April 1978 and announce for the NBA draft. The Kings had the number two overall pick in the upcoming draft, having lost a coin flip with the Portland Trail Blazers.

In a short time, Johnson would hear from other clubs discreetly interested in luring him to the pro game, although the serious bid would come from Kansas City. And Johnson himself was quite serious, serious enough that during Michigan State's team banquet a few weeks earlier—jam-packed with more than fifteen hundred Spartan fans paying the suddenly inflated price of $12 each to attend—he had even broached the subject, telling reporters if the money was right, "I'd probably have to go."

The message seemed designed to juice up interest from more teams. An unnamed source, likely Charles Tucker, was later quoted in the *Lansing State Journal* that Johnson "was almost 70 percent sure that he wanted to go. . . . He's not going for peanuts."

Peanuts it wasn't. The money had begun seriously changing for NBA players in recent seasons, and Johnson was in line to fill up his bank account, despite his shaky performance in the Mideast Regional.

Kings executive Joe Axelson was quite sure that this Magic guy was the real deal and wanted to have serious discussions in person so Johnson and Tucker flew out to Kansas City for a Saturday meeting before the Tuesday deadline for declaring hardship.

"At the end of his freshman year he was supposed to go pro," Tucker recalled in 2019. "So him and I went to Kansas City to see if he was going to go pro. We talked to coaches and everything. They were allowed to bring him down, so we went down."

Teams were not, however, allowed to offer college players inducement to turn pro. Still, time was obviously short so the two sides jumped right into negotiations. "When we left Lansing, I could sense his dad really wasn't comfortable with him trying to go to the pros at that time," Tucker recalled. "So he didn't push it at all. Nor did he go against it. I wasn't pushing it. The only one really pushing it was Earvin. He wanted to do it. The reason he wanted to do it wasn't for money. He just wanted to play at the next level."

Actually, Johnson would later reveal that he was also very interested in the money. There was a belief that he could gain a multiyear contract worth a million dollars, and that was a whole lot of money in 1978, when the starting salary for a public school teacher fresh out of college was about $10,000 a year with no guarantee of health insurance.

Big Earv was still grinding long hours at Fisher Body and running his trash-hauling business on the side late at night for about $20,000 a year. Yet the father obviously had no interest in living off his son's wealth, Tucker recalled. "So in my mind, I just went down there to Kansas City and sat it out a little bit, just listening. And they made an offer to him, but the offer wasn't what we really wanted at that time. It would have been decent enough to take."

Tucker remembered the first offer ran about "250,000 or 300,000, something like that over several years."

The total of the proposed deal was more than one million dollars.

"I told them they were going to have to come up with a better offer," Tucker said, adding that the Kings ended up raising it considerably, "a lot of money," in a phone conversation the next day when he and Johnson were back in Lansing. The offer was probably equal to or better than what both Johnson and Bird received when they later turned pro, Tucker suggested in 2019. Johnson was quite eager to take it.

"They called that night and kind of said you got to take this," Tucker recalled.

Soon after, Johnson phoned Tucker, eager to find out if he had a deal.

"Did they call? Did they call?" Tucker remembered him asking. "I said, 'Yeah.' I had talked to his dad first, and his dad said, 'Nah. He don't need to go.' But he let Earvin make that decision. I didn't support it either."

Essentially, the process repeated Johnson's wrangling to make a decision to attend Michigan State. His father wouldn't tell him what to do, yet Johnson knew what his father wanted. Ultimately, he declined to make a move without his father's approval, no matter how badly he wanted to go.

"From the sixth grade on, I told him what I thought," the father would say later. "When it came time to decide about the pros, I couldn't say that I wanted him to stay or go."

The decision would prove immense for all of basketball. If he had turned pro, there would have been no monumental clash with Bird the next season that hyped the game of basketball to unprecedented levels, which in turn would translate into huge interest in their rivalry when both players did eventually turn pro, a huge public interest, it could be easily argued, that changed the game in many ways. In retrospect, the entire future of basketball had hinged on the quiet opposition of the father to his son taking the money that April of 1978.

Tucker, as usual, was also involved in shaping the events of Magic Johnson's life, an influence that had grown steadily and dramatically since the two had met in the spring of Johnson's ninth-grade year. Tucker's role in events was secured by the relationship he had built with Big Earv.

"Earvin wasn't too happy about it," Tucker said in 2019 of Johnson's recognition and silent questioning of what role the psychologist played in turning down the money. "He kind of looked at me over that."

"They offered him $1.2 million for five years," Heathcote would marvel a few months later.

"Tucker was a huge influence on him," Tim Staudt recalled. "He had been a huge influence along with Earvin's dad."

Johnson hadn't spoken with Jud Heathcote for the three weeks as he deliberated the pros and cons of his choice. The coach would later explain that he had trusted that Johnson's parents would help him make the choice, which included the quiet influence of Tucker behind the scenes. The psychologist had likewise built a strong relationship with Heathcote just as he had with George Fox, made all the stronger by Tucker's deft touch in handling Johnson's storming out of practice that freshman season at Michigan State.

At literally every phase of Johnson's teen life, the psychologist had been there, arranging the furniture of the young star's career. No matter how much he loved the game, no matter how many times he tried out for pro teams, Tucker hadn't been able to arrange his own destiny in pro basketball, other than his decision to gain the graduate degrees that allowed him to use his wisdom to influence events.

Mick McCabe would continue to observe these events and wonder, "What does Tucker want?"

"It was the hardest decision I have had to make in my life," Johnson told Fred Stabley that week in confirming that he would return to Michigan State for his sophomore year after turning down Kansas City. "Choosing a college was small stuff compared to what I've been going through the last couple of weeks. This decision concerns my future, my life. And they were talking a lot of money. One coach called me at twenty minutes to midnight. I really wanted to go hardship."

If his father was reluctant to tell him what to do, that wasn't the case with many others in the community who phoned him up or caught him on the street and told him he needed to stay. The pressure he felt was enormous, but the only thing that really seemed to matter to him was the silent presence of his father. That Tuesday afternoon he had played a pickup game in Jenison with Greg Kelser and Terry Donnelly, who were both looking for a sign he was going to stay. He couldn't assure them he wouldn't be gone.

Johnson pointed out the decision came down to the heart of what was literally his lifelong dream to play in the NBA. He had gone back and forth right up until ten minutes before midnight on Tuesday, April 25. How big was the moment and the decision? Years later, in 2023, Johnson would speak of it at his father's funeral, revealing that Earvin Sr. had told him, we've been poor for a long time; we can be poor a little longer.

The letter renouncing his college eligibility had been written. All he had to do was agree to go. George Andrews, who would become Johnson's lawyer that year, was of the opinion that if Kansas City hadn't "low-balled" Johnson he probably would have turned pro.

Heathcote had been almost certain Johnson wouldn't leave because of the bad taste left by his poor play in the Kentucky defeat.

In the aftermath of the decision, Dale Beard noticed a new clarity in his friend. "I felt like he matured after that first year," Beard recalled, "because he knew what he was chasing and that was a college national championship."

Before that could happen, however, there was more of the world to see. The summer brought tryouts for the U.S. National Team, the core unit for the 1980 Olympics, coached by Bill Vining of little Ouachita Baptist in Arkansas, which was scheduled to play an August tournament in Moscow.

Johnson and the National Team prepped for their trip overseas by playing against a collection of American NBA players, which allowed Johnson to test his skills and think a bit about his decision to turn down the money. In Denver, going against pro players, he tied his career high with 14 assists. He loved the open floor and the pace of the pro game, loved the talent level, and pondered just how well he would fit in.

Coach Bill Vining would relay a development to McCabe. The team also included Gene Banks and Mike Gminski of Duke, who were fresh off a loss to Kentucky in the national championship game.

"These guys were overseas and the coach told me that Duke's Gene Banks was having a shit fit because he wasn't starting," McCabe recalled. "He said he wanted to start or he was going home. He was all pissed off. Earvin overheard the conversation. So after Banks left he went up and said, 'Coach. I don't want to start anymore. You don't have to start me at all. I just want to be on the floor when the game's being decided.'"

Vining "already liked Earvin," McCabe said, "but he loved him after that."

The trip to Moscow provided Johnson yet more evidence of the matchup problems he would cause against top-level talent as the Americans rolled to four straight wins featuring his 27-point performance against a Czech team to land the U.S. club into the championship against the Russians.

"There aren't any blacks in Russia that we saw," Johnson would say when he got back home. "And we were pretty tall, so we stood out wherever we went. People would come right up to us walking down the sidewalk and stop in our path just to stare at us. We kind of smiled and stepped around them. We were on show everywhere we went. Some people spoke English but few could understand it. We could go anywhere we wanted and nobody stopped us."

The Americans ended their trip with a close loss in the tournament finals despite the fact that many locals openly rooted for them. "They gave us a standing ovation for at least five minutes when they had the awards ceremonies after the tournament," Johnson told Fred Stabley. "And there were so many people gathered around our bus when it was over that we couldn't leave for a while."

Johnson was clearly elated by the experience, boasting, "I'm getting a chance to see the world without even spending a dime. A couple of years ago I didn't know much about traveling. And what I did know, I didn't like. But now I've been in quite a few places and can't wait to get going again."

That would be soon. Upon his return from Moscow, Johnson faced just days in Lansing before turning around and heading to Brazil with Michigan State for twelve days. Johnson was exhausted and privately told Heathcote he didn't want to go.

Publicly, he presented the trip as a great lark. "We're going to be right on a beach and I think we're going to have a lot of fun."

Heathcote had said he could cancel the entire trip but that Michigan State wasn't going without him.

Johnson grudgingly agreed and soon found himself faced not just with two tournaments, but nights of disco clubbing into the wee hours in São Paulo.

"We bonded down there for like two weeks," Ron Charles remembered. "We had fun. The guys, we all hung together. We went to the movies together. Everything we did we did together. We'd go out at night. We were already close, but that kind of brought us a lot closer. And those games were tough, hostile crowds and a hostile country and all. That helped us develop for the next season."

The Spartans finished second in the first tournament they played, then captured the Governor's Cup in São Paulo against the blazing hot shooting of Oscar Schmidt, who scored 32. Johnson, meanwhile, had a triple-double with 18 points, 10 rebounds, and 15 assists, his new career high.

"I finally made that fifteen," he shouted out on the bus afterward. "Thank you, team. Thank you, team."

The fact that he now measured his worth in assists showed that he had begun to inhabit almost fully a point guard state of mind. And, having turned down the pro money, he clearly seemed emboldened to own the leadership of the team in ways large and small.

"The players followed him and, frankly, I think he loosened Heathcote up," recalled longtime hoops writer Dick Weiss. "Heathcote really wanted his players dressed for breakfast and Magic came down one day in sweats. And Heathcote didn't say anything. It just became an okay thing to do. Magic liked to have a good time. I mean, from the time he was in high school he loved the idea of going out. On that one trip to Brazil, Jud had always had a curfew. But Magic and a couple other guys went out to two o'clock in the morning, and they ran into Heathcote in the lobby the next day. Nothing was really said. I think Jud was smart enough to realize not to make a big deal of it."

Johnson returned home early that fall to find younger sister Evelyn tearing up the basketball world in Lansing. She had scored 56 points in a single game, breaking her big brother's city record of 54, and was on her way to a college basketball scholarship. "It's nice to be compared to him," she told reporters. "Who wouldn't be to someone like Earvin? But I also would like to be known as Evelyn, not always 'Earvin's sister.'"

When there were no conflicts for his time, Johnson would find his way to her games and had even been coaxed into a game of H-O-R-S-E at Everett's gym the previous season as a fundraising event. With the new city record, she had staked out a little piece of her own territory just as Johnson was looking to expand his own domain and up his profile. Little did he realize the crazy way that was going to happen.

16

THE GREAT SALT LAKE

In 1978, Larry Bird had been named a consensus first team All-American after averaging 30 points a game for Indiana State, a school that millions of basketball fans had never heard of, while Johnson was mostly relegated to All-America third teams. That was certainly enough to get the whole thing going.

It was said that many fans, as well as players on other college teams, assumed Bird was Black, perhaps an understandable conclusion considering the limited TV coverage of the sport in that era.

Yet things began to change abruptly for Bird that fall as he returned to the college game. His being drafted by the Celtics with the sixth overall pick in the first round the previous spring had piqued fan and media interest in his story. Turning down an immediate leap to the pros seemed a highly unusual move for a guy who was one of seven children from a desperately poor family. Theirs was the kind of poverty that had played a part in Bird's father, a Korean War veteran, committing suicide just two years earlier as Bird was set to begin playing for Indiana State. Bird had been raised in the small community of Biden Springs, Indiana, which sat next to another very small community named French Lick, which would lead to his eventual nickname, "The Hick from French Lick." The circumstances, as they became known, begged the question from fans and media alike: How and why does a player from a poor background, set to turn twenty-two that December, turn down millions from the esteemed Boston Celtics to play for some college team named the Sycamores?

With that question largely unanswered, the circumstances then ignited into a much broader cultural story as this poor kid from Indiana proceeded to lead his unknown school on a 33–0 win streak over the 1978–79 season and eventually to the number one ranking in the major college polls.

As the Sycamores rose in the public eye that season while winning game after game on the back of one outstanding Bird performance after another, he became a hero, actually not just a hero but, as fans gained clarity about his race, a white hero. Huge numbers of fans—many of them in the massive baby boom generation—who for years had been tuning out basketball as an increasingly Black sport, suddenly became very interested in Larry Bird. They began following him through the various wire service stories distributed across America in local and regional newspapers. They began following the published box scores of his games and just about anywhere else they could get even a piece of information about him.

This great public interest in Bird was made even more intense by his refusal to speak with the various print reporters covering his games. Considering that the broadcast presence was so light in that era, his disinclination to speak to print reporters essentially meant he was declining to speak to just about all reporters covering his team, a factor that deepened the mystery about him personally while at the same time contributing to his great swell of popularity even more, to the point that the "Bird Man," as Jud Heathcote called him, had a profile that far eclipsed the "Magic Man."

It wasn't that Johnson was without his own media coverage. After all, he had taken his team to a nationally televised regional final in the NCAA tournament while Bird's Sycamores had been relegated to the much lower profile of the NIT, where they had lost in the early rounds.

Better yet, that fall of 1978 Johnson had gotten a huge boost when the dominant American magazine *Sports Illustrated* had come to East Lansing to photograph him for the cover of its college basketball preview issue, which would be devoured by millions of fans late that November as the season was set to open.

Sports Illustrated dressed Johnson in formal attire, tails and a top hat, and had him jump up to the rim nearly two hundred times as its photographer snapped away while requesting again and again that Johnson make another leap in the outfit. Not once did he complain or even sigh. Instead, he smiled. Again and again and again. In some ways, the cover photograph likely contributed to the coming cultural divide. Bird would never have posed in such attire, would never have been asked to, would never have been nicknamed Magic.

The public wasn't making such comparisons, yet, but they were building.

Johnson knew the cover would be fantastic, and sure enough, he went out looking for it in a campus store. It seemed that everybody read the college basketball preview issue so it provided him with another grand introduction to the nationwide audience, as had *Playboy* magazine weeks earlier when it named him to its preseason All-America team.

Yet even with the help of these developments, Johnson would still have no great national recognition or following across the country that season to match that accorded Larry Bird. The clear and simple reason for the difference was that Larry Bird resonated as something of an unarticulated "Great White Hope," a phrase taken from the title of a Pulitzer Prize–winning play in 1969 and a major motion picture in 1970 about the circumstances of African American boxing legend Jack Johnson and the white boxer tabbed to try to defeat him.

Only occasionally would Bird himself actually be referred to that season as a Great White Hope, but that was the obvious dynamic that was developing and how he would come to be seen later as a professional. Many things seemed to make Bird uncomfortable that 1978–79 season—he didn't like reporters, for example, to come into the locker room to speak only to him while ignoring his teammates—and certainly the idea that he was some sort of Great White Hope was among them.

None of this would be an immediate factor in Johnson's life until the end of that season, when he stepped into the national spotlight as the Great Black Foil to Bird's Great White Hope. Rarely, if ever, would anything represent an American zeitgeist as well as the impending showdown between Larry Bird and Magic Johnson.

The Guard

The season certainly started off well enough for the Michigan State Spartans. "We thought we were good," Ron Charles recalled. "The guys thought it would be an easy year."

Heathcote had confidence, too, but it would soon sink as the revelations unfolded one by one, the biggest being the influence of the past on the present. The lack of media attention for Johnson's first year of college had aided the Spartans immensely in going 15–3 to win the conference championship, made possible in part by the fact that opposing teams had no clear view of Johnson and Vincent and how the two freshmen were going to change things for Michigan State.

Indeed, Heathcote himself hadn't known. His biggest questions had begun with how good was Johnson really, and how would veterans Bob Chapman and Greg Kelser respond to his huge presence and leadership? Even more important, how would the team play on offense and defense? Now, for the second season, Heathcote had a much clearer picture of his team, but so did all of his opponents in the Big Ten. They had played against Johnson's unique style. They had game film of him. Those who studied him closely could see that he wasn't the same every night. Some teams had been able to slow him down. Better yet, opposing coaches had seen how Kentucky handled him in the NCAA tournament, all of which would serve to make Johnson's sophomore run through the gauntlet of the Big Ten much more difficult.

The second year also brought obvious advantages. Heathcote now understood him better, knew more about his talents, which meant Johnson's second college season would produce much greater clarity. Mick McCabe recalled talking to Johnson before the first season about the topic of him playing point guard. Johnson didn't seem all that eager to embrace such a role but told McCabe that Heathcote had suggested he think about it because playing the position could prove valuable to him in professional basketball.

His busy summer schedule had pushed Johnson further along in such thinking for his second season, to the point that he would no longer be officially designated as a forward. For 1978–79, he would be listed as a guard, which he had already been much of his basketball life without having it clearly defined as such.

To go along with this identity shift, Johnson had improved dramatically as a player with all of the international competition over the 1978 off-season. In addition, he had worked diligently on his outside shot and had sought to improve his balance as he motored into the lane to shoot or dish off. There had also been growth and maturity, leading to his becoming more adamant in not listening to the advice of his teammates. As always, he had his own vision for how to run the team and kept a very close circle of counsel there to include his father, Heathcote and his coaches, and Tucker and not much else. In short, he was evolving even deeper into his own man.

Which meant that as a guard, Johnson wanted and needed more control, and the freedom to pursue it, which in itself would bring him into new conflict with his coach.

Perhaps the biggest concern for Heathcote and his staff for training camp that fall was an obvious lack of energy they saw in the team, particularly in Johnson. Surely, the off-season schedule had added much to his game and his identity, but traveling and playing had taken something of a toll, even on a nineteen-year-old. He would recover, but that sluggishness and the fact that he was no longer under the radar brought certain setbacks. There would be few surprises. The opposition was now more aware of who and what he was, and so was Johnson himself.

November brought a couple of intra-squad scrimmages that drew the fans back to Jenison. In one contest, Johnson had 17 assists, which left his coach observing that the Magic Man was not only stronger and better, he was more patient in finding the right path to victory despite the often high-speed nature of his game.

Next came another Johnson encounter with the Russian national team, which was making its way through a tour playing American college teams. "We are going to have to run and run and run because they are good," Johnson warned. He then put on a show in driving the running game with 13 points and 13 assists to lead a rousing, flashy 76–60 win in Jenison that left the great Soviet coach Alexander Gomelsky smiling and noting his team had been worn down by the schedule.

"I like Johnson," Gomelsky had declared in heavily accented English afterward. "He's beautiful. He's like a conductor on the floor."

Less impressed was *State Journal* columnist Lynn Henning, who blasted Johnson as a "hot dog" for his emotive celebrations after delivering whirlwind plays against the Russians. "He has a tendency to hot dog . . . wave his arms, break into a dance," the columnist complained. Henning also took Heathcote to task as a sideline martinet on full display.

The surprise attack prompted Fred Stabley to respond with a column defending Johnson, as did several fans in letters to the newspaper's editor. "Can you imagine Earvin Johnson making a typically incredible pass that leads to a slam dunk by Gregory Kelser, and simply jogging back down the floor?" Stabley asked. "No dance? No slapping skin? No fist thrust in the air?"

Stabley said he had seen Johnson many times celebrating much the same in an empty gym over a shooting contest in practice. His celebrations simply displayed his love of the game, not some desire to show off, the sportswriter said.

A day later, Stabley wrote a news story saying that Heathcote had mellowed in his fiery approach to his team. Johnson flatly disagreed with that notion while Kelser saw the coach moderating his abrasive style a bit. "No way," Heathcote himself had replied, pointing out that his team now lacked the same sense of urgency that last year's squad had and thus needed his prodding.

The Spartans were a team with a curious emotional balance, a star player turning loose his natural joy on the floor and a coach routinely spitting his anger and frustration in sideline theater. How could they not be headed toward some kind of showdown?

Perhaps sensing this, Kelser had offered a softer view of Heathcote. His players had gotten used to his constant berating of them, the senior forward said. Just having to pull together to deal with his tirades had made them closer, Kelser explained.

Behind the scenes, Tucker quietly supported the coach. And the psychologist had seen it all at practice. In 2019, he pointed out that one factor in the team's emotional equation was Big Earv, whose influence allowed Heathcote more standing room. "Everybody got along well with Mr. Johnson, because he wasn't going to get in your business as long as you were straight with him," Tucker explained. "As long as you're straight with him, you'll be okay. But you can't fool him. There was a thin line if you tried to fool him. Then he would always keep his eye on you. Jud was straight, and he was flexible, not with the world, but with his own little program. He could jump on a kid, but he's not going to let you jump on the kid, whether the kid is right or wrong. You can't come in and give your opinion."

Other than that, the elder Johnson and his family had their own solutions to team chemistry, with their welcoming household and down-home approach, except when Big Earv gathered with his son's teammates at Tucker's house to shoot pool. It was then they all saw where the son got his competitive nature. "Mr. Johnson, he was a pool shark, man," Ron Charles recalled. "He was a great man. Mr. Johnson loved to play pool. You couldn't beat him."

The big guy wasn't alone in his warmth toward his son's teammates, Charles explained. "The whole family, Earvin's sisters and brothers. And Mrs. Johnson? Oh, my God. She was a mama."

Knowing that a number of her son's teammates hailed far from Lansing, Christine Johnson made a mission of having them feel at home. "Come over and eat" was her regular invitation. "And the sisters, they were so nice, all the sisters," Charles remembered with a smile. "But mama always would cook. Me and Greg and all the guys would always go to Earvin's house in Lansing and eat. It was always, 'Let's get some food to eat. Let's get some collard greens, some black-eyed peas.' Stuff that the guys couldn't get. And she would cook and we would eat and sit there and talk with his sisters. It was fun."

The effort helped seal not just team chemistry but personal

chemistry, Greg Kelser recalled in 2019. "Our families were close. I would eat at Earvin's house; his mom was a great cook. He would eat at my house when he came to Detroit. We talked about the teams we hoped to play for, we talked about the cars we hoped to drive and all that stuff. That's what youngsters do. We both liked Mercedes-Benzes and talked about buying them if we had a chance. Where we wanted to live. The thing of it is, I was twenty-one and he was nineteen. These were just things every kid envisions and dreams about."

All of the Johnsons were extra nice, but sister Pearl had a big friendly personality just like brother Earvin, Ron Charles said. "Pearl was my sweetheart, you know, 'cause she was so nice and sweet. Just a good, good person."

The Johnson family in many ways articulated Earvin's approach with the team that so contrasted that of his coach. Johnson wanted his teammates loose, aware, and having fun, an approach that seemed to oppose Heathcote's constant tirades, which were not fun.

Kelser, over the previous two seasons, had identified the coach's basic honesty, harsh as it could be, as a fundamental thing that drove the program forward. And Kelser's perspective would help to modify the growing resentment from Johnson or other players.

A few days after the Russian game, Heathcote made clear his opinion of Johnson. "I think Earvin is the best basketball player in the open court in the entire game, professional, international or college," he said. "Nobody can do the things he can with the ball."

Despite the hullabaloo caused by Henning's column, a serious trend was developing in the sport. Scouts, coaches, and other figures hadn't gained full clarity on it yet, but Johnson was in the process of revolutionizing not just American basketball but the international game as well, by continually putting on displays that set the best minds to spinning. The international teams, in particular, were developing an abundance of tall players from an early age. Suddenly Johnson was giving international coaches new ideas about how to deploy them. In time, the game would come to see the movement as "position-less" basketball, meaning that tall players would no longer be assigned a life of just standing near the goal, that they would be handling the ball and making plays.

After a season-opening win over Central Michigan, the Spartans entertained 17th-ranked Cal State Fullerton, a veteran team that had made a nice showing in the 1978 NCAA tournament. Johnson and his teammates soon took a big lead, then found themselves holding on at the end to win, 92–89.

Four days later, State added a cupcake win over Western Michigan, then prepared to fly down to Chapel Hill to take on North Carolina in Carmichael Auditorium, where Johnson sat after practice the night before the game, gazing around the hallowed building, smiling and declaring it would be a game for "national prestige and pride."

Maybe so, but the game wouldn't even be available on television back in Michigan. The contest presented a classic meeting of coaching styles. Dean Smith had a roster filled with tall, skillful players—such as six-six sophomore Al Wood, coming off the bench no less—who could contend with the third-ranked Spartans' athleticism. The Tar Heels also saw that they could abuse Michigan State's zone and lax attitude about boxing out by finding one offensive rebound after another, led by All-American forward Mike O'Koren, who lived off the offensive glass.

Dean Smith was also eager to see how State's tower of a point guard would fare against his gambling, trapping, constantly switching defense that featured much ball pressure.

"Johnson played better than I've ever seen him play," Smith would say afterward, almost dismissively, in light of Johnson's six assists and eight turnovers. It would have been hard to fathom Dean Smith ever allowing a player with the dynamic approach of Earvin Johnson into his tightly run offensive system.

Johnson showed flashes early in the contest, once working the ball at the top of the key while looking left, then suddenly zinging a fireball of a pass to the right, through the heart of Smith's defense, for a dunk. Moments later, Johnson could be seen sound asleep on the right block in the State matchup zone, allowing a driver to roll right by him for an easy layup. He would awaken quickly to show that his size and quickness provided remarkable close-outs on perimeter shots, not that the Tar Heels would show an overreliance on jump shots that day.

Carolina trapped in the half-court and usually managed to double-team Johnson when he had the ball. Their offensive rebounding allowed North Carolina to develop a nice lead, while Heathcote grew increasingly furious with the refs. Video of the game would show the struggles of a two-man crew in that era to keep up with the pace and activity of the game.

Michigan State would wrestle with UNC's size and cunning inside in the second half. The Tar Heels also moved the ball smartly against State's zone to expand their lead to 36–29 while keeping Johnson under constant pressure in the half-court. Soon enough Smith would send his team into the Four Corners offense, pulling the ball out high, spreading the court and producing a run of buckets off backdoor cuts when the Spartans overplayed.

Yet it also allowed State with Heathcote's short rotation to rest a bit with the slower tempo.

Even though the Tar Heels were the pressuring, gambling defense, it was the Spartans who amassed the fouls deep into the second half, until Heathcote exploded at the refs with just under five minutes to go, pointing out that his team had gotten just two calls in 15 minutes while the Tar Heels enjoyed regular trips to the free throw line. They would make 12 of 17 for the game while Michigan State made seven of the eight shots it was awarded.

Heathcote's tirade drew a technical, which allowed North Carolina to score five straight points, just enough to keep the Tar Heels ahead of State's attempts to push the tempo with a press. With 45 seconds to go, the Tar Heels were still up, 70–65, but Johnson hit one short jumper and Vincent another to cut the lead to a point. The Spartans even stole an inbounds pass that gave Vincent one last great look, an eight-foot jumper, to win, but it fell off, bringing their first loss, 70–69, which came with a feeling they just might meet North Carolina later on in the tournament.

Coming off the loss they recovered with a win before Christmas over Cincinnati in the Pontiac Silverdome—the first college basketball game in the four years of existence for the football facility—before a rowdy packed house of 31,600, all of them eager to see Johnson do his very unusual thing.

On defense, he was a rebounding forward who took the ball off the boards and headed immediately upcourt racehorse style with that high, long dribble. It didn't help that he still operated almost exclusively with his right hand, that he wasn't some profound leaper, that his outside attempts were still most often awkward one-handed push shots.

Yet even on the grainiest of scouting films, it leaped out at the coaches trying to figure out how to defend against him. He covered the court like a giraffe, or a dragster, dropping his tail at acceleration and shooting out of the blocks in almost a crouch, rising as he went, head erect, eyes searching, tall enough to look over the top of the defense to see everything.

The speed with which it happened left people struggling to see it, to understand it.

The unsettling part came with the long loping passes down the floor, when he routinely, yes, magically, in an instant showed he could deliver the ball, sometimes with a wind-up baseball pass, other times with a two-handed fling, or best of all, a long bounce pass laced perfectly through retreating defenders, each of these balls unleashed in full stride, dropped perfectly through frantic opponents to find a teammate racing ahead to haul in his soft missives to score layups and dunks.

The results of the easy baskets he could produce cut the heart right out of opponents, demoralized them, requiring a rethinking of the very idea of transition defense.

It became one of Jud Heathcote's favorite observations that Earvin Johnson could put pressure on a defense from the very first second he touched a rebound. It was like he had a processor for a mind, could read the floor and make expert decisions in a nanosecond.

Johnson and his new syntax had arrived almost overnight and immediately began speeding up the game. And it seemed to catch many in the sport by complete surprise.

At least that was how things worked when the Spartans were on a roll. More and more, opposing coaches saw that trouble came for the Spartans when defenders managed to gunk up Johnson's show. Above all, they had to find ways to keep the ball from getting into his hands.

The first logical adjustment to his presence was that defenses began choreographing a better transition effort, which meant opponents found themselves committing fewer resources to offense just so they could defend against Johnson's passing.

And so they got better at getting back quicker. Sadly, it often hardly mattered. Johnson refused to take his foot off the accelerator and many nights seemed determined to run right through the set, half-court defenses that had managed to get down the floor to await him. In this regard, his tremendous flow was like water running down a hill, finding its way over and around any obstacles.

Yes, he lived by his right hand, and every single soul in the building knew he was headed right as he raced toward a crouched defender ready to slide either way. Yet as he charged in Johnson would oh so slightly shift his weight to the left at full speed, just enough to get the defender to bite—and bite they did time and time again only to see him shift right again at the last instant and blow right by them.

It all allowed him to find and then flow into the seam of almost any defense, and once inside, in that split instant of penetration, Johnson found his truest expression of joy, of complete command, with his height, his vision, his creative passing—no look, behind the back, over the shoulder, dipsy do, whatever brought complete, jaw-dropping surprise from fans, teammates, and opponents alike—he delivered like no one before or after would ever deliver.

In the entire history of the game, such displays became his identity alone, absolutely and completely immune to duplication. If for some reason he could not deliver the ball, he simply gave the moment back to his flow, cut through the final crease in the defense with his length to drop in a simple right-handed layup. Even when his flow took him to the left, he often finished with a twisting right hand.

Taken together, Big Ten coaches had begun to look at the creases in his attack to find a place to deny him the ball. That, in itself, would require substantial effort and adjustment.

The Spartans flew to Portland after Christmas to play in the Far West Classic, where Johnson pulled his teammates together to talk. "We decided to put the past couple of games behind us and start over," he explained later.

Apparently, that worked. They destroyed George Raveling's Washington State team in the first round, which left Raveling ruing that he hadn't tried to control the game's tempo. The showing capped a tremendous homecoming for Heathcote, who had been a Washington State assistant to Marv Harshman for twelve years but was passed over for the head coaching job.

Next, the Oregon State Beavers pressed the entire game and forced the Spartans to fight hard for an eight-point win, which left them facing Bobby Knight and Indiana for the event's championship. Knight had zero answers, and his Hoosiers fell, 74–57.

In the aftermath, Knight averred State was "as good a team as there is in the country."

Longtime *Spokane Chronicle* columnist Charlie Van Sickel went further, writing that "Johnson alone makes the Spartans the most exciting basketball team I've watched since Bill Walton's heyday career at UCLA. Or maybe all the way back to Elgin Baylor's electrifying performances for the Seattle Chieftains 22 years ago."

Then the columnist turned to what would be an eternal truth about Johnson's relationship with his coaches. "Heathcote has gone from an outstanding coach to a great coach with the presence of Johnson," Van Sickel wrote.

On the joyous flight home, weather forced a layover in Denver, where Heathcote informed the team they had ascended to the number one ranking in the polls, the first such distinction in the school's history.

Strangely, their rise had been dogged by a nervous sense among the fans, the media, and the players themselves that the team often seemed to be sleepwalking with a decided lack of energy.

"I'm worried about it," Johnson admitted to Fred Stabley. "We're not even playing. We're just showing up. It's not just one or two players. It's everybody. I have been fired up at times, but it's hard to get everyone else fired up. Last year we all started each game hungry, and I just tried to keep things going, to keep our spirits up and flowing."

He paused his message, then added, "If this keeps up there's going to be some great disappointments come conference time."

Conference time arrived innocently enough with two opening

home wins over Wisconsin and Minnesota, only to see the road bring two huge disappointments, a two-point loss to Ronnie Lester and Iowa followed by another one, to Joe Barry Carroll and Purdue. They returned home and steamed over the setback and Heathcote's anger in practice before again turning Knight's Indiana club into a piñata, 82–58, in Jenison. Then Iowa and Lester took them to overtime where the Spartans won going away. With their legs wobbly, they then lost to Michigan in Crisler on a last-second bucket to leave their league record at 4–3. Johnson's forecast had come to be with stunning accuracy. The NCAA tournament had been expanded to forty teams for 1979, but that in no way eased the pressure. You either won the Big Ten regular season or you didn't go.

And things had quickly come to look like the Spartans wouldn't be going.

Wondering if they were simply plagued by bad luck with all the close losses, they loaded on the bus the next day for a long, snowy trip to Chicago to play Northwestern, a team with a 4–12 record that featured seven straight losses and no victories in the Big Ten. In the midst of such a season, Northwestern had reason to be concerned about Johnson, recalled former Northwestern assistant Walt Perrin, who had evaluated him in high school. Johnson was bigger, stronger, and coming to realize fully his strengths, Perrin said. "He was a guy that could dominate the game even when he couldn't shoot it. He could dominate the game by scoring, rebounding, passing."

Except for that night. By halftime, State was down 10, which left them with the big idea of pressing more. When his teammates began fouling out, Johnson tried to take the full game on his shoulders and ended up shooting seven for 22.

Tex Winter, who had been the coach at Northwestern the previous season, used to have a saying about up-tempo basketball: "You can hurry to a butt whipping." That's what happened to the Spartans. They lost to the lowly Wildcats by 18.

"We just played an outstanding game," Walt Perrin recalled in 2019. "Magic didn't shoot the ball very well. Greg Kelser didn't have a great game. We just did a very good job playing defense and executing, and we just kind of outplayed them. They maybe came in thinking, 'It's Northwestern, and we really don't have to worry about them.' They were struggling a little bit. Our win probably woke them up."

Heathcote once again displayed his fury with a tirade, Ron Charles recalled. "After the game he went off on everybody."

The team then faced a long, angry late-night bus ride home during which a legendary team meeting, an insurrection, was hatched.

"We would usually stop and get something to eat after we played a game," Ron Charles explained, "but coach did not stop. He did not get us anything to eat on the way back."

The players had eaten their usual light pregame meal, and they were hungry, Charles remembered. "We just drove through. We ain't stopping. When we got back later, we had a little meeting."

"When they lost to Northwestern that night, me and his dad was up in the gym waiting on the team to come back from Chicago," Charles Tucker remembered. "Because the team was in disarray. Everybody was against the coaching. Everybody was against everybody that night because they had lost. So they just happened to get beat at the wrong time. We were there when they got back, just me and his dad. They must have gotten back about three o'clock in the morning because they drove the bus that night. We met the bus."

Heathcote, who had begun thinking his team might be facing the NIT, would later reveal his emotion over finding Tucker and Big Earv there to greet them in those bleak wee hours. While that would warm his heart, it wouldn't stay that way long. Sizzling on the agenda were two different team meetings that would be revealed later.

"That was my story," Mick McCabe said of his *Free Press* scoop that revealed Johnson and the other players had confronted their coach over his handling of the team and the need to lighten up. "Jud, I mean, he was pissed at me, unbelievably pissed at me."

It was Johnson who would later reveal the circumstances to McCabe.

"We had a meeting, a players-only team meeting," Charles remembered. "We said that Coach is on us too hard. He's screaming at Earvin, he's a don't-do-this, don't-do-that guy. Every play has got to be a high-low play."

It wasn't exactly the plays themselves, Charles said. "We had great plays now. Our high-low would eat you up alive, but the Big Ten had seen high-low. And they had the size to defend it, to defend Magic."

It didn't matter how sweet the water in the well was if you went to it too often.

Heathcote had his cards he would hold up for calling out the plays, and it often seemed he had begun calling out high-lows almost every time, Charles explained. "We have cards, and he'll call the play every play. And we're playing like robots. We wasn't playing loose, if you know what I mean. Everything has to be choreographed."

Johnson, in particular, seemed to feel his instinctual approach to the game had been taken away from him. Indeed that often appeared the case.

"We had the meeting in the locker room," Charles recalled. "All the guys were like, 'Hey, Coach is this,' and 'Coach is that.' We're going to get together. We're going to call coach in for a team meeting and everybody speaks their gripe."

"Everybody thought it was just a team meeting," Mick McCabe recalled in 2019. "What a great team meeting it was. A players-only meeting. Well, after the players-only meeting, they went to the coaches and said, 'We want to have a meeting.' And that's when they told Jud, 'You've got to get off our backs.'"

Heathcote had answered that they needed to play better, McCabe recalled. "And they said, 'You get off our backs, we'll play better.'"

"Greg was the first one to talk because he was the captain," Charles said of Kelser. "Earvin went second, Jay third. I think I was fourth. Terry Donnelly was fifth."

Others didn't speak, Charles added. "But the only ones who had gripes was me, Earvin, Greg, and Jay, that spoke up about the gripes. That's what I remember. Nobody else griped, no complaints. I don't think a lot of people did a lot of griping. That was the big thing, that we were gonna let our gripes and beefs and dislikes out about how Jud was treating us."

It wasn't entirely clear, but it appeared Heathcote had gotten the message.

"After that meeting I think coach, you know, he let us play again, or allowed us to play freely again, and Magic was able to be Magic again," Ron Charles remembered.

Heathcote would later portray the meeting as more of a clearing-the-air session that brought them all together, but McCabe insisted the message from Johnson and the players was more pointed than that, a view that would take hold in the legend of the moment.

Heathcote explained in 1986 that substitute Mike Longaker, who was much respected by Johnson and all the members of the team, spoke up to turn the focus of the meeting to what the players needed to do to turn things around.

"He was the only guy Earvin would listen to," Heathcote said of Longaker. "The consensus was, 'We haven't worked hard enough; we haven't played hard enough.'"

"Jud's version was not what it was," McCabe said, adding that Heathcote's interpretation was "we just said, 'You guys have to play better.'"

Although the coach and the sportswriter remained good friends for years, McCabe said Heathcote never came clean on the meetings.

"It never got brought up again, but he was pissed," McCabe explained. "He thought that it made him look bad."

Ironically, the leaked news of the meeting made some recruits want to play for Heathcote because the situation made him seem open to give-and-take with his players, McCabe added with a laugh.

The moment further revealed Tucker as a man with an immense sense of when to get involved and when to let things ride. "From the little bit I asked—and I didn't ask much about it—the result was, a 'let us play' type thing," the psychologist recalled, adding that Heathcote apparently responded by saying, "I'm going to let you play, but you need to do this."

"I think they made adjustments on both sides," Tucker said.

Ron Charles, however, suggested the meeting was an attempt to deal with two very different types of leadership.

"I never feared Earvin, not at all," Charles said of Johnson. "He wasn't into fear."

This would appear to stand in contrast to one of the other great team leaders of the era, Michael Jordan, who would later be known for deploying every single element available, including inspiring fear, to drive his teammates.

Much like Jordan's example, it was Johnson's competitive drive always pushing the agenda, Charles explained. "He loved to push you. Now, if you feared being pushed or feared somebody seeing you being pushed, maybe so. But we didn't have fear of Earvin. First, he's not going to take you in the back room and whip you with that type of fear. Jud would want to take you in the back room and try to fight you. That's his type of fear. Earvin didn't have that fear of cursing and belittling you and stuff like that. He didn't do that. But Earvin is a top dog. Earvin hates losing."

Charles, whose nickname was "Bobo," was often Johnson's roommate on the road, and the night before games Johnson would be pushing fervent, urgent reminders at him.

"Come on, Bobo," he would say. "We gotta win this game. We gotta do this."

Yet no matter how badly Johnson wanted to win basketball games he almost never violated his positive approach, Charles said. "He wouldn't get upset, you know, or pout and be babylike. He wanted to win but not that."

For that 1978–79 season, Jay Vincent had lost substantial weight and moved to forward, where his inside scoring ability was all the more effective. Charles, meanwhile, much lighter at six-seven, had moved into the center slot to start the season, where despite his considerable leaping ability and athleticism he was often challenged by the extraordinary size and strength of opposing frontcourts in the Big Ten.

In the midst of these challenges, Johnson never got down on him, instead offering his friend constant encouragement, saying, "You got to do better next time, Bobo. Come on, Bobo."

"Earvin was a unique player in that he would practice hard," Heathcote would later tell Billy Packer. "He and Gregory Kelser were our hardest working players in practice. Jay Vincent and Ron Charles were—I don't want to say lackadaisical—but there were times they just didn't want to practice. I finally got to the point where, instead of the assistant coaches or myself, I'd say, 'Earvin, get Jay and Bobo to practice harder today.'"

Johnson, Heathcote acknowledged, was essentially a coach. It was a position, an influence, that Johnson would assume and had assumed on each of his teams from high school through professional ranks, merely with the way he conducted himself, a control that certainly began with his play, with his passes serving as sweet opportunity and fun for his teammates, but all of it tied to his larger purpose of controlling the proceedings, all, of course, for his often stated goal of having that supremely desired fun.

The smile was the obvious measure of all that he was. And in midseason 1979, Johnson was not smiling.

Yet, taken together, the meetings had revealed a major development in Earvin becoming Magic, with his taking a major action without consulting or relying on either his father's or Tucker's guidance.

One of Heathcote's major adjustments in the wake of the meetings was to replace Charles, an athletic and effective frontcourt player and rebounder, in the starting lineup with Mike Brkovich, a wing player, because opposing teams were now going to great lengths to deny Johnson the ball, whether it was boxing him off the boards or keeping him from receiving an outlet pass. The Spartans needed an additional ball handler with Terry Donnelly to advance the ball and get it to Johnson at the first opportunity.

"He made a lot of change," Charles said of Heathcote in the aftermath. "And he put me back as the sixth man. He said we needed another ball handler because they were doubling Earvin and taking the ball out of his hands."

With the Northwestern loss, the Spartans had returned home to face Ohio State, led by Herb Williams and Kelvin Ransey and owner of an 8–0 record in the conference.

"They needed that game to get into the tournament," Tucker explained.

State had moved to a nine-point lead with about two and a half minutes to go in the first half when Johnson went down with an ankle injury and had to be helped to the locker room, bringing a silence to what had been a rowdy Jenison. A trainer later returned to the bench and told Heathcote that it didn't appear the ankle was broken but rather severely sprained. The coach agreed Johnson shouldn't return to the game. In the second half, Johnson stayed in the locker room while the Spartans lost their lead and Kelser took a seat with foul trouble.

"He was back there on the stretcher," Tucker recalled. "I had gone back there. And the trainer had told him he couldn't play, that he shouldn't. Earvin couldn't make up his mind. He looked up and saw me standing over there. The trainer had gone back outside to tell Jud what was going on, that it wasn't clear. Earvin looked at me and said, 'Get me up out of here. I'm going to play.' He made his own decision."

In a scene that would become a jewel of Michigan State basketball lore, the crowd in Jenison erupted, what many would claim was the loudest they ever heard in the old building, when Johnson limped out of the locker room and headed to the bench.

"So he went back out there," Tucker recalled. "Ohio State was up two or three at that time."

By the time Johnson had taken a seat on the bench, Vincent had scored twice and State had regained the lead.

"I can play," Johnson told Heathcote. Then the Buckeyes regained the lead yet again.

Heathcote sent him back into the lineup with 8:23 to go.

"He came back out and played with a bad ankle and he was limping," Charles remembered.

From there, Johnson drove the Spartans to overtime. He had 15 of his 23 points in the final five minutes.

"He had a game that second half," Tucker recalled. "He went crazy, and they beat Ohio State."

"He made some plays, and we end up winning that game," Charles said. "Earvin, he meant a lot to Michigan State."

For another day, he had kept their slim tournament hopes alive, although next up was Northwestern in Jenison, a chance to reverse their fortunes. Even though Johnson did not play due to his ankle, the Spartans still took a good lead, only to see it dwindle late in the game.

Heathcote turned to Johnson and said, "Earvin, it's time to go in."

"Yeah, Coach," Johnson replied, "time to get in there."

On the bad ankle, Johnson brought the victory home, Heathcote recalled. "He could have cared less that going into the game was going to lower his scoring average a couple of points a game. He cared next to nothing about scoring."

The very next challenge came in Jenison with Kansas, the kind of meeting that attracted NBC. By the winter of 1979, Billy Packer, former Marquette coach Al McGuire, and veteran broadcaster Dick Enberg had evolved into a popular college basketball broadcast team for the network, with Enberg serving as host and play-by-play man and Packer and McGuire often jousting furiously as analysts.

"They had a huge game that we got assigned to up in Lansing," Packer recalled, adding that as part of their typical duties the trio went to State's practice the day before the Kansas game. "Jud had always been really easy to work with. We're sitting there and he walks in and they're really struggling then."

Heathcote surprised the broadcasters by telling them they had to go sit up at the top of the building, Packer recalled. "He didn't want us down near the court.

"And he went after those guys hard," about as hard as Packer had ever recalled a coach going after his players. Then, he added, Heathcote turned his attention to the broadcasters sitting way up high "to the point that about halfway through the practice, even though I know we weren't causing any problem, he told us just to get out of the arena. So, it was serious time for their team."

Like that, Heathcote had kicked the nation's top college basketball broadcast team out of his gym, apparently because they were witnessing his tirades. So much for the idea that Heathcote was going to ease up in his approach, at least as far as practice.

"Nowadays, everybody gives their opinion," Tucker observed in 2019. "Coaches are often swayed to those opinions, trying to be politically correct. Jud didn't. Even back then. I think that was one of his strongest characteristics. He did not tolerate it. He'd tell you in a minute, 'What do you know? That's a dumb question.' You gotta be captain of the ship. And he was. And that made him very popular among coaches. He wasn't afraid."

Even from watching that brief hour of practice, Billy Packer gained a much greater understanding of Earvin Johnson, not related to "his shooting style or anything like that. But his competitiveness jumped out at me even though things were going haywire and it would be very easy to blame everybody but himself. But he was really concentrating on playing."

Whatever the mojo, the Spartans whipped Kansas, 85–61, that February 4. "He played extremely well," Packer said. "Again, the things that I didn't think he could do, he didn't show me all of a sudden that he could do them, but his competitive nature and ability to handle the ball and to rebound were outstanding."

Despite the internal crisis the terrible loss at Northwestern had exposed, the aftermath somehow produced a clarity that from there sent the Spartans off on a 10-game winning streak that left them tied for the conference championship and a ticket to the NCAA tournament. They headed into the end of the schedule facing two final road games while in a tie with both Purdue and Iowa for the Big Ten crown.

"We beat Minnesota, Purdue loses and Iowa loses, and suddenly we're in," Heathcote would remember. The Spartans had miraculously turned their season around. They had to assume one more last-second loss—this time on a 50-foot heave—in their final Big Ten game, at Wisconsin, which gave them five losses in the conference, four of them on buzzer beaters. It didn't matter. They were in with a 21–6 record, not the kind of numbers normally to inspire confidence for a national championship.

Jud Heathcote had stayed strong, Tucker said. "He happened there at the right time, got Earvin at the right time. He cultivated everything, and it came together. And he won. He coached, though. He could coach. And they needed that."

"He listened," Ron Charles said. "He listened and he eased up. We went back to playing again. Being free and doing stuff. And got back to winning."

Riding on the Freeway of Love

Larry Bird and Indiana State would travel a straighter path to the same destination, yet it wasn't without frustrations. In late January of that year, Duke was the top team in the country but was upset by Marquette in a game broadcast by Packer, McGuire, and Enberg. At the end of the broadcast, Enberg asked who should then be the top team in the country. McGuire said the current number three, Indiana State, should be the new number one. Packer, who was scheduled to call an upcoming home game at Indiana State, disagreed, pointing out the Sycamores' schedule featured much lower-rated teams, a comment that infuriated fans.

"There were death threats if I came to Indiana State for that game with Wichita State," Packer recalled. "So they took me off the game."

He would not have an opportunity to broadcast a Sycamores game until the first round of the NCAA tournament in March when they faced Virginia Tech. Even though a couple of weeks had passed, apparently there were still hard feelings. "I'll never forget this," Packer said. "I go out on the court before the game. The players get lined up at half-court, top of the key, all with a basketball, and they all fire basketballs at me as I walk across the floor. And I kind of laugh, but they were serious as hell."

As was much of the rapidly ballooning fan base for college basketball, drawn there by Larry Bird.

Packer broadcast the Indiana State victory that day as well as two subsequent games on the Sycamores' way through the field. "I'm now seeing him play some minutes," Packer recalled of Bird, "and he's slow. He can't jump real well; he's basically playing a lot inside. He's not outside shooting a lot of jump shots. He scores points and rebounds, but he's not phenomenal."

The more the broadcaster observes, the more he asks, "How is he going to be an NBA player? Because he's not big enough to play center and he's too slow in my estimation to be great. He could probably play, but he was older too, a fifth-year senior. So I'm not real excited about him. Then I get them against Oklahoma and Arkansas."

The Indiana State game vs. Arkansas and Sidney Moncrief proved to be a great regional final, Packer recalled. "So now this is the third time I've seen him and I realized, well, he still is slow. But he has great hands. He's an excellent passer. He's got good leadership qualities. And he is mean as shit and loves to compete."

Bird beat Arkansas with a great pass rather than a great shot to win that regional final, Packer emphasized. "He still had no personality off the court whatsoever, but his knowledge of the game and competitive drive, you saw that. It jumped right out at you. And the players loved playing with him."

At the same time, in their lane, Johnson and the Spartans were buzzing right through their competition. After a bye in the first round, they took on Lamar, coached by Billy Tubbs, and blasted them, leaving McCabe and the reporters covering the event with memories of Tubbs coming into the postgame press conference and asking if anyone had gotten a plate number on whatever had run over them.

Laughs aside, the real news was that Jay Vincent had left the game with an injured foot that would trouble him and keep him off the floor for much of the tournament, a worrisome development for the team's all-important third-leading scorer.

At the time, the term "triple-double," or double figures in three statistical columns, was just coming into the broader basketball vocabulary, mainly because Johnson was helping to put it there. He had 17 rebounds, 13 points, and 10 assists against Lamar, a performance that came on the heels of announcements of Big Ten honors. Johnson was named Player of the Year by a vote of the conference's coaches.

But when it came to the All–Big Ten team selected by the media, Joe Barry Carroll of Purdue and Kelvin Ransey of Ohio State were the only unanimous selections, suggesting the team was being picked by scoring average. Ronnie Lester of Iowa also had more votes than Johnson, who shrugged off the Big Ten media snub, saying of such honors, "It's good for me. I'm more of a team-oriented guy, but, if they come, it's beautiful."

Then came the UPI All America team, and it was Bird's turn to outpoint Johnson there as well. "Bird will be all pro the first year he plays," predicted Tulsa head coach Jim King when the UPI team was announced. "He's so far ahead of the other college players it's unreal."

Bird's great year had clearly eclipsed Johnson's in terms of profile, although as the tournament opened the *Los Angeles Times* distributed a feature on Johnson that ran in newspapers across the country. "Magic has been a superstar since he was a sophomore in high school," Lansing businessman Paul Abraham told writer Pete Donovan.

When Donovan asked Johnson himself to address his rise in the game, he provided what could be seen in retrospect as a telling, almost chilling answer: "I love basketball. It is the biggest part of my life. I never tire of playing. Everyone else, including the girls, has to realize that basketball comes first in my life."

"Including the girls" revealed the growing second agenda in his life.

In his interview with Donovan, Johnson described himself as "real loose and very enthusiastic. I jump up and down and like to get the fans excited. And, I guess, I am exciting to watch. What I love most is when the whole court opens up and I have the ball. I just like to take it down and see what happens."

What was happening was a tournament field falling just the Spartans' way, starting with the upsets of North Carolina and Duke in the East Regional. Penn out of the Ivy League, coached by Bob Weinhauer, had upended the Tar Heels. "We absolutely fear no one," Weinhauer proclaimed after the big win.

Neither did the Spartans, having come alive in the Big Ten. A good LSU team fell next, 87–71, a game in which Johnson missed 11 of his 16 field goal attempts. That didn't matter, said Notre Dame's Bill Hanzlik, who had studied the game closely. "You have to look at the total offensive picture. How many assists did he get against LSU? Twelve? Well, there's 24 points for other players. Earvin is just a tremendous player. I don't know if he can be totally stopped."

Hanzlik's coach, Digger Phelps, was likewise a close student of the Spartans, who found himself marveling, "I've never seen a kid do it the way he does. The players listen to him. Sometimes they listen to him more than Jud."

Indeed, the Spartans' victory sent them into the Mideast Regional final against Digger's Irish, loaded with five future NBA stars—Orlando Woolridge, Bill Laimbeer, Kelly Tripucka, Tracy Jackson, and Hanzlik—at Market Square Arena in Indianapolis. Some would call it the true national championship game, although with all the blitzes the Spartans threw on opponents in the 1979 tournament, that would be hard to distinguish.

What the game actually provided was great clarity to the national audience about the astoundingly good combo that Johnson and Kelser made with alley-oop plays, so good, in fact, as to burn the concept into basketball's consciousness indelibly. Sadly, Kelser would later be taken in the first round of the NBA draft, fourth overall by the Detroit Pistons. Johnson would immediately note that the Pistons were not a running team, which would mean that the high-flying Kelser with his intelligence and acrobatic ability to catch and finish would not be allowed to prosper. But for that one shining moment, as the NCAA would begin to promote the image of its tournament, Greg Kelser and Johnson would step into the spotlight with their uncanny ability to hook up, much to the dismay of the Notre Dame Irish, who watched Johnson and his finishers play the game on a level they simply couldn't reach.

It was difficult for the writers to keep up with just how many alley-oop plays the Spartan duo executed that day. Was it six or eight?

"I always look for Greg because he is usually so much quicker than the guy who is guarding him," Johnson would explain to the media afterward. "If the man is overplaying him, look out."

"We've been together quite some time now," Kelser told the assembled press. "I know what he is looking for, and he knows what I'm looking for. All we have is eye contact. There's no sign, no signal. He knows that if he gets the ball near the rim, I'll go get it. It don't have to be a great pass, but it usually is."

The "no sign, no signal" comment from Kelser didn't reflect some sort of animus between the player and his coach. There was none. Kelser was Heathcote's defender. But it delineated the struggle that had unfolded during the season, that would define the age, the continued emergence of the instinct and innovation of players versus the conventional thinking of coaches, a trend that was on its way to defining the game itself in terms of Black culture.

The team of future NBA players from Notre Dame could only watch. Over one four-minute stretch, Kelser would score 14 points.

"Earvin could be one of the greatest to ever play the game," Digger Phelps observed after he had glimpsed the future.

Johnson admitted he had sought to fire up Kelser before the game by telling him UCLA's David Greenwood was a better dunker.

"I think it made him mad," Johnson said with the smile going full wattage. "He came out today to prove himself. I love to see him dunk. I get so fired up. He hangs so long. He creates things in the air. It's like a cartoon."

John A. McGill of *The Lexington Herald* in basketball-crazy Kentucky thought to ask Johnson how he would defend against himself. Kelser interrupted to say he would "say something about his mother and hope he'd hit me so he'd get thrown out of the game."

The moment in the regional final and Johnson's animated response to it afterward began to create the first profound understanding for the national audience as to just what his nickname meant, not only on the floor but off it. This national audience wasn't fully in tune with Johnson's personality. That would develop over time. But the moment would begin to mark the first clarity that fateful spring.

"They dominated the NCAA tournament like had never been done before other than by UCLA type teams with their margin of victories," Packer, who broadcast decades of the NCAA's championship games, said, looking back in 2019. "Michigan State had five losses in the Big Ten, got in the NCAA tournament, and obviously right from the start of the tournament they just blew everybody away that they played."

The emergence of Johnson and Kelser as a duo served to set up an immediate debate as to who was the better player, a debate that would run through much of the tournament and afterward, Packer recalled. "Kelser is their leading scorer and rebounder. Magic, again, because of his flamboyance, is getting a lot of attention with the name Magic Johnson."

As the finisher, Kelser had 34 points that day and Johnson 19, which helped Kelser garner honors as the MVP of the regional. As Packer pointed out, conventional thinking about the game pointed many to Kelser as the more valuable player at the next level. Conventional thinking wasn't quite aware of it at the time, but it was under a tremendous assault.

The Prelim

The story here becomes much more about media than about basketball or even the championship itself. That would have been a hard position to take that late March of 1979 with Michigan State headed to the Final Four in Salt Lake City, Utah, and the community back home in Lansing festooned seemingly everywhere in green and white with lots and lots of good-luck signage and love. Lots of love. Everybody who could possibly commandeer a ticket to the event was soon on the road with them, including Big Earv and Christine, although she was said to have avoided the Saturday semifinal games in observance of her faith.

The Spartans arrived in Utah with an unbridled confidence stoked by their tournament momentum. There awaiting was the next plump item on the menu, Bob Weinhauer's Penn team that "feared no one." Silly them. They stepped up wide-eyed as the greatest Final Four Tasty Cake in the forty-year history of the tournament. By halftime the score was 50–17, like some Amateur Athletic Union mismatch, with Johnson on his way to another triple-double while giving Billy Packer more to ponder.

"Now you see of flamboyance again that is, you know, out of sight with Magic just handling himself," the broadcaster recalled. "He's drawing crowds. Everybody loves the way he acts and he has a triple-double against Penn and again, they're playing no man-to-man defense. They're playing in this zone, and to be quite honest with you, he plays great, scores like 29, but Greg Kelser is 12 for 19. He scores 28 points, has four blocked shots and hell he plays great. It was a time for Magic to show what he can do because there's a lot of flair to his game."

At halftime, Dick Enberg told Packer to back off and let Al McGuire run the immense amount of garbage time left to televise in the second half with his storytelling.

It was time McGuire used to extoll the obvious virtues of Kelser, even as the splendor of Magic was coming into full view, Packer explained, pointing out that in the second half Johnson was playing more inside and rebounding. Heathcote had been in Packer's ear and in the ear of anyone who would listen about Johnson's ability to rebound and to turn defense into instant offense.

"He could take it coast-to-coast as well as anybody that I've seen in basketball," Packer said in 2019. "But I didn't think he could do that when he went to the next level because of the way he dribbled. The ball was coming three feet off the ground."

It would be one thing to project smaller guards with tighter handles taking the ball the length of the court in the NBA, but not Johnson, Packer explained. "But to see this six-foot-nine-inch guy dribble in the way he did, maneuvering the basketball and wanting to make a play as opposed to scoring with it? It was fun to watch, but it didn't seem reasonable if he's going to go to the next level to play. What is he? What position is he going to play? So even though he had a triple-double and they won the game handily, Greg Kelser probably played a game where you can see him fitting into an NBA team very well."

A similar confounding mystery awaited in the other bracket with Bird's team taking on Ray Meyer's DePaul team featuring sensational freshman Mark Aguirre. The Spartans, in fact, had been dismayed, Ron Charles remembered, because they wanted the challenge of playing DePaul, not some Ivy League blowout. They had seen DePaul on TV several times and knew that would be a fun challenge.

The State players had finally gotten to see Bird and Indiana State in one of their regional games, but that gave them no real idea of how good he was, until the DePaul game, Charles recalled. "Larry Bird killed them. You know, he wouldn't miss a shot. He could not miss a shot. It was like, 'Wow!'"

The Spartans were somewhat let down by the outcome, Charles remembered. "Me and Earvin were roommates. We really wanted to play DePaul because I think it would have been a better, more exciting game."

"Bird had an incredible game against much stronger competition," Packer said in 2019 of that semifinal. "It was a far more competitive game, a game that came right down to the wire. And Larry Bird played as good a semifinal game as probably has ever been played, with 35 points, 16 rebounds, and nine assists."

Even with that performance, Packer harbored serious doubts, recalling that "still in my mind the things that jumped out to me were the things that I had already seen. He was an unbelievably tough guy, great hands, great court awareness, but a limited offensive repertoire. There was no way you knew that he was going to become one of the greatest shooters of all time from the outside. He was still slow and didn't jump well. He was a position rebounder, but he also was a real thinker and he was a leader."

For the next day's practice, Heathcote had to find someone to play Bird so that the Spartans could figure out how to line up their matchup zone to stop him. The coach chose Magic for that job of mimicking Bird's game.

"You're going to go to the scout team," Charles remembered Heathcote telling Johnson. "You're going to be Larry Bird. You can shoot it from anywhere."

"Of course, Earvin, doing whatever he wanted shooting, he played really, really well, didn't hardly miss a shot," Charles recalled, adding that the more Johnson scored against the starters the angrier Heathcote got. "It's like, 'Shut up now.' We're mad at him because coach is on us."

"Can't you stop him?" Heathcote asked again and again. "Can't you do it? Can't you?"

"We were trying now, but Earvin was in a zone and was throwin' up stuff and it was going in," Charles said. "Throwing up stuff, and he's laughing because coach was on us."

Laughter aside, after the practice, the Spartans had a clear idea of how to deal with Bird. "We weren't fearful," Greg Kelser explained in 2019.

Charles and Johnson retreated after practice to their hotel room where they spent time calling their girlfriends. Johnson had brought another girl to Salt Lake City, rather than Cookie, who was deeply hurt by the circumstances. Still, it was a carefree evening. After all, as Charles explained, "We were tall and athletic and we had Earvin playing as Bird the day before. So playing against them the next day was easy. We didn't fear Indiana State. We thought we were better than them. We were just a better team."

The Tube Moment

That Sunday morning of the Final Four weekend, NBC had a production meeting to plan for the Monday night championship broadcast. Don Ohlmeyer, the executive producer for the broadcast, was late showing up, so the broadcast team went ahead with their thoughts for the pregame show. McGuire said it would be cool to focus on Indiana State coach Bill Hodges, who had been an assistant for the team until head coach Bob King, who had become seriously ill before the season, which had resulted in Hodges being promoted to head coach. Here was Hodges, heading into the national championship game in his first season with a 33–0 record.

"Ohlmeyer walks in," Packer recalled, "and he says, 'Okay, so I'm late. How you going to start this off?' They explained it to him, and I'll never forget him. He says, 'That's the dumbest damn thing I've ever heard of. You guys have no damn clue what you're talking about. The real story about this game is going to be Bird and Johnson. It's going to be part of basketball history.'"

He and McGuire were somewhat flabbergasted by Ohlmeyer, Packer admitted. "He didn't know shit about basketball."

Yet Ohlmeyer had spent a decade working for Roone Arledge at ABC's *Wide World of Sports*. As writer Seth Davis would observe in his book *When March Went Mad*, Ohlmeyer knew all about story.

"He really had a great feel for the theatrics," Packer admitted.

The problem was, the broadcast team had no access to the teams at practice that Sunday. Packer would have to hustle to the arena with a camera crew to try to catch the two young stars as they came and went.

"We had to go over to the gym hoping to catch the two of them maybe coming off the bus or something like that," Packer recalled, the disgust and irritation still obvious in his voice forty years later. "It just so happened that that's what we were able to do. We caught them both on camera and just kind of pretended like we were having a conversation with them. But we had no ability to sit down and talk about basketball. I kind of thought it was rather stupid."

Packer certainly had his doubts that Bird would even speak with him, but he did, even though eye contact with the Indiana State star remained hard to achieve.

Asked for his thoughts on the big game, Bird replied simply with great insight, "Well, this is probably the biggest game I'll ever play in my life."

And just as Johnson valued the community of Lansing, Bird held high the town of Terre Haute, Indiana, where his school was located, telling Packer, "I just feel like I'm representing not only myself and my team, but we're representing our school and our town, Terre Haute. It means so much to me just to even be here that we're gonna give it all we got, and we're gonna try our hardest to win."

"You know," Packer replied, "a lot of people were surprised yesterday, Larry, when you mentioned you played ball with Magic Johnson in the World Invitational Tournament."

"Well, you know me and Magic played in that game," Bird said, "and you know it's funny 'cause Magic's such a great presser, but he wouldn't give me the ball. And you know I need the ball."

With Bird's team leaving, Packer and the crew then were able to talk briefly with Johnson for their package that would be aired nationwide before the game.

"It's a dream come true, really, for me," Johnson told the broadcaster. "I won a state title [in high school] back in my home state, and then my next accomplishment was going to the NCAA and playing a game like tonight in the finals. I just hope we play up to par and win the game."

Johnson smiled when Packer told him Bird's comment about not getting the ball from Johnson in the World Invitational Tournament.

"Well, I hope he don't think I'm gonna pass it to him tonight, either," Johnson said. "But I thought I passed him the ball. Maybe he forgot."

The contrast between the two became clearer in and around the workings of the game broadcast. Johnson was the kind of guy to "come over and say, 'Hey, how you guys doing?'" Packer recalled. "Larry Bird? I never said hello to him. I never had a conversation with him at all. And I don't know anybody else that did either. Nobody. That night of that championship, if you watched what would happen, there is no damn way that you'd have thought, 'I'm sitting here watching the two guys who are going to change the world in terms of basketball.'"

Packer recalled that he would finally be able to connect with Bird a little better about a month after the season for Larry Bird Day in French Lick, Indiana, where "it was even more depressing how backward he seemed to be."

As for the championship night, the startling factor would prove to be not the game itself, but the size of the audience. Bird vs. Magic would draw a record 24.1 Nielsen rating, meaning about a fourth of all TV sets in America were tuned to the game, a record 35.1 million people. In the four decades that followed there would be not a single basketball championship, in college or pro, that would equal the rating. Game 6 of the 1998 NBA Finals, Michael Jordan's last championship appearance, drew a 22.3 rating, then estimated to represent 35.9 million viewers, reflecting the growth of interest in basketball as well as in the American population over the two decades between the two events.

"Now, the game as played was a terrible game," Packer offered in 2019. "Everybody talks about now it was the most watched Final Four of all time, and I guess it was. I mean you can't argue with a statistic. It was a noncompetitive game almost right off the bat even though Jay Vincent was injured and only played a little."

For the record, Michigan State won, 75–64. From the start, it became increasingly clear that Indiana State had no earthly idea how to deal with the Spartans' matchup zone.

"We skewed the zone to stop a certain person," Ron Charles explained. "So if you only had one good player on your team or two good players, we would put the zone to put more control on you. Now if somebody else beat you then so be it."

Bird wasn't just the leader of the Sycamores but the scoring leader, the force that drove the entire team.

"There was nobody else that's going to beat us," Charles offered. "He wasn't going to beat us by hisself, right? Because the whole team was Larry Bird."

"Michigan State was just too good for Bird, you know," Packer recalled. "He really had a very difficult game. That zone was just all over him."

For a time, Bird moved to the deep left corner, taking several shots that would be considered corner threes under the later rules. He hit one of them. Beyond that, he moved down to the right block and tried to work there. It was as crowded as Main Street.

The result? Bird missed 14 of the 21 shots he took. He finished with 19 points, nine below his average, with 13 rebounds. Even more telling, he was able to produce just two assists. The zone had taken away even his vaunted passing.

"When Bird dribbled, we put a man and a half on him," Johnson had yelled to an interviewer in the noisy arena afterward. "The guard slid over and helped the forward. I think we put a lot of pressure on Larry."

Bird had still managed to produce surprising moments. Johnson smelled blood on one furious break and unleashed a lob from half-court to Kelser flying high at the rim, only to see a retreating Bird rise up to block it. Johnson also posted on an inbounds play and worked a fancy spin to shoot but Bird slapped it away. But it was and would remain forever Johnson's show, from his passing to his scoring and posting, even his hitting a running bank shot at full speed off the wrong foot.

In and around the championship night, America finally got the first full look at this guy called Magic Johnson, a young man with a smile so tall and wide that his cheeks seemed to strain mightily just to hold it all together. This pleasing battle of his face had proved to be absolutely infectious to that nationwide audience. To many fans, he had appeared from nowhere to lead this denial of Larry Bird.

Never perhaps in the history of America's much beloved sporting scene had the public gotten a glimpse of such an infectious countenance. There had been Cassius Clay in the 1960s, who soon became Muhammad Ali, but the boxer talked so much smack and so openly challenged the social order that white people had set up for themselves that the two were very different forces in different moments.

This new Magic Johnson was none of that.

The entire arrangement of that smile sat perched upon his skinny neck and long, lean almost six-foot-nine frame in a way that suggested he was larger than life, distorted even, as if presented to the public through a fish-eye lens, something otherworldly.

Johnson's happily distended face dramatically differed from Bird's stoic appearance afterward that later turned tearful. On the floor after the game, Bird moved past Johnson quickly with a grim look, not saying even a word of congratulations.

For years afterward, it would be recalled that Bird had sat in his team's training room before the game and said, "I just don't feel it tonight." Although he later said he didn't remember such a statement, others confirmed it and he didn't deny it.

He also had an injured thumb, but the greatest injury was clearly the Michigan State zone. The results for Bird stood in great contrast to those of Gregory Kelser, who scored his own 19 points and registered nine assists, numbers that drove the Spartans' momentum well into the second half.

"I think we would have blown Indiana State out, too, if I hadn't gotten in foul trouble," Kelser told the *Free Press* in 1989. "We were up by nine at the half and had scored the first seven points of the second half to go up by 16. Then I got into foul trouble and we got a little conservative after that."

With 10 minutes to play, Bird and his teammates cut the lead to six. "I think we kind of lost our tempo," Johnson explained afterward. "I decided to shoot a little more."

At Heathcote's urging, Johnson provided a moment that countered the conventional thinking that had misunderstood his game. He showed quite well that he could score on demand, finishing the plays that opened the lead, including a dunk that drew a foul for undercutting him for a four-point play that developed as a give-and-go with Kelser.

With two seconds to go, Johnson inbounded the ball and threw a length-of-the-floor pass to Kelser for an emphatic final slam.

Johnson finished with 24 as the game's top scorer and later was named the tournament's Most Outstanding Player. The only cloud that crossed his face after the game came when he thought that Bird had been named the outstanding player but a quick clarification refired the 100-watt smile.

"Magic had his way and Kelser had his way," Packer said in 2019. "They both played extremely well and basically controlled the game. Magic had 24 points, five assists. But in that game Kelser had nine assists and 19 points. He was 7 for 13 and two blocked shots."

Kelser had been critical making plays, and it would have been easy to name him the tournament's Outstanding Player, instead of Johnson, Packer said. "You can make a case for Kelser."

Even with Johnson's performance, the conventional thinking of so many of the scouts and basketball executives watching the event was that Kelser would be the surefire NBA prospect, Packer pointed out. "If you're thinking in the traditional way, he had all the skills at small forward to fit into an NBA game."

The questions, even with his great tournament performance, still dogged Johnson, Packer remembered. "Where the hell's he going to play? You know, he's not big enough to be a center. He's really not a post-up player to play power forward. You can't use him as a two guard because he doesn't have any shot, and he's never going to get away with the crazy damn ball-handling skills that he has because 'real' guards will take the ball away from him in the NBA. So, you know, even though he's had a great Final Four and he's lighting everybody up . . . I'm looking at him trying to analyze him as a player and I'm saying, 'He loves to compete, he's long, but boy, there's some areas of his game that separate him from greatness that are just too hard to overcome.'"

With the Spartans holding a comfortable lead in the second half, Enberg had asked which player would an NBA general manager want to draft. McGuire answered that Kelser would be the guy. Packer recalled commenting that McGuire had misunderstood Enberg's question, that he was asking who would be seen as more valuable, Johnson or Bird? Packer said he had reservations about both, Bird with his limited athleticism and Johnson with his unusual game. While he loved the competitive nature and intangibles of both players, Bird couldn't jump and Magic couldn't shoot, Packer recalled explaining. "I thought that although Magic's rebounding and starting fast breaks in the college game with that high dribble, what the hell's he going to do in the NBA?"

Packer observed that he and McGuire were two guys fully steeped in all of the assembled wisdom of the game over decades, the kind of conventional thinking that Jerry West himself would later acknowledge.

"Here's two guys supposed to know a little bit about the game," Packer said of himself and McGuire. "Here is supposedly the greatest Final Four game of all time. Here was the great showcase of Bird and Johnson and that was our analysis, our honest analysis of these two guys.

"What we did not understand, what we didn't know, what you can't ever judge . . . we didn't know what kind of heart they had," Packer said.

Meanwhile, NBA executives were looking at Bird and Johnson and seeing something very different, explained Jim Chones, who would be Johnson's pro teammate. "The league, they were sitting and watching the NCAA tournament with Magic and Larry, and they said, 'You know what? This is a more exciting style of play.' He would have had a rivalry with anybody. Magic was competitive with everybody. Bird just happened to be his nemesis. In other words, Bird was also a guy who was garnering just as much respect as Magic. Magic was never afraid to compete. He didn't pick his battles. Whatever battle was out there, he would try to overcome it. He was just super-competitive and Bird was in his way."

"They were powerful figures in life," Ron Charles said of Johnson and Bird. "Players will know them forever."

PART II

HOLLYWOOD

17

STRANGE DAYS, INDEED

There was a large pressure system out of Texas that June of 1979, which meant the Santa Ana winds came rushing out of the desert east of Los Angeles and rolled west across the landscape to deliver daytime highs of 105 degrees, breaking a century-old heat record for the city, hardly a good thing, especially if you were stashing a body in the trunk of a Rolls-Royce abandoned in the parking garage of the Universal City Sheraton.

It was still an era when newspaper headlines announced events to the world, with large, bold type reserved for truly cataclysmic developments, such as the death that same month of John Wayne, then the largest box office draw in the history of the film industry, which was a very big deal in the company town that was Hollywood, and it contributed to the sense, as the decade was coming to a close, that the broader world itself was heading for major uncertainty and change.

After all, 1980 was just around the corner, and right behind it was George Orwell's prophetic 1984. Foreboding seemed to rule just about everything in 1979.

The same was certainly true for American professional basketball, if anybody had bothered to notice, not that many did, especially in Los Angeles, where ticket sales for the Lakers had precipitously declined over the previous four seasons, never mind the star presence of Kareem Abdul-Jabbar with the beloved Jerry West as his coach and two recent trips to the playoffs.

Indeed, it's been said there's nothing sadder in all of L.A. than a star whose time has passed, or one who is watching it slip by, unfulfilled, which meant that whatever pro basketball was to the city, it hadn't been enough to attract any sort of passion, either from the shrinking number of fans or from the thirty-two-year-old Abdul-Jabbar himself, seen as an intelligent and gifted but brooding giant.

"I have seen happier faces on guys carrying a casket," legendary *L.A. Times* columnist Jim Murray would say of the 1979 Lakers, a team that had churned out so many rumors about cocaine use over the late 1970s that its former GM, Pete Newell, revealed in a 1992 interview that the front office had employed an off-duty LAPD vice detective to keep track of the off-court activities of the players.

Yet it was hardly fair to lay the decline of pro basketball on Abdul-Jabbar. As the center himself often pointed out, he was simply the biggest target available for whatever emotion or finger-pointing was in play at any given time.

Besides, pro basketball's problems seemed far larger than the Lakers or any team. The league's broadcast partner, CBS, had just reported a staggering drop of 26 percent in the viewership ratings for its NBA games and was already hatching plans to deliver part of the 1980 NBA Finals, the league's championship series, on taped delay, surely a sign of decline that suggested serious trouble for a business that had struggled the entire three decades of its existence.

In June 1979, frankly, no one in Los Angeles was concerned about the TV presentation of the following year's championship series because there was no great sense that the local team had much of a chance of getting to it.

All in all, 1979 would reveal itself as a twisted, macabre, tragic, angry year in the history of the Los Angeles Lakers. Worse yet, it would prove an absolutely horrific period for the coaches of the team, or for people who wanted to be the coach.

Jerry West, whose silhouette emblazoned the NBA's logo, had

spent three torturous years guiding the team from the bench and was at his wit's end. The agony of his coaching tenure had proved a perfect fit to the agony of his 14-year playing career, which saw his Lakers lose seven times in the league championship series before gaining a single victory there in 1972.

West had abruptly ended his playing career during the team's 1974 training camp in a venomous financial dispute with owner Jack Kent Cooke that led to West filing a lawsuit against the team.

As part of the settlement of the lawsuit in 1976, West had been hired to coach the Lakers, only to run into yet another torturous conflict with Cooke, seen by many as an immensely arrogant and impatient man. ("He was the greatest asshole who ever lived," former Laker Hot Rod Hundley had once said of the owner.) With Abdul-Jabbar in the fold, the Lakers had the opportunity to acquire Julius Erving of the rival American Basketball Association's New Jersey Nets just as that league was folding.

Kareem and Dr. J on the same roster?

It was one of those perfect moments when an ultimate basketball solution was miraculously available to West, the man who had suffered so much with the game.

But Jack Kent Cooke refused to make the move, which doomed West to a miserable coaching experience, watching his team struggle through one frustrating episode after another all while Erving performed wondrously for the Philadelphia 76ers.

Finally worn down by his perfectionist nature and the task of coaching an undermanned team, West had indicated many times throughout the 1978–79 season that he intended to leave the coaching job at the season's end. He had almost quit one night right on the spot after a defeat in Boston, the scene of much of his personal disappointment over the years. Yet when that time finally had arrived to step down, West had strangely hesitated, perhaps conflicted by several converging events, the first of which involved Cooke's ongoing attempts for several years to sell the team due to an ugly divorce he was going through.

Cooke's divorce had finally reached a massive settlement that March, estimated at $49 million, which abruptly hastened the pace of the owner's plans to sell the team and other properties to help pay off his former wife of four decades.

Another of the events was a looming April coin toss with the Chicago Bulls to see who would get the number one pick in the upcoming draft that June, a development that keenly interested Cooke and a local real estate developer and playboy (who also held a PhD in chemistry) named Jerry Buss, who was tops among several candidates to buy the team even though he was not the highest bidder.

Buss was something of a financial whiz who had made millions in the Southern California real estate market, which had allowed him to gain an edge among the figures seeking to buy Cooke's West Coast sports empire because he proposed to swap properties with Cooke rather than pay him entirely in cash, thus allowing the team owner to avoid millions in taxes. The question that would long endure is why, why would a man who had worked two decades to earn millions want to risk it all on the business of pro basketball, a venture that was losing millions at the time?

The two men made for an interesting pair negotiating what at the time would become the largest deal in the history of American professional sports. Buss was a young forty-six, and in love with the future, and Cooke, at sixty-six and immensely impatient his entire life, was done with the past. Asked about his basketball team, the owner replied, "Bloody boring. That's what they've been the past two or three years. Bloody boring."

Cooke admitted that after almost two decades of owning the Lakers he was finished with all of pro basketball, saying, "Dr. Buss and I have different ideas on the potential of tomorrow. Dr. Buss sees things I don't see."

Buss, in fact, had calculated all sorts of untapped profit potential for the franchise, including the little-considered notion of huge revenue from pay-per-view television.

One vision the two men did share was the coin flip just days away that April.

Despite being a playoff team, the Lakers had a shot at the top pick because back in 1976, one of their stars, thirty-three-year-old Gail Goodrich, had played out his option with the Lakers and signed a contract with the New Orleans Jazz. As recounted in this author's 1993 book *The Lakers*, under the league rules at the time, the Jazz owed the Lakers compensation for luring Goodrich away, so Cooke had ordered his lawyer to strike a tough bargain with New Orleans. The Lakers demanded and got New Orleans' number one picks in 1977 and 1979 and a second-round pick in 1980. It was a blatantly unreasonable asking price for Goodrich, who would only play parts of three injury-plagued seasons for the Jazz. But Cooke sensed that if the two teams failed to agree on compensation, then league commissioner Larry O'Brien would settle it for them. The Jazz feared that O'Brien, who didn't like one team signing away another's players, would come down hard on them. So they agreed to the crazy deal.

Which, in retrospect, would prove to be the first lucky strike for Magic Johnson.

The Lakers, however, couldn't stand their success, so they then offered the three picks back to the Jazz for veteran power forward Sidney Wicks, which proved to be Magic Johnson's second lucky strike because the Jazz refused that Wicks deal and then helped the Lakers' cause tremendously by finishing last in the league in 1979, thus ensuring L.A. that coin flip with Chicago, the worst team in the East, for the top pick in the June draft, a coin toss that would change the entire history of pro basketball in profound ways.

So, the complicated drama seemed finally to be coming to a close. For almost three years, Cooke had been hiding away as an absentee owner in Las Vegas, where he had gone to take refuge from the monster divorce action his wife had filed against him. Vegas kept him away from the Lakers, but it allowed him to establish residence in a place where the divorce laws were more favorable.

Cooke clearly was a motivated seller. Even so, both he and Buss held a keen interest in the coin toss that would seal the fate not just of Magic Johnson but all of pro basketball itself as well as two of America's biggest and most celebrated cities, indeed you could argue much of the nation's, even the globe's, zeitgeist.

"That's how it was done back then," longtime NBA executive Pat Williams explained, "and your whole future rested on the odds of what a coin is going to do. And so that's what happened."

In those days, legendary Lakers broadcaster Chick Hearn also served as an assistant general manager for the team. Commissioner O'Brien made the flip at the NBA's New York offices while the Lakers and Bulls listened over the phone in a conference call. Cooke was so nervous, he couldn't go in the cramped office where Chick Hearn was taking O'Brien's call.

"Rod Thorn was the general manager in Chicago," longtime Lakers executive Bill Sharman recalled in 1992. "He said they had a big promotion where they had a lot of people in their auditorium when they made the flip. He asked, 'Would it be all right with you if I make the call, because we got all these people here?' I said it's either heads or tails; it doesn't make that much difference."

The Bulls were so excited about the idea of getting Johnson—the Lakers had also started their own "magical" ticket sales campaign—that they arranged a promotion in which the team's fans decided whether to call heads or tails for the flip.

As directed by Chicago fans, Thorn called heads.

Tails it was.

"Chick let up a yell that could have been heard in downtown Los Angeles," Jack Kent Cooke recalled in a 1992 interview.

"I remember being there the day the Lakers won the coin toss for the rights to draft Magic. It was Chick Hearn, Bill Sharman, and myself," said longtime L.A. sportscaster Jim Hill. "We were standing by a speakerphone, and the cameras were rolling and the coin was being tossed back in New York."

Johnson himself had considered playing for Chicago a positive thing because the city was a short distance from his beloved Michigan and because the Bulls had a legitimate center in Artis Gilmore, according to George Andrews, Johnson's lawyer at the time. "Gilmore was playing really well and Kareem had turned like thirty-two and wasn't playing well. The Lakers were a little over .500 and only drawing eleven thousand. Jerry West was about to quit. It didn't look like the ideal situation, and Artis was such a strong guy. It was close to home. I would say it was at least 50–50 if not leaning towards Chicago."

Exciting as it was, the coin toss victory created one last dilemma. Should the Lakers draft Johnson or Sidney Moncrief, out of the University of Arkansas? It might have seemed a legitimate basketball question at the time, but it was going to be settled by Cooke and Buss, two men who were far more focused on the ticket sales that a rookie named Magic could generate.

After all, both Buss and Cooke were rags-to-riches stories, particularly Cooke in Canada, where during the Depression he sold encyclopedias door-to-door, then sold advertising for drab little radio stations that nobody wanted. "There was a toughness to him," Pat Williams recalled in 2019, "and he got into sports with AAA baseball in Toronto and then he moved to L.A. A hockey guy, he wanted to bring hockey to L.A. Then the Lakers were available. He didn't know anything about basketball, but he did notice that there were basketball hoops in driveways all over Southern California. He bought the Lakers at the right time, you know, Elgin Baylor and West were just coming into their own."

As Lakers owner for nearly two decades, Cooke had come to lord over many of the greatest minds of basketball—men such as Pete Newell and Bill Sharman and Fred Schaus (a former Lakers coach) and Jerry West—and treat them shabbily, Pat Williams explained in 2019. "He would just wear those guys out."

Williams would serve first as GM of the Bulls in Chicago, then the Sixers, and finally the Magic in Orlando, but his early days as an executive left him surprised at just how cowed the Lakers executives were.

"I will never forget, these two basketball titans, Fred Schaus and the legendary Pete Newell," Williams remembered. "You're talking to them about players and they'd say, 'Well, I would have to talk to Mr. Cooke about that. It all depends on what Mr. Cooke thinks. Excuse me. I just heard Mr. Cooke wants to see me.' I'll tell you this, those guys were absolutely terrified of him. These were some of the really successful great names in basketball history, but Jack Kent Cooke just terrified them. It was always Mr. Cooke, this, and Mr. Cooke, that. They would wilt before him. Cooke just ruled by terror. He was just very glib."

John Radcliffe had begun as the Lakers scorekeeper in the early 1960s and would hold the post for five decades, giving him a front-row seat to so many things that happened with the franchise. He was quite familiar with how Cooke dominated the team's coaches and executives.

"He yelled at Fred Schaus," Radcliffe recalled of the Lakers coach and executive. "He would really light into Fred. He would yell at people in front of people. Everybody was on eggshells."

All Lakers employees shared that same fear, Pat Williams added. "You did not want to be called into his office. You didn't want that call from his secretary, 'Mr. Cooke would like to see you.'"

Cooke's personality mixed with that of the intense Jerry West was just incendiary, Williams added. "Jerry, maybe one of the most complicated human beings ever to walk this earth, you pick up the phone to get him on the line and he starts talking and you haven't even asked him a question and he begins to unload on everything that's on his mind and everything that's happening in the league and everything going on with your team. And that's the first fifteen minutes."

As for the decision about the draft, the conventional, safe pick was Moncrief, a great guard who would become a Hall of Famer, but the Laker front office hadn't even interviewed him. Those hungry for glittering star potential and ticket sales thought it should be Johnson. The Lakers, for better or for worse, were Hollywood's team in a town that loved its stars.

"Jerry Krause was our scout back then who was very high on this kid Magic," recalled former Lakers PR and marketing man Roy Englebrecht. (Krause would later become general manager of the Chicago Bulls during the Jordan era.)

"There was no question in my mind that we should draft Magic Johnson," Cooke said in a 1992 interview.

Broadcaster Jim Hill recalled the owner declaring, "The name Magic says it all!"

Jerry Buss also made known his strong preference for Johnson. "My dad had watched him in the NCAA tournament and was such a huge fan," Jeanie Buss recalled in a 2020 interview.

And so it was. The decision to draft Magic Johnson was made largely by two men who knew little about the game and were operating on their business instinct, just the kind of circumstances that had created many high-priced failed NBA draft picks over the years.

Having lost the toss, the Bulls then offered to trade their top pick, plus another flashy talent in Reggie Theus, for the rights to the Magic Man. When the Lakers declined that deal, Johnson had secured his third lucky strike in the process.

So with the owner's future and present weighing in, the choice was sealed. Little did they realize then that what would become the Showtime era was close to signing its master of ceremonies.

Dabs

Just days after the coin toss, Johnson, his father, Charles Tucker, and his attorneys from Chicago, George Andrews and his uncle Harold, all went to L.A. to check out the deal.

For a time, Johnson had retained Georgia attorney Jack Manton but then abruptly fired him. "I had him $600,000 a year for five years," Manton would later tell *Sports Illustrated*. "What Magic and his people did was leave $1.5 million on the table. It's sad."

Johnson also flew to Philadelphia, spent a weekend with one of his idols, Julius Erving, to consult about the business of pro basketball, George Andrews recalled, adding that Johnson also visited with Erving's agent and found the man unsuitable.

There was little limit on what percentage agents could take in that era. Some took as much as 30 percent. Johnson's instincts led him to follow the advice of Gus Ganakas, who recommended Andrews and his uncle Harold as lawyers, not agents, paid hourly, not on a percentage. The Andrewses already had some sports clients, but their law practice focused on other things, including representing a string of McDonald's franchisees.

George Andrews and his uncle stepped right to the immediate issue of sorting out a contract with the Lakers.

It might seem strange, looking back, that the outgoing owner would control so much related to the signing of Magic Johnson, but the sale of the team was a tangled, mysterious endeavor that seemed in doubt right up until the very last minute, then remained in limbo awaiting a vote approving the deal by the league's Board of Governors late that June.

In their first contract meetings, a clash quickly developed between the titanically arrogant Cooke and the Johnsons with their humble midwestern sensibilities.

"It wasn't rude, just pretty funny," George Andrews recalled in 2019. "My uncle and Jack Kent Cooke spent about twenty minutes arguing about the parameters for how to pronounce the word *parameter*. We all met Jack Kent Cooke because he was still the owner at the time. Now, we do not know he was having contemporary discussions with Jerry Buss. Cooke took Magic on a tour of the Forum."

As everyone in Los Angeles knew, Cooke was immensely proud of what he liked to call the "Fabulous" Forum, which the owner had built in 1965 as something of an architectural wonder.

As George Andrews recalled, "Cooke was saying, 'Well, what do you think, Earvin? How does it compare?' Earvin goes, 'Well, we got three or four buildings in the Big Ten that are just as good or better.' I thought Cooke was going to shit in his pants because at the time it was pretty much a state-of-the-art facility."

The first day of the two days of meetings, Cooke suggested that to close the deal the entire group should go to a well-known restaurant, while pointing out that "it's really expensive," Andrews recalled. "Jack Kent Cooke was just finishing his divorce. He had just finished giving his ex-wife 49 million dollars. Mr. Johnson goes, 'I don't want to say anything, Mr. Cooke, but if you say it's so expensive and you just gave your wife 49 million dollars, I don't think we can afford to go there.' I mean, it was really funny."

In one of their two meetings, Cooke ordered for them all what was then considered something of an exotic dish, a type of Pacific flounder.

"Before they started negotiating, Mr. Cooke ordered sand dabs," L.A. sportscaster Jim Hill recalled. "Magic said, 'I didn't know what a sand dab was.' He turned to his father and said, 'I don't want a sand dab. I don't know what that is.' Mr. Cooke said, 'Do you know how much a sand dab costs?' He said, 'I don't care how much it costs. I just want a burger and some fries.' So, they laughed about that."

The laughter struggled to break the uneasiness that prevailed. In a 2002 radio interview with broadcaster Larry Burnett, Chick Hearn recalled the introduction and negotiations: "Mr. Cooke said, 'Well, Magic Johnson. Should I call you Magic or Earvin?' Magic said, 'It doesn't matter what you call me, Mr. Cooke, we're going to have to negotiate if I am going to play for your team.' Mr. Cooke said, 'I understand that.' Mr. Cooke took out a big yellow pad and his pen. He said to Magic's father, 'What, Mr. Johnson, do you think I should pay your son to become a Laker?'"

"That's out of my field," Big Earv told the owner. "I can't answer that question."

Known for a prodigious memory, Hearn recalled Johnson interrupting, saying, "I'll answer that question."

The owner told Johnson to go ahead, Hearn said. "So Magic told Mr. Cooke, 'Here's what I think I should get in my first year.' He gave him a big number. Big number! Then Magic said, I should also get compensated for doing this or that. He went through a lot of things."

Cooke asked, "Is that all?"

"That's all I can think of right now," Johnson said.

"So," Hearn recounted to Larry Burnett, "Mr. Cooke drew a line under all those numbers, added them up, and said, 'My God, Magic! That's a lot of money!' Magic, very calmly, said, 'Mr. Cooke, I'm a lot of player.'"

Hearn laughed in 2002, telling Burnett the story.

"And that's when they signed him," the legendary broadcaster recalled. "It was very unusual."

One interesting aside was that Pat Riley, then working as a broadcast assistant to Hearn, was also included in one of the meetings, George Andrews recalled. "We met them for our initial visit when we had lunch with Jack Kent Cooke and Chick and Jerry West. Pat was just kind of like a guy in the room. It was pretty funny. Pat was Chick Hearn's assistant in the broadcast booth. He basically got everybody coffee."

Amidst all the various discussions, the participants managed to get down to a clear figure.

"Mr. Cooke made him an offer, about $400,000 or so," Jim Hill, long a Johnson confidant, remembered. "Magic said, 'I don't know about that offer.' His father was sitting there with him. His father tapped him on the knee and said, 'Come with me.' They went outside, and Magic said his father said, 'Oh, yeah, you gonna take that $400,000.' So they went back inside, and Magic said, 'Mr. Cooke, we've reconsidered . . .'"

It was at that point, Andrews recalled, that "Cooke says, 'Let me sleep on what we agreed on.' And Mr. Johnson goes, 'Well, you know, I got to get back to work. It's costing me money.'" Andrews pointed out that he and his uncle were Johnson's lawyers, not his agents, "because Earvin wanted to preserve his eligibility to go back to school. So, Cooke says, 'Don't worry. It'll be worth your while.' And the next day we made the deal, and then subsequent to that Cooke had to go back to Jerry Buss and get Buss's approval on the contract."

Media outlets would later report a variety of estimates for Johnson's first contract. Johnson himself would later figure that he got about $150,000 a year less than Bird's reported $650,000 a year contract, a development that Johnson was watching intently. That Bird contract, which was still being negotiated, would eventually include a signing bonus of an estimated $375,000.

In recalling the negotiations for Johnson in 2019, Charles Tucker pointed out the sketchy amount of an NBA contract leaked to the public in those days before rookie salary caps. Tucker said Cooke was offering extra money sometimes paid under the table, which somehow helped him in his multifaceted transactions. Agreeing to part of the money being paid under the table required trusting Cooke's word on the deal, Tucker explained, adding that Cooke kept his word about all such monies.

Salaries for rookies were escalating in 1979, driven in part by the tough deal that Bird's agent, Bob Woolf, was pushing with Red Auerbach and the Celtics in Boston. Bird, after all, was a coveted white star, and the Celtics were under the gun to sign him or lose him to immediate free agency.

Meanwhile, the Lakers were reportedly paying an established star like Jamaal Wilkes $300,000 a year. Signing a rookie to more than that, or to more than Abdul-Jabbar's reported $650,000 a year at the time, could create huge headaches.

"One source says Magic received $300,000 a year for four years, plus a $100,000 signing bonus," *Sports Illustrated* would report much later that fall, well after the negotiations.

With at least $100,000 available in immediate cash because of the signing bonus, Johnson signed the contract based on those negotiations with Cooke, although the rookie would come down with a case of cold feet once he was back in Lansing.

Before he could become available to the Lakers, he would have to declare hardship for the draft, which had left Johnson strangely pondering what to do amid many distractions. *Sports Illustrated* dispatched writer Douglas S. Looney to explore why. Looney found the Magic Man in his East Lansing apartment fielding an almost nonstop flow of phone calls from women eager to meet and greet him.

"Donna?" Johnson would answer. "Donna who?"

"Lisa?" he asked, taking a call just a moment later. "Lisa who?"

On it went through the entire interview.

Ah, college life for a star, especially one who listed his phone number publicly, almost as a means of catching the bees. But Michigan State's campus was a mere 45,000 students. Johnson had absolutely no idea of the size of the buzz that awaited him in Los Angeles.

"Magic had to go have his press conference up in Lansing," George Andrews recalled. "He couldn't sleep all night. He said, 'I couldn't make a decision.' But the guy had already decided to go. He had a signed contract. I wasn't at the press conference. Obviously, he was a pretty good actor. He had no choice."

The deadline for declaring hardship arrived on May 12 without Johnson having revealed that he was turning pro. He pushed it right up to the deadline before making the announcement, which broke all the hearts he knew it would break in Lansing and left Heathcote darkly jesting about going off somewhere to puke.

This time, Big Earv offered no silent opposition. "It seemed like he couldn't do no more there," the father said. "They won the Big Ten, then they won the NCAA. After that, there didn't seem like there was anything for him to do."

Meanwhile, back on May 3, just days earlier, reporters had arrived at a press conference to announce the new owner of the Indiana Pacers fully expecting it to be Jerry Buss, who was heading up a group trying to buy the team. Buss, however, had quickly ducked out of that announcement because the Lakers deal had suddenly taken precedence. Instead, Sam Nassi, one of Buss's business associates, and Frank Mariani, Buss's business partner of the past twenty years, showed up in Indianapolis to take control of the Pacers. Buss had stepped out of the way of owning the team, but he still took majority ownership of the long-term lease for Market Square Arena, the home court of the Pacers.

The crazy moment was part of a series of swirling events that would leave observers confused with questions that would go unanswered for years. In fact, Johnson's future and that of the Lakers were set to be tied to two huge mysteries that would never be fully solved. One would involve the aforementioned body in the trunk of the Rolls at the Universal City Sheraton, and the other was the rapidly mushrooming deal for Jerry Buss to buy Jack Kent Cooke's sports empire on the West Coast.

The negotiations over Buss buying out Cooke already seemed to be playing out like a Hollywood script concoction and that was before the murder. Increasingly, the spotlight was turning to Buss himself and he welcomed it for the most part, except for talking about the murder.

"I remember right after he bought the team," recalled Roy Englebrecht, who doubled as PR director and marketing manager for the Lakers. "We had a meeting with some of the executives. I remember his saying, 'Don't book me for any meeting until afternoon. I don't do mornings.' He was a party guy. It was so funny because Jack Kent Cooke was all buttoned up and very coat and tie. Then here at noontime or so Dr. Buss would come down the hallway—this was in the '80s—with his shirt open and a leather jacket and torn jeans and then maybe five minutes later here would come a dynamite-looking girl with a little dog on a leash. Mr. Cooke would have had a conniption, but that was Dr. Buss. It was a complete 180-degree difference on how he managed and how we ran his businesses and how we enjoyed it. That was the precursor to Showtime."

Buss himself had quite a unique narrative. He had grown up the child of divorced accountants, first in Southern California, then in Wyoming. His story featured a harsh stepfather and poverty, icy walks for miles to school, rebellion. Buss first became frustrated, dropped out of high school, worked at manual labor, returned to school and graduated. From this background, he went to the University of Wyoming, earned a degree in two years, gathered momentum, and pushed through Southern Cal to a PhD in chemistry. Thus credentialed, he found work in the aerospace industry, with occasional stints teaching chemistry at Southern Cal. Those were formative experiences but Buss hungered for more. More money. More power. More fun.

On the side, Buss and a work friend from the aerospace industry, Frank Mariani, saved their money and in 1959 bought an apartment building and became landlords, the kind who did a lot of their own maintenance and spent time scheming how to finance even more buildings. Over the next two decades the two men, operating as Mariani-Buss Associates, would build a small empire of hundreds of apartment units, as well as some hotel and resort property.

Rather swiftly, like the Monopoly game that Buss loved to play, the properties had all added up with a perfect timing hastened along by a Southern California real estate boom.

Somehow, he found the time to father four (and would later add two more) children, then separated from wife JoAnn and emerged into his new identity as a budding real estate tycoon and playboy who dated attractive young women and kept photo albums of them, much like his beloved coin and stamp collections. There was a certain hip shadiness about Buss. He wore large-frame glasses with transitional lenses, the kind favored by in-crowd stoners in that era (there is nothing in his narrative to suggest Buss smoked pot regularly although he seemed to sample everything else in the culture). Mainly, he sported dimples that kept all the lines in his pleasing face headed in the right direction. He was outgoing, enthusiastic, and for the most part people seemed to like Jerry Buss.

His leisure moments included high-stakes poker games. Ultimately, however, stamps and coins and beautiful young models weren't enough for Jerry Buss. Neither was the thought of just being a landlord.

He loved going to all kinds of games and events, prizefights and horse races and Southern Cal football games, which had led him to realize he wanted to own a team, which had led him in 1972 to partner to buy the L.A. Strings of World Team Tennis, where he promptly lost a bundle trying to promote tennis at the Sports Arena in L.A. That, in turn, sent Buss looking for a better deal at the Forum. It was there in 1975 that he got to know Jack Kent Cooke, setting in motion the chemistry that would eventually evolve into the deal for the Lakers. Tennis losses ran heavy, but Buss was determined to move into pro sports ownership and began rummaging around for baseball, football, and basketball options. What property could he find that would allow him to get a leg up in the sports world?

"That's what really brought Jack Kent Cooke and my father closer," Lakers executive Jeanie Buss recalled in 2020. "His intention was always to own a sports team. Now, if the Dodgers had been for sale or the Rams had been for sale at that time, maybe he would have ended up with one of those teams. But he really wanted to own a sports team."

Thus, his strange dance with the Indiana Pacers.

"He noticed that Cooke wasn't attending Laker games and felt that there was an opportunity there and worked really hard to make it happen," Jeanie Buss recalled.

Cooke and Buss made for a fascinating pair of business adversaries. One, soft-spoken and intense. The other a loud, overbearing sort, always eager to get the best of every situation. Together they would hatch what was billed at the time as the "largest sports deal in history." Yet, when their talks first started, it was friendly conversations with Buss eager to learn about team ownership from Cooke.

"One day, in the middle of one of our many talks, Cooke mentioned that he might like to sell the Forum," Buss recalled in 1992. "I jumped. It was just the opportunity I wanted, but he was coy. I'd fly up to Vegas every six weeks or so, and we'd talk about it."

Mostly, Buss listened as Cooke told tales of running his two teams, the Lakers and the L.A. Kings hockey club. In some ways, Cooke seemed in retrospect to be slowly grooming his own customer.

"It was a very frustrating time," Buss recalled in 1992. "I guess I always believed that it would happen, although it seemed like forever. I would alternate being down and depressed. Then I'd think it was going to work and I'd be elated. As his divorce proceedings moved along, the sale talks warmed up."

The deal itself, however, remained vague.

"There were times when I felt I'd gotten in a little over my head," Buss remembered. "Jack Kent Cooke was remarkably charming when he wanted to be, and he was a very, very tough-willed man. He may have had the toughest will I've ever seen. It was like iron. And he was very quick to take advantage of turns in the negotiations."

Then, like that, it seemed to be on if Buss could manage to pull together a miraculous, seemingly impossible deal, to buy Jack Kent Cooke's West Coast sports empire, including the Lakers and Kings.

"He asked me, 'How would you like to buy the whole thing?'" Buss recalled. "My heart jumped again. The size of the deal doubled. I told him I'd love to purchase the teams, but I said I'd need time to see if it was possible."

Looking for more liquidity, Buss hurriedly began rummaging through all of the properties he had stacked up, gauging what he could get for them on the market.

"That deal was going to work regardless," Cooke recalled in 1992. "He was so eager to get it. It was just a matter of the price."

"The excitement that he had about it and his love of the Forum and all the things about the Forum," Jeanie Buss recalled of her father, "you could see the passion and the purpose. He was going to do whatever it took to make it happen."

Fortunately, the real estate market was strong in 1979, and Buss soon realized he was in a position to move. No sooner was he set to go all in than Cooke changed his mind again. He wanted the Chrysler Building in New York instead of Buss's properties. Buss laughed, then hustled to find buyers for his buildings. That done, he worked out a trade: his high-rises, complete with buyers to soften the tax blow, for the Chrysler Building.

"Then Cooke decided he wanted to include his 13,000-acre Raljon Ranch in the Sierras in the deal," Buss recalled. "I drove up to the ranch, saw it, came back, and made an offer. I don't think he knew for sure he wanted to sell, but once he made up his mind, things went smoothly."

Sort of.

With everything in place in early May 1979, Cooke told him, "Jerry, we're going to make the deal." Buss would pay what was reported to be $67.5 million for the Forum, Lakers, Kings, and Cooke's ranch. Cooke in return got the Chrysler Building and properties in three states. The high-rises would go to the owners of the Chrysler Building.

Then at midnight on May 17, Buss learned one of the buyers in the Chrysler deal had backed out. Suddenly after all his years of coaxing Cooke to the finish line, he found himself short an estimated $2.7 million to close it all, which was no small change in 1979.

Buss scrambled to get the money together, which would soon spark concern about how he wound up with the cash on such short notice.

As it turned out, Buss somehow pulled things together by the 12:30 closing time the next day.

In the hours after it all finally came together, an exhausted and drained Buss could only muster the energy to go sit courtside in the empty Forum. Then he went upstairs and strolled down the hallway among the photographs of Lakers and Kings. "My players," he thought proudly.

"It announced the ending of my real estate career and the beginning of my sports career," Buss recalled in 1992.

Not exactly. Buss would remain very much a real estate whiz. In fact, as longtime Buss associate Ron Carter would recall, the Lakers themselves with their games at the Forum would long be a major factor for Buss in attracting those high-priced investors for his real estate partnerships. It became a place where the new owner could realize his dreams while finding moneyed partners for his ventures.

He clearly was a man of large appetites and even larger dreams.

The Shark

From the announcement of their deal at the end of May, Cooke and Buss turned to the next chore, hiring a coach to replace Jerry West, who had turned down Buss's earnest appeal that he stay on the bench. Instead, West wanted to move into a player personnel role with the team.

Cooke was selling the team. Why did he care who coached it? Actually, the deal was still far from done and would need approval from the league. Plus Cooke had long wanted to lure Jerry Tarkanian, coach of UNLV's famed Runnin' Rebels, to take over the Lakers. Cooke had tried to hire Tarkanian in 1976 only to have the Vegas coach get strangely spooked and pull out of the negotiations. This time, however, with a deal with Johnson in negotiations, Cooke was eager to pair Tarkanian with the Lakers' new Magic Man, apparently as sort of a move to protect his investment while also boosting his legacy of ownership with the team.

And this time Tarkanian assured Cooke he was ready to come on board, especially with Magic Johnson in the mix, a development that immediately excited Buss as well as Johnson and all his advisors.

In 1976, the deal to make Tarkanian the Lakers' coach had been quashed when UNLV boosters found out about it and pressured him into staying in Vegas, as set out in 1993's *The Lakers*.

"This time we kept it a total secret," Tarkanian recalled in a 1993 interview. "This time I wanted the job."

The first meeting between Cooke and the coach went well, so Tarkanian called in his agent and friend of many years, Vic Weiss, to work out the details with Buss and Cooke.

Because the deal to sell the Lakers was finally headed toward closing, Cooke said in 1992 that he invited Buss into a meeting with

Weiss early that June at the Beverly Comstock Hotel. In fact, the Buss purchase of the Cooke sports empire had been announced publicly about a week earlier.

Weiss, described in news accounts as a fifty-one-year-old San Fernando Valley auto dealer, boxing manager, and gambling figure, drove a white Rolls-Royce to the meeting that day.

Cooke recalled in a 1992 interview: "We hadn't been talking long when Vic Weiss pulled out a roll of bills that would have choked an ox. He rather casually informed me that he always carried $5,000 to $10,000. I was distracted by this, and he calmly put it back in his pocket. I am sure he did it to show us how well off he was."

Steve Springer, the longtime Los Angeles sportswriter who came to enjoy a warm relationship with Buss, recalled the owner often talking about the meeting and Weiss's money clip. "It was just choked with hundred-dollar bills," Springer recalled Buss saying.

The owners and Weiss sketched out a five-year, $1 million contract for Tarkanian to coach the Lakers, but there remained small issues—season tickets and autos for Tarkanian's family—-to be settled. So, Weiss agreed to return the next day with Tarkanian for a final meeting to close the deal.

When Weiss failed to show the next morning, Cooke phoned Tarkanian at his Newport Beach hotel room. He didn't show here either, the coach replied. Then Weiss's wife phoned Tarkanian because her husband hadn't been home the night before.

The fact that Weiss was missing under such circumstances shocked and intrigued sports fans across Southern California, including Charles Tucker and Johnson, who read the story in the *L.A. Times* while they were visiting the city that week working on details about the upcoming draft later in June.

The answer to the mystery came five days later when a parking garage attendant at the Universal City Sheraton noticed a terrible odor that eventually led to the discovery of Weiss's badly decomposed body, stuffed in the trunk of his Rolls. He reportedly was still carrying the rough draft of Tarkanian's agreement to coach the Lakers.

In their investigation, L.A. detectives were said to have discovered that Weiss had been accosted by several men in a car almost immediately after the meeting with Cooke and Buss. Evidence would indicate that in less than an hour after leaving the meeting, the agent would be dead and his body, with both arms tied behind, stuffed in the trunk with his Rolls neatly parked in the hotel garage. It had the markings of a mob hit.

Basketball shoe executive Sonny Vaccaro, who had known both Tarkanian and Weiss for years, recalled being stunned by the ferocity of the killing. "They shot him somewhere else and took him to the hotel parking lot? Whoa," Vaccaro said in a 2016 interview. "They didn't touch nothing, except his life. It was a tremendous shock because he was such a close ally of Tark. Vic was sort of Tark's bag man. All the coaches then had bag guys. Vic got things done. Tark wouldn't have done anything without Vic."

A close business associate of Weiss's was so disturbed by the killing that he packed up and immediately moved to Hawaii, Vaccaro recalled.

Weiss had an array of powerful relationships in Las Vegas, to the point that he once played a role in staging a banquet in honor of Frank Sinatra for $1,000 a seat, Vaccaro remembered. Tarkanian, who was notorious for refusing to pay for anything, didn't want to fork over the thousand for the Sinatra banquet but finally did so after Dodgers manager Tommy Lasorda talked him into it.

Tarkanian was overcome by the murder of his friend. "I didn't know it at the time, but Vic was apparently involved in shady deals with Rams owner Carroll Rosenbloom," the coach recalled in 1993. "I heard he was transporting money for Rosenbloom."

Known for his love of swimming in the surf, Rosenbloom himself had drowned in Florida under somewhat mysterious circumstances just a few weeks before the killing of Vic Weiss. Rosenbloom had long generated suspicion of high-stakes gambling and underworld connections. Reportedly, federal authorities had been investigating Weiss's role in transporting cash to Las Vegas, ostensibly to place bets for Rosenbloom. It was reported that investigators had even surveilled Weiss during a briefcase exchange in a Las Vegas airport restroom, but no connection could be proved.

Another angle that police explored was based on the notion that

Weiss had been caught skimming off money he was moving for the mob.

"Not a lot of people know about Jerry Tarkanian and the agent," Jeanie Buss recalled in 2020. "I know my dad was really shook by that because he drove a very similar car to the car that was the Rolls-Royce. His body was found in the Rolls-Royce."

Indeed, Buss supposedly sought police protection for his family after the incident.

Was Buss spooked that it might have been a case of mistaken identity, that someone was targeting him? Or was there another angle? Sometime after the murder, a dark, tightly held rumor was whispered oh so quietly that Buss had somehow been marginally connected to the hit. For example, longtime Buss associate (and former Laker player) Ron Carter would recall in 2015 that Buss was quite angry with Vic Weiss at the time "for shooting off his mouth" that Buss didn't have the money to buy Cooke's empire. Buss himself had told several reporters that Mariani-Buss was worth about $350 million and that his personal worth was $50 million. What wasn't made clear to reporters was that much of that supposed wealth was on paper, in the form of property deeds, certainly not in available cash.

In a 1992 interview about his purchase of the team, Jerry Buss recalled many details vividly about the deal, although he insisted he remembered absolutely nothing about the meeting with Weiss and questioned if he was even at the meeting. The owner said he remembered almost nothing about Weiss's murder.

Buss's stance in 1992 seemed strange considering that police reported questioning him and Cooke about the murder at the time, as the two owners were the last people known to see Weiss alive.

During an interview in 1992, Cooke said Buss was clearly at the meeting with Weiss. Numerous news accounts reported Buss was there, and the owner never sought to correct those accounts at the time. Yet over the years Buss came to deny he was present.

"They both shied away from it," Steve Springer said in 2019 of the discomfort that both Buss and Cooke felt in discussing the case. "But the fact of the matter is that when Buss took over, the target for head coach was Jerry Tarkanian. And so they began talks with Weiss."

"I've heard that story," said a reliable source with Vegas connections who knew both Tarkanian and Weiss.

Only a select group of people knew about the Buss rumor, the source said. "It wasn't common knowledge."

L.A. police could never produce evidence that the murder was anything other than a mysterious mob hit, a position that never changed with years of subsequent investigation by the LAPD. The department acknowledged doing DNA testing on the case as late as 2015.

"The investigation really stopped there," Sonny Vaccaro said in 2016. "I don't think there's any way Jerry Buss did it. Buss would never hurt anybody himself."

Even so, Vaccaro, himself a longtime figure in Vegas gambling circles, didn't buy entirely the story that Weiss was skimming the mob's money, explaining that it seemed highly unlikely the mob would allow a figure like Weiss from Los Angeles to handle any of its money.

"Vic loved Tark," Vaccaro said. "But Tark was always afraid of Vic. They had been friends for years."

The two had been close since their high school days in Pasadena, California. In those days, college basketball coaches needed someone to "push the envelope across the table," in other words, present a prized recruit with illegal cash. Weiss had always been that guy for Tarkanian, Vaccaro said.

While his denial about the meeting seemed unusual, Buss, from all accounts, was as shocked and horrified by the turn of events as anyone else. The new team owner would soon evolve into a beloved figure in Los Angeles. He was the man who would bring championships to the Lakers, and as such was the object of immense love and respect as well as curiosity for his unabashed joy at dating young women and collecting their photos in albums, a practice he would boast about. In another age and another place, such behavior might have been scandalous. But in Los Angeles of the late twentieth century, no one person or group or even media organization (except for a brief discussion of the circumstances on NBC's *Today* show) made a big deal about it, just as they made no big deal about one of Buss's idols, *Playboy* magazine publisher Hugh Hefner and his Playboy Mansion, a fixture in the city.

Despite his approach to dating young women and boasting about it to the reporters covering the team, there was no evidence in the record of Buss's behavior over the decades of public life to suggest that he could have been involved in any way with the Weiss murder other than the fact that he was disturbed because it cut very close. Still, the rumor had quietly persisted. Taken together the circumstances did leave Buss with the aura of a man not to be trifled with. Obviously that aura also came from the fact that he was very bright and successful and rich, attributes that spoke well in any town, not just Los Angeles.

"I'd rather have a handshake deal with Jerry Buss than a signed contract from someone else," George Andrews said in 2019, an opinion repeated often in and around pro basketball over the years.

Charles Tucker, too, would be absolutely taken with Buss's sincerity and compassion and soon enough would become close with the owner, to the point that years later when Johnson cut ties with Tucker, Buss would put him on the payroll as a Lakers scout. As for the Weiss murder, the psychologist never got any indication that the situation involved either Cooke or Buss. "The timing of it was crazy," Tucker said in 2019. "Some rumors had it that something else was going on, even in Vegas. So much was going on at that time in Vegas, period. That was a hot time. They would get rid of you. They didn't ask why."

The swirl of events with Buss purchasing the team would draw scrutiny, however. Los Angeles–based *Sports Illustrated* writer Paul Zimmerman would recall in a 1992 interview that the deal between Cooke and Buss was so complicated that the magazine, acting on a tip about alleged underworld involvement in the financing, employed an accountant to try to figure it out.

In all likelihood, the tip came from inside the league offices. After all, the events in and around the sale of the Lakers had to be deeply disturbing to the NBA, which was poorly run and weak in that era, with many of its teams losing money. The circumstances had put the NBA Board of Governors under considerable pressure in facing the decision to approve the Cooke-Buss deal just after Weiss's murder and Buss's strange dance with the Pacers.

The league could ill afford the lawsuits that would follow if it openly challenged Buss and Cooke. It seems logical that someone within the NBA would turn to *Sports Illustrated* to investigate. The magazine was owned by Time Inc., and certainly had the resources in that era to conduct something of an investigation.

Paul Zimmerman recalled in 1992 that when the magazine's accountant had trouble figuring out the deal, more accounting help was brought to the task. The writer explained that the magazine eventually gave up at the complexity of it all.

"It wasn't complicated at all to me," Cooke would respond to the circumstances in 1992.

"No one could figure it out," explained the Las Vegas source. "Where did Buss get the money?"

The concern, it seemed, was that perhaps the underworld was somehow laundering money in the deal. The record would eventually show that Buss was able to make up the cash shortfall with loans from his partner Frank Mariani (who would become treasurer of the Lakers), from Sam Nassi, and from Donald Sterling, another Buss associate, who would soon purchase the San Diego Clippers.

Nassi, in particular, would soon get added scrutiny from *The New York Times,* which would describe him in a profile as a "corporate mortician" who operated with large sums of cash buying up the distressed assets of bankrupt department store chains, then selling off those assets for a nice profit. There were lots of chains going under in the 1970s, as evidenced by the fact that Nassi had spent better than a billion dollars buying up their assets.

A billion dollars was a lot of money to be handing out in the 1970s.

With its investigation proving unfruitful, *Sports Illustrated* would issue a glowing profile of Jerry Buss, although the piece was listed as a staff report rather than under a byline. The magazine described Buss as "an amiable and intelligent Los Angeles multimillionaire who extravagantly admires, among other things, M&M candy, French existentialists, any and all USC football teams, any and all *Playboy* centerfold girls, rare coins, rare stamps, rare cars and rare bargains in real estate."

The magazine did note that among the books on Buss's shelf was Irving Wallace's *The Nympho and Other Maniacs.*

Thus, the deal between Jerry Buss and Jack Kent Cooke would be approved by the NBA governors late that June.

Ron Carter was already beginning to work for Mariani-Buss Associates by then and offered in a 2022 interview that he saw neither nefarious activity nor overtly malicious characters in that era, although he pointed out the offices of Mariani-Buss in Santa Monica did burn mysteriously not long after the sale, with the loss of many records.

Nassi was a nice man, as were Frank Mariani and Buss himself, Carter recalled.

Soon enough, two NBA teams were being operated out of the offices of Mariani-Buss Associates, Carter would also recall. And soon enough, the NBA would call for an investigation of the off-court activities and business connections of Buss, Nassi, Mariani, and Donald Sterling.

No NBA investigation, however, would ever touch on the mystery of the body in the trunk. With the mob-style hit on Weiss, someone had been sending a message, observed Sonny Vaccaro. Rarely in the history of basketball, in the history of coaches and their agents, had underworld figures ever brazenly cut things that close, not even in the sport's numerous point-shaving scandals. The assassination of shamed former NBA player Jack Molinas, a fixer of college games, just four years earlier in Los Angeles was one example. But killing a coach's agent immediately after he met with team owners? Those who couldn't understand it didn't know what to say, and those who did know weren't talking.

Starry, Starry Nights

Before most could comprehend what had happened with the Weiss murder, the draft was upon them that June 26. Johnson and his parents went to New York for the event.

"The draft then wasn't as hyped as it is now," recalled Sidney

Moncrief, who had fun at the event hanging out with Johnson. "Nobody really cared about the draft. There wasn't a lot going on. There wasn't a ton of interviews. I think there were about fifteen, twenty media people. And back then I think only six or seven players were invited. And you didn't have social media; you didn't have people tweeting, you didn't have any of that. You didn't have the type of pressure they have today. We were calm. It wasn't that big of a deal."

Johnson wore a three-piece suit and was pictured with his smile at full wattage while making an A-OK sign for the cameras. Afterward, his mother gave him a huge hug, matching their smiles cheek to cheek. Soon after he was off again to L.A. to meet Jerry Buss and make plans for his new life.

"He flew in from Michigan, and Bill Sharman brought him over to meet my dad," Jeanie Buss remembered in a 2020 interview. "At that time, I was living with him in Bel Air."

The doorbell rang, and Jerry Buss jumped up and asked his daughter to answer it and offer his guests a drink because he had to go upstairs and change clothes.

"I'll come down in a few minutes," he told his daughter.

"I opened the door and I'll never forget it," recalled Jeanie. "I'm like seventeen and Magic's nineteen. We're basically the same age. I opened the door and there was literally like this smile that had like stars, you know, coming out of it. It was just lit up. It was a show-stopping smile. Opening the door and seeing him, I was just blown away."

Johnson was accompanied by Sharman, the Lakers GM.

"Bill Sharman was so sweet," Jeanie Buss recalled. "I brought them in, making small talk and asking to bring them a soda, whatever they would want to drink. And we started this conversation. Earvin said, 'I'm really so happy that I got drafted by the Lakers. This is really nice. But I'm only gonna stay here three years because I really want to go back to Detroit and play for the Pistons.' And when I heard that I was like, 'Uh oh.' I go, 'Excuse me for a second.' I ran upstairs to my dad and I said, 'Dad, you're not going to believe this, but he said he's only going to stay three years.' And my dad didn't miss a beat. He just said, 'You know, the second he puts on a

Laker uniform and steps on the floor at the Forum he's never going to leave.' And that's exactly what happened."

Steve Springer, who later wrote a book with Jeanie Buss, pointed out that the owner also made mention that the city's abundance of beautiful young women, many of them drawn there by Hollywood, would also serve to keep Johnson a Laker.

"Once he got there, he was all in," George Andrews said of Johnson. "We met Buss right after Jack Kent Cooke sold him the team. Buss was a really big factor in Magic's life from like Jump Street."

Charles Tucker had long found it necessary to make swift, silent judgments about the white people he encountered. Were they inclined to accept Black people? The decision on Buss was easy. "He was way before his time as far as relationships and problems," Tucker said in 2019. "He didn't know nothing about that. He didn't know what Black and white relationships were. He just dealt with people. He was for real. Some people have to think about it. Should I do this? Who's watching? Who's listening? Can I get away with it? Do I have good reason not to do it? You know, all the tangibles. But Buss didn't have any. He didn't even think."

Some would see it as strange that Johnson, who had such a fine father back in Lansing, would adopt Buss as his second father in Los Angeles, two men who were so different in many ways, yet alike in their interpersonal honesty.

"He always called him Magic. Never called him Earvin," Jeanie Buss recalled of her father. "And so as soon as he met him, it was like magic. He hugged him and couldn't have been more excited that he had Magic Johnson on his team. They were close from the very first minute they met until the end. There was just something. They were each other's soul mates in some ways."

Broadcaster Jim Hill was among the press at the Forum to greet Johnson that week in his new basketball home. "They brought Magic out after the draft," Hill remembered, "and we did interviews with him. He and I sat in the stands in the Forum. I remember him saying, 'I can just see myself now, running up and down this floor, diving into the stands for loose balls, hollering and screaming.' The enthusiasm in his eyes right then told me that this was going to be special."

Asked in 2004 about those early times, Johnson recalled weeping the first time he ever put on his Lakers uniform.

Such emotion aside, the immediate issue would be housing, with both Johnson and his father stunned at the dramatic difference in costs between Michigan and California.

"Buss had all these apartment buildings and we just went in to meet him," George Andrews recalled. "He's in the cowboy boots and blue jeans, just a nice, nice man and happy as hell to have Magic."

"I'll find you a place," Buss told Johnson.

"He ended up putting him in a place over in Culver City," Andrews remembered. "Earvin had his name and phone number in the phone book, and the girls were crawling into his apartment. We straightened that out."

Or so he thought, perhaps.

At the time, amidst the shock of the murder and the wheeling and dealing, all the major parties still clung to the hope that Tarkanian was going to be the team's coach. He soon informed them that he would have to decline. The turn of events had cost Johnson the opportunity to be coached by Tarkanian, who believed deeply in the running game. News reports of the murder tipped UNLV backers that their coach was planning to leave.

"A bunch of Vegas boosters got to me and put the guilt trip on me," Tarkanian recalled in a 1993 interview. "It got to me, really got to me, so I turned it down. I told Jerry Buss it was gonna be a big mistake for me to turn it down. Going in with Magic would have been something."

"Jerry was scared shitless," Sonny Vaccaro said of Tarkanian in the wake of the murder. "Everybody was."

When West declined to remain coach, the Lakers turned to Jack McKinney. Although he had never been a pro head coach, McKinney had been a college head coach in Philadelphia, then an NBA assistant for five seasons. Buss had preferred a coach with an established record and wasn't sure about McKinney's credentials, but he came highly recommended. For an assistant, McKinney hired Paul Westhead. The two coaches had worked together during summers in the

Puerto Rican basketball leagues, where the running game was highly prized. That would prove a profound influence on both men.

Thus came Magic Johnson to the busy and seemingly bizarre hub of Southern California in 1979, even as the place was abutting the grip of a large and intense negativity.

"He was the first pick and he was coming off a great year in college," Jim Chones, Johnson's teammate in Los Angeles, recalled in 2019. "He had just been part of the most viewed basketball game of all time with Larry Bird. Everybody was excited. Magic was just nineteen years old and he was the toast of the city. Even though he was fresh out of college, everybody knew he could play; they just didn't know how good he could become."

His first introduction to the Lakers came in the L.A. pro summer league, although neither McKinney nor Westhead had joined the team by then. Instead, Jack McCloskey, who had been an assistant to Jerry West, ran the team. Johnson missed the first two of the Lakers' three games that summer but was able to make the third. Summer league games in the balmy gym at Cal State Los Angeles were usually laid-back and sparsely attended.

Bill Duffy, his friend who played for Minnesota, decided to drop by to check Earvin out. "So, there's a lot of hype with him being the first pick for his first game," Duffy recalled in 2019. "I go to the game and I'm telling you, the people knocked the doors down—literally. On the baseline, there were big doors and, after some person opened the door from the inside, people barnstormed in. They literally just blew open all the doors to get into the gym."

Jack McCloskey had had the Lakers' other first-round draft pick, Brad Holland, in the starting lineup the first two nights, and McCloskey asked Johnson to come off the bench for his only appearance in the league, George Andrews recalled. "He goes, 'Earvin, you're playing this one game and Brad has been here every night. Would you mind not starting and letting Brad start?' The gym's totally packed, and they're all there for Earvin. There hadn't been ten people at the other games. Earvin goes, 'Fine. No problem whatsoever. Brad's here, let him play.' And he did. And when he came into the game the people in L.A. went nuts. He was just slicing and dicing in there."

That didn't prevent a defender from plucking Johnson's high dribble for a fat breakaway right off the bat. Nonplussed, he went right back to work.

"The gym was packed," Bill Duffy remembered. "People are standing all around the court and he's doing the same things he did in Oakland when I played against him two years earlier, going behind his back and doing all the things that only Magic could do. They were playing Detroit, and Magic just annihilated everybody."

The *Los Angeles Times* reported the crowd of 3,600 in the small gym broke an attendance record for the nine-year-old league as Johnson led the Lakers with 24 points, eight assists, and four steals in beating Detroit.

Afterward, Johnson made a point to invite the fans out for Lakers games once the season started, where he promised more fun ahead.

Was it possible that a soon-to-be twenty-year-old with a big goofy grin could somehow save a major city in a few short months, especially one as deeply encrusted in cynicism as Los Angeles?

"He brings the Los Angeles Lakers something they badly need. A smile," *Times* columnist Jim Murray wrote that next week. "Some teams need a power forward. Others need an outside shooter or someone to bring the ball up court. The Lakers just need somebody to dispel the gloom."

Just from that one summer league appearance, the team's fan base was already coursing with a new energy. But the gloom wasn't over just yet. Nor was the heartbreak for the men who dared to coach the Lakers.

18

WE HAPPY FEW

Paul Westhead got to Los Angeles that August, missed just about all of summer league play, then walked into one of the Lakers' rookie practices at Inglewood High School before training camp and was immediately greeted by Earvin Johnson running across the court to give him a huge hug. Westhead was taken aback just a bit. He didn't even know the guy, making the greeting so over-the-top as to seem almost surreal.

Westhead didn't know all that much about pro basketball either, had absolutely no history with that very insular world. He was a college coach, a Philadelphia guy, who had guided La Salle and Jellybean Bryant, Kobe's dad, to the 1975 NCAA tournament.

"One of the most likable guys you'll ever find," former Philadelphia 76ers GM Pat Williams said of Westhead in a 2019 interview. "He became absolutely known for his love of Shakespeare. Which always to me was cool, you know. Here's this college coach and now this pro coach with his great love and knowledge of Shakespeare."

Westhead himself would caution anyone describing him not to cover him up in just Shakespeare. There was Robert Frost's poetry, too. Indeed, he dearly loved the subtlety of language and had taught

English. This love combined with an intense, experimental mind in basketball?

"I mean, what a combo," Pat Williams offered. "That just made him even more colorful. Westhead was a lifer."

Lifer or not, quoting Shakespeare in the NBA proved unwise and would be used later to suggest that he was a poor fit for the pro game.

"I am a kind of quirky guy," Westhead admitted in 2019 while looking back on his long coaching journey.

Being an old-school Philly guy suggested tough teams steeped in the motion offense, making five passes before shooting, controlling tempo, working slowly for an opening. But Westhead and his friend and mentor, new Lakers head coach Jack McKinney, had both coached those summers in the fast-paced Puerto Rican league, which had blown up their ideas about the running game.

In 1972, as the head coach at La Salle, Westhead had watched Joe "Jellybean" Bryant, almost six-ten, snare defensive rebounds for Philly's John Bartram High, then power out with a dribble and head upcourt with a very bouncy, fun-filled, showboating style of play. Joe Bryant was a singular player at the time, and Westhead was the singular coach perfectly willing to deploy him just as he played naturally, even though Bryant himself would be frowned upon in that era as a big man out of place handling the ball.

Several coaches would gain credit years later for encouraging their players to "power out" with their rebounds on the dribble, but Jellybean Bryant was one of the first big players to display the move, which, of course, by 1979 was a signature part of the game of this kid Magic Johnson, whom Westhead was just now meeting.

After that rookie practice session, Johnson would explain his over-the-top greeting, revealing that they had a mutual friend in Chuck Daly, another great Philly coach, who would go on to fame as coach of the Detroit Piston Bad Boys and the 1992 Dream Team.

"Chuck Daly had talked to him about me saying that he would like me, that I was a good guy and we should be able to get along," Westhead said in 2019.

The greeting certainly seemed like the beginning of a beautiful relationship. The important thing to note here is that McKinney, the Lakers' new coach, and later Westhead, had played in college at St. Joe's for Dr. Jack Ramsay, another Philly guy, known widely as "Dr. Jack" and considered to be the sage of pro basketball coaching in that era with his Portland Trail Blazer teams.

Jack McKinney had been an assistant to Ramsay in Portland. Better yet, McKinney had also been an assistant in Milwaukee when Kareem Abdul-Jabbar played for the Bucks, a connection that had helped him land the job with the Lakers.

Upon looking at the task he faced that fall, McKinney had consulted with his old boss Ramsay about this very unusual rookie. The moment allowed the top mind in coaching to evaluate the premier young talent just coming into the game.

"I didn't think Magic could be a point guard. Jack McKinney did," Ramsay recalled in a 2004 interview.

McKinney told Ramsay that fall that he disagreed, that he was going to make Johnson his point guard.

"Good luck," Dr. Jack had replied.

"I thought he was going to be more of a small forward," Ramsay admitted in 2004. "But, you see, Magic worked on his game. His first year he couldn't dribble with his left hand. I remember a game in Portland we got nine turnovers from him by forcing him to the left side of the floor and making him play with his left hand."

The kind of confrontation that Ramsay and Portland would set up for Johnson was just the sort that cut short the careers of many young would-be stars who couldn't adjust and became busts as draft picks.

Indeed, that very question would linger over the coming months while Johnson sorted out the pro game based on his instincts and experience. Taken together, this would result in a somewhat complicated, almost mysterious, rookie season in the NBA.

First of all, Johnson had joined an immensely talented roster that was led by two men entirely focused on trying to outthink their opponents, an approach that called for a minimum of emotion. As such, both McKinney and Westhead mostly avoided making the player-coach relationship any type of friendship, which meant that

Magic Johnson, who would come to be seen as the most emotional player in the history of the game, was now partnered with two men who took a diametrically opposite approach. They sought to be good people in dealing with their players, but they weren't looking to be buddies.

Which also meant the first hug with Westhead might well have been the last.

Johnson would make an impressive effort to fit in with these circumstances that first year, but the rookie had his own agenda, Westhead would reveal. Without being overt about it, Johnson sought to keep the tempo of the game to his liking, under his control. The good news was that pro basketball had a shot clock, which fit Johnson's game like the spandex he was so fond of seeing on his growing number of lady friends.

Buck

Jerry Buss was quite excited to host his new Lakers for training camp at the classy Palm Springs resort, the Ocotillo Lodge, that he and Frank Mariani had purchased in 1969 from movie and singing star Gene Autry. The Lodge had been the scene of numerous staged events, celebrity parties, and whatnot that Buss had held there to raise his profile. Now his bringing the Lakers to the Lodge would spark a dramatic upgrade in that profile. The team would hold its camp at the nearby College of the Desert, quite an upgrade for Palm Springs, one of Buss's favorite places.

He was already planning a major retail development project there, a huge gamble that would cost him millions, and he figured the raised profile the Lakers would bring would be very good for business.

As for the new owner's own profile, it had jumped off the charts as news organizations such as *The New York Times* and *The Washington Post* hustled to L.A. to check out the playboy with his shiny new toys.

The *Post*'s hockey writer, Jeffrey Kaye, found Buss hanging out at his mansion with a gorgeous, "leggy" young model named Autumn Hargis, who attentively wiped his brow and made sure his carefully coiffed hair weave stayed in place during a ride in his company's powder blue Lincoln.

Buss had no problem boasting about the photo albums he collected of the attractive young women he dated. "I like one type," he told Kaye. "Beautiful."

"I don't know very much about hockey," Buss admitted to George Maguire, the GM of the Kings, a declaration similar to the one he made to Bill Sharman, GM of the Lakers.

He did know money and he did know real estate and he projected immense confidence that he would certainly figure out how to operate his teams.

Meanwhile, Johnson would arrive in Palm Springs that September still harboring considerable doubt about just how he would fit into the NBA. McKinney, his new coach, had made clear his plan to make him the team's primary point guard, a complicated development in that the Lakers already had an excellent point guard in Norm Nixon, all of six-two with a tight handle and a sweet shot. Furthermore, Nixon had made a big splash in the league in just two years, the Associated Press pointed out. "Nixon has developed into one of the leading guards in the league, leading all backcourt men in field goal shooting percentage (54.2 percent) while finishing third in steals and assists."

Nixon also toted around a substantial ego, an ability to lead, and his own magnetic presence. He was known as "Mr. Big" to his teammates. "It's an interesting backcourt combination the Lakers will put on the floor this season," the *Times*'s Scott Ostler noted as the preseason games got underway. "Nixon has proven his skills in two NBA seasons and Johnson has been sometimes spectacular and always entertaining in preseason games."

As with most rookies, Johnson found other veterans eager to send him a message, notably Ron Boone, a physical guard, who had played every single game of his 11-year career, a mark of 908 consecutive contests, the all-time NBA record at the time, this from a player who had been an 11th-round pick in the 1968 NBA draft out of Idaho State. Boone was an intensely proud underdog of a man who soon walloped Johnson in the back of the head, knocking him to the floor, in an early training camp exchange. Johnson had made sure to respond and later went right back at him. Set to be the Lakers third guard that season, Boone would be shipped off to Utah before the month was out.

There would be no bullying of Jerry Buss's prized rookie.

Faced with such immediate challenges, Johnson was in need of an ally and soon found one in a little-known second-year swing player out of the University of New Mexico named Michael Cooper, who was fighting for his basketball life in training camp. At least part of Cooper's competition was seen as Ron Carter, another second-year swing player out of Virginia Military Institute. Johnson quickly recognized that Cooper, who had been limited to playing just one game his rookie year because of injury, was a spectacular dunker with lots of raw athletic talent and defensive energy. Cooper was the very picture of wiry, with just 185 pounds spread over his six-foot-seven frame.

Johnson, meanwhile, was espousing the same dictate that he had delivered to teammates at Everett High and Michigan State. "In training camp, he always used to say to the rookies, 'Whenever you get around the basket keep your hands up,' because he'd knock your head off, because he'd get the ball there when you didn't think he could get it there," Cooper recalled in 2004.

As the competition in camp intensified, Johnson supposedly had breakfast with Cooper to tell him not to worry, that things would work out, much as Johnson had encouraged Dale Beard at Everett.

Cooper made the team. Carter did not and would long contend that Johnson started a fight with him in training camp for the sole purpose of eliminating him from the competition. After playing a stint with the Indiana Pacers (a quick connection arranged by Buss), Carter would go on to work for almost a decade for Jerry Buss in his real estate endeavors, which necessitated him going to Johnson's residence a couple of years later to get Johnson to sign some papers for a property deal.

"I thought I cut you already," Carter remembered Johnson remarking when he showed up at Johnson's place with the papers.

It seemed that Johnson had taken the team's personnel matters into his own hands, even as a rookie, much as he had on the outdoor courts of Lansing, where he had trusted in good role players more than guys who thought they were stars. Role players made for winning chemistry. "You get all those big scorers or the one-on-one players and the game breaks down," Johnson explained to writer Joseph Dalton that rookie season. "Everybody gets mad because one guy's trying to show off for all the women. But the team that was a team always won. My team won all the time."

In the case of Cooper, Johnson had found an alley-oop partner to replace Greg Kelser. The Magic Man's hookups with this guy from training camp would become the treasured "Coop-a-Loops" in Laker lore, known for igniting the Forum crowd's delight with spectacular finishes.

However, the majority of Johnson's focus in training camp would go to the always-difficult-to-read Kareem Abdul-Jabbar. Johnson got the early vibe that his approach might have left the center with the impression that he was trying to take over the team as a mere rookie, prompting Johnson to assure him that wasn't the case.

"What I tried to do in exhibition and during the season was to try to learn where every player wants the ball, where he can operate best from," Johnson would recall a few months after his first season in Los Angeles. "It takes a little more time with the Big Fella than everybody else because he's in only a certain area of the floor, which is down low. You have to really watch him to see where he puts his hand. Once he puts his hand up, that's where he wants the ball."

That would be Johnson's study work for the entirety of his first season.

Training camp was also notable in that McKinney put in an offense that called for the two point guards to share the floor and the ball. Whoever got the defensive rebound could simply outlet the ball to either Johnson or Nixon. Johnson, of course, used his excellent rebounding skills to assert that he often enough had the ball in his hands.

"I don't want either one of them to have the ball exclusively," McKinney told reporters.

The idea worked well enough although it would create a bit of tension between the two, a situation that would begin with the first exhibition games that October, which provided opposing teams their first good look at this Magic.

Kevin Stacom, a six-three ball-pressure guard struggling to stay in the league, found himself matched against Johnson in an exhibition game that rookie season. "I remember picking him up full-court and it was pretty unnerving," Stacom explained in 2019. "Usually, I could find a way to bother people. That's what I did at that level. But my brain was like a software package that was overloading. This guy I was guarding, Magic, was as big as the center I played with . . . and he was handling the ball."

The NBA had decided to give the three-point shot a limited one-year tryout that season, and the Lakers got their first lesson in the preseason against Denver. They were up by three points with four seconds left and chose not to defend David Thompson, who rose up and hit a 25-foot three to tie the game. Nonplussed, the Lakers called a timeout they didn't have, which gave Denver a technical free throw that won it.

It was during the preseason that both Nixon and Abdul-Jabbar took to calling Johnson "Young Buck," later shortened to "Buck," because of his virtually unprecedented energy and zeal. It was a nickname that had surfaced on occasion earlier in his life but served to mark that most unusual rookie season.

As would the direction of the relationship with Abdul-Jabbar, which would emerge famously in the very first regular season game that fall, at San Diego against the Clippers (who were paced by World B. Free's 46 points). Cooper got a steal with two seconds left, which allowed Kareem to win it at the buzzer with one of his astounding 18-foot skyhooks.

"Everybody was laughing and screaming and jumping up and down, and Magic runs over and jumps on Kareem and hugs him around the neck and is actually kind of choking him right out there on the floor," broadcaster Jim Hill recalled in 1992. "They get in the back and Kareem pulls Magic aside and says, 'Hey, we got 81 more of those. You don't have to hug me like that.' Magic with that enthusiasm and that passion says, 'I'll tell you what. You make that game-winning hook shot like that 81 more times, I'm gonna hug you like that 81 more times.' Kareem, who had always had that stoic look about him, just had to break down and laugh himself."

As an indication of just how high the league's hopes were for the Magic impact, the game was broadcast nationwide by CBS that Friday night, October 12. "I did Magic's first game in the NBA in San Diego, the night he jumped in Kareem's arms," longtime network broadcaster Brent Musburger recalled in 2004. "We kept taking tight shots and there were big smiles on his face. The smile never really faded."

"Everybody was shocked, but I was used to showing my emotions," Johnson explained later.

Perhaps that would prove the biggest adjustment for those around Johnson—from Westhead to Kareem—learning to deal with his freely flowing emotions. Lost somewhat in the drama was the fact that in his first pro game Johnson had scored 26 points with eight rebounds and four assists, a performance quietly noted with great interest by opponents.

With their new rookie leading the way, the Lakers seemed set to roll out of the gate in 1979 while cautiously sensing a very bright future. Westhead, the new assistant, was truly amazed by everything he would see in the early going. "He's like an artist," he raved to one reporter. "He creates basketball as he goes along."

Jim Chones, who had just arrived to the Lakers in a trade, noticed immediately that being on the floor with the rookie and his potential to make a fun play had raised the anticipation of nearly everyone on the roster.

Then abruptly, reality struck in the season's third game, at Seattle. Johnson sprained his knee and was taken from the floor on a stretcher, the pain obvious on his face. He would be shocked when a doctor looked at it afterward and declared he might be out six weeks. He was terrified by the news. The team quickly chartered a flight to take him back to Los Angeles.

The injury had also sent a jolt of panic through the staff for the Lakers, Roy Englebrecht would recall. For several years, the team had been hamstrung by personalities. Jerry West, who had been the coach, was so hung up about winning that he could be impossible in dealing with the press after a loss. Englebrecht would recall spending many nights in the team training room literally begging West to come out and speak with reporters in the hallway. And Abdul-Jabbar? He could be coaxed into talking, but it simply wasn't something he cared to do. Problem was, the media had no interest in talking to players beyond those two.

Johnson, on the other hand, just flowed into conversation with anyone he met, including reporters, flowed much as he did running a fast break. But now he was going to be injured for what seemed at first like a long time.

Fortunately, Dr. Robert Kerlan, the team physician, examined the rookie and told him to chill, that the injury wasn't so serious. He would miss nine days, time enough to contemplate just how different the physical challenge the NBA would be with its 82-game regular schedule filled with road trips all over America.

"Goooddaaamn, I swear I always get hurt," Johnson would tell *Inside Sports* later that season. "I used to never get hurt; now I always get hurt. I might be a little brittle, but that's the way I play—as hard as I can. And I don't mind taking the charges."

Another Bike Ride

Johnson had just started working his way back into the lineup 13 games into the schedule when tragedy struck again. The Lakers had opened with nine wins and four losses and seemed primed for big things. Jack McKinney's offense was offering something for everyone. The ball moved and the players moved, as Johnson would recall. It would obviously require adjustments, but the atmosphere was open and getting better with every game.

Then out of nowhere the coach jumped on a bike to ride to a tennis match near the apartment he had rented in Palos Verdes and on the way wrecked and suffered a serious head injury.

Like that, Westhead, the college guy who had barely gotten his toes wet in the NBA, was the interim coach of a very good pro team.

"The initial opinion was that Westhead was going to be in that position a very short amount of time and McKinney would be back," Lakers reporter Steve Springer recalled. "Then the opinion was that he would be back sooner rather than later. Then it just became obvious as time went on that he would face months of convalescence."

For a while, there were fears that McKinney might even succumb to his injury.

Among his considerations, Westhead pondered selecting Pat Riley, then serving as Chick Hearn's broadcast color man, to become his assistant coach.

"Riley was a good color man. I liked Pat," Hearn told broadcaster Larry Burnett in a 2002 radio interview. "I had to talk him into it. He wouldn't go. I said, 'They want to talk to you. Go!' 'No. No. No. I don't want to do that. I want to stay in the booth with you.' I said, 'Geez. You can stay here all your life, but you can't get an opportunity like this in a sport that you love so very, very much. Go on. Try it.'"

Westhead recalled that Jerry Buss was against adding Riley to the staff, but after pondering the matter for almost a week the interim coach chose him anyway. After all, Riley was about the only person Westhead knew in the NBA. In their short time together, Westhead had observed Riley's deep understanding of the emotional side of the game for pro players. Plus, in those early days of video, Riley had become skillful at the quick editing of tape, which would prove good for explaining mistakes at halftime and scouting chores, an innovation well ahead of much of the opposition.

Riley certainly needed the money, not that Lakers assistants, or broadcast assistants, banked all that much. The Lakers as a team had long earned the reputation of being notoriously cheap in regards to its employees.

Roy Englebrecht recalled that Riley in those days was a regular in his office, looking for any sort of speaking engagement or small gig that paid anything. He had been a role player for years in the league, which in those days was no path to wealth.

The son of a longtime minor league baseball manager, Riley would step in and provide immediate help with the burden that Westhead faced.

"It was difficult for many reasons," Westhead said in 2004 about the loss of McKinney. "Jack was the reason I came to the Lakers. He brought me out to work with them. It was his team that he assembled in training camp. He put in all the fundamentals and the basic offenses and defenses. And we're off and running and playing pretty good. He has this disastrous bicycle fall and really isn't able to function for some weeks. He gets out of the rhythm of the team. So, it was an incredible misfortune for Jack."

In the aftermath, Westhead set his course by what McKinney had planned to do, and the Lakers quickly resumed their pace. As many like Jack Ramsay suspected, Johnson would prove he was far from exempt from rookie growing pains. The quickness of NBA guards would require an adjustment on both sides of the ball.

Despite all that, Johnson would recover from his knee injury and the loss of his new coach to ignite what would be remembered for the most part as dramatic, joyful change that season.

"His enthusiasm was something out of this world, something I had never seen prior to him and something I haven't seen since," Jamaal Wilkes, a small forward on that first team, recalled in a 1992 interview. "It just kind of gave everyone a shot in the arm."

"With us he was just Magic," Jim Chones said in 2019 of that first season. "He never changed. He was always positive; he was always happy. He just had a great spirit, and when you're around him, you feel it. And it had nothing to do with his accomplishments. You look into his eyes, and he looks you in the eyes. He stands straight. You talk and he listens. That's the type of person he is. No environment, no event, has ever been too big for him."

Long forgotten about the era, observed former Lakers marketing director Roy Englebrecht in 2019, was the fact that before Johnson they were a .500 team struggling to draw ten thousand fans in a building that held 17,500.

"That was until Magic came," Englebrecht said.

The Lakers sorely needed his energy and enthusiasm, which went well beyond the "smile" that columnist Jim Murray had prescribed. No one player had or would ever offer both qualities in the abundance that Earvin Johnson did beginning that fall in the very first minutes of training camp.

Later, Michael Jordan would marvel at his own life and declare, "Timing is everything." Those around Johnson would make similar declarations about his life, how after all the good fortune of his prep work in Lansing he had landed on an exceptional Lakers roster in 1979, with a brand-new ownership and a giant city eager to love him dearly, to please him in every way imaginable, please him beyond imagination really, far beyond what all those in Lansing had done to please him. And they had done a lot.

"The people get off on you," Johnson would say that rookie season.

What They Saw

The first thing center Tom McMillen had noticed that season when his Atlanta Hawks went up against the Lakers was how smoothly and rapidly the rookie took control of the entire flow.

"Wow," McMillen remembered thinking.

"He had tremendous control of the game," he recalled in a 2019 interview. "And they played at a very fast pace. It was all led by and orchestrated by Magic. He was the conductor. They had an extraordinary team."

Reggie Theus recognized the control, too. As a six-seven point guard playing for the Chicago Bulls, Theus himself offered more living proof that size was one of the key things that mattered at the position.

"I was a big guard, just like him," Theus recalled in a 2019 interview. "The size allows you to see things on the floor in a way the average, smaller point guard can't see. The anticipation you have, the ability to project three or even four seconds prior to the play. . . . You can see the play way before it happened. By the time you've crossed half-court you already know exactly what's going to happen. On a fast break as soon as you touch the ball, you've already taken that picture of the floor and it's going to develop exactly the way you see it."

His size helped provide Johnson a wild quality, that "Young Buck" element, at age twenty, as if he were already stalking a place he knew others couldn't reach. And that would include negotiating the tricky terrain with Nixon as to who would be in control.

Fortunately, as Jud Heathcote had projected, Johnson also filled in nicely as a pro forward, which helped take the pressure off his relationship with Nixon.

"He and Norm Nixon were kind of tandem guards together," Westhead recalled in 2019 of that first year. "If you saw our team working on offense it was almost like a coin flip. Magic had it one time; Nixon had it another. That first year it was like a shared responsibility. They were the guards, and however the ball was dealt to them, they took care of it accordingly. The one thing I want to say to you about Magic Johnson with his play that year, he really stood out in his rookie year not so much as a future point guard. He was a very strong body in the paint, and he went in and got more than his share of rebounds in his search for his role that first year. He carried the load for our team when we needed him to go in and get a second shot. So, he was a nice complement to our team, not so much in the beginning for his signature passing but for his very tough-minded rebounding."

When Johnson did play the point, it required an adjustment as veterans began to complain that he was controlling the ball too much, keeping it to himself. And his no-look passes kept catching teammates unaware, leaving some of them angry that he was making them look bad. It was one thing to do that in college. Doing it in the pros had the potential to cost teammates money at contract time if they lost status by fumbling passes. In that regard, playing forward offered a safter territory for him. "I don't know if he did that intentionally, but it's a nice way of winning your team over," Westhead would recall. "Because we had guys shooting the ball, Norm Nixon, Jamaal Wilkes, or Kareem. Magic would go get their misses and put it back, or give it back to them, so everybody loves somebody who's gonna go to the offensive glass and get your missed shot."

Even that approach couldn't cloak his passing and flashy game. The fan response alone told much of that story, along with the body language of teammates when things were going well, when he could whisk the ball out, get it back, and find a teammate on a full-court break for a finish with the ball hardly touching the floor. With plays like that, Johnson soon had seemingly all of Los Angeles jumping with excitement. After years of boredom in the Forum, fans quickly fell in love with the way this Magic guy seemed to take on life as one big, joyful disco, a trip from one jam to another.

"I'll never forget walking through airports with him," Norm Nixon would recall later. "He'd have his Walkman on, and all of a sudden you'd hear somebody singing, and there he'd be—stopped in the middle of the airport, singing his song and dancing with himself."

Sometimes his youthful charm might be as ostentatious as wearing a full-length fur coat and chartering a helicopter as his personal limousine. Usually, though, it was as simple as his countenance.

Eddie Doucette, the Hall of Fame broadcaster for the Milwaukee Bucks, was a Michigan State grad who was quite eager to track Johnson's adjustment to the pros. "I just wanted to see just how good this guy could be," Doucette recalled in a 2019 interview, "and how he would draw his teammates to him in a leadership role. He was coming to a team that was laden with veterans. It's not always easy to exert your influence and style on other people. When you're a young guy, you really have to display some leadership qualities and you got to put it all together on the floor. And he did all of that. As a result, he was so good—and I was hoping this would happen—the older guys on the team, the veterans, ceded their authority to him almost immediately.

"He illuminated everything that he did," Doucette said. "When he was playing, everything kind of lit up. When he was being interviewed, he lit up. He was a rare individual because of who he was. There was no sense of arrogance, no sense of I'm better than you. When I first interviewed him, it was, 'Hey, I'd like to get to know this guy better. This is a fun guy, I'd like to be around him.'"

Since the Lakers franchise moved from Minneapolis to Los Angeles in 1960, the team had found favor with a small group of movie stars and celebrities drawn to courtside seats for games. Yet even that had always been sort of sleepy.

"The celebrities at that time had their front-row seats," Roy Englebrecht recalled. "Jack Nicholson had his seat, but it was different back then. They came and nobody really bothered them. There wasn't TMZ back then and gawkers and stalkers and all that. I mean, Jack was in his seats and Doris Day and Billy Crystal were in their seats back then and that was about it." When halftime came they would all get up and trudge up to concessions for a drink. Nicholson was long known to retire to his favorite closet in the building for a toke.

In retrospect, it seemed like it took about a nanosecond for word to get out that this rookie Johnson was electrifying the atmosphere at Lakers games. Very quickly all sorts of people realized they didn't want to miss an opportunity to see and be seen.

"The moment Magic smiled, I guess L.A. started smiling," recalled Lou Adler, the world-famous record producer and Nicholson sidekick and longtime Lakers fan, in a 2004 interview. "The city before had not really gotten into the team, even though they had won that championship in 1972. But these were younger guys, they were more outgoing, they were out around the town. They brought the town into the game."

Another longtime Lakers observer, sportswriter Doug Krikorian, agreed with that assessment in a 2004 interview. "When Magic got here, Hollywood descended on the Lakers. And they became the new in thing in L.A. My gosh, in that Forum press lounge, you'd see Sean Penn, Rob Lowe, Francis Ford Coppola, Robert Towne, the screenwriter for *Chinatown*—you saw all of these stars there. It was compelling and it crossed over. Sports crossed really over then. The explosion of basketball as entertainment happened during Showtime."

And it ignited pretty quickly that fall. Whether Johnson was the official point guard or not, he still often found a way to end up with the ball on the break where he could orchestrate those finishes that fans had never seen before.

"He pushed the ball and was a penetrating guard who was a

passer first and a scorer second," explained teammate Jim Chones in 2019. "And he had that undeniable enthusiasm and all the other intangibles. And he worked hard in practices. He was always smiling because he loved the game. He was physical. He would do whatever it took to win. I always remember his interviews with Chick Hearn. And he'd say, 'Chick, I just want to win. It's not about me. I just want to win.'"

"Basketball as entertainment" was the phrase just beginning to bubble into the pro basketball conversation as Johnson stepped into the spotlight. Boston's Red Auerbach, the old guard of the league, despised the very idea of it. He refused any of the trappings of entertainment, certainly no dancing girls or any such silliness. To Auerbach it was about the basketball and only the basketball. Jack Kent Cooke would go so far as to allow music, but only organ music, certainly no pep bands or rock bands. Jerry Buss, of course, was out to change all of that, which would soon set in motion the era known as Showtime that was just beginning to emerge that season, made possible by the new guy.

The California Star

Along with those fanciful and fraught first days would come the deep homesickness that Johnson sought to cure with massive phone bills, almost $400 a month, an ungodly cost at the time. But he was still Christine's baby boy, and he had been away from home for four whole months, something he had never done before. He ached for Lansing and admitted it, idolized his carefree youth, those nights spent hanging on the corner singing out of tune or loading up the Deuce and heading over to a party at State and turning on the smile for the college girls.

He called his feelings "homesick burned."

Johnson soon enough found some down-home comfort at the desk of longtime Lakers administrative assistant Mary Lou Liebich, who had served as an official mother figure to many rookies over the years.

Liebich, in a 1992 interview, couldn't recall a rookie who spent more time at her desk than Johnson. "Earvin would come in grinning, talking a mile a minute," she remembered with a laugh. "He always said, 'How ya doin', Sweets?'"

Johnson would visit there, then head over to public relations for more small talk. The Lakers had no players lounge in those days so Roy Englebrecht's office became a gathering spot of sorts for lonely players and assorted people hanging around the team.

Perhaps most important, that office was where Johnson got to know Lon Rosen. Even then Rosen was putting forth the narrative that he had been caught sneaking into a Lakers game a few years earlier and somehow wound up with an internship with the team. It all sounded highly unlikely. A New Jersey transplant, Rosen was the son of an ad executive. Why the hell would he need to sneak in anywhere? But the story was true, Roy Englebrecht confirmed years later. He had caught Rosen sneaking in, then wound up making him an intern who would hang around for years. After all, the team's marketing and publicity operations had zero staff.

It meant that Rosen had a perfect timing of his own that would flow quite well into Johnson's own substantial perfect timing.

And it all began with the popcorn, Englebrecht remembered. "What happened once the season started, Magic loved popcorn before he would play. For some reason he needed popcorn, and Lon became his designated popcorn getter."

When concessions would crank up the popcorn machine before a game, Johnson would want it fresh. And not just once. He would have to replenish it. At the time, Rosen would have a lot of other duties before games. And when Englebrecht couldn't find him, it was usually because he was fetching popcorn for Johnson.

Rosen would later take exception to that memory, maintaining in 2023 that it was never his job to fetch Johnson's popcorn. It occurred to Englebrecht at the time that his intern was quite aware that getting to know Johnson might be important for him. Actually, Rosen had been in the business of getting to know everybody in his seasons as an intern, all of the Hollywood personalities with their requests for game tickets and whatnot. There were a lot of important people coming and going, but Johnson was clearly a priority.

"Lon was still a college student at USC," Englebrecht said. "He bonded with Magic and was kind of Magic's guy there at the Forum, running around for him. He was his gofer."

It so happened that Johnson's lawyer George Andrews had made a point of getting to know Englebrecht as well, in part to coordinate the rising number of appearances and promotions requests for his client, which quickly grew in scope.

There, too, Rosen thus became the natural option to accompany the young star to his promotions and events. Rosen was near Johnson's age and knew the city. When Johnson had to be somewhere, Englebrecht would often dispatch Rosen to take him.

Thrown together, the two, as Rosen would long tell the story, "had nothing in common and everything in common, a Black kid from Michigan and a Jewish kid from L.A."

Emotionally, Johnson was something of an open book and Rosen, while calculating, wasn't too far behind him. "Earvin really didn't know what to do with himself," Rosen recalled.

An instant millionaire who had always been perfectly happy without any money, Johnson was lost in the expanse of the city with a college wardrobe that had mostly included sweatsuits and T-shirts and jeans.

It was obvious he didn't have anything to do.

Rosen knew the hot spots, the way to find fun, the tricks to coping with the city's oppressive traffic. They went to Southern Cal football games and Dodger baseball games and movies and nightspots together. It was easy fun.

"We didn't know that Showtime was just around the corner," Englebrecht recalled. "I think those were some of the happiest times of Magic's life, those first years, because this was the start of his professional experience. I don't think there was a lot of pressure on him then. It was just a whole lot of fun. He eats that popcorn in the Laker dressing room before the game, you know, and he and Lon Rosen went on to do great things."

As much as he seemed to appreciate every little thing, Johnson needed much more that rookie season. Mainly, he wanted company from back home. Jim and Greta Dart jumped at the opportunity to visit. For years, Jim Dart had seen every single game he had played only to be cast suddenly into a broadcasting netherworld, left to hope for a nationally televised Lakers game some weekends. Otherwise, it was a matter of searching through two-day-old box scores in the agate type of the newspapers. Lakers games finished so late that eastern papers could only report delayed results. In some ways, it seemed like Johnson was playing on the moon, an exotic one for sure, but from the Lansing perspective, the West Coast posed as some foreign realm, separated not just by time and space but reality itself.

Big Earv, who had spent those Sundays with his young son pulled close watching NBA games on TV, now had to hope to catch a good look at his game on the color set and then talk about it on the phone afterward. For years, Johnson would tell the media, "I don't care what you guys say. I don't care what the fans say. When the game's over, I go in the back of the locker room and call my dad. I want to know what he thought."

Johnson wasted little time in getting his parents a nice, comfortable home, which left them with a balancing act, having a wealthy, quickly famous son and nine other children who weren't. The Johnsons, of course, would show over time they were built for such challenges.

Asked about his famous son's money that season, Big Earv offered, "You know it made a difference, but let's just say this—it didn't make me no bigger than I already am."

As for the Darts, who were childless, they had longed to have Johnson in Lansing throughout his college years. He had been so good to them with the craziness of the NCAA Final Four, had made sure they had a spot on the charter plane to Utah. And when he came off the floor with the net draped around his neck, they were hit with the realization that he would leave. He had told them as much when he agreed to go to State out of high school.

That rookie season he welcomed them to his new life, which reportedly left them a bit wide-eyed and sad, too.

Others from Lansing had visited him in Los Angeles, but this was the Darts' first trip to witness him as a young, exploding California star. "He asked us to come out," Jim Dart would say at the time.

"We're staying at his place. How many of these guys would do that? And how many of them should? He's going to outgrow us, someday."

In time Johnson would outgrow his entire life from back home, but that would never prevent him from cherishing it, to the point that he would own two sets of clothes, one for California, the other parked in a closet back home so that he could move back and forth, unencumbered with luggage, as his schedule allowed.

His first trip home that January, on a Thursday to play the Pistons on a Friday, turned crazy pretty quickly. Charles Tucker had picked him up at the airport and chauffeured him swiftly back to Lansing only to realize he had media obligations back in Detroit, an embarrassment settled when a TV station helicoptered him back to his press interviews five hours late. It hardly mattered. His homecoming at the Pontiac Silverdome drew 28,000 adoring fans, better than twice the best crowd the Pistons had previously managed to draw to the cavern. Johnson was slowed by a painful groin pull, obviously hampered, but the crowd loved him anyway as he limped around and the Lakers won easily.

Even though he had hustled west after college, three time zones away from eastern media coverage, his face would soon enough come alive nationwide on 7Up commercials, as would Larry Bird's in his own set of spots for the soft drink company. Johnson's presence in Hollywood would soon have him on *The Mike Douglas Show*, where he enjoyed playing a goofy hoops contest and hanging out and competing with other guests such as Helen Reddy, Neil Sedaka, and Danny Thomas.

Mostly, though, the NBA life was hoop here, hoop there, all while teams matched up their schedule with an array of crazy connections on commercial flights that had them in and out of airport crowds.

And just as Dr. Jack had predicted, teams were quite eager to test the rookie night after night. "If you watched some of the films of Magic and the Lakers back then, he, for the most part, would have the ball behind him a little bit when he dribbled," recalled former NBA journeyman Junior Bridgeman in 2019. "And most of his passes were with his right hand, kind of coming across his body. So, what we would try to do is keep our left hand up, which may change what he wanted to do and maybe we would even get a deflection. Pressuring him, picking him up full court, trying to tire him out . . . just little things like that with the hope you might throw him off his game. That was part of the scouting report."

Obviously, Johnson had what he thought was a useful left hand, but going up against pro-level players meant that everything would be tested to the max, tested far more in the 82-game grind of the NBA than in college or high school.

"The next year you couldn't do that," Ramsay said of his coaching efforts to make Johnson go left as a rookie. "Each year he added something to his game. Magic was such a great competitor he knew what he had to work on and did it."

None of that, however, was yet established with Johnson just coming into the pro game, where his coaches were trying to figure out how to deploy his unique talents and opposing coaches were likewise trying to find how to defend against them.

What Johnson did not have to adjust was his competitive mindset, Junior Bridgeman recalled. "Even with the big smile, and his love for the game, he would still cut your heart out on the court. And you have to have that mentality in order to be successful. He had that killer instinct."

The competitive nature would prove a huge challenge for other teams from the very start.

Johnson had given the entire league an indication of that challenge in late October when he registered a rare triple-double, one of seven he would have over that first season.

The fact that it would all be cloaked in a unique joy created some confusion among opponents, Bridgeman explained. "He wasn't a trash-talker. He didn't do that. But there was a true love for what he was doing, for playing basketball. You kind of felt that or saw it every time you were on the floor with him. It was almost as if you were playing against a kid, like it was his first time playing basketball."

"Confident. He was very confident," teammate Jim Chones said of Johnson's rookie demeanor. "And he was unselfish and worked his craft. Every day he put in the work. He wasn't a good shooter but after every practice, he worked on his shot. He worked on ball handling before practice, up and down the floor, change of pace, changing direction EVERY day. And the more physical the game, the more rougher the games, the better he was. He was a warrior, man. He was our best rebounder. He was our most physical player."

February brought the All-Star Game at the Capital Centre in Landover, Maryland, where Johnson became the first rookie starter since Elvin Hayes more than a decade earlier. He played well but it was Bird who provided the showboat highlights, pulling a rebound off the front of the rim at one end, then driving straight up the center of the floor to whip a behind-the-back no-look among an array of his dazzling passes that evening.

Asked about Johnson that season, Bird left no question about the hierarchy. "He's a great all-round player and a better passer than I am, no doubt," he said. "He has the enthusiasm and the hustle to be the greatest ever."

Both had gotten their careers off to sizzling starts, but it was now Bird's turn to be the man in green as he and Johnson kept track of each other through the box scores.

What those box scores revealed were two teams on the rise, suddenly, profoundly elevated by their rookie stars and seemingly on their way to another championship meeting. "How delightful would that be?" basketball fans across America asked each other.

Also in February, the Lakers descended on the Knicks in Madison Square Garden, where Johnson celebrated his first appearance there with a triple-double and afterward charmed the New York media with his youth and charisma and patience in making sure all the many questions were answered, a performance that hinted at his future of many appearances on the league's all-interview team, back in an age when the NBA sorely needed its players talking and constantly selling the sport. It was clear that Johnson wasn't just infusing the Lakers with his very special mojo. The entire sport was getting a facelift from the alternating styles of its two unprecedented rookies, with Johnson's chuckles and charm and Bird's homespun hick act.

Both of them had found substantial challenge defensively in their first 40 pro games. "Early on, they were eating him up," Bird's coach,

Bill Fitch, said frankly in assessing Johnson. "But he's made much better adjustments to defense from the beginning of the year."

As he would throughout his career, Bird jumped quickly to have Johnson's back, replying when asked about the issue, "Ah, they always talk about rookies and defense. If he does make a mistake on defense—which all of us do—he can come back and make some guy who has maybe been in the league nine years look bad."

A showdown over rookie of the year was looming between the two, with Boston showing an unprecedented turnaround with Bird's presence. Atlanta coach Hubie Brown, already an opinion leader, would soon weigh in that the award should go to Bird because Johnson had landed on a team much more talented with the likes of Abdul-Jabbar, Jamaal Wilkes, Norm Nixon, Chones, and company, among an array of opinions that Johnson acknowledged with his smile.

"We're becoming so close, man," he told the New York media when asked about his Lakers. "You wouldn't believe it. All of them are showing their emotions now—Kareem is definitely fired up, smacking hands. We doing a lot of things, and that's part of the team I want to be on."

After dancing with the New York media, Johnson would pull on his long fur coat and take in the infamous Studio 54, leaving Charles Tucker, who had come along on the trip, to tend to more prosaic chores. It wasn't beneath the psychologist to serve as everything from errand runner to pickup basketball sidekick to master career strategist to counselor to the star—and family—he obviously loved so deeply.

After all, Tucker would say, never mind that the scene had shifted to a much larger world; it was his job to take care of business.

Steve Springer would spend decades as a sportswriter in Los Angeles, much of it with the *Times,* but Johnson's rookie season had brought Springer's first time on the Lakers beat for a suburban newspaper. The Lakers would quietly pay the air travel costs of the writers working for the suburban papers as a means of broadening their publicity, which allowed Springer a close-up view of Johnson in his formative moments as a pro, starting with the team bus on road trips. "He'd have his big boom box," Springer recalled, "and he'd sit in the back right in the middle of the back row and play music loud. His thing was 'EJ the DJ,' and he would do his imaginary radio show and play the music. He was obviously the loudest on the bus, but everybody sang along. He was very outgoing for a twenty-year-old kid. He quickly moved to the head of the class."

Part of that was due to Johnson's ease in dealing with reporters, Springer explained in 2019. "He was always available. He was always on, you know. That smile never seemed to leave his face. He never dodged a question. He sometimes said more than he probably should have said, but he was just a really easy, easy guy. Some guys, they see a sportswriter coming and they just clam up. He had that smile and he was like, 'How you doing?' Whatever. He was just so accessible in contrast to Kareem, who was a total jerk to us. It was just so much easier to deal with Earvin."

It helped that it was still that era where teams and their media flew commercially together, stayed in the same hotels, and often dined together.

"We were the media and they were the players, but on the road we were just all tourists together," Springer recalled. "It was amazing going out to dinner. I remember we went to a club, maybe in Portland, and Earvin took the microphone. The spotlight was on him, it was like almost like rap. He'd introduce the players but then he'd do the writers. 'There's Steve Springer.' 'There's Scott Ostler.' We were just all part of the group. That didn't stop us from being sportswriters. It didn't stop us from writing what we had to write, but they understood. It was easy to be lured into his circle."

Especially when you had a press seat to watch him do his routinely amazing thing.

"We're in Madison Square Garden," Springer remembered, "and Earvin gets this rebound and he is looking at the backboard and throws it over his head all the way down the court. Norm Nixon has broken for the fast break. It's one bounce and Norm lays it in. So, I was talking to Earvin in the locker room and I said, 'How did you know? How did you know Norm was breaking?' He said, 'I saw him.' I said, 'No, you didn't.' He said, 'Yeah. I saw him breaking.'"

"Your head never moved," Springer recalled telling Johnson.

"You were looking straight at the basket. Your head never turned and you threw it over your head. How did you know where he was?"

"I guess I saw him in my mind," Johnson replied.

"Stuff like that would happen all the time," Springer said in 2019. "How do you know? How can you do that?"

19

GAME 6

For all of his basketball life, Earvin Johnson had dominated every team he had ever played on, to the point that all his teammates were forced to play the game the way that Johnson dictated. Finally, in Los Angeles, he had encountered a player who wasn't going to succumb to his immense will and charm.

"It took Magic just a minute to figure that out," former Laker Ron Carter said of Kareem Abdul-Jabbar's outsized presence. "Once he did, he stopped pushing, because Kareem was not going to bend. Magic figured it out like everybody else. When Kareem said jump, you asked how high. Nobody would ever correct or chastise Kareem in any way."

Not even Lakers coaches.

By 1980, Abdul-Jabbar had followed a long path to cynicism from what was essentially a life as basketball's first childhood star. Very tall and very shy, he had discovered early enough that a withering, blank stare worked pretty well in putting off the intrusions of his many questioners. Including teammates.

"He said over and over and over again that he was an introvert and he didn't want to get along with people," remembered his fellow Milwaukee Bucks star Oscar Robertson when asked about Abdul-

Jabbar in a 1990 interview. "I guess that was okay. But after a while, he assumed this posture."

He would carry it seemingly everywhere he went in life.

Born Ferdinand Lewis Alcindor, Jr., on April 16, 1947, Abdul-Jabbar had been raised in Manhattan, the only child of "Al" and Cora Alcindor. His mother was a singer, and his father studied the trombone at the Juilliard School of Music while working as a Transit Authority cop, among other jobs, to support the family.

On the surface, it may have been hard to discern any traits shared by the very different personalities of Abdul-Jabbar and Johnson, but actually there were several, perhaps the main one being the relationship both men treasured with their fathers.

"I got my work ethic from my Dad," Abdul-Jabbar explained in a 2004 interview. "Between the time when I was in grade school and high school, when I was living at home, my Dad missed work one time. He had the flu, and he was down for a week. I had to go pick up his paycheck. That was the only time he missed work. He was stoic. He said, 'I got a job to do.'"

As a Transit Authority cop there was money to be made by simply looking the other way.

"A whole lot of people might be tempted to be corrupt," Abdul-Jabbar said, looking back at the life of his father. "People tried to get him to sell his badge. He wouldn't do that. He had an incredible amount of integrity, and it was something I just adored."

As recounted in this author's 2006 book *The Show*, by thirteen, young Lewis was already six-eight and the darling of New York's considerable hoops culture when he conducted his first newspaper interview. Quiet and bookish, he had decided he wanted to be an engineer. "I know I can't play basketball forever," he explained to a reporter.

His years at Power Memorial High would produce two national high school titles and a 71-game winning streak. By the spring of his senior year, college coaches everywhere wanted him, and they weren't alone. "I'll trade two first-round draft picks for him right now," quipped Gene Shue, coach of the old Baltimore Bullets.

But it was UCLA's John Wooden who won the prize, and together they formed the heart of the Bruins' college basketball dynasty. "I always related to him," Abdul-Jabbar said of Wooden. "He was about what you had to do to win games."

Which, of course, was another critical trait he would share with Johnson.

John Wooden and his great center did plenty of winning, claiming three straight NCAA championships, which prompted the college rules committee to adopt the outrageous "Alcindor Rule," outlawing dunking over his final two seasons, a rule that would stain all of basketball for a decade.

As Wooden often pointed out, Alcindor was the most valuable player ever. The coach emphasized that most valuable didn't necessarily mean most talented. It simply meant that Alcindor was the kind of gifted, versatile center who could take a team beyond the sum of its players, yet another key trait he shared with Johnson. Both played their careers as force multipliers.

From UCLA, he catapulted to the Milwaukee Bucks, then a year-old expansion team. Even to the wise old tough guys of the NBA, he presented an immediate mystery. Just how tall is he really? they asked. The answer in college had been seven-foot-one. The official word from the Bucks was seven-two, but nobody believed it. "You could start the guessing at seven-four," said Nate Bowman of the Knicks, "but his arms seem to be eight feet long."

Whatever his size, it was big enough to take the Bucks to the Eastern Conference finals his rookie season. They lost to New York, but for 1970–71 Milwaukee added the great Robertson, and the two of them marshaled their teammates on a businesslike march to the title in just the team's third season of NBA operations.

That championship season also marked the completion of his conversion to Islam, which he had pursued since 1968. Just before the 1971 All-Star Game, he had quietly changed his name and married a woman named Habiba.

The new name, Kareem Abdul-Jabbar, meant noble, generous, powerful servant of God, yet the task of living up to it seemed quite a test. In October 1972, he was jailed briefly in Denver for suspicion of marijuana possession, only to be released after teammate Lucius Allen was charged. Three months later, in January 1973, seven people, including five children, were murdered in Abdul-Jabbar's Washington, D.C., town house. The victims, who belonged to the orthodox Hanafi Muslim sect, were the family of his close friend and advisor, Hamaas. The matter involved stemmed from conflict within the sect and had no direct connection with Abdul-Jabbar (they were supposedly merely living in the town house he owned and provided), but repercussions from that incident soon left him stunned and separated from his wife and living a monastic life in his Milwaukee apartment.

The Bucks, meanwhile, had traded or released key members from the 1971 championship team, moves that led to playoff losses in 1972 and '73. They had mustered the effort to challenge the Celtics for the 1974 championship but lost in an intense seven-game series. The next season, his last in Milwaukee, he broke his hand, smashing it against a basket in anger. He missed long stretches with injury, and the Bucks sank to 38–44 in 1974–75. Afterward they finalized the deal he had requested and traded him to the Lakers.

His years in Milwaukee had produced three league MVP awards and yet another name when Bucks play-by-play man Eddie Doucette tagged his bread-and-butter shot the "skyhook," certainly a worthy weapon for a noble, generous, powerful servant of God.

The California drug culture was in full bloom when he arrived there in 1975. Having experimented with cocaine and heroin in college, he would recall having little interest in the coke crowd that sought him out. Even so, he soon became a symbol of pro basketball's atmosphere of decline in the 1970s. The ABA was on its last legs, and the NBA was viewed as adrift, a second-rate sport. As the NBA's top star, his brooding image did little to help the situation. His last season in Milwaukee had been his first ever as a loser, and many sportswriters read his unemotional response as a lack of interest. Laker fans, however, mostly remembered Big Lew of UCLA fame, the Dominator. They welcomed him and expected great things.

The troubles, of course, began almost immediately. As team GM Pete Newell explained, the Lakers had given up most of their young talent and their draft picks to get him, leaving a mishmash of a roster to greet him.

He won the rebounding title with a 16.9 average and scored 27.7

points per game, all good enough to bring his fourth league MVP award. But the 1975–76 Lakers could not win on the road and finished 40–42, out of the playoffs for the second consecutive season. The 1976–77 season would bring his fifth MVP award, but again bad luck and a thin roster kept the Lakers from postseason success. "Those teams in the late 1970s would have been lucky to win 20 games without him," Jerry West said of Abdul-Jabbar. "Yet we were always in the playoffs. We just didn't have enough pieces."

"I recall being the scapegoat," Abdul-Jabbar explained in 2004. "I was the best player on the team. I got a lot of things done, so they just used me as the focus for why the Lakers weren't successful. That was very frustrating. It was one of the worst times in my basketball life because I couldn't win. I was the dominant player in the league. I won three MVP awards in that span. It wasn't good enough. But I wasn't the problem. The problem that people had with me was that I wasn't into giving interviews or spending a lot of time with the press. And they didn't like that. I got into a test of wills with . . . people who were writing."

By the spring of 1980, Abdul-Jabbar was facing his thirty-third birthday yet still reigned as the game's greatest offensive weapon and was well on his way to becoming the NBA's all-time leading scorer.

Just as impressive as his massive scoring totals over the decades was the style in which he rang them up, with his unreachable sky-hook, which he could hit seemingly from all over the floor. It wasn't enough.

"Kareem had that look and that reputation of being very standoffish, very sullen," explained Roy Englebrecht, who ran both the marketing and public relations efforts for the Lakers in that era, adding that he personally found the great center to be cooperative. That, however, wasn't a view shared by many in the media who had to interview him.

"At that time, Kareem seemed to be going through a peculiar questioning in his life," *L.A. Times* sportswriter Ted Green said in a 1992 interview. "He seemed to be wondering if he wanted to continue playing basketball. He was often lethargic and apathetic on the floor. Many nights he operated on cruise control. One night in Madison

Square Garden he scored 24 points and had only one rebound. I wrote a story and called him Kareem Abdul-Sleepwalker. He got very upset and didn't speak to me for several months."

"Understanding me meant that I was supposed to come around to the writers' point of view," Abdul-Jabbar explained in 1992.

Like Robertson, other observers said that Abdul-Jabbar brought much of the situation upon himself.

The arrival of Johnson had ignited a new narrative that credited the rookie with stirring the great center's competitive fire, an interpretation that itself soon enough irritated Abdul-Jabbar. He would acknowledge that Johnson was influential, but another big factor was that the Lakers teams he played on before Johnson had lacked a power forward for various reasons, which always left him paired with two small forwards, a fatal flaw.

Beyond Johnson's influence that rookie season, what mattered greatly, Abdul-Jabbar would point out, was the team's addition of two power players, Spencer Haywood and Jim Chones, to help him in the frontcourt. Even in that sense, Johnson also provided a lift because he did so much rebounding work as a forward for the Lakers.

Still, opponents had a certain clarity when it came to assessing the hierarchy of the Lakers that season. First of all, it wasn't like other teams were scheming to stop the rookie Magic Johnson, explained Lloyd Walton, another NBA journeyman, in a 2019 interview. "He played with Kareem. We were more concerned about stopping Kareem. Magic was a great player, but he didn't get that kind of attention. Certainly not in his first year. Magic made everybody better, but he wasn't going to score a lot of points like Kareem."

Even so, there had been the growing sense across the league that season that the giant had been awakened.

Tom McMillen had come out of the University of Maryland in 1974 as a Rhodes Scholar, studied in Europe for a year, then came home to an 11-year NBA career before going on to enter politics and serve in Congress. Tall and studious, McMillen identified a bit with Kareem, which left him curious as to the effect playing with Johnson would have on the big guy.

"It was a different Laker team than when Kareem was there

without Magic," McMillen remembered. "It was more plodding and not as fast-paced. Magic just immediately up-tempo-ed the whole thing. I think they were fortunate to play with each other. Obviously, Kareem is an unbelievable talent. But having Magic took pressure off him, and Magic always got him the ball. It was just a gift from above. There was just a discernible difference with the Lakers once Magic got there."

Meanwhile, Johnson's associates, George Andrews and Charles Tucker, were well aware that his relationship with Abdul-Jabbar would be essential and that it would prove a challenge because the center could be quite gnarly and difficult to read. During the season Christine Johnson would join the cause, quietly forming a friendly relationship with the center and then pursuing their good personal vibe to keep the lines of communication open. Mostly, she baked her famous sweet potato pie for Kareem upon request, and requests were reportedly frequent.

Time would reveal a rarely articulated thorniness to the Kareem-Magic partnership over the years, but Jim Chones chose to see the similarity between the two that ultimately served them so well. "He's the smartest player I've ever played with," Chones said of Johnson in 2019. "And then I think Kareem was next, a close second. They thought in different ways. I think, in a way, Magic was more detailed, more grassroots, as far as understanding how things were done and how they should be done."

Charles Tucker had settled in rather comfortably with Johnson as a Laker, making time to be there for training camp, then traveling back and forth between Los Angeles and his work in Lansing, using his time on the West Coast to gain a surprising closeness with Buss, Bill Sharman, Jerry West, and other team figures, hanging out with them, playing pickup ball anytime a game was available, doing all sorts of things, but most important of all, sitting back and quietly observing this new landscape of personalities in this very different culture that his young charge must now negotiate. Kareem was at the top of that list.

"He was different but a good guy," Tucker observed in 2019, adding that the big man would have been better appreciated if his personality hadn't gotten in the way. One of the dominant images from that era was Kareem sitting in a chair in the locker room, his back turned away from his teammates as he read a book.

Fortunately, Tucker would point out, Johnson had enough charisma for both of them.

George Andrews also watched with curiosity as to how things would develop only to realize that Johnson's hypercharged desire to win would push him to a smart solution on the Kareem riddle. Bad things could happen when a player wasn't totally focused on winning, Andrews observed in 2019. "But Earvin was all about winning. It was a situation of 'I want to do whatever it takes to win.' And he sublimated his own ego to Kareem. You know, that was a very mature thing to do for a twenty-year-old kid. He was very deferential, and it wasn't always appreciated."

Once his playing career was over, Abdul-Jabbar wouldn't present such an obtuse personality, Andrews explained, but at the time he offered a challenge for Johnson.

From the early days of that season, Johnson had fallen in line with accommodation.

"Kareem represents the franchise," he had told *Sports Illustrated*, "so I guess I wanted to be accepted by him more than anybody else. I had heard that he was unemotional, that he didn't work hard. But the stories I heard weren't true—he cracked jokes, he got mad, and he worked hard. The guy has got feelings."

As Jim Murray had said, the smile alone would be quite useful, and Johnson agreed while talking to *SI*.

"I'm going to keep on smiling because that's how I live," he promised. "When I get up in the morning, I'm grateful to see the sun. I'm just going to go on being happy old Earvin because that's what people seem to like. And it's fun to be liked, the funnest thing of all."

In the end, it all came together to produce pleasing results. Kareem won the league's MVP for an unprecedented sixth time (Boston's Bill Russell had won five), and the Lakers topped the Western Conference with a 60–22 record.

"I think Magic has led us," the center acknowledged late in the season. "He's playing the same game, but he's getting smarter—

throwing away the ball less. He's just like me—I was never a rookie and Magic was never a rookie."

During the regular season he had averaged 18.0 points, 7.7 rebounds, and 7.3 assists while shooting 53 percent from the floor. He would up those numbers during his 16 playoff games that spring of 1980 to 18.3 points, 10.5 rebounds, and 9.4 assists.

It would be enough to impress the tough old birds like Dr. Jack and Jerry West and all the other conventional minds that had wondered if Johnson could find a role in the NBA.

"By the end of that year, by the time they played Philadelphia in Game 6," Ramsay would say, "Magic was doing everything."

The Rookie Vote

Thus, it was no great surprise that L.A.'s team was surging that May. Abdul-Jabbar was playing his best ball in years, and it showed as the Lakers ditched Phoenix in the first playoff round. Hall of Famer Paul Westphal, then playing for the Suns, battled the Lakers in that series and even scored 37 in a critical Game 3 loss. Asked in a 2019 interview what he considered most memorable about Johnson that first season, he replied, "Just watching him lead the break. He had such exuberance. You could see it in his eyes that he was looking for the most exciting play and, at the same time, the most effective play."

Westphal laughed at the memory, then added, "I just think he loved competing and he loved the bright lights and the stage, and winning and putting on a show. I think he was just special in that regard and that he embraced the spectacle of the NBA as well as anybody ever has."

There, awaiting Johnson at the end of the season, would be plenty of bright lights and a wide-open stage begging for his best.

Next up after Phoenix were the defending champion Seattle Supersonics in the conference finals. Led by Gus Williams and Dennis Johnson, the Sonics were a team that had taken the Western Conference crown two years in a row at the personal expense of the Lakers and their center.

Seattle promptly stole Game 1 against the Lakers in the Forum, but with Abdul-Jabbar determined to exact revenge on a Sonics team that had authored his embarrassment the Lakers fought back, with Abdul-Jabbar producing surprising locker room emotion in the clinching game of the series, which Johnson helped control with a triple-double despite playing with a 101 degree temperature. He delivered the ball early and often to Kareem (who would average 30.6 points, 11.6 rebounds, 3.8 assists, 1.6 steals, and a whopping 4.2 blocks in the five games) as the Lakers made a statement, winning four close games in a row, leaving Seattle fans to fuss for eternity that Johnson was allowed to double-dribble nearly every time he handled the ball.

From there the Lakers stepped up to battle for the top prize, the league championship, in a series known officially as the NBA Finals.

Larry Bird, meanwhile, had offered up his deadpan delivery against Johnson's beaming personal charm. In reality, they spoke different versions of the same broken English, all while sharing a superior basketball intellect, so much so that players, much like fans, also followed Bird's progress, especially as it appeared more and more like he and Johnson were headed toward another epic meeting, this time for an NBA title their very first year in the league. For many, the anticipation of a Bird-Johnson matchup had become palpable that spring. Bird had led the Celtics to a 61–21 finish. The Boston forward had averaged 21.5 points in helping his team to what was then the best turnaround in league history. The year before Bird arrived, Boston had finished 29–53. That upswing of 32 wins resulted in Bird being named Rookie of the Year, an insult that would be announced before the championship series opened, results that would leave Johnson with plenty of incentive.

Especially when he learned the vote tally. The twenty-three-year-old Bird had outpolled him, 63–3. But that wasn't the only insult. Bird was the third leading vote-getter for the All-NBA first team (Abdul-Jabbar led all candidates by snaring 130 of 132 votes).

There were two Johnsons selected for the second team and neither of them had a nickname. Dennis of the Sonics and Marques of the Bucks had made the cut.

Magic had not.

Privately, as Buss PR man Bob Steiner had revealed in 1991, Lakers ownership had recognized that Bird was two years older and thus had a more mature body and approach that first season. Buss was sure that given just a little time, Johnson would quickly eclipse Bird. Johnson himself was merely eager to demonstrate his superiority for a nationwide audience.

The circumstances would have created an amazing showdown between Bird's Celtics and the Lakers, with Johnson full of the kind of fire that had fueled their 1979 meeting in Salt Lake City. Alas, Bird couldn't make it. His hopes ended when Boston ran aground against Julius Erving and the 76ers in the Eastern Conference finals, losing four games to one.

Billy Cunningham's 76ers had finished 59–23, two games behind Boston during the regular season. They brought to the league championship series an array of talent with a veteran Dr. J still at the top of his high-flying game. "I don't think about my dunk shots," Erving had said during the Boston series. "I just make sure I have a place to land."

Sixers

Dr. Jack had warned Lionel Hollins that he was about to be traded that February of 1980 and then it happened, and he was on a Saturday night red-eye to play in a nationally televised game that Sunday afternoon with his new team, the Philadelphia 76ers.

About all he could remember four decades later from the dizzying turn of events that weekend was that he started the game, the Sixers won, and his tenure with the club was off to a good beginning.

Philly had seen enough of Hollins in the 1977 NBA championship series when the Sixers had taken the first two games in Philadelphia only to watch Bill Walton, Hollins, and the Trail Blazers take four straight games to steal it away from them. The Blazers had traded Walton and his injury troubles to the Clippers before that 1979–80 season and were now breaking up the rest of that championship roster to rebuild.

As GM of the Sixers, Pat Williams had come up with a marketing phrase for the fans in the wake of that disastrous '77 collapse—"We Owe You One," a promise the club was still trying to fulfill three seasons later, which was why Pat Williams had traded for Hollins.

Sixers guard Doug Collins had suffered a knee injury and Hollins was the answer. At six-three, he had good size for a point guard in that era. He, too, was a basketball lifer. Played in college at Arizona State. Enjoyed a long, productive NBA career, a smart player who then went on to enjoy a much respected coaching life, first in college, then the pros.

In February 1980, Hollins was provided an inside view of the Sixers, the immensely talented team that would confront Magic Johnson and his Lakers three times in the league championship series in four years, a confrontation that would prove to be the foundation of Johnson's legacy. The Sixers were coached by former North Carolina and NBA star Billy Cunningham.

"We practiced that Monday and a lot of guys weren't going all out," Hollins recalled of his first forty-eight hours in Philly. "I remember going all out and Darryl Dawkins yelling at me saying, 'Why are you playing so hard? It's just practice,' and 'You can't win a championship at practice.'"

"That's why we beat you guys," Hollins shot back at Dawkins, referring to the '77 championship. "We got it every day. We didn't wait till we got to the championship moment."

Dawkins's attitude reflected the values of that Sixers team that featured the famed Dr. J, Hollins recalled. "It played to the level that it needed to win and it won a lot of games. We were a very good team, but the commitment to each day of climbing the stairs to set a standard of excellence was not the biggest drive for that team. Julius was a pro. He came and he worked, but it wasn't all Julius. You had a lot of personalities on that team."

Cunningham was known to take something of the old pro approach to coaching, sort of rolling out the ball in practice and letting the grown men make their way. "In a lot of ways Billy Cunningham was from a different era," Hollins explained. "He didn't push as hard in practice. There was a lot of times when we didn't practice when we won."

As for playing for Dr. Jack, he may have had the scholarly professor image, but he offered a toughness beneath that sheen, Hollins explained, recalling a trip to practice in "D.C. and the bus driver getting lost on the way to shoot around."

Ramsay told the driver to pull over at an elementary school and had his team go at it outdoors on the concrete, Hollins remembered. "So those were different personalities and philosophies of coaching then. With Dr. Jack, we would fly home from New York or wherever on a Sunday afternoon and go straight to a high school to practice."

Playing for Portland the first half of the season, Hollins had gotten some experience going up against Johnson but hardly found it memorable, much like Dr. Jack, his coach. "I mean, Magic wasn't Magic," Hollins recalled, adding that Johnson would sort of turn and back you up the floor, leading with his butt. "He wasn't giving you a whole lot attacking you at that stage of his career, but he was talented and big and he could see the court. He could pass."

Well steeped in the Dr. Jack mind-set, the Lakers coaching staff seemed obviously pleased with Johnson but also measured in their approach even though the excitement could overtake them on nights when he showed the greatness that was coming. "Down to the wire, Magic wants the basketball," Westhead offered as the season entered its final weeks. "He wants the loose ball in the lane, wants the follow. And he'll put it in somebody's face. It's over for the rookie stuff."

Others around the league, meanwhile, employed less restraint in their reviews, beginning with George Gervin, who had played against and observed Johnson since he was a young teen. "He hasn't surprised me," the Ice Man said. "He can score big when he wants, and he makes the team look sharp."

Elvin Hayes went so far as to lump the rookie in with the all-time greats, saying, "The way he brings out the best in a team reminds me of Dave DeBusschere, Bill Russell, Bob Cousy, Walt Frazier . . ."

Dennis Johnson, another bigger guard in the Western Conference in those days before his tenure with the Celtics, declared, "Magic does exciting things. The Hop, the No-Look, the Hesitation . . ."

Dennis Johnson would cite Magic's court awareness, then add, "What impresses me most is his intelligence. He recognizes situations on-court very well. For any young player to come into this league and understand what's going on as well as he does is amazing."

Even so, new as it all was, Magic's performances couldn't always find a comfort level with the play of Norm Nixon, who had continued to give up some of the point guard role and moved to shooting guard at least half of the time. Some would even describe Nixon's presence as a crutch for Johnson as he adjusted that season.

"In that rookie year, Nixon had more assists than Magic did," Dr. Jack would note.

"You talk about people that weren't given their due. Norm could handle the ball as well as Earvin," Abdul-Jabbar would say in 1992. "Norm was faster up the court, and he had just as good a vision. But Norm couldn't get to the basket like Earvin because he didn't have the size. But when other teams tried to pressure Earvin and he gave the ball to Norm and let him run the break, then Norm and Jamaal, that was an incredible break right there. If the other teams tried to stop Earvin, that gave Norm and Jamaal the open court. They got us a lot of points. We went to two world championships that way."

Ron Carter, a friend of Nixon's, had gotten an early look at the relationship during training camp and preseason games, then kept track through Nixon. "Magic and Norman don't get along," Carter recalled in a 2004 interview. "I mean, they get along, but it's always about the court. So there's always this little petty inside thing going on . . . the kind of stuff that's going on every day between Norm and Magic. Just little digs trying to get at each other. It got ugly. . . . The problem was, in that locker room it was Norman's locker room. As long as Norm Nixon was there, it was gonna be Norm's locker room because of Norm's persona. It wasn't just about having the ball. It was always about, 'Who you gonna follow, me or Norm?' Kareem in a very discreet sort of way made it clear that Norm was his guy. Just subtly. Westhead might say, 'All right, run the play.' And Magic would grab the ball to run the play, and Kareem would slap it out of his hands and hand it to Norm. Just little stuff like that. You could see it irritate Magic. Eventually there was going to be this rift. You could see it coming."

Not everyone drew the edges of the relationship quite that sharply.

"Magic had to learn to keep everybody in the game," Nixon told *The New York Times* late that rookie season. "He was losing 'em. He had to make an effort, and he did. I like playing with him much more now. We complement one another."

Despite the tension, opposing coaches saw clearly that the Lakers had the best backcourt in the league. Combined with a dominant offensive center, they presented a formidable challenge.

"It was Jack McKinney's feeling that they should share the guard role," Paul Westhead emphasized in 2004. "So they would play off each other. It was kind of an even deal. At least half the time Nixon was free to run the team."

Taped Delay

The Sixers were returning to the championship series for the first time since their '77 collapse, Lionel Hollins recalled. "In 1980 we got to the Finals and everybody was just thinking that we were going to win the championship. Nobody was looking at Los Angeles as this super formidable team."

The Sixers knew they faced an unusual matchup with Johnson, Hollins said. "It was like, 'We can't let the Lakers get in an up-and-down game.'"

After all, they reasoned, "How many six-nine guys can handle the ball well enough and quick enough to get by you?"

The answer was exactly one. More players with size would soon be handling the ball, but they all would struggle to get the ball up the court, Lionel Hollins offered. "Magic never really struggled to get the ball up the court. You had to keep Magic in front of you. Once he got on the side of you, he was so big and he just kept going. He was definitely a force to deal with."

It was Johnson's unique combination of features that took him to another level, Reggie Theus explained in 2019. "The thing about Magic, you got to pick him up before he crossed half-court. If you didn't pick him before he crossed half-court, he'd go downhill on you, and there's no way you could stop him. If he got to the top of the key, forget about it. He's got you in his back pocket."

Handling the ball, Johnson sought physical contact with the defender once he got across half-court, Theus added. "In those days, the physical contact is what you wanted. The more pressure you applied, the more physical you were, the more Magic liked it. Then, he'd spin off of you to create scoring opportunities for himself. His ability to see the floor, his ability to push the ball for his size, his ability to attack the basket were some of his assets, but the biggest thing about Magic was his leadership. His competitiveness. All of those things were what made Magic."

No one would ever display the unique ability to drive the agenda the way Johnson was doing as a rookie that spring.

For all the focus on Johnson's very different game, what became immediately apparent as the series unfolded was that as a team, the Sixers seemed to lack an answer for Abdul-Jabbar, who quickly overmatched their centers, Caldwell Jones and Darryl Dawkins, which put L.A. in position to win the championship. In Game 1 in the Forum that May 4, Kareem scored 33 points, with 14 rebounds, six blocks, and five assists, to push the Lakers to a 109–102 win. Nixon had 23 points and Wilkes finished with 20 while doing an excellent double-team job on Erving. "Every time I caught the ball I had two people on me," the 76ers star said afterward.

Johnson provided an almost quiet difference with 16 points, nine assists, and 10 rebounds, somewhat under the radar as the games unfolded.

Down the stretch of the season, Westhead had begun playing Johnson at power forward on offense, while Nixon and sixth man Michael Cooper ran the backcourt. "That's our best lineup," the coach told reporters.

Long trained to recognize his own tremendous advantage, Abdul-Jabbar scored 38 in Game 2, but the Sixers managed to contain the Lakers' fast break and did it without fouling. Philly led by as much as 20 in the fourth period, but the Lakers raced back, trimming the lead to 105–104 late in the game. Then the Sixers' Bobby Jones hit the money shot, a jumper with seven seconds left, enough for a 107–104 win that tied the series at one-all and provided Philly with the home-court advantage.

Part of the loss was blamed on the "distractions" of Spencer Haywood, who had fallen asleep during a stretching exercise and exhibited other strange behaviors. The former ABA star had spent much of the season as a Lakers reserve. Haywood stated publicly that Westhead's reasons for not playing him more were "lies." Fans in the Forum loved Haywood, who had taken to encouraging their affection by waving a towel during games to urge their chanting his name. It would later be revealed that cocaine abuse had unraveled Haywood's life. The loss in Game 2 ended his run with the team, however, after he supposedly picked a fight with rookie teammate Brad Holland. Afterward Westhead suspended Haywood for the remainder of the season, which left the Lakers thin in the frontcourt just when they needed the help.

In that age of strictly man-to-man defense mandated by the rules—over time the Lakers would develop a carefully disguised zone press that would leave opponents complaining that it was a rules violation—Westhead made two key defensive switches for Game 3. First, he gave Jim Chones the task of covering Dawkins. That left nonshooting Caldwell Jones for Kareem, who parked his big frame in the lane to protect the rim. Then Westhead switched Johnson to covering Hollins on the perimeter, which stifled Philly's outside game. The result was a 111–101 Lakers win in Philadelphia in Game 3, which allowed Los Angeles to retake the home-court advantage with a 2–1 series lead in the best-of-seven playoff format. Once again, Abdul-Jabbar had provided the 76ers a matchup headache—33 points, 14 rebounds, four blocks, and three assists. And once again the center got plenty of help from Nixon, Johnson, Wilkes, and others.

As explained in 1993's *The Lakers*, Philly lashed back for Game 4. The lead bounced back and forth through the first three periods, then the 76ers took control down the stretch. Julius Erving unleashed one of his more memorable moves, scooting around Lakers reserve Mark Landsberger on the right to launch himself. In midair, headed toward the hoop, Dr. J encountered the Lakers' towering rim protector. Somehow "the Doctor" moved behind the backboard and freed his right arm behind Kareem to put the ball into the basket. Sitting on the bench near the baseline with Cooper, Johnson couldn't help but erupt with delight at the elegance of his role model. The move served as Philly's own variety of magic and the 76ers went on to even the series at two-all with a 105–102 win.

These events served to set up a marvelous Game 5 back at the Forum. L.A. clutched to a two-point lead late in the third quarter when Abdul-Jabbar twisted his left ankle and went to the locker room. At that juncture, he had 26 points and was carrying the Lakers despite an uneven performance from Johnson. It was then, however, that the rookie scored six points and added an assist to move the Lakers up by eight.

It was all just enough to buy time for Abdul-Jabbar, who limped back into the game early in the fourth period. His appearance stirred the L.A. crowd, and despite the bad ankle, he acknowledged their embrace of him by scoring 14 points down the stretch. With the game tied at 103 and 33 seconds left, the great center scored, drew the call, and finished Philly by completing the three-point play. L.A. won, 108–103, and took the series lead, 3–2, with Game 6 in Philadelphia.

It was both a remarkable and gutsy performance by the center. But the cost of it soon became apparent, when the Lakers arrived at Los Angeles International Airport for their flight to Philly and learned that "Jabbar" wouldn't be making the trip. His ankle was so bad, doctors said he should miss Game 6 and stay home in hopes he might be able to go if the series made it to a Game 7. If the center missed both of the last two games in the series, the Lakers seemed sure to lose it all. Westhead was understandably concerned about the effect the news would have on the team.

Johnson, however, was ready with an answer.

His teammates heard him before they saw him that day with the boom box shouldered and blasting. He boarded their United Airlines flight to Philadelphia and plopped himself down in the first-class seat always set aside for Abdul-Jabbar.

"It was like a sacrilege to sit in Kareem's seat," recalled Ted Green of the *L.A. Times*.

"People thought he was crazy," broadcaster Jim Hill remembered, laughing. "He looked back at everybody and said, 'Have no fear, EJ is here. We're gonna go win this game.'"

Actually, several accounts offered that he declared, "Earvin Magic Motherfuckin' Johnson is here."

"He sat back in Kareem's chair and started laughing," Jim Hill recalled. "There are certain things you don't do. That was Kareem's domain. They were like, 'Young buck, you don't know what you're talking about.'"

"Could you imagine a twenty-year-old kid having the wherewithal to do that?" Lon Rosen asked in 2022, still animated four decades later about Johnson's response.

The looming issue on the flight became what to do with the starting lineup.

In a 2002 radio interview with broadcaster Larry Burnett, Chick Hearn remembered it this way: "We flew commercial in those days. I was sitting with Paul Westhead, the coach, and Magic came up and said, 'Coach. I want to ask you a favor.'"

"Yeah," Westhead said. "What do you want?"

"Magic said, 'I want to start at center,'" Hearn recalled. "The coach said, 'Whaaat?'"

Hearn laughingly recalled that Westhead initially rejected the idea of Johnson at center.

"Magic left and went back to his seat," Hearn recalled. "Westhead said to me. 'Can you imagine that? Him asking me to start at center?' I said, 'I think it's a hell of an idea.'"

Whatever the genesis, the answer began to gain clarity.

Westhead then went and sat with Jerry Buss and asked his opinion. The owner was decidedly against Johnson jumping center or playing center, Westhead would later recall. And when the coach said he was likely going to do it, Buss said he wouldn't try to stop him, but if Westhead made the move and it backfired and cost the Lakers the series there were going to be consequences.

Once in Philadelphia, the matter was again addressed in practice. "I asked him at practice, can you play center?" Westhead remembered in 2019.

"I can do it," Johnson answered. "I did it in high school. That was only a couple of years ago."

"Paul's fear was that we couldn't match up with Dawkins and Caldwell Jones," Johnson recalled in 2004. "I told him I could play Caldwell Jones, and he looked at me like, 'Jesus, he's seven feet tall!' He couldn't believe that I could match up. I told him, 'Coach, on the other end, what are they gonna do with us? Who's gonna guard the guys we're gonna have?' "

"He did start him, and the rest is history," Hearn told Burnett.

Fans in Philly never really bought the story that the Lakers had left their star center back in L.A. One radio station reported regular sightings of "Jabbar" at the airport. One taxi driver was sure he had driven the center to his hotel.

The atmosphere seemed further tilted because the game was not going to be broadcast live that night but on "taped delay" across the country. "It just showed where the league was," Pat Williams said in 2019. "The league had not arrived, you know, literally just was not on the cutting edge of the sports media world."

CBS wasn't willing to invade its prime-time lineup for pro basketball, Williams explained. "The network just wasn't going to do that. It just wasn't. They didn't want to cancel the evening news, not for the NBA. There was no ESPN. There was no Fox Sports. There was nothing else in those days. The feeling was the Lakers couldn't survive and Philly was going to take them now, you know. Our feeling was, 'Boy, what a break. What a break we just got.' The whole city was that way. The basketball fans of Philadelphia came to the game that night ready to celebrate."

First of all, the public had gotten the idea that Johnson was entertaining, but network executives didn't foresee his impact and stardom, Pat Williams said. "Magic had had a good rookie year. He was a good player, but nobody really could have anticipated what happened that night in Philadelphia where the Lakers come to town severely, severely limited because the great Kareem had gone down with an ankle sprain in Game 5."

In retrospect, the evening would be explained in terms of psychology. "I don't care who you are, if you're a fan or a player, and you go to a game and you've heard that their best player's out tonight," the former Sixers GM added. "How often does it happen and your feeling immediately is, 'We're gonna have a much easier time tonight'? Psychologically the players, they let down a little bit whether they realized it or not. 'Oh boy. We got an easy game tonight.'"

The Lakers themselves, meanwhile, were almost too loose, their coach feared. Johnson was his normal euphoric, dancing, rookie self. About the only thing that punctured his mood was reporters' questions about his thoughts for Game 7.

"They all figured that if they lost that game, Kareem would be ready to play in the next home game," Chick Hearn said. "That was not a fact. Kareem had a badly sprained ankle."

It's all perfect, Johnson told his teammates. Nobody expects us to win here. In reality, most of the Lakers had their doubts. But when they arrived at the Spectrum that Friday evening, there were the carpenters building an awards presentation platform. The NBA rules required that Philadelphia provide some facility to present the trophy, just in case L.A. happened to win.

"It should be interesting," Westhead told his players before the game. "Pure democracy. We'll go with the slim line."

Which meant Johnson, Chones, and Wilkes in the frontcourt while Nixon and Cooper took care of things at guard. Abdul-Jabbar, who was sprawled on his bed back at his Bel Air home, was reported to have sent a last-minute good luck message. In those days of no cell phones, thus no text messages, not even emails, it was never clear exactly how the center would have sent the good wishes. Perhaps he reached them on a nearby pay phone. Or a smoke signal.

By game time, the Lakers' big plan was hardly a secret. Johnson announced to the TV audience just what was coming in a sideline interview with former Laker Hot Rod Hundley.

"I will be playing some center and forward, depending on certain plays," Johnson said, smiling broadly.

The Lakers then took the floor, only to find more confusion, even disarray.

"We were going out for the center jump," Westhead recalled, "and we said, 'Let's go.' The last thing, Jim Chones looked at me and said, 'Now, coach, I'm jumping center, right?' I said, 'No, Magic is jumping center.' We wanted it to appear that he was the center."

"I remember," Jim Hill would later offer, "Brent Musburger was doing the play-by-play. He started laughing. 'And the rookie Magic Johnson from Michigan State is going to be in the center circle to jump ball.'"

Johnson was said to be smiling as he stepped up to jump center against Dawkins. He lost the tip, but the 76ers seemed puzzled. L.A. went up 7–0, then 11–4.

"On the first play, he came down in the low post and took a turnaround hook shot," Westhead remembered. "He took a Kareem hook shot. What happened the rest of the game, he played everywhere. He played guard. He played forward. Everyone sees him as playing center. It was a psychological thing. Everyone saw Magic as the center. That helped us. People forget Jamaal Wilkes had 37 points in that game."

"At the start of the game, I'm thinking to myself, 'Nobody thinks this young guy is going to be able to fill the shoes of Kareem and be as successful as Kareem,'" NBA journeyman Lloyd Walton remembered. "But my eyes got bigger and bigger and bigger as the game went on."

Johnson was hot early and the shots kept coming—and falling—from an early jumper right of the key to a left-handed hook shot driving left on Erving. He then posted Erving on the left, and when the Philly star jumped the passing lane looking for a steal, Johnson attacked and scored, drawing a foul on Dawkins.

He then posted on the right, drew a double-team, and hit Chones for a jumper. A short time later, he sold a pump fake, then motored right to make a short pullup jumper. Then he moved back to the right post and finished with a startlingly sweet hook.

The Sixers clearly seemed discombobulated by the display, which allowed him to uncork a hesitation dribble that froze the entire defense, which then opened up the floor for him to roll right down the lane and score unchallenged.

And all of that was in addition to what he did in the running game.

"Magic got into the flow," Lionel Hollins said in 2019, pointing out that Kareem's absence from the lineup created awkward matchup issues for Philadelphia. "He was running unattached most the time."

If the game slowed to half-court sets, there was usually somebody near Johnson to guard him, Hollins explained. "But he was ahead of the pack a lot more often and he was making plays and he was getting rebounds, you know. He had 15 of them in the game. And he also had assists and he scored a lot of points. I think that was the one thing that probably wasn't thought of, was Magic's ability to score from the perimeter versus just being in the post."

Mostly, though, it was the running game that brought an edge.

"Once we got the ball, we were gone," Johnson said, looking back in 1992. "We beat Philadelphia in the transition game because they couldn't keep up."

The situation came about, in part, because of assumptions Billy Cunningham made about the matchups, Hollins recalled. "Because Kareem wasn't playing, Billy figured Magic was going to post up more and Norm Nixon was going to handle the ball more. So he took me off of Magic and started Julius on him. But Magic handled the ball and pushed the ball just as much as he did when Kareem was playing. It didn't change, and that wasn't a good fit for us because Julius was down in the low post trying to score. And you know Magic would get a rebound and he'd be out and he's off on the attack and Julius was behind Earvin. It was just a bad matchup. Magic was a guard and Erving was a forward."

It was the blend of Johnson's unique skills that drove the Sixers' confusion that night, indeed would drive the soul of a glorious decade in American pro basketball that was unfolding that very night. On taped delay.

Beyond running, Johnson did plenty of posting, attacking from the block with spinning moves both right and left. With that, the Lakers gained the momentum and a nice lead early, Hollins said, adding that subbing Bobby Jones helped the Sixers slow the Lakers' momentum. "Once we got behind, we were playing catch-up to try to put the best matchups together."

Philly broke back in the second quarter and took a 52–44 lead. Westhead stopped play and told them to collapse in the middle. Steve Mix had come off Philly's bench to knife inside on his way to 16 points. The Lakers squeezed in and closed to 60-all at the half. Then they opened the third period with a 14–0 run, keyed by Wilkes's 16 points in the period. At 66–60 Johnson had sensed Wilkes to his left, so he took a step right and pulled the defender with him, which opened the lane for Wilkes to take in his pass off the weak side and score.

Early in the third Johnson had hit a baseline jumper to give the Lakers a six-point lead, which was soon followed by a bounce pass to Cooper cutting from the weak side.

The big run wasn't all offense, however. Johnson's speed getting back on the Philly break allowed him to steal a Henry Bibby pass, followed by a defensive rebound that he hurled full-court to a streaking Brad Holland for an easy lay-in.

Adding to his display, Johnson hit a long jumper to push the score to 72–60.

Too good to collapse, Philly had pulled back in it by the opening of the fourth. After a timeout, Cunningham had moved Bobby Jones back on Johnson, which the rookie answered with a set shot in the rangy defender's face.

Another signature moment found Johnson dribbling at the top of the key, looking right over his shoulder, his back to Jones, craftily, patiently waiting for Philly's best defender to make a move. When Jones finally reached, Johnson instantly spun left and rolled right down the center of the lane for an easy bucket.

"Earvin gets a lot of credit," Hollins said. "He had a fantastic game. He didn't play center. He jumped center. They could have had anybody jump center with Kareem out. You know, they had Jim Chones. I mean, it wasn't like they didn't have guys who could jump center. I think a lot more was made out of him playing center. He was the point guard in that game. If he got by you, he was gone. Because of the matchups, he was played by a forward who couldn't really get to him quick enough nor stay in front of him consistently. And he was able to get to the basket and score, and he got to the free throw line. He was aggressive and attacked. And it wasn't because he was playing center and posting it up. He got 'em rolling, but the people who won the game for them in the end was Jamaal Wilkes with his 37. He made every big shot that was needed to be made in the fourth quarter. Brad Holland from UCLA came off the bench; he made some big jumpers. And then Butch Lee made some shots. And then Jim Chones had a heck of a game. Magic was great. Don't get me wrong. And he was a catalyst of them getting out and running and playing the way they played. I mean, he was a bear to deal with in the open court. But in this last game, he was a bear to deal with in every facet of the game."

The Lakers played differently than they had all year, Hollins concluded. "Magic was smart enough and wanted to win and he knew how to stay in his lane and let Kareem do his thing. But in that game, there was no Kareem. And Magic was in all the lanes."

With only five minutes left, it was 103–101, Lakers. Westhead called time again and made one last attempt to charge up his tired players. They responded with a run over the next 76 seconds to go up by seven. Then Johnson with all of his youthful energy scored nine points down the stretch to end it, 123–107.

"He just took over . . . and against Philadelphia," Lloyd Walton concluded. "You're talking about Doc, you're talking about Bobby Jones, you are talking about some really good guys, big Darryl Dawkins, Caldwell Jones, and he just dominated them like he had been in the league for 10 years. That kind of performance is legendary. Period. . . . Legendary. Oh, my God, he dominated that game."

Alas, the Lakers were too exhausted to celebrate. Wilkes had a career-best outing, scoring his 37 points with 10 rebounds. And

Chones lived up to his vow to shut down the middle. He finished with 11 points and 10 rebounds. He held Dawkins to 14 points and four rebounds.

For the Lakers, Mark Landsberger also had 10 boards. And Cooper put in 16 points.

Johnson had rung up an astounding 42 points, including all 14 of his free throw attempts. He had 15 rebounds, seven assists, three steals, and a block.

"It was amazing, just amazing," said Erving, who led Philly with 27.

"Magic made a pass one time in that '80 series against Philadelphia," Cooper recalled in a 1992 interview. "He threw a bounce pass three quarters of the court on the run to Jamaal Wilkes. He threw it between about five players, and to this day, I still don't know how he got it there."

The late Phil Jasner, longtime *Philadelphia Daily News* basketball writer, pointed to the weight of the moment in a 2004 interview. "With Magic that night, you knew you were watching history. . . . After a while his performance became psychological. He took that game over, whether he was bringing the ball up the court, rebounding, blocking a shot. He was mesmerizing."

Back in Lansing, George Fox had found a fuzzy radio signal that had allowed him to follow in real time.

"I was listening to it," Fox recalled in 2019. "When I got through, I was going nuts. So I called Earvin's dad."

"Earvin, how do you like that?" Fox blurted immediately.

"What?" Big Earv responded.

"Earvin's the MVP," Fox announced, "and they won the national championship."

"Are you serious?" the father responded.

"Well, yeah. I've been listening to it," Fox told him.

"He said, 'Well, we still got a few minutes to go on TV.' So he went in and woke up his wife, Christine. Now that's a story. That's how things have changed in the NBA since 1980."

"That's when he emerged," Pat Williams recalled. "Everybody woke up the next morning because most people had missed the game and then they're thinking, 'This guy did what?' And, 'This young guy, what did he do'? Well, he went for 42 and 15. 'Oh my gosh. Oh my gosh.' I think that was probably the reaction. I think the people who saw it were sitting home watching the game late on taped delay and they couldn't believe it."

Rick Barry grabbed Johnson for a quick interview as the game ended and told him, "A lot of people didn't know if you could make it in this league. You certainly made a believer out of me."

"The whole season has been just great," Johnson replied. "It's been beautiful."

Johnson's outburst had been prompted in part by the fact that he was going up against Erving, one of his idols, Pat Williams would say. "He also had an enormous amount of respect for Julius. And, you know, I think with that in mind, he came over to pay tribute to one of his boyhood heroes, Julius."

The Lakers' joy hadn't fully erupted before the controversy began sizzling behind the scenes. As the clock was winding down, the broadcast team announced that Johnson had been named the series MVP, the first and only time in NBA history that the award went to a rookie. The selection seemed to ignore Abdul-Jabbar's huge performance in the first five games.

Johnson had been asked how his team had managed without their great center. "Without Kareem," he said, "we couldn't play the half-court and think defensively. We had to play the full-court and take our chances."

In the postgame interview on national delayed television, Johnson turned to the camera and addressed Kareem back in Los Angeles. "We know you're hurtin', big fella," he said. "But we want you to get up and do a little dancin' tonight."

Jerry Buss, in fact, was already jumping. He hadn't been a pro basketball owner a full year and already he was on national television, soaked in champagne and accepting a championship trophy. It was something he'd worked for a long time, he told CBS, comments that brought chuckles. There had been owners sitting around the league forever during the lean years enduring the fact that the bloodthirsty Boston Celtics and the great Bill Russell had won 11 championships in 13 seasons, with coach and GM Red Auerbach crowing and literally blowing cigar smoke in their faces the entire time. And now this guy Buss wins it in his first year as owner and he's talking about his long, hard road to a title?

Yet for Abdul-Jabbar, the MVP was another insult. He began seething as he sat at home and watched stupefied as Johnson was given the award. He suspected that CBS had tampered with the voting process so that there could be a presentation after the game. Johnson would later admit as much.

"He was robbed of it," admitted Lon Rosen, Johnson's longtime friend. "Kareem should have been the MVP."

"I had to give away the MVP," Abdul-Jabbar said in a 1992 interview. "I had won it. The writers voted me for the MVP, and then somebody from CBS went and asked them to change their vote so they could give it to Earvin. Earvin talked to me right afterwards. He said, 'Hey, I should give this to you. I didn't deserve this.' But I wasn't going to get into a thing with Earvin about that. I was thrilled with everybody else that he did what he did and we ended up with a World Championship. I was able to put it behind me, but it was one of the things that happened to me in my career that makes me bitter. It all came from me not being popular."

"It was a media selection," Westhead said, looking back years later. "It had nothing to do with our team or our feelings. Magic was spectacular that night. If you were voting for the MVP that night, well, he certainly deserved it. If you were voting for MVP of the series, we nonetheless would not have gotten that far if not for Kareem. If there was ever time for a co-MVP, that was the time to do it."

"I kind of see it like the Chrysler Building," the center said more than a decade later. "You can't build a building like that without an incredible foundation. My game was the foundation which enabled . . . all these guys to do their thing on the perimeter while I created what I created inside. We played off that, which is what teamwork is all about. Because of Earvin's special charisma the story was written a different way. It was always what he did. It got to the point that I had no real belief in the objectivity of the press. I guess I was a victim of my success, the team was a victim of its success, and Earvin was the victim of his success. We compounded each other's successes and difficulties. I should emphasize that I would rather be dealing with these problems than dealing with the problems of not ever winning a World Championship."

It happened to be a championship with many major contributors, Michael Cooper offered in 2004, saying, "You know what? Magic had 42 points, 15 rebounds, and gobs of assists, but you forget that Jamaal Wilkes had a career-high 37 points, Michael Cooper had a career-high 16 points, Jim Chones had a career-high 14, 15 rebounds, so there was a lot of things that went on, but the limelight was on Magic because he made it fun for everyone."

As Alex Wolff, the longtime *Sports Illustrated* writer and basketball historian, pointed out in 2020, that Game 6, taken along with Johnson's role in the 1979 NCAA championship a year earlier, had created this transformative moment for position-less basketball.

"There were no shackles on the guy," Wolff said. "There were no boundaries. He's going to be free to do whatever he wants."

Johnson was making a statement that the old ways of playing the game didn't have to be the things that "took basketball through the rest of the century and into the twenty-first century, that there's a whole new way of doing it."

It may have been driven by Johnson's unique mix of persona, size, and skill, Wolff said. "He's kind of like a ringmaster almost as if he was inviting all of these others to the party. He was famously friendly with so many of them, and it was almost like, 'Hey, we can do this together.' And that was so very much a part of his personality."

"I honestly believe this," Cooper would say a quarter century later. "If we hadn't won that championship I don't think we would have been as successful as we were. We would have won a couple of titles, but to win five within a 10-year period and to get to the Finals nine times, that's an impressive record. I don't think we would have been as successful because it would have hurt us mentally. What it showed us was that we could win under severe adversity. That's what it brought out. As Kareem went down, and Kareem was our main focus for the whole season, when he went down and we were able to get that game, we pulled together as a team. And we did it against a very talented Philadelphia team. Darryl Dawkins, Doc, Bobby Jones. By all rights, that Game 6 with Kareem not with us, that should have been their game and possibly their series. But we fought through that, and it showed us that if we worked together as a team and kept with the team concept, you could accomplish anything in this league."

"Game 6 was definitely a platform for everything else that we did," Johnson said much later. "That's what ignited Showtime. That game actually coined the phrase Showtime, because our best dominant big man, the best big man in the game, was down. We're on the road against the most dominant team in the East, and we end up winning. We won because we ran up and down the court. That was the most unbelievable game that we all had been in because of the circumstances. We knew that we had to run and gun, and that's what we did."

Ron Charles would have a memory that he was watching the replay of the game at the apartment of his girlfriend, who happened to room with Cookie Kelly, Johnson's on-and-off girlfriend.

"I was sitting there and watching the game with them," he recalled. "I knew who won because I listened to it on the radio. I hear a knock on the door. It's 12:30. Who's knocking on the door? I opened the door. It was Earvin. After the game, he flew back to Lansing that night."

Johnson had somehow slipped away and showed up in the wee hours? It never happened, Johnson would say in 2022. He did not board a private plane and fly to Lansing after the game, stay a half hour with Cookie Kelly, then fly back to Philadelphia for a flight home the next morning.

In a night of pure fantasy, the clearly implausible had found a place in people's minds. In fact, the whole season and its ending had been the most implausible in the history of the game, Buss PR man Bob Steiner would say, looking back in 1992. Westhead had been pulled in with no head coaching experience in the NBA. Riley had been “pulled out of the broadcast booth” with no coaching experience on any level.

If you added in all the other bizarre events, from murder to losing the great Kareem before the deciding game, the word *implausible* would have to be stretched out considerably just to try to cover it all.

Unable to enjoy the championship moment was Jack McKinney, whose recovery from head injury had been slow. Against doctors' advice, he decided to attempt a comeback during the spring of 1980. When the Lakers questioned the wisdom of his move, he became frustrated and criticized Buss in a newspaper story. After the championship series, the Lakers had informed McKinney that Westhead would remain head coach. The decision left McKinney embittered at the team and Westhead, his longtime friend. Buss quietly arranged for McKinney to go to the “other” team being run out of the offices of Buss-Mariani, the Indiana Pacers (where McKinney would win NBA Coach of the Year for 1981). It would take many years for him to eventually acknowledge that the Lakers made the right decision, that he was still debilitated when he attempted to return.

“He had some memory loss for a while,” former Lakers GM Bill Sharman recalled in 1992. “It was just kind of a no-win situation for the team.”

“It was difficult on one hand because Jack was an integral part of what we had done,” Westhead recalled in 2004. “Somehow he kind of got left aside on it.”

The remaining immediate problem that weekend was how to celebrate. Roy Englebrecht recalled the team had worked up some generic hats and T-shirts that interns took to local radio and TV stations that night so that the team could begin offering them for sale.

Earlier, Englebrecht himself had gone to the airport to make arrangements to get the team back if they did manage to somehow win it in Game 6, he recalled. “They laughed at me for ten minutes, talking about, ‘Wait a minute. Kareem's sitting here in L.A. You're not going to go back to Philadelphia and beat Dr. J and Dawkins.’”

Now the Lakers' tiny staff suddenly found themselves having to make up plans for a parade on the fly, Englebrecht remembered with a laugh in 2019. "We had a crowd at the Forum to meet the team. There hadn't been a downtown parade in L.A. for decades. We had no map for standard operating procedure for a championship parade. We got cars and we put players in cars. I look back now, and the crowd just enveloped the cars. I forget what street we came down in downtown L.A. It might have been Washington Boulevard or La Cienega. Even looking at some pictures now, there was very little security. We just got overwhelmed. We didn't know what sort of crowd we were going to have. I've got a great picture of me walking next to Kareem's car and there's Magic. Kareem was the first car. Magic was in the second car and I'm standing there with kind of my hand on the car and the crowd is right there. Everybody's smiling and I'm looking up with no idea, like, 'I hope we can get to the end of this, but this is crazy.' There was Kareem with his girlfriend at that time in the car. We didn't have any buses; we didn't have any semis or flatbed trucks which they use now to kind of keep the players insulated from the fans. Back then I needed fifteen convertibles. I got them. We took the players in a bus from the Forum to downtown. We got everybody in a car. We put placards in the front of each on the windshield to say who it was in there."

In that first year, the fans knew who Kareem and Magic and a few others were, but not all the players, Englebrecht explained.

There, in the second car behind Kareem, was Magic, the PR and marketing man recalled with a laugh. "He has the biggest smile on his face. You got to realize, you know, he comes to L.A. and eight months later he's driving in a world championship parade downtown."

"When the Rams first came here before my time, they were the first pro team," Steve Springer recalled, looking back on the 1980 title. "But then when the Dodgers got here it was all Dodgers, Sandy Koufax and Don Drysdale for all those years. Before the Showtime Lakers it would be unheard of for a Lakers playoff game to get a higher rating than a Dodger spring training game. I mean, the Dodgers owned this town, lock, stock, and barrel. The '72 Lakers team, that won 33 in a row, that created this great excitement, but it was just a one-year thing. But starting in '80 the Lakers took over this town."

What had been Johnson's expression? Do it for love?

Sure enough, the love was coming, headed for him and borne by a legion. Events would show he had neither the inclination nor the desire to get out of the way.

20

THE STORM SURGE

Thinking that the Lakers would lose Game 6 on the road without Kareem, many of their key support people hadn't made the trip to Philly for the event, but George Andrews had decided to fly down from Chicago to be there for his young client.

"Nobody went to Philly except me among his family and his entourage, which was really a small entourage," Andrews recalled in 2019. "They watched him on taped delay. They said, 'Well, we can't win without Kareem. We'll watch it here.'"

Andrews instead figured, "I'm going because it's more important to be there when you lose."

The lawyer's reward for that effort was a cherished moment toasting the championship with orange juice, not champagne, with Johnson in the locker room afterward. The atmosphere around them was strangely subdued for a title celebration, largely attributed to the utter exhaustion of the players.

"He turns to me," Andrews recalled of Johnson in that moment, "and asks, 'You think we might get some more offers? You think we'll get some endorsements now?'"

Johnson was immediately aware that his big night meant his life was going to change and was wondering if that, in turn, was going to translate into a bounty of sweet deals.

"Yeah," the lawyer answered quietly with a smile.

"It was just a great moment," Andrews recalled in 2019. "I was so happy for him because he had showed the full array of what he could do."

Neither of them was aware of it at the time, but they had just entered the giant sweepstakes of the age, and the outcome would be a sore subject for both of them for a long time.

Lawyer and client could already guess perhaps that Johnson's top rival on the court was going to be Larry Bird. What neither of them could have possibly understood then is that Johnson and Andrews would both be measured forever by an off-the-court competition with a player who was only finishing his junior year in high school at that moment, Mike Jordan, the North Carolina kid who would soon have the "Magic Mike" vanity plate on his car.

This race between what would become the top two icons of American basketball in the era wouldn't be measured in points scored or rebounds or assists. Or even wins and losses.

It would be measured in endorsement deals and marketing power and influence, and ultimately in the long run, wealth.

"We were different," Andrews said in 2019 of the effort and strategy in finding Johnson endorsement deals. "We were very selective."

The retort, of course, would be that Jordan, too, was selective. He selected all the deals that made him far richer and far more powerful than his idol.

Andrews pointed to another factor in what would become the disparity in global marketing power between the two stars.

"He really didn't want to spend the time," the lawyer said of the twenty-year-old Johnson. "I mean, you could have gotten all the personal appearances he wanted in L.A. for $25,000 an hour and he wouldn't do it. He'd rather be back in Lansing playing softball with his buddies."

Actually, the record would show that Jordan himself as a young man wouldn't be all that savvy about deals or endorsements in his own pro debut. As Sonny Vaccaro, who would be the driving force behind

Jordan's 1984 landmark shoe and apparel deal with Nike, pointed out in 2013 interviews, Jordan's mother deserved the credit for pushing her son to go to Portland, Oregon, with her to strike the Nike agreement. Young Jordan himself didn't even want to make the trip.

In that strange way, the competition between the two superstars would ultimately come down to the influence of their mothers, two women who had emerged from North Carolina's enormously difficult sharecropper culture at just about the same time in the 1950s.

The difference was that Mrs. Jordan's father, Edward Peoples, was a hard-nosed businessman, one of the rare, rare North Carolina sharecroppers, Black or white, to win at the agricultural game that was absolutely and completely rigged against them. Edward Peoples came to own his own land, farmed for himself, not another man, and had all sorts of side ventures, including the cash crop of making and selling illegal "moonshine" liquor. Deloris Peoples Jordan, with the business acumen and drive of her father, pushed her son into the Nike deal.

Vaccaro would describe Mrs. Jordan as "one of the most impressive people I've ever met."

Christine Johnson, meanwhile, was obviously impressive to many people as well. However, she appeared far more concerned with her son's spiritual well-being as opposed to his endorsement deals and his investment portfolio.

Who's to say ultimately which woman was right?

In all fairness, no one in the shoe industry was looking to build a global marketing and apparel campaign around a young Black male in 1979 as Vaccaro would push Nike to do with Jordan just five years later, before he had played even a minute of NBA basketball, a fact that would come to annoy Magic Johnson to no end.

Obviously in 1979, no one had dared to think of such a novel idea, that a Black man would be every bit as deserving as any other figure, that in fact a Black man would prove far superior for the task. Actually, shoe deals were far from the rage, no matter your skin color, in 1979.

Lawyer George Andrews recalled that Johnson had worn Bata Wilsons in college, liked the people there, and wanted to work a pro shoe deal with them. Unfortunately, Bata Wilson had launched a signature John Wooden shoe in 1977 only to find itself with ninety thousand unsold pairs, recalled Andrews, who handled all deals for the first eight years of Johnson's career.

Bata Wilson did manage a competitive deal for Johnson by adding in equipment revenue, but Converse countered with a better deal by including an equipment agreement with Spalding.

Shoe deals for NBA players in 1979 were measured in tens of thousands of dollars. And no one received a shoe deal that offered a player a percentage of the profits, which is what fell into place for Jordan in 1984, a multiplier that would bring him hundreds of millions of dollars in royalties over the years and ultimately his own brand with Nike.

Andrews was able to negotiate a combined shoe and equipment deal for Johnson in 1979 that put him at or near the top in shoe money, a reported $100,000, although Andrews said in 2022 that the contract was larger than that. Whatever it was, it still would compare poorly with what Jordan would receive in 1984.

The issue would only gain relevance years later as millions in the global basketball fan base began comparing the wealth, power, and influence ultimately amassed by the two competitors. Such thinking coincided with the growing recognition that top American pro basketball stars, once considered somewhat obscure in terms of celebrity, suddenly began looming as major cultural figures with their media appeal to a vast and growing audience, with their sports apparel and shoe deals driving the fashion industry.

Soon enough, the issue between Johnson and Jordan wasn't just who was the greater player but who owned a bigger cultural and marketing footprint. It was a competition that caused immense frustration in the Johnson camp, as a younger Jordan rose with his decided marketing advantage driven by his groundbreaking Nike contract. After all, this off-court competition proved to be merely another means the two men had of keeping score with their natural inclination to seek to upstage each other.

The competition would reach absurd heights, beginning in 2017 as Johnson would come up with a story that Nike had actually offered him a shoe deal in 1979 that was to be paid in shares of Nike stock, which was cheap at the time with Nike still a relatively young company. Johnson's story was reported widely and even included in the 2022 HBO series about the Lakers, *Winning Time.*

Such an offer was never even discussed and certainly not offered, George Andrews said in 2022. "We never talked to Nike. Nike was never in the conversation. It never happened."

"He was just in error," Andrews said of Johnson's assertions that he had been offered and turned down a stock deal from Nike that would have been worth billions later. "He just must be confused. Nike really wasn't a player at that point. They didn't become a player until several years after that."

Sonny Vaccaro, who at the time was a primary figure in Nike basketball, also agreed that there was no such deal offered to Johnson.

Johnson himself had often extolled the excellence of his own memory, but the record would show that it was selective. Was he engaging in wishful fantasy that somehow he had been offered a Nike deal after all? Lon Rosen wasn't representing Johnson at the time, so he professed to have no idea.

Nike had moved into college basketball in the late 1970s by using Vaccaro to pay college coaches under the table to have their teams wear Nikes. "It was feeble," Vaccaro recalled of Nike's approach in 1979. "They didn't have money to do anything. It would have been impossible. I was the only guy at Nike then who understood basketball."

Other Nike basketball figures wouldn't arrive until the Jordan shoe explosion in 1985. Rob Strasser, who oversaw Nike's small basketball operation, had not considered a Johnson deal, Vaccaro said. "Rob Strasser never asked me, 'What do you think of Magic Johnson?' They would have asked me."

And Vaccaro was a friend of Johnson's at the time.

This is not to say that Johnson didn't come into immense power and influence in 1980, even without a mega shoe deal. Indeed, the conclusion to his first NBA regular season had brought a rise in his confidence that would grow into something like a storm surge through the playoffs, a moving, fluid wall of self-belief that the people around him began to sense well before it arrived in its full power.

What made the power of both Johnson and later Jordan unique was that they came into the possession of it as young Black males in the 1980s, a development that white American culture had worked fearfully for centuries to preclude. The example of both men, how they would gain a unique power and how they would come to wield it, would rebuke decades upon decades of racism, providing a profound context for their accomplishments.

The power that Johnson accumulated swiftly that spring of 1980 also stood in dramatic contrast to the power of his teammate Abdul-Jabbar as well as that of earlier dominant sports figures, including his childhood idol, Wilt Chamberlain, and Boston great Bill Russell, all of whom came to the fore in aggressively racist times. Both Abdul-Jabbar and Chamberlain, as well as an array of great Black figures in sport, had long desired the sort of deep adulation that Johnson and Jordan would inspire.

Chamberlain had worked in an era when many sports fans simply weren't going to give him the kind of allegiance that Johnson would earn. San Francisco Warriors owner Franklin Mieuli would declare as much when he deployed Chamberlain as a star in the mid-1960s only to discover that the center did not display a great drawing power at the gate.

Chamberlain simply wasn't easy to love, the owner would declare later in deciding to trade "Wilt the Stilt" to the Philadelphia 76ers. That same absence of love had haunted Kareem and numerous other early Black pioneers of sport along their path to greatness as competitors. There was love for Abdul-Jabbar as well as Chamberlain when he became a Laker in 1969, to be sure, but nothing like the adulation inspired by Johnson.

Still, it would grow increasingly obvious over the seasons that the pairing of Johnson and Abdul-Jabbar would enhance their shared power. Yes, Johnson would boost Abdul-Jabbar tremendously, but the center was correct in his later assertions. His own huge presence would do wonders for Johnson, perhaps an even greater gift to the younger player.

In identifying Jordan as the first Black man to ascend as the godhead of a global sports-merchandising empire, beginning in 1984, Vaccaro would declare that a young Jordan had the "it" factor, that almost undefinable combination of charisma and talent that wowed the mass audience regardless of race.

Johnson, too, had the obvious "it" factor, Vaccaro acknowledged in a 2019 interview. Yet, over time, the major questions would remain unanswered. Was Jordan's "it" factor more appealing to audiences than that offered by Johnson? Or was it merely that the culture in terms of race had changed that much in those five short years? Or did Jordan simply benefit from the heavy rotation worldwide of ads such as the famous Gatorade campaign "If I Could Be Like Mike"?

"I've seen them all," Jerry West would say in 1992. "I've seen every great player you want to talk about. No one else even came close to having charisma like Earvin Johnson."

Obviously, Jordan would be "packaged" for widespread public consumption far better than Johnson. Then again, he was arguably packaged far better than any athlete in history, a function of Jordan's immaculate timing, his great gifts, and the work of many in sustaining American pro basketball through the decades until it could flourish in the 1980s and '90s.

Whatever the answers to those questions, the difference between Johnson's entering the NBA in 1979 and Jordan five years later would be that Jordan would accumulate a wealth estimated at well over a billion dollars while Johnson would fall somewhere below half of that, an estimated six hundred million by 2022, according to various estimates.

The comparison itself tends to overlook perhaps the most important factor, that both men would become successful businessmen capable of amassing such fortunes because their parents and relatives had engaged in successful small businesses, setting in motion a standard for both Jordan and Johnson. The comparison would also overlook a key hidden personal trait the two shared. The record would show that both were superior listeners, thus armed with the keen wherewithal to learn from all that they encountered on their path to basketball greatness.

Thus, timing and background allowed both players to find the sort of widespread love and acceptance and thus power that others before them had not. Pat Williams, for example, mused in 2019 about the power that a supremely talented entertainer and classy personality such as Julius Erving might have found if he had broken onto the scene a decade or so later, or even in the twenty-first century, rather than in 1972 in the American Basketball Association.

Dr. J would have had immense exposure and power, Williams observed, adding that the decades had dramatically altered fan interest in the NBA, much of it driven by the rise of Magic, Bird, and Jordan in hand with growth in media and technology and marketing power.

Back in the 1970s, even with a star like Erving, "we had a lot of empty seats on a lot of nights," Williams recalled of his days as Sixers GM. "The big games sold, you know, Philly, Boston, L.A., New York. But we had many nights where we were pulling out all of the promotional stops trying to drive people into the Spectrum. If you woke up from a time machine and saw what's going on in Philly basketball now, you would be blinking hard. They're packed every night. They have a waiting list on season tickets. 'You got to be kidding,' that would be the reaction if you just woke up from a long sleep."

This curiosity of timing and culture and family would be quietly underscored over Johnson's rookie season with his emotional intelligence overflowing as he intoned that certain phrase, out loud or to himself, on the team bus or in practice while encouraging a teammate, or whenever the moment happened to strike him.

"Do it for love," Johnson would tell those around him over and over that season, saying far more than he, or frankly anyone, understood in 1980.

"He traveled early in his career with the Jackson 5 and some other groups because he loved music," Jim Chones recalled. "He had that rhythm and pace. He would have his music playing and it would be playing loud and nobody said anything. The crazy part of it is that he would sing, or call it singing. He knew I loved singing and one of my favorite artists at the time was Bobby Caldwell. And Bobby Caldwell had a song called, 'What you won't do, you'll do for love.' And I used to always sing it in the locker room and then, every once in a while, we would look at each other and sing, 'What you won't do' and we'd point at each other and everybody would start laughing."

As the playoffs had unfolded, "the love" rode the storm surge of confidence right along with Johnson, swelling in its flow as he grew in the public mind, launched there by his succession of feats, defeating Larry Bird, then replacing Kareem in Game 6 to defeat Julius Erving, each feat bringing more clarity.

Doug Krikorian, longtime sports media personality in Los Angeles, sat often with Buss during games in that era, marveling at how the owner surrounded himself with a collection of pretty young women and celebrities. Krikorian had covered the Lakers dating back into the 1960s and he saw that something changed with Johnson's overnight success in 1980. The Lakers weren't just about sports anymore, he observed in a 2004 interview. "It was compelling and it crossed over. Sports crossed really over then. Don't get me wrong. Danny Kaye and Cary Grant went to Dodger games. You had it. But not to the extent that Hollywood came out for the Magic Era. The explosion of basketball as entertainment happened during Showtime. He was so entertaining, the way the guy played. Every game he put on this great act. The way he orchestrated things was really fun to watch. He played the way John Wooden would concoct a game, but Magic did it on the fly."

Johnson's presence awakened something in the Lakers, Krikorian explained. "They're in the middle of the entertainment capital of the world, so it's not surprising they became the most glamorous team in basketball and that glamorous people from Hollywood would start coming to the games."

Years later, in January 1990 in a late-night conversation, Johnson would be asked to look back at that moment. He was already an extremely confident young man by that 1980 off-season, but the confidence would surge in the wake of that title.

"It enabled me to believe in myself," he admitted, "that all the things they were saying about me were not true. I already had the confidence. I already knew what I could do, basically, because I'm a confident person. I thrive under the pressure, under the gun. What happened, people didn't think I could shoot from outside. They didn't think that I could do this or that. And all that game just showed them I could do it under the pressure."

In truth, most doubters he had were not there in his failed big moments at Everett or even Michigan State in 1978. The biggest doubts he had quelled were his own.

And it was also important for his teammates to see him in that moment, he said, because it elevated their belief in him, "not just for myself but for the whole team."

It was a belief that would travel quickly well beyond the team to the point that it would eventually overcome the many sports-minded citizens of Southern California, indeed the growing Lakers fan base, leaving them first blinking in wonder, then filled with joy as his confidence washed over everything and everyone that fell in the path of their twenty-year-old wonder man.

Unfortunately, he said in 1990, he wasn't able to truly enjoy that moment very long because then, as always, the next season would be looming with a fan base now ravenous for another such moment.

"What happens is, they want it again," he said, looking back and laughing. "And they want more than that."

Certainly no one would prove more ravenous than Johnson himself. Beginning that first night after the championship he would return to his room to watch the entire game again, a measure that he would use again and again over the years to slake his hunger.

Asked that night in 1990 how many times he had watched Game 6 over the decade, he laughed a big laugh, not quite uncontrollably but almost, before admitting that the number of times he had watched it was "in the thousands. Easily."

It would always be there, whenever he needed a reminder. "It charges me up and gets me ready. You smile, you laugh and jump up. Yeah! You get those chills," he said, still cackling. "You'll have that, the beauty of it, forever in your life."

It would always remain that "beautiful thing," but also like a storm surge, this power and confidence would then keep rising that fall of 1980, feeding on itself, growing beyond imagination into a rawer power that would soon reveal, like all power, a decided harshness at its edges.

The Other Game

Offstage from this crossover, Johnson lived a somewhat monastic life as 1980 turned to 1981, except when he didn't. He had become somewhat estranged from Cookie Kelly during this period and was said to have begun seeing a relative of one of his Michigan State professors, who would enter med school in Los Angeles in that era. Then again, as George Andrews pointed out, Johnson, monastic or not, was seeing a lot of women. The two-bedroom apartment he rented from Jerry Buss in Culver City provided a quiet escape except, of course, for those times when it could quickly transform into a beehive.

Two young women who had graduated from Michigan State, friends of his who had professional jobs in the city, had been provided an apartment in the same Jerry Buss building and in return would help Johnson with the fundamentals of life, especially as his public began to overwhelm him. George Andrews, his lawyer, recalled that like Big Earv, Johnson liked to keep a wad of cash in his pocket and often had thousands of dollars in checks from the Lakers and his business activities just lying around the apartment. Going to the bank had become burdensome with so many fans now eager to engage him. So his friends from Michigan State would help him with deposits and other small chores.

"They weren't like housekeepers or anything like that, you know," Lon Rosen recalled of the two women. "They would help him out with some things when he was on the road. They were really helpful. I think once in a while they cooked him a home-cooked meal. But these are professional people. They had jobs and everything. They were just very close. He was also very close to Jerry Buss. Jerry introduced him to a lot of people, but Earvin was never one of those guys to have like tons of people back then that he would hang out with. He was really focused on playing. I mean really focused."

Dale Beard came to Los Angeles and stayed with his friend during this period and was amazed that Johnson seemed so unaffected by the fact that his smiling face now seemed to be on signage and advertising, billboards and buses, seemingly everywhere you turned.

"He lived in that little two-bedroom apartment not too far from the Forum," Lon Rosen recalled. "He'd play in the games. You go pick up food after the game and you go home. He wasn't out there a lot. He'd go to some parties obviously, but he was a homebody. He would sit there and watch TV and watch game tapes. That was early on. He didn't do a whole lot. He didn't venture out in the beginning around L.A. a whole lot."

That all would prove short-lived.

Led by Magic Johnson, owned by Jerry Buss, eventually managed by Jerry West, the Lakers soon assumed the image, the essence, of cool, first in Los Angeles and then across the country. In that process, Johnson became the orchestra director of cool, what you might call the Duke Ellington of a new jazz with his passing growing into a rage.

Without that spark, boosted by the public's anticipation of his rivalry with Larry Bird, it's hard to imagine performances from others at that exact time that would have elevated the game in such singular fashion. Even that couldn't prevent a disturbing number of NBA teams from losing money each year, but the presence of Johnson and Bird and even Jerry Buss allowed the sport to see a future.

Johnson seemed to power it all, this growth in interest in American pro basketball, first in Los Angeles and then for the greater audience. As a result, his power, sheathed in that L.A. cool, would prove unprecedented. He would be the first blinding flash of light, wielding a charisma that would help ignite, later, Jordan, and then the evolving age of player power that would flame brightly decades later, in the twenty-first century, laying a groundwork that afforded Kobe Bryant, LeBron James, Steph Curry, Kevin Durant, and several of their key contemporaries unprecedented power as players and public figures.

For much of the 1980s, Johnson and Jordan would share a similar power rooted in their astounding abilities. Where Jordan derived further power from his product endorsements, Johnson gained much of his standing with his unprecedented relationship with Buss, who absolutely loved him, a love sealed by that 1980 title, which delivered Buss his dream in making him an immediate success as a sports owner.

"Magic was his guy," George Andrews would say of Buss.

Nobody would have a relationship with her father like Magic Johnson, Jeanie Buss observed in 2020. "Not even Kobe."

"Dr. Buss was approachable," Jim Chones recalled. "He was just a great guy. He and Magic were exceptionally close. And we had never seen that before, where an owner would take to a player like that."

The owners in that era, Chones recalled, "were always standoffish, but what Magic had done was transcend from being an employee to being an asset. And his asset wasn't necessarily being on the floor. L.A. embraced Magic. He was part of them. He was a midwestern kid that they totally accepted because of his honest nature and Dr. Buss recognized that."

"Jerry sort of looked at Earvin as an extension of his family in a certain way," Lon Rosen recalled. "He really took him under his wing. You know, he talked to him about business. He took him to different places, but not all the time. It wasn't like they hung out every day, but he showed Earvin some of the places in Los Angeles. They had a really unique owner-player relationship and it stood really till the day Jerry passed away."

Buss had swiftly moved into hosting boxing at the Forum, which provided yet another opportunity for Johnson and the owner to get away together and talk, along with USC football games and other sporting events. Or it could be as simple as Johnson dropping by Buss's place to shoot pool and talk up their ambitions deep into the night.

"I suspect that off the court they were developing a friendship," Paul Westhead recalled of Buss and Johnson, "but I was not aware of that. He was an owner who on one hand loved the team and was obviously passionate about them, but Buss was not someone who would be hanging around practices and trying to get a feel of how the team was doing or how any player, Magic Johnson included, was doing."

In part, Buss's comfort in keeping that distance was built on the fact that he was already being briefed on the team by his most trusted source.

As Johnson's story unfolded in 1980, the revelation of this power, his connection with the new owner and the fans, would leave his teammates, who had all gotten their own small taste of such love during their time in Los Angeles, to fall into two basic categories: 1) those who could embrace Johnson's status, and 2) those who could not.

Even before his team won the title, Buss had swiftly made it known that he was ready to party.

"I remember the first interview I did with him," sportscaster Jim Hill explained in 2003. "He said, 'Oh, yeah, Jim, we're going to have a lot of fun.'"

He soon endeared himself to players, media, and just about anyone else hanging around the Lakers.

"When Jerry Buss bought the team, everything changed," the late Joe McDonnell, a longtime L.A. sports radio personality, recalled. "You had an atmosphere like you were part of a rock and roll show. I can't tell you how many times we'd sit in the press room after a game with Jerry Buss and Bob Steiner and other media people and we'd play Trivial Pursuit till seven or eight o'clock in the morning. We'd walk out and the sun would be shining. Everybody was drinking and having a good time. Buss was just a really good guy."

The package, as the owner saw it, was to build the team image on his own keen sense of celebrity—and sexuality. As a younger man, he had fallen in love with a routine at a Southern California nightclub, the Horn, where every night the lights would come up and singers would rise among the crowd to sing "It's showtime!"

He and Frank Mariani may have bought the Ocotillo Lodge together in 1968, but afterward they began promoting the resort's constant schedule of events in the *Desert Sun* newspaper as "Jerry Buss's Ocotillo Lodge," much like before it had been Gene Autry's Ocotillo Lodge. In 1971, Buss began running ads in *The Desert Sun*

"Jerry Buss Introduces 'Showtime,'" a music show every Monday at the lodge's lounge.

His purchase of the Lakers allowed Buss to take his Showtime fancy and his desire for celebrity to a whole new level. Nothing emphasized this more immediately than game days. Where Jack Kent Cooke had dressed the Forum staff in cheesy togas for games, Buss brought in the dancing, scantily clad "Laker Girls."

"Everything changed. Magic's first year is when we introduced the Laker Girls," recalled Roy Englebrecht. "We introduced the live music. That was the beginning of it."

"Buss built them that way," Joe McDonnell recalled. "He wanted the Laker Girls and the uniforms and Showtime and having a guy like Magic with a great infectious personality as the main guy. Buss wanted things to be that way. That's where the Laker Girls came from. Was it a novel idea to have cheerleaders? No. But to dress them like that and make them an important part? A very novel idea. Jerry Buss, if you look, never did any marketing. His marketing was all on the floor. He used sex to sell the Lakers."

Indeed, Buss would dress the entire franchise in a sexy new vibe. The forty-six-year-old owner took great delight in dating those attractive young women, usually no older than twenty-two, usually dating them only once or twice each, but he enjoyed keeping their pictures in albums, which in those early days he proudly showed to visitors and friends, including media representatives.

Scott Ostler, then a reporter for the *L.A. Times,* would be offered a look at the owner's photo albums, and later recalled Buss as a nice guy but clearly a case of "arrested development."

"Buss was very open about his women," journalist Steve Springer recalled in 2019. "And so right from the beginning he was portrayed as the playboy who owned the team and he never hid it ever, you know. One of the great parts of covering the team was the press lounge. I mean, we would go up there after a game and everybody would be there. We'd be there till three or four in the morning."

And Buss would be there over in the corner with two or three what were commonly referred to at the time as "bimbos," Springer noted.

"He liked the girls," recalled Ron Carter, the former Laker who went to work for Buss. "The girls were always around. They were always very young. That took some doing."

Buss, on occasion, towed along a small entourage, Carter said. "We went everywhere. We did everything. The girls, the jets, the fun. It was nothing for Jerry to say, 'Hey, I feel hot. Let's go to Vegas.' And get his pilot to crank up his jet and shoot over to Vegas. That kind of stuff. A crazy, crazy life. It was Showtime. Anywhere that we went, we were the party."

Buss could also be seen simply jumping a commercial flight to Vegas, leaving the impression he didn't always have to go large to have a good time. Meanwhile, it didn't take Johnson long after arriving in Los Angeles in 1979 to learn that he had come to the land of the limitless casting couch, according to circumstances laid out in 1993's *The Lakers*. Hollywood offered an abundant supply of young women, many of whom were eager to get to know a basketball star or a team owner. It wasn't a phenomenon particular to Johnson or Buss, far from it.

The movie industry and its stars, of course, had been wallowing in sexual excess and scandal for decades. Film legend Mae West in the early days of Hollywood built her image on a purported immense sexual appetite that drove her to bed a wide array of male stars, including Cary Grant and George Raft. Clara Bow, another sexually liberated starlet, was rumored to have exceeded even West's dalliances by taking on the entire University of Southern California football team. Many Hollywood historians scoffed at that claim. Regardless, the tendency toward frivolity was well established long before Jerry Buss or Magic Johnson came to the fore.

California itself had led the charge into the American sexual revolution. As fate would have it, the Lakers moved from Minneapolis to Los Angeles in 1960, just as that revolution was first unfolding.

In all fairness, it should be pointed out that hypersexuality evidenced itself in other sports and pastimes, in other cities. L.A., though, clearly offered its own special environment.

"I could tell you Dodger stories for a year and tomorrow about stuff going on down in little rooms at the clubhouse before the games. It's prevalent in all sports," Joe McDonnell explained in 2004. "In baseball, it can happen during a game. In basketball, it always happens after a game."

As the 1970s wore on, Lakers GM Pete Newell retained an off-duty LAPD vice detective to keep track of the drug usage and questionable behavior of the team's players, a ploy first initiated by Lakers GM Lou Mohs in the early 1960s. "We were reluctant to get involved," Newell recalled in a 1992 interview, "although we were all appalled by the women who just flaunted themselves. The players just kind of passed these gals around. There was no deterrence about AIDS and sex in those days. The players just didn't have as much to lose."

With Jerry Buss, sex would become the Lakers' image, their tradition, part of why fans loved them and him, a continuing theme evidenced in part by daughter Jeanie Buss posing nude for *Playboy* in the team offices in 1995 (the only issue of the magazine that her father said he would never read).

Ron Carter recalled coming to the team in 1978, well before either Buss or Johnson, and being stunned by the veteran players' attitudes and sexual habits. "All the old-school guys—these guys were like sex addicts," Carter recalled in 2004. "They were crazy with it. It was there and it was available. Actually, it was a part of the mentality that the veteran players would teach you how to manage the women."

Understandably, the circumstances made players from other teams eager to visit L.A. Some observers said it was the Lakers' true home-court advantage, with the distraction of beautiful women and Hollywood stars in the crowd.

"You're going out to L.A. and coaches worried about that," former NBA player Kelly Tripucka recalled in 2004. "You're so hyped up to be into it and to play against Showtime, and you're sitting over there looking at whoever may be walking by, and your head's doing a little swivel. You're not concentrating. You're not into the game. You really had to have blinders on like those horses at the track across the street. As far as coaches, they really sweat it, playing the Lakers in that particular environment. If you didn't have your team's entire concentration for forty-eight minutes, you could get embarrassed out there."

Just about every night, the primary assumption was a loss for the visitors, Herb Williams said of the intimidating place and circumstances. "You never really had to look at the score. You knew that people were getting blown out, because everybody was looking in the stands or at the floor. They had an incredible team. They could run, they could post. You name it, they could do it. And they had probably the best point guard ever to play the game running the show."

This was the atmosphere Buss wanted to build on, and Johnson stepped right in as the charismatic figure he needed to lead it. Later, when the depth of Johnson's problems became public, many of his old friends from Lansing would assume he had come under the unfortunate influence of Jerry Buss. And there is no doubt that the owner influenced Johnson greatly. Yet there were other influences, as teammate Butch Carter, who arrived as a rookie in the fall of 1980, witnessed as Johnson headed into his second season.

At the time, Johnson wasn't even considered the busiest Laker. That designation went to Norm Nixon, for whom Johnson perhaps served as an understudy. Butch Carter recalled in the fall of 1980 Johnson marveling at the popularity of Nixon. Kareem may have been the captain, but "Mr. Big" was its leader, Ron Carter recalled. One day Johnson walked through a hotel lobby and three women had given him their phone numbers—to take up to Nixon's room.

"At the time, Norm Nixon was the king of L.A.," Butch Carter recalled with a laugh in 1992. "When we'd go out somewhere, the women would ask, 'Where's Norm? Where's Norm?'"

With the 1980 championship, however, Johnson had begun to alter that dynamic. Even before the big victory, Johnson's size and energy and unique game had slowly begun nudging Mr. Big out of his leadership role.

More to the point, as Ron Carter would observe, Johnson had arrived in Los Angeles with a decided agenda. Indeed, he first discovered the connection between women and his magnetic on-court play back in Lansing in high school when he and Reggie Chastine took to eyeing furtively the hot ladies in the crowd, then dispatching a team manager to deliver a message to them about getting together after the game. Moving to his dorm and then apartment in East Lansing only multiplied the opportunity.

Los Angeles, particularly Hollywood, presented a different level, a different abundance. "I mean, you had women with no panties. Women with women," Johnson told writer Charles Pierce in 1993.

In 1980, America was entering its third decade of sexual revolution and Johnson was hardly alone in his youthful experimentation, except in that he was in that unusual position reserved for high-profile figures across the spectrum of popular culture, the stars of music and film and sports, all especially idolized in an erogenous zone such as Los Angeles.

"I wanted to be a part of that," Johnson told Charles Pierce. "There was Earvin, but it was Magic who wanted to be a part of that Hollywood life. Magic is the side where you go to Hollywood and live that Hollywood life and so forth."

That Hollywood life, so to speak, had generated more than its share of "sex addiction" cases over the years, the only problem being that mental health officials couldn't seem to agree among themselves if sex addiction, also known as "compulsive sexual behavior," or satyriasis, could be classified as a true addiction.

The World Health Organization would only go so far as to classify it as an impulse disorder.

Part of the trouble in defining it was the complexity of human sexual behavior. For example, some humans simply have a greater libido than others.

One study suggested that "compulsive sexual disorder" affected between 3 and 6 percent of the American population.

True addiction or not, the behavior was said to often include certain negative factors, such as a recklessness in regard to sexually transmitted disease, as well as relationship issues. Some who suffered from the condition have described hellish experiences similar to those endured by drug or alcohol or gambling addicts.

Some have speculated that the process of Johnson's "addiction" would be influenced by his earliest experiences as a Laker in Los Angeles and his most unusual relationship with Buss. The owner and his young star fast became companions hanging out in Los Angeles, often in the roped-off VIP sections of the various clubs where they went to talk about life. That also happened to be the setting where they engaged in a mutual interest, the pursuit of a seemingly endless supply of attractive young women seeking some sort of presence in Hollywood.

"My dad loved to dance. My dad was so young at heart," Jeanie Buss recalled, adding that her father often "begged" her to head out on the town with them, but that club life was not something that interested her at the time. Which left her father and Johnson to prowl together. "And so they went all over town together," she recalled. "Whatever, whether it was going to dinner or to a dance place, whatever it was. My dad would include him, invite him to go along with him, although my dad was attending a lot of the hockey games at that time."

Buss hadn't purchased just the Lakers. He also now owned the Kings, which required his attendance. Their clubbing often came later, after Buss was done with hockey games or other commitments.

"They both liked to go to the clubs," Johnson's lawyer, George Andrews, explained. "They enjoyed each other's company. Magic had a great dad so it wasn't a father figure but kind of like an uncle when they would talk about stuff."

"It was authentic and real," Jeanie Buss would say in 2019 of the relationship she witnessed between her father and Johnson. "That's who my dad was. That wasn't to make money or exploit or anything. It was, he truly loved him and their bond was very much student-teacher, father-son, best friends, whatever you want to call it, but they adored each other."

As for any undue influence the owner might have wielded on his young star, Lon Rosen cautioned against reading too much into it. "He showed him things, introduced him," Rosen said in a 2019 interview. "But other people did, too, not just Jerry Buss. It's funny. I've heard this for so many years. Oh, Jerry Buss, you know, brought him down to the Playboy Mansion. Yeah. He did. He brought him here to this club or that club. Other people brought him to the clubs, too. And other people brought him to clubs when he was in college, so, no, it wasn't completely new to him. The truth was, when Earvin was in college he went to clubs, right? He was a DJ."

Johnson had always had his own mind about things, Rosen pointed out. "Jerry Buss drank. He didn't drink in excess. Earvin doesn't drink. . . . No one taught Earvin how to think. Earvin is a self-made thinker. You can show him things and he might say I like it or not like it."

There was much to like, and not just female companionship.

Their conversations would last the long life of their relationship. And they weren't about just their sexual conquests or proposed sexual conquests, far from it. Buss was a businessman eager to share his knowledge, as demonstrated by his sending of former Laker Ron Carter to Pepperdine for graduate studies.

To go along with his two strong parents, Johnson already had one extremely influential mentor in Charles Tucker, and now the second such figure had entered his life in Buss. It was no coincidence that the team owner and Tucker shared such a high regard for each other. They both shared a deep love for Magic Johnson.

And like all great mentorships, the learning did not flow one way. As Tucker had learned from Johnson and his family, Buss charged in with Johnson, eager to gain knowledge of this wonderful new toy the owner had acquired, the Lakers.

Buss and Johnson were new kids on the block together, having rocked pro basketball in a single season, jumping the broom and heading all the way to a title. Looking back in 2019, Jeanie Buss offered that the instant success her father shared with Johnson made them both targets of sorts.

Thus, Buss may have won a championship immediately, but he was very aware that he was new to basketball, and while he obviously had some great ideas about how to sell the game, he was a neophyte. And he was seeking to mine Johnson's understanding of the team and its players. This relationship between the two men would be a running foundation of the Lakers franchise throughout Johnson's playing career, and far beyond. In the twenty-first century, when Phil Jackson and top assistant Tex Winter were coaching

Shaquille O'Neal and Kobe Bryant, Winter would explain that the staff was quite aware that Johnson "was in Jerry Buss's ear," advising the owner on team issues.

"He became such good friends with Earvin early on," journalist Kelly Carter offered. "So the two of them could do a lot of things together, which helped him report on the team, gave him some insight access to what was going on."

Part of what drove the Buss-Johnson relationship was how soon it became virtually unbreakable, Jeanie Buss explained. "My dad could look at Magic and say, 'He would do anything for me. Like I know he has my back.' He felt that their relationship was reciprocal. And he trusted Earvin, you know, to give him information about how he's feeling about the team and about, you know, just the direction that the team was going. He felt like Earvin wanted to win just as bad as my dad wanted to win. My dad trusted Earvin and the feedback that he got from him because it came from a place where there was no double-talk. It was no manipulation. It was just they both wanted the Lakers to be great."

As far as the owner fancying himself a great dancer, that, too, fed the early relationship. In the 1950s, when Buss was in school, he loved the cha-cha, the polka. "But the rage was the jitterbug," Buss would say in a 1992 interview. "I loved it and did it all the time."

When the late 1970s came along, he got caught up in the *Saturday Night Fever* craze. "I took disco lessons and tried to imitate John Travolta," he said with a laugh.

That effort had prepared him to hang out with Johnson in the clubs, once his star became old enough to gain admittance. Johnson quickly came to love the club scene every bit as much as the owner.

"He would dance, I would dance," Buss explained.

In 1980, Johnson's teammates were quite aware—and somewhat alarmed—that Johnson had quickly developed a relationship with the owner that they and other players simply could not have. For example, Johnson, Norm Nixon, and Michael Cooper had begun hanging out together on the team's road trips, but in Los Angeles, much of Johnson's hang time was reserved for the owner.

"Jerry and Earvin, they had their own relationship," Steve Springer recalled in 2019. "When Earvin went out with Buss that was just the two of them. That didn't include Norm and Coop."

"I think the thing with Earvin and Dr. Buss, the thing that brought them together really was their lifestyle and their attraction to having lots of women around them," explained Kelly Carter, who went to the clubs herself and observed the two together there, who were obviously interested in the numbers of women. "It wasn't enough to have one. They had to have many. So they were always surrounded by them and I think that's what brought them together. They had a very special relationship because of that."

By all reports, there didn't seem to be a lot of coercion involved, although Buss apparently employed a younger male protégé to scout and sort through potential "dating" targets.

As for Johnson, there was no need for a scout.

"He's in L.A.," recalled lawyer George Andrews, who witnessed Johnson's off-court life in that era. "He's famous, rich, good-looking, a virile young guy, and there's millions of women throwing themselves at him."

It was astounding how attractive many of the young women were, but word soon spread among the NBA player population jokingly that Johnson was no discriminator. He seemed on a mission to sleep with the array of women who approached him.

"One was more beautiful than the next," Andrews recalled. "As for his shot selection, it was just superb. Let's just put it that way."

Still, the lawyer acknowledged that Johnson would "swing at anything, you know, and that's just how it is. I think that was his philosophy. I think that was something, and I'm not trying to make any value judgments, right? He was single so in my own mind, it was all right. It wasn't my lifestyle. I think we had girls, they would have offered to have sex with me as a plan to get to Magic. I said, 'Well, this really doesn't work that way. I am married but thank you.' Anyhow, I mean, holy crap, you know, it was tough."

And perhaps even tougher on the road, where women could seemingly drop in from anywhere, including finding their way into

Johnson's hotel room even before he checked in, Andrews recalled, explaining that he would meet Johnson on the road at various locations to discuss business and "having naked women sitting in bed for him because they paid the bellman to let them in."

On one such occasion, Andrews asked Johnson if he should come back later only to have him reply, no, the woman could wait.

Sometimes the business meetings might happen in Johnson's room after a game, Andrews said. "The girls would be knocking on the door, calling him all night long. He took the phone off the hook so we could finish our business. He said, 'Well, if they really want me, they'll come back.'"

As Ron Carter, who worked for Buss, would explain, the owner began using the Lakers and the Forum as a honeypot to attract well-heeled investors for his real estate deals, inviting them to dinner before the game at the Forum Club and having them sit with him in his reserved area during games, which raises the question, was Johnson also one of his honeypots in the club scene to attract young women?

"It was an endless list of young women," Ron Carter said in 2022. "I couldn't even begin to . . . You know, this is way before MeToo. When you're the owner of the Lakers, or you're a Laker and you are coming out of this era, women are falling out the sky, you know. You don't have to recruit. You select."

Ron Carter confirmed reports that Buss had an associate who sometimes screened the young women, saying, "That was pretty much his job is to sift through the weeds and buying whatever the flavor of the day is. I don't know how that worked. I didn't get involved in that part of it."

"A lot of people didn't know him," recalled journalist Kelly Carter. "You know he was Dr. Jerry Buss. You know he was a smart guy. People would see him and see all these young pretty girls around him and probably kind of dismiss him for that. But the man didn't get to where he got in life by having young pretty girls around him. He was a smart businessman, but he was quiet. I never remember Jerry, you know, him saying too much."

Kelly Carter later wrote a story about Buss and Johnson and the club scene, she recalled. "I knew one of the women he had slept with. She talked about that time and she talked about being a groupie and her self-esteem and all that."

Later, after it had all crashed down for Johnson, he would offer estimates that he spent his career sleeping with three to five hundred women a year, an astounding number that, much like Wilt Chamberlain's estimate that he slept with thousands of women over his career, begged the question, how did Johnson manage it, what with all the time he spent playing and practicing basketball, what with public appearances and other commitments? Just scheduling and managing such a throng would seem to require the organizational efforts of a small business, except that, as Andrews described, the women seemingly appeared out of nowhere to come at him in droves.

"I think when you talk about a lot of women, people think that's all you're doing," Johnson would tell Charles Pierce in the wake of the outrage over his revelations of three to five hundred women a year. "I wasn't, like, numbers, like a Wilt Chamberlain and thousands of women or whatever. It wasn't even close to that. People don't realize that I was friends with these women, not that I just went out and picked one up and that was it. See, I talked to them because I wanted to know what's up here and, see, people are not getting that, so I guess they think it's one night here and one night there and that was it, and it wasn't like that at all."

Later, Johnson would offer that he "accommodated" all the numbers of women who sought his company, a comment that understandably angered female activists, especially when taken alongside other facts.

Through all the years of sexual activity, he declined to wear condoms or provide any sort of protection, despite what one close associate described as the constant battle Johnson waged against every sort of venereal disease. His strategy in this regard, according to the associate, was to procure multiple prescriptions to antibiotics through multiple doctors.

"Magic had a real problem with syphilis and gonorrhea," the associate alleged. "He was doing massive penicillin from multiple doctors."

Lon Rosen denied that Johnson ever engaged in the practice of multiple prescriptions from multiple doctors, pointing out that Johnson disliked going to doctors. Frankly, the idea of massive doses of antibiotics certainly wasn't anything sustainable and likely lasted only a short time if it happened at all. If Johnson attempted that at some point, it wasn't something that could become routine practice.

In all fairness, it was an age that was still somewhat casual about venereal disease, yet his persistence in such behavior as the 1980s wore on would later strain credulity. After all, statistics would show that during Johnson's first twelve years playing for the Lakers, 150,000 people in America would die of AIDS and the topic would be the routine subject of headlines.

Another consideration is that Johnson, who had been such an important community figure in Lansing as a teen, came to Los Angeles just a month before turning twenty. He admitted later that he had engaged in a volume of sexual activity from his earliest days as a Laker.

Some saw it as naïveté that he had his number right in the phone book. Others assumed the opposite.

It soon became a frequent saying that Los Angeles had transformed into Magic's own city. More accurately, it would later be identified as his harem, as writers such as Charles Pierce and E. Jean Carroll would point out.

Magic, of course, would come to be seen as his public persona, the fellow who turned in wondrous performances nightly on the floor at the Great Western Forum. Earvin, on the other hand, was his private sanctuary, the person who had been that sweet, chubby adolescent son of deeply religious Christine Johnson back in Michigan.

Earvin was the good guy.

Magic, in time, would be seen as the satyr, as Johnson himself had implied and Charles Pierce would write.

At the time, however, it all passed for the fun of a good red-blooded American male. *Sports Illustrated* had described Jerry Buss as a "serial" dater of young women, and that had hardly raised an eyebrow. The team owner had quickly come to be admired around Los Angeles. For Buss and Johnson, every little thing in those early days seemed part of one sensational joyride. They smiled together.

Trade Kareem?

Whether it was time to play or time to party, Johnson wanted to lead. Whether it was an NBA tipoff or a morning pickup game at UCLA, his passion set the agenda, Kiki Vandeweghe explained. "Whether the lights were on or they weren't, he just loved to play basketball."

It was this immense passion that he shared with Jordan, as time would reveal, a singular passion that would compel the global audience to embrace them and fuel the rise of the game itself, a passion that would prove an impossible touchstone for so many who came after them with one question: Did they display the sort of unquenchable competitive desire that could elevate the game to a place it had never been before?

Butch Carter began to gain an inkling of that in late September 1980 at Lakers training camp. Having come from crazy man Bobby Knight's Indiana program, Carter understandably figured he was fully versed in the definition of an exceptional athlete.

"We had to run a mile after our first practice in Palm Springs," Carter would recall later. "I'm a rookie trying to make the team. I mean, I'm hauling ass; I'm trying to be first, trying to impress the coaches. And I couldn't catch Magic Johnson. This was a guy who had just earned the MVP of the championship series, and he's like 40 yards ahead of everybody else, and I'm asking myself, 'How do you ever make it up?' That's what I'll always remember about him. Not only was he the most talented, he was the hardest-working."

As the 1980–81 season was set to open, CBS brought together Johnson, Abdul-Jabbar, and Jamaal Wilkes for a conversation with Bill Russell, who had anchored the Boston teams that won 11 titles in 13 seasons. Russell had even served as player/head coach for the final two championship seasons in 1968 and '69.

It could be argued that no one in America in 1980 had a better understanding of the key ingredients for championship play. Russell's thoughts on that issue were succinct.

"The key to a great team is chemistry," he told the three Lakers.

Obviously, the Hall of Fame Celtics center had watched the first season of Showtime with great interest. He saw the potential for a dominant team much like his Celtics, but he wanted to test their mind-set because he also saw some conflict on the horizon.

Wilkes had played a prominent role on Golden State's '75 title team and he had seen the physical and mental challenge of trying to repeat that had sunk that Warriors team in '76.

"Kareem is the man on our team, and we have exceptional talent around him," Wilkes said.

Russell then turned to Johnson and asked how he saw his task.

"Just do my role," Johnson replied. "Get in there and rebound, score a little bit, smack 'em on the rear or on the hands, get 'em fired up. That was my role."

Russell asked him what he had learned in playing a hundred games with Abdul-Jabbar.

"Give him the ball," Johnson shot back quickly, grinning broadly.

Russell exploded with his own trademark cackling laugh. He then pointed out that both Abdul-Jabbar and Wilkes were quiet men and "quiet men never complain."

"Believe me," Johnson said, "when they want the ball, nobody is quiet. Jamaal is the type of player to keep his stats up because he's a runner."

"When you run," Wilkes interjected, "and you get the ball and you get it where you want it, where you can do something with it, then there's a tendency to want to run more. With Earvin and Norman, I know if I get out there, there's a good chance I will get the ball."

The answer took Russell to the point of his conversation—probing Abdul-Jabbar's feelings about watching his teammates run off to the other end of the floor without him. Kareem, in turn, was ready with an answer, recalling that Jack Donohue, his high school coach at Power Memorial, had taken him to Madison Square Garden as a teen to watch Russell and Boston's great running team. The young Alcindor asked his coach why Russell didn't run down to the offensive end of the floor with his teammates.

"Don't worry," Donohue replied. "He will when it's necessary."

"I learned that from watching you play," Abdul-Jabbar told Russell. "You can't get in on every break."

His job was to get the defensive rebound and get the ball out for the fast break, Abdul-Jabbar offered, adding that his teammates already had a 20-foot head start getting to the other end.

"He really doesn't have to get down the floor because we're gonna get a shot," Johnson said. "Somebody's gonna get a shot."

The Lakers would have a very good chance of repeating, Wilkes said. "We have exceptional talent and a good coach. And we have the organization behind us."

Russell then looked at Johnson and said, "You expect to win all the time."

"Yeah, I do," Johnson said. "I think we have the team to do it."

It sounded so promising sitting there in October. Russell then said the one thing he knew for sure about the coming campaign: "For the whole season, you'll be introduced as the world champions."

Indeed, once the regular season began, rookie Butch Carter was in for more wide-eyed wonder as the Lakers took to the road, a virtual traveling championship party.

"Every city we went to, there was a party for us, the defending world champs," Carter recalled. "They would provide transportation, everything. That was the tone in every city. What amazed me was our true stamina. People don't understand the godly gift some of these people have. They could stay out all night and be no slower the next day out on the floor."

As Butch Carter saw in training camp, Johnson's championship confidence and bolstered determination set the way for him to conquer the world in the fall of 1980, evidenced by his claiming NBA Player of the Month to open his second season with the Lakers zooming to a 9–2 record.

The operative phrase for Johnson in that moment was "coast-to-coast," his unfettered game of taking the ball off the defensive boards and rolling end-to-end through the traffic to finish with a slam, making things look almost like he was back in Lansing running through the retreat of Sexton or whatever beleaguered high school opposition happened into his path. He ran up 20 points in a half against the Clippers and 18 in another half versus Dallas, to go along with eight steals that contest.

"The next year when Earvin came back, the confidence he had," lawyer George Andrews marveled. "He was going like coast-to-coast and dunking. Earvin would take the ball and go."

As good as things might have looked on the surface, behind the scenes they were already pushing the gauges, Westhead would reveal much later. After asserting that he was not going to bring back McKinney, Buss had reluctantly agreed to give the fill-in coach a three-year contract only after Johnson had declared, "If you don't keep him, I'll go where's he's coaching."

It was the first flexing of his new power, and he liked it.

Obviously, Westhead appreciated the support, but he soon came to believe that Johnson was out of control with his ego, his stubbornness, and his desire to control the team's tempo. Westhead thought about confronting him, but he was playing so hard and so well that the coach decided to let things roll.

The result was a strange Laker vehicle, one foot pushing down on the accelerator, the other hitting the brakes, giving the team a conflicted beauty that was both enthralling and annoying all at the same time.

Thus, the tempo of play posed a quietly simmering conflict for those Lakers, between Abdul-Jabbar, then the best half-court weapon in the history of the sport, and just about all the rest of a lineup that sorely loved to get out and run the fast break, led by young Earv.

"We have three or four guys on our team who can get down the floor real quick," Johnson had told Bill Russell.

The nucleus of the speed mind-set, according to Steve Springer, was Johnson, Norm Nixon, and Michael Cooper, who had taken to hanging out together on road trips. Springer recalled the trio even had matchbook covers printed up that signaled their desire to be free of rolling their eyes and waiting on Kareem to get up the court.

"Back then the players smoked and they all had cigarette lighters or matchbooks or whatever," Springer recalled in 2019. "So, there was this group that was Earvin and Norm and Coop, to some extent Jamaal Wilkes. They wanted to run the greatest fast break of all time. And then there was Kareem."

No Lakers coach during that era was going to get out of the business of Abdul-Jabbar and his great skyhook, his deadly beautiful mode of launching his hook shots from a distance and watching them swish, or his artlessly efficient dunks, raining down and ker-chinging over the course of every game.

"They were not going to ignore the guy who has the unstoppable shot," Springer said of the no-brainer.

Logically, coaches would often want to slow the team down and go for Kareem's high-percentage shot, which annoyed the racehorse faction, Springer explained. "I don't know who started it, but these matchbooks were printed up that said the words on the front, 'Trade Kareem.' All these guys carried these matchbooks, and we'd be in an airport or a hotel or somewhere and they'd pull it out of their pocket, look at me, show me the matchbook, smile, and put it back in their pocket. I don't know if Kareem found out, but that was the Trade Kareem matchbooks. All the young gunners, they all carried the matchbooks."

It was not the sort of toxic topic that many beat writers would have addressed publicly in that era.

Asked if Johnson carried the matchbooks, Springer replied, "They all had them so I believe he did. I saw it often particularly with Nixon and Cooper, but yeah, I think they all did. The guys were all close and all wanted to run and all hated to slow down the offense. They all carried it, yeah."

They would pull these out whenever they got a chance to smoke in airports or lounges. Players toyed with smoking in that era, which was a guilty pleasure left over from a long line of old-school pro players. They would furtively flash the matchbooks and smile. Kareem may have been the team captain, but he was aloof, largely unfriendly, and the target of such feelings for several seasons, which would translate into conflict for Jerry Buss when it came to a new contract for the center.

First, it seemed logical that the results of Game 6 in the championship series without Kareem had fed into such notions.

While there was obvious sentiment against Kareem on the team, longtime Johnson friend and representative Lon Rosen pointed out in 2019 what the record reflects, that Johnson spent the bulk of his career deferring to the Hall of Fame center, the game's all-time leading scorer, to achieve great success for the Lakers.

"Him and Kareem had sort of this relationship on the court," Lon Rosen recalled in 2020. "It was pretty interesting, but more importantly they both realized that they both benefited from each other. Kareem was much older. He came obviously from a different place than Earvin came. But Kareem could have sabotaged Earvin Johnson and in a major way when he joined the Lakers. Let's face it. Kareem was a Hall of Fame player. He's got this kid that's coming in and I watched it firsthand. Kareem's the one. It could have gone the wrong way, ego-wise when it comes to basketball, it could've been a whole different story."

Particularly considering Abdul-Jabbar was encountering in Johnson an unprecedented personality, so young, so driven for control of events, yet so given to joy.

"At age twenty years old," Rosen said, "Earvin Johnson came in and became a leader like almost immediately, which is sort of pretty amazing for a young kid."

That accommodation had begun from Johnson's very first minutes on the team.

"Earvin was Kareem's rookie," Rosen pointed out, talking about the NBA tradition of the systematic hazing of rookies by veterans. "His first year he would be screaming, 'Okay, you got to go get me this at the airport.' Or, 'Go get me a hot dog.' He was his rook. Earvin did it. He didn't care if he was Magic Johnson, he did it."

Johnson did these menial tasks, as rookies were called to do, despite the difficulty of Kareem's personality, so prone to dark moods, so lacking in warmth, so inclined to stare right through teammates and others around him. It wasn't always pretty and it apparently helped translate into little matchbook jokes about having the team captain, the basketball icon, traded.

Then as later, it was almost unfathomable.

Veteran Bob McAdoo would come to the Lakers in late December 1981. Years later, he would confirm encountering that exact sentiment, those feelings against Kareem in 1982. "When I got there I was a sounding board for a lot of players," McAdoo said in a 2004 interview. "Guys would come to me with their frustration over how they were playing. Everything was slow, walk it up the court, throw it in to Kareem. They didn't want to play like that. They wanted to get up and down."

Obviously, the matchbook covers represented no serious rebellion, rather a juvenile attempt at humor, further supported by the fact that Abdul-Jabbar was never traded, although Jerry Buss would seem to have had mixed feelings when it came time to give the center a new contract. Considering Johnson's relationship with Buss and the power he was gaining, if Johnson had wanted Kareem gone that could well have happened.

A far more important factor was Johnson's focus on winning, and as he entered his second season the Lakers were doing plenty of that. By mid-November, they were 15–5, and Johnson was leading the league in assists, an average of 8.6 a game, that while playing alongside another point guard in Nixon. Johnson also was leading in steals, his long arms snaring a whopping 3.4 per game. He was averaging 21.4 points (while shooting 53 percent from the floor) and 8.2 rebounds.

"He does more things well that can help a team than anybody I can think of," Bill Sharman told *The New York Times.*

Before becoming the Lakers' general manager, Sharman had been a starter on four Boston Celtics world championship teams led by Russell and Bob Cousy. Sharman had also coached the Lakers to their 1972 championship. He wasn't speaking lightly.

Johnson was giving opponents all sorts of new headaches to contemplate.

Then, abruptly, all the momentum halted in smoking, steaming confusion.

Officially, the left knee injury came on November 18, a Tuesday night, in the Forum against Kansas City, but Johnson had tweaked it two days earlier in Dallas and even earlier there was supposedly a wrestling match in Atlanta, which occurred when huge Tom Burleson fell on Johnson's knee. The full injury finally came on a defensive cut, and he collapsed immediately. "I went to pick up my man," Johnson said of his injury, "and the knee said, 'I'm not going with you.'"

Team physician Dr. Robert Kerlan confirmed the next day that the cartilage was torn and would need immediate surgery, that Johnson would likely be out better than two months.

"I was there," Charles Tucker recalled in 2019. "I went to the hospital with him, and I sat there all night until he had the operation the next morning. And I stayed out there for two weeks, then went back and forth for a month."

Westhead went to see Johnson before the surgery, the coach would recall. "I pushed the door open and peeked in and there was Magic propped up in the bed with a Dodger cap on backward, a piece of apple pie shoved up under his face, watching a football game, yelling at his father and a bunch of friends playing cards to keep the noise down."

The despair and frustration would come later, whenever he paused to think about what might have been for his second campaign.

"This season was easier," he said in the days afterward. "I knew the league. I knew the ropes. This season could have been my best ever, of any season ever."

"He got hurt, hurt his knee," George Andrews recalled, "and after that his ability to jump was hindered. He never really went that way again. He really had hops at one point."

He would miss 45 games, during which the mojo and momentum he had gained evaporated. "It made me see that, just as fast as you can rise to the top, you can come tumbling down," Johnson would explain afterward. "First they take your ball away. That's bad. And then, not being around the guys, that really hurts. I mean, you're alone now, you see. That's my life, being around the fellas, talking jive, singing on the bus, that's the whole thing. All of a sudden that's all taken away. I don't think missing the ball was that important. Missing the fellas was badder than missing the ball."

Things quickly went down, Tucker recalled. "He said it was about the worst time of his life. He wasn't angry, just disappointed and hurt."

Deal

The timing and situation proved difficult for other reasons, especially since Tucker and George Andrews were in the midst of negotiating a mammoth new contract for their client when he was injured.

The idea for the deal had actually been floated by Buss when he was hanging out with Johnson in the wake of the championship, Andrews recalled. "Buss was offering a one-year extension for a million dollars, which would have brought Magic's average to be more than Bird's."

"You're better than Bird," Buss had told Johnson.

"I'm going to make them pay you more," the lawyer told Johnson.

As Tucker would recall, maybe negotiating wasn't quite the word to use in describing the discussions, because Buss had seemed extremely eager to lock down his new angel in a contract. The owner had not forgotten that first night upon their meeting when Johnson told Jeanie that he was only going to play in L.A. a couple of years before slipping off to Detroit or Chicago.

The championship, however, had swiftly changed that. "When they won, that turned it all around," Andrews recalled in 2019.

No longer was he talking about going anywhere. So, Johnson and Big Earv and Tucker had kicked around the new deal with Andrews, who recalled asking, "Earvin, as long as you want to stay, how much you want?"

"He goes, 'Well, how about a million a year for eight years?'" Andrews remembered. "And his dad goes, 'I want nine million for eight years. I'll be a pig.' I said, 'No it's not even close. The number's twenty-five. Because it's two and a half million for ten years. That's what we now should be getting.'"

These, of course, were huge numbers for that era. Buss, meanwhile, was eyeing the high interest rates at the time, a prime rate well above umpteen percent, and licking his chops realizing he could salt some four or five million away and pay Johnson just off the interest for a long time.

"That was part of it," Andrews recalled. "But the other thing was, we couldn't get more than a million a year because Kareem was making a million and that would upset the whole apple cart."

Abdul-Jabbar was already upset just seeing the endorsement deals Johnson was stacking up in the wake of his Finals performance and MVP award that the center saw as his by rights.

The new numbers would have made Kareem's head explode, if he had known them. The main gist of the agreement was an unheard of $25 million over twenty-five years. Both Tucker and Andrews recalled that the draft of the agreement required almost nothing in the initial negotiation.

Andrews remembered, "Buss and me just sitting there, you know, no notes. He didn't want me to take any notes. I said, 'That's okay, Jerry. I can keep my attention for 25 million.' And we actually approved it, signed off on the deal."

But now, the injury had suddenly threatened to end all talk of a new contract, allowing the owner to wait and see.

"Earvin was in the recovery room after surgery the day we finalized the 25 million," George Andrews recalled, "and I said to Jerry, 'You really want to do this now?' He goes, 'Yeah, the doctor said he'll be fine. We're going to do it.'"

There was, however, an immense need for secrecy. News of such a deal could have blasted apart the team's chemistry that always teetered on the brink, with Kareem considered an extremely touchy situation. It was agreed that the deal would be announced much later, if at all. At no time did anyone in Johnson's camp, especially Johnson himself, think the terms of the deal would ever be disclosed, but they had all misjudged the desire of Jerry Buss to go big and his desire to let everyone know he was going big.

Strangely, however, Johnson sat on it. Looking at what was then the sudden wealth of a lifetime, he held off on signing the agreement, even though they faced a deadline at the end of April that would allow him to have a no-trade clause.

Meanwhile, he spent time on the bench in street clothes watching the Lakers adjust, with Norm Nixon going back to full-time point guard duties. They struggled at first.

"One of the interesting things is the team after getting over him not playing, they played pretty darn good for much of the season," Paul Westhead recalled. "They found a way to win a bunch of games. We won 54 games with Magic's unfortunate injury and us missing him. The team regrouped about as well as they could have."

Finally, Johnson could take no more sitting on the bench.

"He came back to Lansing about a month before he returned, to test it out," Tucker recalled. "We ran every morning in Jenison Field House, inside running the curves and stuff. Man, he was faster than before he got hurt."

Maybe not the same leaper, but faster. And when he came back, he was greeted with a 45-second ovation from the crowd that included Kareem standing and pounding his big mitts together along with everybody else.

Sports Illustrated's John Papanek tried to put it in perspective, citing the return of Mickey Mantle from a horrific knee injury, Tommy John from elbow surgery, Rocky Bleier's foot injury from a grenade in Vietnam. "All Magic Johnson did was have a small piece of cartilage removed from his knee—a relatively minor procedure as knee operations go—and he is only 21 years old, for heaven's sake," Papanek wrote.

Then he pointed out what everyone there felt, that it wasn't about the injury. It was about the love.

"I guess I've been blessed," Johnson told reporters that day. "The strength comes from my father, the smile comes from my mother and . . . well, I just don't know why it's me. It just is."

The Lakers had made a very big deal of the moment, a nationally televised game with a large media contingent, all of which immediately stirred resentment among several of his teammates, especially Nixon, who had gotten comfortable and successful in his old point guard position. They had gone 28–17 in Johnson's absence and were battling Phoenix for the division.

That wasn't the point, Westhead would observe later. Johnson had probably returned too early, but the playoffs were looming. And the doctors had already held him back beyond what Johnson wanted.

"When Earvin came back it was awkward," Steve Springer recalled. "Norm was the point guard, then he lost it understandably when Earvin came along, then he got it back when Earvin was hurt. He kind of grudgingly had to give it up when Earvin came back. And Earvin, I don't know if he was a hundred percent when he first came back."

"As for my observation," Paul Westhead recalled, "I don't know what the doctors would say, but he never got in kind of his physical groove, his basketball groove, at the end of that season and through the playoffs. He was fighting, you know. Fighting within himself."

And they fought with each other.

"They made some statements in the press, a story leading into that miniseries at the end of the season," Steve Springer recalled of the three-game first-round series the NBA used in those days.

The acrimony was relatively mild but clearly disruptive. More serious was the conflict between Kareem and Jim Chones, because it factionalized the team when Westhead decided to bench Chones. Nixon, Johnson, and others felt the coach made the move to keep Kareem happy. "We just lost our best inside player," Nixon told reporters.

"Injuries made it interesting," Westhead would recall. "Our problem was, when we went into the playoffs we were still adjusting to Magic's return, getting into the flow of the game, mixing our old starting lineup with our new starting lineup."

The Lakers lost to a plodding Houston Rockets team that didn't even have a winning record in the regular season (40–42) led by Moses Malone and Mike Dunleavy, 2–1, when Johnson, faced with a last-second shot to tie Game 3, drove into the lane and put up an air ball.

Westhead had called for the final shot to go to Kareem, but Johnson didn't think he could get it to the center and took it himself.

"Magic missed the finger roll down the middle against Houston," Roy Englebrecht recalled. "And we lost at home."

"Everybody," Steve Springer said, "was looking for somebody to blame."

With the season cut short Jerry Buss targeted what he saw as the league's stupid three-game first-round series.

"The league after that realized you really penalize a very good team by playing the best of three," Westhead observed.

The NBA realized it because an infuriated Buss worked adamantly to have the rule changed, Jeanie Buss recalled.

In the interim, the owner took his two guards away to discuss the team's chemistry over a long breakfast. "Buss took Norm and Earvin to Palm Springs," Steve Springer recalled, "and they kind of hashed it out. I think they've got along."

Basically, the meeting produced an avowal from Nixon that he didn't have to be traded, that he could get along with Johnson in the backcourt.

There remained the matter of the contract, a whopping $25 million sitting there on the table, all guaranteed as a personal services contract, a bundle of not just money but pure unadulterated power, for as far into the distance as any mortal could possibly see.

"Earvin wouldn't sign it," Andrews recalled. "This is painful because they got beat in the playoffs early if you remember and he hadn't played that well. He didn't want to sign it."

His lawyer asked him why.

"Well," Johnson was said to have replied, "Jerry Buss is paying for Magic Johnson, but I'm playing like Earvin Johnson."

21

POWER PLAY

Harvey Knuckles counted his good fortune when he was taken 39th overall in the 1981 NBA draft, a second-round pick of the Lakers. That fall in training camp, he got the first taste of being Magic Johnson's teammate.

"He was always energetic, always pushing guys," Knuckles recalled in a 2019 interview. "I remember one time in practice, I kind of raised my hand for a pass and the next thing you knew his pass went flying past me."

"Don't put your hand up if you're not ready and don't want the ball," Johnson admonished him.

"I learned real quickly if I'm calling for it, I better catch it," Knuckles remembered.

Another guy, named Clay Johnson, was also trying to make the team. One day he and Knuckles were shooting around.

"Magic came over, looks at Clay and he says, 'Johnson, right?' And then Magic paused and said, 'Well, you know there's only one Johnson on this team, so you know you're out of here.' We were really surprised, the both of us," Knuckles recalled. "Magic said it jokingly, of course. It was kind of funny. But it was still like, 'Wow.' And, you know what? Eventually, Clay didn't make the team."

Knuckles and Clay Johnson had been afforded a view of the Magic Man that fall just after he had turned twenty-two and was surging with his newfound sense of power, one so tangible that at times it almost seemed to cast off big sparks of static electricity. Get too close, and you could get zapped.

Even so, the 1981 off-season had brought much to annoy Johnson. The loss to Houston would mark the first time for the derisive nickname "Tragic Johnson," but he was well familiar with the feeling that engendered it, the gut-twisting aftermath of an embarrassing playoff loss when it seemed everywhere he turned, people he met had something to say, something cute, or sometimes the straight-up question, "What the hell happened?" Some of them just wanted to know, but others seemed to want it to linger, to revel in his takedown. Either way, the operative vibe in his life in those days after the defeat had been "loser," driven by the very public evidence of it.

Yes, he had played like Earvin instead of Magic, but George Andrews worked away on him about the massive new contract sitting there in front of him. Finally, as the deadline loomed, the lawyer told him, "Bud, you got to sign it."

So, he did. And then it became a matter of waiting for the other shoe to drop. Because he knew something that few else did, something that he had to keep quiet, something he loved very much, the absolute feeling of it, yet something in another sense that he never wanted known. At least not now. It might slowly leak out years later, but not now.

Every time he started feeling good about the money, there was somebody else asking how the hell they had lost to Houston. Plus, there was an even bigger annoyance. Johnson's air ball had allowed Larry Bird and his Celtics to get their first title when they defeated Houston in the NBA Finals.

"It was not a happy summer, following a spring that had not been happy," Charles Tucker remembered in 2019. "I spent it with him. He stayed with me that summer. It wasn't a good one."

Back in Lansing he was cruising around in his new blue Mercedes convertible, revisiting his past while deep in thought. He was flashing the smile for those he encountered all while harboring deep concerns. His son, Andre, had just been born, to a family friend with whom Johnson had had supposedly a brief encounter, but it would take more than two years for Johnson to acknowledge the child and only after paternity tests conclusively showed Andre was his. Still, the situation was very close to home and very problematic.

Thus, his convertible cruising about his hometown in 1981 became a time for him to process the moment, taking the blue Mercedes for a roll down the streets of his youth, over by Main Street School, stopping to take in the yellow house on Middle Street, seeing it all with a new wonder, even clearer than he had seen it before, something he would do over and over again in his life, much like his viewing of the videotape of Game 6, which he would watch again and again and again over the years, seeing it reveal over and over the power of his tour de force in that moment. And who wouldn't revel in every little detail of such an ascension? Just as he would look again and again at the yellow house, fantasizing that he could walk right in the front door and it would be the summer of 1971 again, when his young world was just coming alive, so crisp he could hear the crickets chirping rhythmically on the warm evenings, could sense again the wonder of the streets stalking about with his buddies in search of things they couldn't quite yet see or understand. The thought of it all made his heart ache with joy, and fear too. It was all almost too good, his past. He could drive around and see it, but he couldn't touch it.

"Come home from school, got the homework done, I'm gone. Go play," he would later recall, aching for those things, forget his women and his millions. "Oh, I wish so much it could be that way again. You don't know how much I wish it could be that way."

On one of those 1981 late-spring afternoons in Lansing he had pulled up to a stop sign in the blue Mercedes only to encounter Cookie Kelly strolling with one of his old friends. The two were just budding as an item. Johnson hadn't seen all that much of Kelly in the two years since they had backed off the relationship before he headed to Los Angeles. They had talked some on the phone, brief encounters here and there, but now seeing her with his friend stirred something in him.

Kelly would later recall the two men were among a group headed to play pickup ball that day as if it were some sort of Old West shootout. Her boyfriend had made an unusual request of Kelly, that she come to the pickup games at Jenison, something she had never done. She thought it strange but reluctantly agreed only to get there and witness Johnson's total destruction of her new beau on the floor, a humiliation, Kelly would recall, that ended her new relationship that very day, with Johnson afterward coming to her apartment, where they soon found themselves tangled up on the floor.

There was a temptation to see it as a renewal of their relationship. It some ways perhaps it was. In other ways, however, it would prove to be just another leg of their long and very winding road.

Soon after he made his way back to Los Angeles for a big event.

On June 19, Jerry Buss was honored as a humanitarian by the Bravo Chapter of the City of Hope, staged on the grounds of the famous Pickfair mansion the team owner had recently purchased and was renovating. It was a star magnet of an affair, the grandest sort of 1980s display. Singer Dionne Warwick performed. L.A. mayor Tom Bradley spoke. Regis Philbin covered it live for L.A.'s Channel 7 TV. Buss's hero, *Playboy* magazine publisher Hugh Hefner, came with a Playmate of the Month on his arm. O. J. Simpson showed up with Nicole Brown. As did Zsa Zsa Gabor and a host of others, including Red Buttons and Gabe Kaplan and Leslie Uggams and many more.

All of the stars, however, were "almost prostrate" before young Magic Johnson, the *L.A. Times* reported in a huge spread on the event.

Buss, once a veritable nobody in celebrity-rich Hollywood, was overcome by the attention now directed his way.

"I'm eating this up," the owner told the crowd in receiving the City of Hope's Spirit of Life Award. "I received more attention tonight than I have in a lifetime and I'm really enjoying it."

Such a spotlight was tops among the many reasons that wealthy men owned sports teams. In addition to Buss's four children, business partner Frank Mariani was there, along with another of his business associates, Donald Sterling, identified by the media as "the prince of Los Angeles."

"Buss made it on his own," Johnson told the crowd. "All the millions." Then he paused and added, "And all of the girls."

Hovering overhead, drowning out the yuks, was a large helicopter flashing a message: "We Salute Jerry Buss."

"The shiny tuxes glittered in the light," observed writer Marylouise Oates.

Then it was off to Lansing again for both Johnson and Buss. Tucker had arranged a "roast" of Johnson for twenty bucks a plate, in hopes that it would cheer him up.

As usual, Johnson was late, noted emcee Tim Staudt. "We feel very fortunate to have Earvin here tonight. We told him it started at noon—yesterday."

Staudt gave Johnson a brick, complete with a thank-you note from the Rockets. It was "in honor of that last shot, and all the money you made us," the broadcaster said, diving right in for the tender spot.

Greg Kelser was there, allowing that most of the alley-oops that Johnson threw him at Michigan State were just bad shots that Kelser had cleaned up. "I just made him look good," Kelser said, a quip that didn't seem to sit right with Johnson, apparently still too sensitive to be roasted.

"Ain't that something," Johnson told the adoring crowd, offering perhaps a little too much truth considering that Kelser's once promising pro career seemed headed nowhere. "You try to help a guy make millions, and he comes up here and says something like that about me. Dr. Buss was thinking about trading for you, but now, forget it. You blew it."

Buss, who had come to the event with his own Playmate centerfold on his arm, told the crowd, "I'd like to tell you how Magic has influenced my life. The Forum is now Magic Place. The millions are gone—and so are all the girls. Now I walk down the street and everybody says, 'There goes Magic and what's his name.' But I was told I should concentrate on some of the good things. For instance, his humility. The other day we went to Disneyland. When we came to the Magic Kingdom, he said, 'Aw, they didn't have to do that.'"

Well-intentioned fun aside, the days afterward brought word slowly leaking out about the deal with little snippets of speculation in the L.A. papers. Then it happened. Buss dropped the whole thing like a bomb in a TV interview toward the end of June, not just the money but the fact that it ran for a quarter century, that it was no typical NBA contract but a personal services deal, personally guaranteed by Buss.

George Andrews knew immediately it had happened because his pager was instantly stuffed with media calls to return.

What made it worse was all the gushing the owner did. He talked about Johnson in a management role with the team once his playing days were over, quotes that the wire services distributed, with headlines about Johnson's big haul literally in every newspaper in the country and on radio and TV sportscasts.

"He may even be my coach," Buss had said. "'Or general manager. Or maybe he'll run the team and I'll just sit back and watch. Magic is a bright kid and I plan to make him my protege, teach him the business aspect of sports. I realize this is a very unusual contract because we're talking about a kid whose college class just graduated. But what it comes down to is that Magic is part of the family."

The signing made Johnson just the third NBA player to make a million a year, behind Kareem and Houston's Moses Malone. "The $1 million a year I'm paying covers all his basketball playing," Buss said. "You have to figure the kid has 10 years of playing left. After that, you and I both know he will be a legend. And he'll know plenty about basketball and business because I'm going to teach him."

Johnson himself would be surprised by just how much the owner had to say that day. Teams usually left out the financial specifics when announcing such matters. Obviously, the owner was proud of the deal, proud of the inventive way that he had financed it that would cost him little or nothing.

"I know that $1 million a year past basketball sounds exorbitant," Buss told the media. "But consider this: 14 years from now, the average secretary—not good ones mind you, but average ones—will be making $60,000 a year. So Magic's services, as coach or GM or whichever direction we mutually choose to take, are worth $1 million a year to me."

Hell, the *Chicago Tribune* noted, the *Trib* itself had just bought the entire Cubs franchise for $20 million.

The contract was cited as the largest and longest in sports history. Dave Winfield of the Yankees had recently signed a $24 million deal, and Buss slyly acknowledged that Johnson's was intentionally larger. And for many more years.

Other owners may have been irked and irritated by what Buss had done, but the new Lakers owner enjoyed making the big play in the big spotlight. Some observers would cite the move as problematic. "Buss had created a monster with that long contract and those lavish L.A. promises," Anthony Cotton of *Sports Illustrated* would write. "In the process, Buss served notice on Kareem Abdul-Jabbar, on Jamaal Wilkes, on all the other Lakers, that he played favorites. By going on an emotional splurge, beyond the big money Johnson obviously deserves, Buss set the Lakers up for a fall."

"It hurt Kareem and my father probably heard from the league and other owners that it made them look bad," Jeanie Buss observed in 2020.

Considering the earlier fear that the Lakers were somehow funded by mob money, the response was understandable. It wasn't long after the big move that the league adopted a salary cap, she added.

Just as predicted, Abdul-Jabbar was hot and let the owner know it, which reduced Jerry Buss to tears, Charles Tucker recalled in 2019. "When Earvin got his contract, the 25 million, Buss felt kind of bad about it because Kareem had complained about it to him. Buss was just in tears."

"That my dad was crying over the hurt feelings of Kareem, I could see that," Jeanie Buss said in 2020 while pointing out that her father crying was a rare occurrence. "He never did anything to like hurt somebody else. He had a lot of compassion for people because of his upbringing and where he came from. He would never want to disrespect anybody. But, as soon as my dad, you know, buys the team he is now best friends with Magic."

It was only reasonable, she said, that someone like Kareem could be asking, "Where did this come from? How did that happen?"

"We sat down and talked about it," Tucker said of Buss. "I just told him, 'Shit, man. You can't worry about that. You've been fair to everybody.' 'Cause he didn't deserve it. Buss is the guy who helped Kareem really. For the longest time, Kareem couldn't get anywhere in L.A. Nowhere."

"Magic was his muse, you know," Jeanie Buss said, "so I don't think he felt bad about doing anything for him."

Muse or not, the matter was said to have soon prompted a players meeting that featured substantial anger and many questions aimed at trying to define the relationship between the owner and his young star. Johnson was once again trying to offer assurances that he wasn't trying to take over the team.

Abdul-Jabbar waited a month to calm down, then called a press conference to question if Johnson had become part of team management, as both the size of the deal and Buss himself had implied in his comments.

"I'll tear up the contract if it's gonna cause problems," Johnson responded.

Instead, Buss would eventually give Abdul-Jabbar a new contract at $1.5 million per season to quiet the complaints, but that only came after Buss acknowledged that he was pondering trading the center. Inside observers wondered just how the guard and center would get along in the aftermath. Abdul-Jabbar had made it clear he thought Johnson and the owner were too close.

"It kind of got to be like a family thing," Kareem said in a 1993 interview, still irked more than a decade later, "where Earvin got to be the favorite child. I think they did a whole thing to placate me. Up until the year I retired, I was the highest paid player in the league. So I don't have any complaints. They paid me well; they appreciated what I did. But I never got to be a part of the family thing, because my own personal integrity made Dr. Buss uncomfortable."

Some observers believed that Abdul-Jabbar intimidated the owner just as he intimidated every other single person in the franchise. Others thought their personal styles were simply different. Buss craved the high profile that his Lakers ownership and the Johnson friendship had brought him. It was great for business, great for his sex life, great for his social life. Each game night he packed his area of reserved seating high up at the Forum with an array of impressive people. Actors. Lawyers. Executives. Intellectuals. Celebrities of all ilks.

"It was Jerry Buss's party, Jerry Buss's night out," Joe McDonnell recalled. "A lot of times you'd look up in his box to see who was up there."

"That was really fun up there," Doug Krikorian said of Buss. "He'd bring young girls. I was single at the time. It was unbelievable, having dinner with Jerry beforehand at the Forum with all his celebrities, and then going up there to his box."

After games, the owner enjoyed taking certain favorites to the locker room to meet his stars. Abdul-Jabbar had absolutely no talent or desire whatsoever for schmoozing and glad-handing. Johnson, on the other hand, loved the Buss menagerie. He unleashed the smile, set them at ease, and made any and all guests feel welcome, which freed Kareem to make a quick exit.

Ultimately, the entire contract proved nothing more than a large, problematic symbol of the owner's relationship with his young star who had been endowed with an unprecedented power. Soon enough, the NBA raised doubts about it due to legal issues.

"When we did the $25-million contract, David Stern wasn't the commissioner yet," George Andrews recalled.

Instead, Stern was one of the NBA's top lawyers, in charge of its entertainment division. The league "bounced the contract," Andrews recalled, which required he and his uncle meet with the NBA's legal team.

"It was Stern and Russ Granik and Gary Bettman," Andrews recalled. "We're in the room and my uncle goes to Stern, 'David, how you doing?'"

"Yeah," Stern replied, "doing great. Why do you ask?"

"Well," the senior Andrews replied, "if Magic is hit by a taxi cab we're suing you personally for the 25 million because you violated the terms of the contract."

The situation required arbitration, according to the NBA's own agreements, the Andrewses argued.

"I thought Dave was gonna crap his pants," George Andrews

recalled with a laugh. "But before we left the contract was approved subject to arbitration."

There were legitimate legal issues that would require major changes. First of all, a personal services contract in California couldn't extend beyond a set number of years, certainly not to twenty-five.

Lon Rosen would point out that the contract was replaced soon after he became Johnson's representative in 1987. Until then, symbolically Johnson remained the $25 million man and the owner's favorite son in just about everyone's eyes. As with anyone imbued with a new power, Johnson would soon show that he was primed to test it.

The Change

God, it was messy, they would all say of 1981 after it was over, that it was messy and emotional and ugly, so much so that they would have to expend a great deal of effort just to pretend that it wasn't messy and emotional and ugly at all. Nor profoundly embarrassing. Lo and behold, they brazenly led others to pretend that it wasn't ugly at all, which was said so often that everybody came to believe it.

There was no doubt that Magic Johnson fired his coach, Jeanie Buss would say with a laugh, looking back in 2020.

But nobody was laughing at the time.

Perhaps none of the big pretense would have mattered if they hadn't won. But win, they would. And experience has long shown that nothing befits believing quite like winning. And, despite the unseemly events of that fall of 1981, Earvin Johnson was well on his way to making the good people of Southern California very big believers.

"If you're an athlete and you win, they forgive you for a lot of things," teammate Kurt Rambis would say in 2004.

In the end, it all confirmed that instinct and genius and immense talent work just like that. They show the way to new rules, new paradigms, and if nothing else, Earvin Johnson was all that.

That ugly, sad, uncertain L.A. of 1979? It would all be gone by the time he was done, inhabited by a new vibe.

"All of a sudden Magic shows up," longtime NBA writer Mike Wise would say in 2004, "and Showtime happens. And it's real. You went into the Forum on a Friday night, and if you were a visiting team, you didn't come out of that building a winner. Everybody knew that's just how it was. It wasn't just about Magic. It wasn't just about Kareem. It was about Showtime. There was an aura around the team that was somewhat bigger than the franchise itself. It's why the stars came out, it's why the town started singing Randy Newman after every game. 'I Love L.A.' It's a corny song, but if you were in L.A. and you were visiting and that song was playing after the game, you were like, 'Yeah. This is a great town.'"

There would be little second-guessing of events, or even values, Jeanie Buss said, "not with a name like Magic. I mean, he was so talented and so entertaining. You're seeing something and you're sharing something with the crowd and, you know, you get to be part of it. And it's like you're all in on this high five. It's unique and you're watching him."

The transformation Johnson started would serve as a defibrillator, jolting the city back to life with this series of events.

"The Lakers then became part of something alive," Mike Wise said. "You get a rental car at the airport, and the guy driving the Avis is like, 'Ah, the Lakers are playin' tonight.' It's a communal thing. L.A. is like this big car culture where you don't know your neighbors and everybody is driving around. But the Lakers made it a town. A small town."

Even the troubles of 1981 would be part of the rebirth, which began in the training camp that fall that Harvey Knuckles had witnessed.

"Magic was an easy person to get along with and he was easy to coach for me," Paul Westhead said in 2019. "The only issue that evolved was when he had the injury and was recovering. He was struggling the season before that fall. He was struggling in the playoffs. We got knocked out early and now with two or three months off. And doing whatever. I don't know what he was doing to recover or rehab. Back in the early '80s when the season ended you might not see any of your players until like four days before training camp. They would just disappear and did whatever they did, went back to their homes."

Westhead pointed out that in more modern times players are often around their teams through much of the year, and their rehab from injuries is routinely watched closely by teams. Not so back in 1981.

"So, you would not have a feel of somebody and what he's doing," Westhead offered. "My take on Magic's return the next season was, there was not any significant improvement in his physical status, in his ability to get up and down the court, the ability to cut and drive and do the things that he did so naturally. He did not seem to have that ready to go."

As for the feelings of the team in that training camp, Westhead recalled, "I did not know the daily interaction of Magic and other teammates and what their feelings were. . . . I think everyone was hoping that we're going to have a great year. It got off to a slow start."

And there was some dissension growing in the ranks.

As the situation unfolded, the coach explained to the Lakers' front office that he was merely trying to install a half-court offense so the team would have an option if the break wasn't available and the tempo slowed, as it often did in the playoffs. But Westhead failed to make this clear to his players, who had been grousing about coaching since the '81 playoffs.

Perhaps the coach didn't realize he was stumbling upon a greater divide in his team than he realized, that his players so resented Abdul-Jabbar they would print up matchbooks about trading him. Ironically, in hindsight, those Showtime teams would be prized because they could do both: 1) run like the wind, and 2) set up the half-court offense and pound opponents' heads in with a dominant figure like Kareem.

"It's really hard to get inside what people were thinking and doing," Westhead said when asked about it in 2004. "Early in that season, Magic was still trying to work out some physical difficulties from his surgery. He didn't have the same quickness and movement that he'd had in the past, so he was being jammed up by defenders where normally it would be easy for him to control. I think he was both physically and emotionally distraught because he wanted to be the best."

Johnson had been among those advocating the acquisition of Mitch Kupchak, but it soon became apparent that Kupchak fed into the team's issues.

"That was Mitch Kupchak's first year, too," former Laker Eddie Jordan explained in 2004. "And Westhead wanted to incorporate Mitch into the offense. Now, we were out there running and Mitch didn't catch up so well. So, Paul wanted to get some post-ups. I think he thought half-court basketball controlled the game. And it did for most teams, but not for those Showtime Lakers."

Actually, Westhead was one of the game's foremost proponents of the open-court attack, but any coach would have wanted to sharpen what the Lakers did in the half-court. Westhead would later acknowledge he didn't realize there was so much resistance among the players, especially Johnson, who could not abide the thought of the Lakers devolving into a slower operation. Even discussing the matter years later, the anger could well up in him. Johnson was thoroughly miserable.

In 2019, Charles Tucker, who seemed to have found every possible way to communicate as an advocate for Johnson over the years, would describe the whole episode as "a failure to communicate."

"What we wanted to do was perform," Michael Cooper said. "We were more of a freewheeling team. We'd run, and if we didn't get it, the ball was popped around. But now it became, 'Get it down and get it to Kareem.'"

Truth? This was hardly a new development. Things had been that way. It was how the Lakers took three of their four victories against Philadelphia in the 1980 championship—on Abdul-Jabbar's shoulders.

In the days after things went down, the writers and other close observers would look back at the first weeks of the season. Some clues they missed. Others leapt out.

"There was a game. I think it was at Houston," Steve Springer recalled in 2019. "It was a couple of weeks to ten days before the blowup in Salt Lake City. It was the typical game where they were all standing around. They hated the offense. They didn't have any freedom. The shackles were on or whatever. And the next morning we go out to the team bus parked next to the hotel. There was a little island in the street with grass on it and a couple of trees and then there was the main thoroughfare of the freeway. So, Earvin's got on his earphones and he's got a boom box. He was waiting for the players to just get on the bus. It was no smiles. It was none of the EJ the DJ. He was in his own world and he gets off the bus while we're waiting and he walks onto that island and he sits down, his back against the tree, his head bobbing up and down listening to music like he's lost in a world. Like he wanted nothing to do with the whole scene. He had walked right by Westhead and Westhead seemed like totally oblivious. Everybody else, we're all looking out the window and now everybody's on the bus except him. And they're not going to move without him and he's just sitting there. Like he just doesn't want to be a part of this anymore. And if you couldn't figure out then that this was not going to end well, you were totally clueless. Eventually he got up and trudged back on the bus and sat down, but it was just the first sign."

With Johnson and Buss synced so closely, it wasn't long before the owner supposedly began planning to change coaches, although even that would come into question later. General manager Bill Sharman had pleaded for patience. Johnson supposedly was among a group of players frustrated with Westhead's new offense. But as the coach had told management, the team was coming around. The new offense just required a little patience.

"There was a meeting on the Sunday before they went to Salt Lake City with Buss, Jerry West, and Bill Sharman," Springer recalled of circumstances that would be offered to him later. "Buss wanted to fire Westhead and they said to give it a little more time. They're agreeing to pause, but Buss was already actively planning this, and Earvin had forced his hand."

If Buss was actively planning it, which seems in doubt in retrospect, then time would show he was doing a terrible job of it, which was very uncharacteristic.

"My dad knew that Earvin wasn't happy with Westhead," Jeanie Buss recalled. "They were having conversations, but they had that game in Utah and my dad basically said, 'You know, go play the game in Utah and when you get back to L.A., we'll sit down and talk about it.' When they were in Utah, that's when he went to the media and said the things that he said."

The mid-November trip to Utah produced a road win, the fifth victory in a row. But Johnson and Westhead argued on the bench.

"Things came to a head in Utah," Bill Sharman would recall in a 1992 interview. "There was a miscommunication between Paul and Magic. The band was playing; Magic was toweling off and seemed not to listen. Paul kind of hollered at him and upset him."

"We didn't know that was happening," Steve Springer said of the four reporters traveling with the team. "It was just a typical game. And so, we walk in the locker room and we walked over to Earvin and asked, 'How'd it go tonight?' He was like a politician who had just finished his speech and was going to get up and deliver it. He stood up and said, 'I'm not having any fun. I want to be traded.' I'm the one who said, 'Earvin, you know what you're saying?'"

"I know exactly what I'm saying," Springer remembered Johnson answering.

"That was the scene in the room," Springer recalled. "So, I look all the way down the room at all the locker stalls. All the players stop what they're doing and they're all looking at us, the four of us around Earvin. And when I turn to look at them, they're all like choreographed. They all turned their backs or went back to getting dressed. All of them were stunned."

"I just sat there and watched the wildfire spread around the locker room as word went around," Kurt Rambis recalled in a 2004 interview for *The Show*. "It was pretty amazing."

"I was the first player to hear it," Eddie Jordan recounted much later. "I went across the locker room and I told Norman, 'Norman, you and I are gonna be starting in the backcourt.' I had never heard a player say the coach has got to get fired or I have to get traded. Then I told Kareem, and Kareem said, 'No, we'll straighten this out. Magic shouldn't have done it.'"

At the time, all Johnson wanted to do was go to a pay phone and call his father. Indeed, it wasn't the first time Johnson had challenged his coaches. The first had come when he called for the walkout over cheerleader selections at Everett High, the second when he stormed out of practice at Michigan State. Tucker had been there with Johnson's father to smooth over and correct the trajectory of both earlier circumstances. This time, both men were back in Lansing. This time, events quickly took on a life of their own. Tucker learned about the situation in a phone call after it happened. Johnson was angry and emotional and seemingly determined to change the equation.

He had told reporters he wanted to be traded because he felt the new offense was stifling the team's creativity. Asked about Westhead, Johnson told reporters, "We don't see eye-to-eye on a lot of things."

The reporters then hustled to inform Westhead of Johnson's statement.

"Apparently what had happened was that in a timeout in a huddle Westhead yelled, claimed that Earvin was looking at some girl walking backwards," Springer recalled. "Earvin was told to keep his head on what they were doing."

Later, there was apparently an exchange in a hotel ballroom, Springer said. "I guess we didn't know any of this at the time. And they had it out in the ballroom, yelling and screaming at each other."

The writers were at the airport the next morning when one of them, Mitch Chortkoff, walked up to the group and said their airline had just made a terrible mistake.

"What's that?" Springer asked.

"They just gave Westhead a boarding pass that says coach," Chortkoff quipped.

Just about all of them began to realize, no joke, that Westhead was gone.

"When you have thoroughbreds, you let them run," sportscaster Jim Hill, a longtime Johnson confidant, observed much later. "I remember the night Magic told Westhead, 'You know what? You might as well trade me.' Magic wasn't used to that. He was a young man used to going and playing and having fun and not getting all caught up in the business aspect or the ego. So now Westhead is telling him,

'You gotta do this, and I don't want you doing that. And sit down and shut up.' And so forth. Magic said, 'Uh-uh. You might as well trade me.' And he was serious."

"Walking off that plane the next morning, it seemed like the coach was fired in flight," former Laker Eddie Jordan would recall later. "We arrived in LAX, and the reporters were right there as soon as we came off the plane. The announcement had been made by the time we got to our homes. It was strange. You knew there were some grumblings, that [there] was some holding back of a team that really wanted to be let loose. But we didn't know it was gonna happen."

"The next day we met them at the airport," sportscaster Jim Hill remembered. "Magic got off the plane, and I asked him if he felt the same way that he did the night before. He was so cool about everything. He said, 'I don't want to make further comment until I talk to Dr. Buss.'"

Westhead recalled he was back at work studying game film when he was called to Buss's office.

Bob Steiner was, according to Lon Rosen, a most loyal and ardent advisor for Jerry Buss. Indeed, Steiner would provide quite a role model for Rosen himself and how he spent his career as Johnson's most loyal advocate. In 1992, looking back on the events of 1981, Steiner would posit that the meeting that day between Buss and Westhead was special, that Buss and Westhead had a great visit, and that Buss came away with tremendous respect and admiration for Westhead.

That was not how the coach himself would recall the moment.

"It was a very brief meeting," Westhead said in 2019. "To be honest I didn't expect it. I guess that shows my intelligence level. I thought we were gonna have some conversation about how we're going to be able to avoid this in the future. He found another way to avoid it in the future. I was willing to sit and have a discussion about having our players being all on the same page, Magic included. He was very quick in saying that 'We're gonna let you go.'"

"The team was not as exciting as it should be," Buss said at the time. "We were in a car and I didn't like where it was heading. Instead of saying, 'Let's find a new way to go,' I decided to change drivers."

Joyce Sharman, Bill Sharman's widow, recalled the events of November 1981 clearly, because she and the Lakers GM had gotten married that very month. Then all of a sudden, the team's superstar had pulled this most unusual move that put Westhead on the firing line?

"They were going to fire him anyway? After he had won a championship?" Joyce Sharman said in 2019, casting doubt on the idea that the entire move was somehow already in the Lakers' plans. "I have to tell you the truth. Bill was kind of mortified about it. When you think about it, they had won the championship, they had a five-game winning streak. Why would you fire him? I think it was more personality."

Johnson would later defend his actions. "Why was it wrong for me to talk?" he asked. "Should I shut up and be unhappy and jeopardize the team, waiting for something to blow up? Ask anyone who saw us. We were the dullest team in the league. I'd look at films and say, 'What is this?' We would get dressed before games and there would be no enthusiasm, nothing; we'd all just sit there."

"We were on a five-game winning streak," Westhead would emphasize in 2004. "People forget that. Usually you don't get fired for five-game winning streaks."

"Yeah," Michael Cooper recalled much later, "but it was a very tough five-game winning streak. We weren't winning like we should have been."

The front office was then caught in confusion over the identity of the next head coach. The company line would quickly become that Buss had planned to fire Westhead all along, but that became highly questionable considering the fiasco of a press conference that followed, which seemed to reveal that the firing was unexpected and that management had no plan ready to move forward. The staff thought that all were agreed that Pat Riley was going to be the new coach, except that Buss stepped to the microphone and said it would be Jerry West, a jolting change in direction.

"When they made this choice with Westhead to let him go, they didn't really have a plan," Jeanie Buss related in a 2020 interview, "and so my dad just wanted to get through the rough patch because he wasn't expecting that he'd be firing a coach in November. So, he wanted Jerry to go in as a head coach until they figured out what they wanted to do. And, of course, Jerry didn't want to be head coach again. And so that's why in that famous press conference Jerry is like, 'No, I'm not coaching. Riley's the coach.'"

West, on the spot in front of the cameras, had contradicted the owner, which required an about-face. On the fly, no less.

"I was working there so I know sort of what happened," Lon Rosen explained in 2020. "You know, Jerry West and Pat Riley and Jerry Buss didn't discuss it enough, what the heck would be happening. So, Jerry Buss kind of winged it at that press conference."

Rosen also emphasized that Buss said, "Well, Jerry's going to be the offense coach and Riley's going to be the defense coach."

"Jerry West said, 'No. I'm just going to assist for a little while,'" Rosen recalled. "Because it was not his intention to come back on the bench. That's not what he wanted."

Buss had not wanted to hire Riley to be Westhead's assistant in the first place, and now the owner seemed to have rejected him again.

"They were like, who's the most familiar with our roster?" Jeanie Buss recalled. "That was Pat Riley because he's been doing all the games. He's broadcasting the games with Chick. He's always been watching them. At least he's aware of who our players are. So that's kind of how they made the decision to make him the assistant coach and put him on the bench."

That, in turn, made him the logical candidate to replace Westhead, Jeanie Buss said.

West, then forty-three, essentially helped the thirty-six-year-old Riley, his former teammate, as an assistant for two weeks, until Bill Bertka was hired. There would be many things that contributed to the success of the Showtime teams, few of them more important than the presence of "Bert," a man possessed of immense basketball wisdom who would come to be considered a treasure for Lakers players for decades.

Johnson and Riley, who had talked basketball frequently in their time together, came to a quick alliance in the aftermath, Lon Rosen recalled. "When Pat Riley emerged as the coach, they became one pretty quickly because Pat realized, 'I better be in sync with this guy.' And I think Earvin realized, 'I better be in sync with this guy because I just went through, you know, a situation with Westhead.' Did Pat need training wheels? I think we all need training wheels when you first start a job. But if there's anybody that took to it, it was Pat. The guy was brilliant."

At the time, Riley said he thought the firing was horrible. For the record, Westhead considered Riley an excellent and loyal assistant, an opinion that did not change in the years that followed. First of all, Riley had been made all too aware of the difficult emotional terrain any coach faced in pulling together the team's two major attributes, one fast, the other slow.

In the Lakers' next home game, Johnson was walloped by a chorus of boos from the Forum crowd. For months afterward he would hear extensive booing on road trips, especially in the arena of the rival Seattle Sonics, where he would be booed every time he touched the ball. "What you must do," Riley told him, "is ride it out and not break concentration. Just play your head off and you'll turn the crowd around."

"The first time he really faced criticism was Westhead's firing," Steve Springer observed in 2019, "and he'd be booed everywhere we went in the league. I mean, let's face it. He was a young Black kid who got the white coach fired. That was part of it."

The ensuing weeks also brought round after round of condemnation from editorialists across the country who labeled Buss a meddlesome owner and Johnson a spoiled, overpaid crybaby. His new contract was cited as part of the problem. The *Los Angeles Times* called him a "glory hog," while the New York *Daily News* said he was a "spoiled punk."

Even Buss's favorite paper, *The Desert Sun* in Palm Springs, called the move "bizarre."

Perhaps sensing that he needed support, Jim Dart organized a trip of Johnson's former coaches and friends, including George Fox and Pat Holland, to Chicago when the Lakers visited the Bulls early in January 1982. Johnson was excited about the reunion and, true to his control freak nature, he even had the seating already arranged when the group went to dine together after his game, where Johnson had again been heavily booed.

The coaches were staying in the same hotel as the Lakers, and after the meal they all returned there to visit some more. The coaches were astounded to see the place packed with women, from the lobby to the hallways in and around the Lakers' rooms. One of the group asked Johnson if all those women were prostitutes. Some were, Johnson explained, but many were simply women eager to share intimacy with an NBA player. Some were businesspeople, even lawyers and other professionals, Johnson said. The moment would come to mind years later when Johnson announced he was HIV positive. Just thinking back to that Chicago hotel packed with women helped his coaches and friends understand how Johnson could have gone astray. It even opened the door to the possibility that Johnson's sudden unpopularity over the Westhead firing had served to accelerate his plight as he became even more involved with groupies to ease the pain of his rejection by crowds that had so readily loved him before. Yet that was only an excuse, and for Johnson's ultimate carelessness no excuse would seem to fit.

The moment did bring him to a reality. Fans could jeer him just as easily as they could cheer him.

"He got booed in a lot of arenas," Kurt Rambis recalled in 2004. "People were coming down on him. The media was always down on him. So, he went from being one of—if not the—NBA's favorite sons at that point to having to deal with a lot of criticism. Everywhere he went before that, everything was positive. Now half of it was positive, the other half negative. He had to grow and learn from that."

When the All-Star voting came that February, Johnson was fifth in the tally for Western Conference guards, the only time he would not start in the midseason event except for injury. He had gone from one of the league's most popular players to one of its most suspect.

"You watch what you say and do after that," Johnson would say, looking back at the pain he felt and the distrust that grew between him and his once adoring public. "You watch them as they watch you. And you say to yourself, 'What are they after?'"

"My only disappointment was that Magic was going through

some personal problems, meaning he couldn't easily recover from his injury, that he knew that he was a superstar and he was struggling to deliver that," Westhead said in 2019. "That caused him, from my perspective, to not be the same player or person to deal with on a regular basis."

In the weeks following the firing, Riley would point to the problematic dynamic that the team faced, a dynamic that had brought down Westhead. "Any time you run an offense with a center in the low post," the new coach told *Sports Illustrated,* "you're going to have trouble with the half-court offense, a lack of movement, and it also tends to put restrictions on freelancing. Even when we won the championship there were players unhappy with the offense."

It was a trend that would continue, even under Riley.

One narrative that emerged, it seemed, to protect Johnson was that he was merely expressing the opinions shared by his teammates who refused to step up and support his assertions in the moment of truth.

"When Magic spoke out, it wasn't because he was crazy or anything," sportscaster Joe McDonnell offered in 1992. "It was because nobody else would speak out. This had been festering for the whole season. They just didn't like Westhead, period. Magic was no dummy. He knew that Jerry Buss would never trade him. It was just his power play, and he got him out of there."

"Later," Steve Springer recalled, "I went to Norm and I said, 'Why don't you back him up?' And he said, 'Because I'd get traded.'"

That, apparently, was the sense of the meeting Nixon and Johnson had had with Buss after the previous season. If Nixon wasn't happy, he could be traded. Nixon had promptly assured the owner he did not want to be traded.

Indeed, Johnson was the one player with the power to make such a move, the one player with an extremely close relationship with the owner. It was dramatic new territory for a player, a power play that would serve as the forerunner of the coming age of player power.

Journalist Roy S. Johnson, who would write a book with Johnson in 1989, doubted in a 2021 interview that Johnson, at age twenty-two, was in any way consciously flexing his new power in that moment, rather he was simply venting his frustration and trying to get away from a style of play that he intensely disliked.

Such an observation certainly had merit. For whatever reason, however, Johnson's move revealed for the first time the major power that a player could wield.

Professional team owners in a variety of sports had long worked to keep such power out of the hands of their players. NBA team owners, who had tightly held power since the league was founded in 1946, had long displayed dramatically mixed results in their decisions, with their frequent mismanagement often far exceeding the successes. As players in the wake of Johnson's big move would later gain their own power, they would also gain their own record of mixed results in the difficult business landscape of pro basketball.

Soon after the 1981 incident, another narrative gained traction, that Westhead had fallen into disfavor because he quoted Shakespeare on occasion.

"One of the lines, I remember after a game, I was talking to Michael Cooper," Joe McDonnell said in 2004. "And he said to me, 'You know what this fucking idiot did before the game?' I said, 'What?' He said, 'He tried quoting Shakespeare to us.' He said, 'Doesn't he understand the brothers don't give a shit about Shakespeare?' And there, I think, was in essence the rift between Westhead and the rest of the team. They felt like he was a cultural snob and they wanted to play basketball and they didn't give a shit about Shakespeare."

George Andrews would point out in 2019 that highly successful Phil Jackson had a different, somewhat odd, intellectual approach that worked quite well with the Chicago Bulls a decade later. Jackson introduced Native American symbolism to his teams. He beat a tom-tom before games. He burned incense in the locker room to ward off evil spirits. He taught his players meditation and mindfulness techniques and used practice time to develop such skills, all things that Jordan greeted with a tilted eyebrow if not outright suspicion.

There was, however, one huge difference between Jackson and Westhead. Jackson had been a pro player himself for years. He understood well the hierarchy of teams, that it was necessary for the head coach to make clear who the top dog was on the roster and to build a great relationship with that top dog. Jackson did that, first with Jordan in Chicago and later with Shaquille O'Neal and the Lakers and finally with a player whom he had long held at bay, Kobe Bryant.

Westhead had failed to do enough to establish that relationship with the top dog, Magic Johnson. Or perhaps more relevantly, he had mistakenly chosen Abdul-Jabbar for the relationship building. The coach and the center understood each other, and the offense that Westhead had been trying to install would have helped the team by helping Kareem. The mistake Westhead made was easy. After all, Kareem was "The Cap," the team captain, but its true leader, by all accounts, was Magic Johnson from the very first day he arrived. In the delicate business of coaching superstars, Westhead likely should have clearly explained to Johnson what he planned to do and tacitly sought his permission by discussing it in detail.

Even that might not have saved his job. In an environment with few easy targets, Westhead had been merely the easy target in a highly emotional time.

"They all hated Westhead," Joe McDonnell said in 1992. "Kareem was the only one who didn't talk too much about him on or off the record."

Indeed, Abdul-Jabbar would later criticize Johnson over the firing in an interview with *The New York Times.*

"I have an interesting coaching style," Westhead said in 2019. "I always thought I was a player's coach and I never try to give players a hard time. I never tried to embarrass them, like on the court, you know. I learned real fast, like if a player turns the ball over you don't take them out the very next play because he feels embarrassed. So, I thought I was pretty confident doing that. But, on the other hand, I never sought to become friends with players. I saw myself as someone who had to help direct them and not get personally involved with them. So, I don't know what Magic's plan was, but it wasn't my plan to be his best friend."

It was likely a fatal miscalculation for a championship coach in the delicate world of NBA relationships.

"This wasn't about 'me,'" Michael Cooper would say. "It wasn't about 'I,' Magic. 'I want to score more,' or 'I want to do more.' After the championship year we had had, we weren't doing the things that won us that sixth game. We were coming back and getting away from a lot of stuff."

Truly, Westhead was catering to the wins that Kareem had delivered in the first three games of the 1980 title series. Frankly, that's just about what any American basketball coach would have done, faced with the circumstances. In fact, it was what Pat Riley would do essentially, although he was better at perceiving and reacting to the emotions of a team.

Some years later, Johnson would include Westhead, among his other coaches, in the dedication of the book he wrote with Roy S. Johnson. But Westhead would say in 2019 that he and Johnson had never addressed the issue of his firing, had never really spoken, since he was dismissed that afternoon in November 1981. Sometime around the airing of Johnson's multipart documentary on Apple TV in 2022, the former coach and Johnson would reconnect, and Johnson would express appreciation for Westhead. But that would come only after four decades of silence.

"I know I'm going to be booed, but I have to deal with it," Johnson would say in the days after the firing. "As long as I know in my heart that I didn't try to get him fired, I can handle it."

"I'm not blaming him, but I'm not excusing him," Westhead would say in 2004.

"The only thing I will say," Westhead said later, "that I want to attempt to clarify, was the explanation that the team wasn't running as much. I said, 'Well, you can fire me for a million things. Take your pick. You didn't relate to the team. All the classic things. You weren't tough enough. You were too tough.' But every practice of my coaching career has been running. So, if that was the reason, that's not a reason, not an accurate reason. Fire me for other things then. That's the only clarification that I requested. Not that it mattered. If you're relieved, then you're relieved. Ultimately, history will look back and see me as the mad scientist who ran more than any other coach, maybe in the history of the game. He might have lost a lot of games. He might have been fired more than anybody in the history of the game, but nobody ran more."

Bob Steiner would say looking back that Westhead clearly had the belief and intent to keep the Lakers a running team, but for some reason that wasn't happening that fall.

Westhead would be hired by the Chicago Bulls after leaving the Lakers and fired again after a single season, although he would go on to leave his mark in coaching.

"Pat Riley was very relatable to players," Joyce Sharman observed. "It was a great era with Pat. It was great and fantastic. In retrospect, thank heaven it happened."

At the time, however, Riley had his hands full with the emotional issues, the ups and downs of the team's play as 1981 became 1982, but he had a clear message for his players. Sort of.

"I told them to wing it—just like I was doing," he said at the time.

Most important, Johnson was born to wing it and thus happy, which meant Buss was happy. The owner, who took great pride in being a gambler, was clearly quite willing to wing it all, to turn over the fortunes of the team and thus the city itself, to the emotional intelligence and instincts of his young protégé.

"This, I think, is the beginning of Showtime," the owner told *Sports Illustrated,* a remarkable insight for that moment. "At least the curtain is up."

22

THE ART OF RILES

It was back in those days when Jeanie Buss was still a student at Southern Cal, still the owner's teenaged beauty queen daughter (Miss Pacific Palisades) feeling her way around his sports operations and helping where she could to run them.

Handsome Pat Riley was making an ascension of his own when she passed him in the hallway at the team offices one day.

"He was Riles, he was Pat," she remembered in 2020. "He had changed his hairstyle. He'd gone to all of a sudden having the slicked-back hair." Buss flashed her own girlish smile and said, "Hey, Riles . . ."

"He stopped me," she recalled. "He said, 'It's Coach now. We have to call me Coach.' He was fully serious."

Soon enough, instead of quoting Shakespeare, he was citing Sun Tzu's *Art of War* and winding the Lakers into one tightly knit operation, the kind of guy who would say, "You gotta totally get out of yourself and into the unity of the team. The spirit of unity does not guarantee you anything, but without it you can't be successful."

Thus began the miracle transformation of Pat Riley, from slim pickings to Master of the Ritz, from longtime NBA sub to coffee getter and special appearance hustler to radio analyst to assistant coach, then abruptly to NBA head coach and from there on to superstar, cultural icon, and then a darling of New York before becoming a multimillionaire president of the Miami Heat.

Beginning in 1981, Riley's personal transformation was one of the fascinating developments of Showtime, recalled Doug Krikorian in 2004. "I covered him when he was the lowest-paid player among the Lakers, the most humble nice guy. I've never known anyone since I've been covering sports to change more dramatically than Pat Riley. He became like this aristocratic, philosophical, serious person. He was just a regular guy, beer-drinking, nice, typical guy, a jock, and all of a sudden he became this very effete person, espousing all this philosophy and principle."

Jeanie Buss recalled Riley later explaining the moment: "'People know me as the guy getting coffee, the former player,' he said. He talked about how when he got the job he asked, 'How am I going to exert authority?' He thought about his dad and about how his dad was the biggest authority figure in his life. His dad had some Brylcreem and so he decided to change his hairstyle to be more like his dad, to like give him that authority feeling, to kind of change the perception of who he was before and who he was now going to be with the persona that he was going to grow into."

Tim Hallam, the longtime PR director of the Chicago Bulls, recalled the moment in 1988 when Riley nemesis Phil Jackson was promoted to coach Jordan. "You had to have some shit with you to coach Michael," Hallam observed. "And Phil had some shit with him."

The same, of course, could be said of Magic Johnson. To coach him, you had to have some shit with you. And Riley would show that indeed he did have that quality among his possessions. Whatever it was, it was an ambitious approach yet grounded in a humble family background—much like Johnson himself—and it worked. In short time, Riley would become the coaching soul mate to Magic Johnson's big run through the NBA and its annals. It wasn't too long before Riley had taken up the practice of phoning Earv Sr. every now and then just to talk, an approach that would have seemed foreign to Westhead or most other NBA coaches, frankly, but it spoke to a Riley emotional intelligence that approached that of his point guard.

Like both Johnson and Abdul-Jabbar, Riley idolized his father.

Riley's old man, Leon, spent years laboring as a minor league baseball manager and coach. He then went into business and failed, requiring that he work late in life as a school custodian, a station that Riley recalled his father carrying with dignity. The youngest son in the family, Riley was a high school quarterback in Schenectady, New York, and Bear Bryant wanted him to play football at Alabama. But Kentucky's Adolph Rupp talked him into basketball in the bluegrass, where he became an undersized All-American frontcourt player who starred on Rupp's all-white team that lost, in a revelatory moment, to Texas Western with its all-Black starting lineup in the 1966 NCAA championship game. From Kentucky, Riley went on to a nine-year pro career over which he averaged 7.4 points.

"Pat made up for his lack of speed with hustle and drive," recalled Pete Newell, Lakers GM in the 1970s.

Riley injured a knee in 1975, and the Lakers dealt him to Phoenix. "I felt betrayed," he said later. "My only pro blood is Lakers blood. They were the only team I cared about or had a passion for."

Now, just a few years later, he had bizarrely found himself as the team's head coach and had to learn, at Jerry Buss's urging, to exert his will over the roster. It would require both determination and nuance.

At first Riley hadn't been sure he should take Westhead's place. After all, Westhead had given him the chance to be an assistant. Riley did not want to show disloyalty. He sought the advice of West, his old teammate. "Yes," West had said. "Take the job."

"I was numb," Riley said later. "I thought the firing was horrible." Not to mention unfair. "Contrary to what people think, Paul was flexible. He was beginning to make changes in the offense. He was aware there were problems, but he was judged too quickly. It seemed to be the feeling of the media, the fans, the players, and the front office that it wasn't happening fast enough. I think it was more of an emotional decision than anything else."

"The change had been made," former Laker Eddie Jordan would recall. "There was nothing you could do. Riley came in and he was good. Right from the beginning, he was good. I liked him a lot because he always said I was the fireman. I guess that's how he always thought of himself when he was a player. The fireman is always ready, whether he's called on every night or every third night, you're always ready to play. He had motivational techniques that were very new and innovative to the league."

"Pat Riley, what he was able to do was to mold and meld superstars together," Lon Rosen explained. "That's a hard job and he did it."

Not always. Sometimes it was as simple as the fact that Riley liked to have a beer in the hotel bar after games, a routine that harkened back to what had been old-school habits of pro players for years, coaches and players bonding after a game with a brew. It was a foreign thought to Westhead at the time, but to those Lakers in 1981–82 it served as a symbol of the freedom that Riley was bringing to things. In truth, it wasn't just Johnson who felt he had been let out of jail. They all did. Riley ultimately may have had the same goals as Westhead, but he moved toward them with that old-school familiarity.

Besides, as Norm Nixon liked to point out over the years, that team was so good and talented, just about anybody could have coached it. Riley himself soon got an inkling of that when he would get excited about something on the sideline and Johnson would look over at him and signal, "Relax. I got this."

In retrospect, the unity that Riley preached seemed a tailored response to the furtive "Trade Kareem" matchbook covers. He knew he had to pull together a roster that faced forces that could pull it apart. Thus, he focused on keeping the group small, the dozen or so players and four or five staffers, which allowed him to focus on the loyalty of those in the circle.

"He called it the family," Rosen, one of Riley's most ardent admirers, would later note.

In succeeding decades, sports teams would be described as families and brotherhoods, but Riley was among the very first to articulate such a notion, albeit with other nomenclature. In retrospect, it seemed perfectly logical, but the internal competition within a team—for status and statistics and endorsements—is often even greater than the external competition with other teams.

Oddly, Riley accomplished this unity without openly attempting to curry any great relationship with Jerry Buss. He accurately read that the owner's affection was Magic's kingdom.

"He was never close to anybody as much as he was close to Magic," Jeanie Buss said of her father.

It wasn't that the owner and the new coach didn't come to have a great appreciation for each other. They did, but Riley's focus was his team. He was quite aware from his own father's experience that there were only certain things you could control, but you better have a firm grip on those.

There were some nice early results, gained from the mere fumes of Johnson's emotion after the firing. "Before we weren't getting any easy baskets," the star told *Sports Illustrated* in the days after the Westhead meltdown. "Now we're getting the layups, the back-door plays, the fast break. That's the way it should be. If we don't play like this, we're just an average team. I think everybody feels more comfortable now. We're all more relaxed and not worried about making a mistake, about cutting the wrong way or passing to the wrong guy. We can make things happen. We're playing well now, but we're going to get even better. When we're running and playing our game, we're one of the top three teams in the league."

Just as important, that early burst of emotion served to snare the allegiance of staff members.

"Pat's preparation was second to none," Rosen, then the team's newly promoted marketing director, recalled in 2019. "Studying the greats, he was second to none. Relationship building was second to none. Innovation? Oh, my goodness. He was innovating before you even knew what the word was. The guy prepared, like, morning, noon, and night. That's why that team was so well prepared. They were a reflection of him, and he was a reflection of them because he knew what he had."

That early Showtime team was awed by Riley's use of videotape replay, that he brought it right onto the bench and then right out onto the court during timeouts until the league made him back off.

"He brought a TV monitor on the court," Rosen recalled. "They made him take it off the court. He was so ahead of his time."

He would need it all.

In December, power forward Mitch Kupchak, for whom the Lakers had spent a bundle of cash, blew his knee out in a game at San

Diego and was out for the season. Just days after Kupchak went down, Abdul-Jabbar suffered a severe ankle sprain. The injuries left the Lakers weakened in the frontcourt, all while the controversy had left them numb. Faced with this adversity, they responded with a short winning streak, much of it coming from Johnson's emotion. But it was clear that enthusiasm could only carry them so far.

The rebounding problems would continue, even after Abdul-Jabbar returned to the lineup, until Lakers assistant coach Dave Wohl came up with a perfect addition—thirty-year-old free agent Bob McAdoo, who while playing in Boston, Buffalo, and Detroit had been branded as selfish. Sharman, though, focused on the talent. McAdoo had a league MVP award and two scoring titles under his belt.

"I was coming off a foot surgery, and I wasn't even sure I was gonna be able to play again," McAdoo would recall. "When I first got there, every time they introduced Magic he was getting booed. I said, 'Wow, this team won the championship a year ago, and now they're booing one of the star players.'"

The other unexpected aid came with the emergence of power forward Kurt Rambis, the supposed Clark Kent look-alike and free agent. Not long after Kupchak went down, Rambis got an unexpected start and responded with 14 rebounds. The Lakers needed his hustle, his defense, his rebounding, and his physical play. Johnson would recall that he just couldn't pass to Rambis on the run because it seemed he would travel every time, but the other chores got done.

Riley astutely made the fast break the team's top option. Still, there were problems aplenty. The Lakers fell back between January and March, barely playing .500 ball.

"Don't be afraid to coach the team," Jerry Buss finally told Riley in one meeting.

That may have seemed like an obvious solution, but Westhead's departure had created a vacuum of sorts.

"I was giving the players too much responsibility," Riley explained later of his move to assert himself, marked when the team lost at home to Chicago on March 12.

"I got fed up," he would explain. "I didn't know what I wanted to do when I took the job. I looked at the players and I respected their games so much and I respected them as people. I gave them too much trust. I said, 'This is their team.' It was their team, but they needed direction. That's my job. It took me three months to realize it, but I have certain responsibilities to push and demand. They have to play. I have to coach. They were waiting for me to put my foot down. That's my nature anyhow."

The players, indeed the entire fan base, seemed relieved.

"Pat was new to the job, but he had done his homework well," McAdoo, a longtime Riley admirer, said in 2004. "He knew the talent because he had been around, seeing the guys from the booth, or seeing them from the bench. He knew what he had, but he kind of freelanced it a lot. He let us show our talents. He didn't get in our way, saying, 'You gotta be here on the court.' He didn't X and O us to death. Things were organized, but we were a freewheeling bunch, because there was a lot of talent out there on that floor. You look back now, I'm in the Hall of Fame, James Worthy's in the Hall of Fame, Magic's in the Hall of Fame, Kareem. You had four Hall of Famers on one team."

From that corrective moment, they finished the regular season with a best-in-the-West 57–25 record. Better yet, they surged as the playoffs opened by showing Jack McKinney's flexibility of using either Nixon or Johnson to run the break, which doubled their potency.

"It was very nice to be able to get the ball off the board," McAdoo remembered. "You didn't have to really look for your point guard. You just turned and you just threw it. It was either Magic or Norm, either one of them. Whatever side they were on, or whatever side you turned to, you just threw it, and our fast break started through one of those two guys. Most teams your fast break started with one guy. In L.A., it was turn and go."

Johnson's emotional firing of his own coach had paid off because Johnson himself had made sure it would. "The crowds still get me going," he said toward the end of the regular season. "They still jack me up. And I still love the game. I don't think I'll ever lose that."

"Magic has become a great player," Jerry West told the writers. "I've watched him go from one level to another, higher level this year.

He's become solid; that's the big thing. He's in control out there. He knows what he's doing every minute he's on the floor."

West was watching him take the final steps in becoming not just a full-time point guard, but a great one. The Lakers won 21 of their final 24 games, fueled by Johnson and lifted by Riley's decision to use McAdoo heavily.

"We had a playoff run that was just unbelievable," McAdoo recalled.

They would break loose, sweeping nine straight playoff games before finally closing out the championship with a record-tying 12 wins against only two losses.

Despite a 63–19 record in 1982, the defending champion Celtics had fallen yet again to Philadelphia, this time in a seven-game Eastern Conference finals, bringing another delay of Johnson and Bird's anticipated meeting in the championship series. Johnson and the Lakers watched this drama on the tube, having dispatched Phoenix and San Antonio, 4–0 each.

The Spurs series had allowed Johnson to face one of his youthful Michigan idols, George Gervin, but it was brief. Their last game against the Spurs ended a full twelve days before Philly finished off Boston. Rather than get rusty, they worked two-a-days in practice and battled each other to pass the time.

"That's the best thing about this team," Riley said, "the work ethic."

This time, the Lakers of 1982 had improved dramatically, former Sixer Lionel Hollins recalled in 2019. "The second time we played the Lakers for the title, they were a much better team. Oh, my goodness, it was incredible. I mean, it was a blur going up and down the court, that second time around. They had added more pieces that fit that style, and they were even better at it."

Julius Erving was thirty-two as the 1982 playoffs opened, and he was making his third trip to the Finals since coming to the NBA in 1976, with his team fighting the perception that his talent was going to waste. For 1982, Erving might have been able to lead his team past Bird, but asking him to then turn around and do the same against an intensely motivated Johnson?

Philadelphia had the home-court advantage in the 1982 Finals, but the Lakers had their nifty zone trap, devised by assistant Bill Bertka, which they produced at just the right time in the opener at the Spectrum on Thursday, May 27. Zone defenses were illegal in that era, so the trap had to be well-enough disguised to avoid a technical foul. As it was, the trap was perfect for Johnson's length and the Lakers' overall athleticism.

The 76ers worked their offense to precision until midway through the third period when the Lakers unleashed their weapons. At the time, Philadelphia led by 15, but over the next 11 minutes or so, Johnson and company ripped through a 40–9 blitz. The overwhelmed 76ers fell, 124–117.

Afterward, Billy Cunningham complained that the Lakers' trap was a thinly disguised zone.

Aware of every little comment in his chess match with the opponent, Riley then decided to back off the trap a bit for Game 2. "The officials read the papers, too," he explained.

"They got away with that zone trap a lot," explained Herb Williams, longtime pro and friend of Johnson, in a 2004 interview. "A lot of people were pissed about that, because they would be playing in zone areas and not playing man. The referees had a tendency not to call things as much against them. You got Magic at six-nine, Worthy at six-nine, Kareem at seven foot, Rambis at six-nine, six-ten. They had a very long and very athletic team. Once they turned you over, you knew the ball was going to 32, and they were pushing it the other way."

So, with the zone trap getting unwanted attention, Riley switched Johnson to cover Erving on defense.

"I've always been his fan," Johnson said of the Doctor. "I respect him. I'm in awe of him."

Erving earned that respect again in Game 2 and brought the 76ers back with 24 points and 16 rebounds for a 110–94 win that evened the series at one-all.

The Lakers then dominated the next two games in the Forum. Nixon led a parade in Game 3 with 29. Again, the zone trap was Philly's undoing, 129–108. In fact, it worked so well, the Lakers employed it again in Game 4 to take a 111–101 win. Down 3–1, the 76ers seemed finished. But they managed in Game 5 to pin an embarrassment on Kareem, holding him to just six points, his lowest total since 1977–78 when he had been ejected from a game for punching Kent Benson. Afterward the Lakers center made his exit without speaking with the media. The league liked to enforce its media protocols, but as Ron Carter said, no one challenged Kareem.

Philadelphia had closed it to 3–2, but had to return to the Forum for Game 6, where the Lakers got the lead early. The 76ers held L.A. to 20 points for the third quarter and several times cut the lead to one. "I had a few butterflies about then," said Jamaal Wilkes, who led six Lakers in double figures with 27. The Lakers held on and then surged to boost their lead to 11 early in the fourth period. Philly again responded and with a little under four minutes to go trimmed the edge to 103–100. But Abdul-Jabbar completed a three-point play to put L.A. up by six. At the end, Wilkes got a breakaway layup to close it out, 114–104.

Johnson had played out the season under immense pressure, having fired his coach and absorbed months of negative reaction. Winning the title had wiped all of that away.

"There were two times in that finals the ball never touched the floor, coast-to-coast," Steve Springer recalled, summing up the Showtime that was emerging before his eyes. "To me, that was the greatest aspect ever, I think. That's also why there was this frustration because you've got the greatest scorer of all time with the most unstoppable shot. But for him to function it has to be a half-court game. So, Riley did it the best. He wasn't going to turn his back on Kareem, but you have the two best approaches ever, and you could use either one."

That was once again emphasized by the MVP selection.

Johnson with 13 points, 13 rebounds, and 13 assists in Game 6 was named the series MVP.

"There were times earlier in the year when I didn't think this would be possible," Wilkes said with champagne on his face. "We had so many unhappy people around here you wouldn't believe it."

Viewed suspiciously by the rest of the league, Jerry Buss had been an NBA owner for three seasons and had won two titles.

By 1982, the league was looking for a solution to the fact that

Buss was basically operating two pro basketball teams out of the offices of Mariani-Buss Associates. *The Boston Globe* published a series that took a deep look at the NBA, which still had an alarming number of teams said to be losing money, even with the presence of Bird and Johnson. The series also highlighted a serious violation of the league's competitive integrity and made public the fact that Frank Mariani was treasurer of the Lakers while owning a minority share of the Indiana Pacers, even as Buss controlled a majority of the lease for Market Square Arena.

With the *Globe* series setting the public agenda, the NBA Board of Governors promptly announced an investigation of Buss and his business associates. Not long after, Sam Nassi and Mariani sold the Pacers.

The NBA had long been a league with its power based in the Northeast, with the media and entertainment centers of New York and Boston and Philadelphia. But Johnson and Buss were well on their way to altering that landscape and shifting the focus west, across the time zones.

Forget any messiness, Johnson's arrival had swiftly transformed L.A. from a mausoleum into a party.

Rich Getting Richer

In the aftermath of another title, another parade, another round of euphoria, all of it with Johnson's smile serving as the headlight on the Lakers' happy train, it soon was time again for Buss to add to his collection of riches.

Because the Lakers had traded Don Ford to Cleveland during the 1979–80 season, they now had the Cavaliers' first-round pick for 1982. For a time, Sharman and West considered high-flying Dominique Wilkins, out of the University of Georgia. He was so exciting, yet, ultimately, they decided North Carolina's James Worthy would be far better equipped with his great variety of skills and ability to play both forwards as well as shooting guard. Best of all were his speed and moves, which would allow him to reach the Hall of Fame as the finisher on Magic Johnson's wide array of feeds and passes.

"It looked like we were going to need a small forward first," Jerry West recalled. "I thought James and Dominique were the two players we should consider. It was very difficult not to take on Dominique Wilkins. Very difficult. Because we played in Showtime, and he was a Showtime player. And a great player."

"I knew it was going to be special as soon as I was drafted," Worthy recalled in 1992. "For two years I had watched Earvin just kill teams with his passing. I used to watch Jamaal Wilkes and Coop get out on the wing, and I knew I was gonna benefit from Earvin. I didn't realize then how much. But I knew it was going to be good running the break with somebody who could deliver it to you at the right time."

"James Worthy was the next big six-nine player who played like a six-two player," Michael Cooper would explain.

The 1982–83 Lakers would thus boast a deep roster. Johnson, Nixon, and Cooper in the backcourt. Rambis, Wilkes, Worthy, and McAdoo at the forwards. Perhaps best of all, Abdul-Jabbar was in the last year of his contract and playing like a man who wanted to reap millions, the only problem being that his agent, Tom Collins, and Buss soon engaged in bickering over a new deal. Each day brought increasing speculation that Kareem's days as a Laker were growing short, that the Trade Kareem matchbook covers might see reality.

The Lakers would run off to a 34–9 start to the 1982–83 season and had just finished a loss to the Celtics in Boston when the bad news came. Abdul-Jabbar's Bel Air mansion had burned to the ground, taking with it his personal sports memorabilia and vast collections of Oriental rugs, jazz albums, and books. His longtime girlfriend, Cheryl Pistono, and their son, Amir, had escaped unhurt. But the loss was in excess of $3 million. The team captain took the next flight to L.A. while the Lakers went on to Dallas. The media immediately speculated that the loss of his home might make it easier for Abdul-Jabbar to leave Los Angeles.

Riley and West figured that Abdul-Jabbar would need at least a week to get his personal life in order. But he flew to Dallas before that Wednesday's game and then scored a season-high 34 points.

"It's absolutely incredible to me that he'd come here under these conditions," remarked West, who was traveling with the team. "You know why greatness endures when you look inside a person."

Showing up meant that the Lakers center was there for the immediate fan response to the disaster. Beginning in Dallas that night and lasting months afterward, people would come forward in NBA cities to present him with records and books to replace those he lost. Josh Rosenfeld, former Lakers PR director, recalled the center being almost stunned that first night in Dallas when a young fan gave him an Ella Fitzgerald record.

"Kareem was showered with a lot of love and a lot of heartfelt concern for the first time in his entire career," Riley said. "I don't think he had ever seen that before."

Yet all the support couldn't prevent the Lakers' momentum from slipping after the fire. They finished 58–24, good enough again for best in the West. But their hopes for a repeat championship suffered dramatically again a week before the playoffs when Worthy jumped for a tip-in against the Suns and fractured his leg just below the knee.

Without him, Johnson and the Lakers were able to stifle Portland and then San Antonio in the Western playoffs. They were up 3–1 against the Spurs and should have ended it in Game 5 in the Forum, but they lost and had to return to San Antonio for a sixth game, where McAdoo got hurt. The cumulative damage added up in the 1983 championship round against Philadelphia. Determined to finally win a title, 76ers owner Harold Katz had acquired Moses Malone, the scoring/rebounding machine, from the Houston Rockets. Thus armed, the 76ers had run through the regular season schedule with a 65–17 record. When writers asked Malone how the 76ers would fare in the playoffs, he offered his famous "fo, fo, and fo" prediction. They had swept the Knicks in the Eastern semifinals and lost a single game to the Milwaukee Bucks in the conference finals before moving on to the NBA Finals to face the Lakers for the third time in four years.

The championship round brought yet more woes, however. Nixon went down with injuries. Without help, Abdul-Jabbar found himself in a situation similar to the one that had frustrated him so during the late 1970s. Malone dominated the boards, outrebounding Kareem 72 to 30 over the course of the series, and the Lakers dropped in line with Philly's other victims.

Magic and company could do nothing to stop the sweep, and in the aftermath, the team decided to trade Norm Nixon, a move that Jerry West, looking back on his life in a 2008 interview, described as his most difficult. It would mean, West said, that Nixon and his wife, stage and screen star Debbie Allen, would hate him forever.

At the time, Nixon and Allen seemed fueled by the notion they were being persecuted for alleged drug use, as Ron Carter and others from the era recalled. But West said he felt he had to make the deal to give Johnson the ball full-time to reach his vast potential. Finally, Johnson was the team's point guard. The timing seemed right.

"Norm Nixon was a very good point guard," Bob Steiner observed, looking back at the tug-of-war between Johnson and Nixon. "That was a struggle. Both guys had to give up something from their games and ultimately that got to Norm. Norm was quoted as saying, 'Look what I had to give up to play with Magic.' Never once did Earvin say, 'Look what I had to give up . . .' That was a dark moment. That was put aside, among the many things in Lakers history. Norm and Earvin were the backcourt of two championship teams."

Largely, the trade was an event mostly defined by what Johnson didn't do. He didn't use his influence with Jerry Buss to stop it.

Summer Runs

The revelation that was Earvin Johnson soon demonstrated that he wasn't just all about controlling the Lakers. Almost immediately, upon his arrival in the city the young phenomenon from Lansing had begun haunting the storied, elite levels of L.A.'s pickup basketball culture. And it wasn't long before he had taken over there, too, in dictating how the games would be played.

"Magic was so difficult to play against," recalled Reggie Theus, who like a lot of pro and college players with Los Angeles connections began running into Johnson at pickup games over at UCLA, something that mirrored the kind of high-test pickup connection that Johnson had discovered at Jenison Field House as a young teen and in his battles with Charles Tucker. Johnson had wanted to play in college at UCLA until his canceled recruiting visit. Now it almost seemed he was out to make the place his anyway.

"For him, losing was not an option," Theus remembered of the pickup version of Magic. "He would do anything to win. You had to call your own fouls, and if you even breathed on him the wrong way, he'd call a foul. If you guarded him tight, you had to throw your hands up so there was no way he could call a foul."

It required a rare persona to get away with such a tactic, Reggie Theus observed. "Magic Johnson is one of the only guys who I've ever been around in my life that when he walks into the room, the energy automatically picks up. When he walked into a gym, the games that were going on automatically started to get more intense. He had that kind of effect on everybody."

"He played at UCLA," remembered Kiki Vandeweghe, who was a pro in that era and also had been a Bruin in college. "We had pickup games in the old gym, which is a tradition they still carry on today. . . . It was an amazing time to be a basketball player in Los Angeles and come there to play in the summer against some great players. He just had a court presence about him. You could tell right away. That's the first thing. The second thing, he was one of the guys. He laughed and joked with everybody. Obviously, he enjoyed playing very, very much. That stood out right away, too. Just the joy he had in playing and being around basketball. But when games started, it was all business."

Especially if you happened to tick him off, which revealed Johnson to be the alpha male of alpha males.

"For the most part, he would pick his team," Theus remembered with a laugh, "and if you didn't play the game the right way, he would actually kick you off the team and pick up another guy. And those guys were all pros. These were all real guys. These were all real players. It was pretty amazing."

Even so, many of the people who played in those summer runs with Johnson considered it a special experience, Vandeweghe explained. "It's hard to describe his love for the game unless you've been on the court with him. Many people who have seen him play can sense the joy he played with. But he just had a special kind of joy that he brought that translated to anybody who watched him play or competed against him. His enthusiasm for the game was just palpable."

Johnson hadn't been in Los Angeles long before the city's hoops crowd knew where to track him down in the summer to watch competition that was every bit as intense as an NBA game, sometimes more so.

"We'd have a gym full of spectators in the men's gym at Pauley Pavilion," Theus recalled. "The great thing about those pickup games was that it was all about winning those games."

Matching up meant not just size but intensity with Johnson, Vandeweghe pointed out. "He came to play every single day. . . . And he came typically with his own team, meaning his teammates from the Lakers. And they played hard. He demanded they play hard and take it seriously every day."

"Every day," Theus said. "And sometimes twice a day. A lot of times, we'd all work out together. We'd do weights, we'd run on the track, run the bleachers, we'd go shoot, we'd go play, go eat. And then come back and do it again. I'm not saying Magic was there all the time, but he was there a lot. You'd have a gym full of players. There was probably fifteen to twenty real NBA players in the gym."

As Johnson aged, his pickup play would become even more important, as Greg Foster witnessed first as a UCLA player later in the decade. "I was privy to those summer runs by just being at UCLA," Foster recalled in 2019. "Our UCLA five would play, and Magic would walk in with the Lakers' starting five. There would be guys from all around the league. So, for a young kid like me, it was like, 'Wow.'"

In some ways, the summer games were a place to witness Johnson's full game, the one he rarely trotted out in an NBA game, the one that had allowed him to take over Game 6 in 1980, recalled Foster, a longtime NBA player and coach. "Everybody thinks of him as a pass-first guy, but I can tell you that in those summer games he could score as well as anybody. If he wanted to score 40 points a game, he could have easily done that. His level of conditioning was second to none. He worked his ass off to be the player he was. Another thing I always remember about him is that he always worked on a facet of his game. Like, one summer, literally, he was working on his left-handed running hook. The majority of his shots that he took around the rim was those left-handed shots. And he was deadly with it. I was really amazed at his work ethic. Every day he worked out. He ran in the mornings and worked out in the afternoons."

For the young guys, either at UCLA or just coming into the league, there was another great benefit to going at it in the summer with Johnson.

"He always had the greatest pool parties in the summer," Foster recalled. "Just incredible parties. At his place. He would clear out all the furniture. His inner circle would be there. A ton of people would show up and hang out."

The parties may have carried a wild image, but, ever the businessman, Johnson had found sponsorship even for his good times. "There were coolers all over the place, and towels," Foster remembered. "They were handing out free Pepsi towels to us. . . . I just remember I had an incredible time at those parties. Again, for a young kid, just fresh to the NBA, I thought I was in heaven."

23

THE LARRY THING

The anticipation had been building for four long NBA seasons. Then in 1984, it finally happened. Two dudes, one Black, one white, who were competitive mirror images of each other, renewed their rivalry just in time to land again in the cultural crosshairs. It proved to be very good for basketball, good for the NBA, good for the 1980s, and immensely refreshing for the world at large.

Most important, the rivalry of Johnson and Bird would reassert itself with another burst of perfect timing for the long, ugly, sorrowful swath that is race in America.

In the many discussions of what would become known as the Showtime era in basketball, the cliché had been offered that the characters were from the pages of a script, that Hollywood couldn't have dreamed up a more perfect plot.

Actually, Hollywood already had, with the 1958 film *The Defiant Ones,* starring Sidney Poitier and Tony Curtis, about two escaped convicts, one Black, one white, chained together on the run, chased by bloodhounds and the judgment of a very racist society. The film, way ahead of the times, won many, many awards.

It was often said of Bird and Johnson over the years, as their battle for championships unfolded, that they were "inextricably linked," chained together, if you will, by their karma, which would become basketball's karma, and ultimately for an important period of time, America's karma.

"We are linked forever," Johnson would say in renewing his vows at his Hall of Fame induction in 2002.

They were both from the middle of the country. Bird with his impoverished background in the basketball breadbasket of Indiana, Johnson with his family climbing out of another sort of centuries-long poverty, represented two forces in the culture that had long clashed for opportunity, jobs, identity, respect, whatever meager gains that were to be had by America's large underclass of workers. It should be pointed out that these battles between Black and white people had been fought in intermittent spasms of riots and massacres and violence that seemed to have played on an endless loop through the entire course of the country's history.

In the midst of this larger tension, the two men would engage in an intense, exemplary, unprecedented, and very public rivalry.

Johnson's friends would recall that he absolutely hated Bird in the early days, a sentiment that the star himself would quietly confirm on occasion. In the end, despite all their differences, their competition would make them first grudging admirers, then slowly and eventually genuine and loving friends.

As the Lakers' scorekeeper for nearly five decades, John Radcliffe was there to witness so many of their showdowns. Basketball was never better, he would say, looking back on the Bird-Johnson battles. "He was a great conversationalist on the floor," Radcliffe said of Bird. "I think Magic got a kick out of that. He thoroughly enjoyed it. It kind of pumped him up even more."

A huge part of their "linkage" would become the infernal vexation they would visit upon one another.

At his Hall of Fame induction in 2002, Johnson recalled a game in Boston Garden where he was injured and had to sit on the bench in street clothes, which made him a perfect target.

"They're warming up down by our bench," he recalled of the

Celtics with Bird in the layup line. "The last time he comes around, he says, 'Magic, don't you worry. I'm going to put on a show for you.' He went out and scored 40 points, got 20, 22 rebounds, nine, 10 assists. Just ate us up. Missed like three shots."

Bird kissed off the performance with a final swish from range, Johnson remembered. "So just after he hits that deep one in the corner, I'm sitting right there, you know that deep three where he just watches it go in?"

"Magic, that one's for you," Bird turned and told him.

Boston's star knew well the depths of such torment.

"Losing to the Lakers was the worst feeling you could ever have," Bird explained as Johnson's presenter for the Hall of Fame ceremony. "I remember flying back all night after a playoff loss being so disgusted I couldn't sleep and couldn't care less if the plane crashed or not."

He remembered seeing Johnson trapped in a similar despair walking away through the parking lot after a Boston victory in L.A. "I could see the pain in his face, the look in his eyes that he was a beaten man that day," Bird recalled. "I was just watching and I'm going, 'Suffer, baby, suffer.' I knew he'd probably go home, shut off all the lights, pull down the blinds and sit in that dark room for hours. I know. Because I've been there."

Through such misery, their relationship remained testy even though the kinship was obvious.

"We were the slowest two guys in the world, and we could jump this high," Johnson said during the Hall of Fame moment, measuring off two inches with his index finger and thumb. "But we knew how to play with our heads. We were winners. If Larry and I had played on the same team, there would have been no championship for anybody else."

He would suffer the mistake of making the same comment nearly two decades earlier, before the 1984 championship series. Before they were real friends. Before they even knew each other all that well. And Johnson would soon rue it immensely.

"Larry and I really appreciate each other now," Johnson had told reporters that May. "The competition was pretty intense. There was definitely something there, but that's over with now. He's a thinking man's player."

The moment brought the opportunity for Johnson to remind the media that he and Bird were teammates on that obscure international exhibition team coached by Kentucky's Joe B. Hall. "Larry and I didn't get a chance to play together much," Johnson remembered then, as he and Bird were about to launch their first battle for an NBA championship. "We were sitting on the bench most of the time. But when Larry and I got in together we did it all. We always took a lead or made it bigger. . . . If we played together now, I think you'd have to give us all the championships."

Fast-forward the two decades, and Bird would recall that same experience at Johnson's Hall of Fame ceremony. He remembered going home after the Joe B. Hall fiasco and telling his brother that he'd just seen the best player ever and that that player was two years younger.

"Get out of here," his brother had replied.

When Johnson and Bird met at the NCAA championship a year later, Bird's brother was there, saw what he had been talking about, and told him, "Yeah, he's a lot better than you."

They would meet just 38 times in the NBA, including 19 playoff games. Johnson went for 20.2 points, 7.3 rebounds, and 12.3 assists in those engagements. Bird put up 23.4 points, 10.8 rebounds, and 5.3 assists. They each won three MVP awards, but a broader measure of their impact would be the number of times they would finish in the top three of MVP voting.

Johnson finished among the top three nine times in his thirteen seasons. LeBron James, as of 2022, had finished in the top three more than anyone, eleven times in twenty seasons. Jordan had managed to finish in the top three ten times over fifteen seasons.

Bill Russell, like Johnson, finished in the top three nine times in thirteen seasons, as did Kareem, who played twenty-one seasons.

Larry Bird would finish in the top three eight times in his thirteen seasons.

For Johnson and Bird, their real measure would be championships.

And whatever their individual rivalry, it would always be cast dead in the middle of what was easily the NBA's greatest team rivalry, brutally dominated by the Celtics during the 1960s only to be revived and challenged by Johnson and his Lakers in the 1980s.

"It was different between the Lakers and the Celtics," Johnson said in 2004.

Former Celtic Jerry Sichting had gotten an indication of the intensity in 1985 when he became Bird's teammate. For years, off and on, the Lakers and Celtics had engaged each other in an extensive preseason series, dating back to the 1960s when the teams traveled about in touring cars.

"The first year I came to Boston, the Celtics and Lakers played each other four times in the preseason," Sichting recalled. "The second game was in the Forum. During that game, Maurice Lucas and Robert Parish got into it. Both benches emptied. I remember that when they began breaking it up, K. C. Jones was at the bottom of the pile and had Michael Cooper in a headlock. That's the first time I had ever seen an NBA coach in a fight with one of the players. But that was the Celtics and Lakers."

"The good thing is, the Celtics did it their way, and we've done it our way," Johnson said in 2004. "It's in a Hollywood style, showy, flashy, yet with a lot of substance. We wanted to run and put on a show. The Celtics and Larry did it their way to help shape and mold basketball."

At the center of the rivalry were two guys dragging around a very complicated chain.

"Alone, they are men," Jeff Jacobs observed in *The Hartford Courant*, a publication that had long preached the Gospel of the Celtics in New England, upon Johnson's Hall of Fame induction. "Together, they are athletic gods. Alone, they were brilliant basketball players. Together, they saved the league."

"You can write this down," Johnson offered. "There's never been basketball like the Lakers and Celtics played. Never. I don't know if there ever will be."

Never would that be more apparent than in the sizzling heat of late June smack-dab in the middle of the 1980s.

The best thing about it was that it was not scripted. It was just basketball, what Celtics boss Red Auerbach had long called the mystery of the game, the smooth floor, the round ball, the two hoops, the 94-foot court. It was a meeting place that required very large hearts. History would show that Bird and Johnson and their teammates were all too happy to provide those.

When It Rained Dimes

"Dime" over the years became the slang in basketball vernacular for an assist.

When Jerry West traded Norm Nixon to the Clippers just before training camp opened in 1983, it meant that Earvin Johnson would become the man to pass out more shiny new dimes over the coming season than ol' John D. Rockefeller himself.

It didn't hurt that the deal sending Nixon and Eddie Jordan to the Clippers had brought the rights to unsigned draft pick Byron Scott. Scott was not as good a ball handler as Nixon, but his presence didn't complicate the offense with two guards in a tug-of-war over the ball. An excellent shooter, Scott knew how to play off the ball and would become a target of many of those Johnson assists. He would soon be known for finding the space to spot up, then waiting for Johnson to drive, then catching the kick pass when Johnson drew the double-team. From there, it was merely a matter of hitting the open shot, which Scott could sure enough do.

Before that happened, however, there was the matter of the Lakers' complicated history. Yes, Johnson and Nixon had their tension on the court, but Nixon was still a figure beloved by all his teammates.

"I caught a lot of trouble," Scott recalled in 1992. "Norm had been traded, and the people in Los Angeles weren't happy about it. And the team didn't seem real happy. They thought they'd been betrayed and were losing a friend."

After all, Nixon and Johnson had come to be considered the best backcourt in all of basketball, with two titles in three trips to the NBA championship series in four years. Breaking up such a winning combo seemed absolutely crazy at the time. When you added Cooper to the mix, the Lakers had broken up a trio that fancied itself as very special.

"It all came down to me, a rookie who had nothing to do with it," Scott recalled. "Earvin and Cooper were the two that gave me the most trouble, because Norm was very close to both of them. Mostly it was just pushing and shoving, things like that. Taunting and talking, trying to make me upset."

As a rookie, Scott faced a traditional hazing that required he run errands and do favors for the veterans. Johnson and Cooper displayed some zeal in their handling of the matter.

"I think they took it a little bit overboard," Scott recalled, "but I never complained and kept doing what I could until one day Coop threw an elbow."

"You throw another one, I'm gonna throw one back," Scott told him.

From that point on, Johnson and Cooper began to offer him little tidbits of respect.

"Earvin told me they had done it, number one, to see if I could play; number two, to see what kind of heart I had; and number three, to see if I could fit in," Scott recalled.

Johnson finally declared that Scott had passed the audition.

The circumstances had made clear to the rookie what anyone ever engaged with those Laker teams came to find, that the man in charge was Johnson, running the entire show and doing it his way.

Scott's presence and the fact that Johnson was now the team's exclusive central playmaker would soon bring a dizzying array of big performances. In mid-November, he notched what was then a career-high 22 assists, scored 23 points, and grabbed a team-high nine rebounds in a home win over Cleveland, bringing his assist average over the first four weeks of the season to a league-leading 14.1 a game.

Even better, his big assist moment marked the sixth win in a row for the Lakers. In five straight home games, Johnson averaged 20.2 points, shot 75 percent from the field, and averaged 16.6 assists and 8.2 rebounds.

"I don't think Magic has improved," Riley told reporters, delivering the message that he knew Johnson wanted him to deliver.

"Don't take me wrong on that. But he showed he can play this well when he was a rookie. We knew all along he was a great player. He just has the ability to turn it on and rise to the occasion, that's what he's doing now. He takes the load of responsibility on his shoulders. We want to keep the ball in his hands, and he's happy to have it. There are a lot of teams in the NBA that just can't defense against Magic."

"I knew I would have to do more when Norm left," Johnson acknowledged during his early success that season. "Pat made that clear to me and I felt I could do more. My main role is to orchestrate the offense, that's what I do best. I never worry about the points, but I've been getting them anyway."

Even with all the gaudy numbers and his sense of total control, Johnson had discovered one huge setback to Nixon's departure. "I can't run wild anymore," he would say of the style that marked his launch into the league. "I can't go to the offensive boards or roam around looking for ways to take over. It's very frustrating right now, but, hopefully, it'll change soon."

His frustration drove his impatience with Scott. "He's been slow," Johnson admitted. "But he'll be all right. This is a learning process for every player when he comes in. Just in my four years, I learned so much about the game, stuff that I never even considered. It's tough. I know what he's got to be going through."

Scott would slowly begin to raise the team's three-point shooting percentage, which wasn't much of a challenge. The year before, the Lakers had set an NBA record for the lowest three-point shooting percentage in a season when they made just 10 of 96 shots from distance for 10.4 percent. Johnson had done his part, missing all 21 of his trey attempts.

If nothing else, the numbers would reflect just how much the game would change in the twenty-first century with the rules and the pace and the use of analytics ushering in an age dominated by the three-pointer.

Back in November 1983, however, Johnson was averaging 15.1 assists a game, good enough to get him named the NBA's Player of the Month. At the time, the league's all-time single-season record was 13.4 assists per game, set by Kevin Porter of Detroit in 1979.

Johnson had also averaged 18.1 points, 8.0 rebounds, and 2.4 steals per outing over that November.

Yet on the very first day of December against Dallas, Johnson suffered a painful dislocation of his right index finger and would be ruled out for weeks, possibly as much as two months again, a development that rocked Jerry Buss.

"I recall specifically that when he injured his finger my dad brought him home," Jeanie Buss recalled, "and he said, 'We have to cheer him up. He's taking this really hard.' And so, my dad was very in tune, not just with the physical part but also the emotional part of Earvin. And he took it upon himself to make sure that his head stayed clear and he didn't get down or didn't get discouraged. My dad had that sense, you know. He knew when Earvin needed to be cheered up or when he needed to put his arms around him to make sure that he didn't lose him."

Her father seemed to sense a fragility in Johnson at that moment, Jeanie Buss recalled in 2020. "I don't think I've ever heard the word *insecure* in conjunction with Earvin. It doesn't even make sense to think of him like that."

But her father, Jeanie Buss said, "just gravitated toward things that other people didn't see. He was a good dad, a good teacher, and he knew when Earvin needed a shoulder to lean on. And my dad was always there for him."

That closeness, however, wouldn't prevent Johnson from responding emotionally just days later in late December when he traveled with the Lakers to Detroit, still injured with a cast on his hand, and was asked about his contract. By that point, the NBA's rapidly changing financial structure had eclipsed what had seemed like Johnson's huge new contract from 1981, even though that contract hadn't even been scheduled to go into effect until 1984.

"I have to be paid what the other top players are being paid," Johnson told *The Detroit News*.

The newspaper and wire services were reporting that Philadelphia's Moses Malone now made $2.16 million a year, that Larry Bird made $2.14 million annually, while Kareem made $1.65 million a season.

"If I'm paid like they are, I'll be happy and everything will be fine," Johnson said. "I don't want to renegotiate now; all I want to do is win the championship. But I do want to be paid what I think I deserve."

Soon enough word would leak out that Buss and George Andrews had been in contract talks since November. "I don't want to sound like I'm rocking the boat," Johnson said. "Our team has got enough problems to overcome without something like this. At this point, I don't want to start nothing."

His comments in Detroit made the wire services, based on the image of his 1981 contract. To the public, it seemed crazy that the Lakers' supposed "twenty-five-million-dollar" star was already asking for more money.

However Buss clearly understood the situation and was again ready to pony up for Johnson.

It was a friendship in an age just beginning to explore a more liberal mind-set. And it was not a one-way friendship. Johnson, too, was keen to complicated events unfolding for the owner that would soon leave Buss charged with racketeering, the sort of charges usually reserved for mob figures and gangsters. It would all serve to enforce three or more parallel narratives in the life of Jerry Buss, one of them being a caring and deeply engaged owner of an immensely talented sports team. That competed with another narrative, that he was a playboy and a card player and a gambler and a womanizer who pushed the boundaries of propriety with his routine, almost antiseptic, targeting of young women. Yet another narrative cast him as a brilliant investor and academic, which in turn dovetailed into yet another narrative, the slightest sense that there could be something very tough, even cold, something almost sinister or menacing about him, a view leavened immensely by his often genuine approach with the people around him.

If Earvin Johnson was a big head-scratcher in terms of his persona, his team owner would long remain an even bigger one.

Steve Springer recalled that as he stepped into the job of covering the team, he began to hear from an anonymous source within the Lakers organization. Springer never disclosed the name of the source that was feeding him information. But one of the informant's early tips was that Buss would soon be charged in Arizona with racketeering. Springer broke the story, which was immediately picked up by a Los Angeles television station, a report that served to embarrass Jerry Buss quite a bit.

"This guy was in the Laker organization," Springer said of his source in a 2019 interview, "and I don't know what his motivation was. He never exactly told me what it was. No one ever found out. I never revealed his name anywhere. He told me to look into Jerry Buss's real estate holdings in Arizona."

Springer went to Arizona and learned the issue involved millions in unpaid property taxes.

After the story appeared, one of Buss's aides called and told Springer, "Dr. Buss would like you to come to lunch at Pickfair."

Buss had wrapped up renovations on the mansion and was living there.

The invitation had an eeriness about it, to the point that before he left to meet Buss, Springer told his wife, "I don't know if I'm coming back."

"I was kind of kidding," he recalled.

The reporter arrived at Pickfair and was seated at a large table that could have easily accommodated thirty-five people. But the lunch involved just four, Buss, his assistant, Springer, and a server wearing white gloves.

"He looked across the table at me and he says, 'You know, if I'd known you had that story, I'd have given you $100,000 not to run it,'" Springer recalled.

"I didn't know what to say," the writer recalled. "Well, Jerry," Springer remembered finally offering, "if it cost you a million, and you are only offering me a hundred thousand, that's kind of cheap."

"He laughed and we became the best of friends," Springer recalled. "He said to me, 'Good for you. You did your job. I admire that. You beat me fair and square, and I won't forget it.'"

And he never did. Two or three years later, Buss would be immensely helpful in a book Springer was writing with Scott Ostler about the Lakers. And years later the owner advised daughter Jeanie to use Springer as a coauthor on her own book.

"He was always there for me, would give me an interview when nobody else would," Springer explained in 2019. "That just amazed me. That was unbelievable."

As for the racketeering charges? They soon enough went away. Buss assistant Ron Carter would explain much later that the incident was largely his own fault for taking excessive tax breaks on large bundles of residential real estate loans that Buss owned in Arizona. An aggressive prosecutor had responded to the situation by hitting Buss with the racketeering charge, which made headlines but disappeared as soon as Buss paid the back taxes.

Carter would explain that Buss wasn't even aware of the details until the charges were filed, that even though the owner was greatly embarrassed, he was quite supportive of Carter. Buss would point out that Carter's efforts had made his company money even after the taxes were paid.

The breaking of the news also contributed to a certain image of Buss as someone not to be trifled with, an image that the owner found could be useful at certain times.

Unfortunately, just a year later, in February 1985, headlines would report that Jerry Buss had encountered serious cash flow issues in his businesses and was behind on about $100 million in bank loans secured by the Forum and his athletic empire. It would later be revealed that the size of the problem was overstated but the cash flow issue itself would remain very real. There were rumors Buss might struggle to make his Lakers payroll, and Johnson apparently stepped up and offered to have Buss hold his checks until the cash flow problems eased, that he could be paid later. In time, the cash flow problems, too, would pass, significant only in that it had been an opportunity for Johnson to show support for his friend, the team owner.

A Sweet March to Disappointment

After missing 13 games with the finger injury as 1983 turned to 1984, Johnson would return to action in cold Cleveland on January 4 with 23 points.

There, covering the game for *The Washington Post,* was reporter

David Remnick, who would go on to literary fame as an author and the longtime editor of *The New Yorker.* Remnick was stunned by one Johnson play in particular, an 80-foot bounce pass for an assist to a streaking James Worthy. Months later, Remnick would ask Johnson about the moment.

"I got the rebound and I turned and looked downcourt," Johnson recalled for Remnick. "The defense was sort of split, two on one side and two on the other, but they were closing in, sort of like a curtain. So, I did the only thing I could do. I had to drop it down between them."

Johnson had actually looked left, seeking a safer option, before making the play, Remnick recalled. "Suddenly, Johnson whipped the ball upcourt, completing a perfect, 80-foot bounce pass between the defenders."

"I took my chance," Johnson would say. "There are times in every game when you can take a chance. You just have to know when to take them."

The play summed up the essence of Johnson's sobriquet, Remnick observed. He was decidedly Magic. And it was a quality that breathed huge life into the NBA everywhere he played. His time away healing from yet another injury would allow many close observers to gain a greater sense of a league without this Magic as opposed to when he appeared, when every single game he played was a big game.

This phenomenon, of course, matched so well Pat Riley's mindset. "It's my particular sickness," Riley would explain quietly one night in 1990, as his time coaching Johnson was coming to a close, "that I believe every game is a big game."

As 1984 unfolded, this "Magic" would prove quite popular, pushing his lead as tops in All-Star voting with a total nearing 800,000, setting him up for a memorable All-Star Weekend in Denver.

The East All-Stars defeated Johnson and the West All-Stars, 154–145, in overtime and Isiah Thomas was named the MVP of the game.

That weekend, Johnson had spent lots of time hanging out with Thomas and Mark Aguirre, his newest, fastest friends in professional basketball, both of whom were clients of Charles Tucker and George Andrews, along with Herb Williams, another good friend in the group. "We hung out and did everything together," Johnson would say of Thomas and Aguirre that weekend. "This is the first time we've all three been here together, and we just wanted to have fun and make the best of it."

It would be hard to convey, George Andrews would say in 2019, just how much both Aguirre and Thomas looked up to Johnson in those days, how much they sought to emulate him. Hardest to grasp for so many in pro basketball was what seemed like the homing device he possessed for winning, how fervently he pursued it, yet how insistent he was on wrapping the whole thing in the biggest sort of fun anyone could imagine. It was almost as if Johnson had cast a spell on the entire league.

Meditations on athletic greatness in American team sports just about always encounter fuzzy evaluations and blurred comparisons, but Johnson had clearly inserted himself into the conversation by the time his team was steaming that spring of 1984 toward a fourth appearance in the NBA championship series in five seasons.

Along that path, there were milestones to consider.

In a February win over Seattle, Johnson spread 23 assists among his teammates, tying the Lakers record set by Jerry West. Johnson had 12 of those assists in the first quarter, tying Boston's Bob Cousy for the most assists in a quarter, a record that John Lucas had tied twice.

Kevin Porter's record for assists in a game, 29, stood there before Johnson as a statistical mountain. As far as numbers were concerned, however, the Matterhorn was Wilt Chamberlain's prodigious mark for career points scored, which Abdul-Jabbar was approaching that very spring.

Reporters asked Johnson if he and his teammates might fight over that honor of making the pass to Kareem for the big bucket, but Johnson was adamant. "No, no. I'm the point guard here. I run the show. I'll call a timeout or steal the ball from my teammates before I let one of the other players pass him the ball."

It happened in a rare game in Las Vegas of all places. Kareem moved past Wilt as the game's all-time leading scorer in an April contest against the Jazz. With a smiling Johnson making the assist, Abdul-Jabbar racked up a total of 31,421 with a skyhook over Utah's Mark Eaton. "I'd like to give thanks to the great Allah for gifting me," he told the audience afterward. "I'd like to give thanks to my parents, who are both here tonight for inspiration and a lot of courage and support."

There was no immediate mention of Johnson, but it didn't matter. He was dominating another important conversation, for the league's Most Valuable Player award, in the running with Bird as the season wound toward a conclusion.

Los Angeles beat Boston in both regular season games. In the second win over Boston, marked by Johnson's 18 assists, the often laid-back fans in L.A. showed a growing new personality, one that romped and stomped and cheered, frenetic even, a dramatic departure from sleepier days.

"Maybe we'll meet again this year," James Worthy said afterward, a reference to the only place they could meet, in the NBA Finals. "They've got to have us on their minds now."

The win was notable for Cooper's defensive work on Bird, which would become a trend, what with Riley constantly focused on Bird and urging Cooper on in his mission to counter Boston's offensive weaponry.

"The other players really liked that quality in him," John Radcliffe would say of Cooper's defense, which was so deeply based on his film study. "When Michael would guard somebody, he knew what they were going to do. He had so much confidence he would allow them to do it."

But when it came to the key moment in the opponent's move, Cooper had that knack for being right there to force a miss or even block the shot.

Even with the loss in the second Lakers meeting of the season, Boston stood at 44–14, with the Lakers chasing at 36–19. Once Johnson put his finger injury behind him, they won 56 of their last 61 games, including a nice little roll through the early rounds of the playoffs.

The Lakers capped their big season by finishing off the Phoenix Suns and taking the Western Conference title. Once again, they were lucky to return to the championship series, having overcome injuries and other problems. Still, they possessed a solid confidence as they prepared for the Finals. Abdul-Jabbar was no longer dominant, but he still gave the Lakers a formidable half-court game when they needed it. Beyond that, Worthy had quietly come into his own as a forward. He had brilliant quickness, and once Johnson got him the ball in the low post, the result was usually a score. He took delight in faking one way, then exploding another. And he had continued to add range to his shot, building consistency from 15 feet out.

And the Lakers again got good frontcourt minutes and scoring from McAdoo. In the backcourt, Michael Cooper had added to his identity as a three-point specialist, while third-year guard Mike McGee contributed 9.8 points per game.

But would this be enough to finally ditch the Lakers' cursed luck in their championship encounters with Boston?

Showdown

Essentially, the collision between the desires and ambitions of Larry Bird and those of Earvin Johnson would play out almost like a heavyweight boxing match that stretched over four NBA seasons, beginning that spring of 1984.

There would be no taped delay for this prizefight.

Over Bird's and Johnson's first dozen years in the league, television rights money alone zoomed from a paltry $14 million per year to more than $100 million.

In sports bars, living rooms, and cocktail lounges across America, the competition spawned a running debate as to who was greater. Beginning in 1984, Bird would be named the league MVP for three consecutive seasons, through 1986. On the heels of that, Red Auerbach went so far as to declare Bird the greatest basketball player ever, greater even than Bill Russell, the five-time MVP who had led Auerbach's Celtics to all those titles. How taken was the public with Bird? On the eve of the 1984 Championship series, Jerry West surprisingly told *Sports Illustrated*, "Bird whets your appetite for the game. He's such a great passer and he doesn't make mistakes. Magic handles the ball more, and he makes more mistakes because he has it more. . . . I would recommend a young player model himself after Bird. He's a genius on the basketball floor."

Yet even as Bird claimed his awards, plenty of observers, including Wilt Chamberlain, thought Johnson was being discounted. "I don't know if there's ever been a better player than Magic," Wilt said.

Bird himself readily agreed. "He's the perfect player," he said of Johnson.

Early in Johnson's career, George Andrews had introduced him to Chamberlain at a UCLA game. "You might not be aware of it, but Wilt and Magic had a very close relationship," Andrews said in 2019.

It began in 1981 when Johnson and his lawyer were at a game in Pauley Pavilion.

"We're there and Wilt walks in," Andrews recalled. "I knew that Wilt was Magic's hero because he'd always said, 'That's where my hook shots came from.'"

Chamberlain was also Andrews's personal favorite as a player, and Johnson had told his lawyer several times about his early years on the playground when he imagined he was Wilt the Stilt.

"Let's go say hello," Andrews had suggested when they spied the legend. But Johnson was suddenly timid for once in his life.

"I can't do it," Andrews remembered Johnson saying. "He's my hero."

"So, I go over there," Andrews recalled, "and I go, 'Mr. Chamberlain, I'm George Andrews and I'm Earvin Johnson's attorney. He'd love to come over and say hi.'"

"Send the young man over," Chamberlain said immediately.

Johnson went over to make the acquaintance, and the two hit it off, Andrews said. "After that, every time the Lakers won, Wilt would say Magic wins the playoffs for Lakers. And every time they'd lose, he'd go, 'Kareem loses the playoffs for Lakers.' That's because Kareem and Wilt had had a falling-out somewhere along the line, and they never patched it up."

It wouldn't be too long before Johnson and Chamberlain took their relationship to the court, remembered Larry Brown, who coached at UCLA from 1979 to '81. "When I was at UCLA, he was playing with four of my freshmen against a team with a fortysomething Wilt

Chamberlain and James Worthy. After Wilt blocked a shot, Magic called goaltending."

The moment erupted in furious debate, Brown later explained to the Associated Press. "Magic won the argument, but Wilt said there would be no more baskets at his goal. Wilt then put on one of the most spectacular performances I've ever seen, and Magic didn't say much after that."

Johnson and Chamberlain, however, would remain "very close," George Andrews recalled.

By 1984, Chamberlain and every other basketball fan in the country were beyond eager to see Bird and Johnson duke it out on the court for the title, none more so than Bird and Johnson themselves.

It had been fifteen years since Los Angeles had last faced Boston in the Finals, yet old-timers needed no reminder of the numbers. The nervous presence of Jerry West at games in the Forum reminded them of that. Seven times the Lakers had met the Celtics for the championship, and seven times they had lost.

As scorekeeper, John Radcliffe had keenly observed those 1960s battles and their impact on the Lakers and their fans. "In the early years, it was, 'What is Boston going to do to us now?'" Radcliffe explained in 1992. "But when Magic came it seemed to be, 'What are we going to do to them?' He gave the same feeling to the fans that he did his own teammates, that he was in charge."

"We had heard a lot about the Boston jinx," James Worthy recalled later, "but it wasn't something we worried about. We knew we could win."

To get to the championship series, Boston had whipped Washington in the first round before outlasting the Knicks in seven games in the conference semifinals in Boston Garden. Milwaukee then fell 4–1 in the Eastern Conference title series.

The Celtics had ended their conference finals series on May 23, while the Lakers didn't wrap things up until Friday night, May 25, after making their way past Kansas City, Dallas, and Phoenix.

With the first game of the Finals set for Sunday, May 27, in Boston Garden, the Celtics' four days' rest was thought to be a major factor.

"It's like the opening of a great play," Jerry West told the writers. "Everyone's waiting to see it."

The foundation of Johnson's game many nights was his ability to rebound and start the fast break from there. *(Steven A. Roseboro)*

From left, Lakers assistant coach Pat Riley, head coach Paul Westhead, trainer Jack Curran, and Norm Nixon on the bench in 1981. *(Steven A. Roseboro)*

ABOVE: Johnson's smiles turned to anguish in the 1984 playoffs. *(Steven A. Roseboro)*

RIGHT: Showdowns between the Boston Celtics and the Lakers immediately became huge events, after Larry Bird and Johnson came into the league as rookies. *(Steven A. Roseboro)*

OFFICIAL CAMERA
LAKERS
33

After years of being dominated in championship play by the Celtics, the Lakers discovered how to celebrate in the Boston Garden during the 1980s. *(Steve Lipofsky)*

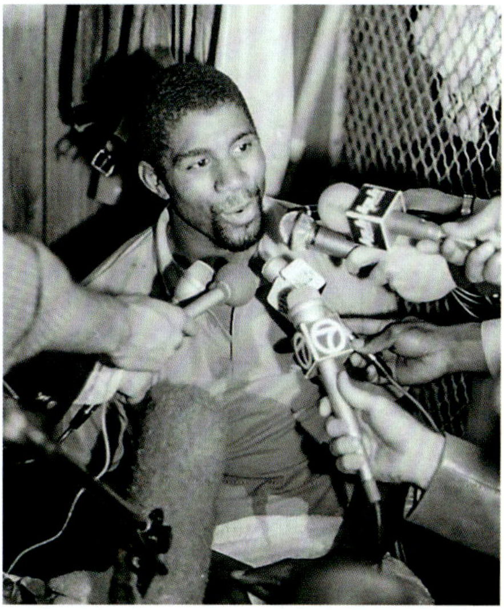

LEFT: The huge presence of Kareem required Johnson's deference. *(Steven A. Roseboro)*

RIGHT: Johnson offered a presence that made him a regular on the NBA's all-interview team. *(Steven A. Roseboro)*

Johnson and Bird, center, on the bench during Johnson's Midsummer Night's Magic charity game in Los Angeles in 1986. *(Steve Lipofsky)*

Johnson and Michael Jordan, shown here in 1989, tested each other in the NBA for parts of seven seasons, before finally meeting in the 1991 NBA Finals. *(Steven A. Roseboro)*

TOP LEFT: Johnson and Isiah Thomas greet each other warmly at the 1992 All-Star Game. Yet, the two men would soon become estranged from each other for almost three decades. *(Steve Lipofsky)*

TOP RIGHT: Johnson and Jerry Buss in an emotional moment at the 1992 All-Star Game in Orlando. *(Steve Lipofsky)*

Johnson scoring over Joe Dumars in the 1988 NBA championship series. ***(Steven A. Roseboro)***

Magic and Riley looking at the court, one of many moments in their competitive partnership. *(Steven A. Roseboro)*

Since the league had been created in those first months after World War II, the NBA had sought desperately to gain the attention of the American public.

For the first time in its history, the league now had some truly legitimate media hype.

As any number of news organizations pointed out, the championship would be a clash of symbols. West versus East. L.A. Cool versus Celtic Pride. But beneath all the symbols and media hooks, at the heart of everything, it was—just as NBC's Don Ohlmeyer had insisted with the 1979 Final Four—mostly about Larry and Magic.

"The number-one thing is desire," Bird said, "the ability to do the things you have to do to become a basketball player. I don't think you can teach anyone desire. I think it's a gift. I don't know why I have it, but I do."

"With Magic, it's a macho thing," West explained. "He wants to be better than everybody else."

Especially the perpetually annoying Bird with his cold-eyed Indiana arrogance and that trashy mouth. Bird talked as tough as he played, James Worthy recalled. "He'd always say, 'Get down!' or 'In your face!' or 'You can't guard me!' Whatever he could use to throw you off balance. That was his biggest weapon over the years. Back then, when I was young and didn't know any better, I thought he was a jerk. But after reflecting back, I realized that was just part of his game. He was measuring and analyzing his opponents, and he would do it from the moment he stepped on the floor. In the layup line, he'd be looking down there at you, just checking out your tendencies and your mannerisms and your posture. He could tell if your confidence wasn't right. He could tell. He could sense the vibe. If you came out on him and really didn't bump him or weren't aggressive with him, he knew. He knew he had you. If you showed any signs of doubt, you were through with Larry."

Riley had fixated on that Bird persona almost immediately. The blond forward was the pale rider who weaponized Boston's old-school mentality, the one that had long earned a hatred in Los Angeles. These new Lakers might not have understood the history at first, but it didn't take long before they understood that Boston took

Late in overtime, Boston reserve forward Scott Wedman hit a jumper from the baseline to give Boston a 124–121 win and a 1–1 tie in the series.

"What will I remember most from this series?" Riley would ask afterward. "Simple. Game 2. Worthy's pass to Scott. I could see the seams of the ball, like it was spinning in slow motion, but I couldn't do anything about it."

"I had the first big blooper of my career," Worthy recalled in 1993. "I threw the ball to Gerald Henderson. We could have gone up 2–0. That set the tone for them."

Angry and aghast, Johnson and his Lakers quickly recovered back home in the Forum. Johnson turned in a Finals record 21 assists, and Showtime rolled to a 137–104 win, which left Bird memorably outraged at Boston's lackluster performance.

"We played like a bunch of sissies," he said afterward.

The Celtics rose the next morning and read in the Los Angeles papers that Worthy just might be the series MVP. The history between the two teams had long hinged on Hollywood's mindless assumptions about their championship play. In 1969, the Lakers after years of losing to the dominant Celtics had finally earned home-court advantage in the series, which came down to a Game 7. Jack Kent Cooke had ordered the staff to put balloons in the rafters of the Forum to be released when they won the title.

Bill Russell was said to have walked into the building before the game, looked up into the rafters, and offered, "Those balloons are going to stay up there an awful long time."

Sure enough, Boston squeezed by in that Game 7, the moment Jerry West would long rue as the final twisting dagger in his agony.

As for the 1984 Celtics, the moment brought a similar awakening, especially for Celtics guard Dennis Johnson, who had scored only four points in Game 3. Coach K. C. Jones, who had been a tremendous ball-pressure guard on many of those Russell teams, adjusted the Boston defense, switching Dennis Johnson to cover L.A.'s Johnson. That didn't prevent the Lakers from taking an early lead. Once again, they seemed poised to run off with the game and the series.

From the Boston bench, reserve M. L. Carr began demanding that the Celtics get more physical, which produced the famous second-quarter moment when Kevin McHale stopped the Lakers cold by clotheslining Kurt Rambis on a breakaway, causing a ruckus to erupt under the basket.

The incident ignited the Celtics.

Afterward, Riley would call the Celtics "a bunch of thugs." This, of course, was long before the word *thug* had taken on another connotation in popular culture.

Boston forward Cedric Maxwell would take his cue from the moment. "Before Kevin McHale hit Kurt Rambis, the Lakers were just running across the street whenever they wanted," he famously told the media. "Now they stop at the corner, push the button, wait for the light, and look both ways."

After the Rambis foul, Bird had posted Cooper deep on the right block when Worthy knocked him to the floor and was called for a foul. Abdul-Jabbar flashed his anger at official Jess Kersey for the call and later threw a wild elbow that caught Bird in the head.

The Lakers center and Bird squared off as the benches emptied, with Johnson pushing Abdul-Jabbar away from the conflict.

In the modern game, the exchange would have resulted in immediate suspensions. In that era, the NBA wasn't about to throw stars like Bird and Kareem out of a highly charged championship series.

Bird then drilled a jumper and scored again on a fast-break followup that cut the Lakers' lead to 109–106.

Abdul-Jabbar later shoved Bird on a rebound at the other end and was called for his sixth foul, while Bird hit both free throws to tie it at 113.

Even with all the high-frequency mental interference, Los Angeles still had managed to hold a five-point lead with less than a minute to play.

That's when Johnson's old demons paid another visit, this time in the form of a bad pass that Boston's Robert Parish plucked away. Not done there, Johnson then missed two key free throws that allowed the Celtics to force an overtime. Late in the extra period, Worthy faced a key free throw. And M. L. Carr crowed loudly from the Boston bench that he would miss. Worthy promptly complied, which inspired Maxwell to greet him with a choke sign.

Bird posted up Johnson on the right block, then turned and shot over him for a 125–123 Boston lead.

Allowed to escape once again, the Celtics veritably floated to a 129–125 win to tie the series again and regain the home-court edge.

The free throw misses and the turnover would be destined for Johnson's personal Hall of Fame of Horrors. "I thought the free throws more than the pass were mistakes," he would say later. "Those were things I—not the team—I should have taken care of. When you miss the shots, you go home and sit in the dark."

It was just the place where Bird had longed for Johnson to be. The Celtics forward and his teammates realized then that the Lakers could be chased out of their fancy game. "We had to go out and make some things happen," Boston's Gerald Henderson recalled in 1991. "If being physical was gonna do it, then we had to do it. I remember in the fourth game that was the turnaround. We had to have that game or we were gonna be down 3–1. We had to have it."

"Cedric Maxwell and M. L. Carr would try to talk you out of your game," Worthy himself would recall years later. "They'd do a good job of it. They made me mad with the choke signs. I really didn't say anything, except 'Forget you,' or something like that. But they were good at taunting you and keeping you disoriented."

Now the series hinged on Game 5 in Boston, where Riley's big idea was to place oxygen tanks on the bench so his players could recover in the Garden's sweltering June heat.

"The so-called 'heat game' in 1984," longtime Boston sportswriter Bob Ryan remembered in 1989. "The fifth game with Los Angeles. It was 97 degrees in the Boston Garden, and the one player that you could have predicted turned this game into a positive was Larry Bird. That sums up Larry Bird. The Lakers were sitting there sucking on oxygen, and Bird is saying, 'Hey, we've all played outdoors in the summer. We've all played on asphalt. We've all done this. Why should this be different? It's just because we have uniforms on and it's a national television audience.' That game and that performance summed up Bird to me as much as anything else he's ever done."

The numbers back that up. Bird was 15 for 20 from the floor for 34 points as Boston won, 121–103. Abdul-Jabbar, on the other hand, had finally taken on the demeanor of a thirty-seven-year-old man running to keep up with a younger game.

How hot was it? a reporter asked him. "I suggest," the Lakers center replied, "that you go to a local steam bath, do 100 pushups with all your clothes on, and then try to run back and forth for 48 minutes. The game was in slow motion. It was like we were running in mud."

"I love to play in the heat," Bird said, smiling as Johnson fumed in the aftermath. "I just run faster, create my own wind."

Once again, Riley was transfixed, locked in on the detail of Bird's every move.

"He was just awesome," the Lakers coach told reporters afterward. "He made everything work."

If nothing else, the series would remind Johnson of the great treachery of dreams, that just as they were coming into your grasp they could dissolve into the worst of nightmares.

The changing series was worlds away from what Johnson wanted. He had lived for this moment and was fighting the sense that it was slipping away, that he had somehow allowed it to squirm out of the control that he had always so fiercely sought to maintain.

Fueled by that, he and the Lakers then answered the Celtics' aggressiveness in Game 6 back in the air-conditioned Forum. In the first period, Worthy shoved Cedric Maxwell into a basket support. From there, Abdul-Jabbar rediscovered his younger self to score 30, and Los Angeles pulled away down the stretch for a 119–108 win to tie the series at three apiece. As M. L. Carr left the Forum floor, a fan pitched a cup of mysterious liquid in his face, enraging the Celtics. Carr said afterward that Los Angeles had declared "all-out war."

Bird suggested that the Lakers had better wear hard hats on the bench for Game 7 in the Garden because the fans might get wild.

The entire city of Boston was juiced up for the event that Tuesday night, June 12, writer Steve Springer recalled. "I remember we pulled up in a press bus. This wasn't a team bus; it was a press bus. We pulled up to the Garden for Game 7, and somebody threw a brick through one of the windows that shattered the glass in our press bus."

The Lakers needed a police escort just to get from their hotel to the Garden. Carr came out wearing goggles to mock Kareem (who had begun wearing the protective eyewear) and told the Lakers they weren't going to win. Not in the Garden.

In the end it was Cedric Maxwell who seized the moment for Boston, demoralizing the Lakers on the offensive boards and, worst of all, drawing fouls. By halftime, he had made 11 of 13 free throws. When the Lakers tried to double-team him, he treated Johnson to a passing display. Maxwell would finish with 24 points, eight assists, and eight rebounds. Bird had 20 points and 12 rebounds, Robert Parish 14 points and 16 rebounds. And Dennis Johnson scored 22 while again covering the other Johnson.

To their credit, the Lakers fought off that barrage and raced back from a 14-point deficit to trail by just three with more than a minute left, which produced the final nightmare for Johnson, who had the ball in his hands. Dennis Johnson knocked it loose, but Michael Cooper recovered it. Rescued, the Magic Man went back to work and spied Worthy open under the basket. Just as he was about to seal the moment with a brilliant assist, Maxwell knocked the ball away yet again. It would be the vision of Worthy open under the basket that Johnson would cite again and again over the dreadful summer that was to follow.

At the other end, Dennis Johnson drew a foul and made the shots, spurring the Celtics to their 15th championship, marked by Bird being named the MVP after averaging 27.4 points, 14 rebounds, 3.2 assists, and two steals over the series. The award might well have been shared with Maxwell's decidedly righteous seventh-game performance. All of which left the Garden crowd launching into the kind of over-the-top celebration that had marked all of Boston's conquering moments over the Lakers in the 1960s. Abdul-Jabbar had made the mistake of retrieving a rebound as the final horn sounded and was caught up in the rush. "People tried to snatch my glasses," he said. One fan jumped on Rambis's back and would later file suit when the

Laker forward slung him off. "There was no crowd control, and they just went nuts," former Lakers PR Josh Rosenfeld would recall.

In the Celtics' locker room, Auerbach enjoyed yet another of his very fat, very special cigars as Commissioner David Stern presented the league trophy. It was as if he had twisted the smoking stogie in the Lakers' eye. For years, every time his Boston teams dumped the Lakers for a title when Auerbach was coach, he would light up the cigar on the bench at the end of the game, an insult the league seemed to have great trouble in preventing. "There were an awful lot of times I wanted to shove that cigar down his throat," former Lakers coach Fred Schaus admitted in a 1990 interview.

The Celtics president clutched the trophy with satisfaction and asked, "Whatever happened to that Laker dynasty I've been hearing so much about?"

Seeking to feast on the carcass, reporters crammed into the tiny visitors' dressing room but had to wait a very long time for Johnson and Cooper, who sat on the floor of the shower, too disconsolate to come out. There for support, Johnson friends Mark Aguirre and Isiah Thomas waited, too, Rosenfeld would recall. "Finally they went back to Earvin and told him, 'Why don't you get this over so we can get out of here?'"

Then the Lakers tried to escape the bedlam in the streets outside the arena, but the crowd spotted their bus headed down the exit ramp.

"People were throwing stuff at the bus and banging on the windows," recalled longtime Lakers equipment manager Rudy Garciduenas. "There was this one guy in a wheelchair shooting us the bird. I remember people laughing at him. He was smiling and flipping everybody off. He was just sitting there so out of it about the Celtics."

"It was a slow exit from the arena down that ramp," Worthy recalled. "The crowd was shaking and hitting our bus."

Because they still traveled on commercial flights in those days, the Lakers faced a sleepless night in Boston, where the air was filled with delirious celebration. Jerry Buss recalled that he spent the night chain-smoking. Michael Cooper was sequestered in his room with his agony and his wife, Wanda.

Riley had brought a white tuxedo he had planned to wear for the championship celebration. He put it away and pushed his thoughts to the next season.

Isiah Thomas and Mark Aguirre spent the night with Johnson, the disturbing sounds of his sobbing breaking the awkward silence. Eventually, he would turn talkative in those miserable hours, reminiscing about anything that popped into his stream of consciousness. Music. Cars. Old times. Anything but the Celtics. If the conversation drifted that way, his friends would quickly steer it away.

George Andrews recalled being right there with them. "Isiah, Mark, and I went out to Boston for Game 7 to be with Earvin," the lawyer remembered. "We were in the hotel, and the four of us stayed up all night and just talked."

The subject turned to a far happier moment—Johnson winning the state title at Everett, and both Thomas and Aguirre seemed amazed at Johnson's experience winning one with his high school buddies, something neither of them had been able to do.

"It was just an amazing conversation that I'll never forget," George Andrews said in 2019. "We stayed all night. When the sun came up, we were still talking."

Isiah Thomas said later, "For that one night I think I was his escape from reality."

Fat chance. There would prove to be no escape from this one, just like the other playoff moments that haunted Johnson, no way to hold the thoughts at bay or run from the memory.

Each of those games in 1984 was very intense, Steve Springer remembered. "But as a reporter you try not to be involved with the emotion and all. But there was so much going on."

The *Boston Herald* the morning after the Lakers lost went big with the victory, Springer recalled. "The front page was just two words. WE WON! I remember leaving the hotel. I was at the front desk getting my bill."

The clerk saw where he was from.

"Ah, Los Angeles," she said.

"We'll be back next year," Springer told her.

"Good," she said. "Come back. And we'll kick your ass again."

24

HEAVEN IS A PAYBACK

For years, apartment life in Culver City had served him well.

"He loved that little place," Rosalie Metcalf would later say of the two-bedroom abode.

Johnson had hired Metcalf and Pam Smith, his two friends from Michigan State, to help with cooking and a little cleaning, to keep him supplied with favorites such as peanut butter cookies and fried chicken. The arrangement proved a sweet tooth of a deal for the women as well, including Lakers tickets, an apartment of their own in Jerry Buss's building, and some living expenses as well as salary.

His apartment had been perfect for small parties and gatherings of his circle of friends, including twin sisters Pamela and Paula McGee, who both played basketball at USC; his old basketball manager Darwin Payton from Michigan State whom Johnson had hired to help with various enterprises; even Greg Kelser on occasion, among others.

The arrival of Payton, in particular, had served as a lifeline to his beloved Lansing and comforted Johnson against the homesickness that had persisted through his first few years in Southern California.

Yet, sweet as the apartment arrangement was, as the calendar had turned to 1984, Johnson had outgrown his cheerful quarters. He wanted a place befitting an NBA star, a palace of sorts where he could spread out and host the kind of larger parties that he had long dreamed of, a place that could accommodate his siblings on vacation (he preferred no more than two at a time) or new friends Isiah Thomas (who would quickly claim his own bedroom) and Mark Aguirre whenever they came in from out of town, a place where they could all hang out and live the sort of big life available to those who had it all.

And by 1984, Johnson certainly had it all. As George Andrews would explain, since Johnson had come into the league, he had sought to live off his endorsements, his deals with Spalding, Converse, 7UP, and others, all while banking his fat checks from playing for the Lakers without touching a cent of that money. Such an approach suited the conservative sensibilities of his own family and his midwestern background. And while those deals would later be minimized in comparison with those snagged by Michael Jordan, Andrews would argue that Johnson was actually the first NBA player to be offered such an array of endorsements that paid him so handsomely, well beyond the relatively scant offers that had been available for the magnificent Dr. J.

To fit his status, Johnson had found a place that he considered almost perfect, built in the English country style, with a racquetball court that he planned to convert into an indoor basketball half-court that he could keep as busy as he desired. It was located on Moraga Drive in Bel Air, as George Andrews explained, "just down the road from Jerry West's place."

The mansion, with fourteen rooms and seventeen telephones (in that age before cell phones), had what was then a mansion-sized price tag, $2.35 million, which presented only one problem. Johnson was flying his parents in to see the place for their approval before he closed on it, and he was concerned that his father might go into apoplexy at the price. (The son would long laugh about his father's earnest early advice that he might have to pay as much as $300 to $400 a month for an apartment in L.A.) So, Johnson recruited Andrews to show the old man around the new digs and soften the blow.

"We walked around," Andrews said of Big Earv, "and then we sat on the hall stairway and his dad was kind of crying. I go, 'What's going on?'"

"I never thought a son of mine could ever have something so magnificent," Andrews recalled the father replying quietly, sitting there in the emptiness of the mansion.

"It was ten thousand square feet, you know. Had a pool overlooking the hills," Andrews recalled.

The place featured hardwood floors (one writer noted a semblance to Boston Garden's parquet), high ceilings, and a thunderous sound system piped into every room that allowed Johnson to slip into EJ the DJ mode, either entertaining friends or simply enjoying his solitude, slow dancing with himself, swaying in his own embrace on afternoons before games, as he once allowed *Sports Illustrated* writer Bruce Newman to witness.

"You play to a beat, on a stride, sort of," Johnson explained of this connecting of his music to his game. "Sometimes if I've been listening to a song, it will come up in my mind during a game. I always listen to music before a game. It gets me going, pumps my blood up. I'll always be more sweaty when I leave home, than I am after warmups. I'm thinking about the game, but I'm into the music. You get too uptight if you're thinking about the game all day. It's there but I'm not focused on it. Cool. By the time I hit my car, I want upbeat because then my adrenaline's flowing."

The Tudor-style home had a Jacuzzi sunken tub that he had dreamed about since he was a kid and had seen a lady in a Camay soap TV commercial soaking gloriously in such a tub. From his tub, he could now stare out into the canyon below.

It was a scenery and a setting that would eventually become soothing in the wake of his humiliating loss to Boston, which had clearly interrupted the flow of rhythm and sound and movement that drove his approach.

The defeat had swiftly brought newer, louder "Tragic Johnson" comments about his play. The moment of failure carried with it yet a new realization of the sharp double-edge of his nickname, the realization of what his father and mother had first feared when Fred

Stabley came up with the sobriquet back in Lansing. "A lot of people treat him like he's supernatural because of the way he plays," Darwin Payton observed at the time. "I've been with him a lot of places, and wherever he is, he's the man. When he's at a club, the stars all come over to see him."

Indeed. Supernatural he was.

Yet NBA players, friends, and other associates with a close-up view of his existence soon recognized the burden it brought. After witnessing all that his daily life had become, other players concluded that such a magnetic, over-the-top nickname wasn't something they desired. In fact, it almost led to the perception that his greatness was so routine, so expected, that fans took it for granted, as Isiah Thomas would point out.

That realization gained greater traction in the wake of the loss, just as it had after the public anger over his "firing" of Westhead in 1981. Despite all of his success, "Magic" again teetered on the brink of substantial derision.

He had returned from the disaster in Boston and moved into the mansion, only the furniture hadn't arrived. His palace sat empty, just Earvin and his bare walls. So, he hid out for three days in his Culver City apartment, which left his mother phoning to see how he was doing.

"Mamma, I just can't talk about it," he replied.

Talking about it meant pulling lots of extremely negative and anxiety-producing thoughts and visions back into his consciousness, the kind that had left him sobbing in Boston. At that particular moment, he wanted them cauterized. And definitely did not want to have to visualize once again his line of hard moments from years of playoff basketball. This one would prove the most profound disappointment of his many-splendored career, one that echoed every agony from the past and allowed self-questioning and disgust to flood back in.

Even his daily dive into the newspapers, one of his usual escapes, proved futile. The *Los Angeles Daily News* had described him as "tarnished" while the *Times* suggested he had disappeared at the biggest moment of his career.

Johnson was mindful that the record books now said he was the record holder for the most assists in a playoff series, having averaged more than 15 over the last five games against the Celtics. It hardly mattered. The conclusions themselves sat right there in his heart, inescapably empty. "We made five mistakes that cost us the series," he would admit later. "And I contributed to three of them."

The experience would go on for months, popping back into his thoughts in unexpected moments like a mainspring wound way too tight. "I'll be sitting somewhere relaxing, and here it comes right up in my mind. I can still see Worthy open," he would say of the Game 7 turnover against Boston, the ball knocked away instead of going for the Magical assist that could have allowed him great joy instead of all this self-loathing.

In time, the furniture arrived, but his misery lingered.

Everywhere he turned there seemed to be something to read about it. The Celtics were having fun with their victory, even growing so bold as to publicly dub him "Tragic Johnson."

Asked about the upcoming 1984–85 season, Bird relished the opportunity to toss a little trash talk Johnson's way, saying of the Lakers, "I'd like to give them the opportunity to redeem themselves. I'm sure they have guys who feel they didn't play up to their capabilities."

Asked if he meant Johnson, Bird replied, "You think we don't love it? Magic having nightmares."

Johnson would retort that he had no need for redemption, but the message was lost in the noise, like an echo in the canyons around his new place.

The Celtics' trash-talking was to be expected, but he was flummoxed by the behavior of the L.A. press that had seemed to love him so much. "I sat back when it was over," he said later, "and I thought, 'Man, did we just lose one of the great playoff series of all time, or didn't we?' This was one of the greatest in history. Yet all you read was how bad I was."

Indeed, the commentary from all sides lacked, in retrospect, any perspective on just what Johnson had done in the playoffs in the first five years of his career, beginning with registering a triple-double in his very first playoff game in 1980.

Since then, he had launched a virtual assault upon nearly every playoff assist record owned by the game's greats, including Wilt Chamberlain, Oscar Robertson, Bob Cousy, Jerry West, and Walt Frazier.

Yet, in the wake of the 1984 playoff loss, such accomplishments seemed almost forgotten, if it had ever gained any clarity at all in the public mind. In 1984 alone, he had set the single-game playoff assist record, with 24 in a win over the Suns.

In the Game 3 win against the Celtics, he had set the NBA Finals single-game assist record with 21, a game in which he also recorded an unprecedented third triple-double in the championship series with 14 points, 11 rebounds, and 21 assists on two turnovers.

In his team's loss the next game, Johnson had entered more new territory with his fourth Finals triple-double with 20 points, 11 rebounds, and 17 assists on seven turnovers, all of it only to be designated as "Tragic."

His idol, Wilt Chamberlain, was the only other player ever to record even two triple-doubles in a Finals series.

It was as if all the people following the NBA hadn't even acknowledged what he'd done.

As Lon Rosen recalled, Johnson's answer to these developments was an intense commitment in the gym, the kind that burned on the vapors of the negativity all around him.

"Magic has had his trials and tribulations throughout his entire NBA career," Michael Cooper would observe much later. "That's the thing I've always admired about him. He's always met them head-on and conquered them to the best of his ability."

He was nearing his twenty-fifth birthday, venturing into his athletic prime and advancing maturity, all just in time to conjure up an answer for all questioners.

Officially Johnson's meeting the challenge began when the Lakers returned to Palm Springs for training camp that fall. He wasn't alone.

"When we walked on the floor that first day of camp, we saw it in everybody's eyes," Byron Scott would remember. "This was going to be a serious year."

They all felt the intense burn of how the previous season had played out, Kareem Abdul-Jabbar would recall later. "That first series that we gave them in '84 really seasoned us. It gave us the mental tenacity that we didn't always exhibit. We couldn't outrun everybody. We had to understand that sometimes there were other ways to skin the cat."

Ouch.

In a later media age, Paul Westhead might have been all over the airwaves saying, "I tried to tell you." But that was neither the moment nor Westhead's style.

It was, however, a moment that led to an even deeper bonding of Johnson to Riley. "Pat Riley would say they would communicate by body language," Lon Rosen recalled in 2020. "Earvin was a coach on the court."

Thus, in the wake of Johnson's power move, their relationship evolved almost as coach to coach, one in Armani suits with slicked-back hair, arms folded, on the sidelines, often crouched in a baseball catcher's stance, the other motoring and directing at will on the hardwood. One reading the personnel, the other reading the floor.

"Earvin would never want to leave games, but he would look at Earvin," Lon Rosen said of Riley, "and if Earvin's lips look like they were purple, he would say, 'I'm taking him out.' That was the unique relationship Pat Riley had with Earvin. They were like one. They had the same brain, it seemed like, when he coached and Earvin played. They were really one."

If they hadn't been that way before the 1984–85 season, the final synapses merged then, beginning in that training camp.

Trainer Gary Vitti was relatively new to the team, had been around athletic competition for years, yet was taken aback by the intensity from Johnson and the group, but especially from Riley.

"Pat was screwed down pretty tight, like a spring," Vitti recalled in a 1992 interview. "And it escalated from there."

"Riles made us aware of exactly what he wanted," Byron Scott would recall. "He let us know from day one, 'I'm gonna work you from the first day of camp to the last day of the playoffs.' He didn't let up. That's the main reason we kept going all year, because we had a coach who wouldn't let us stop."

Like Vitti, Lakers equipment manager Rudy Garciduenas had just been working with the team a short time, a tenure that would last for decades, yet that early window into Johnson as he lashed back at defeat presented a view that Garciduenas would cherish and use as a baseline for his personal evaluation of every Laker through the coming decades on rosters that featured Kobe Bryant, Shaquille O'Neal, and Pau Gasol, among many others.

There would be so many greats on those future rosters, the equipment manager allowed, but it would be hard to think of one who matched Johnson in terms of sheer force of personality.

"He just had a drive to win," Garciduenas recalled. "He had a focus. Back then it was a definite learning experience for me. Magic was the kind of player that didn't let his teammates get out of focus. It was all about the ultimate prize. There were no exceptions. You either won the NBA championship or you did not. You know there was no second place back then. It was all about getting that ring and being successful. Otherwise, you came up short."

Short was nowhere Johnson longed to be, explained Garciduenas, who was fascinated watching the impact on the locker room. "Magic affected everybody that he met. He was definitely a personality and someone that people all looked up to. He knew that and he used it and fostered that kind of character. He knew that he represented to a lot of people what their hopes and dreams were."

NBA photographer Andrew Bernstein, another courtside witness perched most often under the baskets, watched the passion unfold as the Lakers seemed eaten up with the purpose of getting back to the playoffs just so they could go at the Celtics. Relaxing even for a moment seemed out of the question.

"Magic," Bernstein recalled, "it could be a nothing game against Golden State in the middle of January, or a Boston-Laker game or a Finals game, he put out the same effort every game."

That his huge effort every night suggested a routine greatness, yes. But Johnson's sobbing in his hotel room after the loss to Boston confirmed another narrative. Riley read that his team's psyche was fragile in the aftermath of the defeat. They had won two championships on their talent, but the Celtics had challenged them with psychological warfare and won. The Lakers would either have to fight back or fall apart.

Asked in 2004 about the product of that 1985 season, Johnson offered that he and his teammates set aside their despair to bond over the challenge. "That team was awful close," he said. "We were all so tough-minded. We would go on the road and just say, 'Okay, how many games we got?' We'd see there was six. 'We're gonna win all six.' And then we'd go and win all six. We would push each other to make sure. Coop would be on me. I would be on Coop. If the game got tight, Coop would say, 'Buck, take over.' And I'd take over. Or I'd say, 'Kareem, it's time for you to dominate. Take over the game.' And it was just that way. Or we could get on one another. 'Man, your man's beatin' you! What's up?' You would get so mad, you'd just shut 'em down. That was the respect we had for one another. That was the sign of a true championship team, that we could get on one another."

By the 1985 playoffs the Lakers put on the face that suggested they had regained all of their composure and their strength. After all, the frontcourt had been bolstered by the return of Mitch Kupchak and Jamaal Wilkes to go with Kareem, Worthy, Rambis, McAdoo, and Larry Spriggs. The backcourt showed Magic, Scott, Cooper, and Mike McGee. The thing that none of them could articulate was their lingering doubt.

"Those wounds from last June stayed open all summer," Riley said as the playoffs neared. "Now the misery has subsided, but it never leaves your mind completely. Magic is very sensitive to what people think about him, and in his own mind I think he heard those questions over and over again to the point where he began to rationalize and say, 'Maybe I do have to concentrate more.' I think the whole experience has made him grow up in a lot of ways."

Johnson already presented a powerful record of accomplishment at an age when most pro players were just beginning to feel comfortable in the game. In the NBA just six years, he already owned two championship rings, as well as some notable epic failures. Could he add a substantial chapter to his narrative?

Certainly, the Celtics were in a happy place but conceding nothing. With a 63–19 regular season finish, they again claimed the home-court advantage for the 1985 playoffs. The Lakers had finished 62–20. And neither team dallied in the postseason. Boston dismissed Cleveland, Detroit, and Philadelphia in quick succession. The Lakers rolled past Phoenix, Portland, and Denver. In one game against Portland, Johnson rang up 23 assists and then in the Game 5 closeout he scored 34 to go with his 19 dimes. Denver upset the Lakers at home in the conference finals, only to watch Johnson and company explode for a 153–109 closeout game, the 44-point margin taken as a sign that L.A. was eager and ready for Boston.

During this stretch, Johnson surpassed the playoff record of 970 assists of Jerry West to become the league's all-time playoffs assist leader. At age twenty-five.

He presented a veritable picture of size, strength, cunning, vision, desire, command. None of those things was the issue, however. Some demons insisted on lingering.

"We really weren't sure of ourselves," James Worthy admitted. "We got back to the Finals and said, 'Golly, we got the Celtics again. How're we gonna do it?'"

For the first time in years, the Finals had returned to a 2–3–2 format, with the first two games in Boston, the middle three in L.A., and the last two, if necessary, back in Boston. The situation set up an immense opportunity for the Lakers to steal one in the Garden, then pressure the Celtics back in L.A.

There was only one huge problem.

"We just came out and . . . didn't have any aggressiveness," James Worthy would remember. "No killer instinct. We paid the price for it."

Game 1 opened on Memorial Day, Monday, May 27, with both teams supposedly feeling good on five days' rest. The Lakers, however, soon looked like they'd spent the week working overtime with Big Earv in the ol' grinding boot. The thirty-eight-year-old Abdul-Jabbar struggled up and down the court, while Boston's Robert Parish ran easily with his trademark erect posture that so fit his nickname, "The Chief." Often Kareem would just be reaching the top of the key to catch up when all of a sudden the action and Parish raced the other way. Abdul-Jabbar finished the day with 12 points and three boards. Johnson was hardly better with a single measly rebound. A single rebound. In the opening game of a championship series no less.

Riley, of course, would become famous for the saying, "No rebounds, no rings."

With no boards, the famed Showtime running game was left buried in the slow lane. The loss wasn't just bad; it was epic, 148–114, this on top of the fact that the Lakers had spent the entire season nursing the very open wounds of 1984.

"It was one of those days," Boston coach K. C. Jones said, "where if you turn around and close your eyes, the ball's gonna go in."

The Celtics overdosed on delight, then abruptly caught themselves and "ix-nayed" the trash talk, fearing that they had gone too far. "It's definitely time to back off," Cedric Maxwell warned. "It's not like backgammon or cribbage, where if you beat someone bad enough you get two wins."

For the Lakers, the film session the next morning opened with same-old-used-to-be doubt, the kind of moment Riley was born to step into. "After that particular game it wasn't pretty," James Worthy would remember. "It was factual. It was the truth, and it was presented to us in a way we couldn't deny."

Abdul-Jabbar signaled that the loss had gotten his attention, as he moved to the front row for the horror show, rather than reclining in the back as he usually did. Afterward, "the Cap" would go to each of his teammates and offer personal apologies for his effort.

"That horrible game, the Memorial Day Massacre," Kareem would say in 1992. "That was mainly me. I remember watching the film of that game. The camera would follow the ball, and I would always be at the back of the pack. I'd be out of camera range, always bringing up the rear. I realized I simply wasn't keeping up with the play. I had worn down over the course of the playoffs. So, we had like three days before we played. . . . And I did like a mini training camp. I just made myself get my cardiovascular back to where it should be. I told everybody, I promised, that whatever happened on the next game I would give my best, whatever that was. Pat was trying to accommodate me minute-wise, but I don't get into shape unless I work myself into shape. I got to play. So, the more time I spent on the bench, it really wasn't getting the job done. We needed a different way of approaching it."

"A lot of the discussion was pointed at Kareem," Worthy recalled later. "But it was all of us, because none of us played well. But he was our leader. He made a contract with us that it would never happen again. Ever."

All the talk was nice, for sure, because it pointed to the next step.

"We had to go out and do something about it," Worthy said.

As the team boarded the bus before Game 2 that Thursday, Abdul-Jabbar showed up with his father in tow and asked Riley if the old man could ride on the team bus to the Garden. The senior Alcindor was going through difficult personal issues in that moment. Riley had a rule against family riding the team bus, but he consented, and like that the entire moment was reshaped. It led to Riley thinking of his late father and changing his message that day for the team.

"Pat talked about when he was a little boy," trainer Gary Vitti would recall. "His big brothers would take him down to the playground. He was the smallest guy out there, and he'd get beat up every day and go home crying. They'd take him home, and his father would say, 'Take Pat back down there tomorrow.' And the big brothers would say, 'Dad, the guy's getting beat up.' His father said, 'Take him back. At some point, you gotta plant your feet, kick some ass, and make a stand.'"

Just before he died, in his last talk with his son, the elder Riley had reminded Pat that survival would require making a stand. Riley recalled those words to his players.

"Riles is an inspiring guy," Vitti would say in 1992. "I mean, after hearing him, I wanted to go out there and kick some ass, too."

They all did. Kareem, in particular, reasserted himself with 30 points, 17 rebounds, eight assists, and three blocks. Cooper hit eight of nine from the floor to finish with 22 points. Together, they evened the series, 109–102.

"That set the tone," Worthy offered in 1992. "That game was the turning point in Lakers history, I think. We came back strong and Kareem led the way. Riley, too. He stepped forward. It was the turning point in his career, too."

They had merely stolen a game in the hated Garden of Evil and now returned to the Forum for three straight. Would they be able to seize that opportunity, or were there more inexplicable days ahead?

Sitting on the baseline with his cameras, photographer Andrew Bernstein simply had to make sure his strobe lighting was set, then wait for the drama to flow. How would the Lakers answer?

"Those Finals games were epic battles," Bernstein, who spent decades shooting every sort of NBA contest, would recall. "Every game was unbelievable. That Memorial Day Massacre was unbelievable. They came back from that, after 1984 was a tremendous year with the Big Three for Boston, with Coop and Magic and Kareem and Byron Scott and all those guys and Pat on the bench. It was a battle. Larry Bird's mouth really never stopped working. He liked to get into people's heads, and Magic would have none of that. But Larry was working on Coop every time that he was posting up. Every time. And Coop stayed with him and stayed with him. If you look back at '85, Michael was one of the keys to that series. He really helped keep Larry in check. He never shut Larry down, but he never let Larry get into his head, either."

"They expected us to crawl into a hole," Lakers assistant Dave Wohl said of the Celtics. "It's like the bully on the block who keeps taking your lunch money every day. Finally, you get tired of it and you whack him."

"That game was a blessing in disguise," Riley would say of the Massacre. "It strengthened the fiber of that team."

The Lakers hosted the Celtics for Game 3 on that Sunday afternoon and issued a payback for Game 1, 136–111. Johnson had matched his 16 assists with just one turnover, a perfection that he had also posted just days earlier in a Western Conference finals win over the Denver Nuggets. Repeat. Sixteen assists. One turnover. In two different playoff games. Many of those assists delivered on the run, full speed, the floor unfolding faster, far gnarlier than any video game could ever hope to emulate.

This time Worthy was the main target of Johnson's largesse, with 29 points. Abdul-Jabbar had 26 points and 14 rebounds.

Boston had led, 48–38, but Worthy opened up his game in the second quarter and L.A. charged to a 65–59 edge at intermission. In the second half, the Lakers ran away with it, a moment marked by Abdul-Jabbar becoming the league's all-time leading playoff scorer with 4,458 points.

Yes, the curiosity of the Lakers' circumstances had led to revelations of matchbook covers, but the reality of Johnson and Abdul-Jabbar would grow over the years to the undeniable conclusion that they were born to operate together, that they brought out the very best in one another, in the most counterintuitive ways, defined by the fact that they did it despite operating at two entirely different paces, often on two different planes, Johnson with his boom box blasting R&B, Kareem with his effete jazz. Many years later, the center would look back and offer that Johnson had led him to realize that he was actually having fun playing basketball.

Bird, meanwhile, would fall that week into a two-game shooting slump, going 17 for 42. He had been troubled by a chronically sore right elbow and bad back, though observers could see his real trouble was Cooper. The more Bird struggled the more Riley urged Cooper to pile on.

As with '84, the series was marked by physical play, although this time it was the Lakers who gained an edge. "We're not out to physically harm them," Abdul-Jabbar told the writers. "But I wouldn't mind hurting their feelings."

Before Game 4, the league warned each coach that fighting and extra rough play would be met with fines and suspensions. Riley told his players of the warning, but K. C. Jones chose not to. Thus, the Celtics roamed free, and the game came down to one final possession. Bird had the ball but faced a double-team, so he dumped it off. From there, Dennis Johnson drilled the winner with two seconds left.

Boston had evened the series and regained the home-court advantage, 107–105.

It provided little consolation that Johnson had recorded his fifth

Finals triple-double in the loss with 20 points, 11 rebounds, and 12 assists on four turnovers.

The immediate question was just how much their doubt would balloon in Game 5, two nights later in the Forum.

The Lakers went on a 14–3 run at the close of the half to take a 64–51 lead and stretched it to 89–72 after intermission. No matter how well Johnson and his Lakers played, the Celtics always seemed to find a way to answer. Boston closed to within four at 101–97 with six minutes left. Johnson, however, hit three shots and helped feed Kareem for four more. The big guy would post 36 on the day, as the Lakers walked away with a 3–2 lead, 120–111.

"People didn't think we could win close games," Johnson said afterward, addressing the bad taste of 1984.

From there it went back to Boston, the scene of so many Laker nightmares over the years, to the point that Jerry West was convinced he shouldn't make the trip. He didn't want his bad karma against the Celtics spooking the proceedings. His former teammates and other old Lakers, all victims of Boston so many times, held their breath and watched transfixed. After all those painful losses to the Celtics in championship play, this seemed to be the best chance yet to end Boston's domination. To prevail yet again, the Celtics would have to win the final two games. The schedule this time allowed for just thirty-eight hours' rest between games.

Johnson would turn in another floor game for the ages, his sixth Finals triple-double with 14 points, 10 rebounds, and 14 assists on four turnovers.

Abdul-Jabbar was there again, pulling Johnson's passes into his huge mitts to go to work for 29 points, 18 of them in the second half. The score had been tied at 55 at intermission with Abdul-Jabbar sitting for much of the second quarter with foul trouble, while Kupchak worked as his backup. The Celtics had played only seven people in the first half, and Johnson could see that they were tired.

Don't worry about turnovers, Riley told his point guard. Just keep pushing the agenda, keep up the pressure. Find out what they have left.

Johnson knew well how to do that.

And the Celtics rewarded him for it, breaking from their long, proud tradition in their three decades of history. In all that time, they had never given up a championship on their home floor, on the hallowed parquet of smelly old Boston Garden.

It was settled early, almost in silence, 111–100, signaled by the music to Jerry Buss's ears, the audible squeaking of sneakers on the parquet floor set against the numb silence of the usually lusty crowd. Kevin McHale had kept them alive with 32 points, but he was called for his sixth foul with more than five minutes left. And, thanks in part to Cooper's defense, Bird was closing out a 12-for-29 afternoon. Twenty-nine shots, searching for just enough oxygen to get by.

"I thought I'd have a great game today," Bird said dismally afterward.

The Garden crowd slipped away meekly, the same crowd that had so riotously jostled the Lakers the year before.

"We made 'em lose it," Johnson said with satisfaction.

"They fought as dirty as they could until they realized they were gonna lose," Abdul-Jabbar would recall in 1993. "Then they came back with Celtic pride and all this crap. Being able to shut those people up in Boston Garden—that was so satisfying. Even though we came back to L.A. and lost a game, we didn't lose any momentum. That was the first year where James really just started to dominate. He just emerged in such a spectacular, wonderful way. It was a nice thing to see. He could finish the break and he could post up. He was just so versatile. And we had Mitch Kupchak and Bob McAdoo on the bench. It was just great stuff."

Abdul-Jabbar was named the MVP of the series, at age thirty-eight no less, a performance that would leave longtime Celtics beat writer Bob Ryan truly amazed, especially considering how the Lakers center had started the series.

"He defies logic," Riley said. "He's the most unique and durable athlete of our time, the best you'll ever see. You better enjoy him while he's here."

Contrary to appearances sometimes, Johnson had clarity about the great center, recalled his friend Herb Williams in a 2004 interview. "Magic used to always tell me, 'Crunch time? The ball's going to the big fella.' Magic would do all the flashy stuff. He would get all the notoriety and publicity, but he would tell you that in clutch time the ball goes to 33. Period. You knew going in that if you were going to stop the Lakers you had to stop Kareem. And the skyhook? There was no stopping that. He knew that if he could get his shoulders turned and get it over his head, it was usually over. I had to defend that more than a few times. It was really just a hope and a prayer. You were hoping he's not on. And if you got physical with him, he seemed to concentrate a lot more. He was already focused, but it seemed like the more you would piss him off, he would never miss shots. When he got the ball then, it was like you couldn't guard him. You might as well just run on back down the court."

For Johnson, the championship filled the emptiness that had marked his life for twelve months. "You wait so long to get back," he admitted afterward. "A whole year. That's the hard part. But that's what makes this game interesting. It's made me stronger."

No one was more excited than Jerry Buss. "My dad was there and he ended up sitting with Boston ownership in their suite," Jeanie Buss recalled in a 2020 interview, "and when the team won my dad grabbed his jacket to go down to the locker room. He grabbed the wrong jacket. So, he wore somebody else's jacket and got doused with champagne. And then had to give back the jacket."

That merely added to the sweetness of it all.

"The Garden was nearly empty, with the reporters taking notes in the locker rooms and writing their stories," the owner would recall fondly in 1992. "Hampton Mears, one of my old friends, and I slipped out to the center of the Garden parquet. We giggled and exchanged high fives. The most odious sentence in all of sport—the Lakers have never beaten the Celtics—wasn't true anymore."

Broadcaster Chick Hearn remembered Johnson bringing Isiah Thomas to Boston with him that series, even inviting him to the joyous Lakers celebration party that night after the victory. Thomas seemed so awed by the event, Hearn recalled, that he stood back in the shadows, taking in every detail of what it was like to win such a rare prize in such an epic showdown in a place that had long frustrated and humiliated the entire league.

Across the country, it was a prize that left old Lakers feeling as if a weight had been lifted, prompting Steve Springer to do a story on Tommy Hawkins, who had sat and watched the closing game of the series on TV while dressed in his old blue Lakers uniform from the 1960s.

"Without a doubt, that was the Lakers' greatest moment," Johnson would say, looking back in 2004.

Err Jordan

Amidst all the joy of payback and retribution Johnson and his Lakers had gained during the 1984–85 season, events would reveal that another seed of another bad narrative had been planted, beginning that February at the All-Star Game in Indianapolis, where Chicago Bulls rookie Michael Jordan showed up in his fancy new black and red Air Jordan attire, which apparently made his clothing collection and shoes a target in the eyes of many of the league's very best players who were said to view it as representing all the things they never got.

For that season, Nike had pushed hard to make Air Jordan products available for the event in Indianapolis, athletic shoe impresario Sonny Vaccaro would recall in 2012. "We made red and black everything. Wrist bands, T-shirts, everything in the Bulls' colors."

Time would reveal just how much Jordan deserved those things, but at the moment, he was a rookie on a losing team who seemed to be way out in front of any sort of natural order of things, as perceived by some of the league's veterans. At least that would be the motivation attributed to figures such as Isiah Thomas and Johnson, among others.

As George Andrews would explain in 2019, these sentiments were driven in particular by Thomas, a Chicago high school legend now turned Detroit Piston who was annoyed immensely that his hometown had been usurped in a few astounding months by this very explosive rookie. Thomas and Mark Aguirre were among a group of players whom Charles Tucker and Andrews had begun representing in 1981 after the astounding rise of their primary client, Johnson, had driven their fortunes, just as it had driven those of Jerry Buss.

Thus began the plot for the infamous and supposed "freeze-out" of Jordan during the All-Star Game by Thomas and his Eastern teammates and enforced with enhanced defense from the Western Conference squad led by Johnson.

Lon Rosen would offer in 2019 that the freeze-out was between Thomas and Jordan, not Johnson, but that's not how it was perceived and received.

Perhaps there was never such a freeze-out, as some would claim, but those assertions only swirled with the facts at the time and for years afterward. George Andrews, Johnson's lawyer, was long dubious that there was a planned freeze-out. However, Andrews acknowledged in a 2022 interview, "there was such an animus against Michael that weekend because of Nike this and Nike that. Everybody was on Michael. Everybody was looking to put him in his place."

It didn't help, Andrews said, that Jordan's agent David Falk "was a pain in the ass."

There seemed little question at the time that Jordan came to believe there was a freeze-out, and that perception would become a reality that would eventually drive another narrative in Johnson's own life while it also defined his early rocky relationship with Jordan, a relationship that Johnson would make considerable effort to smooth over and repair in the coming seasons.

The other impression left by the incident was that it was certainly beneath those involved.

Supposedly, it was all triggered when Jordan wore his new Nike attire while warming up for the slam dunk contest in Indianapolis. Jordan, bedecked with gold necklaces during the event, famously lost in the dunk finals to Atlanta's Dominique Wilkins, as recounted in 2014's *Michael Jordan*.

Jordan's alleged arrogance was said to have prompted certain veterans, perceived as a group somehow represented or coordinated by Charles Tucker, to engage in that freeze-out treatment of Jordan during the main event, the All-Star Game. The alleged collusion was so subtle that at first even Jordan was surprised to learn of it. For the All-Star Game itself, Jordan had played 22 minutes and taken nine of the team's 120 shots.

The story broke afterward based on comments from Tucker, who was described as an advisor to Johnson, Thomas, and George Gervin. Tucker appeared to have talked about it openly. Charlie Vincent of the *Detroit Free Press* recalled in 2019 that Tucker and one of his associates first mentioned an effort against Jordan in the media hospitality room at halftime of the game.

Later, Charlie Vincent would talk again to Tucker and report the news of the incident.

"The man spreading the rumors of the incident was Dr. Charles Tucker, advisor and confidant to Thomas and Magic Johnson," Vincent reported in the *Free Press*.

"He's got some things to learn," Vincent, a veteran columnist, quoted Tucker as saying about Jordan. "He's got an attitude problem . . . like when he makes a basket. Sometimes he'll shake his finger at the guy guarding him. That don't go."

Vincent would report that news just hours after the All-Star Game, when Tucker, Thomas, and George Gervin were preparing to board a flight. They all appeared to be laughing heartily about the matter, according to reports at the time.

Asked about the laughter, Tucker offered a reply that would be quoted by Vincent: "We were talking about how good they got Jordan. I got together with a bunch of guys Saturday and talked about it. . . . But I think some of the guys thought we overdid it some."

Tucker would also be quoted as saying, "The guys weren't happy with his attitude up here. They decided to teach him a lesson. On defense, Magic and George gave him a hard time, and offensively, they just didn't give him the ball.

"That's what they're laughing about," Tucker explained as he stood near the players waiting to fly out. "George asked Isiah, 'You think we did a good enough job on him?'"

Tucker was also quoted as saying that the veterans thought the rookie seemed arrogant and standoffish. Thomas had supposedly been offended when Jordan had little to say during an elevator ride to a player meeting the first night of the weekend.

The reports apparently left Jordan stunned.

"I was very quiet when I went there," Jordan later explained. "I didn't want to go there like I was a big-shot rookie and you must respect me."

Jordan's agent David Falk explained that his client had been asked by Nike to wear the prototype of the Air Jordan clothing. "That makes me feel very small," Jordan said of the snub. "I want to crawl in a hole and not come out."

Asked about the incident by reporters, Thomas denied any freeze-out of Jordan. "How could someone do anything like that?" the Detroit guard said. "It's very childish."

Responding later to the freeze-out, Bulls teammate Wes Matthews said, "He's got gifts from God. He's God's kid; let him be God's kid."

A few days after his report about Tucker's coordinating the action against Jordan, Vincent received a late-night call from the psychologist, an apparent attempt to soften his comments. "You know the guys weren't serious about doing anything to Jordan," Vincent quoted Tucker as telling him. "They just meant they weren't going out of their way for him. . . . They never did plan on getting him. It was just that they weren't going to let him do what he wanted to do. They played him hard and he didn't get off. . . . They might have felt he was being a little bit cocky."

Vincent then quoted Tucker as saying of his clients, "You know how arrogant Isiah can be, and Magic, too."

Reported by Vincent, Tucker's call would be seen as an effort at damage control, but the damage was already done. Perception perhaps was spiraling into reality.

Jordan would go on to establish a reputation for taking any real or even an imagined slight and blowing it up into fierce competitive motivation.

In retrospect, Sonny Vaccaro saw the incident as a backlash against Nike by athletes who earned comparatively little from Converse. "Nike was the enemy," Vaccaro explained. "It was Nike. We created this guy. It was Nike. It wasn't so much he appeared in the dunk contest and was a fan favorite. Dr. J was a fan favorite. Nobody got mad at Dr. J. It was what we did with him."

The incident was particularly painful for Jordan because Johnson had been his idol in high school. His vanity plates stood as evidence of his wanting to perfect Johnson's ability with the no-look pass. "It started one day in practice," Jordan had told Wilmington, North Carolina, newspaper reporter Chuck Carree in 1981, "when I started doing some freaky things like Johnson does. I made some passes looking away and one of my teammates started calling me 'Magic Mike.' He bought me the license tag on the back, and my girlfriend got me a T-shirt and front license tag with MAGIC MIKE on it."

It wasn't just in high school that Jordan cited Johnson's influence. In the NBA, when his Chicago teammates grew tired of the approach of their coach, Doug Collins, they began encouraging Jordan to speak up about these issues, but he declined, pointing to the public furor that Johnson had stirred up in 1981 by taking on Westhead.

"As a head coach you're walking a fine line with Michael Jordan," Chicago's John Paxson said in 1995. "Not that he would ever do anything like that, but we all knew about the situation with Magic Johnson and Paul Westhead at the Lakers, when Westhead got fired after disagreeing with Magic. That's the power Michael could have wielded if he chose to."

That 1985 All-Star Weekend rang with bitterness for another reason, when it was announced the Bulls were being sold to Jerry Reinsdorf for what would be a relative pittance.

Chicago's franchise troubles would be traced to many factors, but ranking high on the list was the 1979 coin flip for the right to draft Johnson, which would mean NBA championships and profits for the winner. The value of the Lakers during Magic Johnson's first dozen years with the team would grow from about $30 million to $200 million, according to *Forbes* magazine in the 1990s.

Not long after the lost toss in 1979, Jonathan Kovler, one of the Bulls' owners, had ruefully joked that it was a "$25-million coin flip."

"It turned out to be a $200-million coin flip," Kovler would say later.

Actually, the flip likely was a billion-dollar loss or perhaps double that, for the collection of Bulls owners at the time. Reinsdorf bought the team from them for an estimated $14 million, then watched the franchise soar over the years to at least $2 billion in value or more. The Buss family and its partners would enjoy a similar rise from Johnson's sweeping influence on their franchise.

At the very least, the coin flip would stand as perhaps one of the most profound moments in NBA history. What if Chicago had won the right to draft Johnson? Would Jordan have ended up playing out his career in another market? Or would they have been teammates? Whatever the supposed answers to those questions, it became clear that in many ways the entire destiny of the league itself had rested in the heads or tails of Johnson's fate.

During that period, Johnson would astutely observe the magical ingredient that was driving his career, that was driving the business of pro basketball itself. "Winners are attractive to people," he would tell the *Detroit Free Press*. "If I were on a losing team, I would still be the same athlete, but I would never have gotten the exposure. Winning is where it begins. None of this would be possible without that."

No longer Jordan's idol, Johnson would soon loom as an unliked rival, and it wasn't just about winning and shoe deals.

"It's no secret around the league that, even with his championship rings, Johnson harbors something that seems to be more than professional jealousy toward Jordan," Curry Kirkpatrick would write in *Sports Illustrated*. "Commercially, at least, Magic should have been Michael seven years ago when he followed up winning the 1979 NCAA title for Michigan State with a tour de force sixth game in the 1980 NBA championship series, which the Lakers won over the Philadelphia 76ers."

The magazine suggested that it clearly bothered Johnson and other veterans that Jordan's Nike deal and the promotional effort behind it gave him a status above even the league's most accomplished stars.

Taken in total, the perceived snub in 1985 fired Jordan's competitiveness, explained Sonny Vaccaro, who had begun spending substantial time behind the scenes with the Chicago star. "That became his personal crutch," Vaccaro recalled in 2012. "That's why we watched this person turn into the killer on the court that he is. He took them all to task. He never forgot that day. He's smiling today and he's kissing with everybody and all that stuff, but he never forgot that."

Soon enough Johnson himself would acknowledge that Jordan's play was forcing a changing of the guard.

"Everybody always says it's me and Larry," Johnson would say some months down the road. "Really, it's Mike and everybody else."

Jordan, however, was on a much slower track than either Johnson or Bird. Jordan would labor in the league seven seasons before winning his first title, which meant Bird and Johnson would have time to conclude their battle before the rise of Jordan's Bulls.

In the interim, the 1985 All-Star Game would play yet another major role in the Johnson narrative.

At the time, Johnson and Isiah Thomas were making much of their high-profile personal friendship. They and Aguirre were portrayed in numerous stories as an extremely close trio, with Tucker often cast as a power broker in their careers.

"Tucker, who has been called a guru, an adviser, a confidante, a Svengali and a hard-boiled negotiator, is one of the most powerful men in professional basketball," the *Los Angeles Times* had declared just days before that fateful 1985 All-Star Game in citing the hold the school psychologist held over a number of the sport's top players.

"It's a necessary role," Jerry Buss told the *Times*. "And Tucker plays it very well. I came to basketball from tennis, where the players seemed to require a strong-willed person with whom to discuss their personal lives and their playing lives. There is so much hustle and bustle around superstars, whether in tennis or basketball. Tuck has his players' unquestioned faith, 100 percent. He deserves that trust."

The newspaper pointed out that Tucker advised a number of players, including the trio of friends.

"I don't recruit anybody," Tucker told *Times* writer Thomas Bonk. "I let them come to me. I work with people who think like I do. Every week, I get lots of players who ask me to help them. I get people who aren't jealous of each other and what they make. I get good people."

Buss wasn't alone in his praise. Pistons GM Jack McCloskey and

Dallas Mavericks executive Norm Sonju offered their own enthusiastic support of Tucker in other news accounts.

Several news stories pointed out that Tucker worked in conjunction with the Andrewses' law firm, and that both parties often worked on a handshake, not a signed contract.

Tucker explained that he didn't charge his athletes a percentage and worked on whatever fee they wanted to give him. Often, the token of appreciation for his services would arrive in the form of a luxury automobile. As for Johnson, he had Andrews drive a new Mercedes convertible up to Lansing from Chicago and right onto the floor of Tucker's summer basketball camp to surprise him.

"I've given back three Mercedes in the last year when Earvin, Isiah and Mark each wanted to give me one," Tucker told the *Times*. "I don't want 'em because I don't need 'em. Got my own car. A Jeep."

The *Times* pointed out Tucker also owned a 1932 Ford, a 1934 Chevrolet, and a 1973 Jaguar, the car the psychologist had lent Johnson "to take to the Everett High School prom."

In the wake of the All-Star Game, Johnson would imply some irritation with Tucker. The two had always related to each other "like brothers," Tucker had said frequently over the years. But the psychologist had likewise become displeased with Johnson a bit during this period. "I don't like all of that high-pollution attitude," Tucker would tell *Sports Illustrated*, implying that Johnson had acquired some Hollywood-style "glitter" values during his time in Southern California. "That's not the kind of person Earvin is."

The period in some ways marked the highest point of the long-running relationship between Tucker and Johnson, and after the events of 1985 the trajectory of that relationship began a marked decline, caused by many factors, to the point that within two years neither Tucker nor Andrews would be representing the Lakers star.

First, Andrews explained in 2019 that he became distracted by a serious family issue in that period. Plus, the distance was a factor. He lived in Chicago, and Tucker was still working as a school psychologist in Lansing. The lawyer also explained that Tucker began moving away from their relationship as the psychologist sought to become a player agent instead of just an advisor.

Certainly, another factor in prompting Johnson to think about making a change in representation was the fact that 1985 had also brought staggering losses in Abdul-Jabbar's wealth, blamed on bad investments set up by his former agent, which brought home to Johnson the long line of great American athletes who lost their wealth due to bad advice and bad decisions.

Clearly, the 1985 All-Star Game rested somewhere on that list of reasons that he began thinking about making a move, along with an added public embarrassment over poor management of one of Johnson's summer events with Tucker in Lansing. The issue of the freeze-out would surface again.

"I heard all the rumors, most of them coming from my former agent," Johnson would say much later, identifying the agent as Tucker, "and I knew I had to do something to clear the air."

Yet just what that air-clearing "something" would be wasn't obvious in 1985. The answer would take some time.

25

THE LIFE

The first wispy clouds of another storm began gathering in Johnson's life during this period, although they were hard perhaps even for Johnson himself to recognize. If there was a symbol of this slowly growing storm it might have been the mansion itself, seen by some observers to be evolving not just as a vacation spot for Johnson's friends and family members, but as the new owner's party palace, the scene of what several sources would later describe as Johnson's legendary sex parties, where attendees were encouraged to "get busy" with the array of women Johnson attracted to the premises, and likewise where Johnson was said sometimes to prowl the party making sure his guests were indeed getting busy.

Lon Rosen would later discount such claims about his friend and client, saying over the years that he himself would make an appearance at Johnson's parties and rarely if ever witnessed anything unseemly.

Yet his longtime friend and representative would, like so many others, tacitly, sadly, acknowledge the complications that numerous liaisons brought to Johnson's life after witnessing their growth firsthand. As intensely as Johnson pursued victory on the court, his off-court activities surged with their own single-mindedness, to the point that those around him began to marvel about them quietly.

Asked somewhat innocently by writer Bruce Newman about Johnson's relationship with the beautiful women of L.A. in 1986, Rosen recalled an incident from that most disastrous of years, 1984. Rosen was still working as the Forum's promotions director at the time, yet he and Johnson were already tight, so tight that while Rosen was having his car worked on, Johnson lent him his Mercedes, only to have the luxury ride explode while Rosen was running errands.

Uninjured but frightened, Rosen had jumped out of the burning car in disbelief, then frantically phoned and said, "Earvin, I've got bad news. Your car blew up!"

"Were you able to save the phone number that was in the glove compartment?" Johnson asked immediately.

"Earvin, listen to me," Rosen replied. "Your forty-thousand-dollar car is sitting in the middle of the street. It's toast."

Johnson said to forget the car, he'd have somebody take care of it.

"All he kept asking me was, 'Did you save that number?'" Rosen recalled.

It was the perfect punch line to illustrate what was then considered the red-blooded attitude of an All-American ladies' man. Only later would the clues add up on the long trail to his friend's sad disclosure.

Despite the chuckles and asides, the rumors and accounts of Johnson's growing appetites had long been an insider narrative making the rounds of quiet gossip in NBA circles. These tidbits were likewise on their way to making Johnson a legend among the league's legends of sexual consumption, all of which would later become immensely painful to his mother and other loved ones upon the dramatic public revelation of his lifestyle.

Christine Johnson, too, had begun to branch out in the public eye during this period, including NBA events, in the wake of her son's celebrity, this after years of not thinking of herself as the type of person to influence others publicly.

"She would attend events sometimes during the course of those All-Star weekends," former NBA player Terry Cummings recalled. "I played in a couple of All-Star Games, and I even came when I wasn't nominated for the team, because I was brought in to speak or to do something."

Cummings himself was quite focused on faith and soon developed an appreciation for Mrs. Johnson. "She has a pure heart toward God and people," Cummings recalled in a 2019 interview, "and I always thought that she was as intense of a person off the court as Magic was on the court. She showed equal intensity about her relationship with God."

To those who got to know Christine Johnson, her qualities helped explain almost immediately the source of her son's exceptional personal warmth and emotional intelligence. "When you meet her, she's everybody's mama," Terry Cummings explained. "It's something that will stick with you because she's not putting on. It ain't a façade for her, and one of the reasons I kept coming back whenever I knew she was involved was because I trusted what I saw in her heart."

Mark Aguirre would discover that same depth when his mother died at age forty-one during that period. Devastated, Aguirre found Mrs. Johnson to be an unexpected source of comfort.

Her touch also remained huge in her son's relationship with Kareem Abdul-Jabbar. She had an easy way of providing something of an emotional bridge between their diametrically different personalities.

In time, her son's sad revelations would make clear the contrast between her growing public expressions of faith, including her love and sponsorship of gospel music, and his reputation in NBA circles for wild, even reckless, off-the-court activities.

This object lesson would come later for Johnson, upon his realizing all the pain and anguish his lifestyle caused his mother and others he loved.

At the time, Christine Johnson was obviously not aware of the extent of this contrast between her behavior and that of her son, although one of his visits to Lansing over the summer of 1984 had helped to offer some indication of the seriousness of it, as well as the alarming sense that Johnson conducted it all in such a clandestine manner.

Johnson had once again renewed his relationship with Cookie Kelly and would bring her to the fine home he had provided for his parents one day that summer of 1984, only to disappear and return later with a cute three-year-old boy in tow.

It was the first time Johnson had brought his son, Andre, to meet his parents, which left Kelly stunned. She had never heard a word about the child, she would reveal later about the moment.

"This is the first time I've taken him from the home by myself," Johnson told her.

It would be another three years before good friend Greg Kelser learned of Andre and was likewise stunned and left to marvel at Johnson's intense privacy, especially for a person so outgoing and with such a large personality.

On the other hand, others saw it as an important step that Johnson had acknowledged the child and had begun to make him a part of his life, a relationship that would continue as Johnson's career moved along, to the point that it would not be unusual for reporters to see Andre hanging out near Johnson in the locker room after a game.

It should not be surprising that with intense, unfettered sexual activity around public figures, from sports stars to entertainment personalities, the era would produce an array of paternity cases, which would soon be detailed by media reports about professional athletes fathering children with multiple women. With his furtive approach, Johnson somehow managed to avoid being mentioned in such stories.

However, Greg Eaton, his old mentor, would also learn about Andre, which left him cautioning Johnson. "I told him, 'You have to be careful. Your career and everything is before you. People don't want you knockin' up their sisters and daughters. Your image is important,'" Eaton would later recall. "You have to put it in perspective. Most young girls, what do they want? If they are unschooled, they want a baby . . . a young man is very vulnerable to that."

That, of course, would be in addition to the vulnerabilities of young women in the insular world inhabited by groupies and others drawn to attractive public figures such as Johnson.

Indeed, media reports years later would reveal that Johnson himself was the target of other paternity actions—not surprising considering his disinclination to wear a condom, a disinclination that would continue for a full decade after the birth of Andre—although the process and outcome of those paternity cases against him would be obscured from public view by the courts.

Just in the Lansing area alone, Johnson faced two such paternity suits, *The Washington Post* would report in 1991. "He is named in two paternity suits in Ingham County Circuit Court in Michigan, the details of which have been suppressed."

During this period, Johnson became known for his vehicles, a Rolls-Royce, a Mercedes, even a Ford Bronco. As opposed to his early days in the Electra, it was a period where some thought he seemed to withdraw from his old friends in Lansing. Those who followed him closely could see his appetite for shopping sprees for clothing and other items, including the reported purchase in New Orleans of seven pairs of alligator shoes. Whatever Johnson did, it seemed, he did it in volume.

In the wake of Cookie Kelly meeting Andre during the off-season of 1984, the couple's relationship seemed to grow stronger to the point that during a 1985 trip to Lansing, Johnson invited Kelly to Tucker's house for dinner before heading back to Los Angeles to begin training for the 1985–86 season. They sat and talked a bit after the meal and as Kelly prepared to leave, Johnson suddenly produced a ring and proposed, almost casually, on the spot.

Her "yes" may have shattered speed records as did her thoughts and many questions about planning the event. She had made great headway in her career in Toledo as a fashion merchandiser and suddenly faced a multitude of decisions. As she later recounted, she was quite eager to wed the man she loved. Yet working out the details of her life in Toledo and his in Los Angeles would involve complications. Little did she realize just how grandiose those complications would prove to be.

One seemingly harmless development would arise just as the 1985–86 season was set to open when Johnson showed up to practice one day with blisters or lesions on his face. Trainer Gary Vitti took a look at him and sent him to the doctor immediately.

The diagnosis, too, was swift and unusual. Johnson had shingles, also known as herpes zoster, a condition tied frequently to those who had suffered chickenpox in childhood. The vast majority of people it strikes are fifty or over. Johnson was twenty-six, although not much was thought of the matter at the time. He missed the Lakers' season opener and a few other games, then returned to lead the team to another strong start.

Six years later, however, after Johnson announced that he was HIV positive, his shingles episode would serve as something of a red flag and draw more scrutiny.

"Shingles is also common among people infected with the AIDS virus," *The New York Times* reported during the early speculation over just when he had contracted the virus.

"A case of shingles that kept Johnson out of several games in 1985 could also have marked the onset of the pre-AIDS virus," *Newsweek* reported at the time.

In the fall of 1985, the public had no knowledge of the extent and complexity of Johnson's sex life and his exposure to sexually transmitted disease due to his aversion to wearing a condom. Thus, there was no great interest in his shingles. Rather, everybody seemed to be focused on whether the Celtics and Lakers could return once again to the league championship series to resume their legendary battle. After all, even the most casual basketball fans knew well the running score between pro basketball's two great teams of that era. Johnson's Lakers had now won three NBA titles while Bird's Celtics had won two. And the teams had split their two championship meetings.

Despite the team scores, when it came to respect as a player, Bird clearly ranked higher in the public mind. He was on his way to his third straight league MVP award. It was no secret to those around Johnson that he was bothered immensely by the fact that his own play and success had brought no such recognition.

If nothing else, 1985–86 loomed as an opportunity for Johnson to rectify that with another excellent season. Sure enough, once he returned to the lineup, both teams resumed their forced march.

In the wake of the '85 title, the Lakers had waived Jamaal Wilkes and declined to pick up the option on Bob McAdoo's contract. Both were popular with their teammates, but the challenge of sustaining a dynasty franchise in sports had long required keen roster management, since the early years of the NBA when the Minneapolis Lakers of George Mikan and Jim Pollard had reigned with a run of five titles from 1948 well into the 1950s (as well as a sixth pro championship in 1947 in the old National League).

To strengthen the frontcourt after McAdoo's departure, Lakers management signed veteran bruiser Maurice Lucas, calculating that he would give the roster some toughness. His tenure, however, was marked by chemistry issues and would become one of several factors in the Lakers' struggles.

"Winning the '85 title took tremendous energy from our guys," Gary Vitti would recall. "It was really mentally fatiguing to break that Celtic barrier. That next year, we needed an injection of something and it just wasn't there."

The team, however, was making progress and Johnson was engrossed in the challenges he faced. It was quite an undertaking, even for a player like Johnson with such talented teammates, to stay atop the NBA mountain. Indeed, Johnson had two very busy lives, one on and the other off the court. In retrospect, it shouldn't seem surprising that a conflict soon arose because Cookie Kelly, like any bride-to-be, had questions and decisions to address with her fiancé. It didn't take much in the way of questions over this period before Johnson phoned her one winter day.

"I can't do this," he said.

Kelly was stunned that he would break off the engagement in a phone conversation, which prompted her to seek him out in person in January 1986 when the Lakers were in Detroit to play the Pistons. She went to his hotel room to discuss the matter further, but Johnson didn't appear to want to even let her into his room, she would recall, and again he offered nothing more than "I just can't do this."

Like that, their relationship plunged just as quickly as it had risen, leaving Kelly's broken heart like a trail of ether and smoke and debris in its wake. Her only solution, she recalled, was to turn to her faith for answers.

Johnson chose to reveal the breakup in a May story in the *Free*

Press. "Not now," he said of marriage. "Not with a career to keep on top of."

The *Free Press* noted that Johnson then lowered his voice and added, "I want to enjoy the other side of life."

In all fairness, Johnson had always emphasized to Kelly that his first love was the game. It would later be revealed that such love for the game had rules, including no sex before tipoff. As much as he had come to desire it, he wanted nothing to keep him from performing his best.

The sad irony, of course, would be that if, in that moment, Johnson had been able to confront his lifestyle issues and see his way to focusing on Kelly, he might have had a far longer NBA career, might even have avoided being infected with HIV.

Yet the conflict would prove to be simply another round in the protracted push and pull between Johnson and Kelly over their relationship, a push and pull some would come to identify, in retrospect, as the earmarks, if not the trademarks, of addiction.

After all, sex "addiction" seemed an almost unfathomable attachment to a figure like Johnson, who had appeared as such a model teen during his days in Lansing. Addictions of all sorts, however, had gained prominence in that era for what they did silently to kill all sorts of people in many different ways, even the greatest Americans, dogging their greatness like packs of wolves, eating huge gulps of the essence of poor, beleaguered figures until they were often consumed and almost unrecognizable.

Being in love with an any sort of addict can be particularly difficult, explained George Mumford, the internationally known psychologist and mindfulness expert on the staff of coach Phil Jackson, both with the Chicago Bulls and the Lakers. Mumford himself had been a drug addict as a young adult until finally throwing off his addiction after it had nearly destroyed his life.

The difficulty of being in a relationship with an addict, Mumford explained in a 2021 interview, is that "they aren't there. You're by yourself in the relationship. The people who love addicts get addicted to them, in a way. Because when addicts are present in the relationship, they are usually really there, to the point that the ones who love them become almost seduced by how good things are when addicts are present in a relationship. The potential is there, to the point that you will put up with almost anything just to have them there."

What makes matters worse for people in love with an addict is that addicts are extremely manipulative, Mumford explained. "They know what to say and when to say it and how to say it. They set you up for the big fall."

Johnson perhaps had gained some insight into such issues when dealing with his brother Larry's drug issues. Johnson had brought Larry to Los Angeles in an effort to overcome those issues, an undertaking that was later viewed as unsuccessful, although Larry would eventually find the immense strength necessary to throw off his issues and regain his life of good standing and respect among family and friends.

Addicts themselves are often governed by an intense self-love and an intense self-hatred, George Mumford explained. That's why, he added, the nature of a relationship with an addict often becomes a matter of push and pull.

"They're like trying to grasp water."

Cookie Kelly would spend years grasping for that water in her dealings with Johnson, as would others.

Johnson's lifestyle would eventually cause concern among the team's management, according to later reports. The Lakers were said to have gone so far as to contact the NBA in New York for help in dealing with Johnson's issues. The team would later deny that it ever contacted the NBA about Johnson's off-court life. Lon Rosen would long maintain that the Lakers never contacted the NBA about Johnson's off-court activities.

Asked later about the issue, Jerry Buss would say in a 1993 interview that, even with their friendship, he didn't think of reminding Johnson about protection. "Magic was a mature man," Buss explained. "Plus, I didn't realize there was as much activity as there was."

With AIDS fears gaining prominence in the 1980s, Lakers trainer Gary Vitti would recall that he began carrying condoms and making them available to players. Vitti would later say he pointedly asked Johnson if he was taking the proper precaution.

In a 1992 interview, Vitti recalled Johnson replying, "Yeah, everything's cool."

Vitti would admit he knew Johnson was fibbing. And it would later haunt the trainer that he didn't confront the star. "I felt I let him down," Vitti would say in 1992. "I let myself down. I didn't do what I was supposed to do. Somehow, I should've made him more aware, made him understand."

Others, of course, weren't so sure, as laid out in 1993's *The Lakers*.

"Earvin wanted to live his life his way," team equipment manager Rudy Garciduenas would say later. "Once he made up his mind, he wasn't going to change it for anybody."

With Johnson's appetites, Laker players and staff marveled at his durability. And they had all come to believe in his infallibility. He was Magic, the guy who produced miracles on the court.

During one training camp during the period, several players and staffers had discussed sex and social diseases. Inevitably, the discussion turned to Johnson. ("We always talked about Magic and the wild shit that he did," explained one staff member.) And one of the group laughed and said, "Shit. If that motherfucker doesn't have it, you can't get it."

The comment was said to have produced laughs all around.

In some ways, he was seemingly superhuman, so potent that sexually transmitted diseases couldn't affect him. He didn't need condoms.

The comment had legs enough to become something of an inside punch line around the Lakers over the ensuing months.

"If he doesn't have it, you can't get it."

Meanwhile, in his public life he loomed as a virtual master of the universe, able to perform wondrously, to conjure up great feats, all on full display for an adoring public. Yet what seemed to be his good and normal approach to life was wrapped in dangerously excessive behavior.

And Johnson's enormous personal confidence was now leading him to a self-deception of immense proportions.

As for "Magic" Johnson's "addictions," he seemed caught fast in the delightful double meaning of the name itself, unable to pull himself away. His relationship with sex was like cocaine. So much confidence. So much elation and fascination with the many beautiful bodies, with physical form itself. His power, the mastery, the loveliness of it all left him absolutely unable to relinquish it.

In certain circles he pridefully carried the image of the ultimate sexual athlete, able to deliver multiple assists at will.

Still, he managed to control the circumstances somewhat by sticking to his code, refusing on game days to engage until after the game, then gorging on it in the variety of fashion that Hollywood and his station offered. In that moment, he remained strong and filled with false confidence and self-deception, which he would come to see only later when his options were pinned to the floor very publicly by his dramatic stumble.

Until then, he was masterfully sneaky like any good junkie worth his salt, and it was always delightfully there. He would become known for inviting multiple women to his games and having them seated strategically around the arena, where he could locate them, the mere thought of their presence and their intent sparking the first endorphins, building his anticipation for after the game. People hardly noticed, and even if they did, it didn't matter, because he kept smiling. And winning.

At one point, Riley's wife, Chris, a psychologist, would make an appeal to Kelly, reaching out and telling her that Johnson needed a woman and a home in his life. Being the wife of his coach, she likely had heard things. As those around Johnson would later say, they basically knew what he was doing only to realize later they had no idea of the scope and the scale of it.

The least among these perhaps was Kelly herself, who had been dealing with the issue since their first days at Michigan State together. After all, Johnson was quite the exceptional person, a great man with the tendencies of a great human being, and she loved him for it. Only later would they all discover just how much she loved him, for hers would prove to be no shallow, prideful love, as it was first assumed by many observers, but an unconditional love. In retrospect, of the many great gifts in Johnson's life, the love of Earlitha Kelly would rival anything else in his existence. Of all the many varieties of so-called love in the life of Earvin Johnson, hers would prove the most powerful and redemptive. This love she would offer time and again, even as he showed repeatedly that he had seemingly little real value or respect for it. As she would later often point out, she had no earthly idea at the time of the volume and depth of his activity. Yet even when she did come to learn those things, she would give almost without condition.

George Andrews would observe that, in Kelly, Johnson was basically courting his mother, which left him trapped in yet another push and pull, between a single female ideal and a virtual flood tide of whatever he wanted whenever he wanted it.

"He always said Cookie was the only woman he would marry," Andrews recalled.

Marriage, though, clearly rode in the backseat. The sex certainly served as a measure of Johnson's sense of power as did his broad personal appeal. Riley had long described him as "the pied piper," and the 1985 championship had only amplified the relationship between Johnson and his adoring public. Literally everywhere he turned, he encountered worshippers, almost awestruck, regardless of who they were. And once they had been in his presence, they seemed to want to be in it again and again, to be near him. Especially after Laker games.

"After every game, we'd have this entourage, this line of cars behind our team bus, that would follow us to the airport in hopes of getting a glimpse of Earvin, maybe an autograph," explained Lakers broadcaster Stu Lantz. "It was hilarious. We'd look out the window at the line of cars and laugh. That's the kind of effect he had on people, and they weren't all women. There'd be families. There'd be the dad, the wife and two kids, following the bus. We'd pull to the airport runway gates—we'd drive straight onto the runway to meet our charter—and the gates would close, and they'd all get out of the cars and run out to the fence, hoping to see him."

That spring of 1986, Johnson made an appearance at a Southern California high school to make a talk against drug use, and it got out of hand, with a crush of teenaged girls and other fans rushing Johnson, sending him retreating through the adulation to his car, which the crowd gathered around, something of a crazy scene as

Johnson told the driver not to pull away, out of fear that one of the fans might get hurt.

He sat in the car, marked by lipstick prints on his clothing and face.

Vitti, the team's trainer, remembered that Johnson was wearing a white sweatshirt, and when he returned, the sweatshirt was decorated with pink lipstick prints.

"Covered with pink lip prints," Vitti recounted six years later, still in disbelief.

Johnson attracted his partners merely by virtue of his personal charm. And they weren't all strangers. Mixed in the crowd seeking his favors were Johnson's regular partners, old standbys, women who would cycle in and out of this shadow life.

"He's magnetic," Dana James, a TV broadcaster who dated Johnson during this period, told *The Washington Post* in 1991. A morning host for a network affiliate in Los Angeles, James described the Johnson attraction she witnessed during months of dating him: "All people are drawn to him. Any person who ever entered his personal space, he was genuinely kind to."

That he could be lauded for his kindness in the midst of disclosures of what critics considered rampant womanizing suggested the complexity of the central figure. But it was a statement that the reporters who covered him knew to be true. In the world of professional athletes, many of whom were known for being rude or brusque with the press, Johnson was considered unfailingly polite and patient by virtually all who interviewed him. Just about everyone who encountered him came away marveling at his ability to engage.

Yet another woman—who agreed to be interviewed only after insisting on anonymity from *The Washington Post*—offered that her relationship with Johnson when he was a young player in 1981 "was nothing real serious."

"He likes power," the former lover said. "He always had to be a winner. I'm not saying he's disrespectful of women, but how can you respect someone when he's going out and sleeping with women daily?"

The woman, who was a Southern California college student when she was introduced to Johnson, said she could "read the writing on the wall" upon engaging with him and realizing she was merely one of his many lovers. She said she stopped seeing him but only after two years.

His later estimate that he had sexual relations with three to five hundred women annually left friends and associates amazed by the discretion, circumstances, and planning required to ring up such numbers, given his schedule. Johnson's revelations would thus produce an effort by associates to try to explain it to the media. At the time it happened, outside of a small inner circle of Laker staffers and players, few people knew exactly what he was doing.

"When I first started with the team, it was astounding," said Rudy Garciduenas, the equipment manager who would become another good and loyal friend of Johnson's. "But it was an existence, a way of life with Earvin. I came to understand Earvin and the way he did things, his love for women, females in general. That's the way it was. When you're a person of that stature, it's almost expected. All the movie stars get the same attention."

Watching Johnson operate left the equipment manager awed when he joined the team around 1985.

"You'd just have to shake your head," Garciduenas said in a 1992 interview. "Every male wants to be that way, or dreams of being that way for just one night. But with Earvin, it was reality."

Reality certainly was tested by the tales of his exploits. Johnson himself would later boast of all sorts of liaisons. In public places with a prominent TV newscaster. Sex in a movie theater. Sex in an elevator. Sex in a corporate boardroom. Sex in a thousand hotel rooms. Literally sex anywhere Johnson could find to celebrate his Dionysian power.

There was even word that Johnson had sex with a woman in one of the Forum's back rooms just moments after a game, then put on a robe and stepped out to hold postgame interviews for the press. Several Laker staffers suggested such a liaison was nearly impossible.

But Garciduenas didn't think so. "It's difficult to imagine," the equipment manager said, "but Earvin was used to doing anything he wanted, really. And people loved Earvin so much that nothing he did was wrong. It was never really hidden from anybody, what Earvin did. He was always pretty up-front with it. That was part of him. You had to learn to accept it."

Many nights, the women would be waiting in the tunnel when the players exited the floor, Joe McDonnell would recall in 2004. "You would go to the end of the tunnel, and the women would be handing their phone numbers to the ball boy, or Magic would have seen somebody that he liked. Everybody knew what was going on back in the weight room and everything else. It was totally different. The women were just ridiculous. Not only the ones with Buss, but the ones who came to hang around just to try to be part of the scene."

This phenomenon, of course, wasn't exclusive to Johnson, far from it. American culture was quite aware of the power of such attraction for public figures. The pace and frequent travel of the NBA merely made its athletes and coaches, even its front office figures, available in predictable ways for the public. And this was especially true for the Lakers.

The Atlanta Hawks' Dominique Wilkins admitted that he had encountered quite a few ladies over the years. "They want the thrill of being with an athlete," he explained to *Sports Illustrated* in 1991. "And they don't want safe sex. They want to have your baby, man, because they think that if they have your baby, they're set for life. That's the hard fact of it, because if they had a life, they wouldn't be hanging around the hotel or showing up at the back door of the arena trying to pick up a player."

"We don't even have to try," former Phoenix Suns guard Kevin Johnson told another writer. "We come into town, and the women come out in force. They call the hotel, they follow the bus. They hover and wait to get you."

Such reactions were typical of many NBA players in that era, explained Lorin Pullman in a 1992 interview. She had once worked for the Lakers in public relations and later became Abdul-Jabbar's publicist. "They act like these women are such a problem for them. But the guys perpetuate the behavior."

Many women had come to see the pursuit of an athlete or an

entertainment figure as an expression of their own liberation. Robin Power, who identified herself as one of Johnson's lovers, told writer E. Jean Carroll that engaging NBA players was a fun pastime. Once again, Jerry Buss would factor into this equation by creating the Forum Club, designed to keep celebrities at the Forum to party after games rather than repairing to bars and spending their money elsewhere.

The owner had a table at the club where he could entertain an array of celebrities that served as an attraction to rival the Playboy Club in terms of magnetism. The Forum Club, as the arena's dining club and late-night hot spot, created a perfect space for the agenda. Basketball had never seen anything quite like it, and probably never will again. Before Laker games in the 1980s, it became the place for power dinners, the kind of place where Jerry Buss could accomplish his goals in courting investors for his real estate deals. After games, it turned into an ultimate singles bar, throbbing with energy and celebrity at the height of Showtime. During that era, the Lakers usually lost only four or five home games a season, making the Forum Club the place for winners. After games, players from both teams donned their expensive suits for a swing through the club. "Any athlete who walks in there is already spotted," guard Byron Scott explained in 1993. "He's got three, four or five girls who already spotted him and it depends on which one he wants to go with."

The atmosphere was said to be so thick that the wives and regular girlfriends of Lakers players felt compelled to make an appearance. "They had to do that to make sure these women knew their guy was accounted for," Lorin Pullman explained in 1993.

Away from Los Angeles, the hotels offered opportunity for liaisons. "When our bus would pull up to a hotel, you'd see 60 people out there waiting and 40 of them would be women," Byron Scott explained in 1992. "It was like going around with a rock group. It was just amazing."

The "road," meanwhile, was said to leave the wives and girlfriends facing distinct barriers. Under Riley, the Lakers were said to have an "excess baggage" rule, barring family members, wives, and girlfriends of players from traveling with the team because they created a distraction. Riley would later counter that his "excess baggage" distinction didn't mean the wives, yet partners who did travel to away games were said to make an effort to avoid the coaches.

"I always felt that contributed to the excess," Pullman said. "If you wanted your wife or girlfriend along, what was wrong with that? You're not going to walk through the bar or lobby looking for women if your wife is upstairs in your room."

Often, the Lakers didn't have to go to the action in the lobby. It came to them, as George Andrews had discovered in the early seasons when he met Johnson on the road to discuss business matters, only to find those discussions interrupted by the seemingly nonstop efforts of aggressive women to connect with Johnson.

In a game of very competitive people, it wasn't much of a stretch to include "scoring" off the court among the accepted metrics for status among the game's players, coaches, and even front office personnel. Sex had been a game within the game long before Magic Johnson ever arrived on the scene. It had become part of the institutional knowledge within the sport itself.

"I couldn't believe how they all shared notes in the locker room," Lorin Pullman explained. "'My God,' I thought, 'this is like they're still in high school.'"

"He could have all the women. . . . For a lot of men—not just Magic—women become another game," Johnson's friend Pamela McGee would tell a reporter. "Who could have the most women? Who could have the most beautiful women?"

For Johnson, keeping score seemed an additional, impossibly complicated burden, although he wasn't above phoning an old friend back in Lansing to announce the identity of a prominent Hollywood star he had just bedded.

"It didn't do any good to keep count," Rudy Garciduenas said, "because there was always going to be somebody new. It just wasn't any good to count or to try to keep track of any of them."

Johnson, however, would later offer up his code in these endeavors, allowing that he never permitted a woman to stay overnight with him. Supposedly, that honor was reserved for Kelly, a distinction that seemed to end when Johnson called off the wedding, which plunged the couple into an extended estrangement during which Kelly turned to a relationship with a man from Chicago. With that, she removed herself from the impossible equations in his life, and Johnson himself was free to make his way through whatever complications the 1986 season would bring without the "distraction" of her presence to blame.

That perhaps seemed to be a good formula through the first two rounds of the 1986 playoffs. The Lakers swept San Antonio in the first round, then swamped Dallas 4–2 in the semifinals, and faced Houston for the conference title, a series that began with a solid 12-point win in the first game in Los Angeles, prompting *Sports Illustrated* along with just about all the sports media in America to project that Johnson and company were headed to yet another gilded rematch with Bird and company.

"No Shot for the Rockets," *Sports Illustrated* announced after Game 1.

But while the Celtics scorched their way 11–1 through the Eastern playoffs, the Lakers somehow then lost four straight games to Houston, their fate sealed by one last awkward Ralph Sampson jumper that somehow dropped in, surprising everybody in the building in the process.

"We beat them the first game and thought it was going to be a cakewalk," Byron Scott recalled. "Then they caught up and got us in Houston and we never recovered."

"Houston was playing great," Gary Vitti would remember, "and we were going through the motions."

And then, adding to the injury, CBS invited Johnson to be a commentator for Game 2 of the NBA Finals.

First of all, he arrived in Boston just as Bird had been presented with his third straight league MVP trophy. "This year I started out slowly because of injuries," Bird had said in receiving the award, "but once they faded away, I was in total control of my game the second half of the season. I just felt there was no one in the league who could stop me if I was playing hard."

No one in the league? It was enough to send Johnson through the roof. Then he had to sit there as a commentator and watch Houston struggle in the bright lights of the championship series.

"They didn't know what a championship is all about," he would say of those Rockets.

The unspoken narrative was that the broadcasting gig had mirrored that game Johnson had sat out in Boston Garden, there on the bench as Bird tormented him from the floor. The Boston star was well aware of his rival's presence in the broadcast booth and responded with another show, specifically 31 points, eight rebounds, seven assists, four steals, two blocks.

In their deep personal rivalry, Bird and Magic were keyed in on the circumstances, of Bird playing his way to a third NBA title and Johnson having to sit there and watch. They both knew exactly what it was, a jab at Johnson's anguish, a finger in his eye.

None of which escaped the trained observation of *L.A. Times* columnist Scott Ostler, who wrote, "How sad it must have been for Laker fans to see Mr. Magic in a suit and tie, sitting up in the broadcast booth, eye-level with the 15 Celtic championship banners. Watching the game."

Midsummer

The loss was only the beginning of the agony, with the Lakers left to watch on TV as Bird and Boston took another title. Jerry Buss especially didn't like it. Houston's Twin Towers approach had left the owner thinking the Lakers needed more size to battle Hakeem Olajuwon and Ralph Sampson in the conference and strangely went behind Jerry West's back to arrange a deal with Dallas for Mark Aguirre and Roy Tarpley, two Charles Tucker clients.

Buss supposedly then informed West of the deal, telling his GM it was already agreed to. West then supposedly threatened to resign if it went through, which in turn sent the wheels into reverse.

A trade based on emotions was unwise, West had argued. The Celtics, of course, had hoped that Buss would break up the team.

The owner's anger eventually calmed, and Pat Riley began looking for other answers.

There would be much fallout, however, including another harsh blow to Johnson's relationship with Michael Jordan. Things between the two stars would continue to sour, based largely on another perception, that Johnson and Tucker were behind the trade. In an interview years later, Lon Rosen would counter that Johnson was not involved in the move, although there were indications he was aware of it.

"Magic would have loved it because they were two of his buddies," George Andrews offered in a 2022 interview. Plus there were basketball reasons for the move. Aguirre was not only a strong scorer but a gifted passer, and Tarpley could play both center and power forward. And both players were said to intensely dislike playing for abrasive coach Dick Motta in Dallas.

It's easy to see Buss discussing such a move with Johnson, Andrews said, because by 1986 "they were almost father and son."

Jordan, meanwhile, didn't hesitate to express his own theory that Johnson had been behind the plan. "I don't hold anything against him," Jordan told *Sports Illustrated*'s Curry Kirkpatrick in 1987. "I just think he doesn't like players who come from North Carolina."

Somehow, that same busy off-season of 1986, Converse, which had been pushing to get Bird and Johnson to do a shoe commercial together, began pushing harder.

"They were as cordial as could be—for sworn enemies," George Andrews said of the relationship at the time. "It was a situation. Nobody gave an inch between them."

"These guys, they really didn't talk for years," Lon Rosen explained.

Writer Jackie MacMullan would reveal that Bird, convinced that Johnson would never agree, had insisted on the ad being shot at his place in Indiana. To his surprise, Johnson did agree to the concession.

It all fell into place because both players very much liked Converse representative Al Harden, who had approached them with the idea. Plus, there was a precedent of sorts. They had at least gotten together for an earlier photo shoot with a larger group of players who endorsed Converse, but a commercial shoot with just the two of them?

"They both had reservations," Andrews recalled, adding they finally agreed only out of their mutual regard for Al Harden.

It didn't hurt that their personal competition was at least in a temporary balance with both having won pro titles against the other, Andrews recalled. "They weren't the kind of guys to go out and party together because they had totally different personalities."

However, the two would first begin to find some measure of a relationship and appreciation in the off-season at two memorable events.

First, Harden and Converse arranged for a video shoot of a somewhat bizarrely edgy and humorous sneaker commercial that had Johnson going Hollywood by pulling up at Bird's country abode in a limo, only to have Bird greet him by ripping off his own warm-up pants, gritting his teeth, and challenging Johnson to "Show me what you got!"

Johnson had approached the meeting with low expectations only to be surprised by the warmth of Bird's mother, Georgia, with the lunch she had prepared. The special moment would be captured later by MacMullan for her book *When the Game Was Ours*, about the Bird-Johnson relationship, which would later serve as a basis for a Broadway play.

The two competitors talked about many things in the basement of Bird's place that day, including an appreciation of their fathers, both veterans, both hardworking family men. Both held their fathers in great esteem, with the marked difference being that at age eighteen Bird had lost his dad to suicide.

The moment allowed Johnson and Bird the time to talk and for the first time really get a sense of each other. This, despite the gathering notion that they were headed for another showdown that just might determine who was going to lay claim to bragging rights for the ages.

When they finally did start talking, they discovered their own little club of two, Rosen said in 2019. "To this day to hear them talk to each other it's like amazing. I mean, they both have a true respect and love for each other. Again, I don't know Larry Bird that well, but I know him well enough he told me how he grew up. I'm not sure how, but this guy—who grew up in Indiana where the Ku Klux Klan was—he just didn't care if you were Black or white. He told the stories of the reason he became a good basketball player. He worked at a hotel and he would play with the waiters. That were African Americans."

That experience contributed much to his learning of the game, Bird would say.

Later, that August, came Johnson's first Midsummer Night's Magic event to raise money for the United Negro College Fund that would frequently be remembered as beginning in 1985, although it actually began that summer of '86.

"When Earvin started doing the UNCF game the first year, he wanted Larry Bird to play," Rosen recalled.

For that to happen, Red Auerbach required Johnson to phone him to ask personally for permission for Bird to play, another of the Celtic boss's mind games.

"Larry, I think he just got married, he came to the game, he was beet red," Rosen remembered. "They played the first game at Pauley Pavilion. It was a great game. Earvin was more excited to play with Larry than you could imagine. And so was Larry to play with him. There was no disrespect."

That first Midsummer Night's Magic was one of basketball's stolen dreams, outshining the official All-Star Game so badly in terms of pure fun that the NBA would soon move to prevent Johnson's game in subsequent years from being broadcast on TV. Why? Because the sad truth was so obvious. Johnson's spontaneous Midsummer event offered so much of his personal charisma as its maestro, star player, and Hollywood host that the league's suits could never hope to match it with the All-Star Game, no matter what their budget or the events they dreamed up. It was Johnson's starburst vs. their process.

And it featured a nonstop pace of showboating wraparound passes, no-looks, and every kind of whoop-a-doodle sequence the roster of great players could come up with on the fly, complete with uproariously missed dunks and grandly ambitious turnovers, all narrated by the fun-loving Chick Hearn on the Prime Ticket broadcast.

Yes, it was just another vapid all-star-type event, but it obviously mattered deeply to those on the court with Johnson's great pride and competitiveness fusing the moment. He made sure Bird was on his team, which produced some gems that evening. When the two sent some no-look passes to each other on their way to a slam dunk (and some glorious misfires as well), Hearn declared, "That's why he and Bird are ticket sellers. That's why he and Bird make three million a year between them."

The rosters were so stuffed with talent, with Jerry West coaching one team and Bill Russell, with his cackling laugh, coaching the other, Johnson and Bird couldn't even manage to eke out a victory at their own rigged game, their blue team losing to the white, 170–166.

Not to worry, the matchups featured a steady pace of the spectacular, such as a block of a Charles Barkley shot at one end that instantly turned into Johnson speeding at an angle up the court, from the left all the way into the top of the key where he bounce-passed a no-look behind him to a converging Bird on the right who instantly converted a touch pass all the way across the court to a streaking Herb Williams on the left who finished with a reverse two-handed slam dunk.

Or moments later Johnson spotting Bird's blond head bobbing as he raced up the right sideline prompting Johnson to hit him with a 50-foot touch pass of his own.

As if this display wasn't enough for the packed, madly cheering house, the sweat wasn't dry from the main run before Johnson grabbed a mic and launched into his running commentary for the slam dunk contest, which rolled into an over-the-top unscripted throw-down between Dominique Wilkins and tiny Spud Webb, again all executed on the fly.

"Three-sixty," Johnson kept yelling at Wilkins, only to see him suffer a huge miss, as the crowd roared.

"We'll give it another try," Johnson yelled immediately. "We got all night."

At the end of the broadcast, Hearn repeated the final score, then added, "But that really doesn't matter."

It did not. There would be even more scoring the second year, when Johnson sent an invitation to Jordan to come play.

Jordan "tersely" declined, *Sports Illustrated* would report, implying that the All-Star snubbing two years earlier still burned him.

The truth was, Jordan now faced a staggering array of commitments in the off-season, much of it related to his shoe line success that would eternally irritate Johnson. Jordan had laughed the first time agent David Falk ran the name Air Jordan past him. But in less than three years, he had become an unprecedented marketing force.

"First I thought it was a fad," Jordan would say, looking back on the response to the shoe line.

Jordan did agree to play in the 1988 Midsummer Night's Magic game, but by then the league had squelched the broadcasting of it. Not to worry, Johnson would run the event a full twenty years, raising millions for historically Black colleges and universities, before turning the event over to others to run.

As he rolled toward his thirties, Johnson's mojo seemed headed toward a fascinating conclusion, much like a storm, both exhilarating and threatening.

26

THE GUARANTEE

Buck Johnson knew they were out there, watching him. They had scouted his games, then come back and scouted some more. People had told him.

Buck was a senior forward at the University of Alabama that spring of 1986, when college basketball was viewed as relatively plump with talent. A small forward at six-seven, he had stacked up a list of bona fides in the frontcourt for the Crimson Tide in an age when many top pro prospects still played four years of college ball. His athleticism and polish meant that he was identified as a likely late-first-round pick that June. Better yet, Buck Johnson had been told Jerry West and his Lakers scouting staff seemed ready to pull the trigger if he was still available when they selected with the twenty-third overall pick.

The Lakers needed defensive help off the bench and rebounding, and Buck Johnson would be a good fit.

The mere thought of that, of playing alongside the Magic Man, sent the draft prospect's hopes soaring. "I dreamed of being on that wing, running as fast as I could just to get one of those outlet passes from Magic," Buck Johnson said in a 2019 interview.

As a Magic fan, Buck Johnson was disappointed that Houston

had beaten the Lakers that spring of 1986 and then that Bird had won a title, but he had no idea how that event was going to shape his own life. The Rockets next stepped in and selected him with the twentieth pick in the draft before the Lakers could take him.

Like that, Buck Johnson had been snatched away from his impending role with the Magic Kingdom and then consigned to a purgatory of sorts. As a Rocket he would face years of the great point guard's wrath.

After all, there was a pattern. When the Lakers lost to Houston in 1981, Magic had answered with four straight trips to the NBA Finals and two championships.

The second time around, after the Houston loss in 1986, Earvin Johnson and his Lakers would respond again with another four trips to the championship round and two more titles. In getting there, Magic and company would go to great lengths to assure that Houston would never interrupt their progress again. Over the next five seasons, Earvin Johnson's teams would go 24–4 against the Rockets, and the two times his Showtime teams would meet them in the playoffs? Both were sweeps. Earvin Johnson and his Lakers would not allow Houston so much as a single playoff win even though the Rockets were led by Hall of Fame center Hakeem Olajuwon.

What's more, as Buck Johnson explained, the Rockets were quite aware the Lakers' point guard had it in for them and yet they seemed almost helpless to do anything about it.

"Sure enough, the years I was there in Houston, Magic took that thing personally to where we were not going to get past the Lakers again," Buck Johnson recalled. "There was no way. Magic was so infuriated by that, he made sure."

Earvin Johnson was at the height of his mastery at that point in his career and, as Riley explained in 1996, he had determined in his constant study of his star's approach to apply the Lakers running game in five-minute bursts. "You can see how he handles it by himself: his energy, his body, his language. When he's got a five-minute burst in him, he's going to use it all up. The afterburner kicks in. And he's going to be dead tired after five minutes is up. But you can bet on something good that's going to happen. The team's going to run. The other guys get up, too . . . sense his energy. He's in the middle. He's drivin' and he's slashin' and kickin'. And guys are running hard." While Earvin Johnson was well known for his love of the running game, it would be in the half-court game where he left an impression on young Buck Johnson, who quickly found his niche as a defender off the bench, the kind of guy who matched up well with James Worthy, an important half-court weapon for Los Angeles.

"If you wanted to play half-court, they could definitely play half-court with you," Herb Williams recalled of those Showtime Lakers. "It was always like, *pick your poison*. Not only Kareem, but James Worthy. James Worthy was always their first option on the strong side. Then you double-team him and the ball swings with Byron in the corner. So you gotta take Byron out, because he can shoot jump shots. Then you got the greatest center ever to play the game sitting there waiting for the ball on the box, with an unstoppable shot. First it would go to James, then they'd swing the ball and go to Kareem in the post."

When Buck Johnson came into the game, it always seemed that Magic Johnson would zero in on Worthy, going to him three or four or sometimes even five times in a row to get Buck Johnson into foul trouble and out of the game again. It was a mind-set that echoed Magic's own playground tactics that dated back to Charles Tucker. You want to win? You draw the fouls.

"Magic was so smart," Buck Johnson said.

The situation underscored a little-recognized fact about Magic. Yes, he was easily what many saw as the greatest ever running the fast break. But he was also a wizard in attacking in the half-court, seeing and doing all the things necessary to feed the ball to Abdul-Jabbar and the team's other weapons, no matter how well defenses were schemed to stop them.

In particular, Johnson's size and mobility allowed him to become quite adept at running the pick-and-roll game, the oldest play in basketball, dating back to the days when CCNY coach Nat Holman, who also doubled as an early pro player, wrote about "Execution Play No. 8" in his 1926 book, *Scientific Basketball,* according to writer Michael Bradley. The 1940s version of the Lakers with Jim

Pollard and George Mikan executed the screen-and-roll to great effect in winning their six championships. Johnson, too, would later be credited for his part in initiating the play from the wing and using his size to find shooters on the weak side for open jumpers. Johnson's innovations would be credited with aiding the evolution of the pick-and-roll to the point that it would be the offensive scheme that came to dominate twenty-first-century basketball.

As for 1987, the balance between the post game and the running game still gave the Lakers their best chance in what most observers figured would be their continuing battle with the Celtics. Sadly, the number two overall pick in that same draft of 1986, University of Maryland forward Len Bias, taken by Boston, would die of a cocaine overdose right after being selected, a development that would affect the great narrative of the Lakers and Celtics battles for years to come.

As for the Lakers, the Showtime era was now headed into its eighth NBA season with its floor director having turned twenty-seven. In that time, the team had become fairly set in its identity, which remained quite complicated in terms of image vs. reality.

It's interesting, for example, to view where those Showtime Lakers ranked on the list of the NBA's greatest running teams of all time, as measured by points scored per game.

On that list are a number of high-scoring teams that played little defense and never won anything of substance. Then again, the list also includes great championship teams led by great players who made them great running teams. For example, of those top 50 scoring teams, five were led by Bill Russell and his fleet Boston Celtics of the 1960s, all of which averaged between 118.7 and 124.5 points per game and claimed four titles (among the 11 in 13 seasons that Russell's teams won overall).

Wilt Chamberlain had seven different high-scoring running teams on the top 50 list, including the Philadelphia Warriors for three seasons, the San Francisco Warriors for one, the Philadelphia 76ers for two, and the 1972 Lakers for one, with the latter two both winning titles while ranking among the highest-scoring teams in history.

It's worth noting that Kareem Abdul-Jabbar had two teams

among the all-time highest-scoring teams, and neither of them would come from the Showtime era. They would be the 1970 and '71 Milwaukee Bucks.

Which leaves an obvious pattern for the very greatest running and scoring teams of all time—the greatest ones were anchored by great centers, Russell, Wilt, and Kareem, each of whom played as a master defensive rebounder and shot-blocker who could whip the ball out to great guards for fast-break buckets. And Chamberlain and Kareem held their place as the game's greatest scorers as well.

It's not surprising to note that no teams from the 1940s and 1950s were on the list, especially those before 1954 when the NBA adopted the 24-second shot clock.

However, another key point is that more than half the highest-scoring teams in pro basketball history came from the 1960s when there was no three-point shot.

There were eight teams from the 1970s. However, seven of them came before the three-point shot was added in 1979 (meaning that 34 of the top 50 scoring teams in history came without a three-point shot). Eight teams on the list were from the 1980s.

It makes sense that the 1990s had just two teams on the list, mainly because the decade was dominated by more physical defenses, and by Michael Jordan's Chicago Bulls, a team that ran Tex Winter's triangle offense, which was designed to control tempo. "You can hurry to a butt whipping," Winter would say of running teams, although his triangle featured a very effective "controlled" break.

As for the first decade of the twenty-first century, it was again Winter's triangle that dominated the game, this time with the Lakers of Shaquille O'Neal, Kobe Bryant, and Pau Gasol. Mike D'Antoni's "7 Seconds or Less" Phoenix Suns teams of that decade did not make the list of the 50 highest-scoring teams. That era, of course, led to the age of supposed "Pace and Space," but only three twenty-first-century teams placed in the top 50 highest scoring teams of all time, the Milwaukee Bucks of 2020 and 2021 and the 2021 Brooklyn Nets, coached by Steve Nash, the famed point guard of those 7 Seconds or Less teams, with D'Antoni as an assistant coach.

The NBA may have altered its rules to limit defense and to require its teams to push the ball and take lots of three-point shots, yet they couldn't come close to producing the points that teams in the 1960s did.

Why did Johnson's great Showtime running teams not make the list? They were certainly the prettiest running team, and the most entertaining. Their averages ranged between 110.7 and 118.2 points per game during Showtime. That highest average of 118.2 points per game came during the 1984–85 season.

The answer as to why they didn't score more points is that they were that hybrid team, running brilliantly until they slowed down to have Kareem and Johnson attack in the half-court. Indeed, Johnson's ability to control events to make sure Abdul-Jabbar and Worthy got the ball when and where they needed it was masterful.

That mastery and control would require more and more effort and focus as Abdul-Jabbar aged. He was thirteen years older than Johnson and had turned forty heading into the 1986–87 season. The center's retirement seemed imminent, and Riley wanted to begin shifting the burden to other players. He wanted Johnson, and to a lesser degree James Worthy, to become the focus of the offense. So, the coaches began roughing out their ideas of how this transition should work. They took their notions into training camp that fall and were promptly confronted with confusion and frustration.

"By then he kind of felt he was the team," Abdul-Jabbar said in a 1993 interview, implying that Johnson's input and power with both the team's coach and its owner went into the decision. "When we lost in the playoffs to Houston, I was the failure and Earvin was the answer. I was being written out of the mix."

Lon Rosen, Johnson's friend and representative, saw it differently in a 2020 interview.

"Think about what they had to put up with when Earvin became sort of the leader of the team away from Kareem," Rosen said. "It was really a big thing because Earvin respected Kareem. It was like a major thing for three months. Earvin was like, 'I hope it's the right thing.' Earvin knew the difference. He had respect for the guy."

Clearly, Westhead's demise still loomed over the team if not the rest of the league. Riley, too, had second thoughts and told assistant

Bill Bertka that maybe they should junk the idea of transitioning away from Kareem.

No, Bertka replied, now is the time to make the change.

"This was Kareem's team," Johnson recalled in 2004. "He was the dominating type. I played my role, and it was great. I didn't mind it, but it was other people saying things. They figured I couldn't dominate like Kareem."

Tex Winter, who had watched Kobe Bryant struggle while trying to coexist with Shaquille O'Neal, often wondered how Jordan's career arc would have been altered if he had been paired with a great center for much of his early years in the NBA. A similar unanswerable question could be asked in regard to Johnson. What if he had been able to play his entire career as he did in Game 6 in 1980?

Despite the clash of egos in the fall of 1986, the players would find over the coming months a comfort zone in the new hierarchy. Abdul-Jabbar personally reassured Riley that everything was working fine. Johnson's play over the season would confirm it. He became the first guard since Oscar Robertson to win the league MVP award. His scoring zoomed to a career-high 23.9 points per game, and he was tops in the league in assists, at 12.2 per game.

It was not accomplished in a vacuum, of course. His top job was still leading the assembly. Kareem, Worthy, Byron Scott, Cooper, and rookie A. C. Green—all of them wanted to establish the team's superiority. They had the opportunity to prove themselves as one of the greatest clubs in basketball history, all of it hidden by the flashiness of their running game that relied on their deceptively good defense, as Herb Williams pointed out. "A lot of times what they did, they would put Byron on the point guard. Worthy would guard the 2 guard, and Magic would guard the 3. A lot of times that would put Magic right at the basket, so when the ball came off he got a lot of rebounds and they could actually run. And Kareem was always right there in the shot-blocking area. They could bang you around, too. They had Kurt Rambis, A. C. Green, Mychal Thompson, guys who were very physical. You just didn't go in there and rip and run up and down with them."

The next big boost arrived on February 13, when the front office acquired Mychal Thompson from San Antonio. Bird was said to have been left heartsick by the news. How could the Spurs give Thompson to the Lakers? he asked. The six-ten Thompson provided just what the Lakers needed, a backup to Abdul-Jabbar as well as solid minutes at power forward. Better yet, he was an excellent low-post defender, and having played with McHale at the University of Minnesota, Thompson knew better than anyone how to defend against Boston's long-armed forward. It was, Kareem would say later, West's most brilliant move for Showtime, because it made them championship contenders again. With Thompson, the Lakers surged to a 65-win regular season, the best in the NBA.

"We rolled in 1987," trainer Gary Vitti recalled, looking back five years later. "It was almost a piece of cake. It was like, 'Who's next?' Every night we knew we were gonna win. All we had to do was keep it close. Then they could just turn it on and finish."

The 1986–87 Celtics were entertaining thoughts of being the first club to win back-to-back championships since Bill Russell's last team in 1969. Standing in their way was Michael Cooper, still skinny, still known for a zany inferiority complex. Cooper had long shown that he was Showtime's defensive backbone, with Pat Riley constantly urging him on. The '87 season finally brought his recognition as the NBA Defensive Player of the Year. Now more than ever, he made Bird his personal challenge, spending hours studying the Boston forward on videotape, even going so far as to take the tapes on vacation.

In 2021, a discussion would arise as to Cooper's worthiness for the Hall of Fame. His nomination certainly was bolstered by the memories of his teammates and Lakers staff from the era, the people who depended on him. Johnson was at the top of that list.

As far as Cooper's effect on Bird, James Worthy observed in 1993, "Larry didn't talk as much with Coop. Coop would be right back in his face. Most of the time, Coop would get the first lick in. He would come out on the floor and say, 'Nothing tonight, Larry. Nothing for you. I'm sorry.' Then that would get it started right there."

"I never once thought that I got into Larry's head," Cooper offered in 2004. "And he never showed it. That's the thing I loved about Larry. There were situations where he was doing some things to me, and I couldn't let him see the frustration, because if you let that set in, you know the guy's getting to you."

"I learned a lot from Coop in that aspect, because there wasn't any backing down," Worthy would say. "If you got 55 points against him, it was gonna be the toughest 55 you had ever gotten. Coop and Larry had that same talent, because if Coop saw you weren't ready or you weren't gonna work hard, it was history. He'd shut you down in a minute."

"I think it was the mental toughness that frustrated me about Larry," Cooper said. "His shot—he could probably go 1 for 16—but you knew there was going to be that one point in the game where he was going to hit that shot. The same defense, hand in his face, and he knocks it down, and he had this look like he had hit six or seven in a row."

"It wasn't just Bird," Gary Vitti would remember. "Coop talked to everybody out there. The guy was 175 pounds. He was nothing. He was like a feather. He was afraid of no one. We weren't a bunch of bruisers. We were a finesse team. But when there was a fight on the court, Michael was always a part of it."

On offense, he remained Johnson's primo alley-oop partner on a team of great finishers, although his age was just beginning to show. "I came into this league primarily known as a defensive player," Cooper recalled, "but runnin' and jumpin' and dunkin', that's what I liked to do. I think people kind of liked that."

He also played a major role in nourishing Johnson's own mental strength, Vitti observed. "Magic's motivation in many, many ways came from Michael Cooper."

It was hard to overestimate the value of such motivation in a league that played 82 games in the regular season and another 20 or so in the playoffs on a team with the highest of ambitions. The circumstances offered just too many opportunities to lose focus, Vitti said of the chemistry he found fascinating to observe up close. "When Magic wasn't there, it was Coop that was grabbing him by the jersey saying, 'C'mon, Earvin! C'mon, Earvin!' They really thrived off each other in a verbal sense. Kareem and Magic maybe thrived in a mental sense. They were on the same wavelength, but they didn't have to talk to each other. Coop and Magic talked to each other a lot on the court, getting in each other's face."

Over the years as Cooper aged, his legs diminished, and he made himself into a solid three-point threat.

One point, rarely articulated, involved the idea that Cooper was routinely submissive to Johnson, willing to bend his own game to Johnson's command, both on and off the court.

Sports Illustrated writer Jack McCallum was stunned to witness it for the first time during the '87 playoffs. "I just remember being in the locker room and Cooper was talking," the writer recalled in 2019, "and he was going on and on and on in his Cooper-ian fashion. They had lost that day, whatever it was. Magic goes, 'Coop, wrap it up.' And Cooper kept talking. Magic turns to him and again goes, 'Coop, wrap it up.' I was very surprised. I didn't know Magic very well. But he was in the league by this point seven or eight years."

And Cooper, who was a veteran as well, did as he was told.

"It kind of surprised me that Magic had that kind of command," McCallum recalled. "Cooper like shut up. He looked like a little boy. He packed his bag and they got out of the locker room."

Johnson and Bird shared that sort of toughness, McCallum realized. "It was very much like the Bird thing, very much like Bird telling McHale to 'Shut the fuck up. We gotta play. Stop talking.'"

So many times, it seemed, Johnson himself was so effusive, talking to writers and reporters almost as long as they would stand there listening. But 1987 marked a point in Johnson's timeline, where he was completing a long effort at making an ascension. And Cooper was his top deputy in this effort, marked by another of his many talents. Best of all, Cooper had an iron will, reflected in his streak of 556 straight games played, which would end fittingly enough in January 1988 when he was suspended one game for fighting.

It meant that in all those years of getting to the top of the mountain, Magic Johnson knew he could rely on Michael Cooper every single night, an amazing factor in Johnson's prolonged effort to exert a level of control over the NBA.

Taken together, Johnson's relationships with his variety of teammates resulted in the Lakers scorching the landscape as they moved through the 1987 playoff field. Detroit assistant Dick Versace scouted them and came away shaking his head. "They're cosmic," he said. "They're playing better than any team I've ever seen."

That helped explain Johnson finally receiving the MVP award that May, ending seasons of irritation. "It was frustrating like anything else," Lon Rosen recalled in 2019. "He didn't get the MVP for so many years."

He had been the MVP of the championship series twice, in 1980 and 1982, but the overall league MVP had eluded him.

Just seeing the way he reacted to these setbacks intrigued Rosen. "The one that I think bothered him the most was in Seattle," Rosen recalled, at the All-Star Game just a few months earlier in 1987 when Tom Chambers was named MVP. "He was kind of surprised. He loved Tom Chambers. That was a thing. But he was like really happy for the guy. I think everybody knew it should have been him. He was like, 'Okay, let's move on.' He's got a way of dealing with things."

He dedicated his first league MVP award to Big Earv. Johnson received 65 of 78 first-place votes with Jordan—who had just become only the second player in NBA history to score more than 3,000 points in a single season—finishing second and Bird third.

"I'd like to thank Larry Bird for having a slightly off year, and I want to strangle Michael Jordan for putting all the pressure on me," Johnson quipped in accepting the award.

It was a performance mirrored in his playoff appearances.

In the first round, Johnson had 43 assists against just six turnovers as the Lakers swept Denver 3–0. Then Golden State dropped out of sight, 4–1. Seattle, the opponent in the Western finals, went down, 4–0, meaning the Lakers concluded their conference work on May 25, while the Celtics and Pistons fought through a seven-game series. Faced with a week off, Riley set up a minicamp in Santa Barbara to keep them focused. They had a pancakes-and-strawberries breakfast buffet on Saturday, May 30, and watched the Celtics finish off the Pistons.

When the NBA Finals opened three days later, on Tuesday, June 2, in the Forum, many celebrities peppered the crowd. The regulars, Jack Nicholson and Dyan Cannon, were there, but the series also attracted Bruce Willis, Don Johnson, Whoopi Goldberg, John McEnroe, Johnny Carson, Henry Winkler, and many others. Their presence provided Riley a convenient prop. He had begun stewing with the end of the Eastern finals, when the press described the injured Celtics as a blood-and-guts brigade. Riley threw this up to his players as an affront. The Celtics were getting all the respect for being hardworking, while the Lakers were being packaged as much like their Hollywood fans, a bunch of glitzy, super-talented flakes who had somehow managed to glide through their Showtime success without much character or thought, Riley alleged.

Although the team loved having Hollywood's celebrities cheer them on most game nights, Riley had now pivoted, using that as a negative to fire up his team. "A bunch of glitter-group, superficial laid-backs," the coach supposedly spat. "This is the hardest-working team I've ever had, but regardless of what we do, we're minimized . . . we're empty people . . . and most of us aren't even from California."

Truthfully, the days of rest mattered far more than any coaching hype. Either the Celtics would come in game-sharp and take it to the Lakers, or they would come in weary from two straight seven-game battles. The answer was soon measured in wagging tongues.

"The Celtics looked like to me like they were keeping up pretty good," Mychal Thompson quipped after Game 1, "just at a different pace."

Johnson set the agenda right away with 29 points, 13 assists, eight rebounds, and no turnovers. It wouldn't spark anything equal to the Memorial Day Massacre, but as routs went, it was enough. Johnson now had 21 NBA Finals games with at least 10 assists, which broke a Bob Cousy record that had lasted more than two decades.

On the receiving end of many of Johnson's passes, Worthy had 33 points and nine rebounds. The Lakers ran 35 fast breaks in the first two quarters alone and led by 21 at intermission. They settled into a trot thereafter, finally ending it, 126–113.

The Celtics knew they had to stop the familiar locomotive that was Johnson. Which they managed in Game 2. He still had 20 assists, the second time in an NBA Finals game he had turned in better than 20, which ranked right behind his Finals record of 21. As it was, Michael Cooper happened to get hot at the perfect time.

So Johnson just kept feeding him.

Boston trailed by seven in the second quarter when Cooper turned up the pressure by accounting for 20 points himself by either scoring or assisting.

"He was so invaluable," Abdul-Jabbar would say. "Coop could come in for a few minutes and really change everything in a game."

When it was over, Johnson had 22 points to go with his 20 assists, and Cooper had laced in six of seven trey attempts. And the Celtics had spent another day gasping.

Even L.A.'s old trademark balance was a factor. Abdul-Jabbar had flicked in 10 of 14 shots for 23 points. In Cooper's big second quarter, he racked up eight assists himself, tying a Finals series record for assists in a quarter. His six treys broke a playoff record as well. It all added up to a 141–122 rout, Boston's sixth straight road loss in the playoffs.

The entire Boston franchise seemed shell-shocked.

The L.A. papers jumped on Boston's dismal showing, calling the Celtics "Gang Green." Fortunately, Game 3 was in the Garden where the Celtics corrected some of their issues with a 109–103 win. "We're just too good a team to be swept," Bird said, revealing his own level of doubt.

Johnson had done his very best to crush his rival, scoring 32 points in the loss with 11 rebounds, and nine assists against a single turnover. He was playing at a level of near perfection.

The pressure of Game 4 was then shifted a bit, to the Lakers, which blackened Riley's mood. During a closed L.A. practice in Boston Garden, the coach told the cleaning staff to leave the building. "Maybe he thought they had VCRs in their brooms," the Garden security director quipped.

Meanwhile, the Lakers' stay in Boston took on its usual character, which found them sequestered in their hotel rooms, waiting on nightmarishly slow room service and jumping at the fire alarms that always greeted their stays in Boston. Things on the court seemed headed south once again early in the second half of Game 4, with Boston up by 16.

Jack Nicholson, who had talked his way into a seat in the Garden's upper press area, had spent most of the proceedings getting choke signs from Boston fans. The actor famously "dropped trow" in response, Lon Rosen recalled in 2022 with a chuckle. "I got Jack Nicholson tickets, and he mooned everybody in Boston Garden."

Nicholson's smirk deepened as L.A. cut the lead to eight with three and a half minutes to go in the game.

The classic ending unfolded after Riley called time with about 30 seconds left to set up a screen for Abdul-Jabbar. But Johnson told Kareem to fake it if his defender, Robert Parish, attempted to fight through the pick. Kareem should roll to the hoop, Johnson said.

Abdul-Jabbar slipped the screen, and the pass was there. The Lakers took a 104–103 lead.

Bird then answered with a three-pointer, putting Boston up 106–104 with 12 seconds to go. On the next possession, Abdul-Jabbar was fouled and went to the line, where he made the first and missed the second. McHale, though, lost the rebound out-of-bounds, setting up the moment for Johnson, who took the ball on the inbounds pass at the left of the key and paused there to contemplate a 20-footer. When McHale closed out on him, Johnson went to the right around him into the key, where Bird and Parish joined McHale in a trio of extended arms. Parish almost got a piece of the soft hook that Johnson lofted. But the ball rose up and then descended to a swish, the moment frozen forever as a dagger in the fourteen thousand hearts of that frenzied Garden crowd.

At the end of Showtime, the Lakers organization would poll their fans as to their favorite moment from the era. Johnson's hook would claim the top spot, even over his Game 6 masterpiece, according to Bob Steiner.

Many observers would assume the hook was some new wrinkle added to his game, but Johnson's old Lansing friends recognized the shot from his youth.

"See, everybody thought I couldn't score," Johnson said of the moment, looking back in 2004. "I had said, 'You know, I'm just gonna go along, and one of these days it's gonna be my show.'"

With two seconds left, the Celtics got a timeout, and as Pat

Riley would later recall, the Lakers knew that Dennis Johnson would be sending the ball to Bird in the corner, "a play they ran all the time."

Riley watched transfixed as, sure enough, Bird moved to the sideline, pushed off Worthy, and cut hard to the spot right in front of Riley, who could see his face.

"He was wide open," Riley would recall.

And he had just enough time to turn, catch the ball, and fall back to let fly one of his trademark killer threes, just like the one he had hit seconds earlier.

"With my heart in my throat, I watched the ball, and it was straight as an arrow," Riley would recall. "But it was long."

The ball struck the back of the rim, and as the Lakers bench erupted in joy, Bird walked emotionless from the floor. For the slightest moment, he locked eyes with Riley with a look that said, "I can't believe you left me wide open."

Johnson ran off happily, having stolen Game 4, 107–106.

Celtics boss Red Auerbach was furious and chased veteran official Earl Strom off the floor, alleging that Strom had given the game to the Lakers. Strom ducked into the officials' dressing room, then stuck his head back out to tell Auerbach, "Arnold, you're showing the class that you always have."

"People say, 'Relax, the game is over. The game is over.' Well, the game is never over," Auerbach said in a 1989 interview.

Johnson had retreated to the locker room to be lost in his eternal joy. He dubbed the shot "my junior, junior, junior skyhook."

"You expect to lose on a skyhook," Bird said. "You don't expect it to be Magic."

"That shot proved it to everybody," Johnson recalled in 2004, "and that was the year I won the MVP. That's the year Pat said, 'Okay, Earvin, I want you to take over.' And that's what happened."

The moment had altered the balance in his personal stakes with Bird.

"After that, people said, 'It is Larry and Magic,' instead of 'Larry can do this, and Magic can't do that.' You always had to fight that," Johnson recalled.

He would fight it no longer.

Game 5 threatened to be a closeout event for the series. For that reason, the Lakers staff iced down several cases of champagne to be ready to celebrate. But Boston got a second win, 123–108, and the series headed back across the continent.

For Game 6 in the Forum, the Celtics would take a 56–51 halftime lead. Johnson had scored but four points by the break, but he went at them with brutally incisive ball distribution down the stretch, spreading around the opportunity. Worthy finished with 22, and Abdul-Jabbar had 32 points, six rebounds, and four blocks. Mychal Thompson had 15 points and nine rebounds. In the process, Johnson broke Bob Cousy's all-time assist record for the championship series. Although he shot just 7 for 21, his 16-point, 19-assist, eight-rebound showing brought him the series MVP. And the Lakers claimed their fourth title of the decade, 106–93.

"Magic is a great, great basketball player," Bird conceded afterward. "The best I've ever seen."

Finally recognized for all that he brought to the game, Johnson turned his thoughts to the marvelous array of players around him. "This is a super team, the best team I've played on," he said. "It's fast; they can shoot, rebound, we've got inside people, everything. I've never played on a team that had everything before. We've always had to play around something, but this team has it all."

"I guess this is the best team I've ever played against," Bird agreed.

The two men, in their effort to outdo one another, had brought the sport to a grand place.

No one saw it clearly at the time, but the matter had been settled. In the process, American pro basketball had been ushered out of a difficult period and into the spotlight. When the two came into the NBA, the air was rife with the long irrational fear that with so many of its teams losing money, the league was too Black, that the public had lost interest. Such fear had been one of the articulated challenges prior to David Stern taking over as commissioner in 1984.

The answer, of course, was that it should never, ever matter, but that notion seemed to require some reassuring for the public, which was Johnson's other huge role, although that, too, wasn't clearly articulated at the time.

It would be another of the many vital roles filled by Earvin Johnson. First, he had been the teen in Lansing who had helped to calm white and Black fears about busing and integration. As a pro player, he had served as a figure facing the strange and subtle business of again calming the white public's fears about integration. In all, it proved a transformative performance that would be measured in the game's future ticket sales and TV ratings.

"I think that's one of the enduring things that Stern appreciated about Magic," observed Jack McCallum. "I don't know whether they ever had a direct conversation about it, whether Stern ever said to him, 'I need you. I need you to help sell this game.' Nobody did that better than Magic."

No one, McCallum added, until Jordan came along and built on Johnson's impact, although it would take seven seasons for Jordan and his team to mature into a title winner, shoes or no shoes.

In that interim, so much hinged on Johnson. And Bird. They each had played their huge roles in the NBA's social drama of the 1980s.

"I think Magic more than anybody was at the center of that," observed Alex Wolff, the writer and basketball historian, "because personality-wise he was comfortable with it. It was really hard for anybody to dislike him."

Not that either Johnson or Bird spent much time contemplating the larger issue of race in America or their outsize role in it. They were both busy trying to win.

"There was a little bit more pressure for Magic to always be on," Jack McCallum observed in 2019. "You know, we kind of accepted it when Larry was being Larry, when he was moody and wouldn't talk and looked to go off by himself. All that was sort of what Larry was, but you know Magic always had this pressure on him to be Magic and I guess he liked it."

Johnson's moment was much bigger and far more political than people realized, Alex Wolff offered in 2020. "He and Kareem had their difficulties, I think, at various points as teammates. But I think

Kareem would be the first one to say that Magic just wore him down with his enthusiasm, with childlike affection, with his emotion of the team, so there was just this kind of Era of Good Feelings. I know that's a political term from American history. He tries to win them over. In that he was relentless. People said this about Bill Clinton, that he intuitively knew who it was when he walked into a room who was skeptical of him or didn't like him. And he would make a beeline for that person, determined to win that person before the end of the evening. He wouldn't always succeed, but I think Magic in his very own way had a little bit of that instinct. And that's a lovely story."

Wolff's observation would mirror Charles Tucker's view of Johnson as an adolescent at racially charged Everett High School, that he didn't care if you didn't like him because he could make you like him anyway.

"It was never clear that Magic was better than Larry," McCallum recalled of the events leading up to their 1987 battle. "The year before I had written a piece kind of indicating that Bird was the best ever. Then the next year I wrote that Magic was the best ever. He had clearly passed Bird, and the Lakers had clearly passed the Celtics as being the team of the decade."

In establishing that, Johnson had made another major point, that he was arguably the greatest team leader of all time, McCallum said. "I'm not sure anyone felt more comfortable ever doing that than Magic."

Jordan would also come to be known as a great team leader, but he led mostly by instilling fear. Johnson wasn't above that, but he used fear more subtly.

More important, Johnson emerged as an irrefutably superior team leader at a time when American culture still offered a stiff and unfathomably blind resistance to the idea that a Black male could lead as well as anyone else.

"Magic was singular in that, more than anybody I've ever seen in terms of being a leader," Jack McCallum said. "I don't even know whether it's close."

No one, perhaps, was more difficult to win over in all regards than Bird himself, who always seemed wary, as McCallum explained, that

Johnson "was the nice guy, who was then going to plant a knife in him. Maybe he resented—I don't know this—but Magic's ability to charm the press."

Ultimately, that didn't matter, McCallum said, because "Bird was legitimately seduced by that guy's talent at that time."

That partly explains how Johnson vanquished Bird and the entire sport and became "really the king in 1987," McCallum said.

Yet, even in that great moment, Johnson and his team seemed far from a coronation. The pattern had been that Boston would be ready to answer as it had each year after the Lakers won a title.

Pat Riley knew that, obsessed about it, and he was prepared to begin dealing with it even as the celebration overwhelmed the Lakers' locker room. The coach was waiting for a reporter's question, so that he could ignite the moment.

Finally, someone in the postgame interview got around to asking the coach if this Lakers team could repeat as champions, and Riley virtually leapt at the question. "I guarantee it," he said flatly.

The reporters, the players, the staffers all stopped.

Roy S. Johnson, then covering the league for *The New York Times,* was among the reporters gathered around the coach in that moment. "Riley had this mind-set to plant the seed early, clearly without telling his players," Roy Johnson recalled in 2021. "We all left Pat Riley and went over to Magic and said Pat just guaranteed a championship next year.

"He was drenched in champagne," the writer said of Magic. "He was in the middle of the locker room. He was celebrating. He was happy. He was relieved. He was letting it all out. He looked at us and he said, 'What!?!?!?!'"

Then the Magic Man let out a giant laugh.

Winning a pro basketball championship was essentially a matter of taking on the immense pressure that builds over the course of a long season, the goal being to conquer that pressure and ultimately eliminate it. The greater the player, the greater the ego; the greater the ego, the greater the pressure. The reward, for truly great players, was always a summer away from the pressure, a time in which they could say that they'd lived up to their potential.

It was not a time that players wanted to spend contemplating an immense new round of pressure.

"In '87, we win the thing, and then Pat turns right around and lays all that pressure right back on them," Gary Vitti recalled in 1992.

"Just when we thought we'd done everything we could do, Riles makes this guarantee," Byron Scott explained. "I thought he was crazy."

Nineteen seasons had passed since the Celtics had won consecutive championships over the Lakers in 1968 and '69. Many observers had come to the conclusion that the feat couldn't be accomplished in the modern NBA. Riley rejected that notion. He had come to believe that winning again was a test of will, that greatness was available to the team with the mental toughness to fight for it. He knew the Lakers were a team of mentally strong individuals. They just needed someone to drive them to greatness. He was that person.

Perhaps he had realized it even as he did it, but Riley had crossed not just one line but several. One of them led to more glory. And another to sorrow.

27

THE LONG KISS GOODBYE

They both had those smiles that they relentlessly deployed in capturing the hearts of their adoring publics. Earvin's, of course, was that gift from his mother that allowed him to disarm just about all he encountered.

"Magic was a lover, not a fighter," said George Andrews, who would serve for years as the lawyer for both men.

Isiah Thomas, who traveled with "Zeke" as his term of endearment, was the fighter of the two, although you had to study him up close to figure that out. He was just six-one but possessed a grittiness that allowed him to thrive in a world of tall trees. Yes, he was a dribble king with the fancy moves and the sweet shot, but the dude was without fear, able to go in among the seven footers routinely to dig out whatever he needed to keep the proceedings going his way.

He was the little guy facing the tall task of turning the Detroit Pistons from a joke of a franchise into champions.

Thomas obviously had tremendous courage, which was essential to meeting the challenges he faced in the relentlessly physical NBA of the 1980s, especially in leading a team that would come to be known as the Bad Boys.

If it came to a fight, and it often did with the Pistons' bruising style of play, Thomas never backed down, never retreated. Then again, he had lieutenants like Rick Mahorn, Bill Laimbeer, and Dennis Rodman, who seemed to truly relish the opportunity to come to his aid in a skirmish.

Most of all, Thomas was clearly basketball's most calculating guy, with the numbers and factors and options continually ringing in the multiple processors of his mojo.

After all, he had been deployed as the floor general of Coach Bobby Knight at Indiana—and the two of them had produced a national championship by the end of Thomas's sophomore season, after which he smartly moved right away into the 1981 NBA draft.

By 1987, he had fought for six years in the league, during which he had pursued a studied reverence for the big guy from Lansing.

"I've seen every championship series since I've been in the league," Thomas told Shelby Strother, the great Detroit newspaper columnist, in June 1988. "I wanted to learn what it took to be a champion. I observed."

Unlike young Michael Jordan's vanity plate, Thomas didn't want to appropriate Johnson's nickname. Instead, he wanted his trade secrets. To get them, Thomas would spend years stalking and wooing Magic in hopes of absorbing the mind-set.

He was also clearly a good friend, taking the time to be there for Johnson during moments both small and large, such as the death from cancer of Earvin's half-sister Mary in January 1987. When the news hit, Johnson had asked his mother if he should miss that night's game with Dallas, and she had told him to play, that watching it would take Big Earv's mind off his heartbreak. Right after the game, Johnson went to Lansing, consoled his family, and spent a long time on the phone talking to Thomas about his feelings. It was that kind of relationship.

From the beginning, Thomas had made sure to get Charles Tucker and George Andrews as his management team, as did a platoon of players coming out of college in Johnson's wake. What wasn't to like about the whole package? Both Tucker and Andrews offered huge doses of reality for young players and weren't looking to make a major move on their money. That, in a day when there were few restrictions on just how much of a player's income an agent could help himself to.

Yet as the pivotal 1987–88 season opened, Johnson had moved Andrews and Tucker out of his management team in favor of Lon Rosen and a team of powerful advisors, a development that later some would see as a part of the gulf that was about to widen between Johnson and his understudy in Detroit.

For Thomas, however, the relationship had moved beyond the same management team, which had facilitated so much of what he wanted. It came across as a full-fledged "bromance" with Johnson, with vacations together, summer All-Star fundraiser games and youth camps and events galore, an awful lot of them chaperoned by Tucker. In essence, they gave pro basketball its first Rat Pack, a paradigm that would predate an unusual closeness among competing players well before the age of cell phones and social media.

The two men also pursued an aggressive social agenda. As gun violence and drugs consumed Detroit during the 1980s, Thomas created an event to bring attention to the problem, and Johnson immediately came to his aid, the kind of effort that suggested more of Tucker's influence.

Yet the connection between Johnson and Thomas would also provide a study in the limitations of such relationships in an intensely competitive business.

When Johnson finally got his mansion, Thomas had immediately claimed his own bedroom, the one overlooking the pool. To mark his territory, he would leave his favorite coat hangers in the closet there. And each time he'd return he'd go to the closet to make sure the hangers were still there. Upon seeing them he'd smile that smile, secure in the thought that he was still very much in the long game that he was playing.

Yet it wasn't just the visits and vacations where Thomas gleaned knowledge from his friend. The real effort came in his many late-night phone calls in which he would ply Johnson about all the many little things it took to win an NBA championship, asking his opinions about all the thousands of choices Thomas faced in trying to build the lowly Pistons into a contender alongside coach Chuck Daly, long a Johnson favorite.

There had been that wish of Johnson's to play for the Pistons, so it was understandable that he engaged in such talks, feeding his fantasy by turning over and over the Pistons' options and decisions in his mind.

Invariably the conversations between the two competitors would turn to the idea that they might one day go up against one another for a title. "It's been a fantasy of ours for years, playing each other for all the marbles," Johnson would say that June of 1988. "Now, it's reality. Head to head. The marbles, the chips. The money."

In all fairness, Thomas revered winners, loved studying them. Bird. Riley. Boston's K. C. Jones. He wanted to duplicate them in Detroit. Whatever he could steal, he stole. The mannerisms were the easy part. Getting inside their minds proved the real challenge. Johnson was the one who gave him total access. After all, they played the same position, albeit quite differently.

"I hate that I taught him," Johnson would say later, upon realizing that he had aided in his own downfall. "That's the only thing. I should go back and kick myself."

Actually, after having to sit and watch his friend play in so many championship series, Thomas began to consider that the Magic Man might be playing him as much as Thomas was attempting to appropriate Johnson. "Earvin is my friend, one of the best people in the world," he would tell Shelby Strother on the eve of the 1988 title series. "And we have been there for each other a lot. But he's not going to tell me the secret of how to be a champion. It's a secret he and Larry Bird have shared. And neither of them ain't going to tell me how it's done."

The journey for Thomas and his Pistons had proved to be long and oh so frustrating, largely due to the presence of Bird and the Celtics in their path. In the spring of 1987, Thomas and his Bad Boys had come achingly close to vanquishing Boston in Boston. With a one-point lead and scant seconds to go in Game 5 of the Eastern Conference finals, the Pistons were inbounding the ball on the sideline near the Celtics basket, and Thomas wanted the ball from referee Jess Kersey in a hurry.

"Don't you want a timeout?" Kersey would recall asking him.

"Gimme the damn ball!" Thomas supposedly shouted.

So the referee gave him the ball. Thomas passed it in, only to watch Bird steal it and hit streaking Celtics teammate Dennis Johnson for the go-ahead layup. Like that, Boston had a one-point lead with a second left, arguably one of the most stupendous plays in American pro basketball history.

Kersey turned to a crushed Thomas.

"Now do you want a timeout?" the referee remembered asking.

Frustrated in the locker room after the Pistons' eventual Game 7 loss, Detroit's Dennis Rodman said of Bird, "He's not God. He ain't the best player in the NBA, not to me. . . . He's white. That's the reason he gets the MVP award. Nobody gives Magic Johnson credit. He deserved it last year, too. I don't care. Go ahead and tell him. You'll put it in the paper anyway."

Reporters then went to Thomas and asked if he agreed. "I think Larry is a very, very good basketball player, an exceptional talent," he said. "But I'd have to agree with Rodman. If he was black, he'd be just another good guy."

Immediately those comments ignited a furor, prompting Thomas to offer this later explanation to Ira Berkow of *The New York Times:* "What I was referring to was not so much Larry Bird, but the perpetuation of stereotypes about blacks. When Bird makes a great play, it's due to his thinking and his work habits. It's not the case for blacks. All we do is run and jump. We never practice or give a thought to how we play. It's like I came dribbling out of my mother's womb."

The comments of Rodman and then Thomas were awkwardly constructed on the fly and obviously unfair to Bird, yet they would smack at a truth as sad then as it would remain in the twenty-first century, a truth dating back through the harsh, violent history of American racism. Their comments weren't so much about Bird as they were about the context of American culture, which weighed as heavy as all of the dark matter in the universe. Easily the most consistent thing about that culture over the course of its existence had been the total and absolute discounting of Black achievement in virtually every endeavor.

Sadly, Rodman and Thomas had merely hinted at that truth. Just because they introduced it awkwardly, in a locker room after a heated series, didn't mean that this relentless discounting of all things Black wasn't overwhelmingly factual. And it was quickly obvious that neither a predominantly white media covering the NBA nor the league's predominantly white fan base was eager to hear or consider such thoughts. Ultimately, the moment made clear just how badly white America needed to have a larger conversation about race but lacked the wherewithal or perhaps even the desire to do so.

"The main thing is that Isiah's statements don't bother me," Bird said at the time. "If they don't bother me, they shouldn't bother anybody."

With the uproar, however, Thomas faced the grim task of eating his words and apologizing to Bird, then was forced to cancel a summer basketball charity event. Canceling such events was something that Charles Tucker never would normally have even considered, but the comments had created the kind of public relations disaster from which thought and truth were banished.

The Lakers, who were about to face the Celtics for the '87 title, were quickly asked if they thought Bird was overrated, and most of them answered like men who wanted to say nothing that would give Boston bulletin-board material for the series. They uniformly expressed their disagreement with Thomas, except for Johnson, who declined to comment at all, saying he would discuss the matter privately with his friend Zeke.

In retrospect, the moment would be cited as one of the first subtle cracks in the relationship between Thomas and Johnson. After all, Thomas had been Johnson's confidant during all those seasons before Bird and Johnson became friends. Thomas would later say he had heard all the unflattering things Johnson had said in private about Bird. And now Johnson couldn't offer a single public word of support for Thomas, who was caught in a public relations disaster and being humiliated?

"I guess what I found out was where people stood, and not a lot of people came to bat for me," Thomas would tell *The New York Times.*

That fall, just before training camp, Thomas lost his father, and the tepid response from those around him left the Detroit star further feeling the sting of the incident, "that many people in sports media didn't particularly care for me because of the whole Larry Bird situation."

To his credit, Thomas survived such devastating moments and entered the next season more determined than ever. Which matched perfectly Pat Riley's vast psychological ploy of guaranteeing that his team would win the 1988 NBA title. Like two freight trains seeking the same piece of track, the Lakers and Pistons suddenly found themselves on a course for one of pro basketball's all-time collisions, a fresh concept for the Detroiters, but almost an anticlimactic scene for the Lakers after their battles with Boston.

The Push

Lakers trainer Gary Vitti had worked closely with Pat Riley for a few seasons by that 1987–88 campaign and had learned to live with his increasingly uncompromising nature. The Lakers players, however, were still trying to decide if they could contend with the coach. Fortunately, Riley's strongest ally was Johnson, which kept the whole thing locked in, even if the coach's promise of another championship finally had begun to stretch even Johnson's patience.

"He thrives on intensity," Gary Vitti would say of Riley. "He thrives on it. There was always pressure, always pressure."

It stemmed from a desire to win matched only by Johnson's.

"They will sell their souls, sell your soul, whatever it takes," Vitti said of the coach and point guard. "Pat will claw and scratch. He will rip your eyes out."

Johnson may have been more diplomatic about expressing it, but he was every bit as willing as his coach to employ such tactics, smiling all the while.

In the wake of his bold promise, Riley proceeded to raise his focus to fanatical levels about every little detail with the team. The staff members had to report everything to him, because, as the coach insisted, it was the little things that led to winning.

"Behind his back, Kareem began calling him Norman Bates," Lon Rosen revealed.

"If somebody makes you be your best all of the time, puts that pressure on you all of the time, there's going to be resentment," Vitti would explain. "I respect Pat because most of us aren't tough enough to do that. We're not tough enough to piss people off to get 'em to be their best."

Frank Brickowski came to the Lakers in the fall of 1986 and soon gained a view of the team dynamic.

"I've never encountered anything like it before or after," Brickowski would say. "Riley was intense, but Magic and Kareem only let him get away with so much stuff. When it came to a point of drawing a line, they would not have a part of something. The first day I was there, they had just gotten done playing back-to-back preseason games. We were sitting in a circle at the start of practice, and Riley said we'd go for two and a half hours and get out of there. Magic stood up as we were ready to break and said, 'All right, an hour and a half and we're outta here.' Riley said, 'No, I said two and a half hours.' Magic said, 'Oh, I thought you said an hour and a half because we're tired because we played the last two nights.' There was a dead silence. Then Riley said, 'All right, if we do this and that, we'll be out of here in an hour and a half.'"

Johnson had the fun face but could turn on the hard edge in a flash.

Chip Schaefer, who would later become the team trainer for Michael Jordan's Chicago Bulls, used to watch Laker practices at Loyola Marymount during Showtime and came away astounded at how quickly and vigorously Johnson could jump on a teammate's case if one of his passes was mishandled. Riley could have played all the mind games he wanted, but it wouldn't have mattered if Johnson himself hadn't been firmly in control of the team's mind-set.

Abdul-Jabbar would be 41 that 1987–88 season, and while he still offered some of the presence the Lakers needed in their half-court game, he simply couldn't carry the load that he once had. Much of that burden would fall on Johnson's and Worthy's shoulders, but also Mychal Thompson's off the bench.

Without a doubt, Johnson drove the Showtime machine, but Worthy, at six-nine, was the forward who finished off plays to his point guard's great pleasure. Johnson's approach had always required expert finishers for his laser passes, and Worthy would head the bunch of them dating all the way back to Everett.

"Earvin can push the ball up-court at an incredible tempo," Riley once explained. "But he needs someone even faster than himself to break for the wing and fly up-court. James is the fastest man of his size in the NBA. In terms of finishing the fast break creatively and swiftly and deceptively, no one else compares."

And when the game slowed down a bit, Johnson liked to find Worthy in the low post because the forward had continued to perfect his skills at attacking there as well. In fact, Worthy was so good Detroit's Dennis Rodman took to studying him on videotape much like he studied Larry Bird. That season would mark the crescendo of Worthy's career, sealing his reputation as "Big Game" James.

Other Lakers stepped forward as well. Byron Scott had labored to find his shot during the 1987 Finals, but the 1987–88 season brought new confidence. He led L.A. in scoring, averaging 21.7 points over the regular season while shooting .527 from the field.

Also vital was A. C. Green at power forward. He didn't shoot much, but when he did the selection was good. He also rebounded and defended the low post. Plus, Green provided the perfect off-the-court contrast to Johnson by carrying a Bible everywhere he went to fend off the incessant female advances. In another world, he was what Christine Johnson might have wished for her son, the steadfast determination that Green employed in keeping to his faith. But Johnson had been swayed long before. Once Johnson had gained that knowledge of his own magnetism, the die had been cast.

Meanwhile, on the floor Johnson once again showed consistently brilliant play, the kind that everyone loved so much yet always took for granted in the routine of his excellence. If anyone needed a reminder, Johnson missed 10 games at midseason due to a groin injury and the team's record plummeted in his absence.

Johnson, too, had gotten ideas from his friend Thomas about slower, isolation basketball. "Earvin does a pretty good job of it too," Riley admitted. "He clears out a side and waves people out of there."

A slower pace meant that Johnson stayed on the floor even longer. He would spend the final four seasons of his career at better than 37 minutes per game, that after several seasons playing less.

"Earvin didn't want to come out of the game anyway," Riley explained one night that season. "I do what he tells me."

The Lakers had started the schedule with an 8–0 run, the finest opening in their history, but from there it had quickly evolved into a test of survival.

"The season was a trainer's nightmare," Gary Vitti would say, looking back. "We didn't know who was gonna play from one game to the next."

After eight seasons, Johnson's all-out approach had left him aching. His back, his knees, his ankles, they all complained to him every single day. For several years he had been saying publicly that with his style of play he didn't see how he could play more than ten or eleven seasons, with no idea how prophetic it would prove to be.

Johnson wasn't alone. Worthy's knees ached. Byron Scott was plagued by patellar tendinitis. And Cooper got hammered by age and his own fearlessness.

"Coop sprained his ankle badly in March in Houston," Vitti would recall. "He was never the same after that. That was really the injury that slowed him down. When he came back from that injury, Karl Malone threw him into a press table and bruised his foot. He still played every single game after that, but he was hurting."

Somehow, they overcame these ups and downs to claim the league's best regular season record at 62–20. "Guaranteeing a championship was the best thing Pat ever did," Byron Scott conceded as the schedule drew to a close. "It set the stage in our mind. Work harder; be better. That's the only way we could repeat. We came into camp with the idea we were going to win it again, and that's the idea we have now."

Johnson and the Lakers dumped San Antonio 3–0 in the first playoff round but then had to fight their way through three consecutive seven-game series, something that no championship team had done before. Next came Utah and a full series battling Karl Malone, followed by seven games with Dallas and Mark Aguirre.

Once again, Magic Johnson's Lakers were back in the title round.

The Original Flu Game

There, suited up to contend for the 1988 NBA championship would be Thomas and the Pistons, who had finally put down the aging Celtics in six. Despite the toughness of the Bad Boys, many observers figured the Lakers would rule in six games. Maybe less.

"We were the peasants," Detroit guard Joe Dumars would recall of the atmosphere as the series opened, "and they were the royal family at that time. They did carry themselves with a tremendous air of confidence, a swagger."

Game 1 at the Forum on June 7, as recounted in 2006's *The Show*, would be known for the huge buzz stirred by the sight of Johnson and Thomas holding hands and kissing before the tipoff of Game 1. It was a display of brotherly love, they explained, but the NBA had never seen such a spectacle.

"If you knew Isiah, if you knew Magic, the kiss was no big deal," Dumars said. "They were going through some tough times because they were both trying to dance with the same girl. And there was only one partner."

His coat hangers might have remained in the closet of the "Isiah Thomas Suite," as Johnson himself called the far bedroom in his mansion. But they would go unused. "He's not staying here," Johnson told Shelby Strother, who noted the absence of a smile accompanying the comment.

It was not a lighthearted matter. The kissing would continue before each game of the series, but not the romance.

In retrospect, the bussing and how it would be perceived was the beginning of a long unwinding of the relationship between the two competitors.

Former *Detroit Free Press* columnist Charlie Vincent, who considered himself a Thomas friend, said in 2019, that Detroit's star would be caught off guard by the physical approach Johnson took in defending him during the series, considering the difference in their size.

That, of course, was largely prompted by the fact that Thomas and his Pistons clearly had no interest in Riley's plans for a repeat title.

With his maddeningly deliberate, ball-stopping style, Detroit's Adrian Dantley posted up to make 14 of 16 shots from the floor, enough to slow the tempo and lead the Pistons to a stunning 105–93 win in the Forum in Game 1. Like that, the media narratives were filled with comments about the Lakers looking old and tired.

"We thought we should have won it when we won the first game," Dantley would recall that summer of 1988. "But their will took over. The first thing we had to worry about was Magic. He had a great series. He had a little bit of a tough time with Dennis Rodman. Dennis played Magic very well defensively."

Rodman had the size, quickness, and athleticism to make the Lakers point guard earn every moment.

It didn't help that Johnson came down with the flu before Game 2, but it provided an opportunity for his own "flu game," although his version never reached the height of legendary hype that would accompany Jordan's flu game against Utah in the 1997 title series. There were no dramatic scenes of a teammate helping a weak Johnson off the floor as with Jordan. But the record shows that Johnson toughed it out and scored 23 points in Game 2. Worthy added 26 while Scott had 24, and the Lakers evened the series with a 108–96 win.

"I don't think there's any doubt Earvin Johnson showed the heart of a champion," Riley said afterward. "He was weak. Very weak. But this is what I call a hope game—you hope you get through it—and we got through it."

The site then switched to the Pontiac Silverdome, the football arena where crowds of 40,000 or more were expected with the Pistons now in the title series after decades of struggling to get there. Johnson always savored playing in front of what he considered the home crowd, but he was still feeling the effects of the flu. Even so, he and the Lakers ignored the huge crush of fans to display a little toughness of their own. They shoved past the Pistons, 99–86, to take the third game and a 2–1 lead, which returned briefly the home-court advantage.

The main damage was done in the third period when the Lakers shot 64 percent and outscored Detroit 31–14 to break open a one-point game.

Despite continuing to battle the flu, Johnson turned in 18 points, 14 assists, and six rebounds that pushed the Lakers along, against four turnovers.

For the fourth game, Johnson again used his size and strength to get to the basket, leaving Rodman to challenge him end-to-end. When all else failed, the Detroit forward tried to knock him down, which left Johnson fuming and complaining.

"Magic is tough because he likes to penetrate," Rodman said afterward. "But I try to distract him, and hopefully he won't be able to look up the court and make one of those great passes."

The tactic obviously frustrated Johnson, who responded at one point by knocking Thomas to the floor with an elbow. It didn't matter. Detroit blew past the Lakers and won by 25 points, tying it at two-all.

Determined to counterpunch, literally, L.A. opened Game 5 with a show of physical intimidation and scored the game's first 12 points. But that approach soon stalled, then backfired into foul trouble. The Lakers seemed to forget what they did best—rebounding and running. "We couldn't contain anyone on the boards," Riley complained.

The Pistons won, 104–94, took a 3–2 lead in games, and now stood to reduce Riley's dream of a repeat to a sad memory. But Detroit would have to claim the championship in the Forum, and that couldn't be accomplished without one immense and memorable effort, which the Pistons were quite capable of producing. They fell behind, 56–48, early in the third quarter of Game 6. Then Thomas scored the next 16 points in trancelike fashion—two free throws after a drive in the lane, then a five-footer off an offensive rebound, followed by four jumpers, a bank shot, and a layup.

But with three minutes to go in the period, Thomas landed on Michael Cooper's foot and had to be helped from the floor. Despite a severely sprained ankle, he returned 35 seconds later and continued the assault. By the end of the quarter, he had hit 11 of 13 shots from the floor for 25 points, setting an NBA Finals record for points in a quarter and driving Detroit to an 81–79 lead. That momentum boosted the Pistons down to the wire, and with a minute left in the game, they held a 102–99 edge.

Sixty seconds from the title, from making the Isiah Thomas dream a reality.

Following NBA protocol, the trophy was rolled into the Pistons' locker room to prepare for the celebration. Attendants brought in the iced champagne that had been oh so carefully concealed. A message was sent to Detroit owner Bill Davidson that CBS needed him in the locker room for the trophy presentation. Minutes later, it would all become a mirage, left in some alternate universe of failed dreams. The trophy would be taken away before Davidson could smudge its sheen with even a fingerprint.

"A minute is a long time," Johnson would say later. "A long time. It's just two scores and two stops and you're ahead."

The first Lakers score came on Byron Scott's 14-foot jumper, to bring L.A. within one, 102–101, at 52 seconds. Thomas then missed an 18-footer. At 14 seconds, Abdul-Jabbar positioned for his skyhook from the baseline, but Detroit's Bill Laimbeer was whistled for a foul that would long infuriate Pistons fans. Even Riley would much later acknowledge that the call was questionable. Kareem calmly made both free throws, giving L.A. a 103–102 lead. Still, the Pistons had the ball and a chance to win it. At eight seconds, Joe Dumars took the shot for Detroit, a six-foot double-pumper. It missed, the rebound slipped through Dennis Rodman's frantic hands, and Byron Scott controlled the loose ball.

"We had 'em on the ropes, but we couldn't get 'em down," Adrian Dantley would lament.

Johnson had rolled his way to a masterful 19 assists and 22 points, against just two turnovers. Between assisting and scoring, he had been responsible for 58 percent of his team's points.

The immediate question for Game 7? Would Thomas play with the bad ankle? "I'm playing—period," he said.

After Game 6, Thomas would begin phoning Johnson and other Lakers figures about being able to use their facilities for treatment on his ankle. His friend Magic never returned his call, Thomas would allege later, which widened the growing fissure in the relationship.

"The amount of intensity and focus was unlike anything I'd ever seen before," Joe Dumars would recall of the deciding game. "The tension was thick out there. I mean thick. Nobody wanted to give an inch. Attitudes were everywhere. And it was great," he said with a laugh in 2004.

Despite limping badly in warm-ups, he scored 10 points in the first half, leading the Pistons to a 52–47 lead. But halftime brought stiffness, and he was no longer effective.

Johnson, meanwhile, hitched the Lakers behind Worthy's low-post scoring and they raced to a seemingly insurmountable lead, 90–75, in the fourth quarter. Facing a blowout, the Pistons fought back with a pressure lineup that began consuming the Lakers' lead. At 3:52 Detroit's John Salley knocked in two free throws to close to 98–92, and the Lakers were in obvious panic. At 1:17, Dumars hit a jumper to make it 102–100.

Johnson then scored a free throw off a Rodman foul, stretching it to 103–100. Detroit had an opportunity, but the nonshooting Rodman took an ill-advised jumper at 39 seconds. Byron Scott rebounded and was fouled. His free throws pushed the lead to 105–100. Dumars then made a layup, Worthy hit a free throw, and Laimbeer canned a trey, running the score to 106–105 with six seconds showing. Green finished a layup, making it 108–105, and although the Pistons got the ball to Thomas at midcourt with a second remaining, he fell without getting off a shot.

The Lakers had in hand their fifth title in Johnson's nine years in the league.

Riley could only exhale. "It was a nightmare to the very end," he said. "I kept saying, 'Please don't let this end in a nightmare.' We were a great team trying to hold on."

Worthy had offered up 36 points, 16 rebounds, and 10 assists, the first triple-double of his career. For that and his earlier efforts in the series, he was named the MVP. A self-effacing Worthy said he would have voted for Johnson.

At last, the league had another repeat champion, a confirmation of Riley's mind games.

"He pretty much got it all out of us that year," Scott said in 1992.

Johnson may have won a fifth title, but he had begun the sad process of losing a friend as his relationship with Thomas would unravel completely over the next three years and remain bitter for decades. "When we got to the Finals, our relationship became very different," Thomas would recall of the 1988 championship series. "It was OK for us to be friends when we weren't competing with the Lakers, but when we started competing with the Lakers, our friendship changed. I remember my son was born in '88 during the NBA Finals and Magic wouldn't even come to the hospital."

On Again

Johnson somehow always seemed to know where she was. Cookie Kelly would be reminded of that during her New Year celebration in Chicago. She was there staying with an old friend, in town to ring in 1988 with a nice man she had been seeing.

For two years she and Johnson had had almost no contact and suddenly here he was, shoving himself into her life again with a phone call. And there she was again, letting him do it.

"I want my girl back," she recalled him telling her.

She listened as Johnson explained that he had ditched the woman he had been seeing. Kelly swiftly informed her Chicago beau that she was out of there. Indeed, she was fired up by a new idea that she and Johnson shared, that she would move to Los Angeles, get her own place, and set about finding out once and for all if she could actually survive life with a superstar.

At least that was how Kelly understood her mission at the time. Only later would she learn that the goal would be amended to surviving with a "sex-obsessed superstar."

She clearly had some inkling, though, as they began talks about getting married somewhere down the road, and she informed him she just couldn't reside in his current mansion, the scene of so many of his memories without her.

Johnson agreed, and soon they set about the business of building a new twelve-thousand-square-foot palace on a beautiful piece of property in the Beverly Park section of Beverly Hills.

However, her move to the West Coast would take time. She had to wind up her job in Toledo while finding new employment and a new place to live. And once there, she would have to settle into the rhythm of being the mate of Southern California's busiest man, one whose wealth was growing. He needed a new insurance policy that year and to get it supposedly took a battery of medical tests, including one to determine if he was HIV positive. It would be rumored to have come back negative, although there would be a scramble in 1991 searching among his health records for documentation that there had indeed been such a test with such a result.

Once she took residence in Los Angeles, Kelly soon enough discovered that she could be useful in comforting him after losses. And there would be some of those.

After all, the "three-peat" pressure had begun immediately after the 1988 title. Forever looking down the road, Riley had heard a phrase supposedly floated by Byron Scott, "three-repeat" for their goal of a third straight championship with the 1988–89 season. Only later would the Lakers learn that their coach had trademarked the term "three-peat."

Such items would be among many, including a *GQ* cover story, amassed as evidence that Riley had changed dramatically in his seasons coaching the team, that he had flowered into a monumental ego out of control, a coach who had settled into the idea that it was much ado about himself.

Johnson, too, could clearly see the road ahead and took matters into his own hands in another direction that off-season. After all, Abdul-Jabbar would be turning forty-two and heading into his last run. Johnson knew that, more than ever, he was going to have to pick up the load.

He began after a needed rest as he always did, poring over videotape of every game from the 1988 campaign, looking for the truth of the matter: What did he need to improve?

There was a list: He needed to rebuild his body and his conditioning. He needed to improve on his 85 percent free throw shooting, which meant spending hours a day in his home gym taking shot after shot after shot. And he had to work on his perimeter game as well.

First to go was the junk food he loved so well, replaced by salads, vegetables, and fruit. He matched that with additional running, much of it on a beach, wherever he happened to be.

When the letter arrived from Riley in the middle of the summer, it confirmed everything Johnson already knew. Riley wrote that Johnson would have to perform at an MVP level if he wanted to take the team to a third straight title.

"I don't know if that little note was any motivation," the coach would say later. "But I felt it was going to take that type of performance to lift up this team."

The first good sign came at training camp when Johnson showed up with a body fat measurement of 4 percent, dramatically reduced from 13 percent the year before.

Even without the coach promising anything this time around, training camp also revealed another familiar development. The pressure was already there and would swirl throughout the 1988–89 campaign, as the drive for victory mixed with night after night of Kareem's retirement tour. He was the game's all-time leading scorer, closing out a great run. The aloof giant had grown more receptive to the adulation that the fans and the press now wanted to send his way.

Still, it would prove an often painful year. His skills obviously diminished by age, he labored through many nights, which led to a flurry of media questions as to whether he was just playing for the money. In retrospect, it seemed a little odd that a team going for a third straight title would have to weather such scrutiny. Yet it was true. If he hadn't lost millions in the business deals arranged by his former agent, he might not have been required to play so long. Some of Kareem's nights were difficult, but he would still manage to average 10 important points a game at that advanced age. There were supposedly even discussions with Jerry West about an abrupt departure. However, wisdom prevailed. Kareem stayed, and the Lakers prospered.

The celebrations went on in every city the Lakers visited with gifts and tributes for the legendary center, leading Johnson to lean over one night and whisper in Gary Vitti's ear during the national anthem, "Just imagine what it will be like when they do this for me."

After all, Abdul-Jabbar was moody and gruff as ever while Johnson remained everybody's sweetheart. Given that, what would Johnson's retirement party look like?

The only disruption came with a hamstring injury that caused Johnson to miss several games, including the All-Star Game in Houston. Although Abdul-Jabbar was clearly struggling, the NBA decided that the all-time scoring leader should replace Johnson in the event.

Soon enough the hamstring mended, and the Lakers were back on track to claim the supposed "three-peat." With each day that spring of 1989, hope grew that they could send Abdul-Jabbar out with another ring. They finished with a 57–25 record, once again the best in the West, yet well short of the Pistons' 63–19 mark. Detroit had gotten a spark heading into the season by sending Dantley to Dallas for Mark Aguirre, thus reuniting Thomas with his old Chicago friend and making Charles Tucker quite pleased.

Even though he no longer represented Johnson and was no longer a factor in his decisions, it hadn't taken Tucker long to realize that if he merely showed up at certain events he could come face-to-face with Johnson. They had been friends for so long, there was no way they weren't going to talk. And sure enough that would translate into the occasional conversations that still afforded Johnson the psychologist's unique counsel.

They would always have that friendship, that love, based on the fact that Tucker had been there in just about all of the moments large and small in Johnson's rise, although increasingly he kept the psychologist at arm's length.

As for the Lakers in the spring of 1989, they had confidence that they could win in Detroit and leave no doubts as to their supremacy. In fact, they would all look back on the team that season as one of their very best, based on how they came alive on a run through the playoffs. Johnson would later aver as much, as would Byron Scott in a 2002 interview with Lakers broadcaster Larry Burnett.

"We were just loose with confidence and we knew that we had the best team in basketball," Scott would recall. "We just felt like it was our time. We were playing so well. Everything was going so well for us."

Burnett himself would soon become a symbol of the new vision and ambition of Jerry Buss, as the team owner had moved into major media ownership with Prime Ticket as his network to deliver Lakers games and other primo California sports to a cable audience, with Burnett, a former ESPN anchor, as the face of the network. Stock market troubles had translated into continued issues for the Buss real estate and sports empire, but that in turn would lead him to sell the naming rights to the Forum to Great Western Bank, thus making Buss a leader in pioneering the development of such revenue for all of sports. Even as he pushed through these struggles, Buss kept eyeing the landscape and would even make an unsuccessful run at buying the Dallas Cowboys.

As for the Lakers in 1989, they gathered momentum as they advanced in the playoffs, sweeping their way along to an 11–0 run to the NBA Finals, leaving good Portland, Seattle, and Phoenix teams in their wake.

The string of playoff success meant that Riley needed only one more victory to become the winningest coach in three decades of league playoff history. Detroit, too, had made its own impressive run. In Boston, Larry Bird had spent the season on the sidelines after constantly struggling with back issues and undergoing heel surgery in November. As a result, the Pistons easily pushed aside the Celtics in the first round, 3–0. The same despair befell the Milwaukee Bucks in the second round, 4–0.

Johnson's role in the Lakers' process earned him his second league MVP award that May, outpointing Jordan for the second time in three seasons in a media vote. It was the closest ballot in eight seasons, with Johnson taking 42½ first-place votes and 664.5 points, 65.7 points ahead of Jordan, who had 27½ first-place votes.

The moment marked the escalation in a coming showdown between the two great players, not so much on the court but in the hearts and minds of a generation of players and fans. An American coaching in China and looking back on the period would later send a note to a basketball writer, lamenting that he was trying to encourage his players to emulate Johnson, to keep their heads up and see the floor, yet all they wanted to do was be Jordan, to keep their heads down and attack the basket.

In Akron, Ohio, another youth coach, Frank Walker, was keenly watching the developments and just a few years later would begin teaching a talented young LeBron James to focus more on Johnson, not on Jordan, to keep his head up, to see the floor, to make his teammates better.

It would become a global conversation that would haunt both players, Jordan in the short term, because he faced the issue as a popular complaint, that he couldn't win a championship because he didn't make his teammates better. It would haunt Johnson in the long term, because his time was coming to a close and he would soon hopelessly watch Jordan swarm the planet with his acrobatic, energetic style.

"He plays in the air. I play on the floor," Johnson said prophetically of Jordan in accepting the MVP award. "We're two different types of players, but we mean the same thing to our teams."

Johnson called it the best of his 10 seasons in the NBA.

He had finished second in the league in assists with 12.8 a game, had averaged 22.5 points and 7.9 rebounds, had claimed the free throw percentage title at 91.1 percent, and had made a career-high 59 three-point shots.

Riley parsed the issue by saying the league should think about giving two awards. "The one who deserved it more, for all he did in the regular season, was Earvin," Riley said. "I swear, if there was ever a person who walked out of an alien spaceship, it's Michael Jordan. The guy is the most outstanding in pro basketball. But that doesn't always mean that the most outstanding is the most valuable. I think Earvin deserves this one."

Johnson obviously agreed. He admitted voting for himself, then doubled down on that by dedicating the season to himself, saying, "I guess this time, since I worked hard during the off-season to take off all that body fat and work on my free throws . . . I'll keep it for myself. Nobody was out there running the laps for me."

The real place to settle such matters about the debate between who had the greater value, himself or Jordan, would be the league championship series. He hoped to meet Jordan there soon, he said. "If we both made it, the NBA and the fans would go crazy, no question about it. It'd be a record-breaking watched series."

It didn't happen in 1989. But Jordan and his Bulls did influence events by managing to win a pair of playoff games against the Pistons in the Eastern finals before falling, 4–2. Which meant that the Lakers, having punched an early ticket to the championship series, were left with time on their hands before the Pistons advanced. So, Riley took his players to a mini-camp in Santa Barbara and worked them hard. The lunacy of that would soon be obvious, especially considering that Johnson had already been sidelined at midseason with the hamstring issues.

"The thing that upset us more than anything was how hard we worked," Byron Scott would say three years later. "It was like training camp all over again. We didn't feel that we really needed that."

"The '89 Lakers team was the best I ever saw," longtime Southern California sportswriter and media figure Doug Krikorian would offer in 2004. "They were 11–0 going into the Finals against Detroit. Magic was in his prime, just primed to go. Orlando Woolridge was playing great ball. They had Mychal Thompson playing great ball. Byron Scott had his great season. They were tremendous. Riley should never have taken them to Santa Barbara."

That would begin to become devastatingly clear before Game 1 in Detroit, when Scott suffered a hamstring injury. He was out for the series, and like that, Riley's hard workouts became an issue in the minds of his players.

Johnson and Thomas revived their oddity of kissing before tipoff, but that would quickly become an afterthought. Without Scott to help contain the Pistons' guards in Game 1, Detroit led late, 97–79, and glided from there to a 109–97 win. The Lakers had plans, however, for Game 2, and sure enough, they snapped right back to pound the boards and take a 62–56 lead at intermission.

Yet events turned miserably upside down in the third period. With about four minutes left, Detroit's John Salley blocked a Mychal Thompson shot, starting a fast break. Johnson dropped back to play defense and, in so doing, injured his hamstring. Knowing immediately what had just occurred, he punched the air in frustration. An entire year of work in remaking his body and his game had simply evaporated.

"I felt a twinge early in the third quarter but thought everything was okay," he said later.

Even with Johnson out of the game, Mychal Thompson led an L.A. comeback. Down 106–104, the Lakers had the ball with eight seconds left when Worthy was fouled and went to the line. He missed the first and made the second, leaving the Lakers short at 106–105. Thomas hit two free throws with a second remaining for the final, 108–105. Down 2–0, L.A. was suddenly short on options. The immediate speculation centered on Johnson. Could he play in Game 3 in the Forum? He tried but left the game in the first quarter with the Lakers leading 11–8. "I wanted to play so bad, but I just could not," he said afterward. "I could not make the cuts, defensively, that I had to make."

Without Johnson, the Lakers made a redoubled effort, but found themselves unable to prevent the sweep, as the once promising season collapsed all around them.

"We had won like eleven in a row going into Detroit," Scott told Larry Burnett. "We could've made history."

Actually, they already had.

In the closing seconds, with the game clearly over, Riley substituted for the team's longtime captain. Johnson came out to meet

Kareem, a moment to celebrate the great partnership they had managed to form and somehow maintain.

Washed in the crowd's applause, the moment was large and warm, and the Pistons all stepped onto the floor, faced the Lakers bench, and joined the celebration.

"Kareem! Kareem! Kareem!" the crowd intoned over and over.

Some would argue that the curtain closed on Showtime with his departure. Others would say that Johnson's style and personality had defined the era. It hardly mattered. What had been accomplished had been accomplished together in their nine seasons. Like other great Lakers tandems who had their conflicts—George Mikan and Jim Pollard in the 1940s and '50s; Shaquille O'Neal and Kobe Bryant at the turn of the century—the Showtime duo had still managed to lord over the game in grand fashion.

Despite whatever events came along to irritate the process, Johnson and Abdul-Jabbar had always found a way to move past them, to set them aside, in the name of teamwork and winning. Riley would point out they did this willfully, almost silently, without having to talk all that much about it, without having to be asked to do it.

"It's an attitude," Riley would say. "It's the attitude that great players have."

End of the Run

By August, the hamstring was healed and Johnson was able to play in his own Midsummer Night's Magic game again, where he displayed his usual caginess by making sure that Michael Jordan was on his team. Johnson turned thirty that month, and while the previous year's effort to remake his body hadn't brought another title, it had prepared him for a new decade.

The Lakers, meanwhile, had begun remaking their roster by finding a steal late in the first round, Serbian center Vlade Divac, who would make his way to America with limited English language skills but a fluid game. Soon enough, the affable young center found himself undergoing trial by Earvin fire. Determined to speed up the process of his adjustment to the NBA, Johnson was all over Divac in an effort to hardwire his acclimation from European basketball to what was then a far more physical NBA.

The season would soon enough reveal just how badly the loss of a young talent like Len Bias had hurt the Celtics. Bird soon acknowledged that the Lakers were a much better team, which left Magic and company again focusing on the Pistons as their measuring stick out of the East. A January victory in Detroit further stoked the hopes of the Lakers.

While the season had brought success, it had left many of the team's stalwarts struggling to adjust to the absence of Kareem, Riley pointed out in a frank conversation after the Sunday Lakers victory on national TV.

"He was our anchor," the coach said. "He disciplined us as an offensive team. He disciplined us in the locker room. He was there, and his presence was always felt. We no longer have that anchor and that presence."

To help fill the void, Johnson had taken to using even more half-court, clear-out isolation situations that marked basketball in that era of mandated "man" defenses. Teammates would clear out of the way and allow Johnson to go one-on-one. Yet the real adjustment came at the other end.

Two years of facing the Pistons in the NBA Finals had left Riley with a deep appreciation of their defense that used intense physicality to limit their opponents. After all, the Bad Boys had been brutally physical in corralling the talented Jordan. Who couldn't see that such defense would rule the league?

"We learned from the two teams we had to compete against in the '80s, Philly in the early '80s and Boston in the mid '80s," Riley explained. "And now Detroit. Detroit has taught me something about really being a consistent defensive team. They're the best defensive team in the league and we're trying to pride ourselves on being a good one."

Johnson acknowledged that in the past when the Pistons came at the Lakers physically, they would back down. That had to change.

Riley and Johnson had pushed on in rebranding the team in Detroit's image. Even Chuck Daly was impressed, telling reporters that watching the Lakers was almost like looking in the mirror at his own team in their style of play.

It would come at a cost, however.

In revealing these things that day, Riley spoke wistfully, as if he was aware that his relentless pushing had already done irreparable damage, that he had burned out his relationships with his players.

"That's my insanity. That's the problem with me," he said.

Not everyone saw that narrative. Asked about Riley that January of 1990, Mychal Thompson observed, "He's coaching the same way, letting Magic run the show most of the time. That's what you do when you have a floor general like Magic Johnson, just let him take over and run the show. Of course, Riley puts his input into the game as we go along, depending on what we need."

Riley's secret? "He's very knowledgeable," Thompson offered. "He knows what guys think about, how they approach games. He lets us play, lets us be our own men on the floor, as long as we play hard."

That view of the coach was shared by longtime scorekeeper John Radcliffe, who had spent years watching Riley work and had come to admire him deeply, how he had managed to find ways to motivate the various personalities.

Thompson didn't acknowledge that some of his teammates were growing increasingly weary of the coach, but he spoke as if presenting a contrary view.

Their coach, he said, was "more of a motivator and a soother," then admitted Riley had engaged in "more yelling than usual, trying to get us pumped up and to keep us pumped up."

The bottom line for the Showtime Lakers, even as the conflicts gained a foothold, he said, "We always want to win."

Johnson, at thirty with almost a full decade working with Riley, didn't need much of his soothing. Detroit's Joe Dumars, who had spent two straight seasons battling Johnson and his teammates in the championship round, would marvel that spring at his drive and focus. Rather than being a know-it-all, Johnson seemed to be working harder than ever to keep learning the game, Dumars declared.

Told of Dumars's opinion, Johnson would reply that he had no choice but to keep learning because the game was changing so much.

Indeed, coaches had come up with a major new defensive strategy that was changing the game. It was a strategy that would help to ignite a chain of other dramatic changes in basketball over the coming decades, changes that would rock the game to its foundation.

"It's amazing the things that happen," Johnson said in that late-night conversation in January 1990, "because the defense is always changing. You used to come off the pick and roll and nobody would trap you. Now, they trap you, and you have to make another decision. It's so complicated now, and you have to make sure your teammates are in the position they have to be in."

If anything, the changing game had prompted him to look even more at the big moments of his career on videotape. "It's so enjoyable to sit back and look at where you were then as to now," he said, "to see how you've changed as a player. I got better and better with maturity."

That maturity had brought for him an appreciation for all of it, even for the failures that once tortured him so. "I enjoyed all of them," he said of his moments battling for the championship. "Even when we lost. Being in the championship series was a high in itself."

In his first 10 seasons, he had driven the Lakers to the championship series eight times, almost a train wreck of success, one season quickly upon another. "What happens," he said, "is the next deal comes so quick, and then the next one and the next one that you don't get to enjoy that one. Because I haven't really enjoyed or gotten to know the impact of that game and that series. Because we move on to the next season and the next championship. And now here comes a new championship. I don't think I get to enjoy any of them like I really want to."

Even watching so many replays of his big games didn't allow him to sop up all of the emotion of each moment, even as that reviewing of his personal greatness did serve to recharge his batteries and stoke his desire to go back through the grind of another long season in search of another.

"Oh, yeah, it charges me up and gets me ready," he said of watching and rewatching himself.

Because he ran the team in real time from the floor, managing every little detail, the grind he faced was far more than that of his teammates. Then again, so was his fire.

February would bring the All-Star Game in Miami, where he was again named the MVP, even though the East blasted the West, 130–113. He seemed stunned at his selection, and for the first time in his career, almost speechless.

More significantly, he had rented out a soul food restaurant in the city during the weekend festivities and invited an array of family members to a private dinner there, where he produced a magnificent ring and once again asked Kelly to marry him. The new mansion was nearly complete. Joy was in the air.

Yet, almost on cue a few months later, he would demand she give the ring back, another breakup, this after Kelly had given up her old life to move to Los Angeles. Infuriated by his games, she refused to return the ring and dug in her heels, backing off a bit all while holding on to the relationship, despite Johnson's ensuing frequent demands that she give the ring back.

The turmoil in his private life apparently cloaked professional issues, revealed first by the fact that the Lakers would lose their first opening round playoff game in seven years, to Houston no less, although they finished the Rockets off, 3–1.

Jerry West had long believed pro basketball to be a players' game. The coach was merely there to give the players the mix of freedom and structure that allowed them to be creative. Yet West had spent the season fielding many complaints that Riley's iron will was choking the life out of the roster.

"It got to the point where we'd heard this speech before and to the point where he got tired of saying it," Byron Scott would recall two seasons later.

Riley flashing his anger and stamping his feet on the sideline had gotten them to a league-best 63–19 record, but it could take them no further. In their first season without Abdul-Jabbar, the coach had been determined to make the transition. But the acrimony thickened with each passing day, until they collapsed, and the Phoenix Suns ended their anguish, 4–1, in the second round of the playoffs. It was an ugly series loss that shook the franchise to the core.

Johnson was again named the league MVP, but this time he would receive the award after his team had already been ousted from the playoffs. The vote itself had been another strange, close one. Philadelphia's Charles Barkley received more first-place votes than Johnson, 38–27. Johnson, however, had 636 total points to 614 for Barkley. Jordan finished third with 564 points and 21 first-place votes.

Johnson dedicated the award to Jim and Greta Dart.

"They're like my godparents," he told reporters.

The award presentation itself was conducted under a cloud of uncertainty over Riley's future with the team.

Asked about it, Johnson joked, "You didn't know? I've just been named player-coach. We're going to move Jerry [West] up to president and I'll be GM and player-coach."

Johnson also told the media he planned on playing just four more years, which prompted Jerry West to say, "Magic, don't quit before your time."

Then West broke his own rule of never comparing players publicly to add, "In my days as a basketball player, I've never seen a greater player, or winner in my life than Magic."

The team's 63 wins for 1990 had brought some satisfaction for Johnson, but the sour playoffs meant two straight years of frustration.

"I just can't watch a whole game," he said of the playoffs. "I'm angry and upset that we're not in it. So now I have to get up and walk away. I have all this energy and no way to burn it off."

Now all the questions were again about the end of Showtime, Johnson said. "I'm used to that. For the last five years, it has been over for us. It was over last year when Kareem left. And we won 63 games. We're looking forward to getting back there next October and showing people."

If they were going to do that, it was looking increasingly like they were going to have to do it without Riley.

"By the end of the season, the fire was not there," James Worthy later said. "As far as the team was concerned, the locker room was dead. For the first time since I had been with the Lakers, it was a job."

"That year was ugly," offered one prominent Lakers staff member. "By the end of the year, Byron and James wouldn't even talk to the guy. Pat would come in the locker room and ask a question, and they wouldn't respond. It was his personality. Then he finally left, and it was like everyone in the whole organization rejoiced."

When the season ended, Riley had told reporters that he was considering leaving his post. Team staff members figured the coach was fishing for entreaties to stay from West and Jerry Buss. Neither, however, was about to suggest that. Seeing he had no support, Riley knew it was over, explained one Lakers staff member.

"Pat Riley was a great coach who wore out his welcome in L.A. and was fired," Doug Krikorian, who had covered the team for years, would explain in 2004. "He did not go out on his own. It was not Jerry West. It was the players. They rebelled against him. They said they did not want to go on another season with him. Magic went to Buss. Pat was fired. They gave him some money and everything and told him goodbye. Riley went to New York and made a lot of money, and now he's a multimillionaire down in Miami. In the NBA, when you're a driving coach like him, the players can only take it so many years."

Yet any rejoicing over Riley's leaving was mixed with mourning. An era had ended. And after they had time to reflect on it, his players would realize something special had passed through their lives. In nine seasons, Riley had coaxed and pressured them into four championship performances and got them close to three others. But the human possibilities had been exhausted.

"Was he fired by Jerry Buss?" Lon Rosen said in 2019. "Yeah, he's finally admitted he was."

He would attend the press conference announcing that he was leaving but before he did, he made one stop.

"Pat went to Earvin's house," Rosen said. "They cried on his porch together. This was before the press conference so that tells you about a relationship of two men, you know. He didn't resign. He was fired. It wasn't sort of written that way. All the players sort of had had enough of Pat, and Pat had had enough of them."

"I'm not searching for the meaning of life in the NBA, okay?"

Riley would say at the time. "But it gives me a feeling of being totally alive every time I'm on the floor. If you don't feel alive for that competition out on the floor, then you're not part of what basketball and sports are all about it. Competition brings out the best and it brings out the worst. And when you're in the middle of it, there is no other experience at all."

He would become a broadcaster with NBC for a season, while the Lakers hired Mike Dunleavy to replace him. Michael Cooper left, too, in 1990, asking to be waived so that he could play in Europe. Meanwhile, Thomas and his Pistons advanced to the league championship series where they defeated Portland to win a second straight title. Johnson was said to have had a hard time witnessing that.

That summer of 1990, promoters thought it would be great to stage a one-on-one game between Johnson and Jordan for pay-per-view television. Jordan, who had spent his life challenging people to one-on-one, liked it. But the NBA nixed the idea—which would have paid big money to the participants—after Isiah Thomas, who was then the president of the Players Association, had objected. Jordan had lashed out at Thomas's intervention, charging that the Detroit guard was jealous because no one would pay to see him play. Thomas made no response to Jordan's comment.

Johnson said he would love to play the game, but he declined to get involved in the scrap between the two. "That's their thing," he said.

Johnson did, however, speculate over the outcome. Actor Jack Nicholson said that if he was a betting man, he'd put his money on Jordan, the premier individual player in the game, as opposed to Johnson, who was considered pro basketball's consummate team player.

Johnson, though, refused to concede. "I've been playing one-on-one all my life," he said. "That's how I made my lunch money."

Asked his best one-on-one move, Johnson said, "I didn't have a best move. My best move was just to win, and that's it. I did what I had to do to win."

That August of 1990, Jordan had agreed to play again in Johnson's Midsummer charity all-star game but tried to consume too many golf holes the day of the event, and it was feared he would be late. Rather than start the event without the star of the league, Johnson at first thought he would have to delay it to give Jordan time to be there for tipoff, which reportedly infuriated Thomas. Apparently, Lon Rosen dispatched a car and got him there just on time to avoid trouble.

All of it helped provide a needed diversion for Johnson. Already prognosticators projected the demise of the Lakers in the coming season, figuring they might finish as low as sixth or even eighth in the Western Conference. Kareem and Riley were gone, Johnson had aged, and there was indeed the thought that Showtime was done.

PART III

ACROSS THE GREAT DIVIDE

28

LAKER RED

As another NBA season neared in the late summer of 1990, Earvin Johnson's life was descending tighter and tighter into a vortex, a swirl of complexity that on the one hand featured abjectly low behavior, for which he would eventually have to work to forgive himself, behavior that would astound and repulse and deeply disappoint virtually all who knew and loved him. Yet on the other hand, that same swirl of that same vortex flashed in the very same moments a portrait of the absolutely brilliant, intensely human traits that would form the crux of his legacy, a vast personal gift that warmed and inspired nearly all who knew him.

As Johnson turned thirty-one, he stood in the eyes of many coworkers as the ultimate professional, entirely superior in his wisdom and approach.

And that's how Jimmy Eyen found him upon joining the Lakers' staff as an assistant coach and advance scout late in Johnson's career. Eyen was entering his second season in the NBA, and just like that he was "coaching" Magic Johnson, so who knew what to expect?

"Earvin was just terrific to me," Eyen recalled in 2019. "I couldn't have asked for anything more. He made it very easy for me to assimilate into the system."

That was oh so welcome because Jimmy Eyen was doing everything possible to fit in with an imposing outfit such as the Showtime Lakers.

"With Earvin, it was more like a consultation," Eyen explained. "Scouting and game preparation were what I basically brought to the table for the Lakers. I'd go scout a game and then go back the following day. When I would be at the shootaround, Magic was really engaged. He was like a member of the coaching staff in preparing and seeing things. He was such a student of the game. He undoubtedly watched the game that I had just scouted the night before. There was no doubt about that. After I had been around a while, he'd come up to me and we'd start talking and he'd say, 'Were you at that game in Phoenix?' and I'd say, 'Yep.' And then he'd say, 'Yeah, I watched.' So then we would talk some more, we'd discuss how we'd deal with the Kevin Johnson–Tom Chambers pick-and-roll. Then we'd do the walk-through."

To share that intense mission with a star of Johnson's magnitude proved fascinating for Eyen, who would go on to be an NBA assistant and scout. "As a young coach, I not only was providing this report," he said, "but I also had another level to go through with the Magic litmus test. I had to have all my ducks in order. Because he was so in tune with the walk-throughs and what I did, that it created a conduit between us."

Soon he and Johnson were in regular consultation in preparation for each upcoming game, Eyen recalled. "I'd like to know what he saw; he wanted to know what I saw."

In looking back over his friend and client's professional life in 2020, Lon Rosen cautioned not to be misled by Johnson's obsession with his sex life. Whether it was in his early apartment or later his mansion, as Johnson's career evolved, he spent many nights alone, studying game tape. As with the select few of the game's greatest, Johnson's busy schedule did not prevent him from a disciplined study of opponents. Much like Kobe Bryant and Dennis Rodman, or his own teammate Michael Cooper, Johnson would commit to substantial preparation for each upcoming game. Such prep before each contest was exceptional in a league that played 82 games a season.

In Johnson's case, it meant that no matter how easy he made things appear on the floor, they had become more and more the product of intense preparation. No matter how often one team faced another, the best NBA coaching staffs constantly sifted through nuances, looking for one subtle advantage or another that might make a difference in that night's outcome.

"He wanted to know play calls," Eyen said of Johnson. "To good defenders over the years, play calls were important to them because they would hear the play call and they would recognize and anticipate what was coming from the other team. There was one game where he asked me about play calls before a game—whoever it was, Detroit or somebody—and I told him they liked to run 3-down or 4-side or whatever it was and he goes 'Okay.' So, we're in the game and they make that play call. He heard it, I yelled it out. We communicated and he ended up stealing the pass and getting a layup. On his way back down the court, he points to me, and I point to him with a thumb up. That exchange, as a young coach, is what it's all about."

Eyen had gone to work for the team in Pat Riley's last season and then stayed over to serve on the staff of new Lakers head coach Mike Dunleavy. In those two years with Johnson, Eyen would come to marvel at many things about him, including his capacity for what clearly seemed an immense charm.

"When I was in my first year there with the Lakers, being from Oakland, when we would go to play the Warriors, my family would come to visit," Eyen explained. "You would play the game and then afterward, outside the locker room, my family would be there, and we'd have a chance to talk before we left town again. I hadn't been with the Lakers very long and I'm out there with my mom, my brother and sister and their kids. And so, Magic comes out of the locker room and they start saying, 'Ooh, there's Magic. . . . There's Magic.' I didn't say anything, and I didn't ask him to come over. But he sees me with my family and he comes over and says, 'Jim, this must be your family. Your brother looks just like you.' And then he says, 'This must be your mom.' And then he introduces himself and says, 'I'm Earvin Johnson' to my mom. And then my mom looks up at him—she's about five-four—and she goes, 'Magic, I know who you are.' He starts to laugh with that big smile and stands there and he talks to us for fifteen, twenty minutes. Obviously, my mother was his biggest fan, particularly after that."

Between regular visits to the Warriors and a playoff series against them in his second season, Eyen had lots of family time during that period in his life. "And every time my family would be waiting after the game," the assistant recalled, "and he would go and give my mom a big hug. That's what I remember most about Magic: His personality and how personable and respectful he was with my mom and my family."

In many ways, he was still very much the ambassador of goodwill who had crossed racial lines as a teenager at Everett High, only now as an adult this had evolved into a more conscious effort, particularly in his sensitivity to race, Lon Rosen explained. It wasn't that Johnson, like anyone else, wasn't prone to annoyance at the seemingly constant racial slights and indignities that life in America seemed to produce.

Spectator sports, such as the NBA, are about far more than race, however. They often display their own peculiar class systems, where a big guy like Paul Mokeski can labor for more than a decade in the lower reaches, setting picks, grunting for rebounds, swapping sweat, coming off the bench in life, and never once coming close to stepping into the spotlight reserved for the upper echelon.

"Obviously, I was never at his level as a player," recalled Mokeski in a 2019 interview. "Part of the reason I survived for 12 years in the NBA was because I knew what I was and how I could help a team win. There's a pecking order in the NBA; there always has been. Magic Johnson was obviously a super, super superstar, but just like the fans could relate to him, other players like myself on another team that was a backup player, he treated with respect. Every time.

"Every time," Mokeski repeated. "Even to this day. I saw him last fall at a preseason game against the Warriors. My son was standing with me, and he came up and gave me a hug and said, 'Mo, how you doing?' Dr. J does that all the time. That means something. And I noticed that early. Back in the '80s, there were guys like that, high-level guys, that treated other guys like me like shit. They'd say, 'Hey, you're lucky to be in the league.' Yeah, I knew that. But Magic was never one of those guys."

There seemed to be few calculations of any equations in Johnson's manner, but his natural, loving inclinations infused his great leadership in many ways. Tony Brown came to the Lakers as a free agent veteran that fall of 1990 and would go on to a long career in coaching. But by Thanksgiving of that year, he was another of the league's transient substitute players, stuck in another new city, often living in a hotel, not really knowing many people there.

"At Thanksgiving I had nowhere to go," Brown recalled in a 2019 interview, "and he invited me to his house. Obviously, we were teammates—I get that—but I didn't know Magic well. But he made it a point that I was with someone and had a good meal on Thanksgiving. I was from Chicago, and he knew I wasn't going to be with my family. That impressed me as well: Here's a larger-than-life guy, a multimillionaire, living in Beverly Hills in a big mansion and living this fabulous life, and he's concerned about me."

From an equipment manager like Rudy Garciduenas, an NBA lifer working in the locker room, to the secretary in the front office, Mary Lou Liebich, to the array of people around him, Johnson made the routine effort with all of them, taking the quiet, friendly moments to check in on their lives, inquiring how they were really doing, leaving in his manner and approach the impression that emotionally he had all of their backs, all of them, the many people in and out of his orbit over his entire time in Los Angeles. It would later leave them in awe as to how he did it. And they quietly loved him for it. For it left them with the distinct feeling that whatever he did—and he did so many big things night after night—that they were an important part of it, that they were important to him.

In an age when the sport was falling deeper and deeper into the grip of statisticians who endeavored to break down every phase of basketball's end-to-end action on the floor and to find a way to measure it mathematically, which in turn would be calculated into the millions of dollars for player contracts and endorsements, for the entire value that human culture placed on competitive behavior, Earvin Johnson had brought an overwhelming abundance of the unmeasurable thing, the elusive sense of togetherness that had made millions of people fall in love with basketball in the first place.

"Something else about that Thanksgiving," Tony Brown said. "When I got to his home, I felt welcome and not like a stranger. He made me feel at home. He made it like a typical holiday gathering. We played cards, we had great food. It was a wonderful time. I'll always remember that."

Make no mistake, Johnson's generosity and compassion had long proved immense, but on another level, the most important level that drove everything, he was all business. That, too, came through in his persistent manner.

A veteran of life in pro basketball's cold cities, Tony Brown had been amazed that the Lakers went to Hawaii for training camp that year. He'd never been to the island paradise and marveled at the entire arrangement.

"I was juiced up about joining the Lakers," Brown admitted in 2019 in recalling that camp. "I remember the first meeting. The coaches talked about what the season was going to be like, what their goals were, blah, blah, blah. After Mike Dunleavy was done talking, he opened it up to the floor and asked if anyone wanted to say anything. And I'll always remember Magic was the first one to stand up. And then he said, 'If we don't win the championship, it's a lost season.' He was the only one that spoke. There was nothing else to say."

Johnson would soon find himself in the business world, sorting through a dizzying array of endeavors and operations, theater chains, radio stations, food services, and an array of contracting business, even dabbling in his beloved music and media, all of it conducted in an environment often fraught with failure and loss, yet it amounted to a small empire that he had begun building with the help of his advisors over the years, to the point that Johnson would amass a fortune.

Quite simply, everywhere Earvin Johnson, Jr., went—and he would go many places in conducting his business operations over the decades of his life—he went with his gift of being able to reach into the lives of many of the employees and customers he encountered in his various operations to make them feel an important part of who he was and what he was doing. As with basketball, a life in business would offer the array of stats to measure his accomplishments. And Johnson was as aware of those stats, measuring them like the pure gold that he considered each one of his assists in basketball. Yet, whatever these statistics were measuring, they all came down to that fundamental equation that Johnson had zeroed in on with laserlike instinct as a teen in his battles with Tuck.

It was the winning that mattered, the great force of the moment and the sustained effort, all for the winning, the pride and accomplishment that could stir the people of a community to their feet to shout and high five and be a part of something. "My music," as he called it, the celebrations he incited play after play after stupendous play. He had to know they were dancing and joyful, that the whole building saw and felt something.

That was his much beloved "winnin' time."

That fall of 1990, in his 12th campaign, he set out in search of it again, this time with a new coach, with a guy who had just wrapped up his playing career, a guy who was quietly bold enough to coach Magic Johnson. Jerry West, who had come to be known as the great guardian of the Lakers, had selected Mike Dunleavy carefully. He wanted somebody with a deep understanding of the game and the emotional road to victory in the NBA, yet somebody who knew the moment, knew that it wasn't about himself.

In West's eyes, the moment for the Lakers was now all about Johnson. West himself had spent the last years of his own great career distracted by an ugly battle over money with Jack Kent Cooke. He wanted to avoid any sort of distraction at all costs for Johnson. After all, this once-in-a-lifetime competitor had before him what was thought to be a precious few seasons left to gather all the greatness possible. No distractions. All eyes on the prize.

Dunleavy, at age thirty-seven, brought a realism to the proceedings. The team's new coach had played alongside at least a dozen

Hall of Famers in his career, but he'd never encountered anyone as competitive and motivated as Johnson that fall of 1990, made all the more so by the ugly exit the Lakers had made from the previous playoffs. Even then, a decade later, just about everyone in the NBA remained quite familiar with Paul Westhead's fate in dealing with Johnson. As a rookie head coach, Dunleavy was mindful of the history. But he knew he would have to deliver a certain message early in his relationship with the team.

"I looked at those guys and told them they weren't necessarily 'Showtime' anymore," he recalled in a 2019 interview.

The ceiling didn't immediately fall in so Dunleavy proceeded. "You guys are slowing down; you're showing your age," he recalled telling them. "We got to play better half-court defense."

As a guy who had just ended his playing career, he approached things almost like he was opening a discussion with his own teammates. He had played for several coaches who welcomed any and all questions from players. That would be his approach. It would be the give-and-take that mattered. He had been hired to bring some defensive ideas to the job. As he had with the Bucks, he wanted the Lakers to trap in the low post, to rotate with energy. His approach offered a new set of coverages, and it would take time for those to be processed by the roster.

At first things seemed to be going okay. Then the team got off to a 1–4 start and Dunleavy found himself playing Johnson heavy minutes just to try to get some wins before things got out of hand. "I can just tell you from the standpoint of a rookie coach coaching Magic Johnson," he said, "and coaching a team that had been knocked out the year before by Phoenix, trying to introduce a new system and getting off to a tough start, I would tell you I probably overplayed him, probably didn't take him out of the games we had already won because I was just making sure we'd win."

Dunleavy figured that he'd make that up to his superstar leader with practice time off.

"Hey, Earvin, why don't you just drop out of practice once we get to the contact stuff?" he recalled telling Johnson, to which the team's star immediately replied, "If I don't play, if I'm not the guy who goes hard the whole time, that gives everybody else an excuse not to go hard for you. That ain't happening."

"I've played with a lot of guys and a lot of guys would have taken up the coach on that offer," Dunleavy observed. "But he wanted no part of it."

Those late days of Showtime began to leave Johnson's teammates pondering the idea that it was all coming to a close, which in turn left them thinking about his unique example. "Earvin was one of those guys to challenge people individually," journeyman Larry Drew, who had been brought in as a backup point guard for Johnson, would recall. "He would set the tone in practice, and once he set the tone, it was up to everybody else to follow the lead. If you didn't, he let you know. That's why he was so successful. Teams would die to have people like that on their roster. It was just unbelievable. I've been with teams where we thought we had leaders. But when I came with the Lakers, Earvin started in training camp. He just demanded perfection."

By 1990 James Worthy had spent years witnessing much the same.

"His leadership qualities were unique," Worthy would recall. "Here's a guy who didn't mind getting on you. Some guys can do that; most can't. Plus, Earvin had energy all the time. Energy at shootaround, energy on the bus, energy in the locker room, energy while he slept. He was just that type of guy. He would not let you get down. He would not let this team lose."

Johnson certainly had been there for a while by the fall of 1990. He knew it all in terms of directing a team down the path to winning, but he also displayed a trait that would later be attributed to Michael Jordan himself. No matter how good he was, when you encountered him in practice, Jordan was playing with everything he had, going all out, harder than anyone else on the floor, like he was some rookie just trying to make the team.

That didn't always endear Johnson to teammates, especially in those moments where he might be channeling a little Charles Tucker. Tony Smith was a rookie that fall of 1990, a second-round draft pick out of Marquette.

"In practice, he'd cheat all the time," Smith recalled in a 2019 interview. "There were times when the second team would play the starters. You know how it is. We're all basketball players. Some days we, the second teamers, would be kicking ass. That's just how it is. But unless you blow him out, you're never going to win because when the game gets close, he's going to cheat. He's going to call fouls because he calls his own fouls. And Dunleavy isn't going to overrule him. So, you can't win in a close game. I distinctly remember one time in a close game, I'm guarding him and he's trying to back me down in the post, right. He goes to shoot his little right hook. I had seen it a million times. I sneak behind him, block it, and he calls a foul. And everybody is like, 'What? Are you kidding?' He just turns his lip up and walks to the free throw line. And Dunleavy and none of the coaches are saying anything. And I'm like, 'You can't win against that guy.'"

That included the seemingly incessant card games that accompany NBA life, Smith explained. "One time we were playing cards on the bus, and the game got out of control. It was a heated game and he was mad. The stakes were getting like crazy out of control. It was a game called 'Tonk.' Usually, you'd play Tonk for five, ten dollars right? We were on a long-ass bus ride and we were playing for a long time. And the stakes got really high. Because he was losing and he wanted to win so bad, the stakes were up to $100, $200 by the end of the game. Now, it's getting really out of control and I'm like, 'Come on, I can't afford this stuff.' But the thing was, I was kickin' their asses and there's no way you can all of a sudden jump out of the game."

Problem was, Smith had won his money in five- and ten-dollar hands, but Johnson had raised the stakes trying to get his losses back and come out a winner.

The main lesson? Don't play cards with millionaires, especially winning-addicted millionaires, no matter how innocent things seemed. There was a flip side to that, however. Smith was Johnson's "rookie," charged with getting up early each morning and getting the star a newspaper, then reappearing around noon to go fetch lunch for Johnson, who always handed him a hundred-dollar bill to pay for a twenty-dollar sandwich and told him to keep the change.

The sandwich and the change had nothing to do with winning, which opened the door to Johnson's well-documented generosity.

Tony Smith wasn't a guy who loved the club scene like Johnson, but he did go out with him a few times, both on the road and in L.A., enough to see what life was like behind the velvet ropes of a VIP section with a guy who was literally worshipped like a god by fans and aggressive women alike. It was all just enough to leave Smith marveling at how Johnson managed to approach his everyday life around the team in such a down-to-earth manner.

Tony Brown, the veteran free agent, saw the same going out to eat with Johnson during that training camp in Hawaii, watching fans approach their table during the meal seeking autographs, and Johnson telling them patiently to please wait till they finished eating and he would comply.

They always seemed to wait, Brown said.

That same patience, that gift from his mother as Tucker had called it, was evidenced in Johnson's dealings with a new coach and a new system. In truth, said Jimmy Eyen, Dunleavy wanted only slight adjustments from the Riley approach, still seeking to run when the opportunity presented itself, just making sure to find efficiency in the half-court.

Whatever this new edition of the Lakers did, Dunleavy wanted to keep much of the decision-making in Johnson's hands.

It wasn't just that Johnson made his coaches better. He had spent most of his career getting concessions out of his coaches at every level. They wisely allowed his mind to control the game, without creating a constant tug-of-war over who was in charge. Sometimes he had to work harder for those concessions, as at Michigan State, but he would eventually get them, as he did readily over the 1990–91 season.

Oscar

By early March 1991, the Lakers were struggling through not one but two ten-day road trips, something that Dunleavy in his many years in the league had never seen before, a team sent on the road for twenty out of twenty-three days.

In the midst of it all, the Lakers happened into Washington with their only three-game losing streak of the season, all while battling injuries and exhaustion. Meanwhile, Johnson was rapidly approaching Oscar Robertson's all-time NBA career assist record, among the things the crowd of reporters wanted to discuss with him after the game.

As it happened, 1990 had brought renewed interest in the idea of female reporters in men's sports locker rooms, a practice that had been around in limited fashion since the mid-1970s. For more than a decade now, the team had been Jerry Buss's traveling sex symbol, with forward A. C. Green as the lone holdout, carrying his Bible to ward off the advances of what could seem at times like a small horde of women.

That night in Washington, Green was standing with a towel around his waist after the game when a female reporter appeared in the visitors' dressing room at the Capital Centre.

"Lady in the locker room," Green announced loudly.

"I got my eyes closed," the reporter quickly promised.

"I just gotta let my teammates know," Green explained in a moment that framed the growing cultural dissonance that Johnson's Showtime Lakers presented as the world was changing.

This edition of the Lakers had played better and better defense as the season unfolded, but the issue had become the offense due to February injuries to starting center Sam Perkins that left him struggling for much of the spring. The Lakers still ran when the opportunity presented itself, but their pace had obviously slowed, which left Johnson posting up more as the team's half-court weapon.

Johnson, in particular, showed just a trace of age on that road trip, although he had been exuberant about handing out five hundred tickets to the game that night for the employees and their families from one of his business interests.

"It's well worth it," he said of the cost. "You got to reward them."

What that reward had allowed them to see was Johnson, when he wasn't in the game, standing on the sideline coaching young backup point guard Tony Smith.

"You just got to help Tony out," he explained afterward. "I'm here to make sure we can get him better and better. We got to develop him for the playoffs. It's the little things. Who to get the ball to when we're struggling."

The Lakers had gone three straight offensive possessions without Worthy touching the ball, Johnson pointed out. "Maybe he don't know, but I can see it and I can tell him."

Also on the agenda that night was Robertson's all-time NBA career assist record of 9,887, which had stood unchallenged since he set it in 1974. Johnson was closing in on both it and Robertson's career steals record.

"I love passing," he said. "That's what I love to do. So if I'm going to have a record, I'm happy it's this one. Now, nobody can ever replace him because he's the all-time greatest all-around player when you're talking about points, rebounds, and assists.

"That's where I got my tools from," Johnson said of the Big O. "I always admired his game, also him as a person. Oscar's got his own businesses. I really respect him off and on the court."

In that regard, Robertson and Julius Erving were the two who influenced him not just as players but as people, Johnson said that night.

Having been fascinated over the years by Robertson's contests against West and his teammates, Lakers scorekeeper John Radcliffe would observe, "Oscar was more deliberate. He slowed the game down."

West was more like Johnson in terms of pace, Radcliffe pointed out. "Jerry liked to push the ball and take the shot off the movement. Oscar liked to set up and shoot. He set the tempo of the game, and he knew what he was doing all the time."

Johnson and Robertson were alike in their command, Radcliffe opined. "Oscar was amazing in his ability. He was the general. He was running the show. The other players on his team knew that."

Robertson and West both started their careers well before the term "point guard" came into broad use, Radcliffe pointed out. "Oscar was the first real point guard in the game."

West himself wouldn't take over the chief ball-handling duties on the Lakers until late in his career, in the fall of 1971, at age thirty-three.

The opportunity to break Robertson's assist record itself wouldn't come for another six weeks, in mid-April, on a lob pass to Terry Teagle, as Johnson ran up 10 assists in the first 14 minutes of a game at Golden State.

In leading up to the moment, Johnson had offered up some spectacular highlights early on—completing a three-quarter-court baseball pass to Worthy for a layup and a half-court bounce pass to A. C. Green for another breakaway.

Johnson also recorded 11 turnovers that night, reported to be his career high.

"I've never been so nervous before a game," he said afterward. "I don't think I've been this nervous since I played my first game at San Diego and tripped over my warmups."

Jerry Buss had ordered up a special crystal trophy for Johnson and had Jerry West present it during an eleven-minute stoppage in play.

"It's been one of the great thrills of my life, watching a great player who has competed every night he stepped out on this court," the team's GM said.

Johnson took the microphone from West and thanked the "Magic makers," his parents. "I know they're both sitting at home watching," he said. "I know my dad is in his favorite seat—the same seat where he told me how to really play the game. If you're listening, Dad, I just want to tell you I love you so much."

Asked later about the moment, Johnson said, "You think of all the times you played shirts and skins, running around as a kid, hoping one day to get to the NBA, not knowing about this day. . . . I think I cried for all those times, maybe, when I was out there shoveling off in the snow, shooting half-court set shots against my father, him beating me with that old set shot."

RUN, TMC

The season would prove good enough for a 58–24 record, second in the West behind Portland's 63-win finish. And the playoffs brought new insights about how Johnson could elevate his mind-set to meet the moment, Tony Smith recalled. "He's not letting you believe that you're gonna lose. So, you go into wherever you are, it's like, 'We're winning this game.'"

After another first-round sweep of Houston, the Lakers faced the infamous "Run TMC" version of the Warriors in the second round. It was a marketing takeoff on Run-DMC, the iconic force in hip-hop making its mark in that era. Johnson rang up 21 points, 10 rebounds, and 17 assists with zero turnovers in leading the Lakers to a Game 1 win, 126–116. The 17 assists were the most without a turnover in a playoff game in Johnson's career. He went on to average a triple-double in that series against the Warriors that May with 25.8 points, 10 rebounds, and 12.8 assists against 3.2 turnovers.

The Warriors tied the series with a 125–124 win in Game 2, a contest that featured Johnson's all-time career playoff high of 44 points. The total included him going 20 for 22 from the line, making him only the fifth NBA player at the time to score 20 or more points from the foul line.

Then the series switched to Oakland.

"They had the Run TMC, right?" Tony Smith recalled. "Tim Hardaway, Mitch Richmond, and Chris Mullin. And Magic got pissed after warm-ups. They did this whole dramatic thing in the playoffs with Run-DMC at their place and they're doing their thing. And so Magic gets us in the huddle and he's like legit pissed. Sometimes, you get guys who will do things to get a team fired up and get the fake hype going. This wasn't the fake hype. He was like, 'These motherfuckers think they're going to celebrate on us and have a concert on us.' I'm like, 'Whoa. Dude. Is he serious?' And he was serious. He was pissed that they had the nerve to try to have a concert on us. He had everyone hyped up. It was unbelievable. . . . We crushed them."

Magic Mike

Clyde Drexler and Portland had just turned in a 63-win season, but Johnson drove the Lakers past them to victory in the conference finals in six games, and once again a team he led was advancing to the NBA championship series. This time, Michael Jordan would be there waiting. The Bulls had finally run off Thomas and the Pistons.

Like that, the city of Chicago, that had struggled for many years in pro basketball, was hosting the opening of a dream of a matchup for fans, Michael vs. Magic, the Bulls vs. the Lakers. Bulls ticket manager Joe O'Neil soon found himself in a nightmare trying to come up with enough tickets for all the demand at old Chicago Stadium with Hollywood and the Lakers coming to town.

"We were about four days out from the Finals starting and I was overwhelmed," O'Neil remembered. "I didn't have enough tickets. Michael needed this, and everybody needed this. I remember going home, getting home about seven that night and walking in to my wife and saying, 'Susan, I don't think I can do this. I'm overwhelmed. The whole world is coming after me. It's Michael vs. Magic. I don't have enough tickets.' My wife said to me, 'I have an idea. Why don't you take out the garbage?' So, I walked out and took out the garbage. I'm pulling it out to the street, and the light goes on across the street and the guy runs out, hands me a credit card and says, 'I hate to do this to you, Joe, but can you get me two?' I go back in the house and tell my wife, 'I got an order for two taking out the garbage.'"

With the championship series, Magic Mike of Laney High was finally coming face-to-face for a title bout with his hero. As if that wasn't trip enough down Memory Lane, Jordan also faced his two college teammates from his 1982 UNC national championship team, Worthy and Sam Perkins. Worthy had suffered a badly sprained ankle in the series against Portland, which greatly reduced his mobility. Some insiders figured Worthy's injury would cost the Lakers the series. Others, including Pat Riley, who was broadcasting the series for NBC, projected that the Lakers would prevail with their experience.

The biggest story line of all involved Jordan's struggles to win a title. He was the one-man show who couldn't seem to keep from referring to his teammates as his "supporting cast," no matter how many times he was reminded not to do it.

"He was hyped. Oh, yeah, he was hyped," recalled Scott Williams, who played for Chicago in that series. "For years Jordan had led the league in scoring, but he hadn't won a title yet. So, the knock on him was that he wasn't the kind of player that could win it all."

Williams was another North Carolina alum, but he had grown up in Los Angeles with Johnson as his schoolyard hero. "All of us kids idolized Magic," he recalled. "The way he was clutch in big moments, his infectious smile. He was a big kid having fun. Magic was the man."

In his pro life, Johnson had already faced three great teams—the 76ers of Julius Erving, the Celtics of Larry Bird, and the Pistons of Isiah Thomas. Now, as his career was nearing its end, he was coming up against a team that would prove to be perhaps the best of them all, Jordan's Bulls. The moment left many fans wishing it was the great Showtime team that Johnson was leading against Chicago. It was not.

Worthy played in Game 1 despite the ankle, which limited his mobility. Jordan and his Bulls played nervously out of the gate but still managed a two-point lead at halftime. The second half, however, became a matter of the Lakers' post game, run through Sam Perkins, Vlade Divac, and Worthy, versus Chicago's jump-shooting. That, in turn, pushed the Lakers' free throw totals to 34 against the Bulls' 18. Even so, it came down to jump shots at the end. Perkins hit an unlikely three-pointer while Jordan missed an 18-footer at the buzzer, and Los Angeles claimed Game 1, 93–91.

"We won the first game, we said, 'Hey, we can beat these guys,'" Byron Scott recalled.

Jordan had scored 36 with 12 assists, eight rebounds, and three steals on 14-of-24 shooting from the floor, but even this magnificent performance left some of his teammates quietly fuming about his shot selection and one-on-one play. Although his team had just lost the home-court advantage, Phil Jackson actually seemed relieved after the game. The Bulls coach had seen that Los Angeles struggled anytime Johnson was out of the game. Jackson figured that the heavy minutes Johnson would have to play would prove too great a burden for a player at the end of his career.

There was another development that Jackson hadn't foreseen, as explained in 2014's *Michael Jordan: The Life*. He had begun the series with the six-six Jordan defending the six-nine Johnson. And in Game 2, that effort brought Jordan two early fouls. Jordan's time on the bench meant that the taller Scottie Pippen would move over to cover Johnson.

At the time there was an assumption that the twenty-five-year-old Pippen would struggle to handle basketball's wiliest veteran. Just the opposite happened. The long-armed Pippen glued himself to Johnson, and suddenly the momentum shifted. Taking turns guarding him, Jordan and Pippen harassed Johnson into four-of-13 shooting from the floor while Pippen scored 20 points with 10 assists and five rebounds as the Bulls won Game 2 in a swarm.

"It's true," Phil Jackson said in 1998 when asked if the switch of Pippen covering Johnson was entirely accidental.

"We started to see that we were wearing him down from a physical standpoint," Pippen happily recalled, "especially myself being able to go up and harass him and trying to get him out of their offense. He wasn't as effective as he had been in the past against some teams, being able to post up and take advantage of situations. I saw the frustration there."

"Some of it was to rest Michael," recalled former Bulls assistant Johnny Bach in 2004. "We didn't want him on Magic all the time. Scottie went in, and suddenly we realized that he was so long and so big that Magic could not throw those over-the-top passes. We called them halo passes, right over the top of the head of the defender. He would throw the ball right past littler guys. But now Scottie was in front of him. He was really a little taller than the six-seven he said he was. Scottie had long arms and big hands. And Magic was starting to fade. He was getting older. Youth doesn't wait for the aged."

The Bulls shot better than 73 percent from the floor, and the result was a blowout, 107–86. Jordan made 15 of 18 from the floor to finish with 33, plus 13 assists, seven rebounds, two steals, and a block. Remembered even better than the numbers was "the move" he executed with a little under eight minutes left in the game, taking a pass at the top of the key and attacking the basket head-on through traffic. He rose with the ball outstretched high in his right hand to dunk until he encountered a defender, then switched to his left at the last instant and reached around the left side of the goal to flip in a bank shot that left the building buzzing.

What really hurt the Lakers was trouble defending the perimeter. Chicago guard John Paxson went eight for eight from the floor. "Does Paxson ever miss?" Sam Perkins asked afterward.

Perhaps the thorniest issue was Jordan's taunting of the Lakers' bench after made shots as the blowout unfolded, pumping his arms or appearing to give the dice a shake and a roll after made baskets. They would file a complaint about him with league offices, and even his teammates attempted to restrain him.

Even with the loss, the Lakers had little room for displeasure. They had gotten a split in Chicago Stadium and were headed home for three straight games in the Forum and a huge advantage in experience over the Bulls.

The first order of business for the Bulls before Game 3 was a videotape Jackson had prepared showing Johnson sagging off Paxson to play a zone and create havoc for the Chicago offense. Jordan had to recognize this and give up the ball to the open shooter, the coach emphasized, a message he would repeat after each of the next two games.

Pulling out his best Magic Mike imitation, Jordan would average better than 11 assists during the series. Johnson himself would average 12.4 assists, a Finals record 62 for a five-game series. In Game 1, he had recorded his seventh triple-double in a championship game, with 19 points, 10 rebounds, and 11 assists against five turnovers.

Faced with the challenge Johnson presented, the Bulls' coaching staff decided to begin pressuring his ball handling to see what that could produce, Williams explained in 2020. "We started to use what we called 'Laker Red.' That's a term a lot of teams use now, which is kind of funny. But we started that. Teams play a different style now, but back then teams would walk the ball up the floor. Scores were lower. But Magic and the Lakers always wanted to run. They were the Showtime Lakers. So one of the things we would do is have one of the bigs, after the ball was inbounded, to not really trap but to shadow Magic in a way that he felt your pressure."

The extra pressure from a taller player was just enough to slow him down, and the tall player would quickly retreat back on defense.

"It turned out to be Pippen most of the time in that series after the first game," Williams remembered. "We wanted to slow him down in the backcourt and make him use a little more time and exert a little more energy in the backcourt. That was one of the techniques I remember that was pretty effective in helping Pippen stay in front of Magic in advancing the ball and slowing the Laker attack down."

The Bulls had experimented with it a bit against the Pistons in the Eastern finals, but circumstances against the Lakers would make it even more effective as Worthy's ankle continued to give him trouble. Worthy, with his size and ball-handling skills, was a key aid to Johnson against the pressure. Without him, Johnson began wearing down, as the Bulls had hoped.

Having Pippen defend Johnson in Game 3 in Los Angeles backfired on Chicago in the second half as the Lakers moved to a 13-point lead when center Vlade Divac found it easier to score over the shorter Jordan. The Bulls narrowed the lead to a half dozen at the end of the third, and trouble caught up with Los Angeles from there. Johnson continued to show the effect of the heavy minutes he had to play (he would average 45 minutes a game in the series), and Worthy's ankle finally became the factor the Lakers coaches had feared it would.

The Bulls closed the gap, and Jordan would hit a jumper with 3.4 seconds left to send Game 3 into overtime. There, Chicago ran off eight straight points for a 104–96 win and a 2–1 lead in the series. Jordan was elated, but cautioned that the Lakers had plenty of experience in coming back.

Yet experience proved no match for the Bulls' young legs. In Game 4, Jordan and company harried the Lakers into shooting 37 percent from the floor and managing a total of 30 points over the second and third quarters. Perkins, in particular, found the going difficult in the low post while shooting one of 15 from the floor.

Jordan, meanwhile, had turned in yet another stellar night in his first championship series, with 28 points, 13 assists, five rebounds, and two blocks.

"I can't believe this is happening," Johnson told reporters afterward.

"It's no surprise the way they've been defending," Dunleavy said of the Bulls. "They are very athletic and very smart."

The Lakers in that moment glimpsed their fate, Johnson would recall years later in explaining that he was still able to score against Jordan with a bit of one-upmanship in an exchange on the court. In the 1980s, Johnson had seen that he and Bird were leading all players in T-shirt sales, prompting him to call Commissioner David Stern to inquire about the size of checks they would be receiving. Uncomfortably, Stern informed him there would be no royalties because the NBA Players Association had taken those image and likeness rights for itself.

Johnson said he was upset enough by the news to form a company—Magic Johnson T's—that became the first player-owned apparel business licensed to sell NBA merchandise. Jordan was talking trash with Johnson about how the series was going to end, when Johnson informed him that as he played Jordan was making money for him. Johnson then pointed to the tag on the shirt Jordan was wearing. It read Magic Johnson T's.

Even if Johnson's tale was true, his T-shirt sales were a small factor against the shoe and merchandise empire that Jordan had inspired. It was more telling that Johnson had to find some measure of victory in the moment.

As for the series, Jordan and his Bulls were on the verge of the improbable, but they'd have to be patient. "We went up 3–1 and had a long wait, from Sunday to Wednesday, for Game 5," recalled Bulls equipment manager John Ligmanowski. "Those three days took forever. Before we had even won it, Michael would get on the bus and say, 'Hey, how does it feel, world champs?' He knew. That was a pretty good feeling. We just couldn't wait to get it over with."

The Bulls then took their third straight in the Forum to close the series, 108–101. The moment was met by the numbed silence of the crowd, recalled Bulls broadcaster Jim Durham in 2011. "The one thing I'll remember is the Bulls dancing off the floor and everybody else just sitting there watching it."

Despite Laker Red, Johnson had racked up a whopping 20 assists and recorded his eighth career triple-double in championship play with 16 points and 11 rebounds in Game 5, which provided no consolation whatsoever.

Afterward, he sought out Jordan to offer his congratulations. Earlier in the series, he had approached Chicago's rising star and told him that they needed to drop the silliness of their differences. The event was the true beginning of their friendship, Jordan would say later. "I saw tears in his eyes," Johnson said of their moment after the final buzzer. "I told him, 'You proved everyone wrong. You're a winner as well as a great individual basketball player.'"

The Elusive Knot

In the many months since Johnson had created that beautiful engagement moment in Miami in February 1990 and then soon followed it up by cruelly demanding the ring back in March—a demand that he would repeat over the coming months—Cookie Kelly had managed to hold on to her relationship with him by backing off into her own life, taking the time to try to read and understand him, this superhero who had been her long-distance beau off and on for years, until finally his demands quieted and they began to settle into something of a comfortable routine. By the spring of 1991, Johnson had reached the point where for the first time in his years of pro basketball, he did the unthinkable. He invited Kelly to follow along with the other spouses and girlfriends as the Lakers made their way through the playoffs.

It would have to be from a distance, of course. Pat Riley and his rules about "baggage" were gone, but the pro basketball mind-set was still very much the same. Whether you labeled them "baggage" or not, family and significant others were not to be distractions when the season was on the line.

Even though she would have to give up her job in order to do the extended traveling required, which meant losing her independence and finally having to trust that Johnson was truly ready this time to get married, Kelly was elated, as were Johnson's parents, who were likewise invited to tag along, apparently for the very first time, for a playoff adventure.

In the past, when people asked why Johnson's parents were never at his games, much was made of Big Earv's disinclination to travel. And that was certainly true. But there was also a matter of an invitation. When Johnson finally got around to asking his parents in 1991 to come along, they jumped at the chance with so much glee that Christine Johnson and Cookie Kelly would hug in delight over the circumstances. After all, the new mansion was completed and the seemingly happy couple had moved forward together with the thought that this time it just might happen.

Then came the dose of reality vs. Jordan and the Bulls, followed by Johnson immediately launching into plans in the aftermath for his usual summer bacchanalia, inviting all his rowdy friends to another of his grand parties, no spouses or girlfriends or wives allowed, which in turn created the usual furor among those spouses. This time, they took their complaints to Kelly, alerting her to how unfair it was of Johnson to hold such an event. She tried to do something about it, which created another door slammer that yet again closed any thoughts of matrimony.

Johnson was adamant in his plan to go ahead with the party, which was said to feature in its tamer elements various bikini and wet T-shirt contests for the women who were invited.

Kelly recalled making a full run of tearful entreaties to get him to call the thing off.

"I'm having a party, Cookie, and we don't have to get married," she remembered him saying before hanging up on her.

He also planned to head off alone again for his usual Bahamas vacation not long after the party. Kelly was understandably crushed yet again by the push and pull of his infatuation with "the life."

Undeterred, she continued to phone him and harangue him about the party, each call seemingly ending with a sudden dial tone. Alas, despite her pleas, he threw his big stag event and headed off for the Bahamas that July.

It was from the islands that he first phoned her days later and said, "I think I can get married."

He told her that hanging out with her in the playoffs had finally convinced him that she could be a part of his world. Her friends, even his family, had come to see that the relationship with the frequent doings and un-doings of matrimonial plans had passed the point of ludicrous long ago. And so, in yet another chapter in their intense personal drama, Johnson once again began reeling her back in.

Only much later—after it became clear that this was a mere prelude to the grand drama that was to come—would most reporters and other media figures realize they had never had so much as a conversation with Johnson about Kelly.

"He always kept that separate," explained Steve Springer in 2019. "He kept that away from us. And that was fine. I mean, he was very private. He made it very plain that Cookie was his private life and that was something he wasn't going to do, to deal with us with."

Having done just as he pleased with his party and vacation plans, Johnson set the wedding plans in motion once again that August with his phone call to Kelly.

She was understandably cautious. Are you sure? she asked.

"This is it," he said. "I want to do it."

Not just do it, but do it right away. This time, she wouldn't have to worry about a thing. He promised he would take care of all the details and all she had to do was show up at the church in her wedding dress. It seems Big Earv had gotten involved this time, telling his son that if he didn't marry Kelly "it would be the biggest mistake of his life."

That didn't stop her stress levels from soaring into fitful sleep and lost weight. Was she being set up yet again for another epic disappointment?

"They had to hurry it up," recalled New York Knicks forward Herb Williams, Johnson's old friend. "So, she didn't get time to set up a big wedding or anything."

There was, however, time to negotiate and sign a prenuptial agreement in which Kelly gave up claims on what was then his estimated $100 million in wealth. Such harsh details aside, they assembled a quick wedding in Lansing.

All of which served to catch old friend Dale Beard off guard.

"Next thing you know, I get a call," Beard remembered in 2019. "Earvin said, 'Hey, man, I need you to be the best man in my wedding.'"

"Huh?" Beard replied. "Me?"

Stunned, his old Everett teammate did a quick inventory in his mind. Johnson had his brothers. He had NBA hotshots like Isiah Thomas and Mark Aguirre. He had Greg Kelser from Michigan State.

"I just wasn't expecting, you know, to be the best man," Beard recalled. "I mean, because he had his brothers or, you know, some of his other friends, but I was pretty honored for it."

Early in Johnson's career in Los Angeles, Beard had gone out and spent a week with him in his apartment, marveling at his friend's big new life.

"I mean, you had billboards and bus stops, you know, with his picture on the benches at the bus stops and on the buses. 'Welcome to Magic's World,' all kinds of stuff with his name on it," Beard recalled, laughing. "He just thought it was part of how this thing was supposed to be, you know. He never said, 'Wow. Hey, man, this is crazy.' He never reacted like that. He just felt like this was how this thing was supposed to be, and I gotta roll with it."

After Beard's week staying with Johnson in his apartment, they would still have their phone conversations several times a year, Beard said. "I understood, you know, he was busy. I just didn't really bother him a lot. As the years went on, I got busy. He got busy."

The wedding had to happen that September because Johnson had to go to Europe in October for the McDonald's Invitational Tournament and then back home for training camp, followed by an absolutely insane preseason schedule.

Four days before the September 14 wedding, the couple went to the offices of Johnson's longtime Lansing physician, Dr. Tom Jamieson, for premarital counseling and to review medical paperwork. Jamieson asked them if they wanted to do any blood chemistry tests, which were no longer mandatory in Michigan. And the state had yet to require an AIDS test.

"Would you guys want to have that done?" Jamieson recalled asking, in a 2019 interview.

"You can have it," the doctor told them. "You don't have to."

Jamieson recalled, "Magic said, 'Yeah, we could do that. That would be okay, or we don't have to. It doesn't matter.'"

The question would come up later in Jamieson's deposition in a legal matter regarding whether Johnson knew he was HIV positive that September.

"I actually was brought into depositions over that because I had gone to Magic," Jamieson said, "and he was trying to prove that he didn't know. He did not know."

Later, Jamieson would wonder to himself, what if they had done the tests and Johnson had found out at that time?

"My statements in those depositions were, 'There's no way he knew it,'" the physician recalled. "He would have told me at that point, 'Don't do any of that.' He'd have known."

Instead, the wedding party gathered that weekend in Lansing. "All of us got up that morning of the wedding," Dale Beard recalled, "and we went out to Jenison Field House, man. We played some hoop for a couple of hours. Me, Earvin, Greg Kelser, Isiah, Mark Aguirre, we were all out at Jenison, man."

They played for two hours, as they had done so many times over the past decade, this particular group of friends, not realizing just how special this little run was, that it would be the last time they would ever join together as friends and get lost in the carefree moment. Then they grabbed lunch and went back to their hotel rooms for a nice nap before the five o'clock nuptials at Union Missionary Baptist Church.

Kelly was waiting there, filled with unbearable anxiety about whether Johnson would back out yet again, this time leaving her standing there at the altar like the all-time sucker of suckers.

Her worry eased when word circulated around the church that indeed he was on the premises.

"His wife is perfect for him," broadcaster Tim Staudt recalled. "I remember his wedding. She told us at his wedding she wasn't getting married to him before she was convinced in her own mind that he had all these boyhood things that he was going to do, date the girls, chase the girls, do what he was going to do in L.A. And when she was convinced that absolutely had run its course and that he was absolutely ready to settle down and get married, that's when she finally said yes."

The joy and relief were obvious in Kelly's eyes, Herb Williams would recall in 1993. "She's a nice girl. She has a nice head on her shoulders. She had a nice job. I mean, she could have had a whole lot of other guys, whoever she wanted. But she had always been there for him, no matter what."

It was a smallish affair with Williams, Thomas, and Aguirre, among others, serving as groomsmen.

The gathering of 275 or so included so many of the old friends. Greta Dart was there. And Darwin Payton. And Stan Martin of Quality Dairy stores in Lansing, the man who gave Johnson his first job as a teen. Absent was Lon Rosen, whose wife had delivered a son just the day before. Johnson would leave the next day and fly to Los Angeles to visit his agent and see Rosen's child.

In reporting on the wedding, *People* magazine noted that Thomas was on the sideline this time and not being kissed by Johnson, who was described as "one of the sports world's most eligible bachelors."

Kelly's white gown featured a sweetheart neckline with a full skirt and train, and her bridesmaids were decked out in black velvet. Johnson went for the white, double breasted look with black trousers. They made a beautiful, radiant couple. The groom's parents greeted the moment with serene smiles, channeling emotions that ran all the way back to that August day in 1959.

"I think he just was ready to do it, you know what I mean?" Dale Beard said of his old friend. "He wasn't nervous to me, you know, and I just thought the whole thing was great, man. It was a great wedding. It rained that morning and then it was really burning up by the time the wedding started."

Once the vows had been said and the songs sung, the wedding party retreated to a reception that featured red-trimmed white lilies on each table, all of it set up by Johnson with the help of his sisters.

"The most magical thing about the wedding may be that it happened at all," *People* noted, pointing out the couple's long trail to the altar.

"No more marriage. No more talk about it," Johnson had said tersely that March of 1990 after the big announcement of the engagement a month earlier. Now, Kelly was finally wed to the man she loved so dearly.

Those who notice such things pointed out she was wearing her five-carat marquise-cut diamond in a white gold setting as she left the church that day.

"Everything went great, man," Dale Beard recalled.

If only it could have stayed that way. But it would not. Yet if anything was steady in the arrangement, it would prove to be Kelly, who was built to endure, to hold on through the intense darkness, once again biding her time until she could make things good. Johnson had come to be seen as a force of nature over his magical career, yet time would reveal that she was every bit the match of that and more.

29

ABSOLUTELY POSITIVE

His life for so many years had been quite the show in lights, with the overwhelming emotion of one sizzling game night after another, all staged end to end for a dozen thrilling seasons, unlike anything Los Angelenos had ever seen, even more spectacular than John Wooden's iconic UCLA teams. Johnson and his Showtime Lakers had risen to become the unrivaled sensation in all of American sport by 1990. Yet very soon all of that sparkling gathered imagery would collapse, almost like used fairy dust, and his life would become a matter of fact. Suddenly people wanted to know what happened when. And where? And how?

His answer, the answer of what was basically a very private man living in a very public eye, was to try to explain the inexplicable.

It was all made even more difficult to understand because of his happy image. The American public had hardly a clue about his secret life. What's more, his troubles came down out of sequence, with perhaps the largest revelation not arriving until months later, in 1992, when one of his old friends from Lansing would file a $2 million lawsuit against him for infecting her with the HIV virus, first reported by legendary sportswriter Frank Deford for *Newsweek* and picked up by news organizations around the globe.

In her legal filing, the woman was identified as "Jane Doe," although eventually the judge in the case would order that she be identified by her real name, Waymer Moore, a health care analyst who had attended Michigan State at the same time as Johnson.

Her lawsuit, which would eventually be settled out of court, offered a timeline that was very different from that put forth by Johnson and the early media reports of his infection.

In her legal action, Moore claimed that she had phoned Johnson in late July 1991 and told him about her situation, that she had been diagnosed with HIV a month earlier, and that she hadn't had sex with another man since her congress with him eight months earlier, back in late 1990.

Moore claimed that Johnson said he would get back with her later but never did. Moore said that she then wrote him in late August 1991, about two weeks before his wedding, explaining again that he had infected her with HIV. Through his lawyer, Johnson would deny ever receiving the letter.

However, in her filing, Moore claimed that she went to Jenison Field House where he was playing ball the Thursday evening before his September 14 wedding. She said that Johnson dismissed the other players and talked with her, during which he acknowledged receiving the letter.

Newsweek would later publish details from her August 1991 letter to Johnson, which she wrote eight weeks before his November announcement that he was HIV positive and two weeks before his wedding.

The letter opened with "Dear Earvin" and admonished him to "read Deuteronomy 5:17. God bless."

"I have no idea when the bottom will fall out," Moore wrote, "so I must prepare now. So, you see, I can't be a silent voice any longer, not even for you, Baby Boy."

She stated that she only could have contracted the virus from Johnson.

At the time, Moore had a four-year-old daughter and was divorced from a former Michigan State quarterback. She also revealed that she had first been tested for HIV as far back as 1986 and had three negative tests before testing positive in June 1990.

"I'm compulsive. I keep track of everything," she wrote. "I once told you I didn't put my love on the street and it's a fact that cannot be denied."

The legal strategy of Johnson's lawyer would be to suggest otherwise, that she could have had relations with a variety of men.

Johnson's legal team did concede his having sex with Waymer Moore the one time she alleged.

"My Baby Boy," Moore had written to him, "I wish you peace and I give you my love. Although you did not have the courage to face me, you will one day soon have to account for it."

The Long Ride

The Lakers opened the season just two weeks after his wedding with an abbreviated version of training camp in Palm Desert, California. Now thirty-two, Johnson showed up in poor shape with the idea that he would build his conditioning during the team's twice-daily practices. From there, the Lakers jetted to Boston for two quick exhibition games with the Celtics, then on to Paris to play in the McDonald's Open, an international exhibition tournament.

In France, seemingly everywhere the Lakers went there were crowds chanting, "Ma-jeek! Ma-jeek!" Such moments brought incredible affirmation for his life and career, moments that might have been even more uplifting if he wasn't dogged by a growing anxiety, a gnawing foreboding that monumental trouble was closing in on him.

Yes, at least one of his former lovers had notified him that she was HIV positive. Were there others?

The mere thought of that would have been enough to plunge many into overwhelming distress, but not Earvin "Magic" Johnson, Jr., whose unsinkable nature had carried him far into what seems, looking back, like virtually impenetrable denial.

He looked across those Paris crowds, heard them calling his name, and stood there, absorbing all that energy that bolstered his immense confidence even further, if that was possible, telling him, yes, he was moving at the upper realm of human existence, that he could negotiate that realm with the ease with which he threw those miracle passes on the Lakers' fast break. It was the kind of adulation that confirmed for Johnson just how much he deserved to hang at those elite clubs back in L.A., the kind of places where he or guys like Prince or Rick James could hold court in the VIP sections. The fans in France offered living proof to Johnson that he, too, was indeed a rock star.

Thus, his sense of power surged that week, never mind that the Lakers barely beat a Spanish team, Joventut Badalona, for the exhibition championship. Yes, he had played in Europe in his college days and even on occasion afterward, but the response had never been anything like this.

Still, it left him strangely teetering at the mountaintop of his playing career, on one side looking back with awe and wonder at all that had been in his life, but then gazing to the other side to a flashing, frightening glimpse of the abyss that lay ahead.

That elation and terror were fusing in that moment to become his fate.

The trip also helped serve as preparation for Team USA's new plan for no longer using amateur athletes exclusively, meaning that the team for the 1992 Olympics in Barcelona could deploy professionals from the NBA. Johnson was expected to be a key figure for what would come to be known as the Dream Team. The crowds in France helped him taste just how delicious that might be.

It was in Paris that Cookie Kelly Johnson learned she was pregnant, from a home-test kit, which further tightened the screws on her new husband's big, unarticulated anxiety.

Soon enough the Lakers were jetting back across the Atlantic to an unanticipated new reality, one coming at them like a train. By then, the grind of playing himself into shape while crossing time zones had begun to show on Johnson, and the fourteen-hour plane trip home offered little relief from his thoughts.

He arrived in Los Angeles with a weary face, but there was little time to rest. Back home, the Lakers faced two more exhibition games in the GTE Everything Pages Shootout, where they again beat Boston, then lost to the Milwaukee Bucks.

From there, the schedule called for them to fly to Utah for another game, then to head off to Vancouver, British Columbia, the night after for yet another game the next night, against the Seattle Supersonics. From there, they were scheduled to fly back to Los Angeles in order to hold practice the next morning at the Loyola Marymount University gym, their regular practice facility at the time.

It was an impossibly chaotic schedule, seemingly arranged with absolutely no thought for an aging roster.

"Earvin really didn't want to go with the team," Lon Rosen recalled in 2019 of the game in Utah. "It was a long training camp. He wanted to sort of take off that game. They said no, just go and play a quarter."

So, ever dutiful, he frowned and went anyway.

"I sat with Magic on the plane," Chick Hearn would recall in an interview with Larry Burnett, "and, like we always did, played gin rummy all the way. We had a good time and a lot of laughs. By the time we got to Salt Lake, he was much richer and I was much poorer. We got to the hotel, went to the counter to get our keys. Magic was first ahead of me in the line. I'll never forget it. The young lady that gave him his key said, 'Mr. Johnson, there is an emergency call for you.'" Johnson went to his room and learned from Rosen that he had to return home immediately.

"I didn't think anything of it," Hearn recalled. "I got my key and was turning to go to the elevator to go to my room. Magic came walking by towards the door. I said, 'Where are you going?' He said, 'I've got to go back to L.A.'"

For all intents and purposes, the era known as Showtime ended in those moments.

Gary Vitti's response was disbelief when Johnson informed him that he was headed home, as reported in *The Lakers*. The trainer first suspected that Johnson had arranged a doctor's excuse to miss the rest of the trip. But Earvin wouldn't do something like that, Vitti quickly realized.

So the trainer called Dr. Michael Mellman, one of the team's doctors, and asked what was up.

"I can't tell you about it at this point," Mellman said. "Something has shown up abnormal on Earvin's physical exam. He has to come home."

The league's salary cap had dissuaded the team from increasing Johnson's $2.5 million annual contract, yet his salary had become eclipsed by younger players coming into the NBA whose agents were negotiating what were then megadeals of $3, $4, and $5 million per year. To compensate Johnson more fairly until the team cleared room under the salary cap to increase his pay, Jerry Buss had arranged to give his favorite player a $3.6 million low-interest loan.

Getting the loan required that Johnson have a life insurance policy. To get the policy, he had to undergo a rigorous physical exam. And now the results were in.

After speaking with Mellman, Vitti asked Johnson what was going on.

"Gary, I don't know," he replied.

Vitti knew something had to be wrong, and as the trainer he had to be on top of each player's health, especially that of the Lakers' biggest star. The whole mysterious development set his mind to spinning.

As laid out in 1993's *The Lakers*, Mike Dunleavy was also confused by Johnson's sudden departure. To find out what was wrong, the coach phoned Mitch Kupchak, the team's assistant general manager.

"Mike," Kupchak said, "I don't know anything about it. All I know is I got a call from Lon Rosen and he said he was scared to death."

"When Mitch said that to me, I immediately didn't have a good feeling," Dunleavy recalled in a 2019 interview. "I thought it was cancer or AIDS. I don't why. But it hit me like that: Bam. Holy crap."

Indeed, Rosen himself, usually calm and collected in taking on the events of Johnson's career, had been overcome with foreboding. In the two hours before Johnson was scheduled to arrive back in Los Angeles, the agent had sat in Jerry West's office, talking with the general manager trying to figure what was up. Rosen thought his friend and client had cancer. After all, Johnson's half sister Mary had died of cancer almost five years earlier.

Back in Utah, Gary Vitti wondered if it was a heart condition. That was the fear with big men like Johnson. But over his years in the league, Johnson had aced many stress tests. His heart was sound. For hours, Vitti was dogged by the unknown. Finally, in the middle of the game with Utah that night, the trainer was struck with the answer.

"It's like somebody hit me in the head with a sledgehammer," Vitti recalled in 1992. "Bang. He's HIV positive."

He wasn't entirely sure. But Vitti had long been the guy trying to persuade Johnson about the absolute necessity of wearing condoms. Vitti was the trainer. When he told Johnson to seek treatment for one ailment or another, the star always dutifully followed the advice. Except for this. Except for protecting himself in the busiest activity of his life other than basketball. Despite his decade-long trail of sexually transmitted diseases. Despite all the doctors' prescriptions to treat those STDs. Despite the refrain, "If he doesn't have it, you can't get it."

Meanwhile, Rosen and others around Johnson were going through a similar process toward their own realization of what was unfolding before their eyes.

"I get this call from the doctor saying, 'Hey, you have to get Earvin back here,'" Rosen recalled in 2019. "He gets on a plane. And I never would pick him up at the airport, but I figured it's pretty important. So, I went to the airport, picked him up, met him at curbside, and then drove him to the doctor's office."

Mellman's practice was located in El Segundo, close to the airport. On the ride over, Johnson phoned his wife, according to her memory.

"I'm coming home early because I have to tell you something," she would recall him telling her. "I have to talk to you, but I'm on my way to the doctor's office right now. I'll tell you what's going on when I get home, Cookie. I can't tell you over the phone."

Dread flooded her thoughts. It's important to note that the conversation came before the meeting with the doctor, which indicated that Johnson was perhaps aware of the news that would greet him.

"What's wrong, do you have AIDS or something?" she asked him.

His only answer was silence, she would later remember. And her immediate supposition of the problem would ring like a bell. It was telling perhaps that so many around Johnson, including his wife, had leapt to that conclusion long before any announcement, and curiously telling considering that at that moment in American culture, HIV, or AIDS, was considered a disease that largely struck gay or bisexual males. Sure, it also had ensnared intravenous drug users and prostitutes and unfortunate blood transfusion victims. And, in Africa, the disease had spread in the population largely through heterosexual activity. But that was not the case in America, nor would it become that in the decades after.

At the time, for Johnson's wife, the circumstances were familiar, except she had yet to comprehend the absurd numbers of his problem, which she would later learn in a crushing moment sitting beside her husband as he talked about his infection in a live interview on nationwide TV, all of it in the dramatic unwinding of his other life that was about to unfold in a medical consultation in El Segundo.

"We walk into the doctor's office," Rosen said in 2019, "and the doctor says, 'Earvin, come on in my office right now.' And Earvin turns to me and said, 'You better come in with me. You're going to hear about it anyhow.' And the doctor just sat us down. He opened up his desk drawer and pulled out a FedEx packet and said, 'Earvin, you tested positive for HIV.' At that point, I can't say we knew too much about HIV, but, you know, the thought was, 'This is a death sentence.'"

Johnson didn't weep or cry out in stunned disbelief at the news, Rosen recalled. "He was concerned and he listened and he asked questions and then we left."

Chick Hearn would recall in 2002, "When he came out of Dr. Mellman's office that day after getting this horrible information, when he went out the door, there were three college girls standing there and they asked for his autograph. Under that duress, he stopped and signed them all. That's Magic Johnson."

A Magic Johnson struggling to process the devastating confirmation of the darkness that had been stalking him.

"He decided he needed a moment to let it sink in before he went home," Rosen remembered, "and he said, 'Let's go to dinner.' I was obviously in a state of shock, and we went to a restaurant in Santa Monica. The drive was tough. At that dinner, which was bizarre, a woman comes up to our table. This is a little restaurant. 'Oh, Magic, I'm a big fan of yours.' She has a business card and goes, 'Hey, I'm out doing a fundraiser for AIDS. Could you donate something?' This was like an hour after the doctor just gave him this information."

They ate and talked until, finally, they could delay no longer. Rosen drove Johnson home to deliver the news to his pregnant wife.

"That ride home was the longest ride of my life," Johnson would say later.

"After I dropped Earvin off," Rosen recalled, "I went right to Jerry West's house and told Jerry. And then I called Jerry Buss from Jerry West's house."

Johnson would come up with a line from that experience that he would often use later in a monumentally lame attempt at levity: "I always tell people, the toughest thing I thought I would have to do was play against Michael Jordan and Larry Bird, but it was actually to go home and tell my wife I had the HIV virus," he told Charlie Rose in a 2005 interview on public television.

Obviously, there was little that was lighthearted about the moment, nor about Cookie's response.

"When you usually do something wrong, it affects everybody that you love, not just yourself, but everybody that you love and care about," he would explain later. "So how am I going to tell the one person who has believed in me my whole, you know, since I met her, also my best friend at the same time. And so, it was a difficult time. And so, I just sat her down, and I was trying to tell her, and it really just came out that I had the HIV virus. She began to cry, and then, also the biggest problem that I had is, I didn't know if she had the virus or my baby, because—or our baby—because she was pregnant with our son, E.J."

The news would ignite her overwhelming fear about the life of her unborn child, about her own life. Cookie would later describe the period as her "personal hell," a time that found her alternating between profound numbness and fits of clarity that left her trying to quell her soaring anxiety.

After breaking the news to his wife that first night, Johnson then went in another room and sat down to call all the many women he could reach to warn them about his condition. He would concede there were many, many names he could not recall. He never discussed the anguish and anger and fear he would hear in the voices on the other end of the line as he dialed one after another to hand out as many devastating notifications as possible, messages that must have poured forth like a fountain from his own grim news, a misery that would surely keep on giving.

All of it would be absorbed as part of the massive, multifaceted blow that would stagger Cookie with its scope and intensity. She later recalled slapping him that evening after he suggested she leave him.

"The next morning Earvin and Cookie came to my house at six, for breakfast," Lon Rosen recalled. "And it was very emotional with Cookie just pregnant with E.J."

In those early hours, his friend and client talked of dying, Rosen said in 2019. "That morning, we went on a walk for like three hours and just talked about everything, life, what the future would be. At that point, his life expectancy was pretty short. I think he probably had to prop me up as much as I had to prop him up."

Johnson even talked briefly of suicide during their walk, Rosen would reveal much later.

Another very difficult call would be the one to Lansing that morning. No fool, Johnson chose Saturday morning to make the call, when he knew his mother would be at church.

Big Earv answered the phone.

Always the steadiest of advisors, the father listened to the news and absorbed it enough to tell him, "It isn't the end of the world. You can deal with it."

It sure sounded good, but when Christine got home later that day she found her husband strangely crawled back up in bed, an empty, lost look on his face.

She asked if he was sick, she later told *Sports Illustrated* writer Gary Smith. Her husband didn't answer, so she asked again if he was ill.

"Sort of," he finally replied. "Talked to Earvin on the phone. He's . . . he's got HIV."

"That was the worst moment of my life," she would later tell Steve Springer. "Oh, my Lord."

Her answer was to get back in the car and drive around, just trying to absorb all that the news meant and all that it would mean. "I didn't know where I was going," she would recall of that lonely ride. "I didn't know what to do."

She went to see an ill friend, which helped calm her somewhat. Finally, she decided she needed to fly to Los Angeles to support her son.

"No, Momma, don't come," Johnson told her when she phoned. "This is something I have to do by myself. Just pray for me."

For years, she had pursued the faith provided by her own mother, and she now found herself in that moment where she needed all that she could muster.

"It's in God's hands," she finally decided. "All of us are going to die of something. He won't die until his time."

Yet Another Flu Game

After losing in Utah that night before, the Lakers boarded the team plane for Canada, all of them wanting to know what was wrong with their leader.

Vitti told them he didn't know.

The trainer's hotel phone rang in Vancouver at eight the next morning. It was Dr. Mellman.

"Mickey, you don't have to tell me a thing," Vitti said quickly. "I already figured it out. Earvin is HIV positive, isn't he?"

"I knew you would figure it out," the doctor said. "Earvin wanted you to know. We're only telling a few people. No one is to know. No one. No coaches. No players. Absolutely no one. Earvin said he wanted you to know and he said he would meet you early in the morning before practice at Loyola."

The locker room at Loyola was empty the following morning

when Vitti and Johnson met around eight. They cried together. Speaking in an emotional 1992 interview, with events still fresh in his mind, an interview interrupted with his quiet sobs, Vitti told of how he and Johnson wept together. Their belief in that moment was that everyone died of AIDS. No one survived.

"You're gonna beat this thing," he told Johnson. "I'm gonna help you. You're gonna eat right, sleep right, exercise. I'm gonna keep you healthy."

In a time of very bad news, supposedly, the good news was that perhaps Johnson had found out early, which meant he could take medication to slow the spread of the virus. People usually didn't learn they had AIDS until they became symptomatic, until symptoms of the disease appeared. Otherwise, the virus worked insidiously. Regardless, Vitti knew that eventually Johnson would develop AIDS that would take over his body. The right regimen was known to slow the onset of the disease. Some people had tested positive, then lived as long as a decade without becoming symptomatic. But Vitti knew these cases were the exception, far from the rule.

The bigger immediate concern was how to handle the news. Johnson needed time to consult with counselors, lawyers, doctors, family. He needed time to realize his options and come to terms with them.

"We came up with this bullshit that he had the flu," Vitti remembered.

The media were told that Johnson would miss some practice and games. That lie would buy them about ten days to figure out a plan.

Even then Johnson didn't make the ruse easy for Rosen, who had to answer reporters' questions about his condition. During this time, Johnson appeared at a Los Angeles Rams game and sat on the sideline. How does a person sick with the flu go to a football game and seem to have a good time? It didn't make sense to the media.

The situation left Rosen phoning Vitti to go over the details. "I had to confide in somebody," the agent explained.

They disliked lying to the media, but felt they had no choice. After a few days, the flu story began to wear thin. So Rosen again called the trainer. "Veets," he said, "I've decided to announce that Earvin has begun light workouts under supervision."

"What the fuck does that mean?" Vitti shot back.

"I don't know, Gary," Rosen replied. "What are we gonna do? We've got to tell them something."

These stories clearly didn't add up for Dunleavy. Concerned about the strange situation, the coach went to Mitch Kupchak's office. "Something's not right here," he told the assistant GM. "This is way off the wall. If Earvin has cancer or AIDS and you know it, you better let me know. I've got about a week before the season starts, and if he's not going to be in the lineup, I've got to start making some plans."

Dunleavy was told that something very bad had come up, that it would have a major impact on the team. The coach would begin changing things swiftly for an offense with no Magic. "Some players were scratching their heads, wondering what the hell I was doing," he recalled.

Fortunately, the team had traded for veteran Sedale Threatt, an NBA journeyman who could fill in at guard.

Amazingly, Johnson's circle of friends, family, and advisors—even the sexual partners he had supposedly phoned—kept his secret for almost two weeks. Beyond Johnson's family, Cookie's family also had the infuriating news. Plus, the doctors and a few other select counselors. But few in that group understood the implications of it all, including Johnson himself. For most of the time, he and the people around him thought that testing HIV positive meant that he had AIDS. They would soon learn the difference, but at that moment there was much to sort out.

Johnson and Cookie's first thought had been to say nothing publicly. It was his own personal health matter. Rosen soon convinced him that wouldn't work.

"There was no way to know what was correct," recalled Rosen in an interview months later. "But very quickly Earvin knew that keeping it quiet was impossible. We knew it would get out."

"He absolutely had to go public with it because of the thousands of women that he'd had sexual relations with," Vitti said a year later. "Even if only one of them was HIV positive because of him, and you had sex with that woman and became HIV positive, indirectly, you could hold Earvin responsible because he knew that he had it and didn't notify the woman. He had a moral and ethical responsibility."

Any moral considerations would be quickly swamped by another consideration. After years of not protecting himself, he now needed to take steps to protect himself legally.

First, he was tested yet again to make sure the original results were correct, and Cookie was tested. "It took me about a week to find out," Johnson would recall. "And so, you're talking about the toughest week of my life, too, not just telling her, but waiting for those results to see if she was—had the HIV virus.

"When that news came back, that she didn't have the virus or the baby, you know, you just wanted to say, 'Oh, man! God bless me.'"

Her negative results helped calm his mind a bit. But it sometimes took months for the symptoms to show up, meaning that Cookie during that time suffered almost constant anxiety about her future and that of her child.

"He gets HIV from whatever he was involved with previously," Lansing broadcaster and old friend Tim Staudt said in 2019, "but she was a rock for him at the same time. Absolutely a rock for him."

Somehow, "rock" couldn't quite cover the obvious depth of her commitment. Cookie Kelly was a bright, intuitive woman long painfully aware of at least the nature of Johnson's secret life of satyriasis, certainly not the extent, but clearly the nature of it.

"All of us are lax in not giving his wife credit," Chick Hearn would say some years later. "Think of that. He comes in and says, 'I've got something to tell you.' Boy, she has stuck. She has nurtured. She is a wonderful, wonderful lady."

Once Johnson realized he had no choice but to go public, his advisors began making plans for a press conference. On Thursday morning November 7, Rosen began making phone calls from his home, notifying Johnson's key relationships, Bird, Jordan, Riley, among others. In each call, he stressed the necessity of confidentiality. Everyone understood.

That morning, Rosen got a call from a radio reporter asking if the rumors about Johnson's health were true. Rosen asked him to hold the story until he could notify the team that it was about to break.

The team was practicing at Loyola Marymount when Vitti got a call from Jerry West.

"Gary," West said, "get everybody out of the gym. Get them in their cars. Tell them to go home and change and be back at the Forum at two o'clock. I don't care what they have to do. I don't care what their schedule is today. Tell 'em no matter what it is to cancel it. Get them out of the gym now. We have a leak, and the press are on their way to Loyola to interview them about it."

This presented a problem because the players had not been told of Johnson's plight. A few had figured it out on their own, but there had been no official word on it. And there had been surprisingly little chatter.

The players began complaining about this abrupt change of plans and odd directive from team management.

"Hey, look," Vitti told them testily. "No matter what you've got to do, cancel it. We've got a press conference today. Believe me, this is going to change your life."

Before leaving, Byron Scott and James Worthy paused to shoot free throws. "What do you think this is about?" Worthy asked.

"I don't know," Scott replied. "It's probably about Earvin."

He recalled pausing, laughing nervously and saying, "He might have AIDS."

Then he and Worthy looked at each other. "Naw," Worthy said. "I hope that's not the case. I pray to God that's not it."

"I hadn't heard anything," Scott later recalled. "Something just made me say it. We were there with him as far as on the road and had seen all the girls and what he did."

On the way home, Scott and several others heard noon radio broadcasts that Johnson had AIDS and was retiring. Still, two or three players arrived at the Forum unaware of what was about to unfold. "Well, Earvin wanted to tell you himself," Vitti said, "but since the other guys know, it's pretty ridiculous that you don't. Earvin has tested HIV positive. That's why he hasn't been with us."

The events of that day would grow stranger by the minute.

"It was one of the worst emotional experiences I've ever been through," equipment manager Rudy Garciduenas said, "because we felt that it was such a loss, because there's such a stigma that follows this disease around, because it's life-threatening. . . . But Earvin came down and told us before the press conference. We all got to be with him for a little while."

Johnson first met privately with Dunleavy and, his voice breaking, told the coach that his career was over, that things would be all right, that he would get through the circumstances as best he could.

From there, Johnson went to his teammates in the locker room.

"He came in," Vitti said in a 1992 interview. "He had on a blue suit and a white shirt and he looked really good and distinguished. I can just see him so vividly. He told the team that he had this virus, you know. 'I got this virus.' You know the way he talks. 'I can't play basketball anymore.'"

"The emotion in that locker room was unbelievable," Dunleavy said in 2019.

Again, weeping as he spoke, Johnson paused to talk about the "wars" he had been through with his longtime teammates, Worthy, Scott, and A. C. Green, and how special those wars had been. Then he moved around to pause with each of the twelve players and the coaches and Vitti and Garciduenas, hugging them and talking privately with each one.

"To have him confirm it was like somebody had just reached in and grabbed my heart and pulled it out," Byron Scott would recall.

"The guys broke down crying, the whole room," Dunleavy said. "Everybody felt for Earvin. We felt like we had lost somebody, and yet he was still there."

Flowing with all the emotion was the flood of questions. What was HIV positive? Did Earvin have AIDS? "It's really something we didn't know that much about," Garciduenas said months later. "Once you mention the word, or that somebody you know has it, basically people write them off and don't understand that people still have a life to live and they can prolong their life and it's not gonna happen for years down the road. But once you mention it, everybody just associates it with death. That's why it hit everybody on the team so hard. Everybody who had been involved with Earvin for any period of time just couldn't handle it. It was devastating."

A throng of media upstairs awaited Johnson, with CNN and ESPN planning live feeds of the press conference to their cable audiences.

"Earvin went in the bathroom and washed his face," Vitti recalled, "and went upstairs and got in front of those cameras like it was nothing. He went from this huge emotional scene to going up there and standing in front of the world, like the strongest man that ever lived. He did what he had to do."

Before he went on camera, Johnson was reminded that he did not have AIDS, but had merely tested positive for the human immunodeficiency virus, HIV.

Chick Hearn recalled, talking with Larry Burnett in 2002, "I didn't see how he could possibly make any words come out, but he did. He made some very valuable words come out."

"Good afternoon," Johnson told a worldwide audience moments later. "Because of the HIV virus that I have obtained, I will have to retire from the Lakers today. I just want to make clear, first of all, that I do not have the AIDS disease. I know a lot of you want to know that. I have the HIV virus. My wife is fine. She's negative, so no problem with her."

He also offered assurances for his own health, saying, "I plan to go on living for a long time, bugging you guys like I always have. So you'll see me around. I plan on being with the Lakers and the league, and going on with my life. I guess now I get to enjoy some of the other sides of living that I've missed because of the season and the long practices and so on. I'm going to miss playing.

"I will now become a spokesman for the HIV virus. I want people, young people, to realize they can practice safe sex. Sometimes you're a little naive about it, and you think it could never happen to you. You only thought it could happen to other people. It has happened. But I'm going to deal with it. Life is going to go on for me, and I'm going to be a happy man. . . . Sometimes we think only gay people can get it, or it's not going to happen to me. Here I am, saying it can happen to anybody. Even me, Magic Johnson."

"I was there," Steve Springer recalled. "That was devastating. . . . When he said that 'I'm going to beat this, I'm going to be back,' I said to someone, 'This isn't the Boston Celtics. He's not coming back. We're gonna have to watch this guy die in public.' It was the only press conference I've ever been to where reporters were crying when we left. Jerry Buss backstage collapsed in Kareem's arms sobbing. It was devastating."

The Laker players and staffers watched these strange events unfold, heard the follow-up questions from the overflow crowd of reporters, and sat around in shock as the session wound to a close.

"He was smiling," *L.A. Times* columnist Mike Downey would write of Johnson. "He was the only one."

Friends and Otherwise

Joe "Jellybean" Bryant and his family had been sound asleep in Europe in the wee hours that November night when the phone rang with news that Magic Johnson was going to die. Magic was Bryant's idol, which meant Magic was also the idol of Joe's thirteen-year-old son.

It was staggering news, so staggering that the Bryants packed up their lives in Europe, where Joe had played for eight seasons after his NBA career, and returned to America. One of the stars in their firmament was threatened.

"I was just trying to understand," son Kobe would later remember. "I cried. I didn't know what it was about. I read some books, rented a movie on it. To see. As a kid you just don't know what to do. Hoping I could help him out in some type of way. It was very difficult."

With the news, young Kobe would fall into a period of serious mourning, almost inconsolable.

Johnson, of course, would influence millions of young admirers over his career, but none more important than Bryant. When his boy was a mere three, father Joe had told *The Philadelphia Tribune*,

"I've taken Kobe to Lakers games and introduced him to players. He's a Magic Johnson fan."

The son had spent much of his childhood studying video of NBA stars, especially Johnson.

"I wanted to see Magic," Kobe would recall in a 2000 interview. "Just the enthusiasm he had for playing the game. He just loved playing, you could tell. Plus his forward passes used to drive me nuts."

Johnson and Rosen were aware the news would have a similar impact on many people. In the hours before the announcement, they had rushed to identify the key people who would need an advance warning so as to avoid a similar shock.

In 1989, Johnson had thrown a thirtieth birthday party for himself and invited five hundred of his "closest friends." But two years later he had no trouble paring that group down to a few who needed to be notified before the bad news broke. The list included Jordan, Pat Riley, Arsenio Hall, Larry Bird, Michael Cooper, Abdul-Jabbar, Isiah Thomas, and Kurt Rambis. Johnson asked Rosen to make the calls.

Each was understandably shaken by the news. Hall wanted to cancel the taping of his late-night talk show, but Rosen talked him out of it.

Riley, who had been hired as coach of the Knicks, first thought to miss his game against the Orlando Magic that night and hop a plane to L.A., but Rosen pointed out there wouldn't be time. Instead, Riley and the Knicks held a moment of prayer before tipoff in Madison Square Garden.

Kurt Rambis, who was then playing with the Phoenix Suns, left practice to fly to Los Angeles for the press conference. Abdul-Jabbar asked Rosen what he could do to help. "Why don't you come over to the Forum and support Earvin?" the agent suggested. So he came to show support.

Recalling the moment in a 1992 interview, Abdul-Jabbar said he had observed Johnson's transformation during their years playing together. "Back in October 1979, Earvin was innocent, just a wide-eyed kid with very special talent," Kareem would confide. "No hidden agenda. He just wanted to have some fun. He was where he wanted to be. Having it go from that to where it ended up was tragic. I'm angry at myself, because I guess somehow I feel I should have warned him. I didn't do anything, or couldn't do anything. He was very much a man who was gonna live his life the way he wanted to live it."

With the news, however, Johnson's life was no longer going to be about just the way he wanted things to be. Lon Rosen quickly realized the same thing. There was nothing to prepare him for the deluge that followed the announcement. The agent recalled that the two fax machines in his office began spewing out messages from around the world and would go on nonstop for days.

Before the announcement, Rosen had phoned Commissioner David Stern for help. The commissioner was on a flight to Utah but instead went to Los Angeles for the press conference. The agent and Johnson would be faced with a massive public relations debacle. Stern didn't hesitate.

"He's very sharp," Rosen would say later of the commissioner. "Magic having AIDS was a crisis that could have ripped the league apart if it wasn't handled correctly, and he knew it."

Stern went after this problem much like he addressed the drug problem when he took over in 1984. "The big problem was no longer the NBA and drugs," Rosen said. "It was excessive sex."

An entire crisis driven by a titanic and willful failure to practice safe sex.

The obvious choice to help with the PR in the aftermath was Josh Rosenfeld, the NBA's newly named director of international public relations. A former Lakers public relations director, Rosenfeld was a close friend of both Rosen's and Johnson's. He would spend two weeks helping Rosen control the damage.

In the few days after the announcement, an estimated 100,000 letters flooded the Lakers' and Rosen's offices for Johnson. There were people with AIDS, people who knew people with AIDS, people who wanted to send donations to the Magic Johnson Foundation, hastily formed to raise money to battle the disease.

Then there were the urgent messages Rosen got the night of the announcement from other players on other teams. "Ten prominent NBA players phoned that night," the agent said, "most of them asking 'What can I do? How can I get tested?' They were scared to death."

In the United States at that time, AIDS was thought to be largely a disease for fringe populations that few bothered to care about. The culture at large was not only still very much racist and sexist, it had also long been decidedly homophobic. Of the 45,506 new AIDS cases reported to the Centers for Disease Control in 1991, approximately 52 percent involved homosexual males. The newsflash that Thursday in November ignited considerable speculation that Johnson himself might be in that demographic.

In the wake of the announcement, *USA Today* basketball columnist Peter Vecsey was asked during a television network interview if Johnson was a homosexual. Vecsey, a former Green Beret who had been known for years as the league's juiciest insider columnist with the *New York Post,* replied that he didn't know for sure because he wasn't always with Johnson.

Rosen recalled that he heard the exchange and phoned Vecsey at home that Saturday and demanded to know why he hadn't taken up for Johnson. Rosen said he pointed out that over the years, the Lakers star had come to think of Vecsey as a friend and had always taken the time to talk to him, to offer his perspective on the many inside stories the columnist brought his readers, the kinds of stories that were considered must-reads.

How could you not defend Earvin? Rosen asked. "You know he's not gay."

The agent recalled Vecsey replying that he couldn't be sure, telling Rosen he'd heard rumors for years that Johnson had been seen frequenting gay bars.

Johnson loathed the idea that people would think he was gay. He and Rosen knew they should move quickly to counter the speculation generated by the announcement. Johnson's first thought was to appear that Friday night on Arsenio Hall's nationally syndicated late-night talk show. Plus, he decided to do an interview with L.A. sportscaster Jim Hill, an old friend, and to write an article for *Sports Illustrated* with writer Roy S. Johnson, coauthor of his book, *Magic's Touch*.

"We knew," Rosen explained, "that by going to the people Earvin felt comfortable with, people who would protect him, that the message would get out."

Arsenio Hall and Johnson had grown close the previous four years after Hall had moved into the late-night talk show circuit as a replacement in 1988 when the Fox network fired Joan Rivers. It was a short-term assignment, and Hall's staying in the business required his selling the idea of his own show to the brass at Paramount.

With the studio bosses planning to attend his show one night, Hall had asked Johnson to come on as a last-minute guest. Johnson's appearance, Hall reasoned, would demonstrate for Paramount that he could deliver big-name personalities. Johnson was all smiles and hugs and handshakes that night (Little Richard and Mike Tyson also appeared), all helping to pave the way for Hall getting his own show.

With his world collapsing around him, Johnson now wanted to defend himself, and he was calling in the favor. He asked to go on Hall's show and explain his situation.

Rosen recalled that Hall hesitated with concern that the appearance would be a disaster. Never mind Johnson, Hall didn't think that he as host could hold up under the emotional duress. Hall even made several phone calls to get Johnson and his advisors to change their minds. But Johnson was determined.

Contrary to Hall's worries, the appearance was a success for both Johnson and the ratings. His smile beaming, Johnson walked onto the set of *The Arsenio Hall Show* that night in a cream double-breasted suit and was met with a rousing standing ovation that ran well over two minutes before morphing into a chant: "Magic! Magic! Magic!" Once the audience settled down, Hall didn't ask Johnson directly if he was gay but merely mentioned the topic, which prompted Johnson to respond that he was "far from being a homosexual." The audience applauded.

Johnson called for people everywhere to practice safe sex, a plea that later brought criticism because Johnson hadn't pointed out that the best protection against sexually transmitted disease was abstinence. Johnson would soon amend his messages to add that option.

Johnson did his interview with Jim Hill in the dressing room at Hall's show, then sat down and talked with Roy Johnson for the *Sports Illustrated* piece. "By now I'm sure that most of America has heard rumors that I am gay," he wrote. "Well, you can forget that.

Some people started the talk during the NBA Finals in 1988 and '89 when I kissed Isiah Thomas on the cheek as a pregame salute to our friendship and our respect for the game. But actually I've been hearing that kind of talk for a long time. . . .

"I sympathize with anyone who has to battle AIDS, regardless of his or her sexual preference, but I have never had a homosexual encounter. Never."

He said that he hadn't matched Wilt Chamberlain's claims of sleeping with twenty thousand women—claims that would later be dismissed as mostly hype to sell a book Chamberlain was publishing—but the story offered the opportunity for Johnson to present the circumstances as merely a "bachelor lifestyle."

"I am certain that I was infected by having unprotected sex with a woman who has the virus," he wrote. "The problem is that I can't pinpoint the time, the place or the woman. It's a matter of numbers. Before I was married, I was never at a loss for female companionship. . . . I confess that after I arrived in LA in 1979, I did my best to accommodate as many women as I could, most of them through unprotected sex."

This public relations effort received decidedly mixed results. That became clearer as Rosen heard from Johnson's endorsement partners. At first, the agent had barely had time to consider the financial implications of the announcement, or what kind of impact it would have on his endorsement deals, then estimated to be worth about $5 million a year. Rosen had planned to contact the key people at each of Johnson's corporate affiliations. Converse. Campofrio (the Spanish meat company). Nestlé. Pepsi. Spalding. Kentucky Fried Chicken. Tiger Electronics. Virgin Electronics. But when the news leak blew the announcement schedule, Johnson's rep had time to reach only four of the companies on the list—Pepsi, Converse, Spalding, and Nestlé.

The announcement sparked speculation that the corporate world would begin dumping Johnson. Whether contacted or not, all of his corporate affiliations phoned or faxed back messages of support, to Rosen's relief. But within days, Nestlé quietly dropped plans to air a commercial with Johnson that had already been produced, a somewhat basic ad that featured Johnson shooting a ball with the standard Nestlé's candy message, "It's scrumptious."

"Their feeling was that it wasn't the right thing to do," Rosen would say. "We disagreed, but it was certainly within their rights to change plans."

Converse soon announced that it was supportive of Johnson, but the message meant little. Some months earlier, the shoe and apparel company had ceased including him in its marketing plans, although it continued to pay him a seven-figure sum each year. The situation loomed very large in Johnson's mind, with Jordan's own Nike line booming. Johnson had even asked to make commercials for Converse, and although the company wouldn't have to pay him any more money, it declined. So, he asked to be released from his contract, which the company also declined. Converse's parent company, Interco, had filed for bankruptcy protection in 1991, and Johnson was left standing in line with other creditors. He couldn't get out of his contract because the bankruptcy court counted his relationship among Converse's most valuable assets. Although the shoe company regained its good standing and resumed sending checks to Johnson, it still owed him several missed payments. (As Rosen would later explain, Johnson and the shoe company eventually settled any differences. Johnson, however, never really settled into a major shoe deal after that. For a time, he attempted marketing his own shoe, but his focus soon turned to other business interests.)

Adding to the misery was the fact that the shoe contract had been reworked into a long-term deal. Johnson was caught in Converse's clutches through 1995. That, of course, seemed just fine with Nike and Reebok, the competition in the shoe industry. If they couldn't have him, both Nike and Reebok told Rosen they'd rather Johnson be with Converse, where his name wouldn't be used to take some of their market share.

Within days after the announcement, condom companies and a pharmaceutical firm made offers for Johnson's endorsement. But Rosen and Johnson decided that striking a deal there would make them seem eager to exploit the health issue. But Johnson did soon sign a $5 million three-book agreement with publishing giant Random House, which suggested that of the estimated 11 million people in the world who had tested HIV positive, he was perhaps the only one to turn his status into financial gain.

In the days after the announcement, Johnson retreated to a rented beach house in Maui with his wife and four of his friends and their wives. The doubt had already begun to grow in his mind. Had he made the right decision? He certainly didn't feel sick. His life, always a storybook, had changed abruptly, sending his destiny spinning off in a strange direction. He knew he wasn't ready to retire. His nature demanded that he be busy with something.

Soon there was another distraction. The tabloids had tracked him to Maui. He spent some time around the pool at the Westin Hotel, until the paparazzi sought him out there, enough to send him off in another direction.

Lansing

Contacted by a reporter, Charles Tucker admitted profound sadness at the news, yet had immediately offered an upbeat prediction: "Heroes continue to carry on, even though their back is against the wall. His back is against the wall now, but he's a hero. He'll go on now and help people in other ways."

Dale Beard, Johnson's best man, wasn't among the friends notified early about his medical situation. This slight seemed to have been linked to the fact that among Johnson's long list of dreaded things that November was how this news would be received in Lansing. (For years afterward, George Fox would say that Johnson had simply "taken too many field trips" with Jerry Buss.)

Christine Johnson would recall being taken aback by the comments she heard in those days and stunned by just how cruel people could be.

On the other hand, there were friends like the affable Beard, who remembered the moment well in a 2019 interview. "He called, you know, his friends Michael Cooper and Pat Riley," Beard said. "He called the people that he thought that he should tell right away.

Once he told them what was going on, they felt like, 'Hey, you know, I've told people I needed to tell.'"

As for Beard, he learned all about it from TV. He was shocked but didn't want to call Johnson about it right away because he figured his friend was overwhelmed at the moment. Instead, Beard waited a couple of days, and he might have waited longer except that the media were swamping him with calls for comment and on-camera appearances.

They all wanted to hear about Earvin from his best man and old friend.

The biggest money offer was $600,000 to appear on Oprah Winfrey's show, Beard remembered. "Winfrey's people called me that Friday and wanted to fly me to Chicago to be on the show. I thought it was a prank."

The producers, however, had his flight ready to go. One of the tabloids worked an offer for $150,000, he added. "I was like, 'Nah, I can't do it. I can't do it.'"

For grins, he added up all the offers later and figured he had missed out on millions and laughed about it. Many were news organizations that offered nothing in the way of pay, including what seemed like every radio and TV station in Michigan.

After a couple of days of being bombarded, Beard finally broke down and phoned Johnson, reaching him in Hawaii. The *National Enquirer* wanted to fly Beard to Hawaii in hopes of catching Johnson there.

"The media was just going crazy," he remembered. "I called him up and I said, 'Hey man, you know, I've got all these tabloids calling me, offering me a hundred and fifty thousand for this.' You had *Star* magazine and the *National Enquirer*. You had the *Chicago Tribune* and *The New York Times*, all these people calling me. I don't even know how they got my number. So, I called Earvin and told him, 'I haven't answered anybody.' He said, 'Well, you know what? If they continue calling, just say, "Hey, I have no comment."' He said they'll just back right off. I could have made almost three million dollars, shoot, just if I wanted to be a whistleblower."

Faced with his own tide of media attention, Johnson finally decided to seek his one true refuge. "He called me back and said that he's coming to town, back for a while to Lansing to kind of get away from the hoopla," Beard said, "and so I did meet him when he came back, a lot of us, at his parents' house."

Johnson had built his parents their dream home, with seven bedrooms and a circular driveway, all of which served as the perfect retreat. Beard didn't want to hover at the place, but he did want to show up, offer any help he could, but to make sure not to crowd his old friend.

"We just talked," he recalled. "It wasn't like he, you know, could go anywhere and not have somebody say anything. But he kind of wanted to just get back here and be around the family and get out of the spotlight and think about what he had to do, what he needed to do, because this was something big."

Mostly, Johnson could bask in the embrace of home without feeling judged. "They were really rooted in their family at that house, man," Beard remembered. "They were just showing love, man, you know, a lot of love. Nobody knew what to expect because at that time everything was new. When you first heard about it, people thought you get the virus and die the next day. Nobody was educated enough to know what was going on with it. Knowing Earvin, the guy was strong-hearted, strong-minded, and he was gonna do what he had to do to overcome all this stuff."

As for all of the media attention, "it was kind of sad because I don't think they really cared about how this guy really felt, what he was going through," Beard said. "They just wanted the story."

The time in Lansing helped, but Johnson couldn't escape the feeling that he shouldn't have quit. When he returned to Los Angeles, he picked up some of his old routines, arriving early at the Forum before Laker games, dressing in his playing gear and going through his shooting warm-ups, with the ushers and early-bird fans there to cheer him on. He'd then shower and dress, and for a time he even sat on the bench with the team. But that was too close to the action. He wanted the game. On the bench, it was in his nostrils. So he backed off and moved up into the stands.

His doctors, however, had said from the very start that they wanted him to continue exercising. He had begun taking AZT, the medicine that helped to slow the spread of the virus, and his physicians were eager to track his adjustment.

He missed his daily playing fix so much that he settled for pickup games at Sports Club/LA. Spreading the virus by playing basketball was virtually impossible, his doctors said. At the club he tried to find satisfaction by mixing with the usual pickup crowd and a smattering of former college players.

Instead of Worthy on the wing, there'd be a thirty-one-year-old banker, with a million-dollar pass smacking him in the face. It didn't matter where, Johnson didn't like to miss an assist. But at the club, he forced himself to smile. After all, these people accepted him. They boxed out on rebounds and played hard defense. There was no AIDS fear here. Once he found that, he locked in on it and was like a kid on Main Street playground again.

Yet ultimately, all it did was stoke his habit. He wanted the game. His departure had been too abrupt. The lights. The media. The crowds. The autographs. The locker room. The fellas. The team. The travel. The purpose. It had all been there one moment, then gone the next. He hadn't been able to squeeze it one last time.

He wanted to play again, maybe full-time. And if not full-time, he at least wanted some type of goodbye, maybe a farewell tour like Kareem in 1989.

After a couple of weeks of playing pickup at the club, he decided to put together a group of skilled players, mostly former pros and college players, who could offer more of a challenge. This group included Mike Dunleavy, Larry Drew, and former Syracuse star Stevie Thompson. They became Johnson's unofficial support group, and most of them managed to meet him whenever he could get a free gym. 7 A.M. 10 P.M. It didn't matter. They just wanted to help.

This higher level of competition served to drive his desire up a notch. By late December, Johnson was phoning Rosen nearly every day to discuss a comeback. The agent stalled. Johnson also repeatedly discussed the issue by phone with Big Earv. If you feel good and you want to do it, go on back to playing, his father told him.

In early January, Johnson phoned Rosen. "Just tell them I'm coming back next week," he ordered. But Rosen again found a way of stalling. In the days after the announcement, the agent had flown to New York for a parley with the NBA's top executives—Stern and assistants Gary Bettman and Russ Granik. Earvin will want to play in the All-Star Game in Orlando, Rosen told them. After all, his name is on the All-Star ballot, and this will be an excellent farewell.

Stern and his associates instantly agreed. That would be a very good idea, they said. After all, Johnson had been monumental to the league's success. There wasn't one good reason not to let him play.

If all the rest could only have been so easy.

The folks who knew him well had seen Earvin Johnson dumped out of his very big life in what seemed like record time. But they would have to give him credit. There was no question that Johnson had done himself tremendous damage with the public with his revelation. Still, it didn't take him all that long to find his new best friends, the growing global population of AIDS victims.

Admittedly, Johnson fell in at the head of their parade rather uneasily after his announcement. But once he got going, he made much of the new position.

With his revelation, he had announced his intention to become "a spokesman for the HIV virus." Which, he would quickly discover, was sort of like heading up Hell's Own Chamber of Commerce. To his credit, he studied hard, learned about the disease, and began to play his own oversized part. Where other celebrities with AIDS had chosen to fight the virus in private, as was their right, he attacked the circumstances with all of his positivity.

He hadn't inhabited his new status long when he was asked if the virus had brought him "bad days."

"I'm not a bad day person," he replied. "Every day I wake up, I'm happy. I'm ready to go do something. The virus can only make you have a bad day if your frame of mind is like that. So I'm not down about it. I'm not trying to say, 'Why me?' I'm going on. It's happened, and I'm dealing with it. But it hasn't stopped me from living and enjoying life."

AIDS hotlines across the country had been jammed with callers seeking information and counseling in the days after his announcement. The cards and letters to his foundation filled a large storeroom at the Forum, with bags of mail packed to the ceiling. It would take platoons of volunteers weeks to open each piece, discarding the small amount of hate mail to focus on the frantic pleas for help from some writers and the support offered by others. In the first two weeks after the announcement, his Magic Johnson Foundation took in more than $500,000 in unsolicited donations. NBA player Rex Chapman alone sent a $50,000 check, even though he hardly knew Johnson, who drew encouragement from the public outpouring of love.

He had fallen into a rather casual relationship with his faith over the years of his stardom, but that began to change with his diagnosis. Now confronted by death, Johnson began to rediscover his spiritual life a bit. With pro basketball's Sunday games and practices, he had never found much time for churchgoing. But with his abrupt departure from the game, he had time for church again. He and Cookie quietly began attending worship services in Los Angeles.

And Johnson soon began repeating what others were saying about him. He must have been selected by God to fight this disease. Thus, Johnson set about the business of making good on his promises to join the AIDS fight. In addition to setting up the Magic Johnson Foundation to raise money for AIDS research, he lent his name to a book, *What You Can Do to Avoid AIDS*. And he and Arsenio Hall produced an AIDS awareness video, *Time Out,* for distribution in the public schools. He also joined broadcaster Linda Ellerbee for a well-received AIDS special for children on the Nickelodeon network (which Nestlé supported).

Johnson avowed that he especially wanted to reach "the young people, because I'm trying to make sure that what happened to me doesn't happen to them."

He continued his other charitable work as well, including benefits for the United Negro College Fund, the American Heart Association, and the Muscular Dystrophy Association. That February of 1992, Johnson again held the annual dinner he sponsored for the Muscular Dystrophy Association. "It was overwhelming," said Bob Gile of the MDA. "We had more people than ever before."

Yet Johnson also soon discovered that unlike his other charities, his AIDS involvement went beyond the realm of feel-good. Shortly after the announcement, he had agreed to serve on President George

H. W. Bush's commission on AIDS, and in mid-January Johnson went to Washington to attend his first commission meeting. There he encountered New York AIDS activist Derek Hodel, himself sick with the disease. Hodel talked of the immense power that Johnson had brought to the AIDS fight, how the basketball player overnight had attracted publicity to the issue that activists hadn't been able to garner in a decade of work. "Mr. Johnson, already you have given people with HIV great hope," Hodel said. "By your will to live, by your will to beat this thing. Your taking control of your illness and your positive attitude show great courage. Sadly, they will not be enough to keep you alive."

Hodel's speech and his criticism of the Bush administration for weak support of AIDS research deeply affected Johnson. He had been nervous about going to Washington, about commenting on this very complicated issue. He didn't want to mess up, especially not in front of the bank of media covering the commission.

That night, when he got back to his hotel room, Johnson phoned Rosen in Los Angeles. He told his agent that Hodel had opened his eyes for the first time to the frustration, to the reality that people with AIDS face. He had learned more from that simple speech than all the other literature he'd read.

"That struck a nerve in Earvin," Rosen said. "It was a reality check."

"They had all these charts," Johnson explained. "They showed the African American numbers from 10 years ago up to now, and in every category they just kept going up and up and up. We lead in every chart. Children. Adults. Women. I just had to sit back and take a deep breath."

But if AIDS shocked him, it also broadened his public. Everywhere he went, he electrified crowds like never before. "I never had to be escorted into places," he said of the attention. "Now you gotta come in with six guys on you, trying to get through the crowds. It's been different."

Soon Johnson began limiting his public appearances. Without realizing it, he had become a poster child, the patron saint of the disease. Over time, he would become increasingly uncomfortable with that role. Just why was difficult for him to explain. But this much was true. He wanted his old life back. And he wanted to live.

30

SHELTER FROM THE STORM

Johnson was oh so eager to rush out and embrace the game again, but that notion soon brought a deeper realization. Not everyone welcomed the news that he would play in the NBA's 42nd All-Star Game in Orlando in mid-February 1992. Some were struck by the fear of an infection. Still others simply seemed to be weary of his dominating the NBA narrative.

That would certainly include the Lakers, who had to soldier on without him. John Radcliffe had spent three decades by then observing the team's crowds and fan base. "They were spoiled," Radcliffe observed that early winter of 1992. "Since Earvin's been here they are very, very difficult to please. They expect a great play every time down the court. That's what they've had for the last ten years. That's what they've seen every time. Now we don't have that anymore."

The Lakers issues aside, one thing seemed certain. It wasn't going to be just another boring All-Star Game. Magic was headed to the Magic Kingdom for a very big show. It was supposed to be his Grand Finale, the farewell event to say goodbye to the league and his fans.

It would provide an opportunity for AIDS awareness. The game would be broadcast worldwide in ninety countries, and more than 960 journalists would be there, covering it in person, all to see an

HIV-infected athlete compete. If only for a brief time, AIDS victims worldwide could emerge from the shadows and feel that they, too, were being welcomed back to society. One of their own was playing on a world stage.

Not surprisingly, with so little known about the infection, a number of NBA players weren't prepared to embrace the idea of competing against Johnson. After all, basketball was an up-close business, a contact sport played in close quarters. Sweat was swopped, as the saying went. Players fought for rebounds and loose balls. Scratches, cuts, fat lips were on the menu.

About a month before the event, Cleveland guard Mark Price and Portland forward Jerome Kersey voiced their concerns about the safety of the situation. Johnson wasn't happy, but they weren't his teammates or close friends. After all, just months earlier Johnson himself had little knowledge of his infection.

Then, A. C. Green and Byron Scott told reporters they didn't think Johnson should suit up for the game. Scott said he was concerned about Johnson's health. Green simply questioned how Johnson could be honored as an All-Star if he was retired.

"It made it clear to me that 'OK, you're not a part of this team anymore,'" Johnson told reporters. "I had felt like I was a part of it up to that point, but that just put the 't' on the end of retirement."

For the first time, he began to grasp the ostracism that other AIDS victims lived with daily.

Then came a gesture during this low point. Johnson had dressed out and was shooting around before a Lakers home game in January with the Heat when Miami center Rony Seikaly asked if they could play one-on-one. For Johnson, it was like one of those happy moments on the playgrounds back home. Pro players normally only dabbled a bit at one-on-one during warm-ups, and the games were little more than silly shooting contests. But Seikaly seemed intent on making things competitive. He played defense and tracked down rebounds. Johnson didn't know him very well.

"He took me right out there and played," Johnson said of Seikaly. "People were putting fear in other people's minds. He had no fear at all. We just played."

The NBA didn't go light with the matter either, backing up Johnson's appearance with a massive information campaign, for both athletes and the media. In the coming months, the league would establish a policy for bleeding players. If someone sustained a cut or scratch in a game, time would be called and the player removed until the bleeding was stopped and the wound bandaged. Team trainers would treat all such cases wearing latex gloves. Afterward, only one question remained for the players: If it's so safe for us to compete against an infected player, then why is the trainer wearing gloves?

Despite the early concerns, the All-Star Game in Orlando proved a resounding success in the eyes of many. First, the league teamed with Walt Disney World to throw a rousing party. On Friday night of All-Star Weekend, the Magic Kingdom was opened to the media and the NBA's special guests. There were marching bands and Disney characters and free shows and an endless flow of booze and seafood and hors d'oeuvres at the theme park.

In the morning hours before the Sunday night game, Johnson sat in the locker room, quietly talking to a small group of reporters. Someone handed him a dozen roses, and the cameras flashed.

"You look like you just won the Kentucky Derby," one writer quipped.

Johnson told the media gathered around him about how wonderful the day was going to be, how it would be a triumph for AIDS victims everywhere. "No matter what negative comes, I've always been a positive person, always been upbeat," he said. "As long as you have your family and friends supporting you, that's all you need. I have to be out there for myself and I have to be out there for a lot of people, whether they have disease or handicaps or whatever, and let them know that they can still carry on."

Leadership was clearly the strongest among Johnson's many strengths, observed teammate James Worthy, who had watched him struggle since November. "He's a very courageous person. This is not the first time he's met controversy. In my observation, he's handled this like he handled things five or six years ago. He's trying to say the right thing and do the right thing and think optimistically, and not let the barriers and obstacles get in the way of what he wants to do."

Later, in the arena before the game, Jerry Buss stood courtside, a pretty young brunette at his side, looking on as Johnson was warming up. His old friend saw the owner and came over, smiling. He shook hands and draped a long arm over his shoulder and gave a squeeze.

For the past dozen years, they had celebrated championships and weathered hard times together, all of it now punctuated by the staggering news about Johnson. In some regards, the owner took it worse than anyone. Each day for two weeks after the diagnosis he had phoned Rosen to check on Johnson, always breaking down sobbing during the conversation. "Just tell me what I can do for Earvin," he told the agent.

Rosen suggested that the owner simply give him a call.

Buss just couldn't bring himself to do that. We have to meet in person, he said. When they did, Buss was again overcome by grief. He assured Johnson that although the agreement was unsigned, the team would honor his new mega-contract, a sign of good faith for all the years Johnson had played on a contract below his real worth as a player. They both knew what the All-Star appearance meant to each of them.

As with many of his big games over the course of his life, Johnson had been nervous, sleepless, anxiety-driven the night before. This was going to be one of the biggest moments of all. He had not played against pro competition in almost four months. He did not want to make a fool of himself in front of the world.

"Just kick it, man," Worthy told him. "Don't worry about it. If you shoot an air ball, people are going to boo. Just laugh with 'em and have fun."

Kick it, he did, and the Orlando Arena that evening answered with an outpouring of love, 23,000 people showering him with their appreciation. It began before he took the floor.

Johnson blinked back tears as Michael Bolton finished the national anthem. Led by Isiah Thomas, the East players came over, breaking that barrier between opposing teams, and took turns hugging him.

Rubbing his hands nervously, Johnson led the West starters out for the opening tip. Very quickly it became clear the game wouldn't be much from a competitive standpoint, but it would offer lots of garbage time, perfect for those playground moments he had so loved as a youth.

For the record, the West won, 153–113, but the Magic moment had nothing to do with the outcome. With just under three minutes to go in the game, Johnson first took on "Zeke" one-on-one as the other players cleared out of the way. He stopped Thomas on defense, then hit a three-pointer at the other end as the crowd whooped it up. Then he found Dan Majerle of the Phoenix Suns with one of his patented no-look assists, with the fans loving that, too. Last came a one-on-one with Michael Jordan. Johnson got a quick stop on defense, then lofted another trey at the other end that set off the arena yet again when it swished.

There were 14 seconds left when Thomas grinned and picked up the ball. The game had to end on that Magical note. For his style and charisma and 25 points and nine assists, for the emotion of a very big moment, Johnson was named the game's MVP, although Portland's Clyde Drexler had performed very well.

"I will cherish this the rest of my life, no matter what happens," Johnson said. "I'm in a dream right now and I don't ever want to wake up."

A week after the All-Star Game the Lakers retired his number 32 in another emotional ceremony at the Forum. The two events did nothing but feed his overwhelming desire to return to playing. But his advisors and friends again urged him not to, and he listened. Instead, he served as a broadcast analyst for NBC. As for his playing urges, Johnson focused his attention on preparing for the upcoming Olympic summer games in Barcelona, where he had been cleared to play on the "Dream Team."

In April, Los Angeles erupted with riots in the wake of the verdict in the Rodney King police brutality case, creating a nightmarish spectacle that was broadcast live by the networks. The fires and violence and looting left more than fifty people dead and resulted in billions of dollars in damages. The violence spread within blocks of the Forum, with some Laker players and staffers watching television inside the arena's offices as the troubling events happened outside. Somehow that spring, even without Johnson, the Lakers managed a late win that miraculously put them in the playoffs for the 16th consecutive time. The riots forced the team to move its home games to Las Vegas in the first-round series against Portland, which the Lakers lost three games to one, which immediately turned the focus to the 1992–93 season and the big question: If Johnson was going to play in the Olympics, did that mean he would attempt a comeback?

In early June, his NBC broadcasting schedule for the playoffs conflicted with the due date of Cookie's pregnancy, so they agreed to induce labor, which allowed Johnson to perform as Lamaze coach during the delivery. Earvin Johnson, III, arrived healthy, wide-eyed, and complete with an HIV negative blood test.

Elated and relieved, Johnson returned to his busy schedule. His autobiography, *My Life,* with writer William Novak, was on a rush schedule. Charged with advance promotion, Johnson attended the American Booksellers Association convention in Anaheim, where he hobnobbed with the publishing industry's power buyers. He was greeting a line of well-wishers at a reception when a forty-three-year-old woman with a drink in her hand gave him a pair of her daughter's ballet slippers to sign. When he complied, the woman was obviously thrilled.

She thanked him, turned, walked a few feet and collapsed, instantly dead of a heart aneurysm.

Johnson was stunned. Did she die because of the excitement of meeting me? he asked. Rosen assured him that wasn't the case. Johnson wrote her family anyway, offering his condolences.

Could his life get any stranger? he asked.

A Dream of a Team

There was no way the questions that confronted Earvin Johnson in 1992 would not loom over the Olympic Games. Crowds everywhere in Barcelona greeted him with the familiar chant, "Ma-jeek!" His answer was to avoid them and the media's seemingly endless queries about AIDS. The first day he told them he would answer health questions just that once and from then on it would be only basketball.

Still, he was infected with the world's disease. The populations of Africa, India, Asia, Europe, and North America were threatened by the spread of AIDS, according to the World Health Organization. And Johnson was easily the most visible of all the victims. Wherever he took a step, they took a step. Whenever he played, they played. Yet he seemed to be empowering AIDS victims and trivializing them all at the same time.

Skeptics abounded with many questions, and only time itself would help produce the answers.

"It was the greatest moment of our lives," Johnson would declare in 2005, adding, "I always wanted to play with Michael and Larry, and I finally got my chance. That's the perfect game and moment for a point guard, look to your right, there's Michael; look to your left, there's Larry. You don't know who to pass to. I mean, the greatest collection of talent assembled. Patrick Ewing, Karl Malone, John Stockton, Drexler, Barkley. All these great guys. And Pippen and David Robinson. . . . We were going to show the world why we have the best."

Such a conclusion was in doubt in those months leading up to the Games beginning with Jordan being named to the team. Getting him to play was a huge coup for Team USA that came after negotiations in which Jordan was adamant that he would not agree to play if the roster included Isiah Thomas, due to the long-simmering hard feelings between the two. Jack McCallum of *Sports Illustrated* had broken that story with unnamed sources who were on the selection committee for the team.

McCallum reported that the committee decided not to invite Thomas due to questions about how he might affect the team's chemistry. The story suggested that neither Olympic coach Chuck Daly nor Detroit GM Jack McCloskey, who was on the selection committee, had put up much of a case for including Thomas.

So, Jordan agreed to play, and the group in red, white, and blue would be feted across the globe as the men who elevated the game to a level that left their opponents gawking like schoolboys in search of autographs and audiences breathless at their prowess. Time would reveal that the spectacle was extremely good for the global popularity of the sport, but it would say much that their most competitive moment in terms of the game itself would come in an intra-squad scrimmage. They made quick work of everybody else and did much showboating in the process, reducing the supposedly hallowed Olympic contests to pointless, mismatched affairs. Jordan knew all of this heading in and wasn't shy about saying it.

"When you look at the talent and the teams we're supposed to play against, it's a massacre," he had said months before the event.

Blowout games had often been a regular feature of previous Games, even when the United States was using solely amateur players who were volunteering their time. Now, American professionals were lining up to be paid between $600,000 and $800,000 each for their much hyped appearances. The U.S. Olympic Committee, which had provided the payments, discreetly approached each player about donating his salary back to the Olympic cause. Some hesitated, then gave all or part of it back. And the casinos in Monaco, where the team made a promotional visit on the eve of the Games, certainly took a share, too.

The experience began with the team's training camp in La Jolla, California, where the evening card games in Johnson's Torrey Pines hotel suite became part of the legend. One witness recalled that every time Jordan put money in the kitty, Johnson would needle him about his "tennis shoe" cash. They may have become "friends," but Johnson clearly still struggled to get over Jordan's big Nike deal, the gift that kept on giving.

Soon enough, according to witnesses, women showed up to distract the card players, which cast the evenings as what would prove to be a run of party nights.

The Olympics afforded the NBA's top stars their first real opportunity to spend time together and to get to know each other better. Johnson was like most every other fan in the world, marveling about the collection of talent—Ewing, Bird, Jordan, Pippen, Karl Malone, John Stockton, Drexler, Barkley, David Robinson, Chris Mullin, even the lone amateur, Christian Laettner.

"It was," said Chuck Daly, the team's coach, "like Elvis and the Beatles put together."

The Americans played 14 games in winning the gold, and their smallest margin of victory was 32 points.

The subtext for the gathering was the continuing rivalry of Jordan and Johnson. Johnson seemed intent on asserting his dominance as the game's best, never mind that his Lakers had lost convincingly in 1991. He and Jordan resumed their jawing over the matter, then settled it during an intra-squad scrimmage when the team stopped over in Monaco before heading to Barcelona. The scrimmage was closed to the press, but the competition featured one team led by Johnson and the other by Jordan, detailed in Jack McCallum's book *Dream Team,* celebrating the excess twenty years later.

Johnson's "Blue" team, featuring Barkley, Mullin, Robinson, and Laettner, jumped out to a big lead, with Jordan and Johnson talking away. Jordan's team, with Pippen, Malone, Ewing, and Bird, managed to storm back to a win over a furious Johnson, who grew angrier afterward as Jordan was said to serenade him with the song from his new ad.

"Sometimes I dream . . . If I could be like Mike."

"It was the most fun I ever had on a basketball court," Jordan would say later.

Magic Mike had again conquered the hero of his youth.

The affair had turned heated, but in the end, even Johnson had to acknowledge that his time had passed. Years later, he would laugh and recall Jordan floating past David Robinson for an emphatic 360 dunk, after which he supposedly declared that Magic and Bird had had their time, that now it was his turn to rule. They had taken their turn being "the man," and now it was his turn.

"And we all bowed down," Johnson would recall three decades later, laughing.

In another anticlimactic contest, Team USA claimed the gold with a 117–85 win over Croatia on August 8, 1992.

"They knew they were playing the best in the world," Daly said afterward. "They'll go home and for the rest of their lives be able to tell their kids, 'I played against Michael Jordan and Magic Johnson and Larry Bird.' And the more they play against our best players, the more confident they're going to get."

Johnson stood on the awards platform and acknowledged the roaring crowd with a bow and a smile. He who wanted to win everything now possessed the only trophy he didn't own.

That sense of celebration with Johnson apparently wouldn't extend to all on the roster, however. McCallum would report that Clyde Drexler, his rival from Portland, had clearly seen and had enough of Johnson, recounting that Drexler would deploy his best Magic impersonation in recalling the Lakers star some years later: "Magic was always, 'Come on, Clyde, come on, Clyde, get with me, get with me,' and making all that noise. And, really, he couldn't play much by that time. He couldn't guard his shadow."

Drexler, McCallum reporter further, would say that, with the diagnosis, "you have to understand what was going on then. Everybody kept waiting for Magic to die. Every time he'd run up the court everybody would feel sorry for the guy, and he'd get all that benefit of the doubt. Magic came across like, 'All this is my stuff.' Really? Get outta here, dude. He was on the declining end of his career."

Johnson's appearance had robbed Drexler of the MVP of the All-Star Game, and it seemingly continued to rub him the wrong way on the Dream Team, just as it had irritated him all those years the Lakers had dominated Portland and the rest of the Western Conference. Both Drexler's talent and career had been frustrated by Johnson's presence as a result.

"If we all knew Magic was going to live this long, I would've gotten the MVP of that game, and Magic probably wouldn't have made the Olympic team," Drexler would tell McCallum.

Drexler disputed McCallum's reporting, releasing a statement noting, "I have reached out to Magic, to assure him that I did not say those things and to apologize to him and his family for even having to respond to something as baseless as this."

"Clyde is a good guy," Lon Rosen said in 2022. "He called me to apologize for the whole thing. Him and Earvin have a pretty good relationship. Clyde and Earvin like each other."

Meanwhile, the importance of the Dream Team's role in spreading the popularity of the game would grow increasingly obvious as the decades passed. "It kind of set it in stone on an international basis," basketball historian Alex Wolff said of Johnson's effect of the Dream Team experience.

The position-less basketball that Johnson had so dramatically initiated in the 1980 NBA Finals was now being deployed nearly everywhere, in a process that would only grow in influence over the coming decades, Wolff said. "It became a worldwide standard."

Once More

With the Olympics over, Johnson began wrestling in earnest about returning to play again in the NBA for 1992–93. His decision dragged out for weeks, with all sorts of complicating factors, the biggest of which was his family, followed by his health and the ongoing negotiations over a new contract that would be designed to reward him for years of being underpaid as a player.

As weeks became months, Jerry West gently pushed for a decision, phoning Rosen regularly to inquire. If Johnson wasn't coming back, the Lakers needed to sign a major guard and Rod Strickland was available.

Still, it dragged on.

As usual, the contract negotiations would prove to be the easy part. Jerry Buss and Johnson had been discussing them in one form or another for years.

In the 1980s, Buss began promoting prizefights at the Forum. Often, he and Johnson would attend them together. "He enjoyed the fights," Buss said at the time, "and we'd have dinner together. A lot of the talking Magic and I do is at the fights. I told him in one of those talks that I would take care of it. He could have complained about his pay. He could have caused a lot of problems. But Magic Johnson is too professional to do that. Because he treated me so honorably, I returned the favor."

During the 1991 off-season, Johnson had been offered $20 million to play a season for a Spanish pro team. In September 1991, Rosen met again with Buss at the owner's house to discuss the new contract. "I used the Spanish offer as leverage," he recalled.

But he asked Buss for much more than $20 million. "It was a huge figure," Rosen said with a chuckle. "Jerry said, 'That's very high. A lot of money. More than I'm willing to pay him. But we'll keep talking.'"

Buss and Rosen had first begun talking at training camp about a new deal in Hawaii in 1990, although under league rules a new contract couldn't actually be signed until after the 1992 playoffs.

By November 1991, the deal was taking shape only to be pushed aside by HIV. Despite a deep emotional funk that had forced him into virtual seclusion, Buss told Rosen, "Look, I'm still giving him his contract."

With Johnson pondering his return, the matter was no longer a business deal. Buss was operating on pure emotion, much as he had on Johnson's first huge deal. In fact, the new contract made absolutely no business sense because it jammed the Lakers against the salary cap, making it more difficult for Jerry West to arrange trades and other player deals for another three seasons.

"Jerry Buss had no obligation whatsoever to do that for Earvin Johnson, but that's the way he is," Rosen said of the deal they would eventually strike.

Some would later question his wisdom, Buss said in a 1992 interview. "But I don't think people looked at the way Magic handled himself. At no time in his career did you see that he was unhappy with his contract."

For a while, Johnson had made the money he deserved, Buss said. "But then basketball contracts went into the stratosphere and Magic was left behind."

Buss had always told Johnson that he would be the highest-paid player on the team. But that hadn't been the case. Johnson never complained, although Buss sensed that he expected something to be done.

The final answer was a one-year, $14.6 million contract extension, bringing Johnson's guaranteed income to $19.6 million, at the time the largest single-year contract in the history of pro basketball. To reach that figure, Buss and Rosen had looked at past Laker payrolls to determine just how much Johnson had been underpaid. "This was Buss's way of paying Earvin back for all those years," Rosen said.

The owner and the agent reached an agreement shortly after the Olympics and notified the league office, as NBA rules required, the only problem being that Johnson still didn't know if he wanted to come back. Rosen decided to delay the announcement of the new deal until after he made up his mind.

Either way, Johnson couldn't lose. If he decided not to play, Buss still guaranteed his money.

While he took his time, Johnson did the training he needed to prepare for an NBA season. As he had promised, Gary Vitti took charge of getting him ready. First thing each morning, Vitti, Johnson, Byron Scott, and Duane Cooper, the Lakers' second-round draft pick, would head over to the UCLA gym for some quality hoops competition, where Johnson had been king of the court for years, organizing and figuring the sides so he could win. "He ran the show," Vitti said. "Just like the old days."

Each day after their sessions at UCLA, they'd head to World's Gym to lift weights. "He filled the gym," Vitti said at the time. "He'd walk up to people he didn't know, people who were lifting, and pump 'em up. Motivate 'em. 'Push it! Push it!' He was so full of life. He was so happy."

The only downer was the decision. Cookie and most of his advisors weren't hot on the idea. You have nothing to prove, Arsenio Hall told him. His doctors did not advise for or against playing, although they suggested that if he did play, not to attempt to cover the full 82-game schedule, which would make Johnson something akin to the game's original Load Manager. He planned to avoid back-to-back games and long road trips, anything that might weaken his immune system and hasten the onset of AIDS symptoms. Johnson hoped to play about 60 games on the schedule.

In Boston, Larry Bird had briefly contemplated being a part-time player and rejected it. He wouldn't want to approach the game without a complete effort, he said. So he announced his retirement. The same problem remained for Johnson.

"Every time Earvin looked at the schedule, he changed his mind about something else," Gary Vitti said.

At first he was going to play no back-to-back games. Then it was some back-to-backs. Should he travel to Boston? What about New York? His doctors reminded him that a set plan would be difficult. Much of what he did would depend on his health.

Although he hadn't announced it, his comeback intentions seemed clear to many, including new Lakers coach Randy Pfund.

"Earvin doesn't say much to anyone," Jerry West explained. "He does things by the way he feels. But if you've been around him long enough, you get to know what he's thinking."

Chuck Daly, his Olympic coach, came to Los Angeles on business and heard that a group of pro players was moving from court to court around the city to avoid crowds of spectators. Daly was told that if he appeared at a certain public court early he might actually catch the action. Daly was there at nine the next morning, just in time to see Johnson going at it. Daly saw the fire in his eyes and didn't need to see anymore. Johnson would be back.

"A lot of people didn't know what to expect," Rudy Garciduenas said. "But a lot of people knew that Earvin couldn't be without the game."

Cookie knew, too, and finally consented.

"I'm back," he announced, with his wife and Dr. Michael Mellman at his side at a news conference at the Forum that September 29. God had put him here to play basketball, he said, admitting that at first his doctors had been opposed. "But they've never dealt with anyone as big and strong as I am. I continued to work out and do what I was supposed to do, and now I'm in a position to come back and play, so here I am."

It began again with training camp in Hawaii. And Earvin Johnson, point guard, team leader, Magic Man, knew just how he wanted everything to be. To ensure that, he went to Honolulu a few days early, with team management, to survey the familiar gym at the University of Hawaii, to bounce the balls on the rack, to take those early shots, to put everything in his universe in order.

He was alive with it.

Yet the high and the promise of that opening session wouldn't last long. The first jarring clue came when columnist Dave Kindred of *The Sporting News* urged Johnson "to tell the whole truth about how he acquired the AIDS virus. . . . He said unprotected heterosexual sex did it; numbers say that's highly unlikely."

If Johnson was hiding the fact that he acquired the virus through homosexual activity, and his lie caused research money to be diverted into the wrong areas, then that lie would be "reprehensible," Kindred wrote.

Lon Rosen likely wouldn't have even seen the column if an L.A. radio station hadn't picked it up.

"KMPC started it," Rosen said at the time. "They called me. If the radio station hadn't brought it up, we wouldn't have made an issue of it."

Soon other reporters were calling, Rosen was infuriated, and the agenda of controversy was set in motion and would pick up energy at each step along the way during the coming preseason.

Kindred, a veteran, well-respected sportswriter, had based his column not on any specific information that Johnson was bisexual, but on statistics of the disease in America. The odds are roughly one in five hundred that a man can get the virus through unprotected heterosexual activity, Kindred quoted one study as showing.

However, AIDS worldwide was largely a heterosexual disease (75 percent of the millions worldwide had gotten it through heterosexual activity). In Africa, India, and Asia, an estimated 98 percent of all victims were thought to have been infected with the virus heterosexually. Rosen believed that Kindred had misunderstood the statistics and had failed to take into account the worldwide picture. That, health officials had told both Johnson and Rosen, was an important message in the United States, where AIDS was wrongly considered a gay problem.

In Hawaii, Johnson read the faxed column and was infuriated. "The thing about it is, if he knows something, why didn't he say it?" he told a small group of sportswriters that afternoon. "Why didn't he come out like a man and say it?"

The *Sporting News* story would be followed by others on the issue, and within days, Jan Hubbard, *Newsday*'s NBA writer, would produce a story saying that a prominent NBA player was spreading rumors about Johnson's sexual preference.

John Black, the Lakers' director of public relations, knew the firestorm was about to begin. "Everywhere we go," he said, "there are going to be the same questions. Over and over."

Added to the uncertainty were the questions over Johnson's status. Which games would he play? On what days would he take off? If he took off, did that mean he was sick? Suddenly every little thing required an explanation.

As Lakers officials feared, the media interest in Johnson began to swell with each passing day of the exhibition season. At every turn, there were new questions to be answered. It soon became apparent that the only practical solution was to hold a press conference before each preseason game, which Johnson quickly came to detest. He longed for the way things were, the good old days, when he could have quiet time in the locker room before each game. Time to read fan mail. Time to think about the game. Time with his teammates. Time, even, for an occasional chat with a writer or two. And, yes, time for his beloved popcorn. But that all disappeared in a swirl of controversy.

In its place was a press conference in every city with a new group of reporters with the same questions. Johnson, the smoothest of media creatures who had always been comfortable with the limelight, was no longer comfortable.

His first big step back came October 16 in Honolulu's sold-out Neal Blaisdell Arena with the opening exhibition game. Johnson played 27 minutes and finished with 14 assists, five points, and four rebounds as the Lakers defeated the Trail Blazers, 124–112. A night later, the teams met again, but Johnson sat out and the Lakers lost by 29 points. That, unfortunately, would emerge as something of a pattern in the preseason. When Johnson played, the Lakers won. When he didn't, they lost. Still, the exhibitions confirmed that Jerry West had assembled a deep roster, the kind that could win another title.

"With Magic back, they can be very good," said writer Mitch Chortkoff, who had covered the team for years.

The Lakers returned home to play Philadelphia on October 20 in the first round of their annual preseason tournament, the GTE Everything Pages Shootout. Before the game, Johnson told a small group of writers that a well-known NBA player was smearing him around the league as a bisexual. Johnson said he had confronted the player twice and each time the player denied it.

On the court that night, he again held form: 14 assists, 12 points, and five rebounds. They won by 27, the only disappointment being that merely 12,600 showed up at the Forum to see Johnson's official homecoming after a year off. Although he said little about the five thousand empty seats, the team's staffers sensed it hurt him. The next night he sat out and the Lakers lost to the Knicks.

Two nights later, the Lakers moved south to San Diego to play the Sacramento Kings. Again, he played, this time passing out 13 assists, and again they won, by 16. Still, he faced adjustments on the floor. For years, he had made his living pushing his big body through the seams of opposing defenses. Now, those seams were closing up before he got there. He had lost a step. Plus he had forgotten other little things, such as the touch it required to loft a shot over big defenders. In the past, he usually found a way to fool them. Now they blocked his shots.

While the Lakers were in San Diego, news reports had identified Isiah Thomas as the prime suspect in alleging Johnson wasn't being truthful about his sexual activity. Actually, the rumors themselves were an old item in NBA gossip circles. About three weeks after Johnson first announced his infection, Gary Vitti had gotten a call from another NBA player, a former Laker, who told Vitti that Thomas had phoned the player's teammate and told him that Johnson was bisexual. The former Laker had called Vitti to confirm it.

"I got a little nasty," Vitti said. "I told him, 'You know, if I had heard something like that, I would never, ever repeat it. If it's true—it's not—but if it is, so what?' This guy said, 'But I just thought you should know.'"

Vitti decided not to tell Johnson about the phone call. First of all, he hadn't actually heard Thomas tell anyone anything. Second, he didn't want to unload more troubles on his friend. Johnson would find out soon enough, he figured. Later in the 1991–92 season, Vitti had dinner with Mike Dunleavy and learned that coaches from other teams had passed along details about the gossip to Dunleavy, who relayed them to Johnson.

As if the Thomas news wasn't enough that morning in San Diego, the media intensity thickened yet again when Phoenix Suns president Jerry Colangelo told broadcaster Jim Lampley that Johnson should not compete because other players feared his infection. Colangelo's opinion made big news. He was one of the league's most powerful figures, and he seemed dead set against Johnson's return.

Both team officials and Johnson surmised that the Suns executive feared that Johnson's return meant the Lakers would again rule the Western Conference. Colangelo had traded for forward Charles Barkley in the off-season with the hope that Phoenix might finally win an NBA title. Johnson now threatened Colangelo's plans, so he was attacking, they said.

More than the Colangelo challenge, Johnson confided to one team official how disappointed he was about Isiah Thomas. Johnson revealed they were no longer close.

Herb Williams, however, considered both Johnson and Thomas close friends and had known them since their days playing basketball in college. He was a high-scoring freshman at Ohio State while Johnson was the freshman star at Michigan State. When their teams first met in Lansing, Johnson had come up to Williams after the game and offered to show him the town. That night, they toured all the local hot spots. "We just hung out," Williams said. "I had read a lot about Magic and was watching to see if he was ego-tripping. But he was just a regular, down-to-earth guy."

The friendship grew and came to include Mark Aguirre, then

later Thomas, who was two years younger than the others. Soon the four of them made a tight group that spent their off-seasons together looking for fun.

With George Andrews and Tucker as their representatives, they mixed business and pleasure, took vacations together with wives and girlfriends, and appeared at each other's camps and benefit games. Particularly Johnson and Thomas. "I've seen how close they were and the different things they did together," Williams said. "When Isiah was dating his fiancée [wife, Lynn], when he wanted to go see her, Earvin would go with him. He would stay in the hotel while Isiah was out there visiting with his fiancée. They was always together in the summertime."

Often they'd gather in Lansing. "We'd play Jenison Field House in Lansing in the summer," Williams recalled. "There'd maybe be fifty guys there hoping to play, and there'd be four or five thousand up in the stands watching. It would always be me, him, Mark Aquirre, and Isiah. We'd play four-on-four. We were always on the same team, and we never lost a game." Afterward, they'd pay a visit to Tucker's house where they'd relax in the basement with a cold beverage and attempt to be regular guys, as much as young millionaires could be. At night, they'd go to the local clubs, where crowds would gather around Isiah and Johnson, while Williams and Aguirre would hang back, just out of the limelight, amazed at the attention their friends could draw.

"What hurt that relationship more than anything else," Williams said, "were the championships. Once you win them, and as many as Earvin did, you become so big-time, you have so many people around you that do certain things for you."

These people often aren't the best to deal with your friends because things get miscommunicated, Williams said. In Williams's opinion, after the Pistons beat the Lakers in 1989 things began to sour. Obviously, Johnson didn't like losing, even to a friend. And the always emotional Thomas got caught up in his team's accomplishment. "It seemed like, 'You were the man. Now I'm the man. I don't need you,'" Williams said.

When the Pistons had come to Los Angeles to meet the Lakers for that 1989 title, Thomas found that Johnson had changed his phone number. So he drove to Johnson's house and ran inside to speak with him. They spoke for about ten minutes. Johnson had an injured hamstring, and the Pistons were marching to the title, awkward circumstances for stars who would be friends.

One of their last truly friendly visits had come at the All-Star Game in Orlando, when Herb Williams found them laughing and joking in Johnson's room. Johnson invited both of them to a party one of his friends was having, and they both showed up. But the crowd was large. Johnson sat in a private section, and Thomas sat there with him, seemingly wanting to visit, Williams said. "But Isiah had his wife and his mother with him, and I really don't know if he wanted to be in that situation. People kept crowding around and they really didn't have a chance to talk."

After a short time, Thomas left.

Then came the rumors. Johnson told a small group of writers that the reason he was upset was that the player he suspected of talking—he wouldn't identify him as Thomas—was one who had spent a lot of time with him socially and knew that he wasn't bisexual. "Those guys know me," he said. "I'd been hanging out with them. That's what ticked me off. I don't know what I'm going to do about it."

Thomas denied that he was the culprit. Privately, he told Detroit sportswriters that there was no way he would spread rumors about Johnson, because those same rumors concerned him and were related to their pregame kiss before the 1988 Finals tipoff.

"I didn't hear Isiah say anything," Herb Williams said. "I just heard people say that when they heard Earvin had the virus, the first thing that popped into their minds was, 'Is he gay? Well, him and Isiah was real tight, so what about Isiah?' So then Isiah said, 'We're not that tight.'"

The Thomas denial somehow got twisted into the rumor, Williams suggested. "That made things pull apart. Even if he didn't say it, once things hit the papers, somebody should have called. Either Earvin should have called him or Isiah should have called. They should have talked it over, because the first thing Earvin thought, 'Man, this is my friend. Me and Isiah were tighter than anybody.' For him to say something, that's got to really hurt, especially at a time when you need somebody. They would have sat down and talked it out."

Ultimately, Williams said in a 1993 interview, "The people around them kind of tore them apart, because they didn't sit down and talk when the frustration first started. And that's a shame. Because it's hard to find a good friend, and when you do, you shouldn't let anything come between you, especially nothing petty like he said, or she said, or whatever."

The split would be so profound that a quarter century would pass before Thomas and Johnson could bring themselves to a reconciliation.

On the Road

As the exhibition season rolled along toward a close, Johnson bypassed a game in St. Louis and flew to Chicago with his wife and Rosen for a taping of *The Oprah Winfrey Show* to mark the launch of his promotional efforts for his book, *My Life*. The unofficial agenda, however, was to defend his sexuality, and the book publicity tour offered what seemed to Johnson a good opportunity to offer details of his many encounters. The strategy would soon prove to be a disaster, because in several key interviews Johnson told far more than the book revealed. Even worse, he detailed the nature of his off-court life as his wife sat beside him, obviously stunned and humiliated by what he was saying.

"He was surrounded by so much controversy it destroyed the hero," Gary Vitti said in a 1993 interview. "When he started talking about six women at a time on the Oprah Winfrey show and stuff like that, he lost a lot of people. He felt he had to say these things about six women. He felt he needed to defend himself. He didn't want people to think he was gay."

Rosen recalled watching as Johnson launched into similar detail during an interview with ABC's *Primetime Live*. "He looked so sad," the agent said of his friend and client in 1993. "I felt really bad for him."

Rosen and Johnson had discussed the need to limit what he said about his affairs, but he was his own man. What had been Johnson's spontaneity and light manner with the media over the years suddenly became extremely problematic as he attempted to explain and describe his behavior.

"He said it," Rosen said, "and I knew it was gonna cause a lot of shit."

It wasn't long before the agent notified the publisher, Random House, that Johnson wasn't going to continue with the promotional efforts for the book. It simply wasn't in his best interest.

While they were waiting to tape the Winfrey show, Rosen and Johnson had read more of Colangelo's criticism of his return. Colangelo was clearly campaigning against him. Furious about the comments, the agent phoned Russ Granik, the league's deputy commissioner, and asked him to step in.

Colangelo, however, was free to offer his opinion as often as he wanted.

"They couldn't stop him," Rosen said.

Johnson skipped a game in St. Louis, and the Lakers won for the first time without him. They won another game with him in Memphis, which inspired more confidence that the team and Johnson were finding their footing as they headed into a final exhibition game in Chapel Hill, North Carolina, against the Cleveland Cavaliers on Halloween night.

The publicity stirred by his public appearances for the book had created the expectation that everywhere he went in basketball he would talk about his infection and his sex life.

An editor, Paul Ensslin, with a local newspaper was among those eager to question this brazen figure, Magic Johnson, who not only was HIV positive but a man who had gone on national TV and essentially boasted about his sexual exploits.

Granted his interview, the editor asked a number of questions. The main topic, of course, was AIDS, which was something he preferred not to discuss, Johnson explained. "Because of my celebrity status and my position as a role model, I can understand how people would want to talk about it. It wouldn't be right to totally ignore it, but I've tried not to let it affect me too much."

One issue was Johnson's protest resignation from President George H. W. Bush's commission on AIDS, with the 1992 presidential election just five days away. If Bush won the election, what advice would Johnson offer him? Ensslin asked.

"I'm not a political person, and I'm not one to give advice to the president," Johnson replied. "He's got his own agenda right now, and we'll just see what happens after Tuesday's election."

Johnson said he had tried to be a good spokesman for AIDS awareness, and the editor asked about the video Johnson had made with Arsenio Hall. Directed by Malcolm-Jamal Warner, the video had been roundly criticized. The Los Angeles Unified School District rejected it for use in schools because of distasteful content and a jumbled, overly long format. "It was not initially intended to go to the schools," Johnson said. "It was made for kids to watch at home with their parents. If some people find it shocking, well, AIDS is shocking."

In the interview, which ran for fifteen minutes or so, Johnson said he was healthy, said he hoped to be a Laker for a few years to come, said he had responded to press reports of rumors of his bisexuality and didn't care to discuss them again.

The editor then closed the interview by asking Johnson if he was afraid of dying.

"Why should I?" Johnson said as he turned away. "I just live, baby."

That night, he phoned Rosen and said that he didn't want to go to practice in the morning, a routine shootaround before the game the following night.

When he didn't show, Rosen got a call from Jerry West.

"Something's up," the general manager said. "Earvin didn't go to practice."

Rosen assured the Lakers staff nothing was wrong. "He just wanted a break," he explained. "He didn't want to deal with the press today."

There was little escape, however, from the situation. First, Johnson and his advisors had misjudged how basketball itself would respond to his full-time return. The game simply wasn't ready to deal with the gnarly and misunderstood issue of AIDS. He might have been able to finesse the matter if not for the attempt to publish and launch a best-selling book in the middle of his return to the game. Taken together, the return and the book promotion efforts would prove absolutely disastrous.

Before the game that night, Johnson had to attend a reception hosted by a trading card company. He arrived on time and happily schmoozed with the corporate guests. But afterward, he faced yet another pregame press conference. About two dozen reporters awaited him in the Smith Center's pressroom.

"Did you anticipate the media attention being this big with your return?" he was asked.

"You really didn't know," he said, his reply interrupted by a big sneeze. "Excuse me. I've been dealing with the media for a long time. Whatever happens really doesn't surprise me. They have a job to do. Everybody wants a story. So be it. I'll deal with it. It's fine. Because once you hit the floor, it's all about basketball. I can do this now, but another 45 minutes from now I'll be doing something I love to do."

Another writer asked, "Do you have anything left to accomplish in basketball, now that you've won an Olympic medal, NBA titles, and an NCAA championship? What you're doing now, is it just to be playing, or are you making a statement about the HIV virus?"

"I'm making a statement, but I'm also out to win the Championship," he said. "I just don't play basketball to play it. I play to win, and I've always played to win. I only know how to do that."

With that, the Lakers publicity director ended the session.

"He was composed," one writer observed afterward, sounding surprised. "Very composed."

Marked early by turnovers and missed shots, it would not be one of Johnson's best nights. About midway through the first period, he attempted to back Cleveland's Craig Ehlo down near the goal and drew a foul.

As he walked to the free throw line, Johnson examined first one arm, then the other. Gary Vitti caught the attention of official Ed Rush in front of the Laker bench. "Ed, you oughta check Magic," Vitti told him. "Somebody on our team thinks he has an open wound."

Rush then halted the free throw proceedings to examine Johnson's arms. Obviously annoyed at this intrusion, Johnson told Rush he didn't have any injury. The official walked back over and told Vitti, "He doesn't have anything."

Moments later, during a timeout, Vitti decided to examine Johnson's right arm himself. "He sits down," the trainer recalled. "I get kinda nosy. I turn his arm over. I see this small scratch. No bigger than a fingernail. I could easily have looked the other way. But you're supposed to cover open wounds. I pull a four-by-four gauze pad out of my jacket pocket. I hand it to Magic. I said, 'Put this on your arm and wipe away the perspiration.' I got a cotton-tip applicator and sprayed some benzoin on it, which is a sticky, adhesive substance. I painted his arm with it. Never put my fingers on the wound. Yeah, I held his arm, but I never put my fingers on the side of the wound. I made it sticky so we could put a bandage over it. Then he went back out and played."

With about three minutes left in the half, Vitti decided to put a sweatband over Johnson's small, clear bandage as additional protection. Later, the Occupational Safety and Health Administration would cite Vitti for a safety violation for failing to wear latex gloves during the bandaging.

"I didn't forget to put the gloves on," Vitti explained later. "I chose not to. It was a nonbloody wound in a controlled situation, one that was so small the official couldn't see it. There was a lot of controversy about players playing with Magic. I felt this was the perfect opportunity to make a statement. If I put the gloves on, that would have sent a mixed message to all of these players. 'Gary, you're telling us to play with Magic Johnson because we can't get HIV. But now he has this fingernail scratch. It's a nonbloody wound and you're putting gloves on? Now if I can't get it, why are you putting those gloves on? What are you trying to say? It's okay if he bleeds on me, but not on you?'"

Most people in the arena failed to notice the issue with the scratch. The Lakers' broadcasters didn't notice it, nor did most of the reporters in attendance. Photographer Brad Isbell on the baseline took pictures of Johnson receiving treatment, but outside of that, little attention was paid to it.

As Lon Rosen would explain later, Johnson had also gotten cut during the Olympics, another small cut on his finger, covered by a Band-Aid, and no one noticed then either.

Properly bandaged in North Carolina, Johnson continued to play with mixed results.

A bad pass to Worthy. Another missed opportunity with Sam Perkins.

"Shit," Johnson muttered.

And it seemed like he couldn't get anything to fall.

"God!" he yelled in disgust after missing another shot.

He played 28 minutes and made just one of 10 shots as the Lakers lost. A crowd of reporters asked all sorts of basketball questions afterward. Finally, someone mentioned his arm. "You kinda got nicked a little on the arm," a writer said. "Is that a problem at all?"

"No. No-o-o-o," he replied. "Everybody, anybody who gets cut, not just me, anybody, you just go, get it fixed. Boom. Come right back."

"Nothing special to worry about?" the writer asked.

"No," he said. "That's everybody. Not just me. Everybody in the league."

After several more basketball questions, he was asked, "Does the controversy take some of the luster off your comeback?"

"Naw," he said. "You gotta remember something. People are gonna have their own opinions, and so be it. But once the regular season starts, it doesn't matter. I'm out here tonight. Boom. I'll be out there Friday night, and once you play all that will die down. Everybody needs something to write about right now. It's exhibition time."

"In fact, it's probably good it happened at exhibition time," a writer suggested.

"Yeah, it's good," Johnson said, not sounding convinced. "But it's gonna happen. I knew it when I decided to come back, because even mentioning about coming back, people had their own opinions even then. It's fine. You know, I've handled everything in my life. The majority of it's been good. Ninety percent of it good, 10 percent of it bad."

"You've said God chose you to be the person to do this," another writer said. "Do you still feel that way about coming back? That a lesser person, a lesser talent, couldn't have pulled it off like you have."

"It's been tough," he admitted. "First of all, I'm a strong person. Second of all, I was already financially secure. So you had both of those things working. Anybody else, it was gonna be a problem, see. The best about all of this, I own both of my houses. No mortgage. Everything that comes in to me is mine. When it happened, it wasn't like, 'Oh, man, what am I gonna do now?' It was none of that. I just ran my businesses. Just like when I retire, I'll step into the suits. I'll have to wear a suit every day. That's the only difference."

Then he was asked what kind of impact he'd have as the first NBA player with HIV. "The impact will be just that. Just that. I'm just happy it was me," he said and punctuated the comment with a laugh. "I'm like a guinea pig," he added, his voice turning suddenly serious. "I like challenges. It's fun. It's no fun when you don't have challenges. This is one of them."

Then he was asked about the rising percentages of heterosexual HIV infection. The gay community had gotten the message out to its members about protection, he said. "Now it's just us being blinded by whatever it is."

It was his role to fight that blindness, he said, and playing basketball helped him do it. "Look at this. I'm in North Carolina right now. Boom. The message is out. I'm here. I'm playing. I'm talking to you. Boom. It'll be in the papers tomorrow. Next time I'll be in Philly. I'm gonna be in Cleveland. In Chicago. See? So the message gets out even bigger."

Playing in the Olympics helped broadcast the message? someone asked.

"Oh, man," Johnson said. "That's the whole forum. That's what I wanted. So I got the whole forum.

"We educated them," he said, his eyes gleaming.

Moments later, team officials finally ended the session and the media filed out of the locker room. Most of his teammates had dressed quietly and gone to the bus.

Later, after it happened and they would all be stunned again, one Lakers staffer and players would think back in search of a clue and remember that Johnson strangely went out of his way to sign autographs in the Dallas airport on a stopover on the way home, rather than hiding away to play cards with his teammates.

Go on without me, he said, signing every scrap of paper in sight. In the past when he signed, he tried not to pay attention, because the conversations could drag on and he could become overwhelmed. But on this day, he looked at all of them, taking in each and every sweet wide eye. Smiling. Chatting. Squeezing the moment.

"That's really weird," one Lakers staff member remembered thinking.

When he got home that night, Johnson phoned Rosen and told him he was retiring. Again.

"If you're retiring because you got cut, you're a chickenshit," the stunned agent said.

"No, it's not that," Johnson said. "It's no fun."

He had brought fun to gyms since grade school, but now it had deserted him.

He could see that his mere presence was changing the game with the press conferences, the controversies, the hassle of it all. Even worse, players from other teams feared him, which meant they might not play as hard as they could. And that would hurt the game, he told Rosen. Above all, he didn't want to hurt the game. He said he didn't want to let down all the children with HIV. He knew how many had written him and told him they were counting on him to keep playing. As long as he played, they knew they could play, because other kids wouldn't have an excuse for keeping them out.

"But I can't play," he again told Rosen. "It's no fun."

They met at a quiet restaurant that Sunday morning for breakfast. They had just gotten seated when a man sitting nearby said, "Magic, I just got my season tickets. I'm so glad you're back."

None of this was going to be easy, Rosen thought.

Rosen waited all day hoping he would change his mind, then finally phoned Jerry Buss with the news.

"Is he sure?" Buss asked immediately. "Has he talked about it? Maybe he's just reacting to the cut."

Rosen's next call was to Russ Granik, the NBA's number two

man, who told the agent to get back with Johnson and talk him out of it.

Rosen asked Johnson one final time if he was absolutely sure.

"I'm sure," he said.

Karl Malone of the Utah Jazz had been quoted in *The New York Times* that very morning saying he was concerned about playing against someone infected with HIV, causing some people to think Malone's comments helped force Johnson from the game.

Johnson would explain later that Malone's opinions only reinforced his decision.

"It has become obvious," he would say in a statement released through Rosen, "that the various controversies surrounding my return are taking away from both basketball as a sport and the larger issue of living with HIV for me and the many people affected. After much thought and talking it over with Cookie and my family, I decided I will retire, for good, from the Lakers."

Johnson had forgotten how difficult life is in the NBA, Gary Vitti said in an interview eleven months later. "Then all of a sudden training camp starts and training camp's a bitch. We're all over the place, and he's not playing quite as well as he thought he would. . . . It was like, 'This isn't that great anyway. And on top of it, these guys don't wanna be with me. So what am I doing this for?' And then boom. He just quit."

Steve Springer would long maintain that it was a terrible mistake for Johnson to leave his career early, that he was healthy, just thirty-three, and still able to lead the Lakers into championship contention in the Western Conference. Certainly Colangelo's campaign against Johnson's return aided his Suns. With Barkley, they would make it to the NBA Finals that season.

Journalist Frank Deford, meanwhile, would contend that Johnson was mostly chased from the game by Waymer Moore's $2 million lawsuit, which had become public in the days before he quit.

Johnson showed up at the Lakers' season opener at the L.A. Sports Arena a week later and held a press session beforehand.

"I definitely want to come back," he said, "but I won't. . . . It's a different hurt this year. After going through training camp and knowing what we had on paper as a team, it's more difficult than last season. Am I at peace? I probably won't be until a month or two into the season when I know I'm out.

"I'll never disappear," he promised. "I don't know how to. I love to live."

Years later, NBA commissioner David Stern would look back at the madness and paranoia that had forced Johnson from the game and say, "It was a crazy, crazy time."

"I quit for one reason and one reason only," Johnson would say much, much later to *Sports Illustrated*'s Jack McCallum. "I didn't want to ruin the game that Larry, Michael and I had helped build back up. I would never let someone drive me out. I'm not built that way. But the controversy was hurting the game. Quitting was the right thing to do, but it hurt."

The hurt would add to his already substantial store of motivation—a deeply burning anger that he would carry with him, well hidden, through the wilderness that lay ahead.

31

THE WANDERER

Earvin Johnson's life would be seen as a chaotic struggle in the wake of another abrupt departure from the Lakers in late 1992. For the longest time, his path had been about what fans had joyously seen of him night after night on the floor. Now it would become about things they couldn't see.

They couldn't see his dreams, for example. That's where Reggie Chastine had come to him from time to time over the years, his good ol' friend and Everett teammate Reggie, who had been so vital for Johnson as a teen, pushing and shoving him when he needed to be pushed and shoved. Chastine had seen his greatness before Johnson himself had seen it and had fairly badgered him into stepping into it. Now Chastine was back from the grave, with his trademark feistiness, invading Johnson's nights, leaving him to jump awake with a start, Johnson would reveal to *Sports Illustrated*'s Gary Smith. Those sudden flashes of clarity in the middle of the night would prompt Johnson to rise, shaken out of his slumber, and again view videotape of his greatest moments, something Johnson had turned to quite a bit over the years to stoke his confidence, like a great blazing fire, watching himself in the flames, in the 1979 NCAA championship game or in Game 6 of the 1980 NBA Finals or another moment, all punctuated by his biggest smiles and joy. Johnson would see it all anew then, watching himself attack opponent after opponent. In control. Winning. Reggie's return had helped him see he was now in another such moment in his battle against the virus, which left him in need of his old friend's fighting spirit, literally.

"My whole life has been a challenge," he would then conclude about his battle against HIV, "and this is just another one. I love to shock people. To beat the odds. They said I was too tall to play guard. They said I couldn't shoot. Each time I said, 'O.K., I'm just gonna show you.' And this is just another one of those things."

Quietly then, almost secretly, Reggie's presence was one of the things that would influence this new life with its absurd new challenges.

As the record would eventually show, Johnson may have quit his NBA career, but he was far from done with basketball. Part of his plan had long called for him to step into the life he had quietly pursued on the side—that of a businessman. For years, virtually in every NBA town, he had arranged to meet with influential minds on the side—not about basketball, but about commerce, Johnson always an active learner, always with an eye on his future in business. Yet for so many years his business had been basketball, and that business obviously had been very good. Now, as he began to adjust to his new life, basketball would be there for him again.

The Dream Team in 1992 had basically served as the grand launch for NBA basketball around the globe, one of the most successful branding exercises in the history of branding. Commissioner David Stern had been building toward that for the better part of a decade with media and marketing deals that would prove to work famously to promote the NBA as THE global hoops standard. Having gorged itself on highlights of Bird and Johnson and then Jordan and an array of other players and story lines, the sport was on the verge of unprecedented growth in popularity.

There would be lots of money to be made.

In the early months of 1993, Johnson merely stepped up to meet the immediate demand for more American basketball when he wasted little time in creating a traveling team of recently retired

NBA players. Off and on for years, they would challenge pro teams around the globe in exhibition games and tours.

In that regard, Johnson's new traveling all-star entourage took on a challenge that no NBA team had ever faced—perfection. In so doing, Johnson fell in line with the long tradition of Black barnstorming teams, most notably the Harlem Globetrotters and the Renaissance Big Five, among others, that had begun touring back in the age of segregation in America. In addition to spreading the game internationally, those early touring teams had often provided the first opportunity for white fans to see Black players perform in the United States. Marques Haynes, the first great ball-handling wizard, had starred for the Globetrotters until he won a long court fight for the right to own and operate his own traveling team, called the Harlem Magicians, no less.

In 1993, Johnson set out with his own team with the idea of again spreading the Magic. Old friend Reggie Theus joined the effort with Johnson and saw it firsthand.

"I traveled with Magic Johnson," Theus recalled in 2019. "We went to Venezuela, we went to Europe, everywhere."

Australia, New Zealand, Asia, Finland, Norway . . . the list of stops was long. To borrow from the title of that 1973 Cheech and Chong parody, the world had a "Basketball Jones," and Magic Johnson was determined to delight crowds with a taste of Showtime, delivered by his various versions of the traveling team over the years. In that regard, Johnson would prove to be quite the maestro, both on the floor and in how he conducted the business of his teams. With corporate sponsorships and sold-out arenas, Johnson was able to rake in a nightly personal take of better than $350,000, as *Sports Illustrated* would report, the kind of money that the game's top players would eventually make in the twenty-first century.

Johnson was able to pocket such profit all while sparing little in treating his players in first-class fashion.

"I'll never forget, we were traveling across the continent," Theus said, "and Magic rented three or four Learjets to fly us to our next destination. It was pretty amazing. It was just very cool. Listen, we were all pros, but it isn't like today where these guys rent their own Learjets because they have so much money."

For many of Johnson's touring teammates, the money had just started to grow in the NBA of the 1980s, but they would have nothing of the immense wealth that fell to even the "average" pro players who followed them.

One other thing was clear. Johnson knew that treating his fellow players well allowed him to ask much of them in return. "We were just in awe at how organized and how well he treated us when it came to our travel," Theus recalled. "When it came to working out, our practices were hard. I mean, really hard. Our practices were like full blow. And if you didn't work, you didn't play. He'd even kick you off the team."

Johnson, characteristically, saw the need for perfection and demanded it, Theus explained. "I remember distinctly him having a conversation with me about the thing that made that team special. He told me, 'Reggie, we're only going to be as good as we are as long as we don't lose. If we don't lose, this traveling team will be successful. If we lose, it takes away the whole allure of what we're trying to do.' I didn't play with him the entire time, but the whole time I was with them, we never lost."

Soon enough, Johnson would be promoting his team by touting its 55–0 record. Records show there would be an occasional loss, usually only if Johnson wasn't in the lineup. But those were rare events, even as the team traveled extensively off and on for years around the globe.

Yet, for Johnson, the travel only seemed to stoke his constant thoughts about what he was missing in the NBA, about what might have been. "People would follow our buses," Theus recalled. "That's how crazy it was. The games were all sold out. Basically, it was like a traveling rock band."

Another perk were the little things about a team that Johnson had always craved. "The camaraderie was just so incredible," Theus said, still laughing. "We were big on playing 'Tonk' at the time. It was always so funny because guys gamble with Magic and Magic wasn't going to lose. He doesn't like to lose at anything. If he started to lose, he would just raise the stakes until you had to borrow money from him. Eventually, you'd lose; you just couldn't keep up. By the time you were done playing, you'd be giving him the check you just earned."

The rosters of Johnson's traveling team featured an array of NBA stars and former Lakers, including Bob McAdoo, Michael Cooper, Kurt Rambis, and Mike McGee, along with some all-time greats. Moses Malone, Ralph Sampson, Mark Aguirre, Alex English, and a variety of journeymen were all part of the fun, according to research by basketball historian Robert Bradley and members of the Association for Professional Basketball Research.

Johnson's touring team received almost no attention in the American press, so few NBA fans had even an awareness of the fun and success, not to mention the extensive travel. His determined response to his new HIV status wouldn't be something that basketball fans in the United States witnessed, but his teammates and closest associates all saw it.

The Game Again

He had swiftly launched his new life in 1993, and the international results would end up proving another sad, ironic point. As Steve Springer would offer in 2019, Johnson shouldn't have retired from the NBA after that fraught, disappointing exhibition season in 1992. He should have gone on playing, Springer said. Time would show there was simply no medical reason for him to do otherwise. At age thirty-three, he still had much more to give to the game. The loss wasn't just Johnson's but all of basketball's, not to mention the Lakers and their fans. He could easily have played five or six additional seasons, perhaps more. Imagination can only provide what he could have accomplished in that time.

Essentially, by retiring, Johnson had also surrendered his immense power as an NBA star. He would try to regain it later, but it proved like water slipping through the fingers of his cupped hands. Unfortunately, his own arrogant carelessness plus the lack of knowledge about HIV and its effects had cost him that opportunity to hold on to that power.

Strangely, his HIV status hadn't been an issue for the international teams he faced while barnstorming and it soon became clear there were those in the NBA also eager to welcome him back. Among those was an old standby—Pat Riley—as well as a mysterious new friend. Riley, who took over as coach of the Knicks, wanted Johnson to join his roster so they could revive their success of the past. Johnson checked in with the Lakers about the prospects of that and was told, no, that the Lakers held his rights, and if he was going to play, it would be as a Laker.

The mere thought of the combo of Johnson, at age thirty-three or thirty-four, teaming with Patrick Ewing in New York could have well changed the course of the 1990s, could have erected a roadblock or at least a good speedbump on Michael Jordan's freeway to repeated glory, could have stoked the imagination and delight of Knicks fans for decades, considering how long that franchise had lived off its two titles in 1970 and 1973. Just as important, a New York title in the 1990s would have elevated Johnson's status considerably in terms of his career accomplishments.

Renewing the partnership of Johnson and Riley with Ewing? Jerry Buss had certainly been generous with Johnson, but he wasn't going to be that generous.

It was during this period that Buss allowed Johnson to buy what was estimated to be between 4 and 5 percent of the Lakers at a relative pittance of $10 million, as a recognition for all he had done to build the tremendous value of the franchise. (Jordan was in the process of literally making billions for the owners of the Bulls, yet no such Chicago ownership deal would ever come to him.)

As for the mysterious new friend in Johnson's life, that would prove to be Atlanta Hawks GM Pete Babcock, who stepped up first by seeking to hire Johnson to coach the team that January of 1993, never mind that the club had a winning record and a good coach in Bob Weiss. Babcock merely thought his roster was capable of much more and that Johnson just might be able to get it out of them. If anyone pointed out that Johnson had never coached, Babcock could respond that Johnson had been literally a coach on the floor his entire career.

Johnson was immediately flattered by the interest, Babcock recalled. "I called his agent to run the idea by him and then he called me back and said, 'Yeah, he's actually kind of intrigued by it.' We had a pretty decent team, but I just felt like we were underachieving, so I was just trying to find a way to get us to the next step."

Babcock and Hawks president Stan Kasten flew to Los Angeles to talk it over with Johnson. "All indications were, he was going to do it," Babcock recalled. "His wife was encouraging him to do it and his agent was encouraging him to do it so, yeah, I thought he was going to give it a shot."

Rosen remembered the two Hawks representatives showing up at his house to discuss the meeting in a rare Southern California downpour, their hopes doused first by the rain, then by the answer.

Johnson told them no, that if he was going to coach it would be with the Lakers, a decision he likely made after discussing the matter with Jerry Buss, because a year later, Johnson replaced Randy Pfund and took over as Lakers head coach, in the spring of 1994, which meant that Babcock's idea that the next generation of players was ready to accept Johnson's coaching would be put to the test.

In retrospect, a fresh start in Atlanta might well have been best in terms of the basketball itself. By staying in Los Angeles, Johnson brought the overwhelming specter of Showtime to a mostly new generation of Lakers, who were in the process of moving to a new identity known as the Lake Show, with the influence of point guard Nick Van Exel. Johnson's looming presence would bring substantial pressure to this younger generation.

Johnson came into the new gig with his same old openness with the press, recalled Scott Howard-Cooper, who was covering the team for the *L.A. Times* in those days. "It wasn't unusual to be out after a practice and just kind of shooting the breeze with Magic during his coaching time. There weren't five TV cameras and a dozen internet sites back then. So, you kind of had these different conversations with him, and he had a lot of confidence. I think he went into it really believing that it was going to go."

Reporters on the beat would later recall with a chuckle the day Johnson made his big prediction, Howard-Cooper recalled. "Magic looks at us and says something about 'taking you guys to the Finals,' or 'I'm going to take you guys to the championship.'"

Just a couple of years had passed since his last NBA season, yet the world had changed dramatically even in that time, never mind that the full changes of the technological revolution had hardly begun to fall on society by 1994.

"I'm sure he definitely knew that it was a different era," Scott Howard-Cooper recalled, "and that again one of the big things was a different time in the world, in the NBA world, with its players and cell phones and everyone having different agendas with just everybody's mind going in a different direction. When Magic was playing, there was never any issues about who's on their cell phone. And so here he comes as a coach and it's an entirely different world. And then the losses start coming and his head is exploding and it's just this very strange time."

The Pager

Even in its strangeness, his coaching tenure produced epic moments in Lakers lore. At the time, Danny Schayes was thirty-four and had joined the roster as a backup to center Vlade Divac. The son of Hall of Famer Dolph Schayes, he had played more than a decade in the league and was well versed in the ethos of the NBA. The Lakers, with a 29–38 record, had just gone through a 7–2 run when Johnson took control.

"We were, like, five games out of the playoffs; it wasn't like we were tanking and awful," Schayes recalled of that spring of '94. "But they decide to bring Magic in. The thinking was, 'If we could push toward the playoffs, it would get some momentum for next year.' Ironically, Magic had some scheduled appearances, so he couldn't take over right away. He had to be the keynote speaker at the Michigan State sports banquet or something like that. So, Bill Bertka, the longtime assistant, took over for a couple of games. And then Magic comes in and the excitement, as you might imagine, was ridiculous."

For Johnson's first game as coach, the Lakers entertained the Milwaukee Bucks on Sunday, March 27. "I remember getting ready for our first game at a shootaround," Schayes recalled, "and the PR guy, John Black, comes over at the end of the shootaround at half-court and starts talking about setting up TV shots and recording some B-roll, and Magic said, 'What the fuck are you doing? We're running a practice here.' He was all business. Then we show up for game time and we could barely do warm-ups. There was so many press on the court, filming Magic walking out. We barely could form a layup line. We were completely squeezed by all of the press."

Referee Don Vaden remembered the game in a 2019 interview: "It was his first win as a coach, I do believe. I should have hit him with a technical on that day because he got a little crazy on me, but it was my fault so I had to suck it up and go on. I don't remember exactly what it was about, but I remember he got really vocal. I got a picture at home of me running down the sideline and he's getting all animated. He throws his arm out—I see it right at the very end—so I duck so I don't run into him. That would have been embarrassing, because I knew I missed the play. I kind of put it in my back pocket and said, 'Okay, Magic, I'm going to let you go on this one.' Plus, it was his first game. It's hard to hit a guy on his first night."

Lon Rosen recalled a champagne celebration in the Lakers quarters after that first victory, during which Johnson called him into an office and said, "Get me out of this."

"Earvin really didn't want to do it," Rosen recalled in 2023.

The only reason Johnson had taken the job in the first place, his agent said, was "because Jerry came to me."

"I need a favor," the owner had said that spring. "I need Earvin to coach the team."

Soon enough some of the atmosphere that had enveloped the 1992 exhibition season returned. His traveling all-star team may have finessed the HIV issue with little problem, but the NBA proved another matter. "There were strange moments that just kind of surrounded the team with this circus atmosphere," Scott Howard-Cooper said, adding that he recalled an early road game that reflected "how bizarre this whole setting was. After the game there was sort of this back-and-forth in the postgame interview that Magic's getting questions from the *L.A. Times,* then somebody hops in with a medical question. Then he gets a question from the *L.A. Daily News,* and then it's *The New England Journal of Medicine* with a question.

Here's a guy that one second is being asked about that turnover in the third quarter and the next question is about his cocktail load of medicine that you've been put on for HIV. It was just the strangest thing ever."

Despite such distractions, Johnson got off to a 5–1 start as a coach and his confidence soared as the Lakers moved nearer to making the playoffs.

"We ended up winning a couple of games and getting back into it," Schayes recalled. "And we had a game at Phoenix. It was a pivotal game. If we win it, we're right in it. We were a game or two behind at the time. But we got blown out by Phoenix. We got beat by 30. It was so embarrassing that Dan Majerle ended up shooting free throws lefty at the end of the game just to rub our noses in it. It was bad, really bad."

Johnson couldn't realize it in that moment, but his team was headed into a losing streak to close out the season and his coaching career. There were reports that he began teaming with a couple of benchwarmers and his assistant coaches to take on the starting five in practice some days, that he wouldn't just beat them. He seemed to rub it in by announcing to the guy guarding him where he would go each time he had the ball, then doing it and scoring anyway, exposing his players' inability to do anything about it.

"I would have loved to have played with Magic," Schayes said. "I was an off-the-ball guy, right? I would have had a field day with him. There were a couple of times he would practice with us. We would play the old guys against the young guys. He was, like, thirty-four, thirty-five at the time, and we just lit it up. It was great. I would set a down screen and flash, and the ball would hit me in the face. Bam. It was right there. He was just so damn good."

At least the ploy proved that he could still play.

"The problem we had was this," Schayes recalled. "We had the old guard, all these guys thirty-five and up who had the warrior mentality. They were fighting their asses off. Then, you had the guys of the future who were just going through the motions. They were just waiting for the season to end."

Johnson would bemoan the lack of winning focus, the jovial atmosphere on the team plane after losses, in phone calls to Dale Beard.

Johnson's answer was to take drastic measures, Schayes said. "Magic was super embarrassed and upset. So, he says, 'All right, practice in the morning, 7 A.M. at the Forum and if you're late, you're cut.' So, we fly back, show up at 7 A.M. and we're in the locker room and first Jerry West comes in and chews everybody out. Then Magic starts going off. He starts looking at the guys and says, 'You guys think you're all so cool because you're Lakers, you're having fun, you're fucking the bitches, you're at the parties. Well, you know what? They don't care who you are. It's just because you're Lakers. You know what? Next year, they'll be somebody else's bitches.' And he was just going on and on. I'm one of the old-school guys, right? I'm just enjoying myself watching Magic put on a show and he was putting on a great show."

Yet Johnson's approach wasn't all tirades, far from it, Schayes recalled. "It's got to be one of the craziest stories ever about him. When he was coaching, the game was changing. It was evolving from when he played and he didn't understand it. Like with the game of today and how it's changed from the '90s. He thought totally different about the game than they thought, and it drove him crazy. But one day we were practicing at Loyola Marymount and we were getting our butts kicked and had been on a bad losing streak. He was fed up; guys were frustrated. So, it's a beautiful day outside and we were about to start practice when he said, 'Yeah, let's go outside.' So we all walk outside, not knowing what was about to happen. We didn't know if we were about to run or what. Well, we sat down and he said, 'Take some deep breaths. Take some deep breaths.' So now, we're like what the hell is he talking about? Then, he said, 'No. No. No. Take some deeeep breaths.' So, now we're sitting out there, inhaling and exhaling. And then he said, 'Yeah, that California air smells good, don't it?' And we're thinking like, 'Yeah. Sure. It's just air.' And then Magic said, 'Well, for some of you, it's going to be your last breath in California.' And then we started looking at each other and were saying to ourselves, 'Holy shit.' That was the other side. But once again that side of Magic was about competing and winning."

The new pager and cell phone culture that he confronted and the lack of focus it seemed to engender led Johnson to put in place strict rules about phones and pagers during practices and team meetings. As the losses began to mount the mood around the team grew darker, which came to a head one morning in practice, Schayes recalled in a 2019 interview. "Magic continued talking about the guys' attitudes and, all of sudden in the middle of the meeting, someone's pager started beeping. Now it's 7:15 in the morning. And it might have been even a Sunday. Magic immediately stops talking. He's like a pointer. He's looking around: Where is it? Where is it? We're in a small locker room and the beeper is muffled, like it was in a gym bag or something. So, he can't really pin it down. And the thing wouldn't stop beeping. It was hysterical. I'm laughing my ass off because I didn't have a beeper; I'm not that cool. So, I'm waiting for this thing to play out because it was funny as shit. All of a sudden, we look over, and Vlade has his hands in his pockets, trying to turn the damn beeper off. And he couldn't find the right button to turn it off. Finally, Magic homes in on it, walks over to Vlade and says, 'Vlade, is that your beeper?' And Vlade says 'Yeah.' And Magic says 'Let me see it.' So, Vlade hands him the beeper and Magic throws it as hard as he could against the chalkboard and it smashes into pieces. And poor Vlade's eyes are bulging out of his head. Vlade is stunned beyond belief. Magic then says, 'This is exactly the shit I'm talking about. You're more interested in your beepers and this and that.' I'm biting my lip trying not to laugh because it was so freaking funny.

"The next home game we're in the locker room," Schayes said, "and Magic is with Gary Vitti, the Lakers' longtime trainer, and tells him the story about Vlade and his beeper and Magic's howling, 'You should have seen the look on Vlade's face. Oh, my God.' And we're just cracking up. The punch line was that Vlade's wife was in labor. She was like nine months pregnant. I don't know if she actually went into labor, but she was pretty well advanced. That is why the beeper went off at 7:15 in the morning."

The season ended with a 10-game losing streak. Johnson coached for 16 games and finished with a 5–11 record. *Los Angeles Magazine* would describe the experience as "desultory."

"Obviously coming in at the end of a season like that can be challenging for anybody," Scott Howard-Cooper recalled, "but there was never anybody saying, 'Let's give it a whole season and see how this plays out.' It was, 'All right, we tried it. Bad idea. Next.'"

"I love Magic," Schayes said. "I think he's great. I loved him as a coach. He put out all the messages that I would have put out. He was a winning guy all the way. But he certainly knew how to live the life, the whole Magic persona. But that was only after the work. If you win, you get the goodies. It wasn't the other way."

"He did not want to be a coach," Rosen said.

Over time, it would become clear that the entire process of his HIV diagnosis and his attempts to recover from it had damaged so many relationships, beginning with close friends, such as Isiah Thomas, and extending to other figures across the league. For a time, Rosen and Johnson would pursue an investigation of betrayal, seeking to uncover those who had spread rumors about his sexuality behind his back.

And even with some of those who hadn't talked about him, there was often a new distance. "You'd see people sort of retreating from him," Rosen explained, "and it wasn't the same high fives, the same thing."

Yet the experience had also opened Johnson's eyes to others, such as those who had stepped up to join him on his touring team and those who made special gestures, such as Pete Babcock. Johnson hadn't known the Atlanta executive more than casually, but Babcock's effort in reaching out to hire him in those days after he left the game would weigh immensely.

"We weren't friends," Babcock recalled. "We had talked. But after the coaching situation, when he'd be in Atlanta on business or other things he was doing, he'd call and come to the game and sit next to me and talk about basketball. We became friends after that."

The Return

If it was possible, his whirlwind of a daily routine gathered momentum in the wake of his departure from coaching, as writer Gary Smith would discover while writing a piece for *Sports Illustrated*. Johnson, for example, would rise early for the limo ride to lift weights at Sports Club/LA, which left Cookie thinking that he had taken leave of his senses as he bulked up to an almost cartoonish 255-pound hulking version of himself while pushing his bench press from a little better than one hundred pounds to well over three hundred pounds.

"He's gone nuts," Cookie would declare more than once as her husband moved into a new wardrobe needed for his thicker, broader body.

"I got too big," Johnson would admit later.

"What you found was a man running his life as if it were a Lakers fast break," Gary Smith observed.

Johnson's mornings, Smith would learn, began at daybreak with herbal tea and a scouring of business and sports news, followed by business calls on the way to his weightlifting sessions, which also featured hundreds of sit-ups and other calisthenics, followed by intense shooting drills in the sports club's gym (he had ten spots staked out on the floor from which he would take fifteen shots each followed by animated shooting contests with his workout partner). Then came another limo ride and more phone calls, checking out everything from the progress on his ideas for business to what the Lakers' front office was thinking as far as player moves. With this came a constant array of meetings and presentations and connections for his AIDS foundation and his primary business concern, Magic Johnson Enterprises, his investment firm that was growing at a breakneck pace.

Thrown in next on the daily schedule could be a two-hour practice for his traveling team followed by a quick shot back home for a nap and time with Cookie, Earvin III, and adopted infant daughter, Elisa, then yet more pickup hoops at his old stand-by, the gym at UCLA, where the best players would gather to take on this newer, supersized version of Johnson, who provided amazing displays of his enhanced ability to roll end-to-end with the ball after made baskets. He would finish these dashes with flourishes at the hoop that left those facing him afterward asking again and again, "Man, why are you not in the league?"

Even his annual vacation yachting around the Mediterranean offered no escape from his hyper-competitive nature, as he hauled along his weights and a treadmill to stay on his workout mission, relieved only by every port the yacht would enter, where crowds would invariably gather to chant his name. In between, he would turn loose his pent-up desire to dominate in the co-ed card games aboard the yacht, turning what might have been calm evenings into manifestations of his unquenchable yearning for his next win and the opportunity to crow about it.

The revelatory moments would come back in L.A. on game nights at the Forum when Johnson sat not too far from the Lakers' bench, a spot from where he could address the players on the floor, not unlike a helicopter parent breaking protocol by directing and encouraging his child contrary to the coaching.

"He would sit at the edge of the court, as close to us as possible," Michael Cooper, by then a Lakers assistant coach, would say later. "I could see it on his face, the jitters, the nervousness."

Those moments should have served as ample warning for Johnson's next failure, but they did not. All of his converging whirlwind would produce a double edge that cut Johnson deeply that summer of 1995. It began with his afternoon games at UCLA. The league and its players union had plunged into a labor standoff that put them at odds, meaning that Johnson, the minority team owner, now had to be cognizant of not fraternizing with NBA players in his summer games. So, he quietly moved his afternoon pickup games at UCLA to mornings, but NBA players and adoring crowds soon discovered him there, which only added to his frustration.

Then there was the presence of Jordan in Hollywood that summer making the film *Space Jam*. Studio executives had famously erected a basketball court on a studio lot so that Jordan could meet the demanding schedule for shooting the film while continuing to log many hours playing with an assortment of NBA players drawn to his legendary pickup games. It was just the kind of top-level competition Johnson so desperately craved, but as a minority team owner, he was barred from participating. Only on the last night of Jordan's summer runs, after the labor dispute had been resolved, was Johnson able to put in an appearance on Jordan's special court.

On that night, Gary Smith saw, Johnson had ruled—was unstoppable by some accounts—with his end-to-end dashes to score, which only brought more wonderment at why he wasn't in the NBA.

Johnson himself proved to be fully haunted by the same question. To that end, he would turn to one of the most influential of his many allies in the Lakers organization, old friend Larry Drew, an assistant on the staff of head coach Del Harris, who was on his way to turning around the fortunes of the franchise, which had sagged in recent seasons. As the 1995–96 campaign unfolded, Drew made it known that Johnson wanted to return to the team as a player. The assistant coach suggested that Nick Van Exel and Eddie Jones phone Johnson to welcome the idea of his coming back to the team.

"Coach Drew had been saying that Magic was thinking about coming back and he knew that the players wanted him to come back," Van Exel recalled in a 2019 interview. "But nobody had talked to him, nobody said anything publicly about it."

"Yeah, we'll call him," Van Exel remembered telling Drew.

"Me and Eddie Jones called him about a comeback," Van Exel said. "We were on the phone for about an hour, telling him that we'd love to have him back, that we needed him, that we needed his leadership, that he could do this and that. And he actually started crying on the phone. I don't think he knew how we would respond to him coming back. Once we gave him our blessings, like, 'Come on, man, we're trying to win, too. We want to put up a championship banner the way you did.'"

It certainly seemed like a good idea at the time.

A year earlier, Jordan had created a global sensation with his return to the NBA after most of two seasons away playing baseball. Why not Johnson? His announcement in late January 1996 that he was coming back to the Lakers with 40 games left on the schedule likewise created quite a stir, not as big as the Jordan sensation, but a big moment.

"If I were an owner, I would have been sitting up in a skybox with my wife and forty of my friends living it up," Michael Cooper would say of his friend.

It was obvious, though, Cooper added, that Johnson could feel it. So could the crowd. The team had printed up "Welcome Back,

Magic" signs for everyone in the building that night in his return against the Warriors. Yet when the game started, the bulked-up Johnson looked strangely outsized in his warm-ups, and instead of roaring out in the starting lineup, he began by sitting on the bench. When he entered the game, he showed quickly that he could snag defensive rebounds but instead of heading up the floor with the ball, he would dutifully look to pass it off to the point guard and allow Van Exel or one of the other guards to run the game. He had stashed his famous instinct in order to follow the directives of coach Del Harris. And that, to the trained observer, would produce a huge screeching sound of metal, like two trains colliding slowly in a railyard.

History would confirm that Harris was a good coach, but he was notoriously "thin-skinned," as Scott Howard-Cooper recalled. "Magic's personality was so big, and Del was so concerned over what people are saying. That was a bad fit."

Still, Johnson would find ways to have the ball in his hands and get it to the right people. He would have eight rebounds to go along with 19 points and 10 assists in that first contest, as the Forum crowd celebrated a big win.

The second game of the new Magic Johnson era brought the cold reality of Jordan and his searing hot Bulls to town.

"This city is absolutely rejuvenated," Cheryl Miller declared, working as a sideline reporter broadcasting the big game that Friday night. Miller told viewers that with the Rodney King police brutality incident and ensuing riot, the O. J. Simpson murder trial and other woes, Los Angeles in recent times "hasn't had a whole lot to smile about."

But, with the big news, the town was dressed for a party. There had been those rousing cheers and high fives from the crowd his first game back, but this Jordan-driven steamroller would prove another matter. On their way to a record 72–10 season and Jordan's fourth NBA title, the Bulls brought a ridiculous 40–3 record into the nationally televised contest.

"I know he feels like he didn't leave on his own terms the last time," Chicago's star said of Johnson's HIV troubles. "He always wanted to come back to this."

With that 255 pounds of bulk, Johnson played as a reserve power forward, and showed the crowd a display of hook shots and even three-pointers.

Mostly, though, he was thoroughly roughed up by Chicago's Dennis Rodman, who told reporters afterward, "Who cares if he's got HIV, measles, cancer, whatever. I'm going to slam him anyway, and anybody who's got any balls will do the same thing."

Johnson should go back to playing point guard, Rodman suggested.

Johnson himself thought the same, but he wasn't even the team's backup point guard. And therein would lie the failing. He had returned with almost none of his legendary control over events.

"It was just too much to expect that he would turn things around," recalled Scott Howard-Cooper, who covered the season for the *L.A. Times*. "You understood why people got their hopes up because it had been a struggle for so long. They were desperate for anything to latch on to as a life preserver. And Magic was the reminder of everything good that had come before, and 'Magic is back!' So, the good times must be back."

The occasion did offer Jordan and Johnson a moment, which the two giants celebrated with a single microphone at a joint appearance at the podium before the media after the game.

"It was a thrill playing with Michael again," said Johnson, who had been in the Forum for hours before the game, anticipating the tipoff.

"I'm planning on playing a couple more years," Jordan said, "and I hope he'll stay around, too. I'd hate to see it end on this note because we'd like to have a better game."

Harvey Araton of *The New York Times* noted that Jordan punctuated the comment with a trash-talking smile, which prompted Johnson to snatch the microphone.

"You know he'll be dogging me all summer about this," he said.

As it turned out, Johnson would have bigger things to rue. Losing fifteen pounds as he went along, he would play in 32 of the Lakers' final 40 games that season, and the team would gain a false sense of prosperity. With Johnson on the floor, the Lakers went 22–10 and finished fourth in the Western Conference with a 53–29 record.

"Before Magic joined the Lakers, they averaged about 109 points per 100 possessions," writer Shea Serrano observed in looking back at that season for *The Ringer* website. "That put them outside of the top 10 in that category. After Johnson returned, they averaged about 115 points per 100 possessions, pushing them all the way up into third place."

The only teams more efficient were Jordan's Bulls and Shaquille O'Neal's Orlando Magic, Serrano pointed out. Even so, the season soon devolved into a strange storm of drama.

First came what appeared to be an unarticulated chemistry breakdown with Johnson's presence cramping the style of Cedric Ceballos, which resulted in the Lakers' leading scorer and co-captain leaving the team mysteriously without notifying his coaches or management. He missed two games and practices, which led to Ceballos losing his leadership title. He would be traded after the season.

"There were very few guys that Magic could relate to," Scott Howard-Cooper recalled of the team's chemistry issues. "More importantly, these were guys that knew of Magic but didn't care that much about Magic. They weren't going to bow before him and give him much deference. They didn't want to hear the stories about, 'We were in Boston Garden and Pat Riley said to Kareem, 'Here's what we got to do.'

"The players didn't want that, and they didn't care about Showtime," Howard-Cooper explained, adding that Johnson had made the effort to avoid just such a scenario. "I don't think he was stuck in the past. I think that he would talk about it because so many fans and media would ask him about it and he was obviously still connected to it. But maybe there would have been one or two moments that he got the reminder from the guys, that glazed-over look in their eyes. I think he was conscious of not being that guy, but those Lakers were so determined to start their own life, 'The Lake Show,' that anything to do with the previous generations of Lakers was generally met with either boredom or disdain."

It didn't help that a strong Golden Oldie vibe came naturally with Johnson's presence. "He was always singing those old-school songs and we were like, 'Nah. We're not hearing that,'" Van Exel would recall with a chuckle in 2019.

Toward the end of the regular season, Van Exel would get into an explosive dispute with official Ron Garretson. The Laker guard bumped the ref, resulting in a seven-game suspension and a public rebuke from Johnson, all of which would be followed a few games later by Johnson having his own incident with an official that left him with his own two-game suspension.

Johnson was said to be so distraught about the suspension that he apologized to his teammates in tears. Yet the frustration that boiled over in those incidents was a signal of things to come.

It was hoped that the first round of the playoffs would bring a shift in the team's jumbled narrative as the fourth-place Lakers faced the fifth-place Rockets of Hakeem Olajuwon, the two-time defending league champions, a team that had struggled with injuries most of the season but had gotten healthy late in the schedule.

Both Johnson and Van Exel were playing their first games back from suspension as the series opened. Van Exel started the first game at point guard but missed all of his early shots, while Johnson came off the bench to make just one of five shots in the first half.

By the fourth quarter, however, the Lakers held on to a four-point lead only to go scoreless for eight miserable minutes as the Rockets went on a 13–0 run that allowed them to take the first game in the Forum. Johnson finished with 20 points off the bench and 13 rebounds but only three assists. Afterward, he was angry and considered dropping off the team, quitting right on the spot, a moment that brought to mind his frustration with Paul Westhead fifteen years earlier.

"Sometimes I wish I was back at point guard, because you can't see the game as well at power forward," he complained. "At point guard, I could tell you what was happening and what was going to be happening two minutes from now—who was going to be hot, who was going to need to get the ball—because you were running the show. At forward, I don't see that, I don't feel that. . . . There's a smaller space to operate; the whole game changes."

"The playoffs went bad," Scott Howard-Cooper recalled. "He was a bad match with Del Harris in a lot of ways just because of their personalities. That started to come out. In the middle of the playoffs Magic starts second-guessing coaching decisions. Del had this very sarcastic response about, 'Well, he should just go ahead and coach the team,' and 'I guess he knows everything.' Del, you know, just isn't going to handle the criticism very well, but he certainly understood that Magic had this kind of megaphone that could turn a minor issue into a major issue."

Olajuwon descended into rare foul trouble, and Johnson scored 26 points in Game 2 that April 27 to lead the Lakers to a 104–94 victory. But Johnson proved mostly ineffective in Games 3 and 4 in Houston as the Lakers' chemistry soured completely and the Rockets claimed the best-of-five series.

"When Winning Time arrived at the Summit this evening, Olajuwon had a basketball and Magic Johnson had a clipboard," Tom Friend of *The New York Times* wrote.

Johnson had played in 32 games, averaging 14.6 points, 6.9 assists, and 5.7 rebounds.

Immediately, the situation turned to his future, with Johnson slated to be a free agent on July 1. When asked about that, he unleashed his frustration. "If the Lakers say, hey, we want to play Nick Van Exel at the point exclusively and not even have me back him up, I'm a grown-up," he told reporters. "I'll just say, 'Thanks, it's been nice.' I know other teams that want me, so I'll go elsewhere."

Of his teammates, he complained, "They get caught up into the little things of egos, and who's taking the shots and how many points they have."

He also admitted another option would be to retire yet again: "If I'm just fed up. If I can't deal with it. If I say, 'Oh man, I thought I could, and I couldn't.' Maybe if I couldn't make the sacrifices anymore. I'd step away nicely. It wouldn't be anything bad."

The comment seemed short on perspective with his thirty-seventh birthday just months away and left reporters wanting an explanation.

"Listen," he told them. "I know where home is. I know where I want to be. I'm not saying I'll just run off. But I want to win, and I want a chance to taste it one more time. I hope it's here. I'll sit down and see what's best. I'm hoping L.A. and feel in my heart it's L.A. I'm home."

A few days later, after a team meeting, his perspective began to soften. "I don't know what I'm going to do," he said. "As of today, I want to play next year. I can't go out like this, I don't want to. This is not my style, this is not what I came back for."

About a week later, Johnson announced his retirement in a prepared statement through Lon Rosen. "I was satisfied with my return to the N.B.A., although I would have hoped we could have gone further into the playoffs," Johnson said. "But now I'm ready to give it up. It's time to move on. I'm going out on my terms, something I couldn't say when I aborted a comeback in 1992."

"We want what is best for Magic," Jerry Buss said in his own prepared statement. "We supported him in his return, and we support him again in his retirement. Despite the disappointment he and our organization felt during the playoffs, the special relationship Earvin continued to have with fans everywhere, myself included, had to make this past season a rewarding one for him."

Jerry West responded by taking the long view, saying, "From the time he came to this team almost 17 years ago, Earvin Johnson has been a very special part of our lives. While this is a sad day, it's one that we always knew would come, and I would rather look at it remembering all the great moments he brought to this team and our fans."

Johnson then saw John Stockton eclipse his all-time record for assists. In 906 regular season games in his career, Johnson had averaged 19.5 points, 7.2 rebounds, and 11.2 assists, for which he had been paid an estimated $40 million in salary. For those who obsess about numbers, Johnson's career stats don't add up to anything to rave about. Yet the telltale all time stat that he rules, assists per game, is his true measure and tells the story of his mastery. In regular season games, Johnson averaged 11.19 assists per game for his career. Stockton is the only other player in the long history of American pro basketball, both the NBA and the ABA, to average double figures in assists over his career (10.51 per game).

However, it is playoff stats where Johnson separates himself from all the other point guards, NBA or ABA. In the playoffs, Johnson averaged a mind-boggling 12.35 assists per game.

Stockton, the only other player to average double figures in playoff assists, is a distant second to Johnson, at 10.10 per game.

With Johnson's astounding passing, his Showtime teams scored lots and lots of acrobatic layups, Elliott "Mr. Stats" Kalb observed in 2004 after watching the three-point shot overwhelm not just the statistics but the aesthetics of the sport.

"It sure was more fun to watch Magic and Worthy and Cooper get up and down the court," he said.

Yet Johnson's three-point stats over his career suggest that he could have easily adapted to the modern game. He made only 22 three-pointers in his first seven seasons but would score 106 of them in 1990 alone.

Clearly whatever occasion the game presented for Johnson, he had been able to rise to it. To those who saw him play, or even better, to those who inhabited the court with him, what he had brought to the game was beyond immeasurable. For so many, it was very hard to see his competitive life end in such fashion.

"We weren't totally surprised," Del Harris said of the announcement. "We knew that was one of the possibilities. But obviously, we're sad to see one of the great players who ever played the game make the decision not to play. I don't feel there was a particular disruption, other than basically a broken heart."

Athletic competition of all sorts has always come with the truth that whatever game you chase, it will always break your heart at some dreaded point and leave you pining after it like an irretrievably lost love. The more you give a game, the more it breaks your heart. And Earvin "Magic" Johnson had given it a lot, had given it a deep and abiding love that it had returned to him in many splendored and wondrous ways. He finally surrendered to that, and he was never a man who surrendered easily. Finally, though, in fits and starts, his very big heart had come to its breaking.

32

THE MESSENGER

The way Johnson played the game, with such joy and surprise, had always made things seem far easier than they were. The same would be true of his efforts to survive the devastating earthquake in his life. Instead of wallowing in self-pity, he chose to view the disease like it was Larry Bird, a top foe to be vanquished, the kind of challenge that Johnson had always relished taking head-on his entire life.

"I'm not scared of death," he would say. "I'm not worried. Everyone else cried for me. I've never cried over HIV. I'm going to beat it."

That sounded nice at the time, but just days later that November after Johnson's announcement, rock icon Freddie Mercury had died of AIDS, news that stunned those around Johnson.

"Back in 1991, it was a death sentence," Lon Rosen said in 2019. "And that's the difference that he made, probably the most significant thing he's done in his life for sure. He saved people's lives by going public with it, not being afraid to say, 'Hey, I made mistakes.' He made a difference in this world. That's more significant than anything he did on the court." *Sports Illustrated*'s Jack McCallum visited Johnson in 2001, on the tenth anniversary of his announcement, and found the forty-two-year-old still battling furiously on the pickup courts of L.A., only now there was no paranoia about blood and sweat, no public mania about banning HIV-infected children from schools. The world, for the most part, had come to terms with the mysterious virus, which by then was still killing about fifteen thousand Americans a year, down from forty thousand in 1991.

The circumstances provided an advantage that would only gain clarity in retrospect. If everybody thinks you're facing certain death, expectations quickly plummet. That, in itself, proved helpful because Johnson's efforts to remake his life, though admirable, would come off in fits and starts. As a result, the public was sometimes left with the impression that he seemed a sad, almost laughable failure, which was far from the truth.

Yet "sex addiction" remained a trail of broken hearts. Such things don't usually end in storybook fashion, and they didn't for Johnson, evidenced by tabloid headlines and Hollywood rumors that suggested he was vulnerable to ham-handed relapses.

Life, however, is a mosaic that reflects a total of many pieces. Johnson would in fact move on from his NBA career while finding an astounding success that featured all sorts of victories even if some of the pieces of his journey seemed to the casual observer to be ragged and disconnected at times.

For many of his fans, Johnson's narrative alone would easily prove the biggest of the many mysteries that enshrouded his efforts. How could he possibly have survived his HIV infection for so many years, all while it had killed millions of others around the globe, millions of people who had desired to keep living every bit as much as Johnson had? By 2001, Johnson headed up a mysterious new category called "long-term nonprogressors," survivors who were living with the virus.

"Somehow," Jerry Buss would declare finally in 2003, "he seems to have made up his mind that he doesn't have the disease."

For years, Johnson's battle with the virus seemed to mirror what he did on the floor. Keep moving, keep forcing the action, trying to make a play, see what your energy and action can produce in the flow.

As a result, year after surprising year, he somehow remained very much the Magic Man, which would eventually prompt writer Jesse Katz to ponder his essence in *Los Angeles Magazine:* "We know, too, that magic is, by definition, false. It is built on deception, on the secret manipulation of our senses. We do not believe in magic so much as we believe in its power to confound."

It was in this stage of his life that all of the reasons for his parents' concern long ago about his nickname came into full clarity. Yet it also remained his signature, his essence.

"Is there any way," Jesse Katz would ask, "Magic Johnson could have become the oversized creation he turned into—on the court, in the boardroom, in the media, in the bedroom—if he had stayed merely Earvin?"

In 1992, who among those around him would have dared to predict that he and Cookie would go on to enjoy a long and successful marriage; that they would adopt a beautiful daughter; that Johnson would become a global phenom in terms of living with HIV; that he and Cookie would welcome grandchildren; that Johnson would grudgingly learn to accept and then embrace a gay son, his namesake no less; that in the midst of his whirlwind of a life he would fail quite miserably and publicly in his "indulgent" quest to be a late-night talk show host; that Johnson could recover from various such missteps and false starts to become in 2013 the public face of the successful Los Angeles Dodgers ownership group; that he would dramatically grow and expand his business interests over the coming decades, almost like a winning hand of cards, adding bold new ventures, discarding others with smart timing, always fully engaged with the commerce that he had first come to admire as a teen; that in 2018 he would become a top executive with the Lakers and would use that position to entice LeBron James to join the team (then soon resign in 2019 in a head-scratching dispute with the club's management), that he would reconcile tearfully with Isiah Thomas, in a televised special, no less; that he and Cookie would celebrate their sixtieth birthdays in 2019 by inviting hundreds of friends on an exotic European vacation, complete with yacht trips, sumptuous meals, and an array of headlining live music; that out of immense disaster would come a life marked by prosperity, the growing of his fortune from estimates of around $100 million at the end of his playing career to more than $600 million by 2020, according to Money.com and numerous other sources.

How, indeed, could such a bold and improbable narrative find the light of day?

Mostly, the answers to the mystery of his good health were numerous, some of them quite prosaic, others clearly poetic.

If they could be reduced to a word, that word might well be "love," notably Johnson's immense love for himself and the love of all his family, especially his wife.

The glue that held it all together would prove to be his immense will to turn life's negatives into positives, made all the stronger by the iron determination displayed by his wife to rescue him from disaster. Taken together, the actions of Cookie Kelly Johnson would prove a thing of rare, if flawed, beauty. As would their lives together.

"She's a saint," Lon Rosen would say in 2019. "That's what she is. And I kid her about it all the time. She's a saint."

A variety of observers, including several journalists, had marveled that Cookie could harbor such deep affection for her husband despite all that he had put her through.

Sports Illustrated's Gary Smith had probed the deeply emotional connection of the couple's union in a profile on Johnson and discovered that it rested at the junction of their faith, in the case of Cookie a long-functioning part of her personality and with Johnson somewhat more newly rediscovered after years of what appeared to be dormancy.

The focus of that faith would become the West Angeles Church of God in Christ, a long-standing Pentecostal megachurch that *Los Angeles Magazine* would describe as "the cathedral of upscale black L.A." with better than 24,000 members.

As Johnson's reasoning went, God had chosen him as an important messenger for this great fight against this horrific contagion.

"He was the chosen one," Cookie told Gary Smith.

The acceptance of that role, Smith suggested, had in turn allowed Johnson to move on from the guilt of his actions to focus on the mission of his efforts, ordained by God himself.

"God has said, 'I want you to be the messenger,'" Johnson offered by way of explanation. "He was trying to get the message through before, but nobody, including myself, was listening. It was so hush-hush, then I got it. Now you talk openly about it."

Openly, indeed. Some observers may have rolled their eyes at Johnson's declarations about being the messenger, but he was in quite the position to shove the issue front and center for the public. And he would do that in his own fashion all while closely monitoring his health and attacking each day like he was facing some sort of junk defense.

Time Zero

Beyond the abiding love of his wife and family, it would be hard to overstate the presence of Jerry Buss in Johnson's hour of need. The revelation of Johnson's infection had traumatized the team owner, but so would age. Court records would suggest that the legendary Buss sex drive had waned dramatically in his sixties, yet he would keep attractive young women around him and on the payroll, to keep up the appearance of his playboy image, according to those records. Still, in terms of Johnson, there would be little need of appearances. Buss's actions spoke clearly and would leave Johnson realizing just how close he had become with the owner.

"When I announced HIV, I knew he was really a father figure in my life," Johnson would say in eulogizing Buss in 2013. "We cried for hours, him not knowing if I would be here 22 years later, thinking he would lose a son, an adopted son. He picked up the phone and started calling hospitals to make sure that I had the best healthcare possible, the best doctors."

Indeed, that medical care would prove the difference in Johnson's efforts to overcome the infection. "We got the greatest doctors," Lon Rosen recalled. "We got this doctor, Dr. David Ho in New York, probably the preeminent doctor, and he put Earvin on a course of treatment and Earvin stuck to it. And it worked."

How good was Dr. Ho? He would be named *Time* magazine's Man of the Year for 1996 for his work in developing protease inhibitors.

That hope would grow year after year as Johnson lived, yet ironically, it also supported the timing of Waymer Moore's 1992 lawsuit against him. It all involved the concept of Time Zero.

"The biggest unknown is what we call Time Zero—when he became infected," Dr. Ho explained in 1996. "If Time Zero was just a few months before he tested positive, then what we've seen with him isn't that unexpected. There are many HIV patients showing no symptoms after four years; the average time before onset of AIDS is about 10 years. If Time Zero was 15 years ago, however, then what we're seeing with him would be extraordinary."

Johnson, of course, would not just live, but live robustly, suggesting that his Time Zero had indeed been short, sometime reasonably close to his 1991 diagnosis. His schedule alone would suggest that each day over the coming decades.

"Earvin just kept going," Rosen said, looking back thirty years later. "He didn't let up."

Thus, Johnson would proceed, armed with God and science and the substantial love of his wife and family and Jerry Buss.

"He would call me all the time, 'You OK? You taking your meds? You doing what you're supposed to do?'" Johnson would recall of Buss. "That's when I knew this man loved me and cared about me outside of winning championships, outside of making no-look passes. That's who Jerry Buss was. He cared about all of his players, not just on the court, but off of the court as well, as men, as people."

Even more important, Johnson would often cite Buss taking the time to teach him how to take a deep look at a business through its numbers, a huge benefit that couldn't have been bestowed on a more willing or more fascinated student.

In retrospect, a cynic might observe that Johnson's efforts in business would mirror his sex life with its dizzying array of partners over the years. Far more important than that, it would mark his maturity into a man driven by a new purpose. Indeed, it would bring the process of his life and personality and nickname to their natural full iteration even alongside his rapidly spinning evolution into a brand, with an astounding scope of successful Magic Johnson products and endeavors, each seemingly born of his supersized animation and energy aimed at making money while seeking to uplift a Black population long denied opportunity in America.

Later, broadcaster Tim Staudt would articulate the wonder from his old friends in Lansing as to how the Johnson they knew could manage to mature into the successful businessman he became. Surely, he was just a front man, went the suggestion. Yes, Johnson had made unimagined gains in the polish and demeanor to achieve such things, but even that couldn't explain such growth in his portfolio. Yes, Johnson had tremendous help in his business life, a remarkable team, Lon Rosen explained. After all, he was a corporate executive, a position generally supported by lots and lots of smart people, beyond Jerry Buss, the various partners and experts who came to his aid, including powerful agent Michael Ovitz and Joe Smith, who had held Lakers season tickets for decades.

"I've never met a guy like him and probably won't," Joe Smith, who had spent years in the music business, would tell journalist Jesse Katz, "with all these contradictory avenues coming out of him. But that's the nature of the man. He's a rare bird. He's in the business of being Magic Johnson." In addition to years of tutelage from Jerry Buss and studying business everywhere he went in the NBA, Johnson had also soaked up the guidance of his longtime financial manager, Warren Grant, who had all sorts of high-profile clients, folks like Ray Liotta and Cher. None of them pored over expense reports and financial numbers like Johnson, Grant said.

"We had a conversation once," Reggie Theus would recall in 2019, "where we were talking about going from playing sports to the business world and how they correlate and how they parallel each other and why people like to hire former athletes because they understand teamwork, they understand hard work, they understand what fair competition is all about. And he said to me—and I thought this was really great—'Reggie, I'm still the point guard; I'm just the point guard in the boardroom.' In other words, nothing has changed for him. He's just directing his no-look passes or directing his team in another way."

Those no-look passes came often and early to his associates, including what seemed like a revolving door of personal assistants charged with trying to keep up with him. As the years rolled by, his days seemed to start earlier, with him often at his desk at Magic Johnson Enterprises seven floors up in a Beverly Hills office building, from where he could zing the ball to any one of his thirty-five or so employees. That was just in his investment firm. The businesses he owned or controlled would have more than twenty thousand employees, he would boast to NPR in 2003, a number that would grow from there.

Los Angeles Magazine would reveal that occasionally those thirty-five employees in the home office would refer to the operation as the "Magic Johnson Slave Ship."

As the point guard Theus described, Johnson was driven to push those around him.

"I'm Kunta," Ken Lombard, president of the Johnson's development corporation, jokingly told Jesse Katz. "I knew Earvin as a basketball player, so I figured he was a nice guy."

Magic, the point guard, set the tone with their first meeting, Lombard recalled. "Earvin kind of leaned over and said, 'Boy, if you mess up my money, I will fuck you up.' True story. That's Earvin the businessman."

"Anyone who thinks Magic is a success because of his personality doesn't know business," Jerry Buss said. "A lot of famous athletes open one restaurant with their name on it. Compare that to having an empire."

As a point guard, he knew how to rule with fear, but the critical parts, the vision and the singular ideas, came from nowhere but Johnson himself, seeded first in his late grade school years by afternoons parked in a Lansing movie theater munching his beloved popcorn and absorbing the wonders and delight of cinema, an essential part of his education. Generally, Johnson's first big idea was another sort of no-look pass that grew out of his observation that movie theaters weren't located in minority neighborhoods, as Johnson referred to them. He reasoned that if they were, cinemas would find a brisk business environment there.

He offered the same idea to Howard Schultz, the chairman and CEO of Starbucks, a company that did not franchise its stores. Yet Schultz offered a franchise option to Johnson based on his ideas. Soon the Magic Johnson brand offered four dozen coffeehouses in minority neighborhoods, a number that would grow to more than one hundred.

Yet it was the movie theater pitch circa 1993 that truly elevated his business game and brought him into closer contact with Peter Guber, who would become a major business partner over the years.

"He calls to meet with me," Guber recalled in a 2023 interview. "At the time, I was the chairman of Lowe's Theaters, one of the largest exhibition circuits in America, in the world. It was part of Sony, and I was chairman of that as well. We were building these large, really large twenty-screen theater complexes around the world. Manhattan, San Francisco, Chicago, even Germany."

Johnson knew the chairman of Sony a bit socially, so he and Ken Lombard—described by Lon Rosen as the incredibly effective president of Johnson's development corporation—were able to get a meeting. The presentation would prove to be not just a special moment in Johnson's life but in the history of American business. Two Black men were making a pitch to one of the most powerful figures in global media.

"They came to the office and sat down," Guber said. "I had no idea what they were coming to see me about, no idea at all. They came in and said, 'We know you are building theaters all over the world. We also know that what's important to you is that you have an audience that wants to see those films, wants to go to those films, an audience with a movie-going appreciation.'"

Johnson asked, "What if I told you about a place that had an incredible movie appetite, an audience that just loved movies and went to them any time they could, and it was a place that didn't really have any good theaters?"

"It's a place," Guber recalled Johnson saying, "where the theaters are old and not so good, maybe like in the Caribbean, where the theaters are really old barns without decent projection, where the audience tries to come, but it's not a good experience. What if we told you about a land where they love movies and still go constantly, a place where it would be great to build new theaters?"

"I'm ready, man," Guber replied, taking the bait. "A place where there is a good theater-going audience and no good theaters? That's a place where we want to be."

"Well, it's fifteen minutes from here," Johnson told the Sony chairman. "It's Baldwin Hills. That and thirty more places in America where the African American community is completely underserved—with theaters that are not good, all old projection, old screens, poor hospitality."

Baldwin Hills was a neighborhood in South Los Angeles long known as the "Black Beverly Hills."

"I said, 'Wow,'" Guber recalled. "Magic began to show me the numbers and figures about it. It was startling, and it was absolutely true, a place totally missed by the industry."

Although the theater industry was in full expansion mode at that time, it had no plans to build in Black communities. "We got in the car and went down to Baldwin Hills, looked at the theater. . . . It was a startling presentation. And when we brought our other people in, and he made the same presentation to them, our other folks in the Lowes group . . . it was equally startling to them.

"I said, 'You got a deal. We'll make a deal with your company to do it everywhere in America that fits this criteria.' I mean it was a no-brainer. He was so smart in his presentation and so clever in pointing out, 'Why go to Yugoslavia when you have an audience right here, sitting and waiting for an opportunity?' We were looking for places to do it, and it was right here in front of us. But our own narrowness, our own prejudice—I don't mean prejudice in the narrow sense, but prejudice in the broad sense—kept us from seeing it. It was right in front of us. And so we embarked and made a deal with them, a complete deal for their company, Magic Johnson Theaters."

Johnson's big victory would come that summer of 1995, when the first of his "Magic Johnson Theaters"—described repeatedly as a "state-of-the-art 12-screen cineplex in South Central Los Angeles," not far from where the L.A. riots had begun. Johnson's theater soon vaulted into the rankings of the top earners in the industry, the kind of victory that attracted not just accolades but the financing from Sony to launch sister operations in "minority neighborhoods" in Detroit, Houston, New York, and Washington, D.C., every bit of it due to his vision. The instant success launched Johnson into his new life, one based on no-look ideas rather than no-look passes.

"He went from a taste of a deal to being the entrepreneurial leader of the enterprise," Guber said. "He went from designing to execution, to promotion, to success. We went through all of the steps that an entrepreneur with an idea would have to [go through to have] the control that he had. He was the boss."

"I came out of there that night covered with lipstick," Johnson would tell Gary Smith of that first theater opening in South Central L.A. "People telling me, 'I've been in this community for 40 years, and nothing ever happened like this.' Wives crying, thanking me for creating jobs, for changing their husbands' lives. Me crying, too, the happiest day of my life. I felt God was taking me and saying, 'This is what I want you to do.' It was a different love than I got on the court. It wasn't attached to winning. This love's forever.'"

It wouldn't be forever, of course. In time, Johnson would sell the theaters and the Starbucks to move into even more lucrative activities. But at the time it sure felt like forever. More importantly, the point had been made to the business community, and then reinforced when the opening of *Waiting to Exhale* later that year produced eight lines, each estimated to be the length of a football field, of people eager to get into Johnson's theater. "It changed the perspective of a lot of companies toward that marketplace," Guber said. "He understood that marketplace, he understood the moviegoer in that marketplace. He understood entertainment in that marketplace. He understood the Black, African American imprimatur on a business . . . what it could mean. And he took advantage of it, good advantage, for the community, for himself, for the business itself."

The theater success became a major factor in Johnson's very big American life.

"I think it was a seminal experience for him," Guber said, "because, what happened was he found it, had the idea, knew how to sell it, knew how to tell it, knew who to sell and tell it to, had a relationship capital with the people he went to, took advantage of that, and then delivered with his feet, tongue, heart and wallet. He played a full hand of cards, he really did. He could see how his background experience with the African American community, with the business community, became incredibly important to him." Indeed, his money seemed to be growing across the board, with *Sports Illustrated* soon estimating that his 4.5 percent share in the Lakers had soared to a value of $200 million. That was perhaps generous, but the value of his Lakers shares would continue to grow until years later when he would divest them on his way to being the front man for the group that would purchase the Dodgers.

The winding road to Dodgers ownership would begin in the late 1990s, when Guber recruited Johnson to join a long-shot effort in minor league baseball, creating the Dayton Dragons.

"We decided we were gonna build a stadium in a rust belt city, largely African American dominated," Guber recalled. "We knew that he would be a really good partner to have in that marketplace. The journey was long, arduous, and completely uncertain, because building the whole stadium was different from taking over an existing stadium and running the whole business. Building a stadium where there was no team, no proven audience, in a market that was completely rust belt and rundown . . . We were going to build this beautiful new Single-A stadium in Dayton, which was suffering badly."

The challenge and the gamble grew deeper than expected, but Johnson held fast and played another key role, Guber explained.

"He put energy, money, and time into it, reputation, too. We built the stadium, opened it, and held our breath. On opening day, Magic agreed to fly out to Dayton and throw out the first pitch. Everyone wasn't sure what was gonna happen. But, of course, it was a total smash. The Dayton Dragons became synonymous with success for minor league baseball. Broke records for years. Still do."

They later partnered on another minor league club in Frisco, Texas, and after that Guber brought Johnson in to help start the Los Angeles Football Club, a second soccer team for the city. "He put his money up, his time up," Guber said of the soccer endeavor. "He's showed up, and he's made a big part of the success."

This all led to Johnson playing a key role in forming the group to buy the Dodgers in 2012. This time it was Johnson recruiting Guber, who owned a Dodgers minor-league affiliate.

"Magic came to my house with Mark Walter and convinced me to buy the Dodgers with them," Guber said.

Mysteriously, when Guber later became part of a group that bought the Golden State Warriors and that group wanted to add a basketball mind to the partnership, Johnson declined to be part of it.

Instead, the new Warriors owners turned to Jerry West to fill that role. Guber never knew specifically why Johnson turned down the offer, but he guessed it had something to do with Johnson's loyalty to the Lakers.

"The point is," Guber said, "Magic was always willing to participate, add value, and listen. As brilliant as he is, he's coachable. That's part of the reason he was so successful."

Another reason, perhaps, that he turned down the Warriors group is that he had turned to his business endeavors full-time, stuffing his vast energy into every nook and cranny he could find, traveling fifteen, twenty, even twenty-five days a month sometimes in search of the next something that allowed him to reach and touch and feel people, doing every sort of thing to keep it all headed in the right direction.

At the very same time Johnson was expanding his relationship with Guber, he went into business with Howard Schultz and Starbucks, sort of a quid pro quo with Schultz, who wanted access to the NBA world with thoughts of team ownership. "Magic was introducing Schultz to everybody," explained Henry Abbott of *TrueHoop* in a 2019 interview.

During this period, Johnson would also join an unsuccessful effort to bring the NFL back to Los Angeles. He would also form a group to take ownership of the WNBA's Los Angeles Sparks.

Those efforts would be followed in turn by his move into Esports, saying in 2022 that he never dreamed he would be "paying a guy a million dollars a year" to play video games competitively. It all showed a Johnson willing to cross whatever business horizon appeared on the landscape.

Those would be followed by many more business partnerships—a mortgage company, a bank, an insurance company—all of it aimed at serving Black Americans in a financial sector that had long denied and limited their participation in home ownership and other wealth-building activities.

Noted among his grandest successes would be the acquisition of SodexoMagic, his food services contracting firm, in 2008, and his ascension to becoming the controlling shareholder in 2015 of EquiTrust Life Insurance Co., which was well on its way to growing into a $23 billion concern.

The unleashing of his full energy into the business life would leave Cookie longing for the days when he was actually playing. Yes, he traveled then, too, but nothing like the schedule that his business life required, filling seemingly nearly every possible minute.

Yes, he would still wake some nights, jolted from his dreamy peace of mind, to rise and watch it all again, running back the video of himself in those moments, squeezing again everything he could from the dream. Was it real? Had it all really happened like that? Had he conquered the world with his joy, with that smile, with his unbreakable insistence on believing in his own strange genius?

His business life didn't seem so much of an enterprise, as he would call it, but a great searching for the many places to employ his gifts. In the midst of all that, he still relied on his immense sense of joy, and still managed to find time for friends, old and new. That large group would come to include Michigan State coach Tom Izzo, who had followed Jud Heathcote as the steward of Johnson's beloved Spartans, to everything sacred that basketball in Lansing was to him.

"When he comes in, he is so tuned in to our guys," Izzo said of Johnson in 2019. "You can't believe this guy. He must watch every game. He knows everybody on our team by name. A new group of players? It doesn't matter. He's done that a lot. Over the course of his career, he hasn't missed many of our NCAA runs. He used to fly back, once he got his plane, and pick up his dad in Lansing."

Johnson and Big Earv and brother Larry would delight over the years in their adventures following Izzo's teams. Johnson would revel in the entire scene of the college postseason, including sitting in hotel lobbies and happily signing autographs for the MSU faithful. And when the scene would move to the arena? More autographs.

"I'd look across and there'd be a line for him," Izzo said in 2019, chuckling. "The opposing team would go over there and get his autograph. He's such an effervescent people guy."

He found his way to wherever the Spartans unearthed glory. He was there in 2000 when Michigan State defeated Florida for the national title and later in Indy and in Detroit when they beat the University of Connecticut and in D.C. in 2019 when they upset top-ranked Duke and Zion Williamson.

That big win against Duke was special, Izzo recalled. "Earvin was jacked, man. After listening to his pregame speech, I wanted to play."

That same Magic vibe would just keep on rolling through the greater Lansing community over the years, running deep into its bones with the memory that it was a special place. That sense that they had shared in his greatness could often overflow at Thanksgiving over the years at gatherings at one of Gregory Eaton's establishments.

"Everybody loves seeing him," his old mentor Joel Ferguson recalled in 2019. "Every Thanksgiving, he's home. Everyone comes over to Gregory's and plays cards. And it's really a big deal because it's with the people he grew up with in Lansing. It's a gathering where everyone is just down-to-earth. Everybody just comes there to have a good time. There's no caste system. Everybody is the same. And he sets that tone. Nobody is being big-time. These are all his friends and he treats them like he treated them when they were on the playground or shooting baskets at school. There's huge crowds. There'd be an overflow of people, hundreds of people. They're fun. Everybody looks forward to the day after Thanksgiving."

Lansing could always pull him back to who he was, who he had been on the rise, standing tall and doing all the things that only he could do.

All of the moments, making speeches, hugging clients and employees, signing autographs, throwing parties, spreading that rare gift of love from his mother, it all flowed like a river out of Johnson into the world around him.

And when his and Cookie's sixtieth birthdays neared in 2019, it soon became obvious that he had spent lots of time envisioning the special moment in its every detail. It wasn't just any old birthday. No, no. It was nothing like that. It was a statement from the guy who was certain to die, who with the love of his wife had kept living. Johnson was ready with every detail of an over-the-top extravaganza in southern Europe that cost him millions to celebrate their lives while entertaining hundreds of friends and loved ones.

"Unbelievable," said Greg Eaton, the other business mentor from his youth. "I've done a lot of things, I've been to a lot of parties but this one. . . . You had billionaires there. No bodyguards. He had you picked up in a Mercedes. I mean, it was the greatest thing I've ever seen. A-Rod and his girlfriend were there. Spike Lee was there. Cedric the Entertainer. Isiah Thomas was there, Steve Smith was there, the great baseball player Dave Winfield was there, Judge Greg Mathis. It was a who's who. Everybody that was somebody was there. Him and Cookie has been going there for forty years or so. We were there five days. They rented this yacht, which was more than a million dollars a week. He had a party at this beach: a hundred thousand dollars' worth of champagne.

"And they had this big sand thing built for Cookie and Magic and it said 'Happy Birthday.' And they had this castle in Capri, overlooking the water. He took that over and he had a stage built by the side of the mountain and that's where the band was. And then they had this group of performers that swings around, swinging from the mountain with spotlights on them. He had these girls all sprayed gold, naked, serving drinks. I mean, it was just unbelievable. I figured the party cost him about six or seven million dollars."

It was an overwhelming spectacle, Lon Rosen agreed. "They had an amazing sixtieth birthday party. I sat there in Monte Carlo with Pat Riley and all these people saying, 'Just you look at what this guy's accomplished and what she's accomplished because they do it together.' I don't know how many people might have been there, four hundred, five hundred people in Monte Carlo. He put on a show, you know. He wanted everyone to have a great time. He spent a lot of money, but he enjoyed every minute of it."

Back Home

If there was a moment that displayed the full circle of Earvin Johnson's life, it might well have been his visit in March 2022 to speak at

North Carolina A&T University in Greensboro, one of the country's largest historically Black colleges and universities.

He would note for the crowd at the school's Harrison Auditorium that they weren't far from Tarboro, the ancestral home for much of his mother's family, where he spent time as a youth. "I came here every summer to help my aunts and uncles, pickin' peanuts," he recalled. "It was hot, too."

As he spoke, Johnson presented a towering, massively larger-than-life figure, yet almost sleek, nowhere near as sleek as his playing days, of course, but impressively imposing all the same in his finely tailored suit.

Looking across the rows of young, hopeful faces, he unleashed the full wattage of his smile only to cough up an immediate miscue, telling everybody he was happy to be at "North Carolina AT&T."

Instead of trying to swiftly move past it, he stopped abruptly, eyebrows raised in alarm, and declared that he had just committed a "turnover," then shared a good laugh at himself with everyone.

It wouldn't be his only mea culpa of the evening as he talked openly about his mistakes along with his many successes in the world of business. For example, some of his early retail ventures struggled, he said. "I made the mistake of buying things that I liked. Never make your business about you."

He proceeded into a thoroughly engaging performance, the kind he delivered routinely in his dizzying schedule of appearances around the country in support of his investment interests, all of it aimed at touting his gospel of business and markets and free enterprise and how important they were, not only to him and to the next generation but to the Black community at large.

The mere presence of businesses "drives up property values in minority communities," he said. "If somebody else owns the business, a lot of dollars are drained out of the community."

He would reel off a list of his impressive accomplishments from Magic Johnson Enterprises to SodexoMagic to another venture successfully gaining infrastructure contracts renovating major airports.

"Now we employ about 30,000 African Americans across the country," he said, "and I'm proud of that. What keeps me up at night is my brand making mistakes and doing the wrong thing. My whole life is opening the door for other minorities so they can be successful. . . . Cookie and I have sent 10,000 minority students to college. We're proud of that. Building up black America is what I've been able to do."

A lack of access to technology in lower-income neighborhoods was a problem that he and Cookie had attacked, he said. "We built 20 technology centers across the country. New York, Chicago, Atlanta . . ."

Another problem he has addressed is the dearth of WiFi and broadband in those same communities. Many of his goals had been accomplished, he said, with partnerships with "pastors in cities across America."

He said he was scheduled immediately after his talk to fly to New Orleans to close a deal there on a massive contract that will provide even more jobs.

"Before, I was chasing all the deals," he said of his early years in business, but his efforts had brought cumulative change. "Now I get deal flow coming to me."

In his early ventures, he said, he encountered resistance from institutional lenders and potential business partners who tended to treat him like an athlete. So, it was no surprise that among his portfolio of investments were financial institutions focused on serving "minority communities."

His one-hour presentation poured forth straight from his heart, pretty much all of it seamlessly and passionately and succinctly delivered without so much as a single note.

"Here I am, a former basketball player," he told the gathering. "My dreams were not just to play in the NBA. My dreams were to play in the NBA AND become a businessman."

He told them of Lansing's two Black businessmen who had been such powerful role models for him.

"Two men changed my life," he said and explained how he cleaned their offices at night, how he would slip into the executive suite to kick back in the executive chair, put his feet up on the desk and dream of being a big shot.

He filled his talk with facts, noting, for example, that African Americans now boasted as a group $1.8 trillion in spending power.

The problem for would-be entrepreneurs of color was that "building a business requires us to use other people's money," he said, thus his many efforts at creating access to capital for the next generation. Urban America has long been short on both housing and retail, he explained, recalling that he once bought a shopping center in a minority neighborhood for $22 million.

"You're crazy," the previous owner told him as they were closing the deal.

He later sold it for $48 million, he said.

In the question-and-answer period at the end of his talk, one student asked if he had ever been a victim of discrimination and how he had overcome it.

"Of course, I was disrespected. But that's part of it," he replied.

"I sit here with a twenty-three-billion-dollar company," he added, offering a moment of triumph for that epic struggle of his ancestors across the generations.

"I'm proud of being a black man in America."

Lakers Again

The other big event on Johnson's 2022 schedule harkened back to the teenaged Magic taking to the "phone tree" or whatever it was to connect with all of his Everett High teammates, significant or otherwise, to pump them up for a summer league game.

This time around, the matter was Johnson's big idea of getting each and every one of his Showtime teammates to Hawaii in September for a reunion. First, he recruited Pat Riley, who was immediately all in. The two of them would pony up for an all-expenses-paid trip to paradise for six days to kick around the old times. They even got the notoriously stingy Lakers to kick in a little extra support.

The phone tree involved Johnson calling up each and every member of the clan to issue the invitation personally. He eventually tracked Mike Smrek to Canada and even managed to locate Chuck Nevitt. All seemed truly shocked to get a call from Johnson after all the decades.

"The fringe players were just as important to Earvin as the stars," Lon Rosen said, adding that no other team could have pulled off such a reunion. "You couldn't bring the Bulls together, for example. They were so fractured by their last season."

The Lakers in attendance rose and offered moving recollections of the old days, none more powerful than Spencer Haywood, long healed and recovered from the cocaine binge that led to his dismissal in the middle of the 1980 championship series. Now a Hall of Famer and a man in good standing across the basketball community, Haywood spoke of his regret for those low moments, this in the wake of the recent passing of his wife.

The love from all was in abundance, Rosen reported.

Riley again worked his video magic by putting together amazing footage of the era, including a fascinating look at Game 6 in 1980. "Watching these guys watch the highlights of that year was amazing," Rosen said. "They were yelling like it was happening today. All of them. Like kids yelling."

There as the star of that footage was Earvin Johnson, that grinning young rookie, now a tower of success in his sixties.

Yet, looking at all that had been won also sent thoughts of all that had been lost. In so many ways, Johnson's HIV announcement had overwhelmed and obscured so much of the greatness he had managed to conjure up so magically. "It was really bad. It was really sad," said Rosen of those dark days when Johnson's T-cell count plunged into dangerous territory, along with it his image and reputation.

"As time goes on, it grows sadder with me," Rosen acknowledged, in terms of what had been lost of the special light that Johnson had cast for so long. "He loved his job. He loved his fans, and he loved his teammates."

Yes, Johnson's supersized life was the kind of thing that left old friends like Dale Beard reaching for a little perspective. Asked in 2019 for the long view of Johnson's journey and what it had revealed about his most special qualities, Beard had replied, "Man, there's a bunch of them, but you know, just his personality, that love for people, just his enjoyment of seeing other people happy."

Beard cited his own relationship with Johnson as an example of that. After his years of competing and coaching, Beard had wound up in Los Angeles, where Johnson had helped him get a job in the Lakers organization coaching its Development League team for a number of years. It had been great fun, but eventually Beard had come to miss his daughter back in Lansing and decided to return there.

"He's done so much for me that people don't see," Beard explained.

Johnson was disappointed at Beard's decision and hadn't let him forget it, he recalled.

"I've been hearing that for years," Beard said, "but our relationship has been so strong where, even when we cannot see each other for a time, I can see him tomorrow and we never miss a beat. We never skip a beat. And I think that's what's so intriguing to me about him, because there's been times where I wonder how he does it. You know, I mean really. I just don't know. How does he do what he does, you know, with all the business ventures and the traveling, you know, the phone calls and meetings and stuff like that he has to attend to?"

The sheer scope of it alone, all the victory and celebration, all the trials and tribulations, the incredible highs and incomprehensible lows, all the gaudy success, the grandiose mojo of it all is overwhelming just to contemplate, Beard said slowly.

"I look back and just say, 'Wow.'"

"He's earned it," Peter Guber said, summing up Magic Johnson. "He was born under a lucky star. But he's earned it. To be clear. He has earned it. Fully and totally. He deserves it. I always knew that being with that kind of person, good things rub off. It definitely rubbed off on me. I saw the way he comported himself, the way he behaved, the way he was with people. And it made me understand the value of that. It was something that inspired me."

Yet, it's far more than his story, as magnificent as it is. It's Ferebe's and Ben Jenkins's and old man Isiah Porter's and that special woman, Mary Della Jenkins Porter, and Christine and Big Earv—all of them eventually bound magically by a game, by the tall boy who knew at a young age that it was what we do together that indeed matters—just be sure to keep your eyes open and your hands ready, your head up, no ducking allowed, see all that you can, do all you can do, to slip into the great flow, fully inspired to hear what he called "my music."

Nod and bump, smile if you can. Let it play. Let it all play.

ACKNOWLEDGMENTS

"Earvin wants to think it over."

That's how his friend and agent, Lon Rosen, responded in November 2018 when I asked about Magic Johnson cooperating on a book about his life.

"It's not going to take a lot of his time," I told Rosen. "This is a story that's going to be mostly told by those around him, by all the people he encountered over the years."

Earvin takes his time in making these decisions, Rosen explained.

Sure enough, two months passed before Rosen contacted me in early 2019 to say that Earvin would cooperate.

With that, I set about interviewing the array of people who witnessed Johnson's rise to prominence, especially so many people from the formative years of his life growing up in Lansing, Michigan, about which little had been written.

This effort at interviewing the many witnesses to Johnson's career was immensely aided by my friend and longtime NBA journalist Gery J. Woelfel, whose help was invaluable for me in taking on the daunting challenge of writing about Johnson's very big life through the eyes of those who encountered him. Woelfel himself conducted more than three dozen interviews with various figures around the NBA. He brought angles to the story I could never have imagined.

As for the people who afforded me the opportunity to see Johnson through their eyes, high school coaches George Fox and Pat Holland each agreed to dozens of interviews with me about their experiences with the amazing teen that was Earvin Johnson, as did his friend and major advisor, Dr. Charles Tucker, as did his personal lawyer and representative for the first eight seasons of his playing career, George Andrews.

Tucker's love for the Johnson family and his presence in so many important moments literally opened the doors and windows for this project, as did Andrews's sense of humor and lawyerly perspective and absolute dedication to Johnson. With Rosen's immense input, Johnson's trio of ardent advisors over the years had explained so much that was exceptional about my subject.

The recollections of Johnson mentors Gregory Eaton and Joel Ferguson of their relationships with Johnson and his family were most illuminating.

I've often asked myself what is the true fun of my work. It's the interviewing and research over the years that have created the special moments talking with exceptional people about their memories that in turn create special parts of the story on the page.

For this project, there were many talks with Sandra Jones King, a contemporary of Johnson's mother, Christine, in North Carolina, who so ably conveyed what it felt like to be a Black teen in the southern culture of the 1940s and '50s. A career educator and Missionary Baptist minister as well as the wife of a basketball coach and the daughter of a Black farmer, Mrs. King brought a humbling perspective not only to the book but to my personal education.

I can't begin to express those same values that emerged from my many talks with the late Matthew Prophet, Jr., who brought to life the Mississippi culture that he and Johnson's father, Earvin Sr., emerged from in the 1930s and '40s, and the inside view Prophet provided of the efforts to desegregate Lansing's schools in the 1970s. Prophet generously offered me many private interview moments with a man I consider a great American.

There was the delight of two of George Fox's children, Missy and Gary, who provided extraordinary memories of the life of young Earvin, as did his high school teammates Dale Beard, Bruce Fields, and Leon Stokes, whose recollections captured the youthful Earvin's mix of sweetness and fire.

Teammates Ron Charles and Jay Vincent and Gregory Kelser likewise gave us a view of Johnson, the college star, and his relationship with Jud Heathcote, as did Charles Tucker and George Fox and Pat Holland and Bill Duffy. Also key there was my longtime friend and coauthor of five books, the great Billy Packer, who spoke honestly about just how the basketball intelligentsia of the 1970s struggled to understand Johnson's gifts. I owe many thanks to Sonny Vaccaro, another friend and basketball icon, who influenced the game in his own profound ways.

Jack "Goose" Givens revealed the dynamic of Johnson's disastrous 1978 regional final game against Kentucky.

Tremendous contributions were provided by many journalists, who offered their "outtakes" as memories, their experiences with Johnson and figures such as Jerry Buss that never made their newspaper stories or broadcasts. These moments often presented Johnson's true nature.

From Michigan, I am indebted to the generosity of Fred Stabley, Jr., Mick McCabe, Tim Staudt, and Charlie Vincent in their interviews, as well as to the great basketball writer Dick Weiss, in Philadelphia.

As always, I am indebted to psychologist, mindfulness guru, and my dear friend George Mumford and to our mutual friend, the late Tex Winter.

For the Los Angeles part of the story, it's hard to overstate the help provided by Steve Springer, Scott Howard-Cooper, and Larry Burnett (whose lengthy, excellent career as a broadcaster has somehow become overlooked) and the late, great Mitch Chortkoff, who was so gracious in sharing with me his decades of experience covering the Lakers.

Telling the inside story of the Lakers in that era was made possible by Jeanie Buss, who granted four different interviews. In addition, dozens of others—teammates, friends, opponents, media figures—agreed to offer their take on Earvin Johnson, Jr., including Roy Englebrecht, Rosen, Jim Chones, Paul Westhead, Rudy Garciduenas, Pat Williams, Lionel Hollins, Tony Brown, Mike Dunleavy, Jimmy Eyen, Scott Williams, Nick Van Exel, Greg Foster, Danny Schayes, Reggie Theus, Tony Smith, Sonny Vaccaro, and Ron Carter.

I have done numerous projects on the Lakers and the NBA over the past three decades and in that time have built a substantial archive of personal interviews that helped form the basis of my knowledge and understanding of the team, interviews that played a key role in this project, including with Magic Johnson, Christine Johnson, Jerry West, Kareem Abdul-Jabbar, Chick Hearn, Jerry Buss, Jack Kent Cooke, Bill Sharman, Red Auerbach, Bob Steiner, Isiah Thomas, Joe Dumars, Paul Westhead, Pat Riley, James Worthy, Byron Scott, Michael Cooper, Gary Vitti, John Radcliffe, Herb Williams, Mary Lou Liebich, Josh Rosenfeld, Lou Adler, Kevin McHale, and Jerry Sichting, among others included for this project.

As for Johnson's involvement, it wasn't until late 2019 when I went to Los Angeles for my first interview with Johnson himself (I had interviewed him at other times over the decades for various Lakers projects) that I learned that Johnson wasn't so sure about cooperating.

We proceeded with that status over five years, with Johnson occasionally responding to inquiries through Rosen.

Frankly, I wasn't surprised, after I thought about it. Johnson was the Controller. Had been all of his life. It was a huge part of the essence of his greatness. He had found so many ways to exert surprising levels of control over the basketball landscape, even as a young teen.

Cooperating on a biography over which he had little control was a game he just couldn't bring himself to play, much like a pickup game in which he wouldn't be allowed to call his own fouls.

It all reminded me of a comment Johnson made in 1992 after I told him of an interview I did with his mother, who talked about running into one of his grade school teachers. "She shouldn't be telling you my secrets," he told me.

In all fairness, not many figures like being the subject of a biography, an independent account of their lives. After all, Johnson has already done two as-told-to books about his life and career and was at work producing a docuseries about his life.

Cooperate with an independent project, give up control of his narrative? It wasn't going to happen. However, true to his word, Lon Rosen remained involved in this project and granted me literally dozens of interviews, taking the time to mull over major questions, particularly about Johnson's life in Los Angeles.

Beyond Gery Woelfel's huge effort—he conducted more than three dozen interviews—I owe thanks to many for their considerable contributions, first of all to my wife, Karen, for the many hours she put in helping me transcribe interview recordings, reading the manuscript, and so much else. For literally forty-eight years, she has been the sun in my life and those of our three children—Jenna, Henry, and Morgan—and our three grandchildren—Liam, Aiden, and Freya.

Then there's my editor at Celadon Books, Ryan Doherty, who plowed so much work and faith into guiding this massive project along toward publication. Many, many thanks, Ryan, for your patience and diligence and belief and dedication and hard work, but most especially for challenging me in the many facets of this project. And to his assistant editor, Cecily van Buren-Freedman, who kept so many things moving in the right direction.

Deserving special mention is the stalwart and amazing work of copy editor Fred Chase, production editor Jeremy Pink, and production manager Vincent Stanley.

I would be remiss if I didn't cite the entire team at Celadon, including publisher Deb Futter, former publisher Jamie Raab, associate publisher Rachel Chou, Anne Twomey (creative director for the cover), cover designer Erin Cahill, and the marketing/publicity team: Jennifer Jackson, Jaime Noven, Rebecca Ritchey, and Sandra Moore.

Anna Belle Hindenlang was lead publicist, part of a team that included public relations director Christine Mykityshyn, as well as publicist Liza Buell.

I also want to thank Elisa M. Rivlin for her excellent legal review of the manuscript.

Dear friend Larry Burnett dug deep in his broadcasting archive to provide wonderful interviews with the great Chick Hearn.

Xu Li was quite important with detailed analysis of Johnson's statistical record as a pro player, particularly Li's analysis of Johnson's playoffs and NBA Finals records.

Longtime agent and dear friend Richard Kaner used his many contacts in the hoops world to make key interviews possible.

Ramon Maclin with the Charleston County Public Library in South Carolina went out of his way to find research connections, as did basketball lifer and good friend David Solomon.

I am also indebted to the great Mo Howard, Maj. Gen. Cedric Wins, longtime friends Jorge Ribeiro and Bob Benninger and Dan Smith, Neil Sagebiel, and my daughter Morgan for reading portions of the manuscript.

Also, many thanks to that most impressive of pro basketball's great communicators, Boston Celtics media relations maestro Jeff Twiss, as well as the incomparable Tim Hallam, doing the same work for the Chicago Bulls, and to the legendary Arthur Triche, who for years filled the same vital role with the Atlanta Hawks, plus another great basketball PR guy, the late Matt Dobek with the Pistons. The list also has to include John Black, the former PR head for the Lakers. Each of them played a role in guiding my career, as have so many other great figures, all true pilgrims and guardians of the game we love.

BIBLIOGRAPHY

"16 Cage Tourney Games at 16 Centers." *Detroit Free Press,* Mar. 1976, Newspapers.com. Accessed Oct. 2020.

"151 Tickets, That's All Folks." *Detroit Free Press,* Mar. 1978, Newspapers.com. Accessed Oct. 2019.

"1977: The Year's Biggest Stories." *Lansing State Journal,* Jan. 1978, Newspapers.com. Accessed Dec. 2020.

Abdul-Jabbar, Kareem, and Peter Knobler. *Giant Steps: The Autobiography of Kareem Abdul-Jabbar* New York: Bantam, 1983.

Alexander, Jim. "This Year, Magic Is Using Camp to Get into Shape." (Riverside) *Press Enterprise,* Oct. 1989, Newspapers.com.

Alvarado, Yolanda. "Summer Reading Program Uses Dash of 'Magic.'" *Lansing State Journal,* July 1985, Newspapers.com. Accessed Apr. 2020.

Amdur, Neil. "A New Type of Owner in Sports Establishment." *New York Times,* May 1979.

Anderson, Dave. "He Loved the Surf." *San Bernardino County Sun,* Apr. 1979, Newspapers.com. Accessed Jan. 2021.

"Another Title: Spartan Cagers Capture Governor's Cup." *Lansing State Journal,* Sept. 1978, Newspapers.com. Accessed Dec. 2020.

Araton, Harvey. "Pro Basketball; Magic vs. Michael: Coming Back to Reality." *New York Times,* Feb. 1996.

"Area's Lone Hope Everett?" *Lansing State Journal,* Mar. 1976, Newspapers.com. Accessed Mar. 2020.

The Arsenio Hall Show. https://www.youtube.com/watch?v=CkbaBnzmQIY.

Associated Press. "'Busy Day Marred by Failures." *Lansing State Journal,* Aug. 1959, Newspapers.com. Accessed June 2020.

———. "Top Clubs." *Herald-Palladium* (Michigan), Mar. 1976, Newspapers.com. Accessed Oct. 2020.

Auld, Ute. "Tucker's a Troubleshooter." *Lansing State Journal,* Apr. 1974, Newspapers.com. Accessed Nov. 2020.

Bailey, Rick. "Will Flex Their Muscles." *Lexington* (Kentucky) *Herald,* Mar. 1979, Newspapers.com. Accessed Jan. 2021.

Barkin, Jesse. "Injury Keeps Johnsons from Meeting Again." *Los Angeles Daily News,* Dec. 1989.

———. "Scott Hopes Magic Was Not Offended." *Los Angeles Daily News,* Jan. 1992, Newspapers.com.

———. "Scott Undaunted by Magic's Words." *Los Angeles Daily News,* Feb. 1992, Newspapers .com.

"Basketball: Earvin Is Still Magic." (Port Huron, MI) *Times Herald,* Aug. 1978, Newspapers.com. Accessed Aug. 2020.

Battle, George. *The Battle Book.* www.thebattlebook.com/BattleBookOnline/TheBattleBook _Chapter%208_CoolSpring.pdf.

Battle, Kemp Plummer. *Memories of an Old-Time Tar Heel.* Edited by William James Battle. Chapel Hill: University of North Carolina Press, 1945. Accessed Aug. 2022.

Beeman, Richard. "KCC Star Breaks Record in Defeat." *Battle Creek Enquirer,* Dec. 1969.

Benagh, Jim. "Prep's Cage, Magic Already Fits with Pros." *Detroit Free Press,* Dec. 1976, Newspapers.com. Accessed Oct. 2019.

Benner, Bill. "Spartans Played over Irish Heads." *Indianapolis Star,* Mar. 1979, Newspapers.com. Accessed Jan. 2021.

Bennett, Glenn H. "Yankee Come South." *Rocky Mount* (North Carolina) *Telegram,* Aug. 1959, Newspapers.com. Accessed July 2020.

Besch, Edwin. *U.S. Colored Troops Defeat the Confederacy.* Jefferson, NC: McFarland, 2017.

"Bill Russell Interviews Magic Johnson, Kareem Abdul-Jabbar, and Jamaal Wilkes (1980)." www .youtube.com/watch?v=TtGPi3ai2A4.

"Bird, Greenwood Top All-Americans." *Oshkosh* (Wisconsin) *Northwestern,* Mar. 1979, https:// www.newspapers.com. Accessed Jan. 2021.

Bird, Larry, and Bob Ryan. *Larry Bird: Drive: The Story of My Life.* New York: Doubleday, 1989.

Bird, Larry, Earvin "Magic" Johnson Jr., and Jackie MacMullan. *When the Game Was Ours.* Boston: Houghton Mifflin Harcourt, 2010.

Bird, Larry, and Jackie MacMullan. *Bird Watching: On Playing and Coaching the Game I Love.* New York: Warner Books, 1999.

Bonk, Thomas. "Magic Johnson out with Shingles; He'll Miss Lakers' Season Opener Tonight at San Antonio." *Los Angeles Times,* Oct. 1985.

———. "Quiet Adviser: School Psychologist Counsels Several Top Basketball Stars." *Los Angeles Times,* Jan. 1985, articles.latimes.com/1985-01-22/sports/sp-11050_1_school-psychologist.

Brady, Frank. "Travelin' Man: Magic Busy in Off-Season, Too." (Los Angeles) *Herald Examiner,* Oct. 1989, Newspapers.com.

Brady, Fred. "With Jordan as Teammate, Magic Tries to Break Skein in Charity Game." *Los Angeles Herald,* Aug. 1989, Newspapers.com.

Brown, Judith. "Everett Resumes Classes." *Lansing State Journal,* May 1972, Newspapers.com. Accessed Dec. 2020.

Brown, Judy. "Busing, Three R's Vota." *Lansing State Journal,* Dec. 1972, Newspapers.com. Accessed Dec. 2020.

Buss, Jeanie, and Steve Springer. *Laker Girl.* Chicago: Triumph Books, 2013.

Byington, Bob. "Everett's Earvin Johnson." *Battle Creek* (Michigan) *Enquirer,* Dec. 1975, https:// www.newspapers.com. Accessed Oct. 2020.

Caro, Robert A. *The Years of Lyndon Johnson: The Path to Power, vol. 1.* New York: Alfred A. Knopf, 1982.

Carroll, E. Jean. "Love in the Time of Magic." *Esquire,* Apr. 1992.

Carter, Bill. "Magic Loves to Watch Greg Dunk." *Town Talk,* Mar. 1979, Newspapers.com. Accessed Jan. 2021.

"Chastine Killed in Collision." *Lansing State Journal,* Aug. 1976, Newspapers.com. Accessed Nov. 2020.

"Chastine, Reginald T., Obituary." *Lansing State Journal,* Aug. 1976, https://www.newspapers .com. Accessed Nov. 2020.

Cleveland, Rick. "Jack Johnson's Never Been More Proud of Magic." (Jackson, MI) *Clarion-Ledger,* Nov. 1991, Newspapers.com. Accessed Apr. 2020.

"Cluster Bus Plan Affects 13 Schools, 4,500 Students." *Lansing State Journal,* Aug. 1973, https:// www.newspapers.com. Accessed Dec. 2020.

Collins, Bob. "Houdini Couldn't Have Saved Irish." *Indianapolis Star,* 1979, Newspapers.com. Accessed Jan. 2021.

"Cool Spring Plantation, Edgecombe Co, North Carolina." www.ourfamtree.org/location.php/eid /55078.

Cooper, Barry. "Coach Always Adding to Collection of Suits, NBA Titles." *Orlando Sentinel,* 1988.

Cotton, Anthony. "Don't Blame Me, I Just Want to Have Fun! The Lakers Were Winning, but Magic Johnson and the Owner Were Not Enjoying It." *Sports Illustrated,* Nov. 1981.

Cuniberti, Betty. "Michigan St., Penn Progress to Final Four, Magical Duo Dunks Irish." *Washington Post,* Mar. 1979.

———. "Michigan State Confronts Notre Dame Today." *Washington Post,* Mar. 1979.

———. "Penn, St. John's Pull Upsets; Toledo, LSU Fall Short, Irish, Michigan St. Win." *Washington Post,* Mar. 1979.

Cushman, Tom. "Larry Bird Can Talk Too." *Philadelphia Daily News,* Mar. 1979, Newspapers.com. Accessed Sept. 2020.

———. "Spartans' 1–2 Punch Decks Irish." *Philadelphia Daily News,* Mar. 1979, https://www.newspapers.com. Accessed Sept. 2020.

Dalton, Joseph. "Magic." *Inside Sports,* May 1980.

Davis, Seth. *When March Went Mad: The Game That Transformed Basketball.* New York: Times Books, 2009.

Deford, Frank. "HIV Timeline." *Newsweek,* 1992.

Dempsey, Dale. "Soviets Too Tall an Order for Stars." *Journal Herald* (Dayton, Ohio), May 1978, https://www.newspapers.com. Accessed Dec. 2020.

Denlinger, Ken. "A Magic Future; Magic Wants to Clip Bird with Sleight-of-Hand." *Washington Post,* Mar. 1979.

———. "Magic's Spell Not over NBA—Yet." *Des Moines Register,* Mar. 1979.

Dodge, David. "The Free Negros of North Carolina." *The Atlantic,* Jan. 1886.

Donovan, Pete. "Call Him Magic: Michigan State's Earvin Johnson a Legend in Lansing." *Anniston Star* (Anniston, Ala.), Newspapers.com.

———. "Nobody Escapes Spell of Michigan Magician." *Hartford Courant,* Mar. 1979, Newspapers.com. Accessed Jan. 2021.

Dougan, Steve. "Jay Vincent Pours." *Lansing State Journal,* Feb. 1975, Newspapers.com. Accessed Jan. 2019.

Douglas, Looney. "And for My Next Trick." *Sports Illustrated,* Apr. 1979.

"Dr. Tucker's Cage Camp Set." *Lansing State Journal,* May 1977, https://www.newspapers.com. Accessed May 2020.

Dryer, Boby. "A Talent Show—Big Ten Basketball Recruits." *Des Moines Register,* May 1975, Newspapers.com. Accessed Dec. 2020.

Dunlap, Jim. "Gryphons Swamp New Bern with Second Half Blitz." *Rocky Mount* (North Carolina) *Telegram,* Jan. 1973, Newspapers.com. Accessed July 2020.

DuPree, David. "Big Ten Showdown Tonight." *Washington Post,* Feb. 1979.

———. "Bird: Magic Just Did His Act." *USA Today,* June 1987.

———. "In a Year of Amazing Frosh, Michigan State's Johnson Stands Out." *Washington Post,* Feb. 1978.

———. "Kentucky Leads Parade as Playoff Time Nears." *Washington Post,* Feb. 1978, p. D1.

———. "Michigan St. Befuddles Ohio State." *Washington Post,* Feb. 1979, p. N7.

———. "NCAA Openers Pit Top-Ranked Teams; Freshmen Carry Load in NCAA." *Washington Post,* Mar. 1979, p. C1.

———. "Nicknames Point to Differences Between Illinois, Michigan St." *Washington Post,* Dec. 1978, p. D4.

———. "Only Thing Missing from the Magic Man's Act Is a Jumper." *Washington Post,* Mar. 1979, p. C6.

———. "Purdue Belts Mich. State, One Back in Big Ten Race." *Washington Post,* Feb. 1978, p. C1.

———. "UCLA Ready to Resume Top Spot in College Basketball." *Washington Post,* Nov. 1978, p. D5.

"Dwight Rich Cager Rewrites Record Book." *Lansing State Journal,* Mar. 1974, Newspapers.com. Accessed Sept. 2020.

"Earvin Dazzles in Debut, 114–66." *Detroit Free Press,* Nov. 1977, https://www.newspapers.com. Accessed Oct. 2019.

"Eastern Build, Jay Vincent." *Lansing State Journal,* Dec. 1975, Newspapers.com. Accessed Sept. 2020.

"Easy Earvin Scores 45." *Ludington* (Michigan) *Daily News,* Dec. 1976, p. 6, Newspapers.com.

Ebling, Jack. "That Certain Smile: Magic Johnson Reflects Thrill of Beating Celtics of NBA Title." *Lansing State Journal,* June 1985, https://www.newspapers.com. Accessed Apr. 2020.

Edes, Gordon. "Magic Exorcises Garden Ghosts." *Los Angeles Times,* June 1987.

———. "Magic Johnson 1986–87: His Greatest Act Yet." *Los Angeles Times,* May 1987, https://www.newspapers.com. Accessed May 2020.

"Edgecombe County Marriage Records." State Archives of North Carolina, archives.ncdcr.gov/researchers/collections/government-records/county-records-guide.

"Edgecombe's Rural Schools Vanishing." *Rocky Mount* (North Carolina) *Telegram,* July 1952, Newspapers.com. Accessed July 2020.

"Elisha Battle (1723–1799); Later Expanded by His Grandson, James S. Battle (1786–1854)." Cool Spring Plantation, 1747, www.ncgenweb.us/ncstate/plantations/cool_spring_edgec.htm.

"Enjoy, Spartan Fans, but Please Don't Expect Too Much." *Lansing State Journal,* Apr. 1977, Newspapers.com. Accessed Nov. 2020.

"Everett." *Traverse City* (Michigan) *Record-Eagle,* Mar. 1976, Newspapers.com. Accessed Oct. 2020.

"Everett Crushes East Lansing." *Lansing State Journal,* Feb. 1975, Newspapers.com. Accessed Jan. 2019.

"Everett Stops Sexton." *Lansing State Journal,* Feb. 1975, Newspapers.com. Accessed Jan. 2019.

"Everett Whips Adrian." *Lansing State Journal,* Dec. 1974, Newspapers.com. Accessed Sept. 2020.

"Everett Wins 9th in a Row." *Detroit Free Press,* Jan. 1977, Newspapers.com. Accessed Oct. 2019.

"Everett Wins Big, Belts East Lansing." *Lansing State Journal,* Feb. 1976, Newspapers.com. Accessed Oct. 2020.

"Everett's Finale a Breeze." *Detroit Free Press,* Oct. 2019, freep.newspapers.com. Accessed Oct. 2019.

Falls, Joe. "Johnson's Magic Just Wasn't There." *Detroit Free Press,* Mar. 1976, Newspapers.com. Accessed Sept. 2020.

Falls, Joe, and Mick McCabe. "MSU Made Them Look Ordinary." *Detroit Free Press,* Mar. 1979, Newspapers.com. Accessed Sept. 2020.

"Federal Writers' Project: Slave Narrative Project, Vol. 11, North Carolina, Part 1, Adams-Hunter." Library of Congress, Washington, D.C., www.loc.gov/item/mesn111/.

Fleming, Monika S. *Echoes of Edgecombe County: 1860–1940.* Mount Pleasant, SC: Arcadia Publishing, 1996.

Foley, Eileen. "Schools Too Critical of Kids' Speech?" *Detroit Free Press,* Nov. 1974, https://www.newspapers.com. Accessed Nov. 2020.

"Fox Calls Three Years with Magic a Trip." *Lansing State Journal,* Dec. 1976, Newspapers.com. Accessed Jan. 2019.

Freudenthal, Kurt. "Irish, MSU Coaches Expect Physical Game." *The Republic,* Mar. 1979, Newspapers.com. Accessed Jan. 2021.

Gates, Henry Louis. "The Truth Behind 40 Acres and a Mule | African American History Blog | the African Americans: Many Rivers to Cross." PBS, *The African Americans: Many Rivers to Cross,* Sept. 2013, www.pbs.org/wnet/african-americans-many-rivers-to-cross/history/the-truth-behind-40-acres-and-a-mule/.

Gave, Keith. "Spartan Fun Game Lures Sellout Crowd to Everett." *Lansing State Journal,* Nov. 1978, Newspapers.com. Accessed Dec. 2020.

"GM Cutback Trims Olds, Fisher Jobs." *Lansing State Journal,* Dec. 1973, Newspapers.com. Accessed Dec. 2019.

Goldowitz, Michael. "Magic No Worse for Wear." *News Chronicle* (Thousand Oaks, Calif.), July 1989.

Gordon, David. "Magic's Bonanza Far from Limit." *Chicago Tribune,* June 1981, Newspapers.com. Accessed Mar. 2021.

"Grand Rally of the Republican Party of Edgecombe County." Feb. 1886, Newspapers.com. Accessed Aug. 2020.

"Green Paced MSU's Best." *Lansing State Journal,* Jan. 1974, Newspapers.com. Accessed July 2020.

Green, Ted. "Cooke, West, Magic and Jabbar." *Los Angeles Times,* Apr. 1979, Newspapers.com. Accessed May 2020.

———. "Lakers Book a Magic Show at the Forum." *Los Angeles Times,* May 1979, Newspapers.com. Accessed Jan. 2021.

———. "Lakers Suddenly Get Lucky; Is It Magic." *Los Angeles Times,* Apr. 1979, https://www.newspapers.com. Accessed Jan. 2021.

———. "Magic Signs 25-Year Million Deal with LA." *Los Angeles Times,* June 1981, https://www.newspapers.com. Accessed Mar. 2021.

———. "Picking NBA's Best Not an Easy Job." *National Sports Daily,* Apr. 1990, Newspapers .com.

Greenberg, Don. "Magic vs Bird." *Santa Ana* (California) *Register* (morning edition), Dec. 1989, Newspapers.com.

———. "Sad Goodbye to Kareem." *Cincinnati Enquirer,* Apr. 1989, Newspapers.com. Accessed Apr. 2020.

Gross, Bob. "Cage Fever Hits Everett." *Lansing State Journal,* Oct. 1976, Newspapers.com. Accessed Nov. 2020.

———. "Challenge Sold Earvin on MSU." *Lansing State Journal,* Apr. 1977, Newspapers.com. Accessed Nov. 2020.

———. "Dome Show a Flop." *Lansing State Journal,* Dec. 1978, Newspapers.com. Accessed Jan. 2021.

———. "Earvin Finds G. Ledge a Lovely Place to Visit." *Lansing State Journal,* Feb. 1977, Newspapers.com. Accessed Jan. 2019.

———. "Earvin's Headed to MSU." *Lansing Stare Journal,* Apr. 1977, Newspapers.com. Accessed Dec. 2020.

———. "Eastern-Everett Game Sites Announced." *Lansing State Journal,* Dec. 1975, Newspapers .com. Accessed Jan. 2019.

———. "Everett Overpowers Hill, 80–39." *Lansing State Journal,* Dec. 1974, Newspapers.com. Accessed Sept. 2020.

———. "Everett Topples Holt's Rams, 68–58." *Lansing State Journal,* Dec. 1975, Newspapers .com. Accessed Jan. 2021.

———. "Everett's Strong Defense." *Lansing State Journal,* Dec. 1976, Newspapers.com. Accessed Oct. 2020.

———. "Friends Mourn Everett Cager: All Agree, Reggie Was Special." *Lansing State Journal,* Aug. 1976, Newspapers.com. Accessed Nov. 2020.

———. "NCAA Champion Spartans Receive Rousing Welcome." *Lansing State Journal,* Mar. 1979, Newspapers.com. Accessed Jan. 2021.

———. "Red-Hot Vikings Romp, 103–52." *Lansing State Journal,* Jan. 1977, Newspapers .com.

———. "Smooth, Steady Everett Rambles Past Hill, 88–49." *Lansing State Journal,* Jan. 1975, p. 24, Newspapers.com. Accessed Jan. 2019.

———. "Soph Whiz Gets 27 in Everett Victory." *Lansing State Journal,* Jan. 1975, Newspapers .com. Accessed Jan. 2019.

———. "Sunday No Day of Rest for Fox Family." *Lansing State Journal,* Mar. 1977, Newspapers .com. Accessed Jan. 2019.

———. "Trip to North Country Can Wait for Allen Bush." *Lansing State Journal,* Aug. 1978, Newspapers.com. Accessed Dec. 2020.

———. "Tucker Shouldn't Be Vilified Because of Big Ticket Snafu." *Lansing State Journal,* July 1887, Newspapers.com. Accessed May 2020.

———. "Vikings Tip Saginaw, 48–40." *Lansing State Journal,* Apr. 1977, Newspapers.com. Accessed June 2019.

———. "Will History Repeat for George Fox." *Lansing State Journal,* Mar. 1977, Newspapers .com. Accessed Jan. 2019.

Gross, Bob, and Mark Nixon. "First Came Faith, Then the Magic." *The* (Nashville) *Tennessean,* July 1987, Newspapers.com. Accessed Apr. 2020.

———. "They Believed in . . . MAGIC." *Lansing State Journal,* June 1987, Newspapers.com. Accessed Apr. 2020.

Gutman, Bill. *Magic: More than a Legend.* New York: Harper Paperbacks, 1992.

Hadhazy, Adam. "How Has Magic Johnson Survived 20 Years with HIV?" *Live Science,* Nov. 2011, www.livescience.com/16909-magic-johnson-hiv-aids-anniversary.html.

Halberstam, David. *The Breaks of the Game.* New York: Alfred A. Knopf, 1981.

Hall, John. "Time to Go." *Los Angeles Times,* Jan. 1979, Newspapers.com. Accessed Jan. 2021.

Hargus, Taylor R. "Battle, Elisha." *NCpedia,* 1979, ncpedia.org/biography/battle-elisha. Accessed Aug. 2022.

Harris, James. "To Magic, Lansing Still 'Home Court.'" *Lansing State Journal,* Oct. 1981, Newspapers.com. Accessed Apr. 2020.

"Harris, Mary E., Obituary." *San Francisco Examiner,* Jan. 1987, Newspapers.com. Accessed July 2020.

Harvey, Randy. "It's Time to Get Serious About Rambis." *Los Angeles Times,* Jan. 1982, Newspapers .com. Accessed May 2020.

Haskins, James. *"Magic": A Biography of Earvin Johnson.* Berkeley Heights, NJ: Enslow Publishing, 1982.

Hass, Charlie. "Everett Aide a Plain Talker." *Lansing State Journal,* June 1972, Newspapers.com. Accessed Nov. 2020.

Hearn, Chick, and Steve Springer. *Chick: His Unpublished Memoirs and the Memories of Those Who Knew Him.* Chicago: Triumph Books, 2004.

Heath, Thomas, and Christine Spolar. "Magic Johnson's World: A Life of Temptations." *Washington Post,* Nov. 1991, Newspapers.com.

Heathcote, Jud, and Jack Ebling. *Jud: A Magical Journey.* Champaign, IL: Sagamore Publishing, 1995.

Heisler, Mark. *The Lives of Riley.* New York: Macmillan, 1994.

———. "No Mere Passing Fancy: Lakers: Johnson Breaks Oscar Robertson's Assist Record of 9,887 in 112–106 Victory over Mavericks." *Los Angeles Times,* Apr. 1991, www.latimes.com /archives/la-xpm-1991-04-16-sp-55-story.html. Accessed Aug. 2022.

Henning, Lynn. "Coaching Dream." *Lansing State Journal,* July 1976, Newspapers.com. Accessed Oct. 2020.

———. "Dawkins Super Dunk Explosive." *Lansing State Journal,* July 1977, Newspapers.com. Accessed Nov. 2020.

———. "Everett Express Rolls On." *Lansing State Journal,* Dec. 1975, Newspapers.com. Accessed Jan. 2019.

———. "Fun Night for Happy MSU." *Lansing State Journal,* Apr. 1978, Newspapers.com. Accessed Dec. 2020.

———. "Gus Axing Tough on Jud." *Lansing State Journal,* Apr. 1976, Newspapers.com. Accessed Oct. 2020.

———. "How Did MSU Pull It Off." *Lansing State Journal,* Mar. 1978, Newspapers.com. Accessed Jan. 2021.

———. "Wharton's Edret Obeyed." *Lansing State Journal,* Mar. 1976, Newspapers.com. Accessed July 2020.

———. "Orr Just Wild About Earvin." *Lansing State Journal,* Feb. 1978, Newspapers.com. Accessed Dec. 2020.

———. "Quickness, Johnson Called Edge." *Lansing State Journal,* Mar. 1978, Newspapers.com. Accessed Dec. 2020.

———. "Tributes Cap Viking Year." *Lansing State Journal,* Apr. 1977, Newspapers.com. Accessed Nov. 2020.

———. "What a Game! What a Fieldhouse! What an Evening!" *Lansing State Journal,* Dec. 1976, Newspapers.com.

———. "Wildcats Strategy Clicks, Macy Delivers KO Punch." *Lansing State Journal,* Mar. 1978, Newspapers.com.

"Here Are Heat Tips." *Lansing State Journal,* Aug. 1959, Newspapers.com. Accessed June 2020.

Higgins, James V. "Magic Johnson Faces Tough Decision." (Muncie, IN) *Star Press,* Mar. 1979, p. 23, Newspapers.com. Accessed Jan. 2021.

"Historical Notes." *Rocky Mount* (North Carolina) *Telegram,* Feb. 1990, Newspapers.com. Accessed July 2020.

"History of 13th North Carolina Infantry Civil War Index—American Civil War." *Civil War Index,* www.civilwarindex.com/13th-north-carolina-infantry.html.

"History Repeat?" *Lansing State Journal,* Jan. 1977, Newspapers.com. Accessed Jan. 2019.

"Ho . . . Hum State Prep Tourney Is Coming." *Detroit Free Press,* Feb. 1977, Newspapers.com. Accessed Oct. 2019.

Hoerner, Bob. "Spartans Slip by Chip." *Lansing State Journal,* Dec. 1972, Newpapers.com. Accessed July 2020.

"Howard in East-West." *Rocky Mount* (North Carolina) *Telegram,* Apr. 1973, Newspapers.com. Accessed July 2020.

Hughes, Mike. "When News Is Good News." *Lansing State Journal,* Apr. 1977, Newspapers.com. Accessed Nov. 2020.

"Hundreds Flee Flood in North Carolina; Roanoke River Inundates Towns, Damages Plants—Two Dead." *New York Times,* Aug. 1940, www.nytimes.com/1940/08/19/archives/hundreds-flee -flood-in-north-carolina-roanoke-river-inundates-towns.html. Accessed Aug. 2022.

"Isiah Porter, Obituary." *Rocky Mount* (North Carolina) *Telegram,* Sept. 1989, Newspapers.com. Accessed Feb. 2020.

"Isiah's All-Star Fund-Raiser Dropped over Bird Dispute." *Times Herald,* July 1987, Newspapers .com. Accessed May 2020.

"It's Spartans, Brazil in Another Title Game." *Lansing State Journal,* Sept. 1978, https://www .newspapers.com. Accessed Jan. 2021.

Ivey, Guy. "Uncle Ned Was Legislator Who Could Go Back Home in Peace." (Raleigh) *News and Observer,* Feb. 1935, Newspapers.com. Accessed Aug. 2020.

"Jabbar: No Trade Talk Comment." *Lansing State Journal,* Mar. 1975, Newspapers.com. Accessed Jan. 2019.

Jacobs, Jeff. "Johnson, Bird Made Magic Together." *Hartford Courant,* Sept. 28, 2002.

Jauss, Bill. "Kelser's Brillance Shines Through Magic's Shadow." *Chicago Tribune,* Mar. 1979, Newspapers.com. Accessed Jan. 2021.

———. "Magic Act Puts Crown on Michigan State." *Chicago Tribune,* Mar. 1979, Newspapers .com. Accessed Sept. 2020.

———. "Michigan State, Notre Dame Ready for Their Physical." *Chicago Tribune,* Newspapers. com. Accessed Jan. 2021.

"Jeanie Buss Talks About Growing Up with Magic Johnson and Jerry Buss." www.youtube.com /watch?v=jmhcrwBA4LQ.

"Jerry Is Never Behind the Eight Ball. Jerry Buss Has Always Had a Way with a Chick, a Cue and a Buck. Now He'll Have His Way with the Lakers, Kings and Forum." *Sports Illustrated,* June 1979.

"Johnson Hits 34." *Battle Creek* (Michigan) *Enquirer,* Jan. 1970, https://www.newspapers.com. Accessed Jan. 2020.

"Johnson Hits 39 as Everett Romps, 76–52." *Detroit Free Press,* Dec. 1976, Newspapers.com. Accessed Oct. 2019.

"Johnson Scores 27 for Everett." *Detroit Free Press,* Dec. 1976, Newspapers.com. Accessed Oct. 2019.

Johnson, Cookie, and Denene Millner. *Believing in Magic: My Story of Love, Overcoming Adversity, and Keeping the Faith*. New York: Howard Books, 2016.

Johnson, Earvin, and Roy S. Johnson. *Magic's Touch: From Fundamentals to Fast Break with One of Basketball's All-Time Greats*. Boston: Addison-Wesley, 1992.

Johnson, Earvin, and Richard Levin. *Magic*. New York: Penguin, 1983.

Johnson, Earvin, and William Novak. *My Life*. New York: Random House, 1992.

Johnson, Magic. "Magic's Kingdom." (Port Huron, MI) *Times Herald*, Oct. 1985, Newspapers .com. Accessed Apr. 2020.

———. "The Magic Kingdom Is Freedom." *Detroit Free Press,* May 1986, Newspapers.com. Accessed Oct. 2019.

Johnson, Malcom. "Earvin Makes College Choice: MSU." *Lansing State Journal*, Apr. 1977.

Johnson, Roy S. "Halfway Through a 2-Year Quest for Greatness." *New York Times*, Nov. 1987.

"Junior High Roundup." *Lansing State Journal,* Feb. 1973, Newspapers.com. Accessed Feb. 2019.

"Junior High Roundup." *Lansing State Journal,* Mar. 1973, Newspapers.com. Accessed Dec. 2019.

Katz, Jesse. "Master of Illusion. Twelve Years after AIDS Virus Cut Short His Basketball Career, Magic Johnson Continues to Amaze and Baffle." *Los Angeles Magazine,* Oct. 2003.

"Kellogg CC Scores an 88–82 Win." *Battle Creek* (Michigan) *Enquirer,* Jan. 1965, Newspapers .com. Accessed Nov. 2020.

Kelser, Gregory, and Steve Grinczel. *Gregory Kelser's Tales from Michigan State*. Champaign, IL: Sports Publishing, 2006.

Kindred, Dave. "Arkansas, Kentucky Win Final-4 Berths; Strategy Switch Keys Victory for Kentucky." *Washington Post,* Mar. 1978, p. D1.

———. "Kentucky's Macy Injured." *Washington Post,* Mar. 1978, p. G5.

———. "Please: A Bird-vs-Magic Climax; Bird Plus Magic Equals Fun." *Washington Post,* Mar. 1979, p. D1.

———. "Pro Scouts Drool over Hustling Giant." *Washington Post,* Mar. 1978, p. G5.

Kirkpatrick, Curry. "In an Orbit All His Own Whether He's Pouring in Points or Putting Together Business Deals, High-Flying Michael Jordan of the Chicago Bulls Is Out of This World." *Sports Illustrated*, Nov. 1997.

Knapp, Ron. "Earvin Has Ho-Hum Bout; Everett Wins Easily." *Battle Creek* (Michigan) *Enquirer,* Dec. 1975, Newspapers.com. Accessed Oct. 2020.

Labarre, Steven M. *The Fifth Massachusetts Colored Cavalry in the Civil War*. Jefferson, NC: McFarland, 2016.

"Lady Gamecocks Sign Johnson." (Raleigh) *News and Observer,* Mar. 1979, Newspapers.com. Accessed Jan. 2021.

Lakers 2004–05 Media Guide. New York: NBA Properties, 2004.

"Lakers Hand Johnson Richest Contract in Sports." *Palm Beach Post,* June 1981, p. 47. Accessed Mar. 2021.

"Lakers' Rookies Win as Magic Scores 24." *Hartford Courant,* July 1979, p. 12, Newspapers.com. Accessed Jan. 2021.

"Lansing Prep Cager Labeled Among the Best." *Detroit Free Press,* June 1976, Newspapers.com. Accessed Oct. 2020.

Lazenby, Roland. *Michael Jordan: The Life* (New York: Little, Brown and Company), 2014.

———. *Showboat: The Life of Kobe Bryant* (New York: Little, Brown and Company), 2016.

———. *The Lakers* (New York: St. Martin's Press), 1993.

———. *The Show* (New York: McGraw-Hill), 2006.

Lehr, Julie. "Cheerleader Dies." *Lansing State Journal,* Aug. 1976, Newspapers.com. Accessed Nov. 2020.

Lemasters, Ron. "Michigan State Defeats Notre Dame, 80–68." *Star Press* (Muncie, Ind.), Mar. 1979, Newspapers.com. Accessed Jan. 2021.

Levine, Lee Daniel. *Bird: The Making of an American Sports Legend*. New York: McGraw-Hill, 1988.

Lidz, Franz. "Jeanie Buss, She's Got Balls." *Sports Illustrated,* Feb. 1995.

Los Angeles Lakers 1992–93 Media Guide. New York: NBA Properties, 1992.

Lowery, I. E. *Life on the Old Plantation; or a Story Based on Fact*. The State Co. Printers, 1911.

Macfie, John. "Wimberly, Dred." *NCpedia*, 1996, www.ncpedia.org/biography/wimberly-dred.

"Magic Convinces Me." *Lansing State Journal,* Dec. 1976, Newspapers.com. Accessed May 2020.

"Magic Paces All-Star Win." *Herald-Palladium* (Michigan), Aug. 1978, Newspapers.com. Accessed Dec. 2020.

"Magic Scores 20 as Americans Romp in European Tourney." *Lansing State Journal,* Apr. 1977, Newspapers.com. Accessed Nov. 2020.

"Magic Talks About His Decision and Future." *Lansing State Journal,* May 1979, Newspapers.com. Accessed Jan. 2021.

"Magic Year's Top Prepster." *Ludington* (Michigan) *Daily News,* Mar. 1977, Newspapers.com. Accessed Sept. 2020.

"Magic's Parents Shun Interviews." *Pensacola News Journal,* Nov. 1991, Newspapers.com. Accessed Apr. 2020.

"'March Madness' Begins Second Phase This Week." *Lansing State Journal*, Mar. 1978, Newspapers.com. Accessed Dec. 2020.

Mariotti, Jay. "Frazzled Isiah Epitomizes Pistons." *San Francisco Examiner,* June 1988, Newspapers.com. Accessed May 2020.

"Mary E. Harris, Magic's Sister." *Lansing State Journal,* Jan. 1987, https://www.newspapers.com. Accessed Apr. 2020.

Matthews, Dave. "Classy Everett Tops East Lansing, 76–66." *Lansing State Journal,* Jan. 1975, Newspapers.com.

———. "Crowd Oohs and Aahs as Everett Crushes Waverly." *Lansing State Journal,* Dec. 1976, Newspapers.com. Accessed Oct. 2020.

———. "Dream." *Lansing State Journal,* Mar. 1976, Newspapers.com. Accessed Oct. 2020.

———. "Eastern Gets Sexton at Home Tuesday." *Lansing State Journal,* Jan. 1975, Newspapers.com. Accessed Jan. 2019.

———. "Everett Cagers Bow in Tourney Finals." *Lansing State Journal,* Dec. 1975, Newspapers.com. Accessed Oct. 2020.

———. "Everett Crushes Rival Reds, 71–47." *Lansing State Journal,* Jan. 1975, Newspapers.com. Accessed Jan. 2019.

———. "Everett Survives Upset Scare, 55–52." *Lansing State Journal,* Feb. 1975, Newspapers.com. Accessed Jan. 2019.

———. "Everett's CAC Champions." *Lansing State Journal,* Apr. 1976, Newspapers.com. Accessed Oct. 2020.

———. "First Earvin, Jay Show a Big Hit." *Lansing State Journal,* Apr. 1977, Newspapers.com. Accessed Nov. 2020.

———. "Fox: Vikings Better Be Ready." *Lansing State Journal,* Mar. 1976, Newspapers.com.

———. "Free Throws Carry Everett." *Lansing State Journal,* Mar. 1975, Newspapers.com. Accessed Jan. 2019.

———. "Hungrier Everett, Eastern Lead Pack." *Lansing State Journal,* Dec. 1976, Newspapers .com.
———. "Johnson Powers Everett Win." *Lansing State Journal,* Mar. 1976, Newspapers.com. Accessed Oct. 2020.
———. "Johnson Sifts Countless Offers." *Lansing State Journal,* Sept. 1976, Newspapers.com. Accessed Sept. 2020.
———. "Johnson's 50 Points Pace Everett's Victory." *Lansing State Journal,* Mar. 1976, Newspapers.com. Accessed Oct. 2020.
———. "Magic in Hoop Tilt." *Lansing State Journal,* Apr. 1977, p. 37.
———. "Magic Leaves Sexton Reeling in Everett Win." *Lansing State Journal,* Dec. 1976, Newspapers.com. Accessed Oct. 2020.
———. "Magic, the Man on the Go." *Lansing State Journal,* July 1980, Newspapers.com. Accessed Apr. 2020.
———. "Metro Team a Real Dream." *Lansing State Journal,* Mar. 1975, Newspapers.com. Accessed Jan. 2019.
———. "More Tuckers Needed." *Lansing State Journal,* May 1981, Newspapers.com. Accessed May 2020.
———. "Scoring Giants in Prep Feature." *Lansing State Journal,* Feb. 1975, Newspapers.com. Accessed Sept. 2020.
———. "Strong Defense Will Aid Vikes if Offense Fails." *Lansing State Journal,* Mar. 1977, Newspapers.com. Accessed Jan. 2019.
———. "Thanks for the Memories: Seniors Monopolize Metro." *Lansing State Journal,* Mar. 1977, Newspapers.com. Accessed Jan. 2019.
———. "Viking Rally Stop Quakers 86–79." *Lansing State Journal*, Dec. 1976, Newspapers .com.
———. "Vikings Go to Pieces, Lose to Fordson, 58–55." *Lansing State Journal,* Mar. 1975, Newspapers.com. Accessed Jan. 2019.
———. "Vikings Roll . . . Johnson." *Lansing State Journal,* Dec. 1975, Newspapers.com. Accessed Oct. 2020.
———. "Vikings Top Trojans." *Lansing State Journal,* Feb. 1975, Newspapers.com. Accessed Jan. 2019.
———. "Waverly Fired Up for Unbeaten Everett." *Lansing State Journal*, Dec. 1975, Newspapers .com. Accessed Oct. 2020.
McCabe, Mick. "Earvin Brings Magic to Detroit." *Detroit Free Press*, Feb. 1977, p. 28, Newspapers. com. Accessed Oct. 2019.
———. "How Earvin Johnson's Magic Led to His First Championship." *Lansing State Journal*, Mar. 1997, p. 50, Newspapers.com. Accessed Oct. 2019.
———. "How It Goes Earvin?" *Detroit Free Press,* Nov. 11, 1977, Newspapers.com. Accessed Oct. 2019.
———. "Huffman Learned." *Detroit Free Press,* Mar. 1997, Newspapers.com. Accessed Oct. 2020.
———. "It Won't Shock Jud if Earvin Turns Pro." *Detroit Free Press,* Apr. 1977, p. 27.
———. "Lansing's High School Hero." *Detroit Free Press,* Nov. 1991, Newspapers.com. Accessed Oct. 2019.
———. "MSU Phenom Sizzles—Bring on Basketball!" *Lansing State Journal*, Nov. 1977, Newpapers.com. Accessed Sept. 2020.
———. "MSU Wins Battle for Earvin Johnson." *Detroit Free Press,* Apr. 1977, Newspapers.com. Accessed Sept. 2020.
———. "MSU's Tried Not to Hound Him—Jud." *Detroit Free Press,* Apr. 1977, Newspapers.com. Accessed Sept. 2020.
———. "No. 1 Everett Shocked, 70–62." *Detroit Free Press,* Feb. 1977, Newspapers.com. Accessed Oct. 2019.
———. "Now You See Magic, Now You . . ." *Detroit Free Press,* Jan. 1980, Newspapers.com. Accessed Sept. 2020.
———. "The Russians Are Coming!" *Detroit Free Press,* May 1977, Newspapers.com. Accessed Nov. 2020.
———. "The Story Behind Earvin Johnson's First Championship." *Detroit Free Press,* Mar. 1997, Newspapers.com. Accessed Oct. 2019.
———. "To This Day, Smith Remembered for One Thing." *Detroit Free Press,* Mar. 1997, Newspapers.com. Accessed Oct. 2019.

———. "Vincent Finally Gets His Dream." *Detroit Free Press,* Feb. 1977, Newspapers.com. Accessed Oct. 2019.

McCallum, Jack. "Life After Death" *Sports Illustrated.* August 2001.

———. *Dream Team: How Michael, Magic, Larry, Charles, and the Greatest Team of All Time Conquered the World and Changed the Game of Basketball Forever* (New York: Ballantine Books), 2012.

McCellister, Tim. "Michigan St. Magical, 80–68." *Atlanta Constitution,* Mar. 1979, Newspapers .com. Accessed Jan. 2021.

McDermott, Joe. "Another Campy Russell, All-Stater Earvin's Tab." *Lansing State Journal,* Mar. 1975, p. 32, Newspapers.com. Accessed Oct. 2020.

———. "Unanimous All-State Pick Again: Earvin Johnson." *Lansing State Journal,* Mar. 1976, Newspapers.com. Accessed Oct. 2020.

McGill, John. "Only Way to Trick Magic Is off the Court." *Lexington* (Kentucky) *Herald,* Mar. 1979, Newspapers.com. Accessed Jan. 2021.

McManis, Sam. "Magic Is the MVP This Time." *Los Angeles Times,* May 1989.

———. "Same Magic, with a New Outlook." *Los Angeles Times,* Oct. 1989, Newspapers .com.

———. "The Season He Became Point Pivot." *Los Angeles Times,* Dec. 1989, Newspapers .com.

McNeal, Martin. "Thomas Clears Up What He Perceives as Misconception." *Sacramento Bee,* Feb. 2003, Newspapers.com. Accessed May 2020.

"Metro Coach of the Year." *Lansing State Journal,* Mar. 1977, Newspapers.com. Accessed Sept. 2020.

Miech, Rob. "Ex-Aztecs Coach Smokey Gaines Not Slowing Down After Stroke." *San Diego Union-Tribune,* Dec. 2018, https://www.sandiegouniontribune.com. Accessed Mar. 2020.

Miles, Gary, and Mark Nixon. "Magical Wedding." *Lansing State Journal,* Sept. 1991, Newspapers .com. Accessed Apr. 2020.

"Mix, Simpson Among Cage Clinic Stars." *Lansing State Journal,* June 1976, Newspapers.com. Accessed Nov. 2020.

Moore, David. "Footing the Bill; Or, How Shoe Companies Stay a Step Ahead of Competition." *San Bernardino* (California) *County Sun,* June 1981, Newspapers.com. Accessed Mar. 2021.

———. "LA's Johnson Thrives on Doing His Magic." *Fort Worth Star-Telegram,* Mar. 1984, Newspapers.com. Accessed Sept. 2020.

"MSU Wins Battle for Earvin Johnson." *Detroit Free Press,* Apr. 1977, Newspapers.com. Accessed Nov. 2020.

Murray, Jim. "Fiery Canadian Won't Wait for Americans." *Minneapolis Star,* Apr. 1979, Newspapers .com. Accessed Jan. 2021.

———. "Laker Smile? It's Magic." *Los Angeles Times,* Aug. 1979, Newspapers.com. Accessed Jan. 2021.

———. "With Buss' Lakers, Magic, Inmates Run Asylum." *Hartford Courant,* Nov. 1981, Newspapers .com. Accessed Nov. 2020.

"My Goal in Basketball Is to Play in the Pros." *Lansing State Journal,* Oct. 1975, Newspapers .com. Accessed Sept. 2020.

"National Cagers Selected." *Standard-Speaker,* July 1978, Newspapers.com. Accessed Dec. 2020.

"Negroes Plan Achievement Event." *Rocky Mount* (North Carolina) *Telegram,* Dec. 1952, Newspapers.com. Accessed July 2020.

Newman, Bruce. "Doing It All for L.A." *Sports Illustrated,* Nov. 1979.

———. "Magic Faces the Music." *Sports Illustrated,* Feb. 1984.

———. "Together At Center Stage." *Sports Illustrated.* June 1984.

Nixon, Mark. "Johnson on Johnson." *Lansing State Journal,* Oct. 1981, Newspapers.com. Accessed Apr. 2020.

———. "When the Lakers Signed Magic Johnson, They Thought He Could Do Everything with the Ball but Shoot It. Now He Is Scoring as Well as Passing." *Sport Illustrated,* Nov. 1979.

———. "Johnson Shows a Special Touch." *Lansing State Journal,* Oct. 1981, Newspapers.com. Accessed Apr. 2020.

———. "A Legend That Began at Home." *Lansing State Journal,* Oct. 1981, Newspapers.com. Accessed Apr. 2020.

———. "Magic Interview a Will-o'-the Wisp." *Lansing State Journal,* Oct. 1981, Newspapers .com. Accessed Apr. 2020.

———. "Where Dreams Create Stars." *Lansing State Journal,* Mar. 1979, Newspapers.com. Accessed Apr. 2020.

Oates, Mary Louise. "It Was a Magic Evening for Celebrities." *Los Angeles Times,* June 1981, Newspapers.com. Accessed Mar. 2021.

"Open House Set Sunday at New Everett School." *Lansing State Journal,* Aug. 1956, Newspapers .com. Accessed June 2020.

Ostler, Scott. "It's Magic: 31 Points and 13 Rebounds." *Los Angeles Times,* Aug. 1979, Newspapers .com. Accessed Jan. 2021.

———. "L.A. Soaks Up Its 1st Magic Moment." *Los Angeles Times,* July 1979, Newspapers.com. Accessed Jan. 2020.

———. "Lakers Add Some Size and Age." *Los Angeles Times,* Sept. 1979, Newspapers.com. Accessed Jan. 2021.

———. "Lakers Beef Up the Front with Chones." *Los Angeles Times,* Oct. 1979, Newspapers .com. Accessed Jan. 2021.

———. "The Magic Kingdom; He's Got It All—Disco, Tub and Home-Court Advantage." *Los Angeles Times,* Jan. 1985.

Ostler, Scott, and Steve Springer. *Winnin' Times: The Magical Journey of the Los Angeles Lakers.* New York: Collier Books, 1988.

Papanek, John. "And Now for My Reappearing Act." *Sports Illustrated,* Mar. 1981.

———. "Arms and the Man: With the Big Fella Out, Magic Johnson Was the Man." *Sports Illustrated,* May 1980.

Pearlman, Jeff. *Showtime: Magic, Kareem, Riley, and the Los Angeles Lakers Dynasty of the 1980s.* New York: Gotham, 2014.

Pierce, Charles. "Magic Act: The Making of Earvin Johnson, AIDS Saint." *GQ,* Feb. 1993.

Pierson, Phil. "Everett Cagers After the Ultimate." *Lansing State Journal,* Dec. 1976, Newspapers .com.

Pilgrim, Michael E. *Compiled Military Service Records of Volunteer Union Soldiers Who Served with the United States Colored Troops: 1st Through 5th United States Colored Cavalry, 5th Massachusetts Cavalry (Colored), 6th United States Colored Cavalry.* Washington, D.C.: National Archives and Records Administration, 1997.

Plaschke, Bill. "To Magic Johnson, Jerry Buss Was Friend, Mentor and Second Father." *Los Angeles Times,* Feb. 2013, Newspapers.com.

Platt, Larry. "Magic Johnson Builds an Empire." *New York Times,* Dec. 2000.

"Playboy Tabs Magic All-American." *Lansing State Journal,* Oct. 1978, Newspapers.com. Accessed Dec. 2020.

Pope, Edwin. "Magic in Liberty City." *Miami Herald,* Feb. 1990, Newspapers.com.

"Prep Cage All-Stars to Play Pros Tonight." *Lansing State Journal,* 1977, Newspapers.com. Accessed Oct. 2019.

"Progress in Conetoe." *Tarbourough* (North Carolina) *Southerner,* May 1894, Newspapers.com. Accessed July 2020.

Puscas, George. "Earvin Has Learned All He Can Playing for Spartans." *Detroit Free Press,* Mar. 1979, Newspapers.com. Accessed Sept. 2020.

"Rain to Halt Heat Briefly." *Lansing State Journal,* Aug. 1959, Newspapers.com. Accessed June 2020.

Remnick, David. "Lakers Are Blessed with a Magic That Is No Illusion." *Washington Post,* May 1984.

"Republican State Convention." *Weekly State Journal* (North Carolina), May 1884, Newspapers .com. Accessed Aug. 2020.

"Rich, French Share Junior Grid Title." *Lansing State Journal,* Nov. 1973, Newspapers.com. Accessed Dec. 2019.

Riley, Pat. *Showtime: Inside the Lakers' Breakthrough Season.* New York: Warner Books, 1988.

———. *The Winner Within: A Life Plan for Team Players.* New York: Berkley Books, 1994.

Robbins, Danny. "Then, It All Disappeared as if by Magic." *Philadelphia Inquirer,* Mar. 1979, Newspapers.com. Accessed Sept. 2020.

"Rockettes, Cagers to Play in National Tournament." *Lansing State Journal,* Mar. 1976, Newspapers .com. Accessed Oct. 2020.

Rose, Charlie. Interview with 12-Time NBA All-Star, Magic Johnson. *The Charlie Rose Show,* Nov. 2005.

Rosen, Byron. "Pros Strikeout at Midnight." *Washington Post,* Apr. 1978, p. D3.

Ryan, Bob. "Earvin Johnson Show." *Boston Globe,* Mar. 1978, Newspapers.com. Accessed Sept. 2020.

Ryon, Ruth. "A Magic Act to Gain More Space." *Los Angeles Times,* Oct. 1989.
"Saginaw Class an Underdog." *Ludington* (Michigan) *Daily News,* Mar. 1976, Newspapers.com.
Schram, Hal. "2 Super Athletes Talk of State." *Detroit Free Press,* Jan. 1975, Newspapers.com.
———. "All-State to All-American." *Detroit Free Press,* Mar. 1976, Newspapers.com. Accessed Oct. 2020.
———. "Everett-Sexton Duel Tops Big Prep Cage Weekend." *Detroit Free Press,* Feb. 1977, Newspapers.com. Accessed Oct. 2019.
———. "Everett Walks into 'A' Finals, 48–40." *Detroit Free Press,* Oct. 1977, freep.newspapers.com. Accessed Oct. 2019.
———. "How We Reported It March 27, 1977." *Detroit Free Press,* Mar. 1977, Newspapers.com. Accessed Oct. 2019.
———. "It's Magic! Earvin Johnson Shows Detroit His Tricks." *Detroit Free Press,* Feb. 1977, Newspapers.com. Accessed Oct. 2019.
———. "Lansing Everett Uses Its 'Magic' to Attain No. 1." *Detroit Free Press,* Jan. 1977, Newspapers.com. Accessed Oct. 2019.
———. "On Top Now, Everett Once Had to Struggle." *Detroit Free Press,* Mar. 1977, Newspapers.com.
———. "Prep Stars Duel." *Detroit Free Press,* Dec. 1976, Newspapers.com. Accessed Oct. 2020.
———. "Snow Can't Stop Prep Semifinals." *Detroit Free Press,* Mar. 1977, freep.newspapers.com. Accessed Oct. 2019.
Seanor, Dave. "Celt Great Puts Earv with Elite." *Lansing State Journal,* Feb. 1978, Newspapers.com.
———. "Spartans Look Ahead After Brazil Victories." *Lansing State Journal,* Sept. 1978, Newspapers.com. Accessed Jan. 2021.
Senyczko, Ed. "Earvin Johnson's Other Side." *Lansing State Journal,* Mar. 1976, Newspapers.com. Accessed Nov. 2020.
———. "Jud's Been There Before." *Lansing State Journal,* Feb. 1978, Newspapers.com. Accessed Dec. 2020.
"Sexton Stops Earvn's Magic." *Detroit Free Press,* Mar. 1977, Newspapers.com. Accessed Oct. 2019.
Shaikin, Bill, and Bill Plasche. "Magic Johnson Intends to Bid for Dodgers." *Los Angeles Times,* Dec. 2011.
Shook, Richard. "Cagers Hit Quarterfinals." *Ludington* (Michigan) *Daily News,* Mar. 1975, Newspapers.com. Accessed Sept. 2020.
———. "Earvin Johnson Named Top Prep Cager." *Traverse City* (Michigan) *Record-Eagle,* Mar. 1976, Newspapers.com. Accessed Oct. 2020.
———. "Easy Earvin' . . . Class-A All-Star." *Ludington* (Michigan) *Daily News,* Mar. 1976, Newspapers.com. Accessed Oct. 2020.
———. "A Game Rated Even." *Petoskey* (Michigan) *News-Review,* Mar. 1977, Newspapers.com. Accessed Sept. 2020.
"Slashing Rainfall Hits Here." *Lansing State Journal,* Aug. 1959, Newspapers.com. Accessed June 2020.
Slave Narratives: A Folk History of Slavery in the United States from Interviews with Former Slaves'. https://lccn.loc.gov/41021619.
Smith, Gary. "True Lies. All Along, Magic Johnson Insisted He Wasn't Coming Back. Was He Kidding Us, His Family—or Himself?" *Sports Illustrated,* Feb. 1996.
"Spartans' Fast Start Wins, 78–73." *Lansing State Journal,* Sept. 1978, Newspapers.com. Accessed Jan. 2021.
"Spartans' Magic Act Makes Irish Vanish." *Palm Beach Post,* Mar. 1979, Newspapers.com. Accessed Jan. 2021.
Spencer, Lyle. "Scott, Without Magic, Finding Game Difficult." (Riverside) *Press Enterprise,* Mar. 1982.
"Sports; FanFare." *Washington Post,* May 1977, p. D5.
Springer, Steve. "The Big Fill-In." *Los Angeles Times,* May 2000, Newspapers.com. Accessed Apr. 2020.
——"A Comeback with a Smile." *Los Angeles Times,* July 1984, Newspapers.com. Accessed May 2020.
———. "Could It Be Magic." *Los Angeles Times,* June 2002.
———. "Through the Years, He Stayed the Same." *Los Angeles Times,* Nov. 1991.

Stabley, Jr., Fred. "18th's Great to Spartans." *Lansing State Journal,* Jan. 1978, Newspapers .com.
———. "At Least, State Proved Something." *Lansing State Journal,* Mar. 1978, p. 45, Newspapers .com.
———. "Big Ten Is Tops." *Lansing State Journal,* Nov. 1978, p. 65, Newspapers.com. Accessed Jan. 2021.
———. "Can MSU Shatter N.C. Home Magic?" *Lansing State Journal,* Dec. 1978, Newspapers .com. Accessed Dec. 2020.
———. "Can Spartans Surpass Last Year?" *Lansing State Journal,* Oct. 1978, Newspapers.com. Accessed Jan. 2021.
———. "The Clock Strikes Twelve." *Lansing State Journal,* Apr. 1978, Newspapers.com. Accessed Dec. 2020.
———. "Cofield—Johnson Is One of a Kind." *Lansing State Journal,* Mar. 1978, Newspapers .com. Accessed Jan. 2019.
———. "Cross-Town Rivals Clash." *Lansing State Journal,* Dec. 1974, Newspapers.com. Accessed Sept. 2020.
———. "Dawson, Hunter Bask in Johnson's Shadow." *Lansing State Journal,* Feb. 1977, p. 28, Newspapers.com.
———. "Difference in Programs." *Lansing State Journal,* Jan. 1974, Newspapers.com. Accessed July 2020.
———. "Donnelly Not Spectacular . . . But Gets Job Done." *Lansing State Journal,* Mar. 1978, Newspapers.com.
———. "Earvin Is Earvin." *Lansing State Journal,* Nov. 1978, Newspapers.com.
———. "Earvin Who? Vikings Bury Trojans, 109–54." *Lansing State Journal,* Dec. 1976, Newspapers.com. Accessed Mar. 2020.
———. "Earvin's AAU Trip Was Magic." *Lansing State Journal*, July 1977, Newspapers.com. Accessed Nov. 2020.
———. "Evelyn Another Magic." *Lansing State Journal,* Nov. 1978, Newspapers.com.
———. "Everett Crushes Parkside." *Lansing State Journal*, Jan. 1975, p. 29, Newspapers.com. Accessed Jan. 2019.
———. "Everett, Johnson Reply to Challenge." *Lansing State Journal*, Feb. 1976, Newspapers .com. Accessed Oct. 2020.
———. "Everett Turns 'Shadow' Loose on Sexton, 72–51." *Lansing State Journal*, Feb. 1975, p. 15, Newspapers.com. Accessed Jan. 2019.
———. "Everett's Defense Shines in 62–53 Win." *Lansing State Journal*, Dec. 1974, Newspapers .com. Accessed Sept. 2020.
———. "Fullerton Big Challenge." *Lansing State Journal*, Dec. 1978, Newspapers.com. Accessed Jan. 2021.
———. "Ganakas Takes Firing in Stride." *Lansing State Journal,* Mar. 1976, Newspapers.com. Accessed July 2020.
———. "Heathcote Yells Less, Team Listens More." *Lansing State Journal*, Nov. 1978, Newspapers .com. Accessed Jan. 2021.
———. "How Sweet It Is—MSU's a Champ." *Lansing State Journal,* Feb. 1976, Newspapers.com. Accessed Dec. 2020.
———. "In Viking Romp." *Lansing State Journal,* Dec. 1974, p. 31, Newspapers.com. Accessed Sept. 2020.
———. "It's Krazy Klowns vs. Jumping Jacks." *Lansing State Journal,* Nov. 1978, Newspapers .com. Accessed Dec. 2020.
———. "Johnson, Vincent on Same Team—AP All-State." *Lansing State Journal,* Mar. 1977, Newspapers.com. Accessed Jan. 2019.
———. "Johnson, Vincent Set for Providence." *Lansing Stare Journal,* Mar. 1978, Newspapers .com. Accessed Dec. 2020.
———. "Jud Heathcote a Real Dr. Jekyll, Mr. Hyde." *Lansing State Journal*, Mar. 1978, Newspapers.com.
———. "Jud Heathcote Just Can't Stop Smiling." *Lansing State Journal,* Apr. 1977, Newspapers .com. Accessed Nov. 2020.
———. "Jud Heathcote Returning to Recruiting Job." *Lansing State Journal,* Mar. 1979, Newspapers.com. Accessed Jan. 2021.
———. "Kelser Ignites Sputtering Spartans." *Lansing State Journal,* Nov. 1978, Newspapers.com. Accessed Dec. 2020.

———. "Let's Tipoff Tomorrow Says Jud." *Lansing State Journal,* Sept. 1978, Newspapers.com. Accessed Dec. 2020.
———. "Magic Convinces Me." *Lansing State Journal,* Dec. 1976, Newspapers.com. Accessed Jan. 2019.
———. "Magic, Jay Let People Know Where Lansing Is." *Lansing State Journal,* Jan. 1978, p. 24, Newspapers.com. Accessed Jan. 2021.
———. "Magic Welcomed Home; Decision Awaited." *Lansing State Journal,* Apr. 1977, Newspapers.com. Accessed Nov. 2020.
———. "Magic's Act Makes True Believers of Big Reds." *Lansing State Journal,* Jan. 1976, Newspapers.com. Accessed Oct. 2020.
———. "Magic's High, Low Night." *Lansing State Journal,* Mar. 1978, p. 25, Newspapers.com. Accessed Dec. 2020.
———. "Michigan State Adds Brazil Trip." *Lansing State Journal,* Aug. 1978, Newspapers.com. Accessed Dec. 2020.
———. "MSU Cage Magic Continues, 71–70." *Lansing State Journal,* Mar. 1978, Newspapers .com. Accessed Dec. 2020.
———. "MSU Cagers Forgiven, Reinstated by Ganakas." *Lansing State Journal,* Jan. 1975, Newspapers.com. Accessed July 2020.
———. "MSU Dazzles Lamar, 95 to 64." *Lansing State Journal,* Mar. 1979, Newspapers.com. Accessed Jan. 2021.
———. "MSU's Tuck Relates to Everybody." *Lansing State Journal,* Jan. 1977, Newspapers.com. Accessed Nov. 2020.
———. "MSU's Wary of Wildcats' Jinx." *Lansing State Journal,* Jan. 1978, Newspapers.com. Accessed Mar. 2020.
———. "Muscle or MSU's Magic—Which Will Prevail?" *Lansing State Journal,* Mar. 1978, Newspapers.com.
———. "Poised Wolverines Nip MSU at Buzzer, 65–63." *Lansing State Journal,* Feb. 1978, Newspapers.com.
———. "Pressure Off, MSU Awaits Michigan Clash." *Lansing State Journal,* Jan. 1978, Newspapers.com. Accessed Dec. 2020.
———. "Sad Day." *Lansing State Journal,* Jan. 1975, Newspapers.com. Accessed July 2020.
———. "'Simple Plan' Nets Super Basketball Victory." *Lansing State Journal,* Autumn 1978, pp. 33, 40, Newspapers.com. Accessed Dec. 2020.
———. "Spartan Cagers Steal Media Spotlight in Big 10 Confab." *Lansing State Journal,* Nov. 1978, Newspapers.com. Accessed Dec. 2020.
———. "Spartan Five Passes Road Test at Illinois." *Lansing State Journal,* Jan. 1978, Newspapers .com.
———. "Spartans Own Medicine Is Poison." *Lansing State Journal,* 1978, Newspapers.com.
———. "Spartan, Michigan Cage Clash Sold Out." *Lansing State Journal,* Jan. 1975, Newspapers .com. Accessed Jan. 2019.
———. "Spartans Cut It Close." *Lansing State Journal,* Dec. 1978, Newspapers.com. Accessed Jan. 2021.
———. "Spartans Devastate Cougars." *Lansing State Journal,* Dec. 1978, Newspapers.com. Accessed Jan. 2021.
———. "Spartans Face Different Test than Tourney." *Lansing State Journal,* Mar. 1978, Newspapers.com. Accessed Dec. 2020.
———. "Spartans Find Tar Heels Gym Hostile Place." *Lansing Stare Journal,* 1978, Newspapers .com. Accessed Dec. 2020.
———. "Spartans Hope Friars Not as Tough as Practice." *Lansing State Journal,* Mar. 1978, Newspapers.com. Accessed Dec. 2020.
———. "Spartans Plan to Run, Run." *Lansing State Journal,* Nov. 1978, Newspapers.com. Accessed Dec. 2020.
———. "Spartans Rebounding Much, Much Better." *Lansing State Journal,* Dec. 1978, Newspapers.com. Accessed Jan. 2021.
———. "Spartans Turned Back by Giant." *Lansing State Journal,* Jan. 1978, Newspapers.com. Accessed Dec. 2020.
———. "Teammates, Foes, Marvel at Kelser's Leaps." Mar. 1978, Newspapers.com. Accessed Jan. 2021.
———. "Third Overseas Trip Still Excites Earvin." *Lansing State Journal,* July 1978, https://www .newspapers.com. Accessed Jan. 2021.

———. "Toledo Humbles MSU." *Lansing State Journal,* Dec. 1973, Newspapers.com. Accessed Dec. 2019.

———. "Ups and Downs . . . Spartans Had 'Em All." *Lansing State Journal,* Apr. 1979, Newspapers.com. Accessed Jan. 2021.

———. "Vikings to Give." *Lansing State Journal,* Dec. 1974, Newspapers.com. Accessed Sept. 2020.

———. "We're Not as Good Admits W. Kentucky Coach." *Lansing State Journal,* Mar. 1968, Newspapers.com. Accessed Dec. 2020.

Stabley, Jr., Fred, and Tim Staudt. *Tales of the Magical Spartans: A Collection of Stories from the 1979 Michigan State NCAA Basketball Champions.* Champaign, IL: Sports Publishing., 2003.

Stauth, Cameron. *The Golden Boys: The Unauthorized Inside Look at the U.S. Olympic Basketball Team.* New York: Pocket Books, 1992.

Stein, Garu. "Stately Battle: Earvin's Magic vs. the Birdman." *Battle Creek* (Michigan) *Enquirer,* Mar. 1979, Newspapers.com. Accessed Sept. 2020.

Stewart, Catherine A. *Long Past Slavery: Representing Race in the Federal Writers' Project.* Chapel Hill: University of North Carolina Press, 2016.

Strasser, J. B., and Laurie Becklund. *Swoosh: The Unauthorized Story of Nike and the Men Who Played There.* New York: Harper Business, 1993.

Strine, Gerald. "De Paul Can Make It Close." *Washington Post,* Mar. 1979.

Stultz, Max. "Michigan Quickly States Case." *Indianapolis Star,* Mar. 1979, Newspapers.com.

Sylvester, Curt. "Spartan's NCAA Title Rocket Blasts Off, 95–64." *Detroit Free Press,* Mar. 1979, Newspapers.com. Accessed Sept. 2020.

Taylor, Derrick Bryson. "EJ Cried with Dad Magic Johnson After Coming Out." Page Six, *New York Post,* June 2018, pagesix.com/2018/06/19/ej-cried-with-dad-magic-johnson-after-coming-out/. Accessed Aug. 2022.

"Team Play Key to MSU Cage Future." *Lansing State Journal,* Mar. 1978, Newspapers.com.

"Thank Goodness the Suspense Is Over." *Detroit Free Press,* Apr. 1977, Newspapers.com. Accessed Sept. 2020.

"Thanks for the Memories . . . Seniors Monopolize Metro Team." *Lansing State Journal,* Mar. 1977, Newspapers.com. Accessed Jan. 2019.

"The General Assembly." *Wilmington* (North Carolina) *Sun,* Dec. 1878, Newspapers.com. Accessed Aug. 2020.

Thomsen, Ian. "Looking Back: First Meeting Between Bird, Magic Had Lasting Impact on Basketball." (Muncie, IN) *Star Press,* Apr. 1989, Newspapers.com. Accessed Sept. 2020.

"Top Ohio Cager Headed for U-M." *Detroit Free Press,* May 1977, Newspapers.com. Accessed Nov. 2020.

Turner, Joseph Kelly, and John Luther Bridgers. *History of Edgecombe County, North Carolina.* London: Forgotten Books, 2015 [1920].

"Turner W. Battle Rites Held Today." *Rocky Mount* (North Carolina) *Telegram,* July 1974, Newspapers.com. Accessed Aug. 2020.

"Two for the Show. The Celtics' Larry Bird and Lakers' Magic Johnson Have the Hottest Hands to Hit the Beleaguered NBA in a Long Time." *Sports Illustrated,* Oct. 1979.

United States Army and Navy Journal, and Gazette of the Regular and Volunteer Forces. Vols. I–II, Aug. 29, 1863–Aug. 19, 1865. New York: Publication Office, No. 39 Park Row, 1863.

Van Sickel, Charlie. "The Dutch Rub: Spartans Are No. 1." *Spokane Daily Chronicle,* Jan. 1979, Newspapers.com.

Vecsey, George. "Sports of the Times; a Power Play, off the Court." *New York Times,* Nov. 1981, p. 23.

Vecsey, Peter. "Magic's Message Loud and Clear." *New York Post,* Nov. 1989.

———. "Point of No Return." *New York Post,* Mar. 1976, Newspapers.com. Accessed Oct. 2020.

Vincent, Charlie. "U-D vs. MSU!" *Detroit Free Press,* Dec. 1977, Newspapers.com. Accessed Sept. 2020.

———. "When Tucker Speaks, Basketball Stars Listen." *Detroit Free Press,* Oct. 1981, Newspapers.com. Accessed May 2020.

Vitti, Gary. *32 Years of Titles and Tears from the Best Seat in the House: What I Learned About Happiness, Greatness, Leadership and the Evolution of Sports Science.* London: Icon Press, 2019.

Voisin, Ailene. "Magic Laments Lakers' Title." *Atlanta Constitution,* Aug. 1989.

Walkden, Jack. "Everett Wins No. 15; Topples Holt, 69–45." *Lansing State Journal,* Feb. 1975, Newspapers.com. Accessed Jan. 2019.

"Wearin' o' the Green Is to Spartans." *Detroit Free Press,* Mar. 1978, Newspapers.com. Accessed Oct. 2019.

Westhead, Paul. *The Speed Game: My Fast Times in Basketball.* Lincoln: University of Nebraska Press, 2020.

"Wildcats Next Opponent for MSU." *Lansing State Journal,* Mar. 1978, Newspapers.com.

Wilkerson, Isabel. *The Warmth of Other Suns.* New York: Random House, 2010.

"Will of Elisha Battle." *Battle Family Wills,* 1856, www.thebattlebook.com/BattleBookOnline/TheBattleBook_Chapter%208_CoolSpring.pdf.

"Will Tarkanian Succeed West?" (Palm Springs) *Desert Sun,* June 1979, Newspapers.com. Accessed Jan. 2021.

"Wimberly, Dred." *NCpedia,* June 1848, www.ncpedia.org/biography/wimberly-dred. Accessed Aug. 2022.

Woelfel, Gery. "Bucks Beat Parker's New Agent Is Familiar Figure." *Racine Journal Times* (Wisconsin), Apr. 2009.

Youngman, Randy. "Laker Helps Make a Fan's Dream Come True." *Orange County* (California) *Register,* 1989, https//www.newspapers.com.

Zeigler, Mark. "Crash Course." *San Diego Tribune,* Jan. 1990, p. H-11, Newspapers.com.

INDEX

About the Author

ROLAND LAZENBY is the author of definitive biographies of Michael Jordan, Kobe Bryant, and Jerry West, among other books. He has spent the past three decades writing about the NBA, interviewing players, coaches, staff members, and other figures. He lives in Salem, Virginia.